COLLEGE
ALGEBRA

COLLEGE
ALGEBRA

Updated Edition

Taken from
College Algebra
Robert Blitzer

PEARSON CUSTOM PUBLISHING
75 Arlington Street, Suite 300, Boston, MA 02116
A Pearson Education Company

Contents

Preface

College Algebra is written for students who need either a liberal arts college algebra course or a prerequisite college algebra course for a calculus sequence. Although the book's prerequisites chapter (Chapter P) reviews the basic concepts of algebra, students using this book should have the equivalent of two years of high school algebra.

The book has three fundamental goals: First, to help students acquire a solid foundation in college algebra, preparing them for other college courses such as calculus, business calculus, finite mathematics, and computer science; second, to show students how algebra can model and solve authentic real-world problems; and third, to enable students to develop problem-solving skills, fostering critical thinking, within a varied and interesting setting.

Key Pedagogical Features

The book's features are based on the recommendations and standards for college mathematics set forth by the National Council of Teachers of Mathematics and the American Mathematical Association of Two-Year Colleges. Consequently, the emphasis of the book is on problem solving, graphing, functions, mathematical modeling, technology, discovery approaches, critical thinking, collaborative learning, and contemporary applications that use real data. These applications are listed in the index of applications that appears inside the front covers. The features of this book are designed to support the three fundamental goals mentioned above.

Functions and Modeling. The book's emphasis is on the use of formulas and functions that describe interesting and relevant quantitative relations in the real world. Functions are introduced in Chapter 2, with an integrated functional approach emphasized throughout the book.

Graphing and Technology. Graphing and graphing utilities are discussed in the book's opening prerequisites chapter. Most examples and exercises use graphs to explore relationships between data and to provide ways of visualizing a problem's solution. Although the use of graphing utilities is optional, they are utilized in Using technology boxes to enable students to visualize, discover, and explore algebraic concepts. The use of graphing utilities is also reinforced in the technology problems appearing in the problem sets for those who want this option. With the book's early introduction to graphing, students can look at the calculator screens in the Using technology boxes and gain an increased understanding of an example's solution even if they are not using a graphing utility in the course.

Problem Solving. The emphasis of the book is on learning to use the language of algebra as a tool for solving problems related to everyday life. Problem-solving steps introduced in the third section in Chapter 1 are explicitly described, and they are used regularly. Since students have such difficulty translating word problems, a great deal of attention has been placed on translating the words and phrases of verbal models into algebraic equations. The extensive collection of applications, including environmental and financial issues, promotes the problem-solving theme and demonstrates the usefulness of the mathematics to students.

Extensive Application to Geometric Problem Solving. Problem solving using geometric formulas and concepts is emphasized throughout the book. Included whenever possible are geometric models that allow students to visualize algebraic formulas.

Detailed Step-by-Step Explanations. Illustrative examples are presented one step at a time. No steps are omitted, and each step is clearly explained. Color is used in the mathematics to show students precisely where the explanation applies.

Collaborative Learning and Chapter Projects. Most problem sets contain group activity problems. These collaborative activities give students the opportunity to work cooperatively as they think and talk about mathematics. The chapter projects at the end of each chapter use challenging and interesting applications of mathematics that not only stand alone as ways to stimulate class discussions on a variety of topics, but also cultivate an interest in independent explorations of mathematics on the Worldwide Web. Using the Worldwide Web, with links to many countries, as well as links to art, music, and history, students are encouraged to develop a multicultural, multidisciplinary approach to the study of algebra.

Interactive Learning. Discover for yourself exercises encourage students to actively participate in the learning process as they read the book. This feature encourages students to read with a pen in hand and interact with the text. Through the discovery exercises, they can explore problems in order to better understand them and their solutions.

Study Tips. Study tip boxes offer suggestions for problem solving, point out common student errors, and provide informal tips and suggestions. These invaluable hints appear in abundance throughout the book.

Enrichment Essays. Interspersed throughout the book are enrichment essays—many utilizing contemporary fine art—that germinate from ideas appearing in expository sections. Providing historical information and interdisciplinary connections, topics of some of the enrichment essays include relativity and the clock paradox, recursive processes, viruses of extraordinary virulence, carbon dating and artistic development, cubist art and inequalities, Halley's comet, and the Hubble Space Telescope.

Contemporary Fine Art. Algebra and fine art enable us to view the world in new and exciting ways. An extensive collection of contemporary, thought-provoking images selected by the author provides visual commentary to the book's unique collection of contemporary applications. The art adds an aesthetic sense to the book's pages, while visually reminding students of how algebra is connected to the whole spectrum of learning.

Extensive and Well-Organized Problem Sets. An extensive collection of problems is included in a problem set at the end of each section. Problem sets are organized into seven categories, making it easier to select homework problems consistent with the role of graphing utilities, critical thinking, collaborative learning, and writing in mathematics in your vision of the course. The categories include:

- *Practice Problems:* These problems give students an opportunity to practice the concepts that have been developed in the section.
- *Application Problems:* These problems include many relevant, up-to-date applications that will provoke student interest. Many of these problems offer students the opportunity to construct mathematical models from data.
- *True-False Critical Thinking Problems:* Several true-false problems that take students beyond the routine application of basic algebraic concepts are included in nearly every problem set. The true-false format is less intimidating than a more open-ended format, helping students gain confidence in divergent thinking skills.
- *Technology Problems:* These problems enable students to use graphing utilities to explore algebraic concepts and relevant mathematical models.
- *Writing in Mathematics:* These exercises are intended to help students communicate their mathematical knowledge by thinking and writing about algebraic topics.
- *Critical Thinking Problems:* This category contains the most challenging exercises in the problem sets. These open-ended problems were written to explore concepts while stimulating student thinking.
- *Group Activity Problems:* There are enough of these problems in each chapter to allow instructors to use collaborative learning quite extensively as an instructional format. It is hoped that many of these problems will result in interesting group discussions.

Chapter Introductions. Chapter introductions present fine art that is related either to the general idea of the chapter or to an application of algebra contained within the chapter.

Learning Objectives. Learning objectives open every section. The objectives are reinstated in the margin at their point of use.

Example Titles. All examples have titles so that students immediately see the purpose of each example.

Chapter Summaries. Inclusive summaries appear at the conclusion of each chapter, helping students to bring together what they have learned after reading the chapter.

Review Problems. A comprehensive collection of review problems follows the summary at the end of each chapter. A chapter test that focuses the review problems so that students can see if they are prepared for an actual class test follows the more extensive set of review problems. In addition, Chapters 2–6 conclude with cumulative review problems. Cumulative review problems covering the entire book appear in the appendix.

Printed Supplements

Instructor's Edition   (0-13-660259-2)   Consists of the complete student text, with a special Instructor's answer section at the back of the text containing answers to all exercises.

Instructor's Solutions Manual   (0-13-746629-3)
- Step-by-step solutions for every even-numbered exercise.
- Step-by-step solutions (even and odd) of the Chapter Review Problems, Chapter Tests, and Cumulative Reviews.

Test Item File   (0-13-761925-1)

Media Supplements

TestPro3 Computerized Testing
IBM Single-User   (0-13-746918-7)
MAC   (0-13-746877-6)
- Allows instructors to generate tests or drill worksheets from algorithms keyed to the text by chapter, section, and learning objective.
- Instructors select from thousands of test questions and hundreds of algorithms which generate different but equivalent equations.
- A user-friendly expression-building toolbar, editing and graphing capabilities are included.
- Customization toolbars allow for customized headers and layout options which provide instructors with the ability to add or delete workspace or add columns to conserve paper.

Printed Supplements

Student's Solution Manual   (0-13-746869-5)
- Contains complete step-by-step solutions for every odd-numbered exercise
- Contains complete step-by-step solutions for all (even and odd) Chapter Review Problems, Chapter Tests, and Cumulative Reviews.

Life on the Internet: Mathematics
- Free guide which provides a brief history of the Internet, discusses the use of the Worldwide Web, and describes how to find your way within the Internet and how to find others on it. Contact your local Prentice Hall representative for *Life on the Internet: Mathematics*.

NY Times Themes of the Times
- A free newspaper, created new each year, from Prentice Hall and *The New York Times*
- Interesting and current articles on mathematics
- Invites discussion and writing about mathematics

Media Supplements

MathPro Tutorial Software
- Fully networkable tutorial package for campus labs or individual use
- Designed to generate practice exercises based on the exercise sets in the text

- Algorithmically driven, providing the student with unlimited practice
- Generates graded and recorded practice problems with optional step-by-step tutorial
- Includes a complete glossary including graphics and cross-references to related words

Videotapes (0-13-746934-9)
- Instructional tapes in a lecture format featuring worked-out examples and exercises taken from each section of the text.
- Presentation by Professors Michael C. Mayne and (Biff) John D. Pietro of Riverside Community College in Riverside, California.

Acknowledgments

I wish to express my appreciation to all the reviewers for their helpful criticisms and suggestions. In particular I would like to thank:

Howard Anderson	*Skagit Valley College*
John Anderson	*Illinois Valley Community College*
Michael H. Andreoli	*Miami Dade Community College—North Campus*
Warren J. Burch	*Brevard Community College*
Alice Burstein	*Middlesex Community College*
Sandra Pryor Clarkson	*Hunter College*
Sally Copeland	*Johnson County Community College*
Robert A. Davies	*Cuyahoga Community College*
Ben Divers, Jr.	*Ferrum College*
Irene Doo	*Austin Community College*
Charles C. Edgar	*Onondaga Community College*
Susan Forman	*Bronx Community College*
Gary Glaze	*Eastern Washington University*
Jay Graening	*University of Arkansas*
Robert B. Hafer	*Brevard Community College*
Mary Lou Hammond	*Spokane Community College*
Donald Herrick	*Northern Illinois University*
Beth Hooper	*Golden West College*
Tracy Hoy	*College of Lake County*
Gary Knippenberg	*Lansing Community College*
Mary Koehler	*Cuyahoga Community College*
Hank Martel	*Broward Community College*
John Robert Martin	*Tarrant County Junior College*
Irwin Metviner	*State University of New York at Old Westbury*
Allen R. Newhart	*Parkersburg Community College*
Peg Pankowski	*Community College of Allegheny County—South Campus*
Nancy Ressler	*Oakton Community College*
Gayle Smith	*Lane Community College*
Dick Spangler	*Tacoma Community College*
Janette Summers	*University of Arkansas*
Robert Thornton	*Loyola University*
Lucy C. Thrower	*Francis Marion College*
Andrew Walker	*North Seattle Community College*

Additional acknowledgments are extended to Professor John (Biff) Pietro and Professor Michael C. Mayne of Riverside Community College, for creating the videotapes for each section of the book; Donna Gerken of Miami-Dade Community College, for writing the chapter projects; George Seki, Terry Lovelace, Cindy Trimble, and the mathematicians at Laurel Technical Services, for the Herculean task of solving all the book's problems, preparing the answer section and the solutions manuals, as well as serving as accuracy checker; Amy Mayfield, whose meticulous work as copy editor put me at my syntactical best; Clare Maxwell, photo researcher, for pursuing permissions for the book's extensive contemporary art collection and helping me to obtain wonderful replacement art when the permissions were not forthcoming; Paula Maylahn and Gus Vibal, for contributing to the book's wonderful look; the team of graphic artists at Academy Artworks, whose superb illustrations provide visual support to the verbal portions of the text; Frank Weihenig of Preparé, Inc. the book's compositor, for inputting hundreds of pages with hardly an error; and especially, Ingrid Mount of Elm Street Publishing Services, whose talents as supervisor of production kept every aspect of this very complex project moving through its many stages.

I am also grateful to Tony Palermino my development editor, who contributed invaluable edits and suggestions that resulted in a finished product that is both accessible and up to date. His influence on the book is extraordinary, with the pace in the text and problem sets a result of his remarkable talents.

Finally, I wish to thank the terrific team at Prentice Hall. Special acknowledgements go to Editor-in-Chief Jerome Grant and Acquisitions Editor Sally Denlow who collectively shaped this book into the culmination of my algebra series, set forth the initial vision for the series' design, and urged me onward in my quest to create the first algebra textbooks with an extensive collection of art. Credit is also due to Linda Behrens, managing editor, and Alan Fischer, manufacturing buyer, for keeping an ever-watchful eye on the production process, and Patrice Jones, marketing manager, and Patrick Murphy, marketing assistant, for their outstanding sales force and very impressive marketing efforts.

As I have done in all the books of this series, I must conclude by extending my heartfelt thanks to the gifted artists who gave me permission to share their exciting work, and, ultimately, their humanity within the pages of this book.

Robert Blitzer

The pages that follow highlight the features of the book discussed in the Preface.

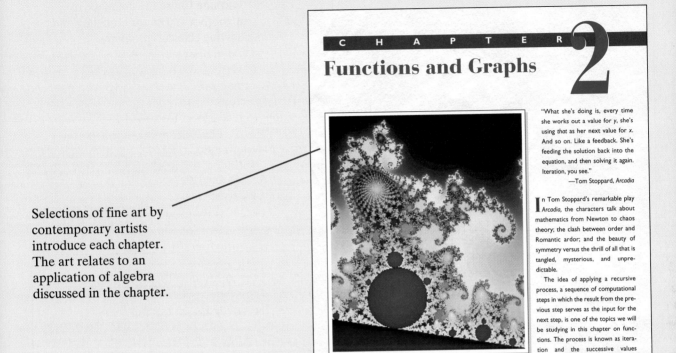

CHAPTER 2

Functions and Graphs

"What she's doing is, every time she works out a value for *y*, she's using *that* as her next value for *x*. And so on. Like a feedback. She's feeding the solution back into the equation, and then solving it again. Iteration, you see."
—Tom Stoppard, *Arcadia*

In Tom Stoppard's remarkable play *Arcadia*, the characters talk about mathematics from Newton to chaos theory; the clash between order and Romantic ardor; and the beauty of symmetry versus the thrill of all that is tangled, mysterious, and unpredictable.

The idea of applying a recursive process, a sequence of computational steps in which the result from the previous step serves as the input for the next step, is one of the topics we will be studying in this chapter on functions. The process is known as iteration and the successive values produced are called iterates. By using a function to define a recursive process to all numbers $a + bi$ in the complex plane, hauntingly beautiful visual images emerge. Reflecting the theme of self-similarity in nature, magnified portions of these images yield repetition of the original overall structure as well as new and unexpected patterns. The most famous of these images, the Mandelbrot set, transforms abstract mathematics into a tangible source of wonder and inspiration, serving as a symbol of the mathematical revolution known as chaos theory.

A magnification of the Mandelbrot set. R. F. Voss "29-Fold M-set Seahorse" computer-generated image. © 1990 R. F. Voss / IBM Research.

Selections of fine art by contemporary artists introduce each chapter. The art relates to an application of algebra discussed in the chapter.

SECTION 2.1 Introduction to Functions

Objectives

Solutions Manual   Tutorial   Video 4

1 Find the domain and range of a relation.
2 Determine whether a relation is a function.
3 Use $f(x)$ notation.
4 Interpret function values for mathematical models.
5 Find function values for piecewise functions.
6 Evaluate a function.
7 Find the domain of a function.

Supplement icons appear at the beginning of every section directing students to the book's supplements, including a series of videotapes created for every section.

Learning objectives open each section and are reinstated in the margin at their point of use.

EXAMPLE 7 Einstein's Special Relativity Models

Einstein's equations relate the mass, time, and length at rest (M_0, T_0, L_0) to the mass, time, and length (M, T, L) for a velocity v. The speed of light, c, is approximately 186,000 miles per second.

$$M = \frac{M_0}{\sqrt{1 - \frac{v^2}{c^2}}} \qquad T = \frac{T_0}{\sqrt{1 - \frac{v^2}{c^2}}} \qquad L = L_0 \sqrt{1 - \frac{v^2}{c^2}}$$

How fast would a futuristic starship that is 600 meters tall have to move so that it would measure only 84 meters tall from the perspective of an observer who looks up and sees the ship pass by?

Solution

$$L = L_0 \sqrt{1 - \frac{v^2}{c^2}}$$ This is Einstein's model for length.

$$84 = 600 \sqrt{1 - \frac{v^2}{c^2}}$$ Substitute L_0 (length at rest) = 600 and L (length at the velocity we must determine) = 84.

$$0.14 = \sqrt{1 - \frac{v^2}{c^2}}$$ Divide both sides by 600.

$$0.0196 = 1 - \frac{v^2}{c^2}$$ Square both sides.

$$0.0196c^2 = c^2 - v^2$$ Multiply both sides by c^2. Remember that c, the speed of light, is approximately 186,000 miles per second.

$$v^2 = 0.9804c^2$$ Isolate v^2 on the left.

$$v = \sqrt{0.9804c^2}$$ Assume that the starship is moving upward, so take only the positive root.

$$v \approx 0.99c$$

If the 600-meter tall futuristic starship moves at 99% the speed of light (approximately 184,140 miles per second), it will measure only 84 meters tall from the perspective of our stationary viewer. A before and after picture of the starship is shown in Figure 1.13. Observe that lengths perpendicular to the direction of motion are unchanged by the effect of speed, so the width of the starship remains unchanged. ∎

600 meters

Starship at Rest

84 meters

Change in starship's dimensions when moving at 99% of light's speed when viewed by an observer

Figure 1.13

The emphasis of the book is on learning to use the language of algebra as a tool for modeling and solving relevant problems.

Average and Minimum Salaries for Major League Baseball Players

Source: Based on statistics from the National Baseball League Players Association

Figure 2.19

EXAMPLE 8 Modeling Average Baseball Salaries

The graph in Figure 2.19 shows average and minimum salaries for major league baseball players. Write the equation that models the data for the line representing average salaries from 1990 through 1994. Then extrapolate from the data and predict the average salary for a major league baseball player in the year 2000.

Solution

The graph indicates that the average salary in 1990 was \$0.6 million, so we will use the data points (1990, 0.6) and (1994, 1.3). To write the point-slope equation of the line, we need two points (x_1, y_1), a fixed point, and m, the slope. Either ordered pair can be taken as (x_1, y_1). Using the smaller numbers, we have

$$x_1 = 1990 \quad \text{and} \quad y_1 = 0.6.$$

Illustrative examples are presented one step at a time, with each step clearly explained. Titles enable students to immediately see each illustrative example's purpose.

EXAMPLE 2 Carbon-14 Dating: The Dead Sea Scrolls

Carbon-14 (C-14) decays exponentially with a half-life of approximately 5715 years, meaning that after 5715 years a given amount of C-14 will have decayed to half the original amount.

a. Find the exponential decay model for C-14.
b. In 1947 earthenware jars containing what are known as the Dead Sea Scrolls were found by an Arab Bedouin herdsman. Analysis indicated that the scroll wrappings contained 76% of their original C-14. Estimate the age of the Dead Sea Scrolls.

Solution

a. We use the exponential decay model and the information about the half-life of C-14 to find k.

$$A = A_0 e^{kt}$$ This is the exponential decay model.

$$\frac{A_0}{2} = A_0 e^{k5715}$$ After 5715 years (t = 5715), $A = \frac{A_0}{2}$ (since the amount present (A) is half the original amount (A_0).)

$$\frac{1}{2} = e^{5715k}$$ Divide both sides of the equation by A_0.

$$\ln \frac{1}{2} = \ln e^{5715k}$$ Take the natural logarithm of both sides.

$$\ln \frac{1}{2} = 5715k$$ $\ln e^x = x$

$$k = \frac{\ln \frac{1}{2}}{5715} \approx -0.000121$$ Solve for k.

Substituting for k in the decay model, the model for C-14 is $A = A_0 e^{-0.000121t}$.

iscover for yourself

The quadratic inequalities in Examples 1 and 2 had solution sets consisting of a single interval and the union of two intervals. However, other possibilities can occur.

The graph of $y = 4x^2 - 8x + 7$ is shown in Figure 1.24. Use the graph to solve $4x^2 - 8x + 7 > 0$ and $4x^2 - 8x + 7 < 0$.

The graph of $y = x^2 - 4x + 4$ is shown in Figure 1.25. Use the graph to solve $x^2 - 4x + 4 > 0$ and $x^2 - 4x + 4 \leq 0$.

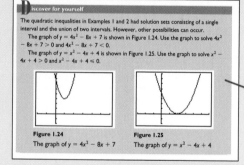

Figure 1.24
The graph of $y = 4x^2 - 8x + 7$

Figure 1.25
The graph of $y = x^2 - 4x + 4$

Discover for yourself exercises encourage students to actively participate in the learning process as they read the book.

tudy tip

The major problem generally encountered in the study of permutations and combinations is the ability to distinguish between each in a given real world situation. Remember that *order is important* when considering a *permutation*. Different orderings or arrangements produce different permutations. On the other hand, *order is not important* when considering a *combination*. A change in order does not produce a new combination.

Permutations	Combinations
$_nP_r = \dfrac{n!}{(n-r)!}$	$\dbinom{n}{r} = \dfrac{n!}{(n-r)!r!}$
Different orderings produce different permutations.	Different orderings do not produce different combinations.
Helpful words: Arrangement, Order, Schedule	**Helpful words:** Selection, Group, Committee, Subcommittee, Subset

Study tip boxes offer suggestions for problem solving and point out common student errors.

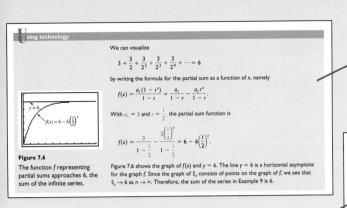
We can visualize

$$3 + \frac{3}{2} + \frac{3}{2^2} + \frac{3}{2^3} + \frac{3}{2^4} + \cdots = 6$$

by writing the formula for the partial sum as a function of x, namely

$$f(x) = \frac{a_1(1 - r^x)}{1 - r} = \frac{a_1}{1 - r} - \frac{a_1 r^x}{1 - r}.$$

With $a_1 = 3$ and $r = \frac{1}{2}$, the partial sum function is

$$f(x) = \frac{3}{1 - \frac{1}{2}} - \frac{3\left(\frac{1}{2}\right)^x}{1 - \frac{1}{2}} = 6 - 6\left(\frac{1}{2}\right)^x.$$

Figure 7.6
The function f representing partial sums approaches 6, the sum of the infinite series.

Figure 7.6 shows the graph of $f(x)$ and $y = 6$. The line $y = 6$ is a horizontal asymptote for the graph f. Since the graph of S_n consists of points on the graph of f, we see that $S_n \to 6$ as $n \to \infty$. Therefore, the sum of the series in Example 9 is 6.

Graphing utility screens enable students to visualize concepts. Visualization is enhanced through optional technology exercises in each problem set.

ENRICHMENT ESSAY

Carbon Dating and Artistic Development

Carbon dating is a method for estimating the age of organic material. Until recently, the oldest prehistoric cave paintings known were from the Lascaux cave in France. Charcoal from the site was analyzed, and the paintings were estimated to be 15,505 years old.

The artistic community was electrified by the discovery in 1995 of spectacular cave paintings in a limestone cavern near Lascaux. Carbon dating showed that the images, created by artists of remarkable talent, were 30,000 years old, making them the oldest cave paintings ever found. The artists seemed to have used the cavern's natural contours to heighten a sense of perspective. The quality of the painting suggests that the art of early humans did not mature steadily from primitive to sophisticated in any simple linear fashion.

Jean Clottes, France's foremost expert on prehistoric cave art, was moved by the sophisticated imagery of the 30,000-year-old work. "I remember standing in front of the paintings and being profoundly moved by the artistry," he exclaimed. "Tears were running down my cheeks. I was witnessing one of the world's great masterpieces."

Jean-Marie Chauvet / Sygma

Enrichment essays connect algebra to the whole spectrum of learning.

TABLE 4.2	Transformations Involving Exponential Functions	
Transformation	**Equation**	**Description**
Horizontal translation	$y = b^{x+c}$	Shifts the graph of $y = b^x$ to the left c units if $c > 0$ and to the right c units if $c < 0$.
Stretching or shrinking	$y = cb^x$	Stretches the graph of $y = b^x$ for $c > 1$ and shrinks the graph of $y = b^x$ for $0 < c < 1$, multiplying y-coordinates of $y = b^x$ by c.
Reflecting	$y = -b^x$	Reflects the graph of $y = b^x$ in the x-axis.
	$y = b^{-x}$	Reflects the graph of $y = b^x$ in the y-axis.
Vertical translation	$y = b^x + c$	Shifts the graph of $y = b^x$ upward c units if $c > 0$ and downward c units if $c < 0$.

Summary boxes organize and highlight key ideas.

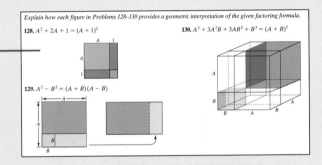

Explain how each figure in Problems 128–130 provides a geometric interpretation of the given factoring formula.

128. $A^2 + 2A + 1 = (A + 1)^2$

130. $A^3 + 3A^2B + 3AB^2 + B^3 = (A + B)^3$

129. $A^2 - B^2 = (A + B)(A - B)$

Geometry is integrated throughout the book.

Problem sets are organized into seven categories, making it easier to select homework problems consistent with the role of graphing utilities, critical thinking, collaborative learning, and writing exercises in your vision of the course.

Practice Problems

1. The graph of a function f is shown in the figure.

a. State the values of $f(-6), f(0)$, and $f(3)$.

b. State the intervals on which f is increasing and on which f is decreasing.

c. State the minimum value of f. At what value of x does this occur?

d. If the domain of f is $(-\infty, \infty)$, what is the function's range?

Practice Problems give students the chance to practice and master the concepts developed in each section.

Application Problems

67. The graph represents the probability of two people in the same room sharing a birthday as a function of the number of people in the room. Call the function f.

a. Explain why f has an inverse that is a function.

b. Describe in practical terms the meaning of $f^{-1}(0.25)$, $f^{-1}(0.5)$, and $f^{-1}(0.7)$.

Application Problems include relevant, up-to-date applications, offering students the opportunity to construct mathematical models from data.

True-False Critical Thinking Problems encourage thinking skills in a format that is not intimidating to most students.

Technology Problems enable students to use graphing utilities to explore algebraic concepts and mathematical models.

Writing exercises enable students to communicate their mathematical knowledge by thinking and writing about algebraic topics.

Critical Thinking Problems encourage students to explore concepts while stimulating rigorous, divergent thinking.

Group Activity Problems allow you to use collaborative learning as a teaching strategy.

Chapter projects at the end of each chapter use challenging and interesting applications of mathematics as a collaborative learning tool, and cultivate mathematical exploration on the Worldwide Web.

Chapter Review

SUMMARY

1. Basic Ideas about Functions
  a. A function is a correspondence between a first set, the domain, and a second set, the range, such that each element in the domain corresponds to exactly one element in the range.
  b. Using function notation $y = f(x)$, the letter f names the function, and $f(x)$, read "f of x" or "f at x" rep-

resents an expression for the value of the function at x. The value y, the dependent variable, is calculated after selecting a value for x, the independent variable.
  c. The domain of a function is the set of all values of the independent variable for which the function is defined. If a function is defined by an algebraic

> Inclusive summaries appear at the conclusion of each chapter so that students can bring together what they have learned.

CUMULATIVE REVIEW PROBLEMS (CHAPTERS P–4)

In Problems 1–2, simplify.

1. $\dfrac{3}{4x^2 + 4x + 1} + \dfrac{x+3}{2x^2 - x - 1} - \dfrac{2}{x-1}$

2. $\dfrac{1 - \dfrac{2}{x}}{1 - \dfrac{3}{x} + \dfrac{2}{x^2}}$

> Chapters 2–6 conclude with cumulative review problems.

REVIEW PROBLEMS

In Problems 1–13, identify each conic and sketch its graph by hand. For ellipses and hyperbolas, find the foci. For parabolas, identify the vertex, focus, and directrix. Use a graphing utility to verify all graphs.

1. $y^2 + 8x = 0$

2. $4x^2 + y^2 = 16$

3. $9x^2 - 16y^2 - 144 = 0$

4. $x^2 + 16y = 0$

5. $(y-2)^2 = -16x$

6. $\dfrac{(x-1)^2}{16} + \dfrac{(y+2)^2}{9} = 1$

7. $\dfrac{(x-2)^2}{25} - \dfrac{(y+3)^2}{16} = 1$

8. $(x-4)^2 = 4(y+1)$

9. $4x^2 - y^2 - 8x - 4y - 16 = 0$

10. $4x^2 - 40x - y + 102 = 0$

11. $4x^2 + 9y^2 + 24x - 36y + 36 = 0$

12. $y^2 - 4x - 10y + 21 = 0$

13. $4x^2 - y^2 + 8x + 4y + 4 = 0$

> Review problems appear throughout the book. Each chapter contains review problems.

CHAPTER 3 TEST

In Problems 1–2, use the vertex and intercepts to graph each quadratic function. Give the equation of the axis of symmetry.

1. $f(x) = (x-1)^2 - 4$

2. $f(x) = 2x^2 - 4x - 6$

3. The function $f(x) = -x^2 + 46x - 360$ models the daily profit ($f(x)$, in hundreds of dollars) for a company that manufactures x VCRs daily. How many VCRs should be manufactured each day to maximize profit? What is the maximum daily profit?

4. A rectangular plot of land along a river is to be fenced along 3 sides using 600 feet of fencing. No fencing is to be placed along the river's edge. Find the dimensions that maximize the enclosed area. What is the maximum area?

5. Consider the function $f(x) = x^3 - 5x^2 - 4x + 20$.

  a. Use factoring to find all zeros of f.

  b. Use the Leading Coefficient Test and the zeros of f to graph the function.

6. Use end behavior to explain why the graph at the top of the next column cannot be the graph of $f(x) = x^5 - x$. Then use intercepts to explain why the graph cannot represent $f(x) = x^5 - x$.

7. The graph of $f(x) = 6x^3 - 19x^2 + 16x - 4$ is shown in the figure.

  a. Based on the graph of f, find the integral root of the equation $6x^3 - 19x^2 + 16x - 4 = 0$.

  b. Use synthetic division to find the other two roots of $6x^3 - 19x^2 + 16x - 4 = 0$.

> Each chapter contains a chapter test so that students can prepare for an actual in-class exam.

Solving Equations and Inequalities

Systematic procedures for solving certain equations and inequalities are an important component of algebra. Problems 1–21 give you the opportunity to review these procedures. Solve each problem, expressing irrational solutions in simplified form and imaginary solutions in the form $a + bi$.

1. $\dfrac{2}{x+1} + \dfrac{3}{2x-3} = \dfrac{6x+1}{2x^2 - x - 3}$

2. $x(4x - 11) = 3$

3. $(x^2 - 5)^2 - 3(x^2 - 5) - 4 = 0$

4. $\sqrt{2x+3} - \sqrt{4x-1} = 1$

5. $x^{1/2} - 6x^{1/4} + 8 = 0$

6. $\dfrac{x-3}{4} + \dfrac{x+2}{3} \leq 2$

7. $-2 < 8 - 5x < 7$

8. $|2x + 1| \leq 1$

9. $6x^2 - 6 < 5x$

10. $\dfrac{1-x}{3+x} < 4$

11. $x^3 - x^2 - 4x + 4 = 0$

12. $3x^3 + 4x^2 - 7x + 2 = 0$

13. $e^{14-7x} - 53 = 24$

14. $e^{2x} - 10e^x + 9 = 0$

15. $\log_2(x+1) + \log_2(x-1) = 3$

16. $\ln(3x) + \ln(x+2) = \ln 9$

17. (Solve using matrices.)
$$\begin{aligned} x - y + z &= 17 \\ -4x + y + 5z &= -2 \\ 2x + 3y + z &= 8 \end{aligned}$$

18. (Solve for x only using Cramer's rule.)
$$\begin{aligned} x + 2y - z &= 1 \\ x + 3y - 2z &= -1 \\ 2x - y + z &= 6 \end{aligned}$$

19. $\dfrac{x^2}{4} + \dfrac{y^2}{16} = 1$
$x - y = 2$

20. $4x^2 + 3y^2 = 48$
$3x^2 + 2y^2 = 35$

21. $3x^2 - 2xy + 3y^2 = 34$
$x^2 + y^2 = 17$

Graphs and Graphing

Throughout the book, we have used graphs to help visualize a problem's solution. We have also studied graphing equations and inequalities in the rectangular coordinate system. Problems 22–36 focus on problem solving with graphs.

22. Use the graphs shown in the figure to describe how the graph of $h(x) = (x+2)^3 + 1$ is obtained from the graph of $f(x) = x^3$. Include the graph of g in your description.

Gender Ratios in the U.S.

> Cumulative review problems covering the entire book appear in the Appendix.

To the Student

The process of learning mathematics requires that you do at least three things—read the book, work the problems, and get your questions answered if you are stuck. This book has been written so that you can learn directly from its pages. All concepts are carefully explained, important definitions and procedures are set off in boxes, and worked-out examples that present solutions in a step-by-step manner appear throughout. Study tip boxes offer hints and suggestions, and often point out common errors to avoid. Discovery boxes encourage you to actively participate in the learning process as you read the book. A great deal of attention has been given to show you the vast and unusual applications of algebra in order to make your learning experience both interesting and relevant. As you begin your studies, I would like to offer some specific suggestions for using this book and for being successful in algebra.

- *Read the book.*
  a. Begin with the chapter introduction. Enjoy the art while you obtain a general idea of what the chapter is about.
  b. Move on to the objectives and the introduction to a particular section. The objectives will tell you exactly what you should be able to do once you have completed the section. Each objective is restated in the margin at the point in the section where the objective is taught.
  c. At a slow and deliberate pace, read the section with pen (or pencil) in hand. Move through the illustrative examples with great care. These worked-out examples provide a model for doing the problems in the problem sets. Be sure to read all the hints and suggestions in the Study tip boxes. Your pen is in hand for the Discover for yourself exercises that are intended to encourage you to actively participate in the learning process as you read the book. The Discover for yourself exercises let you explore problems in order to understand them and their solutions better, so be sure not to jump over these valuable discovery experiences in your reading.
  d. Enjoy the Enrichment essays and the contemporary art that is intended to make your reading more interesting and show you how algebra is connected to the whole spectrum of learning.

As you proceed through the reading, do not give up if you do not understand every single word. Things will become clearer as you read on and see how various procedures are applied to specific worked-out examples.

- *Work problems every day and check your answers.* The way to learn mathematics is by *doing* mathematics, which means by *solving problems.* The more problems you work, the better you will become at solving problems which, in turn, will make you a better algebra student.
  a. Work the assigned problems in each problem set. Problem sets are organized into seven categories. Minimally, you should work all odd-numbered problems in the first two categories (Practice Problems and Application Problems). Answers to most odd-numbered problems are given in the back of the book. Once you have completed a problem, be sure to check your answer. If you made an error, find out what it was. Ask questions in class about homework problems you don't understand.
  b. Problem sets also include critical thinking problems, technology problems, writing exercises, and group activity learning experiences. Don't panic! You are not expected to work every problem, or even all the odd-numbered problems, in each problem set. This vast collection of problems provides options for your learning style and your instructor's teaching methods. You may be assigned some problems from one or more of these categories. Problems in the critical thinking categories are the most difficult, intended to stimulate your ability to think and reason. Thinking about a particular question, even if you are confused and somewhat frustrated, can eventually lead to new insights.
- *Prepare for chapter exams.* After completing a chapter, study the summary, work assigned problems from the chapter review problems, and work all the problems in the chapter test.
- *Review continuously.* Working review problems lets you remember the algebra you learned for a much longer period of time. Cumulative review problems appear at the end of each chapter, beginning with Chapter 2. The book's appendix contains review problems covering the entire course. By working the appendix problems assigned by your professor, you will be able to bring together the procedures and problem-solving strategies learned throughout the course.
- *Attend all lectures.* No book is intended to be a substitute for the valuable insights and interactions that occur in the classroom. In addition to arriving for a lecture on time and prepared, you might find it helpful to read the section that will be covered in class beforehand so that you have a clear idea of the new material that will be discussed.
- *Use the supplements that come with this book.* A solutions manual that contains worked-out solutions to the book's odd-numbered problems and all review problems, as well as a series of videotapes created for every section of the book, are among the supplements created to help you learn algebra. Ask your instructor what supplements are available and where you can find them.

Algebra is often viewed as the foundation for more advanced mathematics. It is my hope that this book will make algebra accessible, relevant, and an interesting body of knowledge in and of itself.

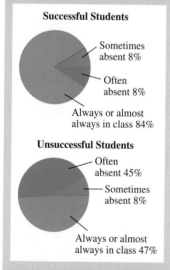

Discover for yourself

What conclusion can you draw from these circle graphs about student success and attending lectures?

Successful Students

Sometimes absent 8%

Often absent 8%

Always or almost always in class 84%

Unsuccessful Students

Often absent 45%

Sometimes absent 8%

Always or almost always in class 47%

Source: *The Psychology of College Success: A Dynamic Approach*, by permission of H. C. Lindgren, 1969

P

Prerequisites: Fundamental Concepts of Algebra

This chapter reviews topics from intermediate algebra that are prerequisites for the study of college algebra. Since the ideas of algebra build in a logical and orderly manner from the fundamentals, it is important to have your feet planted firmly on the ground. By reviewing and mastering topics about real numbers, graphing, exponents, polynomials, factoring, fractional expressions, and complex numbers, you will be ready to advance in your ability to use algebra to solve problems and describe our world in a significant way.

Using algebra to meaningfully describe our world is the primary focus of this book.

René Magritte, "Le Modele Rouge"
© 1998 C. Herscovici, Brussels /
Artists Rights Society (ARS),
New York. Private Collection. Art
Resource, NY.

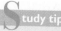
tudy tip

You can use the review exercises at the end of this chapter as a pretest to determine any weaknesses that you might have with the prerequisite topics that are reviewed in the chapter.

SECTION P.I The Real Number System

Objectives

Solutions Manual   **Tutorial**   **Video I**

1 Recognize subsets of the real numbers.
2 Use set-builder and interval notations.
3 Find unions and intersections of sets.
4 Evaluate absolute value.
5 Use absolute value to express distance.

Numbers and their properties have intrigued humankind since the beginning of civilization. In this section, we describe the subsets of the real numbers, using the real number line to order these numbers.

I Recognize subsets of the real numbers.

The Set of Real Numbers

The sets that make up the real numbers are summarized in Table P.1. We refer to these sets as *subsets* of the real numbers, meaning that all elements in each subset are also elements in the set of real numbers.

When we combine the set of all irrational numbers with the set of all rational numbers, we obtain the set of all *real numbers*. Figure P.1 shows a diagram of the subsets of the real numbers.

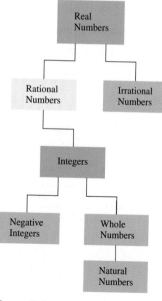

Figure P.I

The real number system

TABLE P.I	Important Subsets of the Real Numbers	
Name	**Description**	**Examples**
Natural numbers	$\{1, 2, 3, 4, 5, ...\}$ These numbers are used for counting and are also called the *counting numbers*.	87 2,369 $\sqrt{36}$ (or 6)
Whole numbers	$\{0, 1, 2, 3, 4, 5, ...\}$ The whole numbers add 0 to the set of natural numbers.	0, 87 $\frac{18}{3}$ (or 6)
Integers	$\{..., -5, -4, -3, -2, -1, 0, 1, 2, 3, 4, 5, ...\}$ The integers add the opposites of the natural numbers to the set of whole numbers.	$-87, -14,$ $-\sqrt{25}$ (or -5), 0, 14, 87

TABLE P.I *(cont.)* Important Subsets of the Real Numbers		
Name	**Description**	**Examples**
Rational numbers	These numbers can be expressed as an integer divided by a nonzero integer: $\frac{a}{b}$; a and b are integers; $b \neq 0$. In decimal form, rational numbers either terminate or repeat.	$\frac{3}{4}$ (or 0.75) ($a = 3$, $b = 4$) $-\frac{3}{11} = -0.2727... = -0.\overline{27}$ ($a = -3$, $b = 11$) $87 = \frac{87}{1}$ ($a = 87$, $b = 1$)
Irrational numbers	This is the set of numbers whose decimal representations do not repeat and do not terminate. Irrational numbers cannot be expressed as an integer divided by an integer.	$\sqrt{2} \approx 1.414214$ $-\sqrt{3} \approx -1.73205$ $\pi \approx 3.142$ $-\frac{\pi}{2} \approx -1.571$

Study tip

The symbol $\approx$ is read "is approximately equal to." The reason that

$$\sqrt{2} \approx 1.414214$$

is that $(1.414214)^2$ is not exactly 2.

EXAMPLE I   **Classifying Real Numbers**

List the numbers in the set

$$\left\{-7, -\tfrac{3}{4}, 0, 0.\overline{6}, \sqrt{5}, \pi, 6\tfrac{1}{4}, 7.3, \sqrt{81}\right\}$$

that belong to each subset of the real numbers:

a. Natural numbers
b. Whole numbers
c. Integers
d. Rational numbers
e. Irrational numbers
f. Real numbers

Solution

a. Natural numbers: The only natural number in the set is $\sqrt{81}$ since $\sqrt{81} = 9$. (9 multiplied by itself is 81.)

b. Whole numbers: The whole numbers consist of the natural numbers and 0. The elements of the set that are whole numbers are 0 and $\sqrt{81}$.

c. Integers: The integers consist of the natural numbers, 0, and the negatives of the natural numbers. The elements of the set that are integers are $\sqrt{81}$, 0, and -7.

d. Rational numbers: All numbers in the set that can be expressed as the quotient of two integers are rational numbers. The rational numbers are -7 ($-7 = \frac{-7}{1}$), $-\frac{3}{4}$, 0 ($0 = \frac{0}{1}$), $0.\overline{6}$ ($0.\overline{6} = 0.6666 \dots = \frac{2}{3}$), $6\frac{1}{4}$ ($6\frac{1}{4} = \frac{25}{4}$), 7.3 ($7.3 = 7\frac{3}{10} = \frac{73}{10}$), and $\sqrt{81}$ ($\sqrt{81} = \frac{9}{1}$).

e. Irrational numbers: The irrational numbers in the set are $\sqrt{5}$ ($\sqrt{5} \approx 2.236$) and π ($\pi \approx 3.14$). Both $\sqrt{5}$ and π are only approximately equal to 2.236 and 3.14, respectively. In decimal form, $\sqrt{5}$ and π neither terminate nor have repeating patterns.

f. Real numbers: All the numbers in the set are real numbers.

The Real Number Line

The *real number line* is a graph used to represent the set of real numbers (Figure P.2). An arbitrary point, called the *origin*, is labeled 0; units to the right of the origin are *positive* and units to the left of the origin are *negative*.

Every real number corresponds to exactly one point on the real number line.

Figure P.2

The real number line

Every point on the real number line corresponds to exactly one real number.

Figure P.3

A one-to-one correspondence between real numbers and points on a number line

Figure P.3 illustrates that every real number corresponds to a point on the number line and every point on the number line corresponds to a real number. For this reason, we say that there is a *one-to-one correspondence* between all the real numbers and all points on a real number line. The real number corresponding to a particular point on the line is called the *coordinate* of the point. If you draw a point on the real number line corresponding to a real number, you are *plotting* the real number.

Ordering the Real Numbers

Figure P.4

a is less than *b*: *a* is to the left of *b*

The real number line is useful in demonstrating the *order* of real numbers. We say that the real number *a is less than* real number *b*, written $a < b$, if *a* is to the left of *b* on the number line. Equivalently, *b is greater than a*, written $b > a$, if *b* is to the right of *a* on the number line (Figure P.4).

The symbols $<$ and $>$ are sometimes combined with an equal sign.

The symbols $\leq$ and $\geq$		
Symbols	**Meaning**	**Examples**
$a \leq b$	*a* is less than or equal to *b*.	$3 \leq 7$ (because $3 < 7$) $7 \leq 7$ (because $7 = 7$)
$b \geq a$	*b* is greater than or equal to *a*.	$7 \geq 3$ (because $7 > 3$) $-5 \geq -5$ (because $-5 = -5$)

2 Use set-builder and interval notations.

Intervals

Inequalities are used to describe subsets of real numbers, called *intervals*. For instance, the inequality $x \leq 3$ describes all real numbers less than or equal to 3. Using *set-builder* notation, we write

$$\{x \mid x \leq 3\}$$

reading this as "the set of all real numbers *x* such that *x* is less than or equal to 3." Using *interval* notation, we write

$$(-\infty, 3].$$

Figure P.5

The interval $(-\infty, 3]$

As shown in Figure P.5, the square bracket at 3 shows that 3 *is* to be included. The negative infinity symbol $-\infty$ does not represent a real number. It indicates that the interval includes all real numbers less than or equal to 3, extending indefinitely to the left.

Let's consider another example of a subset of real numbers that can be expressed in both set-builder and interval notations. The inequality $x > -2$ describes all real numbers greater than -2. Using *set-builder* notation, we write

$$\{x \mid x > -2\}$$

reading this as "the set of all real numbers x such that x is greater than -2." Using *interval* notation, we write

$$(-2, \infty).$$

Figure P.6

The interval $(-2, \infty)$

As shown in Figure P.6, the parenthesis at -2 indicates that -2 is *not* included in the interval. The infinity symbol ∞ does not represent a real number. It indicates that the interval extends indefinitely to the right.

Some inequalities do not extend indefinitely in positive or negative directions. For example, the inequality $-2 < x \le 4$ indicates that $x > -2$ and $x \le 4$. This *double* or *compound* inequality denotes all real numbers between -2 and 4, excluding -2 but including 4. Using set-builder notation, we write

$$\{x \mid -2 < x \le 4\}$$

reading this as "the set of all real numbers x such that x is greater than -2 and less than or equal to 4." Using interval notation, we write

$$(-2, 4].$$

Figure P.7 illustrates that the parenthesis at -2 excludes -2 from the set and the square bracket at 4 includes 4 as a member of the set.

Table P.2 lists the nine possible types of intervals.

Figure P.7

The interval $(-2, 4]$

TABLE P.2	Intervals on the Real Number Line	

Let a and b be real numbers such that $a < b$.

Interval Notation	Set-Builder Notation	Graph
(a, b)	$\{x \mid a < x < b\}$	
$[a, b]$	$\{x \mid a \le x \le b\}$	
$[a, b)$	$\{x \mid a \le x < b\}$	
$(a, b]$	$\{x \mid a < x \le b\}$	
(a, ∞)	$\{x \mid x > a\}$	
$[a, \infty)$	$\{x \mid x \ge a\}$	
$(-\infty, b)$	$\{x \mid x < b\}$	
$(-\infty, b]$	$\{x \mid x \le b\}$	
$(-\infty, \infty)$	$\mathbb{R}$ (set of all real numbers)	

EXAMPLE 2 **Intervals and Inequalities**

Express the intervals in terms of inequalities and graph:

a. $(-1, 4]$ **b.** $[2.5, 4]$ **c.** $(-4, \infty)$

Solution

a. $(-1, 4] = \{x \mid -1 < x \leq 4\}$

b. $[2.5, 4] = \{x \mid 2.5 \leq x \leq 4\}$

c. $(-4, \infty) = \{x \mid x > -4\}$

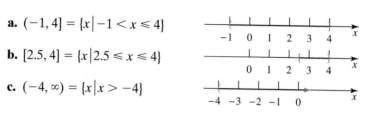

Phrases such as "at most" or "at least" indicate that inequalities are used in everyday language. Example 3 shows how certain English expressions can be written in both set-builder and interval notations.

EXAMPLE 3 **The English Language and Inequalities**

Rewrite each English sentence in the left column in both set-builder and interval notations.

Solution

	Set-Builder Notation	Interval Notation
x is less than 5.	$\{x \mid x < 5\}$	$(-\infty, 5)$
x is greater than or equal to 3.	$\{x \mid x \geq 3\}$	$[3, \infty)$
x lies between -2 and 5, excluding -2 and 5.	$\{x \mid -2 < x < 5\}$	$(-2, 5)$
x is greater than or equal to 2 and less than 7.	$\{x \mid 2 \leq x < 7\}$	$[2, 7)$
x is nonnegative. "Nonnegative" indicates a number is greater than or equal to 0.	$\{x \mid x \geq 0\}$	$[0, \infty)$
x is at most 4. "At most" means $\leq$.	$\{x \mid x \leq 4\}$	$(-\infty, 4]$
x is at least 2. "At least" means $\geq$.	$\{x \mid x \geq 2\}$	$[2, \infty)$
x is positive but not more than 5. "Not more than" means $\leq$.	$\{x \mid 0 < x \leq 5\}$	$(0, 5]$

3 Find unions and intersections of sets.

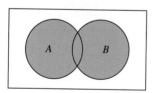

$A \cup B$ is the set of all elements in A or B, or in both A and B.

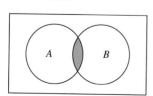

$A \cap B$ is the set of elements common in both A and B.

Union and Intersection of Sets

If A and B are sets, then their *union*, $A \cup B$, is the set containing all elements that are in A or in B (or in both A and B). Their *intersection*, $A \cap B$, is the set containing all elements that are in both A and B.

Figure P.8

$(1, 4) \cap [2, 6] = [2, 4]$

Figure P.9

$(-2, \infty) \cap (3, \infty) = (3, \infty)$

Figure P.10

$(-2, -1) \cap (2, 3) = \varnothing$

tudy tip

The intersection of two intervals is the region where their graphs overlap.

Figure P.11

$(1, 4) \cup [2, 6] = (1, 6]$

Figure P.12

$(-2, \infty) \cup (3, \infty) = (-2, \infty)$

Figure P.13

$(-2, -1) \cup (2, 3)$ is not a single interval

Union and intersection of sets

Union

$A \cup B$ is the set of all elements that are in set A or in set B, or in both A and B.

Intersection

$A \cap B$ is the set of all elements that are in set A *and* in set B.

EXAMPLE 4   **Finding the Union and Intersection of Sets**

Express each set in interval notation:

a. $(1, 4) \cap [2, 6]$ **b.** $(-2, \infty) \cap (3, \infty)$
c. $(-2, -1) \cap (2, 3)$ **d.** $(1, 4) \cup [2, 6]$
e. $(-2, \infty) \cup (3, \infty)$ **f.** $(-2, -1) \cup (2, 3)$

Solution

a. To find $(1, 4) \cap [2, 6]$, we graph each set above the number line and then locate the interval on the number line common to both. Figure P.8 illustrates that numbers common to both intervals begin at 2 and extend up to but not including 4. Thus,

   $(1, 4) \cap [2, 6] = [2, 4)$.

b. Figure P.9 illustrates that numbers common to both intervals are all real numbers greater than 3. Thus,

   $(-2, \infty) \cap (3, \infty) = (3, \infty)$.

c. Figure P.10 shows that there are no numbers common to the two intervals. Their intersection is a set with no elements, called the *empty set* or the *null set*, denoted by $\varnothing$. Thus,

   $(-2, -1) \cap (2, 3) = \varnothing$.

In parts (d)–(f), the union of the two intervals consists of the real numbers that are in either or both of the intervals.

d. To find $(1, 4) \cup [2, 6]$, we graph each set above the number line and then locate the interval on the number line that unites or joins these intervals. As shown in Figure P.11, numbers in either or both intervals are all real numbers greater than 1, extending up to and including 6. Thus,

   $(1, 4) \cup [2, 6] = (1, 6]$.

e. Figure P.12 illustrates that uniting both intervals shown above the number line results in all real numbers greater than -2. Thus,

   $(-2, \infty) \cup (3, \infty) = (-2, \infty)$.

f. Figure P.13 indicates that the union of the intervals consists of real numbers that are either in $(-2, -1)$ or $(2, 3)$. We cannot express the answer as a single interval. Using interval notation, the best we can do is to write

   $(-2, -1) \cup (2, 3)$.

Using set-builder notation, we could express this union as

$$\{x \mid -2 < x < -1 \quad \text{or} \quad 2 < x < 3\}.$$

4 Evaluate absolute value.

Figure P.14

Absolute value as the distance from 0

Absolute Value and Distance

The symbol $|x|$ is read "the absolute value of x." Geometrically, the absolute value of x is the distance between both the real number x and the origin on the real number line (Figure P.14). Algebraically, we can define the absolute value of the real number x as follows.

> **Definition of absolute value**
>
> $$|x| = \begin{cases} x & \text{if } x \geq 0 \\ -x & \text{if } x < 0 \end{cases}$$

The case $x \geq 0$ tells us that the absolute value of a nonnegative number is the number itself. Thus,

$$|5| = 5 \qquad |\pi| = \pi \qquad \left|\frac{1}{3}\right| = \frac{1}{3} \qquad |0| = 0$$

The case $x < 0$ tells us that the absolute value of a real number is never negative. For example,

$$|-3| = -(-3) = 3 \qquad |-\pi| = -(-\pi) = \pi \qquad \left|-\frac{1}{3}\right| = -\left(-\frac{1}{3}\right) = \frac{1}{3}$$

EXAMPLE 5 Evaluating Absolute Value

Evaluate by rewriting as an equivalent expression without absolute value bars:

a. $|13|$ **b.** $|-19|$ **c.** $|\sqrt{3} - 1|$ **d.** $|2 - \pi|$

e. $\dfrac{|x|}{x}$ if $x > 0$ **f.** $\dfrac{|x|}{x}$ if $x < 0$

Solution

a. $|13| = 13$

b. $|-19| = -(-19) = 19$

c. Since $\sqrt{3} \approx 1.7$, the expression inside the absolute value bars is positive. The absolute value of a positive number is the number itself. Thus,

$$|\sqrt{3} - 1| = \sqrt{3} - 1.$$

d. Since $\pi \approx 3.14$, the number inside the absolute value bars is negative. The absolute value of x when $x < 0$ is $-x$. Thus,

$$|2 - \pi| = -(2 - \pi) = \pi - 2.$$

e. If $x > 0$, then $|x| = x$. Thus,

$$\frac{|x|}{x} = \frac{x}{x} = 1.$$

f. If $x < 0$, then $|x| = -x$. Thus,

$$\frac{|x|}{x} = \frac{-x}{x} = -1.$$ ∎

Next, we list several basic properties of absolute value. Each of these properties can be derived from the definition of absolute value.

Discover for yourself

Verify the first three properties in the box on the right for $a = 4$ and $a = -5$. Verify properties 4–6 for each of the following pairs of values:

$a = 4, b = 5; a = -4, b = -5;$

$a = 4, b = -5; a = -4, b = 5$

When does equality occur in the triangle inequality and when does inequality occur? Verify your observation with additional number pairs.

Properties of absolute value

For all real numbers a and b,

1. $|a| \geqslant 0$ 2. $|-a| = |a|$
3. $a \leqslant |a|$

4. $|ab| = |a|\,|b|$ 5. $\left|\dfrac{a}{b}\right| = \dfrac{|a|}{|b|}, \quad b \neq 0$

6. $|a + b| \leqslant |a| + |b|$ (called the triangle inequality)

Distance on a Number Line

If a and b are any real numbers, the distance between a and b is the absolute value of their difference.

Distance between two points on the real number line

The distance between real numbers a and b is

$$|a - b| = |b - a|.$$

5 Use absolute value to express distance.

EXAMPLE 6   Absolute Value and Distance

Express the distance between the numbers -5 and 3 using absolute value. Then evaluate the absolute value.

Solution

The distance between -5 and 3 can be expressed in two equivalent ways, namely,

$$|-5 - 3| = |-8|$$
$$|3 - (-5)| = |8|$$

We evaluate these absolute values as

$$|-8| = 8$$
$$|8| = 8$$

Figure P.15

The distance between -5 and 3 is 8.

Figure P.15 verifies that the calculation is correct. ∎

EXAMPLE 7   **Absolute Value and Distance**

Rewrite using absolute value: The distance between x and the origin is 2. What are the possible values for x?

Solution

Figure P.16

$|x| = 2$ means $x = 2$ or $x = -2$

Using $|x| = 2$, there are two numbers whose distance from the origin on the number line is 2, namely, -2 and 2, as shown in Figure P.16. Generalizing from this example, if c is any positive number and $|x| = c$, then $x = c$ or $x = -c$. ∎

PROBLEM SET P.1

Practice Problems

In Problems 1–4, indicate which numbers in the given set are **a.** *Natural numbers* **b.** *Whole numbers* **c.** *Integers* **d.** *Rational numbers* **e.** *Irrational numbers*

1. $\{-10, -\sqrt{2}, -\frac{3}{4}, 0, \frac{4}{5}, \sqrt{4}, \pi, 7, \frac{18}{2}, 100\}$

2. $\{-5, -\sqrt{9}, -\frac{4}{3}, 0, \frac{2}{3}, \sqrt{7}, 2\pi, \frac{30}{2}, 90\}$

3. $\{-\sqrt[3]{8}, \frac{0}{3}, \sqrt[3]{7}, \sqrt{\frac{4}{9}}, 1.\overline{126}\}$

4. $\{-\sqrt[3]{125}, \frac{0}{6}, \sqrt[4]{7}, \sqrt{\frac{9}{25}}, 3.\overline{47}\}$

In Problems 5–18, express each interval in terms of an inequality and graph the interval on a number line.

5. $(1, 6]$
6. $(-2, 4]$
7. $[-5, 2)$
8. $[-4, 3)$
9. $[-3, 1]$
10. $[-2, 5]$
11. $(2, \infty)$
12. $(3, \infty)$
13. $[-3, \infty)$
14. $[-5, \infty)$
15. $(-\infty, 3)$
16. $(-\infty, 2)$
17. $(-\infty, 5.5)$
18. $(-\infty, 3.5]$

In Problems 19–34, express each English phrase in both set-builder and interval notations.

19. x is less than 6.
20. x is greater than 2.
21. x is greater than or equal to -1.
22. x is less than or equal to -3.
23. x lies between 5 and 12, excluding 5 and 12.
24. x lies between -4 and 7, excluding -4 and 7.
25. x lies between 2 and 13, excluding 2 and including 13.
26. x lies between -7 and 2, including -7 and excluding 2.
27. x is at most 6.
28. x is at least 3.
29. x is at least 2 and at most 5.
30. x is at least -3 and at most 2.
31. x is not more than 60.
32. x is not more than 32.
33. x is negative and at least -2.
34. x is not positive and at least -5.

Express each set in Problems 35–54 in interval notation.

35. $(1, 5) \cap [2, 7]$
36. $(1, 3) \cap [2, 6]$
37. $(-1, \infty) \cap (5, \infty)$
38. $(-3, \infty) \cap (7, \infty)$
39. $(-\infty, 2) \cap (-\infty, 4)$
40. $(-\infty, 1) \cap (-\infty, 5)$
41. $(-\infty, 3] \cap (-\infty, 6)$
42. $(-\infty, 7] \cap (-\infty, 10)$
43. $(-3, -1) \cap [2, 4]$
44. $(-2, 0) \cap [3, 5]$
45. $(1, 5) \cup (2, 7)$
46. $(1, 3) \cup [2, 6]$
47. $(-1, \infty) \cup (5, \infty)$
48. $(-3, \infty) \cup (7, \infty)$
49. $(-\infty, 2) \cup (-\infty, 4)$
50. $(-\infty, 1) \cup (-\infty, 5)$
51. $(-\infty, 3] \cup (-\infty, 6)$
52. $(-\infty, 7) \cup (-\infty, 10)$
53. $(-3, -1) \cup [2, 4]$
54. $(-2, 0) \cup [3, 5]$

In Problems 55–68, evaluate each expression.

55. $|300|$

56. $|705|$

57. $|-203|$

58. $|-109|$

59. $|12 - \pi|$

60. $|7 - \pi|$

61. $|\pi - 12|$

62. $|\pi - 7|$

63. $|\sqrt{2} - 5|$

64. $|\sqrt{5} - 13|$

65. $\frac{-3}{|-3|}$

66. $\frac{-7}{|-7|}$

67. $||-3| - |-7||$

68. $||-5| - |-13||$

In Problems 69–80, express the distance between the given numbers using absolute value. Then find the distance by evaluating the absolute value expression.

69. 2 and 17

70. 4 and 15

71. −2 and 5

72. −6 and 8

73. −19 and −4

74. −26 and −3

75. −3.6 and −1.4

76. −5.4 and −1.2

77. $-\frac{3}{10}$ and $\frac{2}{5}$

78. $-\frac{7}{10}$ and $\frac{4}{5}$

79. $-9\frac{1}{4}$ and $-6\frac{1}{2}$

80. $-12\frac{1}{5}$ and $-2\frac{3}{4}$

In Problems 81–88, use absolute value notation to describe each situation.

81. The distance between x and the origin is 7.

82. The distance between x and the origin is 13.

83. x is at least 6 units from the origin.

84. x is at most 6 units from the origin.

85. The distance between mile marker 72 and mile marker 99.

86. The distance between mile marker 54 and mile marker 76.

87. The distance between y and 7 is no more than 3.

88. The distance between y and −4 is at least 10.

Application Problems

The bar graph shows the average number of times U.S. adults report to have sex per year. In Problems 89–94, you are given the number of times a particular person in an age group claims to have sex per year. Find the amount by which this number differs from the average number shown in the graph.

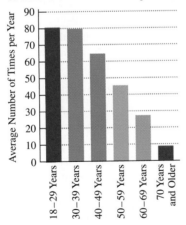

Sex through the Years, by Age
(As Self-reported, the Average Number of Times U.S. Adults Have Sex per Year)

Source: National Opinion Research Council. Adapted from *The Macmillan Visual Almanac.*

	x: An estimate of the average number of times U.S. adults in the designated age group have sex per year	y: The number of times a particular person in the age group has sex per year	$|x - y|$
89. Ages 18–29		180	
90. Ages 30–39		60	
91. Ages 40–49		30	
92. Ages 50–59		100	
93. Ages 60–69		2	
94. Ages 70 and older		85	

The bar graph shows the top ten reasons for doctors' office visits each year in the United States. If x represents the number of visits in millions, write the reason or reasons described in Problems 95–102.

95. $x > 25$

96. $x > 30$

97. x is in the interval $[10, 20)$.

98. x is in the interval $[15, 25)$.

99. x is at least 20.

100. x is at most 20.

101. $15 \leq x < 30$

102. $20 \leq x \leq 25$

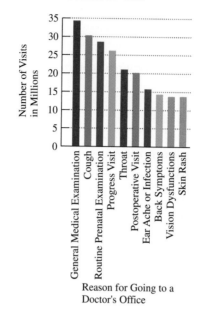

Source: National Center for Health Statistics, U.S. Department of Health and Human Services

True–False Critical Thinking Problems

103. Which one of the following is true?

   a. There are at least two whole numbers that are not natural numbers.

   b. Using interval notation, the set $\{x \mid x < 6\}$ can be expressed as $[-\infty, 6)$.

   c. If a is a positive number and b is a negative number, then $|a + b| = |a| + |b|$.

   d. The least natural number can be expressed as $\left| \dfrac{27 - 5}{5 - 27} \right|$.

104. Which one of the following is true?

   a. Some integers are not rational numbers.

   b. Irrational numbers cannot be located on a real number line because in decimal form they neither terminate nor repeat.

   c. The graph of the union of two intervals can never be the same as the graph of the intersection of the same two intervals.

   d. If $x < -1$, then $\dfrac{|x + 1|}{x + 1}$ simplifies to -1.

Technology Problems

In Problems 105–106, use a calculator to order the real numbers from smallest to largest.

105. $\dfrac{4243}{3000}, \dfrac{873}{618}, \dfrac{55}{37}, \sqrt{2}, \dfrac{112}{80}$

106. $2.23\overline{20}, \sqrt{5}, \dfrac{37,961}{17,000}, \dfrac{111,525}{50,000}, \sqrt{17} - \sqrt{13}$

Writing in Mathematics

107. Consider the rational number $\frac{a}{b}$. Suppose that a is a natural number that does not vary, but b gets large. Describe what happens to $\frac{a}{b}$.

108. Consider the rational number $\frac{a}{b}$. Suppose that a is a natural number that does not vary, but b gets close to zero. Describe what happens to $\frac{a}{b}$.

Critical Thinking Problems

109. Give an example of two different irrational numbers a and b whose product is a rational number.

110. Is there a positive number that is closest to zero on the number line? Explain your answer.

S E C T I O N   P . 2 | **Properties of Algebraic Expressions; Exponents**

Solutions Manual   **Tutorial**   **Video 1**

Objectives

1 Evaluate algebraic expressions.
2 State the property illustrated by an equation.
3 Use properties of exponents.
4 Use scientific notation.

The power of algebra lies in its ability to describe the world in a compact, symbolic manner. When we say "let b be any real number," we condense the symbols for all real numbers into one all-embracing symbol. By writing b^n, where n is an exponent, a symbol is attached to a symbol, condensing all repeated multiplications for all numbers into one compact space. By writing that all the solutions to $ax^2 + bx + c = 0$ are

$$\frac{-b \pm \sqrt{b^2 - 4ac}}{2a}$$

we once again use a compact, symbolic style to present a formula for solving infinitely many different equations. Algebra lets us say infinitely many things at once!

Algebra's power is based on an understanding of algebraic expressions.

Algebraic Expressions

In algebra we use letters, called *variables*, to represent numbers. An expression that combines constants and variables using the operations of addition, subtraction, multiplication, or division, as well as one that contains powers or roots, is called an *algebraic expression*. The following are examples of algebraic expressions.

$$4x^3 - 7x^2 + 5 \qquad\qquad 5(x - y) - (3x - 2y)$$

$$2L + 2W \qquad\qquad \frac{-b + \sqrt{b^2 - 4ac}}{2a}$$

The *terms* of an algebraic expression are separated by addition. For example,

$$4x^3 - 7x^2 + 5 = 4x^3 + (-7x^2) + 5$$

contains three terms: $4x^3$ and $-7x^2$ are the *variable terms* and 5 is the *constant term*. The variable factor of a variable term is the *literal factor*, and the numerical factor is the *numerical coefficient*, or simply *coefficient*. For example, the numerical coefficient of $4x^3$ is 4 and the numerical coefficient of $-7x^2$ is -7.

Evaluating an algebraic expression involves substituting given numerical values for each variable in the expression.

❙ Evaluate algebraic expressions.

EXAMPLE I   Evaluating Algebraic Expressions

Evaluate:

a. $(25t^2 + 125t) \div (t^2 + 1)$ for $t = 3$

b. $\dfrac{-b + \sqrt{b^2 - 4ac}}{2a}$ for $a = 2$, $b = 9$, and $c = -5$

Solution

Expression	Value of the Variable (s)	Substitute	Evaluating the Expression
a. $(25t^2 + 125t) \div (t^2 + 1)$	$t = 3$	$(25 \cdot 3^2 + 125 \cdot 3) \div (3^2 + 1)$	$= (25 \cdot 9 + 125 \cdot 3) \div (9 + 1)$ $= (225 + 375) \div (9 + 1)$ $= 600 \div 10$ $= 60$
b. $\dfrac{-b + \sqrt{b^2 - 4ac}}{2a}$	$a = 2$ $b = 9$ $c = -5$	$\dfrac{-9 + \sqrt{9^2 - 4(2)(-5)}}{2(2)}$	$= \dfrac{-9 + \sqrt{81 - (-40)}}{4}$ $= \dfrac{-9 + \sqrt{121}}{4}$ $= \dfrac{-9 + 11}{4} = \dfrac{2}{4} = \dfrac{1}{2}$ ■

❷ State the property illustrated by an equation.

Algebra's Basic Rules

The basic properties of algebra, listed below, apply to real numbers, variables, and algebraic expressions.

Algebra's basic properties

For each property listed below, a, b, and c represent real numbers, variables, or algebraic expressions.

Property	Example	Description
Commutative Property of Addition $a + b = b + a$	$2x + x^2 = x^2 + 2x$	Order does not matter in addition.
Commutative Property of Multiplication $ab = ba$	$x^2(4 + x) = (4 + x)x^2$	Order does not matter in multiplication.
Associative Property of Addition $(a + b) + c = a + (b + c)$	$(x^2 + x) + 3 = x^2 + (x + 3)$	When we add three numbers (or variables), it does not matter which two we add first.

Associative Property of Multiplication $(ab)c = a(bc)$	$(3 \cdot 7) \cdot 4 = 3 \cdot (7 \cdot 4)$	When we multiply three numbers (or variables), it does not matter which two we multiply first.
Distributive Property $a(b + c) = ab + ac$ $(b + c)a = ba + ca$	$2 \cdot (7 + 4) = 2 \cdot 7 + 2 \cdot 4$ $(4x + y) \cdot 3 = 4x \cdot 3 + y \cdot 3$	When we multiply a number and a sum, we can equivalently multiply the number by each of the terms in the sum and then add the results.
Additive Identity Property $a + 0 = a$ $0 + a = a$	$5x^2 + 0 = 5x^2$ $0 + 7xy = 7xy$	Zero can be deleted from a sum.
Multiplicative Identity Property $a \cdot 1 = a$ $1 \cdot a = a$	$1 \cdot x = x$ $13y^2 \cdot 1 = 13y^2$	One can be deleted from a product.
Additive Inverse Property $a + (-a) = 0$ $(-a) + a = 0$	$17 + (-17) = 0$ $(-4y^3) + 4y^3 = 0$	The sum of a number and its additive inverse gives 0, the additive identity.
Multiplicative Inverse Property If $a \neq 0$, $a \cdot \frac{1}{a} = 1$ $\frac{1}{a} \cdot a = 1$	$7 \cdot \frac{1}{7} = 1$ $(x^2 + 13)\left(\dfrac{1}{x^2 + 13}\right) = 1$	The product of a nonzero number and its multiplicative inverse gives 1, the multiplicative identity.

Algebra's nine basic properties apply to the operations of addition and multiplication. Subtraction and division are defined in terms of addition and multiplication.

Subtraction and division as inverse operations

Let a and b represent real numbers.

Subtraction: $a - b = a + (-b)$

We call $-b$ the *additive inverse* or *opposite* of b.

Division: $a \div b = a \cdot \frac{1}{b}$, where $b \neq 0$

We call $\frac{1}{b}$ the *multiplicative inverse* or *reciprocal* of b. The quotient of a and b, $a \div b$, can be written in the form $\frac{a}{b}$, where a is the *numerator* and b the *denominator* of the fraction.

Study tip

The distributive property can be extended to cover more than two terms.

$a(b_1 + b_2 + b_3 + \cdots + b_n)$

$= ab_1 + ab_2 + ab_3 + \cdots + ab_n$

and

$a(b_1 - b_2 - b_3 - \cdots - b_n)$

$= ab_1 - ab_2 - ab_3 - \cdots - ab_n$

Because subtraction is defined in terms of adding an inverse, the distributive property can be applied to subtraction:

$a(b - c) = ab - ac$

$(b - c)a = ba - ca$

ENRICHMENT ESSAY

Variables and Pronouns

The English language contains all the abstraction and complexity of the compact, symbolic language used in algebra. Consider, for example, the following sentence: "A man once gave his wife something so offensive that she tossed it into her shopping bag and refused to talk about it again, although he occasionally asks her where it is." If we use letters to represent the unknowns, the sentence becomes: "x gave x's wife y a z, and y found z so offensive that y tossed z into a shopping bag and refused to talk about z to x, although x occasionally asks y where z is." This second form of the sentence replaces the variable pronouns with letters, but also contains English words.

Until the 13th century, all algebraic formulas and equations were written out in verbal sentences. Later, abbreviations replaced some of the words. Algebra's current notation, originating near the beginning of the 17th century with the work of the French mathematician René Descartes, utilizes compact symbols without the use of words. In this notation, variables such as x represent any number, with every number condensed into one all-embracing symbol. Using modern notation, mathematicians write x^n, where n is an exponent, a symbol attached to a symbol that condenses all repeated multiplications for all numbers into one compact space.

The symbolic notation used in algebra is the result of a slow and tedious evolution of ideas and symbols. It wasn't until the late 16th century that the French mathematician François Viète came upon the idea of using letters such as x, y, and z to represent numbers in much the same way that English pronouns represent nouns.

Duane Hanson, "Couple with Shopping Bags" © 1976.

Additional Properties of Algebra

The definition of subtraction

$$a - b = a + (-b)$$

states that to subtract b from a, we add the inverse or *negative of b* to a. The following list summarizes the basic properties of negatives.

Properties of negatives

Let a and b represent real numbers, variables, or algebraic expressions.

Property	Examples
1. $(-1)a = -a$	$(-1)3 = -3$
2. $-(-a) = a$	$-(-8) = 8$
	$-(-5x^2y) = 5x^2y$
3. $(-a)b = -(ab)$	$(-5)8 = -(5 \cdot 8)$ or -40
$a(-b) = -(ab)$	$7(-3) = -(7 \cdot 3)$ or -21
4. $(-a)(-b) = ab$	$(-6)(-9) = 6 \cdot 9$ or 54
5. $-(a + b) = -a - b$	$-(3 + 11x) = -3 - 11x$
6. $-(a - b) = -a + b$	$-(3x^2 - 7x) = -3x^2 + 7x$
$= b - a$	$= 7x - 3x^2$

The additive identity property for zero,

$$a + 0 = 0 + a = a$$

was included in our list of algebra's nine basic properties. The following list summarizes other properties of zero.

Properties of zero

Let a and b represent real numbers, variables, or algebraic expressions.

Property	**Examples**
1. $a + 0 = a$	$17x + 0 = 17x$
2. $a - 0 = a$	$14x^2 - 0 = 14x^2$
3. $a \cdot 0 = 0$	$9x^3 \cdot 0 = 0$
$0 \cdot a = 0$	
4. $\dfrac{0}{a} = 0, a \neq 0$	$\dfrac{0}{7x} = 0$, if $x \neq 0$
5. $\dfrac{a}{0}$ is undefined.	$\dfrac{7x}{0}$ is undefined.
	$\dfrac{3}{x - 4}$ is undefined if $x = 4$.
6. If $ab = 0$, then $a = 0$ or $b = 0$. (The "or" includes the possibility that both factors may be 0.)	$(x - 3)(x - 7) = 0$ $x - 3 = 0$ or $x - 7 = 0$

Equations

Throughout this book, we will be working with equations. An *equation* is a statement of equality between two expressions. The basic statement

$$a = b$$

("a is equal to b" or "a equals b") means that a and b represent the same real number.

We will frequently use the following properties when working with equations.

Properties used when working with equations

Let a, b, and c represent real numbers, variables, or algebraic expressions.

Property	**Examples**
Addition Property If $a = b$, then $a + c = b + c$.	If $x - 7 = 5$, then $x - 7 + 7 = 5 + 7$ (so $x = 12$).
Subtraction Property If $a = b$, then $a - c = b - c$.	If $x + 7 = 5$, then $x + 7 - 7 = 5 - 7$ (so $x = -2$).
Multiplication Property If $a = b$, then $ac = bc$.	If $\dfrac{x}{4} = 5$, then $\dfrac{x}{4} \cdot 4 = 5 \cdot 4$ (so $x = 20$).

Division Property

If $a = b$, then $\dfrac{a}{c} = \dfrac{b}{c}$, $c \neq 0$.

If $-4x = 12$, then

$$\dfrac{-4x}{-4} = \dfrac{12}{-4} \text{ (so } x = -3\text{).}$$

Cancellation Properties

If $a + c = b + c$, then $a = b$.

If $a - c = b - c$, then $a = b$.

If $ac = bc$ and $c \neq 0$, then $a = b$.

If $\dfrac{a}{c} = \dfrac{b}{c}$ and $c \neq 0$, then $a = b$.

If $x + 7 = 3 + 7$, then $x = 3$.

If $2x + 6 - x^2 = 10 - x^2$, then
$2x + 6 = 10$.

If $x \cdot 4 = 8 \cdot 4$, then $x = 8$.

If $\dfrac{3y}{17} = \dfrac{15}{17}$, then $3y = 15$.

3 Use properties of exponents.

Integer Exponents

Repeated multiplication of the same factor can be expressed using an exponent.

Definition of a natural number exponent

If b is a real number and n is a natural number,

Exponent

$$b^n = b \cdot b \cdot b \cdot \cdots \cdot b$$

Base b appears as a factor n times.

b^n is read "the nth power of b" or "b to the nth power." Thus, the nth power of b is defined as the product of n factors of b. Furthermore, $b^1 = b$.

EXAMPLE 2   **Evaluating Exponential Expressions**

Evaluate:

a. 7^2 **b.** $(-3)^4$ **c.** -3^4 **d.** $(-2)^3 \cdot 3^2$

Solution

a. $7^2 = 7 \cdot 7 = 49$ 7^2 is read "7 squared."

b. $(-3)^4 = (-3)(-3)(-3)(-3) = 81$

c. $-3^4 = -(3 \cdot 3 \cdot 3 \cdot 3) = -81$ The negative of a number is taken to a power only when the negative is inside the parentheses.

d. $(-2)^3 \cdot 3^2 = (-2)(-2)(-2)(3)(3)$ $(-2)^3$ is read "negative 2 cubed."

$$= -8 \cdot 9 = -72$$

The major properties of exponents are summarized below.

Properties of exponents

For each property listed on the next page, a and b represent real numbers, variables, or algebraic expressions. (All denominators and bases are nonzero.) The exponents, m and n, represent integers.

Property	Example	Description
1. $b^n \cdot b^m = b^{n+m}$	$2^5 \cdot 2^3 = 2^{5+3} = 2^8$	When multiplying expressions with the same base, add the exponents.
2. $\dfrac{b^n}{b^m} = b^{n-m}$	$\dfrac{y^{13}}{y^6} = y^{13-6} = y^7$	When dividing expressions with the same base, subtract the exponents.
3. $b^{-n} = \dfrac{1}{b^n} = \left(\dfrac{1}{b}\right)^n$	$x^{-9} = \dfrac{1}{x^9} = \left(\dfrac{1}{x}\right)^9$	When a negative integer appears as an exponent, switch the position of the base (from numerator to denominator or from denominator to numerator) and make the exponent positive.
4. $\dfrac{1}{b^{-n}} = b^n$	$\dfrac{1}{y^{-2}} = y^2$	
5. $b^0 = 1, b \neq 0$	$(3x^2 + 7)^0 = 1$	Any nonzero number or expression to the 0 power is 1.
6. $(b^n)^m = b^{nm}$	$(x^5)^{-6} = x^{5(-6)} = x^{-30} = \dfrac{1}{x^{30}}$	To raise a power to a new power, multiply the exponents.
7. $(ab)^n = a^n b^n$	$(-2y)^4 = (-2)^4 y^4 = 16y^4$	When a product is raised to a power, raise each factor to the power.
8. $(b_1 b_2 b_3 \cdots b_n)^n = b_1^n b_2^n b_3^n \cdots b_n^n$	$(-3xy)^3 = (-3)^3 x^3 y^3 = -27x^3 y^3$	
9. $\left(\dfrac{a}{b}\right)^n = \dfrac{a^n}{b^n}$	$\left(-\dfrac{3}{x}\right)^3 = \dfrac{(-3)^3}{x^3} = \dfrac{-27}{x^3}$	When a quotient is raised to a power, raise the numerator and the denominator to the power.

EXAMPLE 3   Using the Properties of Exponents

Simplify:

a. $(-3x^4 y^5)^3$ **b.** $(-7xy^4)(-2x^5 y^6)$ **c.** $\dfrac{30a^7 b^4}{-6a^3 b}$

Solution

a. $(-3x^4 y^5)^3 = (-3)^3 (x^4)^3 (y^5)^3$ — Raise each factor in the product to the power.

$\qquad\qquad\quad = (-3)^3 x^{4 \cdot 3} y^{5 \cdot 3}$ — Multiply powers to powers.

$\qquad\qquad\quad = -27x^{12} y^{15}$ — $(-3)^3 = (-3)(-3)(-3) = -27$

b. $(-7xy^4)(-2x^5 y^6) = (-7)(-2)xx^5 y^4 y^6$ — Group factors with the same base.

$\qquad\qquad\qquad\quad = 14x^{1+5} y^{4+6}$ — When multiplying expressions with the same base, add the exponents.

$\qquad\qquad\qquad\quad = 14x^6 y^{10}$ — Simplify.

c. $\dfrac{30a^7 b^4}{-6a^3 b} = \left(\dfrac{30}{-6}\right)\left(\dfrac{a^7}{a^3}\right)\left(\dfrac{b^4}{b}\right)$ — Group factors with the same base.

$\qquad\qquad\quad = -5a^{7-3} b^{4-1}$ — When dividing expressions with the same base, subtract the exponents.

$\qquad\qquad\quad = -5a^4 b^3$ — Simplify.   ∎

Example 3 illustrates the meaning of an exponential expression in simplest form. An exponential expression is simplified when no parentheses appear, no powers are raised to powers, and each base occurs only once. An exponential expression must also contain no negative exponents if it is in simplified form. This involves moving factors with negative exponents from the numerator to the denominator (or vice versa) by changing the sign of the exponent in the last step of the simplification.

EXAMPLE 4   **Simplifying Expressions with Negative Exponents**

Simplify:

a. $\left(\dfrac{4x^2}{y^3}\right)^{-3}$ **b.** $\left(\dfrac{25x^2y^4}{-5x^6y^{-8}}\right)^2$ **c.** $(16x^5y^{10})(-2x^{-3}y^4)^{-3}$

Solution

Discover for yourself

There is often more than one way to simplify an exponential expression. Example 4a can be solved by starting with

$$\left(\dfrac{4x^2}{y^3}\right)^{-3} = \left(\dfrac{y^3}{4x^2}\right)^3.$$

In Example 4b, you can begin by rewriting y^{-8} as $\dfrac{1}{y^8}$ inside the parentheses. Try solving all parts of Example 4 by a different method from the one shown.

Study tip

Be careful when simplifying $(-2)^{-3}$. Change only the sign of the exponent and not the base when moving -2 to the denominator.

Correct: $(-2)^{-3} = \dfrac{1}{(-2)^3}$

Incorrect: $(-2)^{-3} = \dfrac{1}{2^3}$

a. $\left(\dfrac{4x^2}{y^3}\right)^{-3} = \dfrac{4^{-3}(x^2)^{-3}}{(y^3)^{-3}}$ Raise each factor inside the parentheses to the -3 power.

$= \dfrac{4^{-3}x^{-6}}{y^{-9}}$ Multiply powers to powers.

$= \dfrac{y^9}{4^3x^6}$ Move factors with negative exponents from the numerator to the denominator (or vice versa) by changing the sign of the exponent.

$= \dfrac{y^9}{64x^6}$ $4^3 = 4 \cdot 4 \cdot 4 = 64$

b. $\left(\dfrac{25x^2y^4}{-5x^6y^{-8}}\right)^2 = (-5x^{2-6}y^{4-(-8)})^2$ Simplify inside parentheses by subtracting exponents with the same base.

$= (-5x^{-4}y^{12})^2$

$= (-5)^2(x^{-4})^2(y^{12})^2$ Square each factor inside the parentheses.

$= 25x^{-8}y^{24}$ Multiply powers to powers.

$= \dfrac{25y^{24}}{x^8}$ $b^{-n} = \dfrac{1}{b^n}$, so $x^{-8} = \dfrac{1}{x^8}$.

c. $(16x^5y^{10})(-2x^{-3}y^4)^{-3}$

$= (16x^5y^{10})(-2)^{-3}(x^{-3})^{-3}(y^4)^{-3}$ Raise each factor in the second parentheses to the -3 power.

$= (16x^5y^{10})(-2)^{-3}x^9y^{-12}$ Multiply powers to powers.

$= 16(-2)^{-3}(x^5x^9)(y^{10}y^{-12})$ Group factors with the same base.

$= 16(-2)^{-3}x^{14}y^{-2}$ When multiplying expressions with the same base, add the exponents.

$= 16 \cdot \dfrac{1}{(-2)^3} x^{14} \cdot \dfrac{1}{y^2}$ Move factors with negative exponents from the numerator to the denominator by changing the sign of the exponent.

$= 16 \cdot \dfrac{1}{-8} \cdot x^{14} \cdot \dfrac{1}{y^2}$ $(-2)^3 = (-2)(-2)(-2) = -8$

$= \dfrac{-2x^{14}}{y^2}$ Simplify.   ∎

EXAMPLE 5   **Simplifying an Exponential Expression**

Simplify: $\dfrac{(-2x^3y^2z)^4}{-8xy^{-3}z^4}$

Solution

$$\frac{(-2x^3y^2z)^4}{-8xy^{-3}z^4} = \frac{(-2)^4(x^3)^4(y^2)^4z^4}{-8xy^{-3}z^4}$$

Raise each factor inside the parentheses to the fourth power.

$$= \frac{16x^{12}y^8z^4}{-8xy^{-3}z^4}$$

Multiply powers to powers.

$$= \frac{16}{-8} \cdot \frac{x^{12}}{x} \cdot \frac{y^8}{y^{-3}} \cdot \frac{z^4}{z^4}$$

Group factors with the same base.

$$= -2x^{12-1}y^{8-(-3)}z^{4-4}$$

When dividing expressions with the same base, subtract the exponents.

$$= -2x^{11}y^{11}z^0$$

Simplify.

$$= -2x^{11}y^{11}$$

$z^0 = 1$, and 1 can be omitted in a product. ∎

Study tip

Try to avoid the following common errors that can occur when simplifying exponential expressions.

Incorrect	Description of Error	Correct
$b^3b^4 = b^{12}$	Exponents should be added, not multiplied.	$b^3b^4 = b^7$
$3^n \cdot 3^m = 9^{n+m}$	The common base should be retained, not multiplied.	$3^n \cdot 3^m = 3^{n+m}$
$\dfrac{5^{16}}{5^4} = 5^4$	Exponents should be subtracted, not divided.	$\dfrac{5^{16}}{5^4} = 5^{12}$
$(4a)^3 = 4a^3$	Both factors should be cubed.	$(4a)^3 = 64a^3$
$b^{-n} = -\dfrac{1}{b^n}$	Only the exponent should change sign.	$b^{-n} = \dfrac{1}{b^n}$
$(a+b)^{-1} = \dfrac{1}{a} + \dfrac{1}{b}$	The exponent applies to the entire expression $a + b$.	$(a+b)^{-1} = \dfrac{1}{a+b}$

4 Use scientific notation.

Scientific Notation

We frequently encounter very large and very small numbers. For example, a light-year is the number of miles that light travels in one year, which is approximately

5,880,000,000,000 miles.

The large number of zeros in this number makes it difficult to read, write, and say. *Scientific notation* gives us a compact way to display and say this number. In scientific notation, a light-year is approximately 5.88×10^{12} miles.

In general, a scientific notation numeral has the form $c \times 10^n$, where $1 \leq c < 10$ and n is an integer. It is customary to use $\times$ rather than a dot to indicate multiplication in scientific notation.

Definition of scientific notation

A scientific notation numeral appears as the product of two factors. The first factor is a number greater than or equal to 1 but less than 10. The second factor is base 10 raised to a power that is an integer.

EXAMPLE 6 **Converting from Scientific to Decimal Notation**

Rewrite in decimal notation:

a. 1.7×10^3 **b.** 2.31×10^0 **c.** 7.43×10^{-2} **d.** 6.153×10^{-4}

Solution

a. $1.7 \times 10^3 = 1.7 \times 1000 = 1700$
b. $2.31 \times 10^0 = 2.31 \times 1 = 2.31$

c. $7.43 \times 10^{-2} = 7.43 \times \dfrac{1}{10^2} = 7.43 \times \dfrac{1}{100} = 0.0743$

d. $6.153 \times 10^{-4} = 6.153 \times \dfrac{1}{10^4} = 6.153 \times \dfrac{1}{10,000} = 0.000\ 615\ 3$ ■

Observe that when multiplying by 10 to a power, we move the decimal point the same number of places as the exponent of 10. If the exponent is *positive*, we move the decimal point in the first factor to the *right*. If the exponent is *negative*, we move the decimal point in the first factor to the *left*.

You can change the mode setting of a graphing calculator so that numbers are displayed in scientific notation. (Consult your manual.) Once you're in the scientific notation mode, simply enter the number and press ENTER.

Discover for yourself

Study the scientific notation numerals for the numbers in Example 7. Describe a process for converting a positive number to scientific notation without using a calculator.

EXAMPLE 7 **Converting to Scientific Notation on a Graphing Calculator**

Use a graphing calculator to express in scientific notation:

a. 82,000,000,000 **b.** 0.000 000 000 000 000 000 160 2 **c.** 3.7284

Solution

Number		Display	Number in Scientific Notation
a. 82,000,000,000	ENTER	8.2 E 10	8.2×10^{10}
b. 0.000 000 000 000 000 000 160 2	ENTER	1.602 E −19	1.602×10^{-19}
c. 3.7284	ENTER	3.7284 E 0	3.7284×10^0

■

Using technology

Even if you do not set your graphing calculator to a scientific notation mode, it will automatically switch to scientific notation when displaying large or small numbers that exceed the display range. For example use your graphing calculator to multiply

(79,000) (3,400,000,000).

The display shows

2.686E14

indicating that the product is 2.686 × 10^{14}. If you set your calculator to the scientific notation mode, answers to all computations will be displayed in scientific notation even if they do not exceed the display range.

In the Discover for yourself, were you able to state the following procedure for converting a number into scientific notation?

Writing a number in scientific notation

1. Count the number of places n that the decimal point must be moved to obtain the number c, where $1 \leq c < 10$.
2. If the given number is greater than or equal to 1, then its scientific notation is $c \times 10^n$. If the given number is between 0 and 1, then its scientific notation is $c \times 10^{-n}$.

Applying this procedure to the first two parts of Example 7 enables us to write the numbers in scientific notation as follows.

$$82,000,000,000. = 8.2 \times 10^{10}$$
$$\underset{10\ 9\ 8\ 7\ \ 6\ 5\ 4\ \ 3\ 2\ 1}{\uparrow\ \uparrow\ \uparrow\ \uparrow\ \ \uparrow\ \uparrow\ \uparrow\ \ \uparrow\ \uparrow\ \uparrow}$$

$$0.000\ 000\ 000\ 000\ 000\ 000\ 000\ 1\ 6\ 0\ 2 = 1.602 \times 10^{-19}$$
$$\underset{1\ \ 2\ \ 3\ \ 4\ \ 5\ \ 6\ \ 7\ \ 8\ \ 9\ \ 10\ 11\ 12\ 13\ 14\ 15\ 16\ 17\ 18\ 19}{\uparrow\ \uparrow\ \uparrow\ \uparrow\ \uparrow\ \uparrow\ \uparrow\ \uparrow\ \uparrow\ \uparrow\ \uparrow\ \uparrow\ \uparrow\ \uparrow\ \uparrow\ \uparrow\ \uparrow\ \uparrow\ \uparrow}$$

An Application: Black Holes in Space

The concept of a black hole, a region in space where matter appears to vanish, intrigues scientists and nonscientists alike. Scientists theorize that when massive stars run out of nuclear fuel, they begin to collapse under the force of their own gravity. As the star collapses, its density increases. In turn, the force of gravity increases so tremendously that even light cannot escape from the star. Consequently, it appears black.

A mathematical formula, called the Schwarzchild formula, describes the critical value to which the radius of a massive body must be reduced for it to become a black hole. This formula forms the basis of our next example.

Jasper Johns, "Mirror's Edge" 1992, oil on canvas, 66 × 44 in. Photo courtesy Leo Castelli Gallery. © Jasper Johns / Licensed by VAGA, New York 1998.

EXAMPLE 8   An Application of Scientific Notation

Use the Schwarzchild formula

$$R_s = \frac{2GM}{c^2}$$

where

R_s = Radius of the star (in meters) that would
cause it to become a black hole

M = Mass of the star (in kilograms)

G = A constant, called the gravitational constant

$$= 6.7 \times 10^{-11} \frac{m^3}{kg \cdot s^2}$$

c = Speed of light

$$= 3 \times 10^8 \text{ meters per second}$$

to determine to what length the radius of the sun must be reduced for it to become a black hole. The sun's mass is approximately 2×10^{30} kilograms.

Solution

$$R_s = \frac{2GM}{c^2}$$

$$= \frac{2 \times 6.7 \times 10^{-11} \times 2 \times 10^{30}}{(3 \times 10^8)^2}$$ Substitute the given values.

$$= \frac{(2 \times 6.7 \times 2) \times (10^{-11} \times 10^{30})}{(3 \times 10^8)^2}$$ Apply the commutative and associative properties.

$$= \frac{26.8 \times 10^{-11+30}}{3^2 \times (10^8)^2}$$ Apply the properties of exponents. Use the rule for multipying exponential expressions in the numerator. Use the rule for raising a product to a power in the denominator.

$$= \frac{26.8 \times 10^{19}}{9 \times 10^{16}}$$ Use $(b^n)^m = b^{nm}$ on the second factor in the denominator.

$$= \frac{26.8}{9} \times 10^{19-16}$$ $\dfrac{b^n}{b^m} = b^{n-m}$

$$\approx 2.978 \times 10^3$$

$$= 2978$$

Although the sun is not massive enough to become a black hole (its radius is approximately 700,000 kilometers), the Schwarzchild model theoretically indicates that if the sun's radius were reduced to approximately 2978 meters, that is, about $\frac{1}{235,000}$ its present size, it would become a black hole.   ∎

PROBLEM SET P.2

Practice Problems

In Problems 1–12, evaluate each expression for the given value(s) of the variable(s).

1. $x^2 + 5x + 9$; $x = 4$

2. $x^2 + 9x + 6$; $x = 10$

3. $x^2 - 7x + 5$; $x = -3$

4. $2x^2 - 9x - 3$; $x = -2$

5. $3x^3 - 5x^2 - x + 6$; $x = -2$

6. $2x^3 - 4x^2 - x - 7$; $x = -1$

7. $\dfrac{x+1}{x-1}$; $x = -1$

8. $\dfrac{1 - (x-2)^2}{1 + (x-2)^2}$; $x = -1$

9. $\dfrac{2x^2 - 1}{2x^3 + 1}$; $x = -\dfrac{1}{2}$

10. $\dfrac{3^{x+1} - \dfrac{1}{3^{x+1}}}{3^{x+1} + \dfrac{1}{3^{x+1}}}$; $x = -1$

11. $\dfrac{-b + \sqrt{b^2 - 4ac}}{2a}$; $a = 4, b = -20, c = 25$

12. $\dfrac{-b + \sqrt{b^2 - 4ac}}{2a}$; $a = 3, b = 5, c = -2$

In Problems 13–24, state the property that is illustrated by each equation.

13. $7 \cdot 6 = 6 \cdot 7$

14. $3 + (7 + 9) = (3 + 7) + 9$

15. $a(b + c) = (b + c)a$

16. $a(b + c) = a(c + b)$

17. $4(x + 5) = 4x + 20$

18. $\dfrac{1}{(x + 3)}(x + 3) = 1;$ $x \neq -3$

19. $(a + b)(c + d) = a(c + d) + b(c + d)$ **20.** $(x + 4) + [-(x + 4)] = 0$

21. $(x + 3) + 0 = x + 3$

22. $1(y + 15) = y + 15$

23. $\dfrac{3}{\sqrt{2}} = \dfrac{3}{\sqrt{2}} \cdot \dfrac{\sqrt{2}}{\sqrt{2}}$

24. $\dfrac{\sqrt{3} + 7}{\sqrt{5} + 2} = \dfrac{\sqrt{3} + 7}{\sqrt{5} + 2} \cdot \dfrac{\sqrt{5} - 2}{\sqrt{5} - 2}$

In Problems 25–38, use properties of algebra to write each expression without parentheses.

25. $7(x + 3y)$

26. $6(5a - 4b)$

27. $\frac{1}{3}(-12x)$

28. $-\frac{1}{3}(3y)$

29. $4x^2(3x^3 - 2x)$

30. $(5y^4 - 2y)(-6y^3)$

31. $-(-13x)$

32. $(-13x)(2y)$

33. $(-5a)(-4b)$

34. $(-20a)\left(-\frac{1}{20} b\right)$

35. $-(2x^2 - 5x - 6)$

36. $-(-6x^4 - 9x + 17)$

37. $\frac{1}{3}(3x) + [(4y) + (-4y)]$

38. $-\frac{3}{4}\left(-\frac{4}{3} y\right) + [(6x) + (-6x)]$

Evaluate each exponential expression in Problems 39–56.

39. $5^2 \cdot 2$

40. $6^2 \cdot 2$

41. $(-2)^5$

42. $(-2)^4$

43. -2^4

44. -5^3

45. $2^2 \cdot 2^3$

46. $\dfrac{3^5}{3^2}$

47. $\dfrac{4^8}{4^5}$

48. $3^3 \cdot 3^2$

49. $(2^3)^2$

50. $(3^2)^3$

51. $\dfrac{2}{2^{-4}}$

52. $64(-2)^{-5}$

53. $\dfrac{3^{-2}}{3^{-1}}$

54. $\dfrac{2^{-5}}{2^{-3}}$

55. $(3^{19} \cdot 3^{25})^0$

56. $(7^{23} \cdot 7^{96})^0$

Simplify each exponential expression in Problems 57–94.

57. $(4x^2)^3$

58. $(6x^3)^2$

59. $(-3x^4)(-2x^7)$

60. $(-11x^5)(-9x^{12})$

61. $\dfrac{25a^{12}}{5a^6}$

62. $\dfrac{30a^{20}}{10a^{10}}$

63. $\dfrac{14b^7}{7b^{14}}$

64. $\dfrac{20b^{10}}{10b^{20}}$

65. $(2x^2)^3(4x^3)^{-1}$

66. $(5x^3)^2(10x^2)^{-2}$

67. $(-9x^{-2})^{-3}$

68. $(-6x^{-4})^{-3}$

69. $(-2x^3y^4)^5$

70. $(-3x^2y^3)^3$

71. $(-6x^2y^3)(-4xy^5)$

72. $\left(\dfrac{3}{4} xy^5\right)\left(-\dfrac{4}{3} x^2y^3\right)$

73. $\dfrac{25a^{13}b^4}{-5a^2b^3}$

74. $\dfrac{35a^{14}b^6}{-7a^7b^3}$

75. $(-4x^2)^3(2x^3)^{-1}$

76. $(4x^{-4})(3x^2)$

77. $\left(\dfrac{5x^3}{y^2}\right)^{-2}$

78. $\left(\dfrac{3x^4}{y^7}\right)^{-4}$

79. $(-3x^2y^{-5})^{-2}$

80. $(-4x^{-3}y^2)^{-3}$

81. $(5x^3y^4)^2(-3x^7y^{11})$

82. $(2r^3s^4)^3(-5rs^{-14})$

83. $(4ab^3)^3(-3a^{-5}b^8)$

84. $(12x^4y^7)(-2x^{-2}y^5)^{-2}$

85. $(54r^3s^9)(-3r^2s^{-4})^{-3}$

86. $(-x^2y^3z^{-6})(x^4y^{-5}z^3)^{-5}$

87. $(-a^{-2}b^3c)(ab^{-1}c^{-4})^{-3}$

88. $(2x^2y^3)^2(4x^{-3}y^6)^{-2}$

89. $(3x^{-3}y^{-4}z)^3(3xy^{-5}z)^2(-3x^{-4}z^{12})$

90. $\dfrac{24a^{-5}bc^2}{-10a^3b^{-7}c^2}$

91. $\dfrac{-27x^{-8}y^4z}{15x^4y^4z^{-4}}$

92. $\dfrac{(-2xy^3z^2)^5}{16x^{-2}yz^{10}}$

93. $\dfrac{(-4x^4yz^3)^3}{-4x^2y^{-3}z^9}$

94. $\dfrac{(2ab^{-2}c^3)^{-2}}{(4ab^3c^2)^{-3}}$

In Problems 95–98, express each number in decimal notation.

95. 7.13×10^5

96. 5.024×10^9

97. 3.07×10^{-8}

98. 6.573×10^{-7}

In Problems 99–108, express each number in scientific notation.

99. 96,500,000   **100.** 167,300,000   **101.** 7,361,000,000,000   **102.** 5,024,000,000,000,000

103. 7.53   **104.** 9.04   **105.** 0.00016   **106.** 0.0000037

107. 0.007253   **108.** 0.009621

In Problems 109–112, use scientific notation to perform each indicated computation. Write the answer in scientific notation.

109. $(0.00037)(8,300,000)$ **110.** $(0.025)(9,400,000,000,000)$

111. $(4,200,000,000,000) \div (14,000)$ **112.** $(0.00000000124) \div (3,100,000)$

Application Problems

113. The algebraic expression $0.0014x^2 - 0.1529x + 5.855$ describes the percent of income that one contributes to charities, where x represents annual income in thousands of dollars. Evaluate the expression for $x = 10$ and describe what this means in practical terms.

114. The algebraic expression $0.78x^2 + 76.7x + 4449$ describes world population (in millions) x years after 1980. Evaluate the expression for $x = 10$ and describe what this means in practical terms.

115. The algebraic expression $2\pi r^2 + 2\pi rh$ describes the surface area of a cylinder, where r is the radius and h is the height. Evaluate the expression for $r = 6$ inches and $h = 10$ inches. Express the answer in terms of π, and state the cylinder's surface area with the appropriate unit of measure.

116. The figure on the right shows the path of a person who rows across a river (A to B) and then runs along the river bank on the opposite side (B to C). With the distances shown in the figure, and with a rowing rate of 6

kilometers per hour and a running rate of 8 kilometers per hour, the algebraic expression

$$\frac{\sqrt{x^2 + 9}}{6} + \frac{8 - x}{8}$$

describes the total time (in hours) rowing and running. The figure indicates that the running distance is represented by $8 - x$. Evaluate the total time expression for $x = 4$. What is the total time rowing and running and where does the person come ashore?

In Problems 117–120, write each number in scientific notation.

117. A light-year: 5,880,000,000,000 miles

118. Number of pounds of dust from the atmosphere that inundate Earth on a daily basis: 26,000,000.

119. Diameter of a hydrogen atom: 0.0000001016 centimeter

120. One micron: 0.00003937 inch

Use scientific notation to answer Problems 121–126.

121. The mass of Earth is approximately

$$5,976,000,000,000,000,000,000,000,000 \text{ grams}$$

and the mass of the hydrogen atom is

$$0.000\ 000\ 000\ 000\ 000\ 000\ 000\ 000\ 001\ 66 \text{ gram.}$$

If Earth were composed only of hydrogen atoms, how many hydrogen atoms would it contain?

122. If the length of a hydrogen atom is 0.000 000 03 millimeter and the average human foot measures 200 millimeters, how many times as large as the hydrogen atom is the human foot?

123. The tallest tree known is the Howard Libbey redwood in Redwood Grove, California. The tree measures 100,000 millimeters. The distance from Earth to the sun is approximately 150,000,000,000,000 millimeters. How many of the tallest redwood trees would it take to span this distance?

124. Among the planets of the solar system, Pluto is the most distant from the sun, approximately 4.6×10^9 miles. How many seconds does it take the light of the sun to reach Pluto if light travels 1.86×10^5 miles per second?

125. Our galaxy measures approximately 1.2×10^{17} kilometers across. If a space vehicle were capable of moving at half the speed of light (approximately 1.5×10^5 kilometers per second), how many years would it take for the vehicle to cross the galaxy?

126. Pouiseville's law states that the speed of blood (S, in centimeters per second) located r centimeters from the central axis of an artery is

$$S = (1.76 \times 10^5)[(1.44 \times 10^{-2}) - r^2].$$

Find the speed of blood at the central axis of this artery.

True–False Critical Thinking Problems

127. Which one of the following is not true for all real numbers?
   a. $3(x^4 y^3) = (3x^4)y^3$
   b. $2x(y^4 + z^3) = 2x(z^3 + y^4)$
   c. $2x(y^4 + z^3) = 2x(y^3 + z^4)$
   d. $-(-6x^2 y^3) = 6x^2 y^3$

128. Which one of the following is not true for all real numbers?
   a. $(x^2 + y^3)(2z + 7) = (7 + 2z)(y^3 + x^2)$
   b. $5(x - 2y + 3z^2) = 15z^2 - 10y + 5x$
   c. $x(4z) = (x \cdot 4)z = (4x)z$
   d. $7x + (yz) = (7x + y)(7x + z)$

129. Which one of the following is not true?
   a. $2^{-1} + 2^{-1} = 1$

   b. $3^{100} = 9^{50}$
   c. $9^7 9^7 = 81^{14}$
   d. $(0.25)^{-1} = 4$

130. Which one of the following is true?

   a. $\dfrac{3^{10}}{3^{-14}} = 3^{-4}$

   b. $-5^{-2} = \dfrac{1}{25}$

   c. $\left(\dfrac{2}{3}\right)^{-2} = \left(\dfrac{3}{2}\right)^2$

   d. $534.7 = 5.347 \times 10^3$

Writing in Mathematics

131. If $b \neq 0$, we know that $b^{-n} = \dfrac{1}{b^n}$ and $\dfrac{1}{b^{-n}} = b^n$. Express this idea strictly in words rather than using the compact, symbolic notation of algebra.

132. Describe the differences, if any, among, b^2, b^{-2}, $-b^2$, and $(-b)^2$.

133. Discuss one advantage of expressing a number in scientific notation over decimal notation.

Critical Thinking Problems

134. If $b^A = MN$, $b^C = M$, and $b^D = N$, what is the relationship among A, C, and D?

135. Which pair of numbers is closer together: 10^7 and 10^{43} or 10^{200} and 10^{201}? Explain your answer.

SECTION P.3   Graphs and Graphing Utilities

Objectives

1 Plot ordered pairs in rectangular coordinates.
2 Interpret information given by graphs.
3 Find the distance between two points.
4 Find the midpoint of a line segment.
5 Graph equations in rectangular coordinates.
6 Use a graph to determine intercepts.
7 Graph equations with a graphing utility.

Solutions Manual   Tutorial   Video I

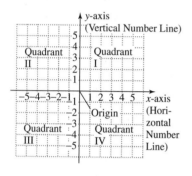

Figure P.17

The rectangular coordinate system

In Section P.1, we saw that any real number could be represented by a point on the number line. We are now ready to graph ordered pairs of real numbers in a plane called the *rectangular coordinate system*. The ideas discussed in this section are those of the French mathematician and philosopher René Descartes. For this reason, the rectangular coordinate system is also called the *Cartesian coordinate plane*.

Points and Ordered Pairs

Descartes used two number lines that intersect at right angles at their zero points (Figure P.17). Each line is called a *coordinate axis*. The horizontal axis is the *x-axis* and the vertical axis is the *y-axis*. The point of intersection of these axes is the *origin*. The horizontal and vertical number lines divide the plane into four quarters, called *quadrants*, numbered in a counterclockwise direction beginning with the upper right. Points on the axes are not in any quadrant.

Each point in the plane corresponds to a unique *ordered pair* (x, y) of real numbers. Examples of such pairs are $(4, 2)$ and $(-5, -3)$. The first number in each pair, called the *x-coordinate*, denotes the distance and direction from the origin along the *x-axis*. The second number, called the *y-coordinate*, denotes vertical distance and direction along a line parallel to the *y-axis* or along the *y-axis* itself. Figure P.18 shows how we locate, or plot, the points corresponding to the ordered pairs $(4, 2)$ and $(-5, -3)$. The phrase "the point corresponding to the ordered pair $(-5, -3)$" is often abbreviated "the point $(-5, -3)$."

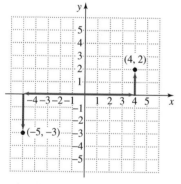

Figure P.18

Plotting points

Plot ordered pairs in rectangular coordinates.

EXAMPLE I   Plotting Points in a Rectangular Coordinate System

Plot the points: $(-2, 3)$, $(5, 4)$, $(-3, -4)$, $(4, -1)$, $(0, 0)$, $(-6, 0)$, and $(0, -5)$

Figure P.19
Plotting points

Solution

See Figure P.19. We plot the points in the following way:

$(-2, 3)$: 2 units left, 3 units up (in quadrant II)
$(5, 4)$: 5 units right, 4 units up (in quadrant I)
$(-3, -4)$: 3 units left, 4 units down (in quadrant III)
$(4, -1)$: 4 units right, 1 unit down (in quadrant IV)
$(0, 0)$: 0 units right or left, 0 units up or down (at the origin)
$(-6, 0)$: 6 units left, 0 units up or down (on the x-axis)
$(0, -5)$: 0 units right or left, 5 units down (on the y-axis).   ∎

2 Interpret information given by graphs.

Interpreting Information Given by Graphs

Magazines and newspapers often display information using graphs in the first quadrant of rectangular coordinate systems.

EXAMPLE 2   The Age at which Americans Marry

Figure P.20 shows the median age at which people in the United States marry for the first time. The data for the years 1997 through 2000 are projections.

a. Estimate the coordinates for point A and interpret the coordinates in practical terms.
b. For the period shown in the graph, what is the minimum age at which men marry for the first time? Approximately when did this occur?

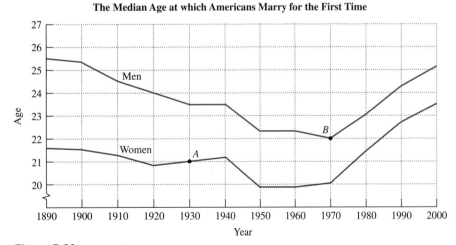

Figure P.20
Source: U.S. Bureau of the Census, *Statistical Abstract*, 1997.

Solution

(Be sure to turn back a page so that you can see both parts of this solution.)

a. A reasonable estimate for the coordinates of point A is (1930, 21). This means that in 1930 women in the United States married for the first time at age 21.
b. For the period shown in the graph for the men, point B is the lowest point on the graph. With approximate coordinates of (1972, 22), this means that the minimum age at which men married for the first time was 22, and this occurred in 1970. ∎

The Distance Formula

We can use the Pythagorean Theorem to find the distance between two points in the Cartesian coordinate plane. Recall that the Pythagorean Theorem involves a triangle with a right angle, called a *right triangle*. The side opposite the right angle is called the *hypotenuse*. The other two sides are called *legs*. Using Figure P.21, the Pythagorean Theorem can be expressed as

$$a^2 + b^2 = c^2.$$

In any right triangle, the sum of the squares of the legs is equal to the square of the hypotenuse.

Now we are ready to find the distance between two points $P_1(x_1, y_1)$ and $P_2(x_2, y_2)$ in the plane. Using absolute value to express the distance between two points on a number line, the distance between P_1 and P_3 shown in Figure P.22 is $|x_2 - x_1|$. Similarly, the distance between P_3 and P_2 on a vertical line is $|y_2 - y_1|$. By the Pythagorean Theorem,

$$d^2 = |x_2 - x_1|^2 + |y_2 - y_1|^2$$

$$d = \sqrt{|x_2 - x_1|^2 + |y_2 - y_1|^2}$$

$$d = \sqrt{(x_2 - x_1)^2 + (y_2 - y_1)^2}$$

This result is the *distance formula*.

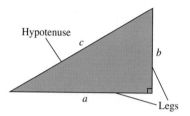

3 Find the distance between two points.

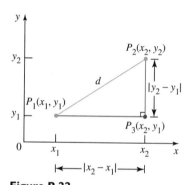

Figure P.21

The Pythagorean Theorem:
$a^2 + b^2 = c^2$

Figure P.22

Finding the distance between P_1 and P_2

Figure P.23

Superimposing rectangular coordinates over a map

The distance formula

The distance d between the points (x_1, y_1) and (x_2, y_2) in the Cartesian coordinate plane is

$$d = \sqrt{(x_2 - x_1)^2 + (y_2 - y_1)^2}.$$

EXAMPLE 3 Using the Distance Formula

A rectangular coordinate system with coordinates in miles is superimposed over a map (Figure P.23). Bangkok has coordinates $(-115, 170)$ and Phnom Penh has coordinates $(65, 70)$. How long will it take an airplane averaging 400 miles per hour to fly directly from one city to the other?

Work Example 3 with

$(x_1, y_1) = (65, 70)$

and

$(x_2, y_2) = (-115, 170)$.

Does the distance formula still give the same result? What can you conclude?

Solution

The distance between the cities is

$$d = \sqrt{(x_2 - x_1)^2 + (y_2 - y_1)^2}$$ This is the distance formula.

$$= \sqrt{[65 - (-115)]^2 + (70 - 170)^2}$$ Let $(x_1, y_1) = (-115, 170)$ and $(x_2, y_2) = (65, 70)$.

$$= \sqrt{(180)^2 + (-100)^2}$$ Simplify.

$$= \sqrt{32,400 + 10,000}$$

$$= \sqrt{42,400}$$

$$\approx 206$$

Because the cities are approximately 206 miles apart, the flight will take $\frac{206}{400}$, or 0.52 of an hour (approximately 31 minutes). ∎

4 Find the midpoint of a line segment.

The Midpoint Formula

The distance formula can be used to prove a formula for finding the midpoint of a line segment between two given points. The formula is stated below and its proof is left for the problem set.

> **The midpoint formula**
>
> Consider a line segment whose endpoints are (x_1, y_1) and (x_2, y_2). The coordinates of the segment's midpoint are
>
> $$\left(\frac{x_1 + x_2}{2}, \frac{y_1 + y_2}{2} \right).$$
>
> To find the midpoint, take the average of the two x-values and of the two y-values.

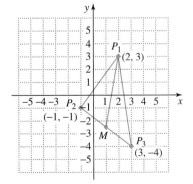

Figure P.24

Median $P_1 M$

EXAMPLE 4 Using the Midpoint and Distance Formulas

The *median* of a triangle is the line segment from any vertex to the midpoint of the opposite side. If the vertices of a triangle are $(2, 3)$, $(-1, -1)$, and $(3, -4)$, what is the length of the median from $(2, 3)$?

Solution

The situation is illustrated in Figure P.24. We can find the length of median $P_1 M$ by first finding the coordinates of M.

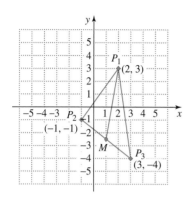

Figure P.24 is repeated here so that you don't have to turn back a page.

$$M = \left(\frac{x_1 + x_2}{2}, \frac{y_1 + y_2}{2}\right)$$ This is the midpoint formula.

$$= \left(\frac{-1 + 3}{2}, \frac{-1 + (-4)}{2}\right)$$ Apply the formula with $(x_1, y_1) = (-1, -1)$ and $(x_2, y_2) = (3, -4)$.

$$= (1, -2.5)$$ Simplify.

Now that we have the coordinates of midpoint M, we are ready to find the length of the designated median.

$$P_1M = \sqrt{(x_2 - x_1)^2 + (y_2 - y_1)^2}$$ This is the distance formula.

$$= \sqrt{(2 - 1)^2 + [3 - (-2.5)]^2}$$ Apply the formula with $(x_1, y_1) = (1, -2.5)$ and $(x_2, y_2) = (2, 3)$.

$$= \sqrt{1 + 30.25}$$ Simplify.

$$\approx 5.59$$

The length of the median from $(2, 3)$ is approximately 5.59 linear units.   ∎

5 Graph equations in rectangular coordinates.

Graphs of Equations

A relationship between two quantities can be expressed as an *equation in two variables*, such as

$$y = 2x - 4.$$

A point (a, b) *satisfies* the equation if the equation is true when a is substituted for x and b is substituted for y. For example, the point $(3, 2)$ satisfies $y = 2x - 4$ because $2 = 2(3) - 4$ or $2 = 2$ is a true statement. We call $(3, 2)$ a *solution* or *solution point* of the equation. The *graph of the equation* is the set of all solution points.

> **The graph of an equation**
>
> The *graph* of an equation in x and y is the set of all points (x, y) in the rectangular coordinate system that satisfy the equation.

The rectangular coordinate system allows us to visualize relationships between two variables by connecting any equation in two variables with a geometric figure, its graph. One way to graph an equation is by plotting points.

> **Graphing an equation by plotting points**
>
> 1. Make a table of some coordinates that satisfy the equation.
> 2. Plot these ordered pairs and connect them with a smooth curve or line.

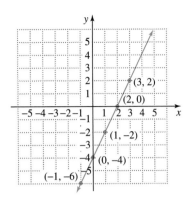

Figure P.25

The graph of $y = 2x - 4$

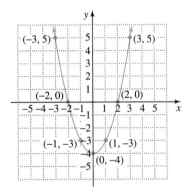

Figure P.26

The graph of $y = x^2 - 4$

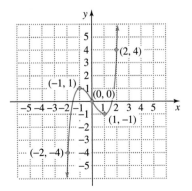

Figure P.27

The graph of $y = x^3 - 2x$

EXAMPLE 5 **Graphing Equations Using the Point-Plotting Method**

Use point-plotting to sketch the graph of each equation:

a. $y = 2x - 4$ **b.** $y = x^2 - 4$ **c.** $y = x^3 - 2x$ **d.** $y = \sqrt[3]{x}$ **e.** $y = |x|$

Solution

a. $y = 2x - 4$

We first construct a table of coordinates by selecting negative, zero, and positive values of x, and calculating the corresponding values of y.

x	$y = 2x - 4$	(x, y)
-1	$y = 2(-1) - 4 = -6$	$(-1, -6)$
0	$y = 2 \cdot 0 - 4 = -4$	$(0, -4)$
1	$y = 2 \cdot 1 - 4 = -2$	$(1, -2)$
2	$y = 2 \cdot 2 - 4 = 0$	$(2, 0)$
3	$y = 2 \cdot 3 - 4 = 2$	$(3, 2)$

Now we plot these points and connect them as shown in Figure P.25. It appears that the graph of $y = 2x - 4$ is a straight line. We'll be discussing the graphs of such equations in detail in Section 2.2.

b. $y = x^2 - 4$

Once again, we begin with a table of coordinates.

x	$y = x^2 - 4$	(x, y)
-3	$y = (-3)^2 - 4 = 5$	$(-3, 5)$
-2	$y = (-2)^2 - 4 = 0$	$(-2, 0)$
-1	$y = (-1)^2 - 4 = -3$	$(-1, -3)$
0	$y = 0^2 - 4 = -4$	$(0, -4)$
1	$y = 1^2 - 4 = -3$	$(1, -3)$
2	$y = 2^2 - 4 = 0$	$(2, 0)$
3	$y = 3^2 - 4 = 5$	$(3, 5)$

As shown in Figure P.26, we plot the seven points and connect them with a smooth curve. In general, the graph of any equation in the form $y = ax^2 + bx + c$ is a *parabola*. We will discuss such equations extensively in Section 3.1.

c. $y = x^3 - 2x$

The following table shows some of the points that satisfy this equation.

x	$y = x^3 - 2x$	(x, y)
-2	$y = (-2)^3 - 2(-2) = -8 + 4 = -4$	$(-2, -4)$
-1	$y = (-1)^3 - 2(-1) = -1 + 2 = 1$	$(-1, 1)$
0	$y = 0^3 - 2 \cdot 0 = 0 - 0 = 0$	$(0, 0)$
1	$y = 1^3 - 2 \cdot 1 = 1 - 2 = -1$	$(1, -1)$
2	$y = 2^3 - 2 \cdot 2 = 8 - 4 = 4$	$(2, 4)$

We plot the five points and connect them with a smooth curve, as shown in Figure P.27.

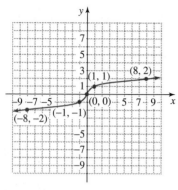

Figure P.28

The graph of $y = \sqrt[3]{x}$.

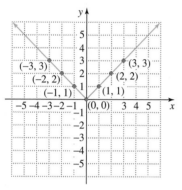

Figure P.29

The graph of $y = |x|$.

6 Use a graph to determine intercepts.

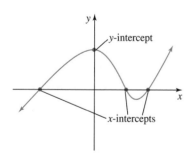

Figure P.30

At all x-intercepts, $y = 0$, and at all y-intercepts, $x = 0$.

d. $y = \sqrt[3]{x}$

In this table of coordinates, we've chosen values of x that are perfect cubes. The graph of $y = \sqrt[3]{x}$ is shown in Figure P.28.

x	$y = \sqrt[3]{x}$	(x, y)
-8	$y = \sqrt[3]{-8} = -2$	$(-8, -2)$
-1	$y = \sqrt[3]{-1} = -1$	$(-1, -1)$
0	$y = \sqrt[3]{0} = 0$	$(0, 0)$
1	$y = \sqrt[3]{1} = 1$	$(1, 1)$
8	$y = \sqrt[3]{8} = 2$	$(8, 2)$

e. $y = |x|$

As before, we first make a table of coordinates.

x	$y = |x|$	(x, y)
-3	$y = |-3| = 3$	$(-3, 3)$
-2	$y = |-2| = 2$	$(-2, 2)$
-1	$y = |-1| = 1$	$(-1, 1)$
0	$y = |0| = 0$	$(0, 0)$
1	$y = |1| = 1$	$(1, 1)$
2	$y = |2| = 2$	$(2, 2)$
3	$y = |3| = 3$	$(3, 3)$

In Figure P.29 we plot these points and use them to sketch the graph of the equation. It appears that the graph of $y = |x|$ is two straight lines that meet at a $\vee$. ∎

Intercepts

The points, if any, where a graph intersects the x- and y-axes are called *intercepts* and are particularly important. Figure P.30 illustrates four such points. The x-coordinates of the points where a graph intersects the x-axis are called the *x-intercepts* of the graph. The x-intercepts are found by setting $y = 0$ in the graph's equation and solving for x. The y-coordinates of the points where a graph intersects the y-axis are called the *y-intercepts* of the graph. The y-intercepts are found by setting $x = 0$ in the graph's equation and solving for y.

Intercepts

Intercepts	How They Are Determined	What They Look Like
x-intercepts: The x-coordinates of the points where an equation's graph intersects the x-axis.	Set y equal to 0 in the equation, and solve for x.	

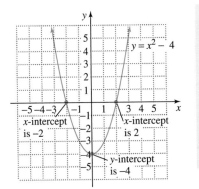

Figure P.31

Intercepts of $y = x^2 - 4$

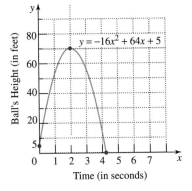

Figure P.32

The height of a ball at different times

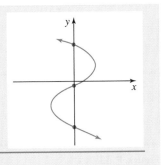

y-intercepts:
The *y*-coordinates of the points where an equation's graph intersects the *y*-axis.

Set *x* equal to 0 in the equation, and solve for *y*.

The graph of $y = x^2 - 4$, obtained in Example 5b, is shown again in Figure P.31. The *y*-intercept is -4, which can be found by setting $x = 0$ in the graph's equation.

$$y = 0^2 - 4 = -4$$

Saying that the *y*-intercept is -4 means that the graph passes through $(0, -4)$.
The graph indicates that there are two *x*-intercepts, -2 and 2. Equivalently, the graph passes through $(-2, 0)$ and $(2, 0)$.

EXAMPLE 6 An Application of Intercepts

A ball is tossed directly upward. The height of the ball (*y*, in feet) at any time (*x*, in seconds) is given by the equation

$$y = -16x^2 + 64x + 5.$$

The graph of the equation is shown in Figure P.32.

a. What is the *y*-intercept and what does this mean in practical terms?
b. What is a reasonable approximation of the *x*-intercept and what does this mean in practical terms?

Solution

a. The graph crosses the *y*-axis at 5, so the *y*-intercept is 5. This means that the graph passes through $(0, 5)$. At time 0, height is 5 feet. This tells us that the ball was tossed from a height of 5 feet.
b. The graph crosses the *x*-axis at approximately 4.1, so the *x*-intercept is about 4.1. The graph passes through $(4.1, 0)$, so at time 4.1 seconds, the height is 0 feet. In practical terms, this means that the ball hits the ground after about 4.1 seconds.

iscover for yourself

Use the graph in Figure P.32 and the equation to determine how high the ball goes.

7 Graph equations with a graphing utility.

Graphing Utilities

Graphing calculators or graphing software packages for computers are referred to as graphing utilities or graphers. The point-plotting method is used by all graphing utilities. A graphing utility displays only a portion of the Cartesian coordinate plane, called a *viewing rectangle*, a *viewing window*, or a *viewing screen*. The viewing rectangle is determined by six values: the minimum *x*-value (Xmin), the maximum *x*-value (Xmax), the *x*-scale (Xscl), the minimum *y*-value (Ymin), the maximum *y*-value (Ymax), and the *y*-scale (Yscl). By entering these six values into the graphing utility, you set the *range* of the viewing rectangle, which is the boundary of the screen.

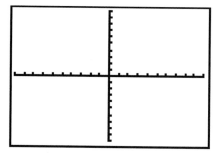

Figure P.33

A standard viewing rectangle for many graphing utilities is $[-10, 10] \times [-10, 10]$.

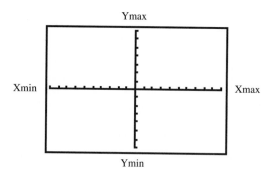

Figure P.34

The viewing rectangle [Xmin, Xmax] by [Ymin, Ymax]

The standard viewing rectangle for many graphing utilities is shown in Figure P.33. This viewing rectangle can be described as $[-10, 10]$ by $[-10, 10]$. On most graphing utilities, the display screen is two-thirds as high as it is wide. By using a *square setting*, you can make the x and y tick marks be equally spaced, which does not occur in the standard viewing rectangle.

In general, the viewing rectangle [Xmin, Xmax] by [Ymin, Ymax] is the set of all points in the Cartesian coordinate plane satisfying $\text{Xmin} \leq x \leq \text{Xmax}$ and $\text{Ymin} \leq y \leq \text{Ymax}$, as shown in Figure P.34. Our work throughout the book will focus on an understanding of equations so that you can determine a viewing window that shows the most important parts of an equation's graph.

Graphing an Equation in x and y Using a Graphing Utility

Graphing an equation in x and y using a graphing utility

1. If necessary, solve the equation for y in terms of x.
2. Enter the equation into the graphing utility.
3. Use the standard viewing rectangle or set the range to determine a viewing rectangle that will show a complete picture of the equation's graph.
4. Start the graphing utility.

EXAMPLE 7   Graphing Equations with a Graphing Utility

Use a graphing utility to graph **a.** $y = 2x - 4$, **b.** $y = x^2 - 4$, **c.** $y = \sqrt[3]{x}$, and **d.** $y = |x|$ in a standard (Xmin = -10, Xmax = 10, Xscl = 1, Ymin = -10, Ymax = 10, Yscl = 1) viewing rectangle.

Solution (Figures appear on page 37.)

a. Figure P.35 shows the graph of $y = 2x - 4$, entered as $Y_1 \boxed{=} 2X \boxed{-} 4$ on many graphing utilities. The line we drew by hand for this equation in Example 5a was straight. Why does the line here seem somewhat bent?

b. Figure P.36 shows the graph of $y = x^2 - 4$, entered as $Y_1 \boxed{=} X \boxed{\wedge} 2 \boxed{-} 4$. Notice that powers are entered using $\boxed{\wedge}$, the power or exponentiation key.

c. Figure P.37 shows the graph of $y = \sqrt[3]{x}$. The equation is entered as $Y_1 \boxed{=} 3$ $\boxed{\sqrt[x]{}} X$. (Consult your manual for the location of the root key, $\boxed{\sqrt[x]{}}$.) You may remember from your work in intermediate algebra that $x^{1/3}$ means $\sqrt[3]{x}$. Thus, the equation $y = \sqrt[3]{x}$ can also be entered as $Y_1 \boxed{=} X \boxed{\wedge}$ $\boxed{(}1 \boxed{\div} 3\boxed{)}$.

ENRICHMENT ESSAY

Cartesian Coordinates: An Historical Perspective

The beginning of the 17th century was a time of innovative ideas and enormous intellectual progress in Europe. English theatergoers enjoyed a succession of exciting new plays by Shakespeare. William Harvey proposed the radical notion that the heart was a pump for blood rather than the center of emotion. Galileo, with his new-fangled invention called the telescope, supported the theory of Polish astronomer Copernicus that the sun, not the Earth, was the center of the solar system. Monteverdi was writing the world's first grand operas. French mathematicians Pascal and Fermat invented a new structure of mathematics known as the theory of probability.

Into this arena of intellectual electricity stepped French aristocrat René Descartes (1596–1650). Descartes, propelled by the creativity surrounding him, felt that it was his destiny to discover a method that would bring together all thought and knowledge using the deductive system of mathematics. Beginning with a simple foundation of rules (axioms),

Descartes believed that all truth regarding nature could be proved in much the same way that the ancient Greek mathematicians proved geometric theorems.

The idea that all knowledge should be presented in the framework of mathematical reasoning appeared in Descartes' book, *A Discourse on the Method of Rightly Conducting the Reason and Seeking Truth in the Sciences*. Descartes concluded his book with three specific examples of how the method could be applied. The third example, a 106-page footnote called *La Géométrie (The Geometry)*, involved the development of a new branch of mathematics that brought together arithmetic, algebra, and geometry in a unified way—a way that visualized numbers as points on a graph, equations as geometric figures, and geometric figures as equations. This new branch of mathematics, called *analytic geometry*, established Descartes as one of the founders of modern thought and among the most original mathematicians and philosophers of any age.

d. Figure P.38 shows the graph of $y = |x|$, entered as Y_1 ⬜ ABS X. (Consult your manual for the location of the ABS [absolute value] key.). ■

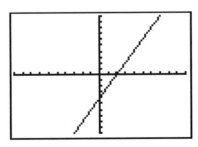

Figure P.35

The graph of $y = 2x - 4$

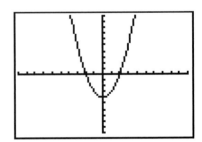

Figure P.36

The graph of $y = x^2 - 4$

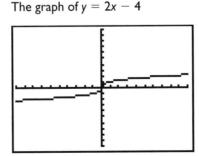

Figure P.37

The graph of $y = \sqrt[3]{x}$

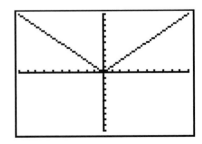

Figure P.38

The graph of $y = |x|$

PROBLEM SET P.3

Practice Problems

*In Problems 1–10, **a.** Plot the points. **b.** Find the distance between the points. **c.** Find the midpoint of the line segment joining the points.*

1. $(4, -3)$, $(-6, 2)$ **2.** $(6, -3)$, $(-4, -5)$ **3.** $(3, 2)$, $(6, 7)$ **4.** $(-3, 7)$, $(5, 7)$

5. $(0, 0)$, $(5, -12)$ **6.** $\left(\frac{7}{4}, -\frac{3}{2}\right)$, $\left(\frac{5}{2}, -\frac{3}{4}\right)$ **7.** $(0, -3)$, $(-3, 3)$ **8.** $(-3, 6)$, $(3, 4)$

9. $(1, -2)$, $(-3, 6)$ **10.** $(5, 7)$, $(2, 3)$

11. Plot the following ordered pairs: $(5, 7)$, $(1, 10)$, and $(-3, -8)$. Then find the perimeter of the triangle whose vertices are the three points.

12. Plot the points $(2, 3)$, $(-1, -1)$, and $(3, -4)$. Then prove that the triangle connecting these points is isosceles (has two sides that are equal in measure).

13. If the vertices of a triangle are $(5, 7)$, $(1, 10)$, and $(-3, -8)$, what is the length of the median from $(5, 7)$?

14. If the vertices of a triangle are $(2, 3)$, $(-1, -1)$, and $(3, -4)$, what is the length of the median from $(2, 3)$?

The converse of the Pythagorean Theorem states that for a triangle with sides of lengths a, b, and c, if $a^2 + b^2 = c^2$, then the triangle is a right triangle. Plot the points in Problems 15–16 and show that they form the vertices of a right triangle. Then find each triangle's area.

15. $(2, 1)$, $(-1, -5)$, $(4, 0)$ **16.** $(2, 2)$, $(3, -1)$, $(-3, -3)$

17. Show that the points $A(-4, -6)$, $B(1, 0)$, and $C(11, 12)$ are collinear (lie along a straight line) by showing that the distance from A to B plus the distance from B to C equals the distance from A to C.

18. The vertices of a quadrilateral are $(-1, -5)$, $(-8, 2)$, $(7, 10)$, and $(4, -3)$. Find the length of the diagonals.

In Problems 19–48, use the point-plotting method to graph the given equation. For each graph, identify all intercepts. Use a graphing utility to verify your graph. (Use the standard viewing rectangle.)

19. $y = 3x - 6$ **20.** $y = 4x - 8$ **21.** $y = -2x + 4$ **22.** $y = -2x + 6$

23. $y = x^2 - 1$ **24.** $y = x^2 - 9$ **25.** $y = 9 - x^2$ **26.** $y = 1 - x^2$

27. $y = x^2 + x - 6$ **28.** $y = x^2 - 4x + 3$ **29.** $y = x^2 - 2x$ **30.** $y = x^2 + x$

31. $y = -x^2 + x + 1$ **32.** $y = -x^2 + 2x - 2$ **33.** $y = x^3 + 2x$ **34.** $y = x^3 - 3x$

35. $y = \sqrt{x}$ **36.** $y = \sqrt{x} - 1$ **37.** $y = \sqrt{x} - 2$ **38.** $y = \sqrt{x} + 4$

39. $y = |2x|$ **40.** $y = |3x|$ **41.** $y = |x + 1|$ **42.** $y = |x + 2|$

43. $y = \sqrt[3]{x + 1}$ **44.** $y = \sqrt[3]{x + 2}$ **45.** $y = |x - 1|$ **46.** $y = |x - 2|$

47. $y = \sqrt[3]{x - 1}$ **48.** $y = \sqrt[3]{x - 2}$

Application Problems

49. Women are taking part in sports as never before. The graph shows participation in high school athletics by women (in thousands). Estimate the coordinates of point A and interpret the coordinates in practical terms.

High School Women Athletes

Source: Women's Sports Foundation

50. The graph on the right shows the height (y, in feet) of a ball dropped from the top of the Empire State Building at different times.

a. What is a reasonable estimate of the height of the Empire State Building?

b. What is a reasonable estimate, to the nearest tenth of a second, of how long it takes for the ball to hit the ground?

Time (in seconds)

Use the figure, which shows the number of accident-related deaths in the United States at home and at work, to answer Problems 51–53.

51. For the period shown, what is a reasonable estimate of the greatest number of accidental deaths that occurred at home? When did this occur?

52. For the period shown, what is a reasonable estimate of the least number of accidental deaths that occurred at home? When did this occur?

53. Describe the trend in the number of accidental deaths that occurred at work.

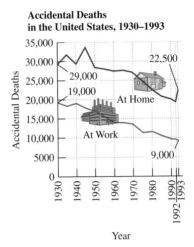

Source: National Safety Council. Adapted from *The Macmillan Visual Almanac.*

A baseball is tossed straight up into the air by a person who is six feet tall. The height of the ball above the ground (y, in feet) depends upon how long the ball is in the air (x, in seconds) and is described by the equation

$$y = -16x^2 + 64x + 6.$$

In this equation, x = 0 corresponds to the instant that the ball is thrown. The graph of this equation is shown in the figure below on the left. Use the figure to answer Problems 54–56.

54. What is the maximum height of the ball? When does the ball reach this height?

55. What is a reasonable estimate of the *x*-intercept for the graph? What happens to the ball for this value of *x*?

56. What is the *y*-intercept for this graph? Explain what this has to do with the height from which the ball was thrown.

57. A photographic light meter is used to measure the brightness of a shining flashlight on a wall. The equation

$$y = \frac{1}{x^2}$$

describes the intensity of brightness (*y*) in terms of the flashlight's distance from the wall (*x*). The graph of this equation is shown in the figure below. As the distance from the light to the wall doubles, by what fraction does the light intensity decrease?

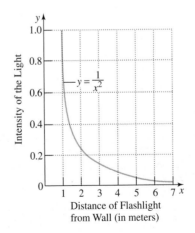

True–False Critical Thinking Problems

58. Which one of the following is true?
 a. If the coordinates of a point satisfy the inequality $xy > 0$, then (x, y) must be in quadrant I.
 b. The ordered pair $(2, 5)$ satisfies $3y - 2x = -4$.
 c. If a point is on the x-axis, it is neither up nor down, so $x = 0$.
 d. None of the above is true.

59. Morphine is widely used in the United States to treat severe pain. Its physiological effects, however, differ for nonaddicts (graph a) and addicts (graph b). Both graphs show the concentration of morphine in the blood following an intravenous injection of 10 milligrams to relieve severe pain. The concentration is measured in micrograms per milliliter (μg/ml). Which one of the following is true based on the graphs?
 a. Nonaddicts receive narcotic effects only when the bloodstream concentration is above 1 μg/ml.
 b. The addict receives narcotic effects for up to 2 hours.
 c. The concentration at which the nonaddict experiences no effects from the drug is the same at which the addict starts experiencing symptoms of withdrawal.
 d. The morphine concentration in the blood over 24 hours differs for nonaddicts and addicts.

(a) Nonaddicts

(b) Addicts

Injecting 10 milligrams of morphine to relieve pain

Technology Problems

60. Use a graphing utility and a standard viewing rectangle to graph each of the following equations. What do you observe?

$$y = 2x + 3, \quad y = 2x + 1, \quad y = 2x,$$
$$y = 2x - 1, \quad y = 2x - 3$$

61. Use a graphing utility and a standard viewing rectangle to graph each of the following equations. What do you observe?

$$y = 4x + 1, \quad y = 2x + 1, \quad y = -2x + 1,$$
$$y = -4x + 1$$

62. Use a graphing utility to graph each pair of equations in the same viewing rectangle.
 a. $y = x \cdot x^2$ and $y = x^3$
 b. $y = x^2 \cdot x^3$ and $y = x^5$
 c. $y = \dfrac{x^5}{x^3}$ and $y = x^2$

 d. What do you observe? What generalizations can you make regarding properties of exponents?

A graph of an equation is a complete graph if it shows all of the important features of the graph. Use a graphing utility to graph the equations in Problems 63–66 in each of the given viewing rectangles. Then choose which viewing rectangle gives a complete graph.

63. $y = x^2 + 10$
 a. $[-5, 5]$ by $[-5, 5]$ **b.** $[-10, 10]$ by $[-10, 10]$
 c. $[-10, 10]$ by $[-50, 50]$
64. $y = 0.1x^4 - x^3 + 2x^2$
 a. $[-5, 5]$ by $[-8, 2]$ **b.** $[-10, 10]$ by $[-10, 10]$
 c. $[-8, 16]$ by $[-16, 8]$

65. $y = \sqrt{x + 18}$
 a. $[-10, 10]$ by $[-10, 10]$ **b.** $[-50, 50]$ by $[-10, 10]$
 c. $[-10, 10]$ by $[-50, 50]$
66. $y = x^3 - 30x + 20$
 a. $[-10, 10]$ by $[-10, 10]$ **b.** $[-10, 10]$ by $[-50, 50]$
 c. $[-10, 10]$ by $[-50, 100]$

In Problems 67–69, find a complete graph of each equation in the same viewing rectangle.

67. $y = |x|$, $\quad y = |x - 1|$, $\quad y = |x - 2|$, $\quad y = |x + 3|$

68. $y = x^2$, $\quad y = x^2 - 1$, $\quad y = x^2 - 2$, $\quad y = x^2 + 3$

69. $y = x^2$, $\quad y = (x - 1)^2$, $\quad y = (x - 2)^2$, $\quad y = (x + 3)^2$

In Problems 70–73, use a graphing utility to graph each equation. Then use the $\boxed{\text{TRACE}}$ feature to move the cursor along the curve to approximate the variable coordinate(s) of the solution point to two decimal places. In some cases, you may need to use the $\boxed{\text{ZOOM}}$ feature to obtain the desired accuracy.

70. $y = \sqrt{6 - x}$ **a.** $(2, y)$ **b.** $(x, 2)$

71. $y = x^2 - 4x + 3$ **a.** $(-0.5, y)$ **b.** $(x, 3)$

72. $y = x^3 - 4x$ **a.** $(2, y)$ **b.** $(x, -2)$

73. $y = x^3(x - 2)$ **a.** $(2.5, y)$ **b.** $(x, 4.5)$

74. The formula $y = -3.1x^2 + 51.4x + 4024.5$ approximately describes the average number of cigarettes (y) per year consumed by Americans 18 and older x years after 1950. The formula describes reality from the years 1950 through 1990, or from $x = 0$ through $x = 40$.

  a. Construct a table of coordinates using $x = 0, 5, 10, 15, 20, 30,$ and 40. Find the corresponding values for y using a calculator and rounding to the nearest integer. Then graph the equation by hand.

  b. Use a graphing utility with the following range setting to check your hand-drawn graph.

    Xmin = 0,   Xmax = 40,   Xscl = 1,   Ymin = 0,

    Ymax = 5000,   Yscl = 1000

  c. Change the range setting so that Xmax = 45. Use your graphing utility to graph the equation for cigarette consumption with this new range setting. Based on the shape of the graph, does the given equation accurately describe reality from $x = 40$ through $x = 45$? What does this tell you about equations that attempt to describe variables over long periods of time?

75. The formulas

$$y = 67.0166(1.00308)^x$$

and

$$y = 74.9742(1.00201)^x$$

describe the life expectancy (y) for white males and females, respectively, in the United States whose present age is x.

  a. Use a graphing utility to graph both equations in the same viewing rectangle. Enter the formulas as

    $Y_1 \boxed{=}$ 67.0166 $\boxed{\times}$ 1.00308 $\boxed{\wedge}$ X

    $Y_2 \boxed{=}$ 74.9742 $\boxed{\times}$ 1.00201 $\boxed{\wedge}$ X

    with the following range setting:

    Xmin = 0, Xmax = 80, Xscl = 1, Ymin = 0,

    Ymax = 100, Yscl = 1

  b. Use the $\boxed{\text{TRACE}}$ feature of your utility to trace along each curve until you reach $x = 40$. What is the corresponding value for y on y_1 and y_2? How long can a 40-year-old white male expect to live? How long can a 40-year-old white female expect to live?

  c. Explain how each graph indicates that life expectancy increases as one gets older. Use the $\boxed{\text{TRACE}}$ feature to reinforce your observation.

Writing in Mathematics

76. The figure shown here depicts actual data points for cigarette consumption in the United States. How does your graph in Problem 74 compare to the one shown here? What does this tell you about mathematical equations that describe variables in the real world?

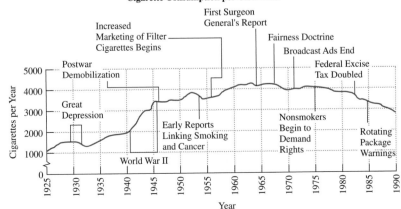

Cigarette Consumption per U.S. Adult

Source: U.S. Department of Health and Human Services.

77. Using a random sample of white Americans (from which we can generalize), sociologists Lawrence Bobo and James Kluegel (1991) studied the extent of prejudice in the United States. Details of some of their research are shown in the graph. Describe the trend shown by the graph in terms of education and prejudice. What is misleading about the scale on the horizontal axis?

Percentage of White Americans Who Favor Segregated Housing

Source: Bobo and Kluegel, 1991.

78. The parentheses used to represent an ordered pair are also used to represent an interval. If you are reading a section in a math book and (3, 4) is mentioned, how will you know if they are discussing the point (3, 4) or the interval for which $3 < x < 4$?

Critical Thinking Problems

79. Show that the points A $(1, 1 + d)$, B $(3, 3 + d)$, and C $(6, 6 + d)$ are collinear (lie along a straight line) by showing that the distance from A to B plus the distance from B to C equals the distance from A to C.

80. Prove the midpoint formula by using the following procedure.

a. Show that the distance between (x_1, y_1) and $\left(\dfrac{x_1 + x_2}{2}, \dfrac{y_1 + y_2}{2}\right)$ is equal to the distance between (x_2, y_2) and $\left(\dfrac{x_1 + x_2}{2}, \dfrac{y_1 + y_2}{2}\right)$.

b. Use the procedure from Problem 79 to show that the points (x_1, y_1), $\left(\dfrac{x_1 + x_2}{2}, \dfrac{y_1 + y_2}{2}\right)$, and (x_2, y_2) are collinear.

SECTION P.4 **Radicals and Rational Exponents**

Solutions Manual   **Tutorial**   **Video**
                                          I

Objectives

1 Find nth roots.

2 Simplify radical expressions.

3 Rationalize denominators.

4 Combine radicals.

5 Evaluate expressions with rational exponents.

6 Simplify expressions with rational exponents.

7 Reduce the index of a radical.

The number of plant species on the various islands of the Galápagos chain is given by

$$S = 28.6 \sqrt[3]{A}$$

in which A is the area of the island in square miles and S is the number of plant species on the island. Radical expressions frequently appear in descriptions of the physical world. In this section, we review such expressions and the use of rational exponents to indicate radicals.

Find nth roots.

Even and Odd nth Roots

Roots in general are related to repeated factors. For example,

$$2^3 = 2 \cdot 2 \cdot 2 = 8$$

so 2 is the *cube root* of 8, written

$$\sqrt[3]{8} = 2.$$

As another example,

$$3^4 = 3 \cdot 3 \cdot 3 \cdot 3 = 81$$

so 3 is the *fourth root* of 81, written

$$\sqrt[4]{81} = 3.$$

Let's generalize from these examples, beginning with the definition of even roots.

Definition of even roots

If n is an even natural number and $b > 0$, $\sqrt[n]{b}$ (the nth root of b) is the positive real number whose nth power is b. Thus $\sqrt[n]{b} = a$ if $a^n = b$.

$$(\sqrt[n]{b})^n = b \quad \text{when} \quad b > 0$$

EXAMPLE 1   **Finding nth Roots When n Is an Even Number**

Find each root, or state that the root is not a real number.

a. $\sqrt[4]{81}$ **b.** $-\sqrt[4]{81}$ **c.** $\sqrt[4]{-81}$ **d.** $\sqrt[6]{64}$ **e.** $(\sqrt[4]{6})^4$ **f.** $\sqrt[4]{\frac{81}{16}}$

Solution

a. $\sqrt[4]{81} = 3$ because $3^4 = 81$.

b. $-\sqrt[4]{81} = -(\sqrt[4]{81}) = -3$

c. $\sqrt[4]{-81}$ is not a real number. There is no real number we can raise to the fourth power and obtain -81.

d. $\sqrt[6]{64} = 2$ because $2^6 = 64$.

e. $(\sqrt[4]{6})^4 = 6$ because $(\sqrt[n]{b})^n = b$.

f. $\sqrt[4]{\frac{81}{16}} = \frac{3}{2}$ because $(\frac{3}{2})^4 = \frac{81}{16}$.

If n is an odd natural number, it is not necessary to restrict b to positive real numbers.

Using technology

Verify the results of Examples 1 and 2 using a graphing calculator, if possible. First consult your manual to locate the root ($\boxed{\sqrt[x]{}}$) key.

Verifying Example 1a: $\sqrt[4]{81}$

4 $\boxed{\sqrt[x]{}}$ 81 $\boxed{\text{ENTER}}$

Verifying Example 2c: $\sqrt[5]{-32}$

5 $\boxed{\sqrt[x]{}}$ $\boxed{(-)}$ 32 $\boxed{\text{ENTER}}$

Definition of odd roots

If n is an odd natural number, $\sqrt[n]{b}$ is the positive or negative real number whose nth power is b. Thus, $\sqrt[n]{b} = a$ if $a^n = b$.

$$(\sqrt[n]{b})^n = b$$

EXAMPLE 2 **Finding nth Roots when n Is an Odd Number**

Find each root:

a. $\sqrt[3]{27}$ **b.** $\sqrt[3]{-64}$ **c.** $\sqrt[5]{-32}$ **d.** $(\sqrt[7]{-6})^7$ **e.** $\sqrt[7]{-\frac{1}{128}}$

Solution

a. $\sqrt[3]{27} = 3$ because $3^3 = 27$.
b. $\sqrt[3]{-64} = -4$ because $(-4)^3 = -64$.
c. $\sqrt[5]{-32} = -2$ because $(-2)^5 = -32$.
d. $(\sqrt[7]{-6})^7 = -6$ because $(\sqrt[n]{b})^n = b$.
e. $\sqrt[7]{-\frac{1}{128}} = -\frac{1}{2}$ because $(-\frac{1}{2})^7 = -\frac{1}{128}$.

Discover for yourself

If n is even or odd, the nth root of 1 is 1.

$$\sqrt{1} = 1, \quad \sqrt[3]{1} = 1, \quad \sqrt[4]{1} = 1, \quad \sqrt[5]{1} = 1, \quad \sqrt[6]{1} = 1, \quad \text{etc.}$$

In general,

$$\sqrt[n]{1} = 1.$$

Can you think of another number all of whose nth roots equal the number itself?

In the Discover for yourself, did you discover that the number is 0, a number with many special properties?

The nth root of zero

If n is even or odd,

$$\sqrt[n]{0} = 0.$$

Mathematicians have a special vocabulary related to even and odd roots.

The vocabulary of radicals

Given $\sqrt{b}, \sqrt[3]{b}, \sqrt[4]{b}, \sqrt[5]{b}$, and so on, the numbers 2, 3, 4, 5, ... are called the *index* of the root. Observe that an index of 2, indicating the square root, is omitted. $\sqrt{}$ is called the *radical sign*. The expression under the radical sign, b, is the *radicand*. The expressions $\sqrt{b}, \sqrt[3]{b}, \sqrt[4]{b}$, and $\sqrt[5]{b}$ are *radicals*.

Before turning to properties of radicals, let's take a moment to summarize our discussion of *n*th roots.

---

*n*th roots

1. If *n* is even: $\sqrt[n]{b} = a$ $(b > 0)$ if $a^n = b$.
   a. Every positive number has two *n*th roots that are opposites of each other. For example, the fourth roots of 16 are 2 and -2.
   b. If $b < 0$, then $\sqrt[n]{b}$ is not a real number.
2. If *n* is odd: $\sqrt[n]{b} = a$ if $a^n = b$.
   a. Every real number has one *n*th root. For example, $\sqrt[3]{8} = 2$ and $\sqrt[3]{-27} = -3$.
   b. The *n*th root of a positive number is positive, and the *n*th root of a negative number is negative.
3. If *n* is even or odd: $\sqrt[n]{0} = 0$.

The following properties will be used to simplify radical expressions.

Properties of *n*th roots

Let b and c be real numbers, variables, or algebraic expressions, and let m and n be natural numbers. In each property, the indicated roots are real numbers.

Property	**Example**
1. $\sqrt[n]{b} \cdot \sqrt[n]{c} = \sqrt[n]{bc}$	$\sqrt[3]{4} \cdot \sqrt[3]{2} = \sqrt[3]{4 \cdot 2} = \sqrt[3]{8} = 2$
2. $\dfrac{\sqrt[n]{b}}{\sqrt[n]{c}} = \sqrt[n]{\dfrac{b}{c}}, \quad c \neq 0$	$\dfrac{\sqrt[5]{36}}{\sqrt[5]{4}} = \sqrt[5]{\dfrac{36}{4}} = \sqrt[5]{9}$
3. $(\sqrt[n]{b})^n = b$	$(\sqrt[3]{5})^5 = 5$
4. If *n* is even, $\sqrt[n]{b^n} = \lvert b \rvert$	$\sqrt{(-6)^2} = \lvert -6 \rvert = 6$
If *n* is odd, $\sqrt[n]{b^n} = b$	$\sqrt[3]{(-6)^3} = -6$
5. $\sqrt[m]{\sqrt[n]{b}} = \sqrt[mn]{b}$	$\sqrt[3]{\sqrt{5}} = \sqrt[3 \cdot 2]{5} = \sqrt[6]{5}$

> **Study tip**
>
> The *n*th root of a sum is *not* equal to the sum of the *n*th roots:
>
> $$\sqrt[n]{b + c} \neq \sqrt[n]{b} + \sqrt[n]{c}$$
>
> Show that this is the case by letting $n = 2$, $b = 9$, and $c = 16$.

2 Simplify radical expressions.

Simplified Radical Form

Properties of *n*th roots are important because they allow us to simplify radicals. A simplified radical expression satisfies four conditions.

Conditions for simplified radical form

A radical expression with index *n* is in simplest form, or is simplified completely, whenever:

1. The radicand contains as few factors as possible. The radicand should contain no factors that are *n*th powers.
2. There are no fractions in the radicand.
3. There are no radicals in the denominator.
4. The index of the radical is reduced.

The first condition for simplified form requires that we remove as many factors from the radicand as possible, using

$$\sqrt[n]{b^n} = |b| \qquad \text{when } n \text{ is even}$$

and

$$\sqrt[n]{b^n} = b \qquad \text{when } n \text{ is odd}$$

EXAMPLE 3   Simplifying Radicals

Write each radical in simplified form by factoring the radicand and removing as many factors as possible.

a. $\sqrt[3]{54}$ **b.** $\sqrt{48x^3}$ **c.** $\sqrt[3]{-16y^4}$ **d.** $\sqrt[4]{32x^4y^6}$

Solution

a. $\sqrt[3]{54} = \sqrt[3]{27 \cdot 2}$ Observe that 27 is a *perfect cube* because its cube root is an integer: $\sqrt[3]{27} = 3$.

$\qquad\quad = \sqrt[3]{3^3 \cdot 2}$ The index is 3, so we want radicand factors that are cubes.

$\qquad\quad = \sqrt[3]{3^3} \cdot \sqrt[3]{2}$

$\qquad\quad = 3\sqrt[3]{2}$ $\sqrt[n]{b^n} = b$ if n is odd.

b. $\sqrt{48x^3} = \sqrt{16x^2 \cdot 3x}$ Notice that $16x^2$ is a perfect square factor.

$\qquad\quad = \sqrt{(4x)^2 \cdot 3x}$

$\qquad\quad = \sqrt{(4x)^2} \cdot \sqrt{3x}$

$\qquad\quad = |4x| \cdot \sqrt{3x}$ $\sqrt[n]{b^n} = |b|$, if n is even.

$\qquad\quad = 4|x|\sqrt{3x}$ $|4x| = |4||x| = 4|x|$

c. $\sqrt[3]{-16y^4} = \sqrt[3]{-8y^3 \cdot 2y}$ The perfect cube factor is $-8y^3$.

$\qquad\quad = \sqrt[3]{(-2y)^3 \cdot 2y}$

$\qquad\quad = \sqrt[3]{(-2y)^3} \cdot \sqrt[3]{2y}$

$\qquad\quad = -2y\sqrt[3]{2y}$ $\sqrt[n]{b^n} = b$ if n is odd.

d. $\sqrt[4]{32x^4y^6} = \sqrt[4]{16x^4y^4 \cdot 2y^2}$ The index is 4, so we want radicand factors that are perfect fourth powers.

$\qquad\quad = \sqrt[4]{(2xy)^4 \cdot 2y^2}$

$\qquad\quad = \sqrt[4]{(2xy)^4} \cdot \sqrt[4]{2y^2}$

$\qquad\quad = |2xy|\sqrt[4]{2y^2}$ $\sqrt[n]{b^n} = |b|$ if n is even.

$\qquad\quad = 2|xy|\sqrt[4]{2y^2}$ ∎

Donald Judd "Untitled" 1967, green lacquer / galvanized iron, 12 units at 9 × 40 × 31 in. Courtesy Joseph Helman Gallery, New York. © Estate of Donald Judd / Licensed by VAGA, New York, NY.

3 Rationalize denominators.

The second and third conditions for simplified radical form do not permit radicals in a denominator. Such radical expressions are simplified by multiplying both the numerator and the denominator by a factor chosen to eliminate any radicals in the denominator. If the denominator contains a square root, you can multiply the numerator and the denominator by the square root expression in the denominator:

$$\frac{1}{\sqrt{a}} = \frac{1}{\sqrt{a}} \cdot 1 = \frac{1}{\sqrt{a}} \cdot \frac{\sqrt{a}}{\sqrt{a}} = \frac{\sqrt{a}}{a}$$

Because we are multiplying by 1, we are not changing the value of the radical expression. Observe that the denominator in the last fraction contains no radical. Removing radicals from a denominator without changing the value of a radical expression is called *rationalizing the denominator*.

EXAMPLE 4 Rationalizing a Single-Term Denominator

Simplify by rationalizing the denominator: $\dfrac{7}{2\sqrt{6}}$

Solution

We multiply the numerator and the denominator by $\sqrt{6}$ because $\sqrt{6} \cdot \sqrt{6} = 6$.

$$\frac{7}{2\sqrt{6}} = \frac{7}{2\sqrt{6}} \cdot \frac{\sqrt{6}}{\sqrt{6}} = \frac{7\sqrt{6}}{2(6)} = \frac{7\sqrt{6}}{12} \qquad \blacksquare$$

Things get a bit more complicated when higher roots appear in the denominator. If the denominator is of the form $\sqrt[n]{a^m}$ with $m < n$, we can rationalize the denominator by multiplying the numerator and the denominator by $\sqrt[n]{a^{n-m}}$.

$$\frac{1}{\sqrt[n]{a^m}} = \frac{1}{\sqrt[n]{a^m}} \cdot 1 = \frac{1}{\sqrt[n]{a^m}} \cdot \frac{\sqrt[n]{a^{n-m}}}{\sqrt[n]{a^{n-m}}} = \frac{\sqrt[n]{a^{n-m}}}{\sqrt[n]{a^{m+n-m}}} = \frac{\sqrt[n]{a^{n-m}}}{\sqrt[n]{a^n}} = \frac{\sqrt[n]{a^{n-m}}}{a}$$

EXAMPLE 5 Rationalizing Single-Term Denominators with Higher Roots

Simplify by rationalizing the denominator:

a. $\sqrt[3]{\dfrac{2}{9}}$ **b.** $\dfrac{7}{\sqrt[5]{8}}$

Solution

a. We begin by writing the fraction as $\dfrac{\sqrt[3]{2}}{\sqrt[3]{9}}$. We note that the denominator can be expressed as $\sqrt[3]{3^2}$. We now multiply the numerator and the denominator by $\sqrt[3]{3}$ because $\sqrt[3]{3^2} \cdot \sqrt[3]{3} = \sqrt[3]{3^3} = 3$.

$$\sqrt[3]{\frac{2}{9}} = \frac{\sqrt[3]{2}}{\sqrt[3]{9}} = \frac{\sqrt[3]{2}}{\sqrt[3]{3^2}} \cdot \frac{\sqrt[3]{3}}{\sqrt[3]{3}} = \frac{\sqrt[3]{6}}{\sqrt[3]{3^3}} = \frac{\sqrt[3]{6}}{3}$$

b. We begin by expressing the fraction as $\dfrac{7}{\sqrt[5]{2^3}}$. We will multiply the numerator and the denominator by $\sqrt[5]{2^2}$ because $\sqrt[5]{2^3} \cdot \sqrt[5]{2^2} = \sqrt[5]{2^5} = 2$.

$$\frac{7}{\sqrt[5]{8}} = \frac{7}{\sqrt[5]{2^3}} \cdot \frac{\sqrt[5]{2^2}}{\sqrt[5]{2^2}} = \frac{7\sqrt[5]{2^2}}{\sqrt[5]{2^5}} = \frac{7\sqrt[5]{4}}{2} \qquad \blacksquare$$

If the denominator is of the form $a + b\sqrt{c}$, we multiply the numerator and the denominator by the *conjugate radical* $a - b\sqrt{c}$. The product of $a + b\sqrt{c}$ and $a - b\sqrt{c}$ does not contain a radical.

Study tip

As we have seen, to rationalize the denominator with square roots, you can multiply the numerator and the denominator by the number in the denominator:

$$\frac{1}{\sqrt{2}} = \frac{1}{\sqrt{2}} \cdot \frac{\sqrt{2}}{\sqrt{2}} = \frac{\sqrt{2}}{2}$$

However, this does not work with higher roots.

Incorrect:

$$\frac{1}{\sqrt[3]{2}} = \frac{1}{\sqrt[3]{2}} \cdot \frac{\sqrt[3]{2}}{\sqrt[3]{2}} = \frac{\sqrt[3]{2}}{2}$$

Correct:

$$\frac{1}{\sqrt[3]{2}} = \frac{1}{\sqrt[3]{2}} \cdot \frac{\sqrt[3]{2^2}}{\sqrt[3]{2^2}} = \frac{\sqrt[3]{2^2}}{\sqrt[3]{2^3}}$$

$$= \frac{\sqrt[3]{4}}{2}$$

$$(a + b\sqrt{c})(a - b\sqrt{c})$$

$$= a(a - b\sqrt{c}) + b\sqrt{c}(a - b\sqrt{c})$$ Distribute each term in the first parentheses over the second parentheses.

$$= a^2 - ab\sqrt{c} + ab\sqrt{c} - (b\sqrt{c})^2$$ Distribute.

$$= a^2 - (b\sqrt{c})^2$$ Simplify.

$$= a^2 - b^2c$$

The significance of this last step is that it does not contain a radical.

Multiplying by a conjugate radical

$$(a + b\sqrt{c})(a - b\sqrt{c}) = a^2 - (b\sqrt{c})^2 = a^2 - b^2c$$

EXAMPLE 6 **Rationalizing Denominators Containing Two Terms**

Rationalize the denominator:

a. $\dfrac{21}{4 - \sqrt{2}}$ **b.** $\dfrac{20}{\sqrt{7} + \sqrt{3}}$

Solution

Discover for yourself

In Example 6a, show that multiplying the given fraction by

$$\dfrac{4 - \sqrt{2}}{4 - \sqrt{2}} \quad \text{or} \quad \dfrac{\sqrt{2}}{\sqrt{2}}$$

does not eliminate the radical in the denominator. In Example 6b, show that multiplying by

$$\dfrac{\sqrt{7} + \sqrt{3}}{\sqrt{7} + \sqrt{3}}$$

does not eliminate the denominator's radicals.

a. $\dfrac{21}{4 - \sqrt{2}} = \dfrac{21}{4 - \sqrt{2}} \cdot \dfrac{4 + \sqrt{2}}{4 + \sqrt{2}}$ Multiply the numerator and the denominator by the conjugate radical of the denominator.

$$= \dfrac{21(4 + \sqrt{2})}{4^2 - (\sqrt{2})^2}$$ $(a + b\sqrt{c})(a - b\sqrt{c}) = a^2 - (b\sqrt{c})^2$

$$= \dfrac{21(4 + \sqrt{2})}{16 - 2}$$ $(\sqrt{2})^2 = 2$. In general, $(\sqrt[n]{b})^n = b$.

$$= \dfrac{21(4 + \sqrt{2})}{14}$$

$$= \dfrac{3(4 + \sqrt{2})}{2}$$ Simplify, dividing the numerator and the denominator by 7.

The simplified radical can be expressed as $\dfrac{12 + 3\sqrt{2}}{2}$.

b. $\dfrac{20}{\sqrt{7} + \sqrt{3}} = \dfrac{20}{\sqrt{7} + \sqrt{3}} \cdot \dfrac{\sqrt{7} - \sqrt{3}}{\sqrt{7} - \sqrt{3}}$ Multiply the numerator and the denominator by the denominator's conjugate radical.

$$= \dfrac{20(\sqrt{7} - \sqrt{3})}{(\sqrt{7})^2 - (\sqrt{3})^2}$$ $(\sqrt{a} + \sqrt{b})(\sqrt{a} - \sqrt{b}) = (\sqrt{a})^2 - (\sqrt{b})^2$

$$= \dfrac{20(\sqrt{7} - \sqrt{3})}{7 - 3}$$ $(\sqrt[n]{b})^n = b$

$$= \dfrac{20(\sqrt{7} - \sqrt{3})}{4}$$

$$= 5(\sqrt{7} - \sqrt{3})$$ Simplify. The answer can be equivalently expressed as $5\sqrt{7} - 5\sqrt{3}$.

4 Combine radicals.

Combining Radicals

Radical expressions can be added and subtracted if they are *like radicals*, meaning they have the same index and the same radicand. We can use the distributive property to add or subtract like radicals. For example,

$$7\sqrt{2} + 5\sqrt{2} = (7 + 5)\sqrt{2} = 12\sqrt{2}$$

$$19\sqrt[3]{5} - 12\sqrt[3]{5} = (19 - 12)\sqrt[3]{5} = 7\sqrt[3]{5}$$

Although at first glance many radicals might not appear to be like radicals, simplification may enable us to add or subtract. Let's see how this works.

EXAMPLE 7   Combining Radicals

Combine:

a. $7\sqrt{18} + 5\sqrt{8} - 6\sqrt{2}$

b. $12\sqrt{\dfrac{1}{3}} - 4\sqrt{\dfrac{1}{12}}$

Solution

a. $7\sqrt{18} + 5\sqrt{8} - 6\sqrt{2}$

$= 7\sqrt{9 \cdot 2} + 5\sqrt{4 \cdot 2} - 6\sqrt{2}$ Begin by simplifying $\sqrt{18}$ and $\sqrt{8}$.

$= 7 \cdot 3\sqrt{2} + 5 \cdot 2\sqrt{2} - 6\sqrt{2}$ $\sqrt{9 \cdot 2} = \sqrt{3^2 \cdot 2} = 3\sqrt{2}$ and $\sqrt{4 \cdot 2} = \sqrt{2^2 \cdot 2} = 2\sqrt{2}$.

$= 21\sqrt{2} + 10\sqrt{2} - 6\sqrt{2}$ Multiply.

$= (21 + 10 - 6)\sqrt{2}$ Use the distributive property.

$= 25\sqrt{2}$ Combine numerical terms.

b. $12\sqrt{\dfrac{1}{3}} - 4\sqrt{\dfrac{1}{12}}$

$= 12 \cdot \dfrac{1}{\sqrt{3}} - 4 \cdot \dfrac{1}{\sqrt{12}}$

$= \dfrac{12}{\sqrt{3}} \cdot \dfrac{\sqrt{3}}{\sqrt{3}} - \dfrac{4}{\sqrt{12}} \cdot \dfrac{\sqrt{3}}{\sqrt{3}}$ Rationalize denominators. The smallest number that produces a perfect square in the second denominator is $\sqrt{3}$, but you can also multiply by $\dfrac{\sqrt{12}}{\sqrt{12}}$.

$= \dfrac{12\sqrt{3}}{3} - \dfrac{4\sqrt{3}}{6}$ $\sqrt{3} \cdot \sqrt{3} = (\sqrt{3})^2 = 3$ and $\sqrt{12} \cdot \sqrt{3} = \sqrt{36} = 6$.

$= 4\sqrt{3} - \dfrac{2\sqrt{3}}{3}$ Simplify.

$= \left(4 - \dfrac{2}{3}\right)\sqrt{3}$ Use the distributive property.

$= \dfrac{10\sqrt{3}}{3}$ $4 - \dfrac{2}{3} = \dfrac{12}{3} - \dfrac{2}{3} = \dfrac{10}{3}$

Discover for yourself

In Examples 4–7, use a calculator to find a decimal approximation for the given number. Then find a decimal approximation for the simplified form of the number. The decimal approximations should be the same, which is a way of checking the simplification.

5 Evaluate expressions with rational exponents.

Rational Numbers as Exponents

We are now ready to give meaning to expressions that contain rational numbers as exponents, such as $27^{1/3}$. You can discover the significance of rational exponents by first working the Discover for yourself with your graphing utility.

iscover for yourself

Use your graphing utility to graph each of the following pairs of equations in the same $[-100, 100]$ by $[-10, 10]$ viewing rectangle.

$$y = x^{1/2} \text{ and } y = \sqrt{x}; \qquad y = x^{1/3} \text{ and } y = \sqrt[3]{x}; \qquad y = x^{1/4} \text{ and } y = \sqrt[4]{x}$$

Based on the graphs of the equations in each pair, generalize and give a definition for $b^{1/n}$.

In the Discover for yourself, did you obtain identical graphs for $y = b^{1/n}$ and $y = \sqrt[n]{b}$? Thus $b^{1/n} = \sqrt[n]{b}$, and rational exponents indicate roots.

Definition of rational exponents

If n is a positive integer and $\sqrt[n]{b}$ is a real number, then $b^{1/n}$ is defined to be the principal nth root of b.

$$b^{1/n} = \sqrt[n]{b}$$

If m is a positive integer that has no common factors with n, then

$$b^{m/n} = (b^m)^{1/n} = \sqrt[n]{b^m} \quad \text{and} \quad b^{m/n} = (b^{1/n})^m = (\sqrt[n]{b})^m.$$

Study tip

The expression

$$b^{m/n}$$

is not defined if $\sqrt[n]{b}$ is not a real number. This can lead to some strange results. For example,

$$(-125)^{2/6}$$

is not defined because $\sqrt[6]{-125}$ is not a real number. However,

$$(-125)^{1/3}$$

is defined because

$$\sqrt[3]{-125} = -5.$$

We refer to $b^{m/n}$ as the *exponential form* and $\sqrt[n]{b^m}$ or $(\sqrt[n]{b})^m$ as the *radical form*. Observe that the denominator n in $b^{m/n}$ denotes the index of the root and m represents a power.

$$b^{m/n} = \sqrt[n]{b^m} = (\sqrt[n]{b})^m$$

EXAMPLE 8 **Evaluating Expressions Containing Rational Exponents**

Evaluate:

a. $64^{2/3}$ **b.** $16^{5/2}$ **c.** $(-125)^{4/3}$ **d.** $-125^{4/3}$

Solution

a. $64^{2/3} = (\sqrt[3]{64})^2 = 4^2 = 16$

b. $16^{5/2} = (\sqrt{16})^5 = 4^5 = 1024$

c. $(-125)^{4/3} = (\sqrt[3]{-125})^4 = (-5)^4 = 625$

d. $-125^{4/3} = -(\sqrt[3]{125})^4 = -(5)^4 = -625$

Using technology

Here are the graphing utility keystroke sequences for Example 8.

a. $64^{2/3}$:   64 $\boxed{\wedge}$ $\boxed{(}$ $\boxed{(}$ 2 $\boxed{\div}$ 3 $\boxed{)}$ $\boxed{\text{ENTER}}$

b. $16^{5/2}$:   16 $\boxed{\wedge}$ $\boxed{(}$ $\boxed{(}$ 5 $\boxed{\div}$ 2 $\boxed{)}$ $\boxed{\text{ENTER}}$

c. $(-125)^{4/3}$: Some graphing utilities do not evaluate $b^{m/n}$ when b is negative.
Enter part (d) as $[(-125)^{1/3}]^4$:

$\boxed{(}$ $\boxed{(}$ $\boxed{(}$ $\boxed{(-)}$ 125 $\boxed{)}$ $\boxed{\wedge}$ $\boxed{(}$ $\boxed{(}$ 1 $\boxed{\div}$ 3 $\boxed{)}$ $\boxed{)}$ $\boxed{\wedge}$ 4 $\boxed{\text{ENTER}}$

d. $-125^{4/3}$: $\boxed{(-)}$ 125 $\boxed{\wedge}$ $\boxed{(}$ $\boxed{(}$ 4 $\boxed{\div}$ 3 $\boxed{)}$ $\boxed{\text{ENTER}}$

6 Simplify expressions with rational exponents.

The properties for integer exponents also apply to rational exponents. For example, by extending the property

$$b^{-n} = \frac{1}{b^n}$$

to rational exponents, we can evaluate an expression such as $81^{-3/4}$ as follows:

$$81^{-3/4} = \frac{1}{81^{3/4}} = \frac{1}{(\sqrt[4]{81})^3} = \frac{1}{3^3} = \frac{1}{27}$$

Example 9 illustrates how we can use properties of exponents to simplify expressions containing rational exponents. Once again, only positive exponents will appear in the final result.

EXAMPLE 9   **Simplifying Expressions Involving Rational Exponents**

Simplify:

a. $(4x - 3)^{4/3}(4x - 3)^{-1/3}$

b. $\dfrac{x^2 + 1}{(x^2 + 1)^{-1/2}}$

c. $\dfrac{32x^{1/2}}{16x^{3/4}}$

d. $\left(\dfrac{7x^{3/5}}{4y^{1/3}}\right)^3$

Solution

a. $(4x - 3)^{4/3}(4x - 3)^{-1/3}$

$= (4x - 3)^{4/3 + (-1/3)}$ $b^n \cdot b^m = b^{n+m}$; Add exponents.

$= (4x - 3)^1$

$= 4x - 3$

b. $\dfrac{x^2 + 1}{(x^2 + 1)^{-1/2}}$

$= (x^2 + 1)^{1 - (-1/2)}$ $\dfrac{b^n}{b^m} = b^{n-m}$; Subtract exponents.

$= (x^2 + 1)^{3/2}$

Study tip

Remember that division by zero is undefined. This means that

$$(4x - 3)^{-1/3} \quad \text{or} \quad \frac{1}{(4x - 3)^{1/3}}$$

must exclude the value of x for which

$$(4x - 3)^{1/3} = 0$$

Thus, x cannot equal $\frac{3}{4}$.

c. $\dfrac{32x^{1/2}}{16x^{3/4}}$

$= \dfrac{32}{16}x^{1/2-3/4}$ $\dfrac{b^n}{b^m} = b^{n-m}$; Subtract exponents.

$= 2x^{-1/4}$

$= \dfrac{2}{x^{1/4}}$ $b^{-n} = \dfrac{1}{b^n}$

d. $\left(\dfrac{7x^{3/5}}{4y^{1/3}}\right)^3$

$= \dfrac{(7x^{3/5})^3}{(4y^{1/3})^3}$ $\left(\dfrac{a}{b}\right)^n = \dfrac{a^n}{b^n}$; Cube the numerator and the denominator.

$= \dfrac{7^3(x^{3/5})^3}{4^3(y^{1/3})^3}$ $(ab)^n = a^nb^n$; Cube each factor in the numerator and the denominator.

$= \dfrac{7^3x^{3/5\cdot3}}{4^3y^{1/3\cdot3}}$ $(b^n)^m = b^{nm}$; Multiply exponents.

$= \dfrac{343x^{9/5}}{64y}$ ∎

7 Reduce the index of a radical.

The final condition for simplified radical form is that the index of the radical is reduced. Rational exponents can be used to reduce the index, as shown in Example 10.

EXAMPLE 10   Reducing the Index of a Radical

Simplify:

a. $\sqrt[9]{b^3}$ **b.** $\sqrt[6]{16x^2y^4}$ **c.** $7\sqrt[3]{25} + 2\sqrt[9]{5^6}$ **d.** $\sqrt[3]{\sqrt{8}}$

Solution

a. $\sqrt[9]{b^3} = b^{3/9}$ Rewrite in exponential form; $\sqrt[n]{b^m} = b^{m/n}$.

$= b^{1/3}$ Reduce $\frac{3}{9}$.

$= \sqrt[3]{b}$ Rewrite in radical form; $b^{1/n} = \sqrt[n]{b}$.

b. $\sqrt[6]{16x^2y^4} = \sqrt[6]{2^4x^2y^4}$

$= (2^4x^2y^4)^{1/6}$ Rewrite in exponential form.

$= (2^4)^{1/6}(x^2)^{1/6}(y^4)^{1/6}$ Raise each factor to the $\frac{1}{6}$th power; $(abc)^n = a^nb^nc^n$.

$= 2^{2/3}x^{1/3}y^{2/3}$ $(b^n)^m = b^{nm}$; Multiply exponents and reduce.

$= (2^2xy^2)^{1/3}$ $a^nb^nc^n = (abc)^n$

$= \sqrt[3]{4xy^2}$ Rewrite in radical form.

c. $7\sqrt[3]{25} + 2\sqrt[9]{5^6}$

$= 7\sqrt[3]{25} + 2\cdot5^{6/9}$ Reduce the index of $\sqrt[9]{5^6}$ by first rewriting in exponential form; $\sqrt[n]{b^m} = b^{m/n}$.

$= 7\sqrt[3]{25} + 2\cdot5^{2/3}$ Reduce $\frac{6}{9}$.

$= 7\sqrt[3]{25} + 2\sqrt[3]{25}$ $5^{2/3} = \sqrt[3]{5^2} = \sqrt[3]{25}$

$= (7 + 2)\sqrt[3]{25}$ Apply the distributive property.

$= 9\sqrt[3]{25}$

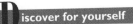

iscover for yourself

Work Example 10d by using exponential form:

$$\sqrt[3]{\sqrt{8}} = ((2^3)^{1/2})^{1/3}$$

d. $\sqrt[3]{\sqrt{8}} = \sqrt[3 \cdot 2]{8}$

$\quad\quad = \sqrt[6]{8}$

$\quad\quad = \sqrt[6]{2^3}$

$\quad\quad = 2^{3/6}$

$\quad\quad = 2^{1/2}$

$\quad\quad = \sqrt{2}$

$\sqrt[m]{\sqrt[n]{b}} = \sqrt[mn]{b}$

Notice that the index (6) and the exponent (3) have a common factor.

Write in exponential form; $\sqrt[n]{b^m} = b^{m/n}$

Reduce the fraction.

Rewrite in radical form.

PROBLEM SET P.4

Practice Problems

In Problems 1–18, evaluate each expression or state that the expression is not a real number. Do not use a calculator.

1. $\sqrt{49}$

2. $\sqrt{100}$

3. $\sqrt[3]{27}$

4. $\sqrt[3]{125}$

5. $\sqrt[3]{-8}$

6. $\sqrt[3]{-64}$

7. $\sqrt{-4}$

8. $\sqrt{-64}$

9. $\sqrt[3]{\dfrac{8}{125}}$

10. $\sqrt[3]{\dfrac{8}{27}}$

11. $\sqrt[5]{-1}$

12. $\sqrt[7]{-1}$

13. $\sqrt{\dfrac{4}{9}}$

14. $\sqrt{\dfrac{9}{25}}$

15. $\sqrt[5]{-\dfrac{1}{32}}$

16. $(\sqrt[5]{-3})^5$

17. $(\sqrt[3]{-8})^3$

18. $\sqrt[6]{\dfrac{1}{64}}$

In Problems 19–34, write each radical in simplified form by factoring the radicand and removing as many factors as possible.

19. $\sqrt[3]{16}$

20. $\sqrt[3]{250}$

21. $\sqrt[5]{64}$

22. $\sqrt[4]{32}$

23. $\sqrt{200y^3}$

24. $\sqrt{40x^3}$

25. $\sqrt{20xy^3}$

26. $\sqrt{45x^4y}$

27. $\sqrt{75xy^2z^5}$

28. $\sqrt{18x^2y^3z}$

29. $\sqrt[3]{32x^3}$

30. $\sqrt[3]{16xy^3}$

31. $\sqrt[3]{-32xy^5z^6}$

32. $\sqrt[3]{-16x^4y^5z^2}$

33. $\sqrt[4]{48y^7}$

34. $\sqrt[4]{32x^{11}}$

In Problems 35–52, simplify by rationalizing the denominator.

35. $\dfrac{1}{\sqrt{7}}$

36. $\dfrac{2}{\sqrt{10}}$

37. $\sqrt{\dfrac{3}{5}}$

38. $\sqrt{\dfrac{3}{7}}$

39. $\sqrt[3]{\dfrac{7}{2}}$

40. $\sqrt[5]{\dfrac{7}{16}}$

41. $\dfrac{6}{\sqrt[3]{2}}$

42. $-\dfrac{8}{\sqrt[3]{2}}$

43. $-\dfrac{6}{\sqrt[5]{8}}$

44. $-\dfrac{16}{\sqrt[5]{4}}$

45. $\dfrac{20}{5 - \sqrt{3}}$

46. $\dfrac{17}{6 - \sqrt{2}}$

47. $\dfrac{13}{\sqrt{11} + 3}$

48. $\dfrac{3}{\sqrt{7} + 3}$

49. $\dfrac{6}{\sqrt{5} + \sqrt{3}}$

50. $\dfrac{12}{\sqrt{7} + \sqrt{3}}$

51. $\dfrac{11}{\sqrt{7} - \sqrt{3}}$

52. $\dfrac{13}{\sqrt{5} - \sqrt{3}}$

In Problems 53–62, simplify where possible and then combine radicals.

53. $\sqrt{50} + \sqrt{18}$

54. $\sqrt{28} + \sqrt{63}$

55. $3\sqrt{18} - 5\sqrt{50}$

56. $4\sqrt{12} - 2\sqrt{75}$

57. $3\sqrt{8} - \sqrt{32} + 3\sqrt{72} - \sqrt{75}$

58. $3\sqrt{54} - 2\sqrt{24} - \sqrt{96} + 4\sqrt{63}$

59. $8\sqrt{\dfrac{1}{2}} - \dfrac{1}{2}\sqrt{8}$

60. $\sqrt{\dfrac{5}{9}} + \sqrt{\dfrac{9}{5}}$

61. $16\sqrt{\dfrac{5}{8}} + 6\sqrt{\dfrac{5}{2}}$

62. $4\sqrt{\dfrac{1}{12}} + 18\sqrt{\dfrac{1}{27}}$

In Problems 63–72, evaluate each expression without using a calculator.

63. $36^{1/2}$

64. $121^{1/2}$

65. $8^{1/3}$

66. $(-27)^{1/3}$

67. $125^{2/3}$

68. $8^{2/3}$

69. $(-27)^{4/3}$

70. $\left(\frac{27}{125}\right)^{4/3}$

71. $32^{-4/5}$

72. $16^{-5/2}$

In Problems 73–92, simplify each expression.

73. $(7y^{1/3})(2y^{1/4})$

74. $(3x^{2/3})(4x^{3/4})$

75. $(3x^{3/4})(-5x^{-1/2})$

76. $(-6x^{2/3})(-8x^{-1/4})$

77. $\dfrac{20x^{1/2}}{5x^{1/4}}$

78. $\dfrac{72y^{3/4}}{9y^{1/3}}$

79. $\dfrac{80y^{1/6}}{10y^{1/4}}$

80. $\dfrac{-60y^{1/3}}{20y^{3/4}}$

81. $(2x^{1/5}y^2z^{2/5})^5$

82. $(3x^{1/4}y^3z^{3/4})^4$

83. $(25x^4y^6)^{1/2}$

84. $(125x^9y^6)^{1/3}$

85. $(16xy^{1/4}z^{2/3})^{1/4}$

86. $(27x^{1/4}y^{2/3}z^3)^{1/3}$

87. $\left(\dfrac{2x^{1/4}}{5y^{1/3}}\right)^3$

88. $\left(\dfrac{7x^{2/3}}{3y^{1/2}}\right)^2$

89. $\left(\dfrac{x^3}{y^5}\right)^{-1/2}$

90. $\left(\dfrac{a^5}{b^{-4}}\right)^{-1/5}$

91. $\left(\dfrac{27a^{-3}}{64b^{-3}}\right)^{-1/3}$

92. $\left(\dfrac{81x^{-8}y^6}{25x^4y^{-10}}\right)^{-1/2}$

In Problems 93–106, simplify by reducing the index of the radical.

93. $\sqrt[4]{b^2}$

94. $\sqrt[6]{b^4}$

95. $\sqrt[9]{(x-1)^6}$

96. $\sqrt[8]{(x-1)^2}$

97. $\sqrt[4]{x^2y^2}$

98. $\sqrt[10]{x^5y^5}$

99. $\sqrt[9]{2^3x^3y^6}$

100. $\sqrt[12]{2^4x^4y^8}$

101. $\sqrt[9]{27x^3y^6}$

102. $\sqrt[4]{81x^2y^6}$

103. $5\sqrt[3]{16} + \sqrt[3]{8}$

104. $2\sqrt{45} + \sqrt[4]{25}$

105. $\sqrt[3]{\sqrt{125}}$

106. $\sqrt{\sqrt{32}}$

Application Problems

107. The formula for the frequency (f) of a note is $f = (2L)^{-1}P^{1/2}m^{-1/2}$, where L is the length of the string, P is the stretching force on the string, and m is the mass of one centimeter of the string. Write the formula in simplified radical form.

108. On a piano, the frequency of the A note above middle C is 440 vibrations per second. The frequency f_n of a note n notes above A should be $f_n = 440 \cdot 2^{n/12}$.

Middle C   One Octave above Middle C

CDEFGABC

Frequency: 440

   a. At what frequency should a piano tuner set the A that is one octave (12 notes) above the A above middle C?

   b. What should be the frequency of middle C, nine notes below A?

109. Archaeologists use the amount of carbon-14 left in a fossil to estimate the fossil's age. The approximate number of milligrams (A) of carbon-14 left in a fossil after 5000 years can be found using the formula $A = A_0(2.7)^{-3/5}$, where A_0 is the initial amount of carbon-14 in the organism. Find the amount of carbon-14 left in a

5000-year-old organism that originally contained 500 milligrams of carbon-14.

110. Meteorologists use the formula $D = 0.07d^{3/2}$ to determine the duration (D, in hours) of a storm whose diameter is d miles. Determine the duration of a storm that is 9 miles in diameter.

111. The formula

$$r = \left(\frac{A}{P}\right)^{1/t} - 1$$

describes the annual rate of return (r) of an investment of P dollars that is worth A dollars after t years. What is the annual rate of return, to the nearest tenth of a per-cent, on a condominium that is purchased for $60,000 and sold 5 years later for $80,000?

True–False Critical Thinking Problems

112. Which one of the following is true?

a. Neither $(-8)^{1/2}$ nor $(-8)^{1/3}$ represent real numbers.

b. $\sqrt{x^2 + y^2} = x + y$

c. $8^{-1/3} = -2$

d. $16^{1/4} = 4^{1/2}$

113. Which one of the following is true?

a. $\sqrt[3]{x^3 + y^3} = x + y$

b. $\sqrt[4]{16} = \pm 2$

c. $\left(\dfrac{9}{16}\right)^{-5/2} - \left(\dfrac{1000}{27}\right)^{4/3} = -\dfrac{28,976}{243}$

d. $b^{-1/n} = \dfrac{1}{b^n}$

Technology Problems

To graph $y = x^{m/n}$ on a graphing utility, enter the equation as $y = (x^m)^{1/n}$ or $y = (x^{1/n})^m$. Many graphing utilities do not store the definition of $x^{m/n}$, so in effect you are telling the utility the definition. Use this idea to graph each equation in Problems 114–116.

114. Graph $y = x^{2/3}$ on a graphing utility by graphing both $y_1 = (x^2)^{1/3}$ and $y_2 = (x^{1/3})^2$.

115. Graph $y = x^{3/4}$ on a graphing utility by graphing both $y_1 = (x^3)^{1/4}$ and $y_2 = (x^{1/4})^3$.

116. Graph $y_1 = x^{2/3}$ and $y_2 = (x^{1/3})^2$ in the same viewing rectangle. Are the graphs that are displayed the same? If not, what difference do you observe?

117. Rationalize the denominator: $\dfrac{2}{\sqrt{x} + 1}$. Then use a graphing utility to graph $y_1 = \dfrac{2}{\sqrt{x} + 1}$ and $y_2 = \dfrac{2(\sqrt{x} - 1)}{x - 1}$, showing that the two graphs are identical.

Critical Thinking Problems

118. Find the exact value of $\sqrt{13 + \sqrt{2} + \dfrac{7}{3 + \sqrt{2}}}$ without the use of a calculator.

119. Press the square root key repeatedly on your calculator, and then enter the number 2. Describe the two emerging patterns. (One pattern is far less obvious than the other.)

120. Place the correct symbol, $>$ or $<$, in the box between each of the given numbers. *Do not use a calculator.* Then check your result with a calculator.

a. $5^{1/2}$ ☐ 5^{-2}

b. $3^{1/2}$ ☐ $3^{1/3}$

c. $\left(\dfrac{1}{2}\right)^{1/3}$ ☐ $\left(\dfrac{1}{2}\right)^{1/4}$

d. $\sqrt{7} + \sqrt{18}$ ☐ $\sqrt{7 + 18}$

121. Rationalize the denominator: $\dfrac{1}{1 + \sqrt{3} + \sqrt{5}}$.

122. If $x + y = 2z$, simplify:

$$\left[\dfrac{(3^{x-y})^y (3^{y-z})^{z-x}}{(3^{z+y})^{z-y}}\right]^{1/z}$$

Solutions Manual   **Tutorial**   **Video I**

SECTION P.5 Polynomials

Objectives

1 Write a polynomial in standard form.

2 Determine the degree of a polynomial.

3 Add and subtract polynomials.

4 Multiply polynomials.

5 Use FOIL in polynomial multiplication.

6 Use special products in polynomial multiplication.

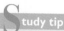
1 Write a polynomial in standard form.

2 Determine the degree of a polynomial.

In this section, we review basic ideas about polynomials and their operations.

The Vocabulary of Polynomials

A *polynomial* is an algebraic expression consisting of a finite number of terms with whole number exponents on the variables. Some examples of polynomials are

$$3x + 7, \; 5x^4 - 9x^2 + 3x + 14, \text{ and } 3x^2y - 4xy - 17.$$

The first two examples are called *polynomials in x* and the third is a *polynomial in x and y*. A polynomial containing exactly one term is called a *monomial*, one with exactly two terms is a *binomial*, and one with exactly three terms is a *trinomial*. Thus, $7x^2$ is a monomial, $7x^2 + 11x$ a binomial, and $7x^2 + 11x + 13$ a trinomial.

The formal definition of a polynomial in one variable illustrates its general form.

> **Definition of a polynomial in x**
>
> A *polynomial in x* is an algebraic expression of the form
>
> $$a_n x^n + a_{n-1}x^{n-1} + a_{n-2}x^{n-2} + \cdots + a_1 x + a_0,$$
>
> where $a_n, a_{n-1}, a_{n-2}, \ldots, a_1$ and a_0 are real numbers, $a_n \neq 0$, and n is a nonnegative integer. The polynomial is of *degree n*, a_n (read "a sub n") is the *leading coefficient*, and a_0 is the *constant term*.

A polynomial in one variable is written in *descending powers* of the variable when the exponents on the terms decrease from left to right. Written with descending powers of x, the polynomial is said to be in *general form*. Three polynomials in general form and their degrees are shown below.

Polynomial	Standard Form	Degree
$5x - 3 + 7x^2$	$7x^2 + 5x - 3$	2
$7x^2 - 6x^5 - 4 + 2x^3$	$-6x^5 + 2x^3 + 7x^2 - 4$	5
17	$17 (17 = 17x^0)$	0

If a polynomial contains more than one variable, the degree of a term is the sum of the exponents on all the variables. For example, the degree of $5x^2y^7$ is $2 + 7$ or 9. The degree of the polynomial is the greatest of the degrees of any of its terms.

EXAMPLE 1 **The Degree of a Polynomial in Two Variables**

Find the degree of the polynomial:

$$7x^6y^2 - 5x^4y^5 - 7xy + 3$$

Solution

We begin by finding the degree of each of the polynomial's four terms.

Term	$7x^6y^2$	$-5x^4y^5$	$-7xy$	3 or $3x^0y^0$
Degree	$6 + 2 = 8$	$4 + 5 = 9$	$1 + 1 = 2$	$0 + 0 = 0$

ENRICHMENT ESSAY

Names, Words, and Meanings

In language, words such as *polynomial* and *degree* (*of a polynomial*) have general agreed-upon definitions. In our work, we are sharing these definitions so that communication within the polynomial realm is possible. However, other words—proper names such as Bob, Alice, Samantha—do not have a meaning other than denoting a particular person.

With the flair of a mathematician defining words such as *polynomial, terms,* and *degree,* Lewis Carroll (*Alice's Adventures in Wonderland* and *Through the Looking Glass*) has his character, Humpty Dumpty, inverting and reversing ordinary linguistic conventions.

"Don't stand chattering to yourself like that," Humpty Dumpty said, looking at her for the first time, *"but tell me your name and your business."*

"My name *is Alice, but—"*

"It's a stupid name enough!" Humpty Dumpty interrupted impatiently. *"What does it mean?"*

"Must a name mean something?" Alice asked doubtfully.

"Of course it must," Humpty Dumpty said with a short laugh; *"my name means the shape I am—and a good handsome shape it is, too. With a name like yours, you might be any shape, almost."*

Alice was too much puzzled to say anything; so after a minute Humpty Dumpty began again. "They've a temper, some of them—particularly verbs; they're the proudest—adjectives you can do

anything with, but not verbs—however, I can manage the whole lot of them! Impenetrability! That's what I say!"

"Would you tell me please," said Alice, *"what that means?"*

"Now you talk like a reasonable child," said Humpty Dumpty, looking very much pleased. *"I meant by 'impenetrability' that we've had enough of that subject, and it would be just as well if you'd mention what you mean to do next, as I suppose you don't mean to stop here all the rest of your life."*

"That's a great deal to make one word mean," Alice said in a thoughtful tone.

"When I make a word do a lot of work like that," said Humpty Dumpty, *"I always pay it extra."*

"Oh!" said Alice. She was too much puzzled to make any other remark.

Robert Arneson "Klown" 1978, glazed ceramic, 37 × 19 × 19 in. Collection of Des Moines Art Center, Des Moines, Iowa. Purchase with funds from the Gardner and Florence Call Cowles Foundation, Des Moines Art Center permanent collection. Photo courtesy of George Adams Gallery, New York. © Estate of Robert Arneson / Licensed by VAGA, New York, NY.

The degree of this polynomial in x and y is 9, the greatest of the degrees of any of its terms.   ■

3 Add and subtract polynomials.

Operations with Polynomials

If we want to add or subtract polynomials, we apply the commutative and associative properties to group terms having the same variables to the same powers, called *like terms* or *similar terms*. We then use the distributive property to combine the similar terms. For example, $-7x^4y^5$ and $2x^4y^5$ are similar terms and their sum is

$$-7x^4y^5 + 2x^4y^5 = (-7 + 2)x^4y^5 = -5x^4y^5.$$

EXAMPLE 2 **Adding and Subtracting Polynomials**

Perform the indicated operations and simplify:

a. $(-9x^3 + 7x^2 - 5x + 3) + (13x^3 + 2x^2 - 8x - 6)$
b. $(7x^3 - 8x^2 + 9x - 6) - (2x^3 - 6x^2 - 3x + 9)$

Solution

a. $(-9x^3 + 7x^2 - 5x + 3) + (13x^3 + 2x^2 - 8x - 6)$

$= (-9x^3 + 13x^3) + (7x^2 + 2x^2)$ Group similar terms.

$\quad + (-5x - 8x) + (3 - 6)$

$= 4x^3 + 9x^2 + (-13x) + (-3)$ Combine similar terms.

$= 4x^3 + 9x^2 - 13x - 3$ Do you find that you're working all these steps mentally?

b. $(7x^3 - 8x^2 + 9x - 6) - (2x^3 - 6x^2 - 3x + 9)$

$= (7x^3 - 8x^2 + 9x - 6) + (-2x^3 + 6x^2 + 3x - 9)$ Rewrite subtraction as addition of the additive inverse. Be sure to change the sign of each term inside parentheses preceded by the negative sign.

$= (7x^3 - 2x^3) + (-8x^2 + 6x^2)$ Group similar terms.

$\quad + (9x + 3x) + (-6 - 9)$

$= 5x^3 + (-2x^2) + 12x + (-15)$ Combine similar terms.

$= 5x^3 - 2x^2 + 12x - 15$ ∎

Study tip

You can also arrange similar terms in columns and combine vertically:

$$\begin{array}{r} 7x^3 - 8x^2 + 9x - 6 \\ -2x^3 + 6x^2 + 3x - 9 \\ \hline 5x^3 - 2x^2 + 12x - 15 \end{array}$$

The similar terms can be combined mentally by adding their coefficients.

4 Multiply polynomials.

The product of two polynomials is the polynomial obtained by multiplying each term of one polynomial by each term of the other polynomial and then combining similar terms.

EXAMPLE 3 **Multiplying a Binomial and a Trinomial**

Multiply: $(2x + 3)(x^2 + 4x + 5)$

Solution

$(2x + 3)(x^2 + 4x + 5)$

$= 2x(x^2 + 4x + 5) + 3(x^2 + 4x + 5)$ Use the distributive property to multiply the trinomial by each term of the binomial.

$= 2x^3 + 8x^2 + 10x + 3x^2 + 12x + 15$ Use the distributive property.

$= 2x^3 + 11x^2 + 22x + 15$ Combine similar terms.   ∎

Study tip

Another method for solving Example 3 is to use a vertical format similar to that used for multiplying whole numbers:

$$
\begin{array}{r}
x^2 + 4x + 5 \\
2x + 3 \\
\hline
3x^2 + 12x + 15 \\
2x^3 + 8x^2 + 10x \\
\hline
2x^3 + 11x^2 + 22x + 15
\end{array}
$$

Similar terms are written in the same column.

$\longleftarrow\ 3(x^2 + 4x + 5)$
$\longleftarrow\ 2x(x^2 + 4x + 5)$
Combine similar terms.

The vertical pattern used in the Study tip becomes convenient if the polynomials we wish to multiply each contain three terms or more.

EXAMPLE 4 Multiplying Polynomials Using a Vertical Format

Multiply: $(x^2 - 5x + 3)(3x - 4 + 2x^2)$

Solution

$$
\begin{array}{r}
x^2 - 5x + 3 \\
2x^2 + 3x - 4 \\
\hline
- 4x^2 + 20x - 12 \\
3x^3 - 15x^2 + 9x \\
2x^4 - 10x^3 + 6x^2 \\
\hline
2x^4 - 7x^3 - 13x^2 + 29x - 12
\end{array}
$$

Write the polynomial in standard form.
$\longleftarrow\ -4(x^2 - 5x + 3)$
$\longleftarrow\ 3x(x^2 - 5x + 3)$
$\longleftarrow\ 2x^2(x^2 - 5x + 3)$
Add similar terms. ∎

5 Use FOIL in polynomial multiplication.

The Product of Two Binomials: FOIL

The product of two binomials occurs quite frequently in algebra. The product can be found using a method called FOIL, which is based on the distributive property. For example, we can find the product of the binomials $3x + 2$ and $4x + 5$ as follows:

$$
\begin{aligned}
(3x + 2)(4x + 5) &= 3x(4x + 5) + 2(4x + 5) \\
&= 3x(4x) + 3x(5) + 2(4x) + 2(5) \\
&= 12x^2 + 15x + 8x + 10
\end{aligned}
$$

Before combining like terms, let us consider the origin of each of the four terms in the sum.

Origin of	Terms of $(3x + 2)(4x + 5)$	Result of Multiplying Terms
$12x^2$	$(3x + 2)(4x + 5)$	$(3x)(4x) = 12x^2$ First terms
$15x$	$(3x + 2)(4x + 5)$	$(3x)(5) = 15x$ Outer terms
$8x$	$(3x + 2)(4x + 5)$	$(2)(4x) = 8x$ Inner terms
10	$(3x + 2)(4x + 5)$	$(2)(5) = 10$ Last terms

The product is obtained by combining these four results.

$$(3x + 2)(4x + 5) = 12x^2 + 15x + 8x + 10$$

$$= 12x^2 + 23x + 10$$

We see, then, that two binomials can be quickly multiplied by using the FOIL method, in which *F* represents the product of the *first* terms in each binomial, *O* represents the product of the *outside* or *outer* terms, *I* represents the product of the two *inside* or *inner* terms, and *L* represents the product of the *last* or second terms in each binomial.

$$(3x + 2)(4x + 5) = 12x^2 + 15x + 8x + 10$$

$$= 12x^2 + 23x + 10$$

EXAMPLE 5 **Using the FOIL Method**

Multiply using the FOIL method: $(5x^2 - 6)(4x^2 + 2)$

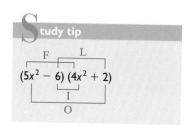

Study tip

Solution

$$(5x^2 - 6)(4x^2 + 2) = (5x^2)(4x^2) + (5x^2)(2) + (-6)(4x^2) + (-6)(2)$$

$$= 20x^4 + 10x^2 - 24x^2 - 12$$

$$= 20x^4 - 14x^2 - 12$$

EXAMPLE 6 **Using the FOIL Method**

Multiply using the FOIL method: $(7x^3 - 2x)(3x^3 - 5x)$

Solution

$$(7x^3 - 2x)(3x^3 - 5x) = (7x^3)(3x^3) + (7x^3)(-5x) + (-2x)(3x^3) + (-2x)(-5x)$$

$$= 21x^6 - 35x^4 - 6x^4 + 10x^2$$

$$= 21x^6 - 41x^4 + 10x^2$$

6 Use special products in polynomial multiplication.

Although it's convenient to memorize these forms, the FOIL method can be used on all five examples in the box. To cube $x + 4$, you can first square $x + 4$ using FOIL and then multiply this result by $x + 4$. In short, you do not necessarily have to utilize these special formulas. What is the advantage of knowing and using these forms?

Special Products

There are several products that occur so frequently that it's convenient to memorize the form or pattern of these formulas.

Special products

Let A and B represent real numbers, variables, or algebraic expressions.

Special Product	Example
Sum and Difference of Two Terms	
$(A + B)(A - B) = A^2 - B^2$	$(2x + 3)(2x - 3) = (2x)^2 - 3^2$
	$= 4x^2 - 9$
Squaring a Binomial	
$(A + B)^2 = A^2 + 2AB + B^2$	$(y + 5)^2 = y^2 + 2 \cdot y \cdot 5 + 5^2$
	$= y^2 + 10y + 25$
$(A - B)^2 = A^2 - 2AB + B^2$	$(3x - 4y)^2 = (3x)^2 - 2 \cdot 3x \cdot 4y + (4y)^2$
	$= 9x^2 - 24xy + 16y^2$
Cubing a Binomial	
$(A + B)^3 = A^3 + 3A^2B + 3AB^2 + B^3$	$(x + 4)^3 = x^3 + 3x^2(4) + 3x(4)^2 + 4^3$
	$= x^3 + 12x^2 + 48x + 64$
$(A - B)^3 = A^3 - 3A^2B + 3AB^2 - B^3$	$(x - 2)^3 = x^3 - 3x^2(2) + 3x(2)^2 - 2^3$
	$= x^3 - 6x^2 + 12x - 8$

The special form for

$(A + B)^2$

can be interpreted geometrically.

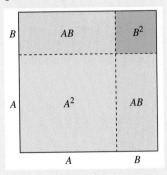

The area of the large rectangle is

$(B + A)(A + B) = (A + B)^2$.

The sum of the areas of the four smaller rectangles is

$AB + B^2 + A^2 + AB$

$= A^2 + 2AB + B^2$.

The area of the large rectangle equals the sum of the areas of the four smaller rectangles:

$(A + B)^2 = A^2 + 2AB + B^2$

EXAMPLE 7   **Multiplying the Sum and Difference of Two Terms**

Find the product of $(6x^2y + 5y)$ and $(6x^2y - 5y)$.

Solution

$(6x^2y + 5y)(6x^2y - 5y)$

$= (6x^2y)^2 - (5y)^2$ The product of the sum and difference of the same two terms is the difference of their squares.

$= 36x^4y^2 - 25y^2$ Square all factors.

EXAMPLE 8   **Squaring and Cubing Binomials**

Find the product:

a. $(4x^2y + xy)^2$ **b.** $(3x - 4y)^3$

Solution

$$(A \quad + \quad B)^2 \ = \ A^2 \ + \ 2 \ A \ \cdot \ B \ + \ B^2$$

a. $(4x^2y + xy)^2 = (4x^2y)^2 + 2(4x^2y)(xy) + (xy)^2$

$= 16x^4y^2 + 8x^3y^2 + x^2y^2$

$$(A - B)^3 = A^3 - 3 \, A^2 \cdot B + 3 \, A \cdot B^2 - B^3$$

b. $(3x - 4y)^3 = (3x)^3 - 3(3x)^2(4y) + 3(3x)(4y)^2 - (4y)^3$
$$= 27x^3 - 3(9x^2)(4y) + 3(3x)(16y^2) - (64y^3)$$
$$= 27x^3 - 108x^2y + 144xy^2 - 64y^3$$

Special products can sometimes be used to find the products of certain trinomials, as illustrated in Example 9.

EXAMPLE 9   Using the Special Products

Find the products:

a. $(7x + 5 + 4y)(7x + 5 - 4y)$ **b.** $(3x + y + 1)^2$

Discover for yourself

Describe how to work Examples 7–9 without using the special products.

Solution

a. By grouping the first two terms within each of the parentheses, we can find the product using the form for the sum and difference of two terms:

$$(A + B) \cdot (A - B) = A^2 - B^2$$

$$[(7x + 5) + 4y] \cdot [(7x + 5) - 4y] = (7x + 5)^2 - (4y)^2$$
$$= (7x)^2 + 2 \cdot 7x \cdot 5 + 5^2 - (4y)^2$$
$$= 49x^2 + 70x + 25 - 16y^2$$

Discover for yourself

Work Example 9b by grouping $y + 1$:

$[3x + (y + 1)]$

Do you still get the same answer?

b. We can group the terms so that the pattern for the square of a binomial can be applied:

$$(A + B)^2 = A^2 + 2 \cdot A \cdot B + B^2$$

$$[(3x + y) + 1]^2 = (3x + y)^2 + 2 \cdot (3x + y) \cdot 1 + 1^2$$
$$= 9x^2 + 6xy + y^2 + 6x + 2y + 1$$

PROBLEM SET P.5

Practice Problems

In Problems 1–8, perform the indicated operations. Write the resulting polynomial in general form and indicate its degree.

1. $(-6x^3 + 5x^2 - 8x + 9) + (17x^3 + 2x^2 - 4x - 13)$

2. $(-7x^3 + 6x^2 - 11x + 13) + (19x^3 - 11x^2 + 7x - 17)$

3. $(17x^3 - 5x^2 + 4x - 3) - (5x^3 - 9x^2 - 8x + 11)$

4. $(18x^4 - 2x^3 - 7x + 8) - (9x^4 - 6x^3 - 5x + 7)$

5. $(5x^2 - 7x - 8) + (2x^2 - 3x + 7) - (x^2 - 4x - 3)$

6. $(8x^2 + 7x - 5) - (3x^2 - 4x) - (-6x^3 - 5x^2 + 3)$

7. $(4x^2 - 5xy + 6y^2) + (7x^2 + 2xy - 4y^2) - (8x^2 - xy - 3y^2)$

8. $(2x^3 - 2x^2y + 3xy^2 + 4y^3) - (4x^2y - 3xy^2 - 5y^3) + (3x^3 - x^2y + 5xy^2 - y^3)$

In Problems 9–26, find each product.

9. $(x + 1)(x^2 - x + 1)$

10. $(x + 5)(x^2 - 5x + 25)$

11. $(y^2 + 7y - 3)(3y^2 - y + 2)$

12. $(2y^2 + 5y - 4)(y^2 - 3y + 2)$

13. $(z^2 + 2)(2z^3 + z^2 - 4z)$

14. $(z^2 + 3)(4z^3 - z^2 + 3z)$

15. $(xy + 2)(x^2y^2 - 2xy + 4)$

16. $(x^2y^4 + 3)(x^4y^8 - 3x^2y^4 + 9)$

17. $(5x + 3)(7x + 1)$

18. $(9x - 4)(3x + 5)$

19. $(9y^3 - 5)(2y^3 + 7)$

20. $(6y^3 - 7)(3y^3 + 4)$

21. $(3x^2y + 4xy)(2x^2y - 5xy)$

22. $(7x^2y + 2xy)(5x^2y - xy)$

23. $(9x^2 + 4)(9x^3 - 4)$

24. $(9y^2 + 5)(9y^3 - 5)$

25. $(2x + 1)(x - 2)(1 - x)$

26. $(2x - 1)(x + 3)(2 - x)$

In Problems 27–56, use the special products to find each product.

27. $(5y + 3)(5y - 3)$

28. $(3y + 7)(3y - 7)$

29. $(4x^2y + 5x)(4x^2y - 5x)$

30. $(5x^3y + 3x)(5x^3y - 3x)$

31. $(-2x + y)(y + 2x)$

32. $(-3a^4b^2 + 5c)(3a^4b^2 + 5c)$

33. $(x + 6)^2$

34. $(x - 5)^2$

35. $(x - 6)^3$

36. $(x + 5)^3$

37. $(3x^2y + 2xy)^2$

38. $(4xy^2 + xy)^2$

39. $(3x + 2y)^3$

40. $(2x - 5y)^3$

41. $(2x^2y - xy)^3$

42. $(4x^2y + xy)^3$

43. $(x^4 + 2x^5)^3$

44. $(3x^6 - x^7)^3$

45. $(3x + 7 + 5y)(3x + 7 - 5y)$

46. $(5x + 7y + 2)(5x - 7y - 2)$

47. $[5y - (2x + 3)][5y + (2x + 3)]$

48. $[8y + (7 - 3x)][8y - (7 - 3x)]$

49. $(2x + y + 1)^2$

50. $(5x + 1 + 6y)^2$

51. $[(3x - 1) + y]^2$

52. $[(2x - y) + 8]^2$

53. $[(3x - 1) + y][(3x - 1) - y]$

54. $[(2x - y) + 8][(2x - y) - 8]$

55. $(x + y - 3)(x - y + 3)$

56. $(x^2 + 3y - 1)(x^2 - 3y + 1)$

Application Problems _____

In Problems 57–59, express the area of each shaded region as a polynomial in general form.

57.

58.

59.

In Problems 60–63, express the area of each plane figure as a polynomial in general form.

60.

61.

62.

63.

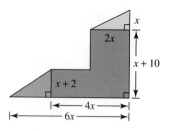

64. Write a polynomial in standard form that expresses:
   a. the difference between the volumes of the two solids shown in the figure.
   b. the difference between the surface areas of the two solids.

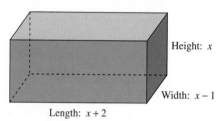

Height: x

Width: $x - 1$

Length: $x + 2$

Height: x

Width: x

Length: x

65. Write a polynomial in standard form expressing the difference between the volume and the surface area of the open box in the figure shown.

x

$10 - 2x$

$8 - 2x$

66. The number of people who catch a cold t weeks after January 1 is $C = 5t - 3t^2 + t^3$ and the number of people who recover t weeks after January 1 is $R = t - t^2 + \frac{1}{3}t^3$. Write a polynomial in standard form for the number of people who are still ill with a cold t weeks after January 1.

67. A rock on Earth and a rock on the moon are thrown into the air with a velocity of 48 feet per second by a 6-foot person. The height reached by the rock (in feet) after t seconds is given by

$$h_{\text{Earth}} = -16t^2 + 48t + 6$$

$$h_{\text{Moon}} = -2.7t^2 + 48t + 6$$

Write a polynomial in standard form expressing the difference between moon height and Earth height after t seconds.

True–False Critical Thinking Problems

68. Which one of the following is true?
   a. $4x^3 + 7x^2 - 5x + 2x^{-1}$ is a polynomial in standard form of degree 3 and contains four terms.
   b. If two polynomials of degree 3 are added, their sum must be a polynomial of degree 3.
   c. There is no such thing as a polynomial in x having four terms, written in descending powers, and lacking a third-degree term.
   d. Suppose a square garden has area represented by $9x^2$ square feet. If one side is made 7 feet longer and the other side is made 2 feet shorter, then the trinomial that represents the area of the larger garden is $9x^2 + 15x - 14$ square feet.

69. Which one of the following is true?
   a. Every algebraic expression is a polynomial.
   b. When simplified, the following expression does not result in a natural number:

$$(y - z)(y + z - x) + (z - x)(z + x - y)$$
$$+ (x - y)(x + y - z)$$

   c. $(x^2 + 8 - 4x)(x^2 + 8 + 4x) = x^4 + 16x^2 + 64$
   d. The special product for $(A + B)(A - B)$ cannot be used to find the product of $\sqrt{a + b} + \sqrt{a - b}$ and $\sqrt{a + b} - \sqrt{a - b}$ because the two factors are not polynomials.

Technology Problems

70. Use a graphing utility to graph $y = (x - 2)^2$ and $y = x^2 - 4$ in the same viewing rectangle. Is $(x - 2)^2 = x^2 - 4$?

71. Use a graphing utility to graph $y = (x + 2)^2$ and $y = x^2 + 4x + 4$ in the same viewing rectangle. What do the graphs indicate about $(x + 2)^2$ and $x^2 + 4x + 4$?

72. Use a graphing utility to show that $(x - 1)(x + 3) = x^2 + 2x - 3$.

73. Use a graphing utility to show that $(x - 1)^3 \neq x^3 - 1$.

74. Use a graphing utility to determine which of the following statements is/are false.
  a. $x^3 - 1 = (x - 1)(x^2 + x + 1)$
  b. $x^4 - 1 = (x^2 + 1)(x + 1)(x - 1)$
  c. $x^2 + 1 = (x + 1)^2$
  d. $x^4 - 2x^2 + 1 = (x^2 - 1)^2$

Critical Thinking Problems

For Problems 75–76, represent the volume of each figure as a polynomial in standard form.

75.

76.

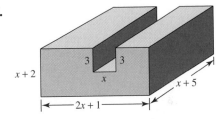

77. Fill in the numbers in fifth, sixth, and seventh positions in the number sequences on the right by using the emerging pattern. Then write a polynomial in x for the number that appears in the xth position.

  a. 0, 3, 8, 15, ____, ____, ____,
  b. 2, 10, 30, 68, ____, ____, ____,

78. Simplify: $(y^n + 2)(y^n - 2) - (y^n - 3)^2$.

S E C T I O N   P . 6

Solutions Manual   **Tutorial**   **Video 2**

Factoring

Objectives

1 Factor out the greatest common factor of a polynomial.
2 Factor by grouping.
3 Factor special forms.
4 Factor trinomials.
5 Use a factoring strategy.
6 Factor expressions with fractional and negative exponents.

In general, factoring involves the reverse of the multiplication process. For example, because we know that $(2x + 1)(3x - 2) = 6x^2 - x - 2$, we can also say that $6x^2 - x - 2$ can be expressed as

$$6x^2 - x - 2 = (2x + 1)(3x - 2).$$

The process of writing the polynomial $6x^2 - x - 2$ as a product is called *factoring*. The *factors* of $6x^2 - x - 2$ are $2x + 1$ and $3x - 2$.

In this section, we review basic factoring techniques.

Introduction

Factoring is the process of writing a polynomial as the product of two or more polynomials. We generally *factor over the set of integers*, meaning that the numerical coefficients in the factors are integers. For example, we will not consider the following type of factoring as factoring over the integers:

$$x^2 - 5 = (x + \sqrt{5})(x - \sqrt{5}).$$

We say that $x^2 - 5$ cannot be factored using integer coefficients. Such polynomials are *irreducible over the integers*, or *prime*.

If the coefficients of a polynomial are rational numbers, we will include factors with rational coefficients. Thus, the factorization of $\frac{1}{9}x^2 - 25$ over the rational numbers is given by

$$\tfrac{1}{9}x^2 - 25 = (\tfrac{1}{3}x + 5)(\tfrac{1}{3}x - 5).$$

The goal in factoring a polynomial is to use one or more factoring techniques until each of the polynomial's factors is prime or irreducible. In this situation, the polynomial is said to be *factored completely*.

We will now discuss basic factoring techniques for factoring polynomials.

■ Factor out the greatest common factor of a polynomial.

Common Factors

In any factoring problem, the first step is to look for the *greatest common factor* (GCF)—that is, an expression of the highest degree that divides each term of the polynomial. The distributive property in the reverse direction

$$ab + ac = a(b + c)$$

can be used to factor out the greatest common factor.

EXAMPLE I Factoring Out the GCF

Factor:

a. $3x^4 + 6x^3 - 15x^2$ **b.** $20x^4y^2 + 10x^3y^3 - 5xy^4$

c. $x^2(x + 3) + 5(x + 3)$

Solution

a. We begin by determining the GCF.

$3, 6$, and -15 have 3 as the GCF.

x^4, x^3, and x^2 have x^2 as the GCF.

Thus, the GCF of the three terms in the polynomial is $3x^2$.

$3x^4 + 6x^3 - 15x^2$

$= 3x^2(x^2) + 3x^2(2x) + 3x^2(-5)$ Express each term with the GCF as a factor.

$= 3x^2(x^2 + 2x - 5)$ Factor out the GCF.

b. Again, we begin by determining the GCF.

$20, 10$, and -5 have 5 as the GCF.

x^4, x^3, and x have x as the GCF.

y^2, y^3, and y^4 have y^2 as the GCF.

Thus, the GCF of the three terms in the polynomial is $5xy^2$.

$$20x^4y^2 + 10x^3y^3 - 5xy^4$$
$$= 5xy^2(4x^3) + 5xy^2(2x^2y) + 5xy^2(-y^2) \qquad \text{Express each term with the GCF as a factor.}$$
$$= 5xy^2(4x^3 + 2x^2y - y^2) \qquad \text{Factor out the GCF.}$$

c. In this situation, the GCF is the common binomial factor $(x + 3)$. We factor out this common factor as follows.

$$x^2(x + 3) + 5(x + 3) = (x + 3)(x^2 + 5) \qquad \text{Factor out the common binomial factor.} \qquad \blacksquare$$

2 Factor by grouping.

Factoring by Grouping

Some polynomials have only a GCF of 1. However, by a suitable rearrangement of the terms, it still may be possible to factor. This process, called *factoring by grouping*, is illustrated in Examples 2 and 3.

EXAMPLE 2 **Factoring by Grouping**

Factor: $x^3 + 4x^2 + 3x + 12$

Solution

Group terms that have a common factor:

$$\boxed{x^3 + 4x^2} + \boxed{3x + 12}$$

Common factor is x^2. Common factor is 3.

We now factor the given polynomial as follows.

$$x^3 + 4x^2 + 3x + 12$$
$$= (x^3 + 4x^2) + (3x + 12) \qquad \text{Group terms with common factors.}$$
$$= x^2(x + 4) + 3(x + 4) \qquad \text{Factor out the GCF from the grouped terms. The remaining two terms have } x + 4 \text{ as a common binomial factor.}$$
$$= (x + 4)(x^2 + 3) \qquad \text{Factor } (x + 4) \text{ out of both terms.}$$

Thus, $x^3 + 4x^2 + 3x + 12 = (x + 4)(x^2 + 3)$. Check the factorization by multiplying the right side using the FOIL method, obtaining the polynomial on the left. $\blacksquare$

Discover for yourself

In Example 2 group the terms as follows:

$$(x^3 + 3x) + (4x^2 + 12)$$

Factor out the GCF from each group and complete the factoring process. Describe what happens. What can you conclude?

Using technology

If a polynomial contains one variable, you can check your factorization by graphing the given polynomial and the factored form of the polynomial in the same viewing rectangle. The graphs should be identical.

We did this for Example 2, graphing

$$y_1 = x^3 + 4x^2 + 3x + 12$$

and

$$y_2 = (x + 4)(x^2 + 3)$$

$y_1 = x^3 + 4x^2 + 3x + 12$

$y_2 = (x + 4) \cdot (x^2 + 3)$

$[-5, 5]$ by $[-50, 50]$ Yscl = 5

as shown on the right. The graphs are the same, so $x^3 + 4x^2 + 3x + 12 = (x + 4)(x^2 + 3)$.

iscover for yourself

In Example 3, group the terms as follows:

$(x^2y^2 + 5x^2) + (-8y^2 - 40)$.

Complete the factoring process by factoring x^2 from the first two terms and -8 from the last two terms. Do you get the same answer as in Example 3? Describe what happens if you factor 8, rather than -8, from the second grouping.

EXAMPLE 3   **Factoring by Grouping**

Factor: $x^2y^2 - 40 - 8y^2 + 5x^2$

Solution

Other than 1, the first two terms and the last two terms have no common factor. Let's rearrange the terms and try a different grouping.

$$x^2y^2 - 40 - 8y^2 + 5x^2$$
$$= (x^2y^2 - 8y^2) + (5x^2 - 40) \quad \text{Group the terms that have a GCF. The first two terms have a GCF of } y^2 \text{ and the last two terms have a GCF of 5.}$$
$$= y^2(x^2 - 8) + 5(x^2 - 8) \quad \text{Factor out the GCF from the grouped terms. The remaining two terms have a GCF of } x^2 - 8.$$
$$= (x^2 - 8)(y^2 + 5) \quad \text{Factor } (x^2 - 8) \text{ out of both terms.}$$

Thus, $x^2y^2 - 40 - 8y^2 + 5x^2 = (x^2 - 8)(y^2 + 5)$. Check by multiplying the right side using the FOIL method, obtaining the polynomial on the left. ∎

3 Factor special forms.

Factoring Special Forms

Certain forms of polynomials occur so frequently that the factors of these forms should be memorized.

Factoring special polynomials forms

Factoring Special Binomials

Factored Form	**Example**
Difference of Two Squares	
$A^2 - B^2 = (A + B)(A - B)$	$x^2 - 25 = x^2 - 5^2$
	$\qquad\qquad = (x + 5)(x - 5)$
Sum of Two Cubes	
$A^3 + B^3 = (A + B)(A^2 - AB + B^2)$	$x^3 + 125 = x^3 + 5^3$
	$\qquad\qquad = (x + 5)(x^2 - x \cdot 5 + 5^2)$
	$\qquad\qquad = (x + 5)(x^2 - 5x + 25)$
Difference of Two Cubes	
$A^3 - B^3 = (A - B)(A^2 + AB + B^2)$	$x^3 - 8 = x^3 - 2^3$
	$\qquad\qquad = (x - 2)(x^2 + x \cdot 2 + 2^2)$
	$\qquad\qquad = (x - 2)(x^2 + 2x + 4)$

Factoring Perfect Square Trinomials

Factored Form	**Example**
$A^2 + 2AB + B^2 = (A + B)^2$	$x^2 + 10x + 25$
	$\qquad = x^2 + 2 \cdot x \cdot 5 + 5^2$
	$\qquad = (x + 5)^2$
$A^2 - 2AB + B^2 = (A - B)^2$	$x^2 - 10x + 25$
	$\qquad = x^2 - 2 \cdot x \cdot 5 + 5^2$
	$\qquad = (x - 5)^2$

EXAMPLE 4 **Factoring the Difference of Two Squares**

Factor completely:

a. $9x^2 - 16$ **b.** $25x^2 - 36y^2$ **c.** $100y^2 - (3x + 1)^2$

Solution

We begin by rewriting each polynomial as the difference of two squares.

$$A^2 \quad - \quad B^2 \quad = (A + B)(A - B)$$

a. $9x^2 - 16 = (3x)^2 - 4^2 = (3x + 4)(3x - 4)$

b. $25x^2 - 36y^2 = (5x)^2 - (6y)^2 = (5x + 6y)(5x - 6y)$

c. $100y^2 - (3x + 1)^2 = (10y)^2 - (3x + 1)^2 = [10y + (3x + 1)][10y - (3x + 1)]$
$$= (10y + 3x + 1)(10y - 3x - 1) \quad \blacksquare$$

In certain situations, we can apply the technique for factoring the difference of two squares more than once.

EXAMPLE 5 **Factoring the Difference of Two Squares More Than Once**

Factor completely: $81x^4 - 16$

Solution

$$A^2 \quad - B^2 = (A + B)(A - B)$$
$$81x^4 - 16 = (9x^2)^2 - 4^2 = (9x^2 + 4)(9x^2 - 4)$$

The factorization is not complete because the second factor is the difference of two squares.

$$A^2 \quad - B^2 = (A + B)(A - B)$$
$$(9x^2 + 4)(9x^2 - 4) = (9x^2 + 4)[(3x)^2 - 2^2] = (9x^2 + 4)(3x + 2)(3x - 2)$$

The complete factorization of the polynomial is given by

$$81x^4 - 16 = (9x^2 + 4)(3x + 2)(3x - 2). \quad \blacksquare$$

EXAMPLE 6 **Factoring the Sum and Difference of Two Cubes**

Factor:

a. $27x^3 + 1$ **b.** $x^6 - 8$

Solution

We begin by expressing the polynomials as the sum and the difference of two cubes, respectively. Then we use the appropriate factoring formula.

$$A^3 + B^3 = (A + B)(A^2 - AB + B^2)$$

a. $27x^3 + 1 = (3x)^3 + 1^3 = (3x + 1)[(3x)^2 - 3x \cdot 1 + 1^2]$ Use the factoring formula for $A^3 + B^3$.

$$= (3x + 1)(9x^2 - 3x + 1)$$ Simplify.

$$A^3 - B^3 = (A - B)(A^2 + AB + B^2)$$

b. $x^6 - 8 = (x^2)^3 - 2^3 = (x^2 - 2)[(x^2)^2 + x^2 \cdot 2 + 2^2]$ Use the factoring formula for $A^3 - B^3$.

$$= (x^2 - 2)(x^4 + 2x^2 + 4)$$ Simplify. ∎

Study tip

Here's how to recognize a perfect square trinomial:
1. First and last terms are positive perfect squares.
2. The middle term is twice the product of the square roots of the first and last terms.

EXAMPLE 7 **Factoring Perfect Square Trinomials**

Factor completely:

a. $9y^4 + 12y^2 + 4$ **b.** $16x^2 - 8x + 1$

Solution

We first express each polynomial in the form of a perfect square trinomial, and then we use the factoring formula.

$$A^2 + 2AB + B^2 = (A + B)^2$$

a. $9y^4 + 12y^2 + 4 = (3y^2)^2 + 2(3y^2)(2) + 2^2 = (3y^2 + 2)^2$

$$A^2 - 2AB + B^2 = (A - B)^2$$

b. $16x^2 - 8x + 1 = (4x)^2 - 2(4x)(1) + 1^2 = (4x - 1)^2$ ∎

The terms of a polynomial can be grouped in several ways. A successful grouping that will lead to a factorization is frequently based on one or more of the special forms.

EXAMPLE 8 **Using Grouping to Obtain Special Forms**

Factor completely:

a. $x^2 + 8x + 16 - 25a^2$ **b.** $x^3 + y + y^3 + x$

Solution

a. $x^2 + 8x + 16 - 25a^2$
$= (x^2 + 8x + 16) - 25a^2$ Group the perfect square trinomial.
$= (x + 4)^2 - 25a^2$ Factor the perfect square trinomial.
$= (x + 4)^2 - (5a)^2$ Express the polynomial as the difference of two squares.
$= (x + 4 + 5a)(x + 4 - 5a)$ Factor the difference of two squares.

b. $x^3 + y + y^3 + x$

$= (x^3 + y^3) + (x + y)$ Group the two terms involving the sum of two cubes.

$= (x + y)(x^2 - xy + y^2) + (x + y)$ Factor $x^3 + y^3$, the sum of two cubes.

$= (x + y)(x^2 - xy + y^2 + 1)$ Factor out $x + y$, the common factor.   ■

4 Factor trinomials.

Factoring Trinomials

To factor a trinomial of the form $ax^2 + bx + c$, a little trial and error may be necessary.

A strategy for factoring $ax^2 + bx + c$

(Assume, for the moment, that there is no GCF.)

1. Find two First terms whose product is ax^2:

$(\Box x + \quad)(\Box x + \quad) = ax^2 + bx + c$

2. Find two Last terms whose product is c:

$(x + \Box)(x + \Box) = ax^2 + bx + c$

3. By trial and error, perform steps 1 and 2 until the sum of the Outer product and Inner product is bx:

$(\Box x + \Box)(\Box x + \Box) = ax^2 + bx + c$

$\underset{\text{(sum of O + I)}}{\underbrace{\quad}}$ I

O

If no such combinations exist, the polynomial is prime.

EXAMPLE 9   **Factoring Trinomials Whose Leading Coefficients Are 1**

Factor:

a. $x^2 + 6x + 8$ **b.** $x^2 + 3x - 18$

Solution

a. The factors of the first term are x and x:

$(x \quad)(x \quad)$

To find the second term of each factor, we must find two numbers whose product is 8 and whose sum is 6. From the table in the margin, we see that 4 and 2 are the required integers. Thus,

$x^2 + 6x + 8 = (x + 4)(x + 2)$ or $(x + 2)(x + 4)$.

b. We begin with

$x^2 + 3x - 18 = (x \quad)(x \quad)$.

Factors of 8	8, 1	4, 2	-8, -1	-4, -2
Sum of Factors	9	6	-9	-6

This is the
desired sum.

Factors of -18	$18, -1$	$-18, 1$	$9, -2$	$-9, 2$	$6, -3$	$-6, 3$
Sum of Factors	17	-17	7	-7	3	-3

This is the
desired sum.

To find the second term of each factor, we must find two numbers whose product is -18 and whose sum is 3. From the table in the margin, we see that 6 and -3 are the required integers. Thus,

$$x^2 + 3x - 18 = (x + 6)(x - 3) \text{ or } (x - 3)(x + 6).$$ ∎

EXAMPLE 10   Factoring Trinomials Whose Leading Coefficients Are Not 1

Factor:

a. $2x^2 + 7x + 3$ **b.** $6x^2 + 19x - 7$

Solution

a. First we factor the first term, $2x^2$. Let's agree that when the first term in the trinomial is positive, we will use only positive factors of that first term. Thus, the only possibility for factors is $(2x)(x)$ (we exclude $(-2x)(-x)$).

$$2x^2 + 7x + 3 = (2x \quad)(x \quad)$$

We must still complete the factorization by filling in the blanks with the correct numbers.

Next, we must find two last terms whose product is 3. The possibilities are $(3)(1)$ or $(-3)(-1)$. Because the signs in the given trinomial are all positive, we will use 3 and 1. Thus, the trinomial has the possible factors

$$(2x + 3)(x + 1)$$

$$(2x + 1)(x + 3).$$

Since we are factoring $2x^2 + 7x + 3$, the sum of the outer and inner products must be $7x$.

$(2x + 3)\ (x + 1)$ $2x + 3x = 5x$, which is not what we want.

$(2x + 1)\ (x + 3)$ $6x + x = 7x$, which is the trinomial's middle term.

Thus, the desired factorization is

$$2x^2 + 7x + 3 = (2x + 1)(x + 3) \quad \text{or} \quad (x + 3)(2x + 1).$$

b. $6x^2 + 19x - 7$ has factors for $6x^2$ of $6x$ and x or $3x$ and $2x$, so we begin with

$$(6x \quad)(x \quad) \quad \text{or} \quad (3x \quad)(2x \quad).$$

The pairs of factors of -7 are 7 and -1 or -7 and 1. This leads to eight possible factorizations.

sing technology

The graphs of

$$y_1 = 2x^2 + 7x + 3$$

and

$$y_2 = (2x + 1)(x + 3)$$

are shown in the same viewing rectangle. With identical graphs, we can conclude that $2x^2 + 7x + 3 = (2x + 1)(x + 3)$.

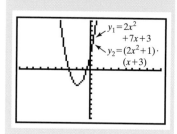

Using technology

The graphs of

$$y_1 = 6x^2 + 19x - 7$$

and

$$y_2 = (3x - 1)(2x + 7)$$

shown in a $[-5, 2]$ by $[-25, 10]$ viewing rectangle, are the same. Thus, $6x^2 + 19x - 7 = (3x - 1)(2x + 7)$.

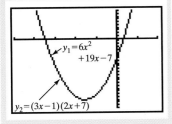

Possible Factors of $6x^2 + 19x - 7$	Sum of Outer and Inner Products (should equal $19x$)
$(6x + 7)(x - 1)$	$-6x + 7x = x$
$(6x - 7)(x + 1)$	$6x - 7x = -x$
$(6x + 1)(x - 7)$	$-42x + x = -41x$
$(6x - 1)(x + 7)$	$42x - x = 41x$
$(3x + 7)(2x - 1)$	$-3x + 14x = 11x$
$(3x - 7)(2x + 1)$	$3x - 14x = -11x$
$(3x + 1)(2x - 7)$	$-21x + 2x = -19x$
$(3x - 1)(2x + 7)$	$21x - 2x = 19x$ ⟵ This is the desired sum.

The last factorization gives the required middle term, $19x$. Thus,

$$6x^2 + 19x - 7 = (3x - 1)(2x + 7).$$

Study tip

You can minimize trial and error by using factoring by grouping in the factoring of a trinomial. For example, to factor

$$6x^2 + 19x - 7$$

multiply the leading coefficient a and the constant c, giving $6(-7)$ or -42. Now find the factors of -42 whose sum is 19. The numbers are 21 and -2, and the middle term can be expressed in terms of these numbers.

Factoring $ax^2 + bx + c$ by Grouping

1. Multiply a and c.
2. Find the factors of ac whose sum is b.
3. Rewrite the middle term, bx, as a sum or difference using the factors from step 2.
4. Factor by grouping.

An Example: $6x^2 + 19x - 7$

$6(-7) = -42$

21 and -2 are factors of -42 whose sum is 19.

$6x^2 + 19x - 7$
$= 6x^2 + 21x - 2x - 7$
$= 3x(2x + 7) - 1(2x + 7)$
$= (2x + 7)(3x - 1)$ or $(3x - 1)(2x + 7)$

5 Use a factoring strategy.

A Strategy for Factoring

The following strategy provides an order for factoring polynomials completely.

> **A factoring strategy: factoring polynomials over the integers**
>
> 1. Is there a common factor? If so, factor out the GCF.
> 2. Is the polynomial a binomial? If so, can it be factored by one of the following special forms?
>
> $A^2 - B^2 = (A + B)(A - B)$ Difference of two squares
>
> $A^3 + B^3 = (A + B)(A^2 - AB + B^2)$ Sum of two cubes
>
> $A^3 - B^3 = (A - B)(A^2 + AB + B^2)$ Difference of two cubes

3. Is the polynomial a trinomial? If it is not a perfect square trinomial, use the trial and error method of Examples 9 and 10. If it is a perfect square trinomial, use one of the special forms:

$$A^2 + 2AB + B^2 = (A + B)^2 \quad \text{or} \quad A^2 - 2AB + B^2 = (A - B)^2$$

4. Does the polynomial contain four or more terms? If so, try factoring by grouping.
5. Is the polynomial factored completely? If a factor with more than one term can be factored further, do so.

EXAMPLE 11 **Factoring Using the General Factoring Strategy**

Factor completely:

a. $2a^3 + 8a^2 + 8a$ **b.** $4x^2 - 16x - 20$

c. $x^2(x - 5) - 4(x - 5)$ **d.** $9b^2x - 16y - 16x + 9b^2y$

Solution

a. $2a^3 + 8a^2 + 8a$
$\quad = 2a(a^2 + 4a + 4)$ Factor out the GCF.
$\quad = 2a(a + 2)^2$ Factor the perfect square trinomial.
b. $4x^2 - 16x - 20$
$\quad = 4(x^2 - 4x - 5)$ Factor out the GCF.
$\quad = 4(x + 1)(x - 5)$ Factor the remaining trinomial.
c. $x^2(x - 5) - 4(x - 5)$
$\quad = (x - 5)(x^2 - 4)$ Factor out the GCF.
$\quad = (x - 5)(x + 2)(x - 2)$ Factor the difference of two squares.
d. $9b^2x - 16y - 16x + 9b^2y$
$\quad = (9b^2x + 9b^2y) + (-16x - 16y)$ Rearrange the terms for factoring by grouping.
$\quad = 9b^2(x + y) + (-16)(x + y)$ Factor within each group.
$\quad = (x + y)(9b^2 - 16)$ Factor out the common binomial.
$\quad = (x + y)(3b + 4)(3b - 4)$ Factor the difference of two squares. ∎

6 Factor expressions with fractional and negative exponents.

Factoring Algebraic Expressions Containing Fractional and Negative Exponents

Factoring techniques can be applied to expressions that are not polynomials.

EXAMPLE 12 **Factoring Variables with Negative Exponents**

Factor:

a. $2x^{3/2} - 16x^{1/2} + 30x^{-1/2}$ **b.** $x(x + 1)^{-3/4} + (x + 1)^{1/4}$

Solution

a. The GCF is the product of 2 and the x with the *smallest* of the exponents in all three terms, namely, $x^{-1/2}$.

$$2x^{3/2} - 16x^{1/2} + 30x^{-1/2}$$ The GCF is $2x^{-1/2}$.

$$= 2x^{-1/2}(x^2) - 2x^{-1/2}(8x) + 2x^{-1/2}(15)$$ Each term is expressed with the common factor.

$$= 2x^{-1/2}(x^2 - 8x + 15)$$ Factor out the GCF.

$$= 2x^{-1/2}(x - 3)(x - 5)$$ Factor completely by factoring the remaining trinomial.

$$= \frac{2(x - 3)(x - 5)}{x^{1/2}}$$ $b^{-n} = \dfrac{1}{b^n}$

b. We factor out the $x + 1$ with the smallest exponent, that is, $(x + 1)^{-3/4}$.

$$x(x + 1)^{-3/4} + (x + 1)^{1/4}$$ The GCF is $(x + 1)^{-3/4}$.

$$= (x + 1)^{-3/4}x + (x + 1)^{-3/4}(x + 1)$$ Each term is expressed with the common factor.

$$= (x + 1)^{-3/4}[x + (x + 1)]$$ Factor out the GCF.

$$= \frac{2x + 1}{(x + 1)^{3/4}}$$ Simplify. ∎

EXAMPLE 13 **Factoring an Expression Containing Negative Exponents**

Factor: $(x^2 - 9)(2x - 1)^{2/3} - (x^2 - 9)^2(2x - 1)^{-1/3}$

Solution

The two terms are separated by a subtraction sign. The GCF involves common factors in each term with an exponent equal to the smaller of the exponents of these factors. Thus, the GCF is $(x^2 - 9)(2x - 1)^{-1/3}$.

$$(x^2 - 9)(2x - 1)^{2/3} - (x^2 - 9)^2(2x - 1)^{-1/3}$$

$$= (x^2 - 9)(2x - 1)^{-1/3}[(2x - 1)^{3/3}]$$
$$- (x^2 - 9)(2x - 1)^{-1/3}[(x^2 - 9)]$$ Express each term with the common factor. (This step is often done mentally.)

$$= (x^2 - 9)(2x - 1)^{-1/3}[(2x - 1) - (x^2 - 9)]$$ Factor out the GCF.

$$= (x^2 - 9)(2x - 1)^{-1/3}(2x - 1 - x^2 + 9)$$ Simplify inside the brackets.

$$= \frac{(x^2 - 9)(-x^2 + 2x + 8)}{(2x - 1)^{1/3}}$$ Continue simplifying.

$$= \frac{(x + 3)(x - 3)(-1)(x^2 - 2x - 8)}{(2x - 1)^{1/3}}$$ Factor $x^2 - 9$. Factor -1 from the trinomial to make subsequent factoring easier.

$$= \frac{(x + 3)(x - 3)(-1)(x - 4)(x + 2)}{(2x - 1)^{1/3}}$$ Factor the trinomial.

$$= -\frac{(x + 3)(x - 3)(x - 4)(x + 2)}{(2x - 1)^{1/3}}$$ Simplify. ∎

PROBLEM SET P.6

Practice Problems

In Problems 1–14, factor out the GCF.

1. $18x + 27$

2. $16x - 24$

3. $3x^2 + 6x$

4. $4x^2 - 8x$

5. $9x^4 - 18x^3 + 27x^2$

6. $6x^4 - 18x^3 + 12x^2$

7. $12x^2y - 8xy^2$

8. $33x^2 - 22xy^4$

9. $7x^3y^2 + 14x^2y - 42x^5y^3 + 21xy^4$

10. $36pq^3 - 12p^3q^2 + 60p^2q^4 - 24p^4q^3$

11. $x^2(x - 3) + 12(x - 3)$

12. $x^2(2x + 5) + 17(2x + 5)$

13. $2x(x - 5)^2 - 3y(x - 5)$

14. $4x(x - 3)^2 - 2y(x - 3)$

In Problems 15–24, factor by grouping.

15. $x^3 - 2x^2 + 5x - 10$

16. $x^3 - 3x^2 + 4x - 12$

17. $x^3 - x^2 + 2x - 2$

18. $x^3 + 6x^2 - 2x - 12$

19. $3x^3 - 2x^2 - 6x + 4$

20. $x^3 - x^2 - 5x + 5$

21. $a^2c + 5ac + 2a + 10$

22. $3y^2 + 4yz + 24y + 32z$

23. $4x^2y + 16xy - x - 4$

24. $5x^2 + 15 - x^2y - 3y$

In Problems 25–36, factor the difference of two squares.

25. $x^2 - 100$

26. $x^2 - 144$

27. $36x^2 - 49$

28. $64x^2 - 81$

29. $9x^2 - 25y^2$

30. $36x^2 - 49y^2$

31. $9y^2 - (2x + 1)^2$

32. $16y^2 - (3x - 1)^2$

33. $x^4 - 81$

34. $x^4 - 16$

35. $9x^4 - y^6$

36. $81x^4 - 49y^6$

In Problems 37–44, factor the sum or difference of two cubes.

37. $x^3 - 8$

38. $x^3 - 64$

39. $y^3 + 27$

40. $y^3 + 125$

41. $64d^3 + 125$

42. $8d^3 + 27$

43. $125 - 8p^3d^3$

44. $64 - 27y^3z^3$

In Problems 45–72, factor each trinomial or state that the trinomial is prime.

45. $x^2 + 8x + 15$

46. $x^2 + 10x + 16$

47. $x^2 - 8x + 15$

48. $x^2 - 5x + 6$

49. $x^2 + x - 30$

50. $x^2 + 14x - 32$

51. $x^2 - 3x - 28$

52. $x^2 - 4x - 21$

53. $x^2 + 4x + 4$

54. $x^2 + 6x + 9$

55. $x^2 - 8x + 16$

56. $x^2 - 10x + 25$

57. $25x^2 - 20x + 4$

58. $9x^2 - 12x + 4$

59. $2x^2 + 9x + 7$

60. $5x^2 + 56x + 11$

61. $4y^2 + 9y + 2$

62. $8y^2 + 10y + 3$

63. $10x^2 + 19x + 6$

64. $5x^2 + 17x + 6$

65. $8y^2 - 18y + 9$

66. $9y^2 - 30y + 25$

67. $4y^2 - 27y + 18$

68. $6y^2 - 23y + 15$

69. $12y^2 - 19y - 21$

70. $16y^2 - 6y - 27$

71. $x^2 + 13x + 9$

72. $x^2 + 17x + 12$

In Problems 73–102, factor each polynomial completely or state that the polynomial is prime.

73. $2y^3 + 8y^2 + 8y$

74. $3y^3 - 6y^2 + 3y$

75. $4x^2 - 16x - 20$

76. $3x^2 - 12x - 36$

77. $3x^4 + 24x$

78. $2x^4 - 250x$

79. $x^2(x - 5) - 4(x - 5)$

80. $x^2(x + 3) - 81(x + 3)$

81. $x^2 + 10x + 25 - 36a^2$

82. $x^2 - 8x + 16 - 49a^2$

83. $c^3 - 16c$

84. $y^3 - y$

85. $9b^2x - 16y - 16x + 9b^2y$

86. $cx^2 + cx + dxy + dy$

87. $x^2 + 25$

88. $x^2 + 1$

89. $y^3 - 2y^2 - 4y + 8$

90. $y^3 - 2y^2 - y + 2$

91. $16x - 2x^4$

92. $7x^5y - 7xy^5$

93. $8x^2 + 40x + 50$

94. $9b^3 - 9b^6$

95. $x^2(x^3 + y^3) - z^2(x^3 + y^3)$

96. $12a^3b - 12ab^3$

97. $3ax + 4bx - 15a - 20b$

98. $63y^2 + 30y - 72$

99. $r^3 - s^3 + r - s$

100. $7by^4 - 7b$

101. $a^6b^6 - a^3b^3$

102. $x^3y^6 - x^3$

In Problems 103–116, factor each algebraic expression.

103. $x^{3/2} - x^{1/2}$

104. $x^{3/4} - x^{1/4}$

105. $4x^{-2/3} + 8x^{1/3}$

106. $12x^{-3/4} + 6x^{1/4}$

107. $3x^{3/2} - 9x^{1/2} + 6x^{-1/2}$

108. $x^{1/2} + 2x^{-1/2} + x^{-3/2}$

109. $(x + 3)^{1/2} - (x + 3)^{3/2}$

110. $(x^2 + 4)^{3/2} + (x^2 + 4)^{7/2}$

111. $(x + 5)^{-1/2} - (x + 5)^{-3/2}$

112. $(x^2 + 3)^{-2/3} + (x^2 + 3)^{-5/3}$

113. $(4x - 1)^{1/2} - \frac{1}{3}(4x - 1)^{3/2}$

114. $-8(4x + 3)^{-2} + 10(5x + 1)(4x + 3)^{-1}$

115. $2x(x^2 + 3)^{-1/2} - x^3(x^2 + 3)^{-3/2}$

116. $\frac{1}{2}(x - 5)^{-1/2}(x + 5)^{-1/2} - \frac{1}{2}(x + 5)^{1/2}(x - 5)^{-3/2}$

True–False Critical Thinking Problems _____

117. Which one of the following is true?

  a. Because $x^2 + 1$ is irreducible over the integers, it follows that $x^3 + 1$ is also irreducible.

  b. One correct factored form for $x^2 - 4x + 3$ is $x(x - 4) + 3$.

  c. $x^3 - 64 = (x - 4)^3$

  d. None of the above is true.

118. Which one of the following is true?

  a. $x^2 + 49 = (x + 7)(x + 7)$

  b. $x^3 + 3x^2a + 3xa^2 + a^3$ can be factored as $(x + a)^3$.

  c. If a rectangular room has a floor space of $2x^2 + 17x + 35$ square feet, and if the room's width is $x + 5$ feet, then there are at least two different polynomials that represent the room's length in feet.

  d. None of the above is true.

Technology Problems _____

Factorizations for algebraic expressions in one variable can be verified using a graphing utility. For example, $6x^2 + 19x - 7$ $= (3x - 1)(2x + 7)$ can be checked by graphing $y_1 = 6x^2 + 19x - 7$ and $y_2 = (3x - 1)(2x + 7)$ in the same viewing rectangle, obtaining identical graphs. In Problems 119–121, use a graphing utility to check whether the given factorization is correct.

119. $x^3 - 5x^2 + 3x - 15 = (x^2 - 3)(x + 5)$

120. $x^3 - 1 = (x - 1)(x^2 - x + 1)$

121. $8 + (x - 2)^3 = x(x^2 - 6x + 12)$

In Problems 122–125, factor completely and verify your result with a graphing utility.

122. $x^2 + 3x - 4$

123. $x^2 - 6x + 9$

124. $x^4 - 1$

125. $x^3 + 1$

126. Computer algebra systems such as *Mathematica, Maple,* and *Derive* will factor polynomials. Graphing calculators, such as the TI-92 with *Derive*, will also allow you to enter a polynomial and use the F2 *Algebra* toolbar menu to display its factored form. Use a computer system or a calculator that can perform symbolic manipulations to verify some of your factorizations in Problems 1–116.

127. Suppose that you are using a graphing utility without the capability described in Problem 126. You have factored $x^2 - 9a^2 + 12x + 36$ as $(x + 6 + 3a)(x + 6 - 3a)$ and would like to verify your factorization by graphing each side of the equation

$$x^2 - 9a^2 + 12x + 36 = (x + 6 + 3a)(x + 6 - 3a),$$

obtaining identical graphs. However, your graphing utility can only graph in one variable. What procedure might you use to convince yourself that your factorization is correct?

Writing in Mathematics

Explain how each figure in Problems 128–130 provides a geometric interpretation of the given factoring formula.

128. $A^2 + 2A + 1 = (A + 1)^2$

129. $A^2 - B^2 = (A + B)(A - B)$

130. $A^3 + 3A^2B + 3AB^2 + B^3 = (A + B)^3$

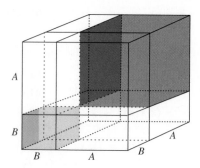

Critical Thinking Problems

131. a. Factor $x^4 + 2x^2y^2 + y^4$.
   b. Factor $x^4 + x^2y^2 + y^4$ by adding and subtracting a term, using part (a) as a guide.

132. Factor $x^6 - y^6$ by two different methods. Use part (b) of Problem 131 to show that the factorizations are the same.

133. Factor completely: $x^4 - y^4 - 2x^3y + 2xy^3$.

134. Factor completely: $(x + y + z)^3 - x^3 - y^3 - z^3$.

135. Express $x^3 + x + 2x^4 + 4x^2 + 2$ as the product of two polynomials of degree 2.

SECTION P.7

Solutions Manual

Tutorial

Video 2

Rational Expressions

Objectives

1 Reduce rational expressions.
2 Multiply and divide rational expressions.
3 Add and subtract rational expressions.
4 Simplify complex rational expressions.

Just as rational numbers play a significant role in the study of arithmetic, fractional expressions and rational expressions frequently appear in algebra. In this section, we review operations with these expressions.

Basic Definitions

A *rational expression* is any expression that can be written as the quotient of two polynomials. The following are examples of rational expressions:

$$\frac{5x^2}{x^2 + 1} \qquad \frac{x^3 - 7x^2 - 18x}{x^3 + 3x^2 + 2x} \qquad \frac{3x^2 + 12xy - 15y^2}{6x^3 - 6xy^2}$$

Reduce rational expressions.

Simplifying Rational Expressions

A rational expression is *simplified* or in *reduced form* if its numerator and denominator have no common factors other than 1 or −1. The following procedure can be used to simplify rational expressions.

> **Simplifying rational expressions**
>
> 1. Factor the numerator and denominator completely.
> 2. Divide both the numerator and denominator by the common factors.

EXAMPLE 1   **Simplifying Rational Expressions**

Simplify:

a. $\dfrac{x^3 - 7x^2 - 18x}{x^3 + 3x^2 + 2x}$ **b.** $\dfrac{x^3 - 125}{5x - x^2}$

Solution

a. $\dfrac{x^3 - 7x^2 - 18x}{x^3 + 3x^2 + 2x}$ This is the given rational expression.

$= \dfrac{x(x^2 - 7x - 18)}{x(x^2 + 3x + 2)}$ Factor out the GCF.

$= \dfrac{x(x - 9)(x + 2)}{x(x + 1)(x + 2)}$ Factor completely. Observe that $x \neq 0$, $x \neq -1$, and $x \neq -2$. A rational expression is undefined if the denominator equals 0.

$= \dfrac{\cancel{x}(x - 9)\cancel{(x + 2)}}{\cancel{x}(x + 1)\cancel{(x + 2)}}$ Divide by the common factors.

$= \dfrac{x - 9}{x + 1}$ Reduce. Although it's obvious that $x \neq -1$, we should restate from above that $x \neq 0$ and $x \neq -2$.

Notice that the restricted values of x in the original expression are also restricted in the reduced fraction, even if these values do not cause division by 0 in the rational expression's simplified form.

b. Before simplifying, we should observe that the quotient of two polynomials that have exactly opposite signs and are additive inverses is −1.

$$\frac{a - b}{b - a} = \frac{-(-a + b)}{b - a} = \frac{-\cancel{(b - a)}}{1\cancel{(b - a)}} = -\frac{1}{1} = -1$$

$$\frac{x^3 - 125}{5x - x^2}$$

This is the given rational expression.

$$= \frac{(x - 5)(x^2 + 5x + 25)}{x(5 - x)}$$

Factor completely. The numerator is the difference of two cubes, $x^3 - 5^3$. Observe that $x \neq 0$, and $x \neq 5$.

$$= \frac{\overset{(-1)}{\cancel{(x - 5)}}(x^2 + 5x + 25)}{x\cancel{(5 - x)}}$$

Two polynomials that have opposite signs and are additive inverses have a quotient of -1.

$$= -\frac{x^2 + 5x + 25}{x}$$

Although it's obvious that $x \neq 0$, we should restate from above that $x \neq 5$. ∎

Study tip

Avoid these common errors in simplifying rational expressions:

You can only divide out, or cancel, common factors that are parts of products. Only when expressions are multiplied can they be factors, so if you can't factor, then don't try to cancel.

Correct:

$$\frac{x^3 + 1}{x + 1} = \frac{\cancel{(x + 1)}(x^2 - x + 1)}{1\cancel{(x + 1)}} = x^2 - x + 1$$

Incorrect:

In Example 1b we used the property that $\dfrac{-a}{b} = -\dfrac{a}{b}$. Properties of fractions, useful in performing operations with rational expressions, are summarized below.

Properties of rational expressions

Let a, b, c, and d be real numbers, variables, or algebraic expressions such that $b \neq 0$ and $d \neq 0$.

Property

1. *Rules of Signs*

$$\frac{-a}{b} = \frac{a}{-b} = -\frac{a}{b}$$

$$\frac{-a}{-b} = \frac{a}{b}$$

2. *Reducing Fractions*

$$\frac{ac}{bc} = \frac{a}{b} \quad (c \neq 0)$$

3. *Writing Equivalent Fractions*

$$\frac{a}{b} = \frac{ac}{bc} \quad (c \neq 0)$$

Example

$$\frac{-x}{5} = -\frac{x}{5}$$

$$\frac{2\cancel{(x + 2)}}{\cancel{(x + 2)}(x + 3)} \quad (x \neq -2, \ x \neq -3)$$

$$= \frac{2}{x + 3} \quad (x \neq -2)$$

$$\frac{2}{x + 3} = \frac{2(x + 2)}{(x + 3)(x + 2)} \quad (x \neq -2)$$

4. *Multiplying Fractions*

$$\frac{a}{b} \cdot \frac{c}{d} = \frac{ac}{bd}$$

$$\frac{3}{x-1} \cdot \frac{x-2}{x^2+5} = \frac{3(x-2)}{(x-1)(x^2+5)}$$

5. *Dividing Fractions*

$$\frac{a}{b} \div \frac{c}{d} = \frac{a}{b} \cdot \frac{d}{c} = \frac{ad}{bc} \quad (c \neq 0)$$

$$\frac{9}{x} \div \frac{5}{7} = \frac{9}{x} \cdot \frac{7}{5} = \frac{63}{5x}$$

6. *Adding or Subtracting*
Fractions with Like Denominators

$$\frac{a}{b} \pm \frac{c}{b} = \frac{a \pm c}{b}$$

$$\frac{5x-1}{x+2} - \frac{2x-1}{x+2}$$

$$= \frac{5x - 1 - (2x-1)}{x+2} = \frac{5x - 1 - 2x + 1}{x+2}$$

$$= \frac{3x}{x+2}$$

7. *Adding or Subtracting*
Fractions with Unlike Denominators

$$\frac{a}{b} \pm \frac{c}{d} = \frac{ad \pm bc}{bd}$$

$$\frac{x}{x-1} + \frac{3}{x-2}$$

$$= \frac{x(x-2) + (x-1) \cdot 3}{(x-1)(x-2)}$$

$$= \frac{x^2 - 2x + 3x - 3}{(x-1)(x-2)} = \frac{x^2 + x - 3}{(x-1)(x-2)}$$

8. *Proportion Principle*

If $\dfrac{a}{b} = \dfrac{c}{d}$, then $ad = bc$.

If $ad = bc$, then $\dfrac{a}{b} = \dfrac{c}{d}$.

If $\dfrac{x}{3} = \dfrac{4}{7}$, then $x \cdot 7 = 3 \cdot 4$. Equivalently,

$7x = 12.$

---

2 Multiply and divide rational expressions.

Operations with Rational Expressions

Multiplication and division can be accomplished using properties 4 and 5 of rational expressions.

EXAMPLE 2 **Multiplying and Dividing Rational Expressions**

Perform the indicated operations:

a. $\dfrac{2x^2 - 13x - 7}{x^2 - 6x - 7} \cdot \dfrac{x^2 - x - 2}{2x^2 - 5x - 3}$ **b.** $\dfrac{x^3 + 8}{x^3 - 5x} \div \dfrac{x+2}{5 - x^2}$

Study tip

To multiply rational expressions:
1. Factor all numerators and denominators completely.
2. Cancel all common factors in any numerator and denominator.
3. Multiply remaining factors in the numerator. Do the same in the denominator.

Solution

a. $\dfrac{2x^2 - 13x - 7}{x^2 - 6x - 7} \cdot \dfrac{x^2 - x - 2}{2x^2 - 5x - 3}$

This is the given multiplication problem.

$$= \frac{(2x+1)\cancel{(x-7)}}{(x+1)\cancel{(x-7)}} \cdot \frac{(x-2)\cancel{(x+1)}}{\cancel{(2x+1)}(x-3)}$$

Factor and reduce.

$$= \frac{x-2}{x-3}$$

From the previous step, notice that $x \neq -1, x \neq 7, x \neq -\frac{1}{2}$, and $x \neq 3$.

To divide rational expressions:
1. Change the division to multiplication and invert the rational expression that follows the division symbol $\div$.
2. Use the procedure in the previous Study tip.

b. $\dfrac{x^3 + 8}{x^3 - 5x} \div \dfrac{x + 2}{5 - x^2}$ This is the given division problem.

$= \dfrac{x^3 + 8}{x^3 - 5x} \cdot \dfrac{5 - x^2}{x + 2}$ Multiply by the reciprocal of the divisor.

$= \dfrac{\overset{}{(x + 2)}(x^2 - 2x + 4)}{x(x^2 - 5)} \cdot \dfrac{\overset{-1}{(5 - x^2)}}{x + 2}$ Factor and reduce. Observe that $x \neq 0, x \neq \pm\sqrt{5}$, and $x \neq -2$.

$= -\dfrac{x^2 - 2x + 4}{x}$ Multiply the remaining factors.   ∎

Rational expressions with like denominators can be added or subtracted using property 6 of rational expressions, namely, adding or subtracting numerators and placing this expression over the common denominator. For example,

$$\frac{2x - 1}{x^2 - 2x + 2} - \frac{3x - 7}{x^2 - 2x + 2} = \frac{2x - 1 - (3x - 7)}{x^2 - 2x + 2} = \frac{2x - 1 - 3x + 7}{x^2 - 2x + 2} = \frac{-x + 6}{x^2 - 2x + 2}.$$

3 Add and subtract rational expressions.

Rational expressions that have no common factors in their denominators can be added or subtracted using property 7, namely,

$$\frac{a}{b} \pm \frac{c}{d} = \frac{ad \pm bc}{bd}.$$

The least common denominator (LCD) is the product of the distinct factors in the two denominators.

EXAMPLE 3   Subtracting Rational Expressions Having No Common Factors in Their Denominators

Subtract: $\dfrac{x + 2}{2x - 3} - \dfrac{4}{x + 3}$

Solution

The LCD is the product of the distinct factors in each denominator, namely

$(2x - 3)(x + 3)$.

We can therefore use property 7 as follows:

$$\frac{a}{b} \quad - \quad \frac{c}{d} \quad = \quad \frac{ad - bc}{bd}$$

$$\frac{x + 2}{2x - 3} - \frac{4}{x + 3} = \frac{(x + 2)(x + 3) - (2x - 3)4}{(2x - 3)(x + 3)}$$ Observe that $a = x + 2$, $b = 2x - 3, c = 4$, and $d = x + 3$.

$$= \frac{x^2 + 5x + 6 - (8x - 12)}{(2x - 3)(x + 3)}$$ Multiply.

$$= \frac{x^2 + 5x + 6 - 8x + 12}{(2x - 3)(x + 3)}$$

$$= \frac{x^2 - 3x + 18}{(2x - 3)(x + 3)}$$ Combine like terms in the numerator.   ∎

When adding and subtracting rational expressions that have different denominators with one or more common factors in the denominators, it is more efficient to first find the LCD, which is the least common multiple of the denominators. This can be done by factoring each denominator and taking the product of distinct factors, using the highest power that appears in any of the factors.

| EXAMPLE 4 | Adding Rational Expressions with Different Denominators |

Add: $\dfrac{x+3}{x^2+x-2} + \dfrac{2}{x^2-1}$

Solution

We find the LCD by first factoring the denominators.

$$x^2 + x - 2 = (x+2)(x-1)$$

$$x^2 - 1 = (x+1)(x-1) \quad \text{Notice that the denominators share the factor } x-1.$$

The LCD is the product of the distinct factors, namely, $(x+2)(x-1)(x+1)$. We now write each rational expression in terms of this LCD by inserting into the numerator and denominator the extra factor required to form the LCD.

$$\frac{x+3}{x^2+x-2} + \frac{2}{x^2-1}$$

$$= \frac{x+3}{(x+2)(x-1)} + \frac{2}{(x+1)(x-1)}$$

Factor denominators. The LCD, the product of each factor the greatest number of times it occurs in any one factorization, is $(x+2)(x-1)(x+1)$.

$$= \frac{(x+3)(x+1)}{(x+2)(x-1)(x+1)} + \frac{2(x+2)}{(x+2)(x-1)(x+1)}$$

Rewrite each rational expression with the LCD. Multiply the numerator and the denominator by whatever extra factors are required to form the LCD.

$$= \frac{(x+3)(x+1) + 2(x+2)}{(x+2)(x-1)(x+1)}$$

Add numerators, putting this sum over the LCD.

$$= \frac{x^2 + 4x + 3 + 2x + 4}{(x+2)(x-1)(x+1)}$$

Multiply in the numerator.

$$= \frac{x^2 + 6x + 7}{(x+2)(x-1)(x+1)}$$

Combine like terms in the numerator. ∎

Study tip

To add and subtract rational expressions that have different denominators with shared factors:

1. Find the LCD by factoring the denominators and taking the product of distinct factors. Use the highest power that appears in any of the factors.
2. Write all rational expressions in terms of the LCD by inserting into the numerator and denominator of each whatever extra factors are needed to form the LCD.
3. Add or subtract the numerators, placing the resulting expression over the LCD.
4. If necessary, simplify the resulting rational expression.

| EXAMPLE 5 | Adding and Subtracting Rational Expressions with Different Denominators |

Combine: $\dfrac{3y+2}{y-5} + \dfrac{4}{3y+4} - \dfrac{7y^2 + 24y + 28}{3y^2 - 11y - 20}$

Solution

Because $3y^2 - 11y - 20 = (3y + 4)(y - 5)$, the LCD is $(3y + 4)(y - 5)$.

$$\frac{3y + 2}{y - 5} + \frac{4}{3y + 4} - \frac{7y^2 + 24y + 28}{3y^2 - 11y - 20}$$

$$= \frac{(3y + 2)(3y + 4)}{(3y + 4)(y - 5)} + \frac{4(y - 5)}{(3y + 4)(y - 5)} - \frac{7y^2 + 24y + 28}{(3y + 4)(y - 5)} \qquad \text{Express all rational expressions with the LCD.}$$

$$= \frac{(3y + 2)(3y + 4) + 4(y - 5) - (7y^2 + 24y + 28)}{(3y + 4)(y - 5)} \qquad \text{Add and subtract as indicated.}$$

$$= \frac{9y^2 + 18y + 8 + 4y - 20 - 7y^2 - 24y - 28}{(3y + 4)(y - 5)}$$

$$= \frac{2y^2 - 2y - 40}{(3y + 4)(y - 5)} \qquad \text{Combine like terms in the numerator.}$$

$$= \frac{2\cancel{(y - 5)}(y + 4)}{(3y + 4)\cancel{(y - 5)}} \qquad \text{Factor and simplify.}$$

$$= \frac{2(y + 4)}{3y + 4}$$
∎

4 Simplify complex rational expressions.

Complex Rational Expressions

Complex rational expressions have numerators or denominators containing one or more rational expressions. Complex rational expressions can be simplified by multiplying the numerator and the denominator by the LCD of all the fractions in the expression.

EXAMPLE 6   **Simplifying Complex Rational Expressions**

Simplify:

a. $\dfrac{\dfrac{1}{x + h} - \dfrac{1}{x}}{h}$ **b.** $\dfrac{\dfrac{1}{x - 2} - \dfrac{1}{x - 3}}{1 + \dfrac{1}{x^2 - 5x + 6}}$ **c.** $\dfrac{x^{-2} - y^{-2}}{x^{-1} + y^{-1}}$

Solution

a. $\dfrac{\dfrac{1}{x + h} - \dfrac{1}{x}}{h}$

The LCD of the denominators is $x(x + h)$. (The h in the denominator has a denominator understood to be 1.)

$$= \frac{\left(\dfrac{1}{x + h} - \dfrac{1}{x}\right)x(x + h)}{h\,x(x + h)}$$

Multiply the numerator and denominator by $x(x + h)$. Because $\dfrac{x(x + h)}{x(x + h)} = 1$ ($x \neq 0$, $x \neq -h$), we are not changing the complex fraction.

Dorothea Rockburne "Noli Me Tangere" 1976, gesso, oil paint, blue pencil and varnish on linen, 55 in. H × 34 in. W. © 1998 Dorothea Rockbourne / Artists Rights Society (ARS), New York.

$$= \frac{\dfrac{1}{x+h} \cdot x(x+h) - \dfrac{1}{x} \cdot x(x+h)}{h \cdot x(x+h)}$$

Use the distributive property in the numerator.

$$= \frac{x - (x+h)}{hx(x+h)}$$

Simplify: $\dfrac{1}{\cancel{x+h}} \cdot x\cancel{(x+h)} = x$ and $\dfrac{1}{\cancel{x}} \cdot \cancel{x}(x+h) = x+h.$

$$= \frac{x - x - h}{hx(x+h)}$$

Perform the indicated operation in the numerator.

$$= \frac{-\cancel{h}}{\cancel{h}x(x+h)}$$

This fraction can be reduced.

$$= -\frac{1}{x(x+h)}$$

Reduce to lowest terms. $(h \neq 0)$

b. $\dfrac{\dfrac{1}{x-2} - \dfrac{1}{x-3}}{1 + \dfrac{1}{x^2 - 5x + 6}}$

$$= \frac{\dfrac{1}{x-2} - \dfrac{1}{x-3}}{1 + \dfrac{1}{(x-2)(x-3)}}$$

Factor. The LCD of the denominators is $(x-2)(x-3)$.

$$= \frac{\left(\dfrac{1}{x-2} - \dfrac{1}{x-3}\right)}{\left(1 + \dfrac{1}{(x-2)(x-3)}\right)} \cdot \frac{(x-2)(x-3)}{(x-2)(x-3)}$$

Multiply the numerator and the denominator by the LCD of the denominators.

$$= \frac{\dfrac{1}{x-2}(x-2)(x-3) - \dfrac{1}{x-3}(x-2)(x-3)}{1(x-2)(x-3) + \dfrac{1}{(x-2)(x-3)}(x-2)(x-3)}$$

Use the distributive property.

$$= \frac{(x-3) - (x-2)}{(x-2)(x-3) + 1}$$

Cancel identical factors in numerators and denominators.

$$= \frac{x - 3 - x + 2}{x^2 - 3x - 2x + 6 + 1}$$

Perform the indicated operations.

$$= \frac{-1}{x^2 - 5x + 7} \quad \text{or} \quad -\frac{1}{x^2 - 5x + 7}$$

Combine like terms.

Discover for yourself

A second method for simplifying a complex rational expression is to combine its numerator and denominator into single fractions. Then find the quotient by inverting the denominator and multiplying. Use this method to simplify the complex fractions in Example 6.

c. $\dfrac{x^{-2} - y^{-2}}{x^{-1} + y^{-1}}$

$$= \frac{\dfrac{1}{x^2} - \dfrac{1}{y^2}}{\dfrac{1}{x} + \dfrac{1}{y}}$$

Since $b^{-n} = \dfrac{1}{b^n}$, then $x^{-2} = \dfrac{1}{x^2}$ and $x^{-1} = \dfrac{1}{x}$. Similarly, the terms involving y are rewritten without negative exponents.

$$= \frac{\left(\dfrac{1}{x^2} - \dfrac{1}{y^2}\right)x^2 y^2}{\left(\dfrac{1}{x} + \dfrac{1}{y}\right)x^2 y^2}$$ The LCD of the denominators is $x^2 y^2$. Multiply the numerator and denominator by $x^2 y^2$. ($x \neq 0$ and $y \neq 0$)

$$= \frac{\dfrac{1}{x^2} \cdot x^2 y^2 - \dfrac{1}{y^2} \cdot x^2 y^2}{\dfrac{1}{x} \cdot x^2 y^2 + \dfrac{1}{y} \cdot x^2 y^2}$$ Use the distributive property.

$$= \frac{y^2 - x^2}{xy^2 + x^2 y}$$ Simplify.

$$= \frac{\cancel{(y + x)}(y - x)}{xy\cancel{(y + x)}}$$ Factor.

$$= \frac{y - x}{xy}$$ Reduce. ($x \neq -y$) ∎

Example 7 involves a fractional expression containing radicals. Although this is not a rational expression, we can use the procedure for simplifying complex rational expressions to rewrite this expression as a single fraction.

EXAMPLE 7 **Simplifying a Fractional Expression Containing Radicals**

Simplify: $\dfrac{\sqrt{9 - x^2} + \dfrac{x^2}{\sqrt{9 - x^2}}}{9 - x^2}$

Solution

Discover for yourself

A second method for solving Example 7 is to use exponential form.

$$\frac{(9 - x^2)^{1/2} + x^2(9 - x^2)^{-1/2}}{9 - x^2}$$

Simplify this expression by factoring $(9 - x^2)^{-1/2}$ from the numerator. Use properties of exponents and make the final answer look like the one in Example 7.

$$\frac{\sqrt{9 - x^2} + \dfrac{x^2}{\sqrt{9 - x^2}}}{9 - x^2}$$ The LCD of the denominators is $\sqrt{9 - x^2}$.

$$= \frac{\sqrt{9 - x^2} + \dfrac{x^2}{\sqrt{9 - x^2}}}{9 - x^2} \cdot \frac{\sqrt{9 - x^2}}{\sqrt{9 - x^2}}$$ Multiply the numerator and the denominator by $\sqrt{9 - x^2}$.

$$= \frac{\sqrt{9 - x^2}\,\sqrt{9 - x^2} + \dfrac{x^2}{\sqrt{9 - x^2}}\,\sqrt{9 - x^2}}{(9 - x^2)\,\sqrt{9 - x^2}}$$ Use the distributive property in the numerator.

$$= \frac{(9 - x^2) + x^2}{(9 - x^2)^{3/2}}$$ In the denominator:

$$(9 - x^2)^1 (9 - x^2)^{1/2} = (9 - x^2)^{1 + 1/2}$$
$$= (9 - x^2)^{3/2}$$

$$= \frac{9}{\sqrt{(9 - x^2)^3}}$$ Since the original expression was in radical form, write the denominator in radical form. ∎

PROBLEM SET P.7

Practice Problems

In Problems 1–10, reduce each rational expression to lowest terms.

1. $\dfrac{3x - 9}{x^2 - 6x + 9}$

2. $\dfrac{4x - 8}{x^2 - 4x + 4}$

3. $\dfrac{x^2 - 12x + 36}{4x - 24}$

4. $\dfrac{x^2 - 8x + 16}{3x - 12}$

5. $\dfrac{y^2 + 7y - 18}{y^2 - 3y + 2}$

6. $\dfrac{y^2 - 4y - 5}{y^2 + 5y + 4}$

7. $\dfrac{y^2 - 9y + 18}{y^3 - 27}$

8. $\dfrac{y^3 - 8}{y^2 + 2y - 8}$

9. $\dfrac{x^3 + x^2 - 20x}{x^3 + 2x^2 - 15x}$

10. $\dfrac{x^3 - 9x}{x^3 + 5x^2 + 6x}$

In Problems 11–24, multiply or divide as indicated.

11. $\dfrac{x^2 - 5x + 6}{x^2 - 2x - 3} \cdot \dfrac{x^2 - 1}{x^2 - 4}$

12. $\dfrac{x^2 + 5x + 6}{x^2 + x - 6} \cdot \dfrac{x^2 - 9}{x^2 - x - 6}$

13. $\dfrac{x^3 - 8}{x^2 - 4} \cdot \dfrac{x + 2}{3x}$

14. $\dfrac{x^2 + 6x + 9}{x^3 + 27} \cdot \dfrac{1}{x + 3}$

15. $\dfrac{x^2 - 1}{(x - 1)^2} \cdot \dfrac{x^3 - 1}{x + 1}$

16. $\dfrac{x^2 - 1}{x^2 - x + 1} \cdot \dfrac{x^3 + 1}{x^2 + 2x + 1}$

17. $\dfrac{2x^2 + 9x - 35}{6x^2 - 13x - 5} \cdot \dfrac{3x^2 + 10x + 3}{x^2 + 10x + 21}$

18. $\dfrac{x^2 + x - 12}{x^2 + x - 30} \cdot \dfrac{x^2 + 5x + 6}{x^2 - 2x - 3} \cdot \dfrac{x^2 + 7x + 6}{x + 3}$

19. $\dfrac{x^2 - 25}{2x - 2} \div \dfrac{x^2 + 10x + 25}{x^2 + 4x - 5}$

20. $\dfrac{x^2 - 4}{x^2 + 3x - 10} \div \dfrac{x^2 + 5x + 6}{x^2 + 8x + 15}$

21. $\dfrac{x^2 + 5x}{x + 5} \div \dfrac{1}{x^3 - 25x}$

22. $\dfrac{y - 1}{y^2 - 3y} \div \dfrac{1}{y^3 - 9y}$

23. $\dfrac{x^4 - 1}{2x} \div \dfrac{x^3 + x}{x^2}$

24. $\dfrac{1 - x^2}{6x + 6} \div \dfrac{x^4 - 1}{6x^2 + 6}$

In Problems 25–44, add or subtract as indicated.

25. $\dfrac{4x - 10}{x - 2} - \dfrac{x - 4}{x - 2}$

26. $\dfrac{x^2 - 4x}{x^2 - x - 6} - \dfrac{x - 6}{x^2 - x - 6}$

27. $\dfrac{3}{x + 4} + \dfrac{6}{x + 5}$

28. $\dfrac{8}{x - 2} + \dfrac{2}{x - 3}$

29. $\dfrac{3}{x + 1} - \dfrac{3}{x}$

30. $\dfrac{4}{x} - \dfrac{3}{x + 3}$

31. $\dfrac{2x}{x + 2} + \dfrac{x + 2}{x - 2}$

32. $\dfrac{3x}{x - 3} - \dfrac{x + 4}{x + 2}$

33. $\dfrac{x + 5}{x - 5} + \dfrac{x - 5}{x + 5}$

34. $\dfrac{x + 3}{x - 3} + \dfrac{x - 3}{x + 3}$

35. $\dfrac{4}{x^2 + 6x + 9} + \dfrac{4}{x + 3}$

36. $\dfrac{3}{5x + 2} + \dfrac{5x}{25x^2 - 4}$

37. $\dfrac{3x}{x^2 + 3x - 10} - \dfrac{2x}{x^2 + x - 6}$

38. $\dfrac{x}{x^2 - 2x - 24} - \dfrac{x}{x^2 - 7x + 6}$

39. $\dfrac{y + 3}{y^2 - y - 2} - \dfrac{y - 1}{y^2 + 2y + 1}$

40. $\dfrac{y - 1}{y^2 + 3y + 2} - \dfrac{y + 7}{y^2 + 5y + 6}$

41. $\dfrac{2}{y^2 - 4} - \dfrac{3}{y^2 - 4y + 4} + \dfrac{4}{y^2 + y - 2}$

42. $\dfrac{y - 3}{y - 2} + \dfrac{7 - 4y}{2y^2 - 9y + 10} - \dfrac{y + 1}{2y - 5}$

43. $\dfrac{4x^2 + x - 6}{x^2 + 3x + 2} - \dfrac{3x}{x + 1} + \dfrac{5}{x + 2}$

44. $\dfrac{6x^2 + 17x - 40}{x^2 + x - 20} + \dfrac{3}{x - 4} - \dfrac{5x}{x + 5}$

Simplify each complex rational expression in Problems 45–62.

45. $\dfrac{\dfrac{x}{3} - 1}{x - 3}$

46. $\dfrac{\dfrac{x}{4} - 1}{x - 4}$

47. $\dfrac{1 + \dfrac{1}{x}}{3 - \dfrac{1}{x}}$

48. $\dfrac{8 + \dfrac{1}{x}}{4 - \dfrac{1}{x}}$

49. $\dfrac{\dfrac{1}{x} + \dfrac{1}{y}}{x + y}$

50. $\dfrac{1 - \dfrac{1}{x}}{xy}$

51. $\dfrac{c - \dfrac{c}{c + 3}}{c + 2}$

52. $\dfrac{b - 3}{b - \dfrac{3}{b - 2}}$

53. $\dfrac{\dfrac{3}{y - 2} - \dfrac{4}{y + 2}}{\dfrac{7}{y^2 - 4}}$

54. $\dfrac{\dfrac{y}{y - 2} + 1}{\dfrac{3}{y^2 - 4} + 1}$

55. $\dfrac{\dfrac{1}{x + 1}}{\dfrac{1}{x^2 - 2x - 3} + \dfrac{1}{x - 3}}$

56. $\dfrac{\dfrac{6}{x^2 + 2x - 15} - \dfrac{1}{x - 3}}{\dfrac{1}{x + 5} + 1}$

57. $\dfrac{\dfrac{1}{x^3 - y^3}}{\dfrac{1}{x - y} - \dfrac{1}{x^2 + xy + y^2}}$

58. $\dfrac{\dfrac{1}{x^3 - 125}}{\dfrac{1}{x^2 - 25} - \dfrac{1}{x^2 + 5x + 25}}$

59. $\dfrac{\dfrac{1}{(x + h)^2} - \dfrac{1}{x^2}}{h}$

60. $\dfrac{\dfrac{x + h}{x + h + 1} - \dfrac{x}{x + 1}}{h}$

61. $\dfrac{2x^{-1} + y^{-1}}{xy}$

62. $\dfrac{x^{-1} - 2(x + 2)^{-1}}{x^{-2}}$

Simplify each fractional expression in Problems 63–68.

63. $\dfrac{\dfrac{1}{\sqrt{x + h}} - \dfrac{1}{\sqrt{x}}}{h}$

64. $\dfrac{\sqrt{y} - \dfrac{1}{4\sqrt{y}}}{\sqrt{y}}$

65. $\dfrac{\dfrac{y^2}{\sqrt{y^2 + 2}} - \sqrt{y^2 + 2}}{y^2}$

66. $\dfrac{\sqrt{5 - y^2} + \dfrac{y^2}{\sqrt{5 - y^2}}}{5 - y^2}$

67. $\dfrac{4y(y^2 - 9)y^{2/3} - 2y^{-1/3}(y^2 - 9)^2}{(y^{2/3})^2}$

68. $\dfrac{y^3(1 - y^2)^{-1/2} + 2y(1 - y^2)^{1/2}}{y^4}$

Application Problems

69. The polynomial $-0.14t^2 + 0.51t + 31.6$ describes the U.S. population (in millions) age 65 and older t years after 1990. The polynomial $0.54t^2 + 12.64t + 107.1$ describes the total yearly cost of Medicare (in billions of dollars) t years after 1990. Write a rational expression that describes the average cost of Medicare per person age 65 or older t years after 1990. Then find this average cost for the years 1995 through 1998.

70. The average speed on a round-trip commute having a one-way distance d is given by the complex rational expression

$$\dfrac{2d}{\dfrac{d}{r_1} + \dfrac{d}{r_2}}$$

in which r_1 and r_2 are the speeds on the outgoing and return trips, respectively. Simplify the expression. Then find the average speed for a person who drives from home to work at 30 miles per hour and returns on the same route averaging 20 miles per hour. Explain why the answer is not 25 miles per hour.

71. If three resistors with resistances R_1, R_2, and R_3 are connected in parallel, their combined resistance R is given by the equation

$$R = \dfrac{1}{\dfrac{1}{R_1} + \dfrac{1}{R_2} + \dfrac{1}{R_3}}.$$

Simplify the complex rational expression on the right. Then find R when R_1 is 4 ohms, R_2 is 8 ohms, and R_3 is 12 ohms.

72. Write a rational expression in simplified form that describes how many times greater the area of the rectangle is than the area of the triangle in the figure at the top of the next column.

73. Write a rational expression in simplified form (and in terms of π) that describes how many times greater the area of the rectangle is than the area of the circle in the figure.

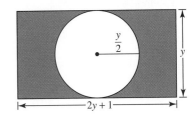

True–False Critical Thinking Problems

74. Which one of the following is true?

a. $\dfrac{x^2 - 25}{x - 5} = x - 5$

b. $\dfrac{x}{y} \div \dfrac{y}{x} = 1$, if $x \neq 0$ and $y \neq 0$.

c. The LCD needed to find $\dfrac{1}{x} + \dfrac{1}{x + 3}$ is $x + 3$.

d. $\dfrac{x}{7} - 1 = \dfrac{x - 7}{7}$ for all real numbers x.

75. Which one of the following is true?

a. $\dfrac{1}{a} + \dfrac{1}{b} = \dfrac{1}{a + b}$

b. $\dfrac{a + b}{a} = b$

c. $\dfrac{a}{b + c} = \dfrac{a}{b} + \dfrac{a}{c}$

d. The rational expression

$$\dfrac{x^2 - 16}{x - 4}$$

is not defined for $x = 4$. However, as x gets closer and closer to 4, the value of the expression approaches 8.

Technology Problems

76. a. Show that $\dfrac{x^2 - x - 6}{x + 2} = x - 3$.

b. Use a graphing utility to graph $y_1 = \dfrac{x^2 - x - 6}{x + 2}$ and $y_2 = x - 3$ in the same viewing rectangle. Do the graphs appear to be identical? Don't be fooled by this; if $x = -2$ then $\dfrac{x^2 - x - 6}{x + 2}$ is undefined, which is not shown on the graph. For all values of x other than -2, $\dfrac{x^2 - x - 6}{x + 2} = x - 3$. (Verify this fact using the $\boxed{\text{TRACE}}$ feature.)

In Problems 77–78, use a graphing utility to answer each question.

77. Is $\dfrac{x}{3} + \dfrac{1}{6}$ equivalent to $\dfrac{2x + 1}{6}$ or $\dfrac{x + 2}{6}$?

78. Is $\dfrac{1}{x} + \dfrac{1}{2}$ equivalent to $\dfrac{1}{x + 2}$ or $\dfrac{x + 2}{2x}$ (assuming $x \neq 0$)?

In Problems 79–83, perform the indicated operations and support your work with a graphing utility.

79. $\dfrac{x^2 - 4}{2 - x}$

80. $\dfrac{2}{x - 1} \div \dfrac{4}{x^2 - 1}$

81. $\dfrac{x}{2} + \dfrac{x}{5}$

82. $6 - \dfrac{5}{x + 3}$

83. $\dfrac{x}{x - 5} - \dfrac{5}{5 - x}$

Critical Thinking Problems

84. Perform the indicated operations:

$$\dfrac{1}{x^n - 1} - \dfrac{1}{x^n + 1} - \dfrac{1}{x^{2n} - 1}.$$

85. Simplify:

$$\left(\dfrac{a^{-2} + b^{-2}}{a^{-2} - b^{-2}} - \dfrac{a^{-2} - b^{-2}}{a^{-2} + b^{-2}}\right) \div \left[\left(\dfrac{a + b}{a - b} + \dfrac{a - b}{a + b}\right)\left(\dfrac{a^2}{b^2} + \dfrac{b^2}{a^2} - 2\right)\right]^{-1}.$$

86. Find the product of the following 199 factors:

$$\left(1 - \dfrac{1}{2}\right)\left(1 - \dfrac{1}{3}\right)\left(1 - \dfrac{1}{4}\right)\cdots\left(1 - \dfrac{1}{x + 1}\right)\cdots\left(1 - \dfrac{1}{200}\right).$$

87. Simplify $(1 + b^{x-y})^{-1} + (1 + b^{y-x})^{-1}$ to obtain the smallest of the natural numbers.

Group Activity Problem

88. As a group, find out as much as you can about computer algebra systems such as *Mathematica*, *Maple*, and *Derive*, or graphing calculators with such systems built in (such as the TI-92). Use such a system to solve five of the practice problems that have appeared in Problem Sets P.5 through P.7. Within your group, debate the issue of whether or not graphing utilities capable of symbolic manipulation should eliminate the necessity for learning algebra's many manipulative skills, such as operations with radicals and rational expressions.

S E C T I O N   P . 8

Complex Numbers

Solutions Manual

Tutorial

Video 2

Objectives

1 Find powers of *i*.

2 Add and subtract complex numbers.

3 Multiply complex numbers.

4 Divide complex numbers.

5 Perform operations with roots of negative numbers.

6 Plot complex numbers.

Some of the numbers that appear in algebra, particularly as the solutions of equations, are not real numbers. In this section, we expand the set of real numbers to include the square roots of negative numbers.

The Imaginary Unit i

In Chapter 1, we'll be studying equations whose solutions involve the square roots of negative numbers. Since the square of a real number is never negative, there is no real number x such that $x^2 = -1$. To provide a setting in which such equations have solutions, mathematicians invented an expanded system of numbers, the complex numbers. The imaginary number i, defined to be a solution to the equation $x^2 = -1$, is the basis of this new set.

The imaginary unit i

The imaginary unit i is defined as

$$i = \sqrt{-1}, \quad \text{where} \quad i^2 = -1.$$

Using the imaginary unit i, we can express the square root of any negative number as a real multiple of i. For example,

$$\sqrt{-25} = i\sqrt{25} = 5i.$$

We can check this result by squaring $5i$ and obtaining -25.

$$(5i)^2 = 5^2 i^2 = 25(-1) = -25$$

A new system of numbers, called *complex numbers*, is based on adding multiples of i, such as $5i$, to the real numbers.

Complex numbers

The set of all numbers in the form

$$a + bi$$

with real numbers a and b, and i, the imaginary unit, is called the set of *complex numbers*. The real number a is called the *real part*, and the real number b is called the *imaginary part* of the complex number $a + bi$. If $a = 0$ and $b \neq 0$, then the complex number bi is called a *pure imaginary number* (Figure P.39).

René Magritte "Portrait" (Le Portrait) 1935, oil on canvas, 28 7/8 × 19 7/8 in. The Museum of Modern Art, New York. Gift of Kay Sage Tanguy. Photograph © 1997 The Museum of Modern Art, New York. © 1998 C. Herscovici, Brussels / Artists Rights Society (ARS), New York.

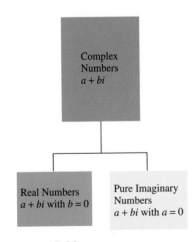

Figure P.39

The complex number system

Study tip

Every real number is a complex number in the form $a + bi$ with $b = 0$.

A complex number is said to be *simplified* if it is expressed in the *standard form $a + bi$*. If b is a radical, we usually write i before b. For example, we write $7 + i\sqrt{5}$ rather than $7 + \sqrt{5}i$, which could easily be confused with $7 + \sqrt{5i}$.

Expressed in standard form, two complex numbers are equal if and only if their real parts are equal and their imaginary parts are equal.

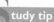

The connective "if and only if" between two statements p and q means

> If p then q.
> AND
> If q then p.

The definition for equality of complex numbers is really two statements in one:

1. If $a + bi = c + di$, then $a = c$ and $b = d$.
2. If $a = c$ and $b = d$, then $a + bi = c + di$.

Equality of complex numbers

$a + bi = c + di$ if and only if $a = c$ and $b = d$.

Powers of i

The fact that $i^2 = -1$ can be used to find higher powers of i.

iscover for yourself

Replace i^2 with -1 and express each of the following in terms of $1, -1, i,$ or $-i$.

$i^1 = i, i^2 = -1, \quad i^3 = i^2 \cdot i = \underline{\quad}, \quad i^4 = (i^2)^2 = \underline{\quad},$

$i^5 = (i^2)^2 i = \underline{\quad}, \quad i^6 = (i^2)^3 = \underline{\quad}, \quad i^7 = (i^2)^3 i = \underline{\quad}, \quad i^8 = (i^2)^4 = \underline{\quad}$

| Find powers of i.

In the Discover for yourself, did you observe that the powers of i rotate through the four numbers $i, -1, -i,$ and 1?

Powers of i

$i^1 = i$	$i^5 = i$	$i^9 = i$	$i^{13} = i$
$i^2 = -1$	$i^6 = -1$	$i^{10} = -1$	$i^{14} = -1$
$i^3 = -i$	$i^7 = -i$	$i^{11} = -i$	$i^{15} = -i$
$i^4 = 1$	$i^8 = 1$	$i^{12} = 1$	$i^{16} = 1$

Although we can use the rotating pattern to simplify higher powers of i, an easier method is to write these powers in terms of i^2 and then replace i^2 by -1.

Discover for yourself

Since $i^4 = 1$, another method for simplifying higher powers of i is to write them in terms of i^4. Use this method to simplify the numbers in Example 1.

EXAMPLE 1   Finding Powers of i

Simplify:

a. i^{12} **b.** i^{39} **c.** i^{50} **d.** i^{1883}

Solution

a. $i^{12} = (i^2)^6 = (-1)^6 = 1$
b. $i^{39} = i^{38}i = (i^2)^{19}i = (-1)^{19}i = (-1)i = -i$
c. $i^{50} = (i^2)^{25} = (-1)^{25} = -1$
d. $i^{1883} = i^{1882}i = (i^2)^{941}i = (-1)^{941}i = (-1)i = -i$ ■

Operations with Complex Numbers

The form of a complex number $a + bi$ is like the binomial $a + bx$. Consequently, we can add, subtract, and multiply complex numbers using the same methods we used for binomials, remembering that $i^2 = -1$.

2 Add and subtract complex numbers.

Adding and subtracting complex numbers

1. $(a + bi) + (c + di) = (a + c) + (b + d)i$
   In words, this says that you add complex numbers by adding their real parts, adding their imaginary parts, and expressing the sum as a complex number.
2. $(a + bi) - (c + di) = (a - c) + (b - d)i$
   In words, this says that you subtract complex numbers by subtracting their real parts, subtracting their imaginary parts, and expressing the difference as a complex number.

EXAMPLE 2   Adding and Subtracting Complex Numbers

Perform the indicated operations, writing the result in standard form.

a. $(5 - 11i) + (7 + 4i)$ b. $(-5 + 7i) - (-11 - 6i)$
c. $4 - (-7 + 3i) + (-11 + 6i)$

Study tip

The following examples, using the same integers as in Example 2, show how operations with complex numbers are just like operations with polynomials.

a. $(5 - 11x) + (7 + 4x)$
   $= 12 - 7x$
b. $(-5 + 7x) - (-11 - 6x)$
   $= -5 + 7x + 11 + 6x$
   $= 6 + 13x$
c. $4 - (-7 + 3x) + (-11 + 6x)$
   $= 4 + 7 - 3x - 11 + 6x$
   $= 3x$

Solution

a. $(5 - 11i) + (7 + 4i)$
   $= 5 - 11i + 7 + 4i$ Remove the parentheses.
   $= 5 + 7 - 11i + 4i$ Group real and imaginary terms.
   $= (5 + 7) + (-11 + 4)i$
   $= 12 - 7i$ Do you find that you're working all steps mentally?
b. $(-5 + 7i) - (-11 - 6i)$
   $= -5 + 7i + 11 + 6i$ Remove the parentheses.
   $= -5 + 11 + 7i + 6i$ Group real and imaginary terms.
   $= (-5 + 11) + (7 + 6)i$
   $= 6 + 13i$
c. $4 - (-7 + 3i) + (-11 + 6i)$
   $= 4 + 7 - 3i - 11 + 6i$ Remove the parentheses.
   $= 4 + 7 - 11 - 3i + 6i$ Group the real and imaginary terms.
   $= (4 + 7 - 11) + (-3 + 6)i$
   $= 0 + 3i$ Equivalently, the answer can be expressed as $3i$. ∎

3 Multiply complex numbers.

Multiplication of complex numbers is performed the same way as multiplication of polynomials, using the distributive property and the FOIL method. After completing the multiplication, we replace i^2 with -1. This idea is illustrated in the next example.

EXAMPLE 3   Multiplying Complex Numbers

Find the products:

a. $4i(3 - 5i)$ b. $(7 - 3i)(-2 - 5i)$ c. $(4 + 3i)(4 - 3i)$

Solution

a. $4i(3-5i) = 4i(3) - 4i(5i)$ Distribute $4i$ throughout the parentheses.

$= 12i - 20i^2$ Multiply.

$= 12i - 20(-1)$ Replace i^2 with -1.

$= 12i + 20$ Simplify. In standard form, the product can be expressed as $20 + 12i$.

b. $(7 - 3i)(-2 - 5i)$

$\quad\quad\;\; \overset{F}{} \quad \overset{O}{} \quad \overset{I}{} \quad \overset{L}{}$

$= -14 - 35i + 6i + 15i^2$ Use the FOIL method.

$= -14 - 35i + 6i + 15(-1)$ $i^2 = -1$

$= -14 - 15 - 35i + 6i$ Group real and imaginary terms.

$= -29 - 29i$ Combine real and imaginary terms.

c. $(4 + 3i)(4 - 3i)$

$\quad\quad\;\; \overset{F}{} \quad \overset{O}{} \quad \overset{I}{} \quad \overset{L}{}$

$= 16 - 12i + 12i - 9i^2$ Use the FOIL method.

$= 16 - 9(-1)$ $i^2 = -1$

$= 25$ We can also write $25 + 0i$. ■

$(7 - 3i)(-2 - 5i)$

Discover for yourself

Work Example 3c using

$(A + B)(A - B) = A^2 - B^2$

with

$A = 4$ and $B = 3i.$

Which method do you find easier?

Discover for yourself

It is not necessary to memorize the definitions for addition and subtraction of complex numbers to perform these operations. The same is true for multiplication, which is defined by

$$(a + bi)(c + di) = (ac - bd) + (ad + bc)i.$$

Show that multiplying $(a + bi)(c + di)$ by the FOIL method gives the preceding result.

4 Divide complex numbers.

Complex Conjugates and Division

In Example 3c, we found that

$$(4 + 3i)(4 - 3i) = 25.$$

Thus, the product of two complex numbers can be a real number. Generalizing from this situation, let's multiply $a + bi$ and $a - bi$.

$\quad\quad\quad\quad\quad\quad\;\; \overset{F}{} \quad \overset{O}{} \quad\;\; \overset{I}{} \quad\;\; \overset{L}{}$

$(a + bi)(a - bi) = a^2 - abi + abi - b^2i^2$ Use the FOIL method.

$= a^2 - b^2(-1)$ $i^2 = -1$

$= a^2 + b^2$ Notice that this product eliminates i.

For the complex number $a + bi$, we define its *complex conjugate* to be $a - bi$. The multiplication of complex conjugates results in a real number.

Conjugate of a complex number

The complex conjugate of the number $a + bi$ is $a - bi$, and the complex conjugate of $a - bi$ is $a + bi$. The multiplication of complex conjugates gives a real number.

$$(a + bi)(a - bi) = a^2 + b^2$$

$$(a - bi)(a + bi) = a^2 + b^2$$

EXAMPLE 4 **Multiplying Complex Conjugates**

Multiply:

a. $(3 + 4i)(3 - 4i)$ **b.** $(7 - 6i)(7 + 6i)$

Solution

$$\underset{\downarrow\ \downarrow\ \downarrow\ \downarrow\ \ \ \ \downarrow\ \ \ \downarrow}{(a\ +\ bi)\ (a\ -\ bi)\ =\ a^2\ +\ b^2}$$

a. $(3 + 4i)(3 - 4i) = 3^2 + 4^2$
$$= 9 + 16$$
$$= 25$$

$$\underset{\downarrow\ \ \downarrow\ \ \downarrow\ \ \downarrow\ \ \ \ \downarrow\ \ \ \downarrow}{(a\ -\ bi)\ (a\ +\ bi)\ =\ a^2\ +\ b^2}$$

b. $(7 - 6i)(7 + 6i) = 7^2 + 6^2$
$$= 49 + 36$$
$$= 85$$ ∎

Discover for yourself

Consider the division problem

$$\frac{7 + 4i}{2 - 5i}.$$

What must be done to both the numerator and the denominator so that the denominator contains only a real number?

In the Discover for yourself, did you observe that multiplying the numerator and the denominator by $2 + 5i$ (the conjugate of the denominator) results in a real number in the denominator? We see how conjugates are used when dividing complex numbers in Example 5.

EXAMPLE 5 **Using Conjugates to Divide Complex Numbers**

Divide: $7 + 4i$ by $2 - 5i$

Solution

We first write the problem as $\dfrac{7 + 4i}{2 - 5i}$. The conjugate of the denominator, $2 - 5i$, is $2 + 5i$, so we multiply the numerator and the denominator by $2 + 5i$.

$$\frac{7 + 4i}{2 - 5i} = \frac{(7 + 4i)}{(2 - 5i)} \cdot \frac{(2 + 5i)}{(2 + 5i)}$$

Multiply the numerator and the denominator by the conjugate of the denominator.

$$= \frac{\overset{F\qquad O\qquad I\qquad L}{14 + 35i + 8i + 20i^2}}{2^2 + 5^2}$$

Use the FOIL method in the numerator and $(a - bi)(a + bi) = a^2 + b^2$ in the denominator.

$$= \frac{14 + 43i + 20(-1)}{29}$$

Replace i^2 by -1.

$$= \frac{-6 + 43i}{29}$$

Combine real terms in the numerator.

$$= -\frac{6}{29} + \frac{43}{29}i$$

Observe that the quotient is expressed in the form $a + bi$, with $a = -\frac{6}{29}$ and $b = \frac{43}{29}$. ∎

Using conjugates to divide complex numbers

When dividing two complex numbers, if necessary express the indicated division as a fraction and then multiply the numerator and the denominator by the complex conjugate of the denominator.

EXAMPLE 6 **Dividing Complex Numbers**

Divide and simplify to the form $a + bi$: $\dfrac{10 + 6i}{5i}$

Solution

The conjugate of $0 + 5i$ is $0 - 5i$, or $-5i$, so we will multiply the numerator and the denominator by $-5i$.

$$\frac{10 + 6i}{5i} = \frac{10 + 6i}{5i} \cdot \frac{-5i}{-5i}$$

Multiply by 1, using the conjugate of the denominator.

$$= \frac{-50i - 30i^2}{-25i^2}$$

Multiply, using the distributive property in the numerator.

$$= \frac{-50i - 30(-1)}{-25(-1)}$$

$i^2 = -1$

$$= \frac{-50i + 30}{25}$$

Multiply.

$$= \frac{-50}{25}i + \frac{30}{25}$$

To write the quotient in the form $a + bi$, divide each term in the numerator by 25.

$$= \frac{6}{5} - 2i$$

Reverse the order of the terms and simplify.

The quotient is in the form $a + bi$, with $a = \frac{6}{5}$ and $b = -2$. ∎

5 Perform operations with roots of negative numbers.

Roots of Negative Numbers

The square of $4i$ and the square of $-4i$ both result in -16.

$$(4i)^2 = 16i^2 = 16(-1) = -16 \qquad (-4i)^2 = 16i^2 = -16$$

Consequently, in the complex number system -16 has two square roots, namely, $4i$ and $-4i$. We call $4i$ the *principal square root* of -16.

Principal square root of a negative number

For any positive number real number b, the *principal square root* of the negative number $-b$ is defined by

$$\sqrt{-b} = i\sqrt{b}.$$

tudy tip

Do not apply the properties

$$\sqrt{b}\,\sqrt{c} = \sqrt{bc} \quad \text{and} \quad \frac{\sqrt{b}}{\sqrt{c}} = \sqrt{\frac{b}{c}}$$

to the pure imaginary numbers because these properties can only be used when b and c are positive.

Correct:	**Incorrect:**
$\sqrt{-25}\,\sqrt{-4} = i\sqrt{25}\,i\sqrt{4}$	$\sqrt{-25}\,\sqrt{-4} = \sqrt{(-25)(-4)}$
$= (5i)(2i)$	$= \sqrt{100}$
$= 10i^2$	$= 10$
$= 10(-1)$	
$= -10$	

One way to avoid confusion is to *represent all imaginary numbers in terms of i before adding, subtracting, multiplying, or dividing.*

EXAMPLE 7 **Operations Involving Square Roots of Negative Numbers**

Perform the indicated operations and write the result in standard form:

a. $\sqrt{-18} - \sqrt{-8}$ **b.** $(-1 + \sqrt{-5})^2$

c. $\dfrac{-25 + \sqrt{-50}}{15}$ **d.** $\sqrt{-12}\,(\sqrt{-3} - \sqrt{2})$

tudy tip

The first thing to do in each part of Example 7 is to express $\sqrt{-b}$ as $i\sqrt{b}$.

Solution

a. $\sqrt{-18} - \sqrt{-8} = i\sqrt{18} - i\sqrt{8} = i\sqrt{9\cdot2} - i\sqrt{4\cdot2} = 3i\sqrt{2} - 2i\sqrt{2} = i\sqrt{2}$

$$(A \ + \ B)^2 \ = \ A^2 \ + \ 2 \ A \ B \ + \ B^2$$

b. $(-1 + \sqrt{-5})^2 = (-1 + i\sqrt{5})^2 = (-1)^2 + 2(-1)(i\sqrt{5}) + (i\sqrt{5})^2$

$$= 1 - 2i\sqrt{5} + 5i^2$$
$$= 1 - 2i\sqrt{5} + 5(-1)$$
$$= -4 - 2i\sqrt{5}$$

c. $\dfrac{-25 + \sqrt{-50}}{15}$

$= \dfrac{-25 + i\sqrt{50}}{15}$ $\sqrt{-b} = i\sqrt{b}$

$= \dfrac{-25 + 5i\sqrt{2}}{15}$ $\sqrt{50} = \sqrt{25\cdot2} = 5\sqrt{2}$

$$= \frac{-25}{15} + \frac{5i\sqrt{2}}{15}$$ Write the complex number in standard form.

$$= -\frac{5}{3} + i\frac{\sqrt{2}}{3}$$ Simplify.

d. $\sqrt{-12}\,(\sqrt{-3} - \sqrt{2})$

$= i\sqrt{12}\,(i\sqrt{3} - \sqrt{2})$ $\sqrt{-b} = i\sqrt{b}$

$= i^2\sqrt{36} - i\sqrt{24}$ Apply the distributive property.

$= (-1)(6) - 2i\sqrt{6}$ $\sqrt{24} = \sqrt{4 \cdot 6} = 2\sqrt{6}; \; i^2 = -1$

$= -6 - 2i\sqrt{6}$ Express the product in standard form.   ■

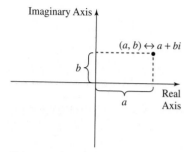

Imaginary Axis

$(a, b) \leftrightarrow a + bi$

b

a

Real Axis

Figure P.40

The complex plane

Plotting Complex Numbers

The *complex plane*, shown above in Figure P.40, consists of a horizontal axis, called the *real axis*, and a vertical axis, called the *imaginary axis*. Every complex number corresponds to a point in the complex plane and every point in the complex plane corresponds to a complex number.

6 Plot complex numbers.

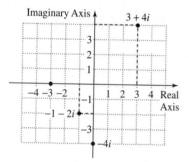

Imaginary Axis

$3 + 4i$

$-1 - 2i$

$-4i$

Real Axis

Figure P.41

Plotting complex numbers

EXAMPLE 8   Plotting Complex Numbers

Plot in the complex plane:

a. $3 + 4i$ **b.** $-1 - 2i$ **c.** -3 **d.** $-4i$

Solution (See Figure P.41)

a. The complex number $3 + 4i$ is plotted in the same way we plot $(3, 4)$ in the Cartesian coordinate plane. We move 3 units to the right on the real axis and 4 units up parallel to the imaginary axis.

b. The complex number $-1 - 2i$ corresponds to the point $(-1, -2)$ in the Cartesian coordinate plane.

c. Since $-3 = -3 + 0i$, this number corresponds to the point $(-3, 0)$. We plot -3 by moving 3 units to the left on the real axis.

d. Since $-4i = 0 - 4i$, we plot $-4i$ by moving 4 units down on the imaginary axis.   ■

PROBLEM SET P.8

Practice Problems

In Problems 1–6, simplify each expression.

1. i^{24} **2.** i^{36} **3.** i^{75} **4.** i^{37}
5. i^{49} **6.** i^{53}

In Problems 7–14, add or subtract as indicated and write the result in standard form.

7. $(7 + 2i) + (1 - 4i)$ **8.** $(-2 + 6i) + (4 - i)$ **9.** $(3 + 2i) - (5 - 7i)$
10. $(-7 + 5i) - (-9 - 11i)$ **11.** $6 - (-5 + 4i) - (-13 - 11i)$ **12.** $7 - (-9 + 2i) - (-17 - 6i)$
13. $6 - (5 - 2i\sqrt{32}) - (11 - 5i\sqrt{8})$ **14.** $7 - (3 + 7i\sqrt{8}) - (-10 - 2i\sqrt{50})$

In Problems 15–28, find each product and write the result in standard form.

15. $-3i(7i - 5)$ **16.** $-8i(2i - 7)$ **17.** $(-5 + 4i)(3 + 7i)$ **18.** $(-4 - 8i)(3 + 9i)$
19. $(7 - 5i)(-2 - 3i)$ **20.** $(8 - 4i)(-3 + 9i)$ **21.** $(3 + 5i)(3 - 5i)$ **22.** $(2 + 7i)(2 - 7i)$

23. $(-5 + 3i)(-5 - 3i)$ **24.** $(-7 - 4i)(-7 + 4i)$ **25.** $(2 + 3i)^2$ **26.** $(5 - 2i)^2$

27. $\left(\dfrac{1}{2} + \dfrac{\sqrt{3}}{2}i\right)^2$ **28.** $\left(\dfrac{\sqrt{3}}{2} - \dfrac{1}{2}i\right)^2$

In Problems 29–42, divide and express the result in standard form.

29. $\dfrac{2}{3 - i}$ **30.** $\dfrac{3}{4 + i}$ **31.** $\dfrac{2i}{1 + i}$ **32.** $\dfrac{5i}{2 - i}$

33. $\dfrac{8i}{4 - 3i}$ **34.** $\dfrac{-6i}{3 + 2i}$ **35.** $\dfrac{2 + 3i}{2 + i}$ **36.** $\dfrac{3 - 4i}{4 + 3i}$

37. $\dfrac{-4 + 7i}{-2 - 5i}$ **38.** $\dfrac{-3 - i}{-4 - 3i}$ **39.** $\dfrac{3 - i}{2i}$ **40.** $\dfrac{4 + i}{3i}$

41. $\dfrac{-4 + 7i}{-5i}$ **42.** $\dfrac{-3 - i}{-3i}$

In Problems 43–52, perform the indicated operations and write the result in standard form.

43. $(8 + 9i)(2 - i) - (1 - i)(1 + i)$ **44.** $(2 - 3i)(1 - i) - (3 - i)(3 + i)$

45. $\dfrac{4}{(2 + i)(3 - i)}$ **46.** $\dfrac{6}{(2 + i)(1 - i)}$ **47.** $(1 - 3i)^3$ **48.** $(1 + 2i)^3$

49. $i^4(1 + i^3)$ **50.** $6i^4(2 - i^5)$ **51.** i^{-17} **52.** i^{-13}

In Problems 53–68, perform the indicated operations and write the result in standard form.

53. $\sqrt{-64} - \sqrt{-25}$ **54.** $\sqrt{-81} - \sqrt{-144}$ **55.** $5\sqrt{-16} + 3\sqrt{-81}$ **56.** $5\sqrt{-8} + 3\sqrt{-18}$

57. $(-2 + \sqrt{-4})^2$ **58.** $(-5 - \sqrt{-9})^2$ **59.** $(-3 - \sqrt{-7})^2$ **60.** $(-2 + \sqrt{-11})^2$

61. $\dfrac{-8 + \sqrt{-32}}{24}$ **62.** $\dfrac{-12 + \sqrt{-28}}{32}$ **63.** $\dfrac{-6 - \sqrt{-12}}{48}$ **64.** $\dfrac{-15 - \sqrt{-18}}{33}$

65. $\sqrt{-8}(\sqrt{-3} - \sqrt{5})$ **66.** $\sqrt{-12}(\sqrt{-4} - \sqrt{2})$ **67.** $(3\sqrt{-5})(-4\sqrt{-12})$ **68.** $(3\sqrt{-7})(2\sqrt{-8})$

In Problems 69–76, plot each complex number in the complex plane.

69. $-3 + i$ **70.** $-4 - 2i$ **71.** $1 - 5i$ **72.** $2 - 3i$

73. i **74.** $-3i$ **75.** 2 **76.** -4

True-False Critical Thinking Problems

77. Which one of the following is true?

    a. Some irrational numbers are not complex numbers.

    b. $i^{-1} = i$

    c. $\dfrac{7 + 3i}{5 + 3i} = \dfrac{7}{5}$

    d. In the complex number system, $x^2 + y^2$ (the sum of two squares) can be factored as $(x + yi)(x - yi)$.

78. Which one of the following is true?

    a. $\dfrac{20}{3 - 2i} = \dfrac{20}{3 - 2i} \cdot \dfrac{3 + 2i}{3 + 2i} = \dfrac{60 + 40i}{9 - 4} = 12 + 8i$

    b. $(\sqrt{-5} + 4)(i - \sqrt{-7})$
        $= i\sqrt{-5} - \sqrt{-5}\sqrt{-7} + 4i - 4\sqrt{-7}$
        $= i \cdot i\sqrt{5} - \sqrt{35} + 4i - 4i\sqrt{7}$
        $= -\sqrt{5} - \sqrt{35} + 4i - 4i\sqrt{7}$

    c. $i^7(1 + i^3) = 0$

    d. $\dfrac{i^4 + i^3 + i^2 + i + 1}{1 + i} = \dfrac{1}{2} - \dfrac{1}{2}i$

Writing in Mathematics

Explain the error in Problems 79–82.

79. $-\sqrt{-100} = -(-\sqrt{100}) = \sqrt{100} = 10$

80. $(\sqrt{-9})^2 = \sqrt{-9}\sqrt{-9} = \sqrt{81} = 9$

81. $\sqrt{-9} + \sqrt{-16} = \sqrt{-25} = i\sqrt{25} = 5i$

82. The only square root of -1 is i.

Critical Thinking Problems

83. Show that $\sqrt[3]{1} = -\dfrac{1}{2} + \dfrac{\sqrt{3}}{2} i$ by showing that $\left(-\dfrac{1}{2} + \dfrac{\sqrt{3}}{2} i\right)^3 = 1$.

84. Perform the indicated operations: $\dfrac{1 + i}{1 + 2i} + \dfrac{1 - i}{1 - 2i}$.

85. Simplify: i^{2n+1}.

86. Simplify: $\left(\dfrac{i}{1 + i} + \dfrac{2 + i}{2 - i}\right) i$.

Group Activity Problem

87. The statement *p if and only if q* is two statements in one. The two statements are

　　If *p* then *q*.
　　AND
　　If *q* then *p*.

Group members should explain whether the connective *if and only if* is used correctly or incorrectly in each of the following sentences.

a. A number is positive if and only if that number is greater than zero.

b. A person is in Washington D.C. if and only if that person is in the United States.

c. Shakespeare is the author if and only if the play is *Macbeth*.

d. *x* is not greater than 5 if and only if *x* is less than or equal to 5.

e. The team won if and only if they did not lose.

f. *a* = *b* if and only if *b* = *a*.

g. A triangle has two sides equal in measure if and only if it has two angles equal in measure.

Group members should now write eight sentences, four which illustrate the correct use of *if and only if* and four that illustrate its misuse. Consult a general mathematics textbook to find two other ways to express *if and only if*. Express your five correct sentences using these equivalent connectives.

CHAPTER PROJECT
Jurassic Math: A Matter of Scale

Looking at numbers describing the physical attributes of a dinosaur is not quite the same as watching a movie filled with fast-moving predators, or seeing a full-scale reproduction in a museum. We may understand an equation in an intellectual sense, yet still feel we are missing some connection to make it real. There is always a human side to presenting information, making it accessible at a level other than an abstract, intellectual understanding. The mathematics in this chapter represents a large amount of information in a compact, symbolic form, but has something been lost in the translation?

For example, judging the size or scale of something is not an exercise in fantasy; it is an important skill for many people involved in the design, construction, or alteration of the landscape around us. To give more information to a client, architects create models of their plans complete with familiar sizes of people and objects. Engineers create models of differing scales as they design new cars, planes, or other objects. For the ultimate model, technological advances make it possible to put on a headset and use virtual reality to walk through a building and investigate how the design will fit into a human scale.

We can explore how the presentation of information affects the assimilation of information. In other words, how do we make the information *real*. We will use something familiar in an intellectual sense, but unfamiliar to most people in a realistic sense: dinosaurs. Given only a list of numbers describing the height and length of a dinosaur, would you be able to make realistic judgments about how this historic creature would fit into your world? Could a Tyrannosaurus Rex peer in the window of a three-story building? Could a Stegosaurus fit in your classroom? How many parking spaces would a Brontosaurus fill?

1. In a small group, select a dinosaur to study. Write the approximate dimensions of the dinosaur in terms of height and length in an uncommon unit of measurement, such as inches, centimeters, or a fraction of a mile. Ask several people to make a comparative estimate of the size of the dinosaur from these measurements. For example, you might ask, "Is it bigger than a car?" or "Is it taller than this house?" You may tell the person if the dinosaur walked on two or four legs, but do not reveal the name of the dinosaur. Record the answers from several sources and compare the results with the rest of your group. How accurate were the answers?

2. Conduct another set of interviews, this time giving the information in a more typical form, such as feet or yards. How does the accuracy of the new estimates compare to the ones in Problem 1? Share your results with other groups in the class. Does the actual size of the dinosaur seem to affect the estimates? In other words, does the size of larger dinosaurs seem harder to estimate accurately than smaller ones or vice versa?

3. Reverse the process of giving out information. Give someone a description of the size of a dinosaur by explaining it in terms of familiar objects. For example, "It is as long as three cars put together." Ask for an estimate in numerical terms. How do these estimates compare with the others? Would you expect different results if you had given the name of the dinosaur?

4. Use a variety of methods to show how a dinosaur would fit into the reality of your school by placing a dinosaur in familiar settings. Your group may use one or more of the following ideas or create your own:
   • Take a photograph of a familiar part of your campus and place a silhouette of your dinosaur, sized to scale, in the picture.
   • Begin with a picture of your dinosaur and insert silhouettes of familiar objects, drawn to scale.
   • Use a small plastic model of your dinosaur and place it in a cardboard model of some part of the campus, constructed to scale.
   • Create a life-sized measurement of your dinosaur. Use the gym or a field and mark the length of the dinosaur on the ground while using a helium balloon to show the height of the head.

5. Discuss with the class how well the methods in Problem 4 presented the reality of a dinosaur. Which style of presentation would be preferred if you stayed inside a classroom? Which presentation would be preferred if a life-sized reproduction was constructed? The weight of a dinosaur was never mentioned. What kind of effect would the weight have on understanding the scale of a dinosaur?

6. Use the numerical data on dinosaurs in each group to put together some of the different styles of equations found in Example 5 on pages 33–34. Each group should be able to create at least three equations, one linear, one whose graph is a parabola, and one with a radical, which give numerical solutions matching the values used for a particular dinosaur. Would solving an equation to obtain the length of a dinosaur give you a better understanding of its length?

Worldwide Web Resources

Go to the Prentice Hall website (http://www.prenhall.com/blitzer) to access other locations on the Internet that will allow you to further explore the concepts presented in this project.

Chapter Review

SUMMARY

(Starting with Chapter 1, a complete summary will be provided at the end of each chapter. For this chapter on reviewing fundamental concepts, we simply refer you back to some of the significant tables and definitions presented throughout the prerequisites survey.)

1. The Real Numbers
   a. Subsets of the real numbers are defined in Table P.1 on pages 2–3.
   b. Interval notation is summarized in Table P.2 on page 5.

2. Algebraic Expressions and Exponents

   a. Algebra's nine basic properties appear in the box on pages 14–15.

   b. Properties of negatives are summarized in the box on page 16.

   c. Properties of zero are summarized in the box on page 17.

   d. Properties that are useful in solving equations are found in the box on pages 17–18.

   e. Properties of exponents and examples are found in the box on pages 18–19.

   f. The definition of scientific notation is given in the box on page 22.

3. Graphing

   a. The distance formula appears in a box on page 30.

   b. The midpoint formula appears in a box on page 31.

   c. Graphing equations by plotting points is reviewed in the box on page 32.

   d. Intercepts are reviewed in the box on pages 34–35.

   e. An introduction to graphing utilities appears on pages 35–37.

4. Radicals and Rational Exponents

   a. Properties of nth roots with examples appear in the box on page 45.

   b. The conditions for simplified radical form are given on page 45.

   c. Rational exponents are defined in the box on page 50.

5. Polynomials

   a. The definition of a polynomial in x is given in the box on page 56.

   b. Operations with polynomials are discussed beginning on page 57.

   c. Special products that are useful in polynomial multiplication are given in the box on page 61.

6. Factoring

   a. A general factoring strategy is shown in the box on pages 73–74.

   b. A discussion of factoring techniques for expressions that are not polynomials begins on page 74.

7. Rational Expressions

   a. Properties of rational expressions with examples appear in the box on pages 80–81.

   b. A discussion of simplifying complex rational expressions begins on page 84.

8. Complex Numbers

   a. Complex numbers are defined in the box on page 91.

   b. Powers of i are shown in the box on page 92.

   c. Operations with complex numbers are presented beginning on page 92.

   d. The use of conjugates to divide complex numbers appears in the box on page 96.

   e. A method for plotting complex numbers is shown on page 98.

REVIEW PROBLEMS OR FUNDAMENTAL ALGEBRA SKILLS DIAGNOSTIC TEST

You can use these review problems, like the review problems at the end of each chapter, to test your understanding of the chapter's topics. However, you can also use these problems as a prerequisite test to check your mastery of the fundamental algebra skills needed in this book. Here are some suggestions for using these review problems as a diagnostic test:

1. *Work through all 74 items at your own pace.*

2. *Use the answer section in the back of the book to check your work.*

3. *If your answer differs from that in the answer section or if you are not certain how to proceed with a particular item, turn to the section and the illustrative example given in parentheses at the end of each problem. Study the step-by-step solution of the example that parallels the review problem, and then try working the problem again. If you feel that you need more assistance, study the entire section in which the example appears and work on a selected group of problems in the problem set for that section.*

1. Indicate which numbers in the following set are **a.** Natural numbers **b.** Whole numbers **c.** Integers **d.** Rational numbers **e.** Irrational numbers (Section P.1; Example 1)

$$\left\{ -13, \ -\sqrt{16}, \ -\sqrt{5}, \ -\frac{2}{3}, \ 0, \ \frac{\pi}{3}, \ 1.\overline{27}, \ \sqrt[4]{16} \right\}$$

In Problems 2–4, express each interval in terms of an inequality, and graph the interval on a number line. (Section P.1; Example 2)

2. $(-2, 3]$ **3.** $[-1.5, 2]$ **4.** $(-1, \infty)$

In Problems 5–8, express each set in interval notation. (Section P.1; Example 4)

5. $(1, 3) \cap [2, 7]$ **6.** $(-1, \infty) \cap (5, \infty)$ **7.** $(1, 3) \cup [2, 7]$ **8.** $(-1, \infty) \cup (5, \infty)$

9. Rewrite each expression without absolute value bars. (Section P.1; Example 5)

     a. $|\sqrt{2} - 1|$ **b.** $|3 - \sqrt{17}|$

10. Express the distance between the numbers -17 and 4 using absolute value. Then evaluate the absolute value. (Section P.1; Example 6)

11. Evaluate: $6x^3 - 5x^2 - 7x + 9$ for $x = -2$. (Section P.2; Example 1)

In Problems 12–13, state the property that justifies each statement. (Section P.2; Box on pages 14–15)

12. $\dfrac{1}{(x - 3)}(x - 3) = 1 \; (x \neq 3)$ **13.** $3 + (9 + 6) = (3 + 9) + 6$

14. Evaluate: $(-2)^4 - 3^2$. (Section P.2; Example 2)

Simplify each exponential expression in Problems 15–18. (Section P.2; Examples 3–5)

15. $(-2x^4y^3)^3$ **16.** $(-5x^3y^2)^3(-2x^{-11}y^{-3})$

17. $\left(\dfrac{2x^{-2}}{3y^3}\right)^{-4}$ **18.** $\left(\dfrac{-10x^2y}{20xy^{-2}}\right)^{-3}$

In Problems 19–20, write each number in scientific notation. (Section P.2; Box on page 23 and example following the box)

19. 98,000,000,000,000   **20.** 0.000362

21. The graph shows the number of juveniles in the United States arrested for marijuana possession from 1980 through 1995.

     a. What are the coordinates for point A? What does this mean in practical terms?

     b. For the period shown in the graph, in approximately what year were arrests for marijuana possession at a minimum? Approximately how many arrests were there during that year? (Section P.3; Examples 1 and 2)

22. Plot $(-3, 7)$ and $(5, 7)$. Then find the distance between the points and the midpoint of the line segment joining the points. (Section P.3; Examples 3 and 4)

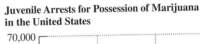

Juvenile Arrests for Possession of Marijuana in the United States

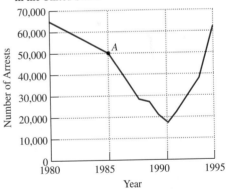

Source: FBI.

In Problems 23–27, use the point-plotting method to graph the given equation. Then use a graphing utility to verify your hand-drawn graph. (Section P.3; Example 5)

23. $y = -3x + 6$ **24.** $y = x^2 - 1$ **25.** $y = x^3 - x$ **26.** $y = \sqrt[3]{x + 1}$

27. $y = -|x|$ **28.** Evaluate: $\sqrt[3]{-27} + \sqrt[5]{32}$. (Section P.4; Examples 1 and 2)

29. Write in simplified form by factoring the radicand and removing as many factors as possible: $\sqrt[3]{16x^3y^8}$. (Section P.4; Example 3)

In Problems 30–32, simplify by rationalizing the denominator. (Section P.4; Examples 4–6)

30. $\dfrac{15}{2\sqrt{5}}$

31. $\sqrt[3]{\dfrac{1}{3}}$

32. $\dfrac{14}{\sqrt{7} - \sqrt{5}}$

In Problems 33–34, simplify by combining the radicals. (Section P.4; Example 7)

33. $5\sqrt{18} + 3\sqrt{8} - \sqrt{2}$

34. $16\sqrt{\dfrac{5}{8}} + 6\sqrt{\dfrac{5}{2}}$

35. Evaluate without using a calculator: $8^{2/3} - 32^{-4/5}$. (Section P.4; Example 8).

In Problems 36–37, simplify each algebraic expression. (Section P.4; Example 9)

36. $(7x^{1/3})(4x^{1/4})$

37. $\dfrac{80y^{3/4}}{-20y^{1/5}}$

In Problems 38–39, simplify by reducing the index of the radical. (Section P.4; Example 10)

38. $\sqrt[8]{16x^6y^2}$

39. $8\sqrt[4]{2} + 2\sqrt[8]{2^{10}}$

40. Perform the indicated operations. Write the resulting polynomial in standard form and indicate its degree:

$(16x^3 - 2x^2 - 5x + 3) - (-2x^3 - x^2 + 4x - 1) + (3x^3 - 7x^2 - x + 1)$

(Section P.5; Examples 1 and 2)

In Problems 41–42, find each product. (Section P.5; Examples 3–6)

41. $(x^2 + 3x - 5)(2x^2 - x + 4)$

42. $(9x - 7)(4x + 3)$

In Problems 43–44, use the special products to find each product. (Section P.5; Examples 8–9)

43. $(4x - 3y)^3$

44. $[5y - (2x + 1)]$ $[5y + (2x + 1)]$

In Problems 45–57, factor each expression completely.

45. $60x^6y^3 - 20x^4y^2 + 10xy^5$ (Section P.6; Example 1)

46. $x^3 - 7x^2 + 9x - 63$ (Section P.6; Example 2)

47. $x^4 - 81y^4$ (Section P.6; Examples 4–5)

48. $x^3 - 1000$ (Section P.6; Example 6)

49. $4x^2 - 20x + 25$ (Section P.6; Example 7)

50. $x^2 + 6x + 9 - 4a^2$ (Section P.6; Example 8)

51. $8x^2 + 2x - 15$ (Section P.6; Examples 9–10)

52. $4a^3 + 32$ (Section P.6; Example 11)

53. $x^2(x - 3) - 9(x - 3)$ (Section P.6; Example 11)

54. $2xy - 2x^{10}y$ (Section P.6; Example 11)

55. $x^4 - x^3 - x + 1$ (Section P.6; Example 11)

56. $16x^{-3/4} + 32x^{1/4}$ (Section P.6; Example 12)

57. $(x^2 - 4)(x^2 + 3)^{-1/2} - (x^2 - 4)^2(x^2 + 3)^{-3/2}$ (Section P.6; Example 13)

58. Simplify: $\dfrac{6x^2 + 7x + 2}{2x^2 - 9x - 5}$ (Section P.7; Example 1)

In Problems 59–66, perform the indicated operations, and simplify if possible.

59. $\dfrac{y^4 - 81}{y^2 + 9} \cdot \dfrac{4y - 20}{y^2 - 8y + 15}$ (Section P.7; Example 2)

60. $\dfrac{x^2 + 9x + 20}{x^2 - 16} \div \dfrac{x^2 + 5x}{4x - 16}$ (Section P.7; Example 2)

61. $\dfrac{3x}{x + 2} + \dfrac{x}{x - 2}$ (Section P.7; Example 3)

62. $\dfrac{x}{x^2 - 9} + \dfrac{x - 1}{x^2 - 5x + 6}$ (Section P.7; Example 4)

63. $\dfrac{4}{a^2 + a - 2} - \dfrac{2}{a^2 - 4} + \dfrac{3}{a^2 - 4a + 4}$ (Section P.7; Example 5)

64. $\dfrac{\dfrac{1}{y + 5} + 1}{\dfrac{6}{y^2 + 2y - 15} - \dfrac{1}{y - 3}}$ (Section P.7; Example 6)

65. $\dfrac{\sqrt{25 - x^2} + \dfrac{x^2}{\sqrt{25 - x^2}}}{25 - x^2}$ (Section P.7; Example 7)

66. Simplify: i^{23}. (Section P.8; Example 1)

In Problems 67–70, perform the indicated operations and write the result in standard form.

67. $3 - (-5 + 11i) + (-17 + 4i)$ (Section P.8; Example 2)

68. $(7 - 5i)(2 + 3i)$ (Section P.8; Example 3)

69. $\dfrac{3 - 4i}{4 + 2i}$ (Section P.8; Example 5)

70. $\dfrac{5 + i}{3i}$ (Section P.8; Example 6)

In Problems 71–73, perform the indicated operations and write the result in standard form. (Section P.8; Example 7)

71. $\sqrt{-32} - \sqrt{-18}$

72. $(-2 + \sqrt{-11})^2$

73. $\dfrac{-18 - \sqrt{-43}}{30}$

74. Plot $-2 - 3i$ in the complex plane. (Section P.8; Example 8)

CHAPTER P TEST

1. Express $(-\infty, 3]$ in terms of an inequality and graph the interval on a number line.

2. Express $(2, 5) \cap [3, 6]$ in interval notation.

3. Find the distance between $(2, 9)$ and $(6, 3)$ in simplified radical form.

4. Graph $y = x^2 - 3$.

5. What property is illustrated by $3 + (7 + 4) = 3 + (4 + 7)$?

Simplify each expression in Problems 6–14.

6. $\left(\dfrac{x^2 y^{-2}}{3}\right)^{-3}$

7. $\dfrac{1}{\sqrt{2} + 1}$

8. $\dfrac{8}{\sqrt[3]{16}}$

9. $4\sqrt{50} - 3\sqrt{18}$

10. $\sqrt{3} + \sqrt{\dfrac{1}{3}}$

11. $\sqrt[6]{16x^4 y^2}$

12. $(x + 5y)^2 - (x + 2y)(x - 7y)$

13. $[7y - (4x + 1)][7y + (4x + 1)]$

14. $\dfrac{4x - x^2}{3x^2 - 7x - 20}$

In Problems 15–18, factor completely.

15. $x^4 - 16$

16. $2x^3 + 128y^3$

17. $x^3 - 4x^2 - x + 4$

18. $(x^2 - 9)(x^2 + 1)^{-1/2} - (x^2 - 9)(x^2 + 1)^{-3/2}$

In Problems 19–22, perform the operations, and simplify if possible.

19. $(y^3 - 8) \div \dfrac{3y^2 + 6y + 12}{3y - 7}$

20. $\dfrac{x + 3}{x^2 - 1} + \dfrac{2}{x} - \dfrac{3}{x - 1}$

21. $\dfrac{1 - \dfrac{x}{x + 2}}{1 + \dfrac{1}{x}}$

22. $\dfrac{2x\sqrt{x^2 + 5} - \dfrac{2x^3}{\sqrt{x^2 + 5}}}{x^2 + 5}$

In Problems 23–25, perform the operations and write the result in standard form.

23. $(6 - 7i)(2 + 5i)$

24. $\dfrac{5}{2 - i}$

25. $14i - (3 + 2\sqrt{-49})$

Equations, Inequalities, and Mathematical Models

Salvador Dalì "The Persistence of Memory" 1931, oil on canvas, 9 1/2 × 13 in. (24.1 × 33 cm). The Museum of Modern Art, New York. Given anonymously. Photograph © 1998 The Museum of Modern Art, New York. © 1998 Demart Pro Arte ®, Geneva / Artists Rights Society (ARS), New York.

"If you could stop every atom in its position and direction, and if your mind could comprehend all the actions thus suspended, then if you were really, *really* good at algebra you could write the formula for all the future; and although nobody can be so clever as to do it, the formula must exist just as if one could."

Tom Stoppard, *Arcadia*

Albert Einstein's (1879–1955) special theory of relativity destroyed fixed notions of time and space. Mass, length, and time are not fixed entities in Einstein's model of reality, but rather are relative to each of us.

The complexities of special relativity can be simplified using algebraic equations. Equations that describe the physical world are called mathematical models and are indispensable as we grasp at the possibilities of nature. Solving algebraic equations is essential in understanding the vastly complicated world just beyond our reach.

SECTION 1.1

Solutions Manual   **Tutorial**   **Video 3**

Linear Equations

Objectives

1 Solve linear equations in one variable.
2 Solve equations involving rational expressions.
3 Solve linear equations involving absolute value.
4 Solve problems modeled by linear equations.
5 Solve linear models for a specified variable.

In this section, we establish the basic techniques for solving equations containing variables raised only to the first power, called *linear equations*. We also consider the solution of linear equations involving both absolute value and rational expressions. These techniques are applied as we answer questions about real world phenomena described in formulas known as mathematical models.

Mel Bochner "Vertigo" 1982, charcoal, conte crayon and pastel on sized canvas, fixed with magna varnish, 108 × 74 in. Albright–Knox Art Gallery, Buffalo, New York, Charles Clifton Fund, 1982.

Equations and Solution Sets

An *equation* is a statement indicating that two algebraic expressions are equal. Examples of equations in x include

$$2x - 3 = 5 \quad x^2 - 3x = 2 \quad 2x + 3x = 5x.$$

The third equation in the list is true no matter what value the variable x represents. An equation that is true for all real numbers for which both sides are defined is called an *identity*.

The first two equations in our list are true for only some of the real numbers. Equations that are true for some (or possibly none) of the real numbers are called *conditional equations*.

Solving an equation in x means determining all values of x which when substituted into the equation result in a true statement. Such values are *solutions* or *roots* of the equation. These values are said to *satisfy* the equation. The set of all such solutions is called the equation's *solution set*.

Conditional equations are neither true nor false until we choose a value for x. For example, the equation $2x - 3 = 5$ becomes a true statement if we substitute 4 for x, resulting in $2(4) - 3 = 5$ (or $8 - 3 = 5$), a true statement. Since 4 is the only number that results in a true statement for this equation, the equation's solution set is {4}.

S tudy tip

The only number that satisfies

$$2x - 3 = 5$$

is 4 because 4 is the only number that when doubled and then decreased by 3 leaves 5.

1 Solve linear equations in one variable.

Solving Linear Equations in One Variable

The most common type of conditional equation, and perhaps the simplest, is a *linear* equation or *first-degree* equation in one variable.

Definition of linear equation

A *linear* or *first-degree* equation in one variable x is an equation that can be written in the standard form

$$ax + b = c$$

where a and b are real numbers and $a \neq 0$.

An example of a linear equation in one variable is $4x + 12 = 0$.

The equations $4x + 12 = 0$ and $4x = -12$ and $x = -3$ are *equivalent equations* because they all have the same solution set, namely $\{-3\}$. To solve a linear equation in x, we use a series of transformations into equivalent equations. Our final equivalent equation should be in the form

$$x = d$$

where d is a real number. By inspection, we can see that the solution set for this equation is $\{d\}$.

In generating equivalent equations, we will be using the following principles.

Generating equivalent equations

An equation can be transformed into an *equivalent equation* by one or more of the following operations.

		Given Equation	Equivalent Equation
1.	Simplify an expression by removing grouping symbols and combining like terms.	$3(x - 6) = 6x - x$	$3x - 18 = 5x$
2.	Add (or subtract) the same real number or variable expression on *both* sides of the equation.	$3x - 18 = 5x$	$3x - 18 - 3x = 5x - 3x$ $-18 = 2x$
3.	Multiply (or divide) on *both* sides of the equation by the same *nonzero* quantity.	$-18 = 2x$	$\dfrac{-18}{2} = \dfrac{2x}{2}$ $-9 = x$
4.	Interchange the two sides of the equation.	$-9 = x$	$x = -9$

As you study the transformations shown on the right, notice that we've actually solved the equation

$3(x - 6) = 6x - x.$

After isolating the variable term on the right, obtaining

$-18 = 2x$

we solved for the variable by dividing both sides by 2.

The following example illustrates the use of these transformation principles to solve linear equations.

EXAMPLE 1   Solving a Linear Equation

Solve for x: $4(2x + 1) - 29 = 3(2x - 5)$

Study tip

The solution on the right illustrates the general steps in solving a linear equation.

1. Simplify each side.
2. Isolate variable terms on one side and constant terms on the other side.
3. Isolate the variable and solve.
4. Check.

Solution

$4(2x + 1) - 29 = 3(2x - 5)$	This is the given equation.
$8x + 4 - 29 = 6x - 15$	Apply the distributive property, thereby removing parentheses.
$8x - 25 = 6x - 15$	Simplify by combining numerical terms.
$8x - 25 - 6x = 6x - 15 - 6x$	Collect variable terms on the left by subtracting $6x$ from both sides. This step is usually done mentally.

iscover for yourself

Solve the equation in Example 1 by collecting terms with the variable on the right and numerical terms on the left. What do you observe?

$$2x - 25 = -15$$

Simplify.

$$2x - 25 + 25 = -15 + 25$$

Collect numerical terms on the right by adding 25 to both sides. Once again, this step is usually done mentally.

$$2x = 10$$

Simplify.

$$\frac{2x}{2} = \frac{10}{2}$$

Solve for x by dividing both sides by 2, usually done mentally.

$$x = 5$$

Simplify.

Check

The proposed solution, 5, should be checked in the original equation:

$$4(2x + 1) - 29 = 3(2x - 5)$$

This is the original equation.

$$4(2 \cdot 5 + 1) - 29 \stackrel{?}{=} 3(2 \cdot 5 - 5)$$

Substitute 5 for x. When checking, be sure to work each side separately.

$$4(11) - 29 \stackrel{?}{=} 3(5)$$

Perform operations in grouping symbols.

$$44 - 29 \stackrel{?}{=} 15$$

Multiply.

$$15 = 15 \checkmark$$

This true statement indicates that 5 is the solution.

The check verifies that the solution set of the given linear equation is {5}. ∎

Using technology

A graphing utility can transform the algebraic solution into a visual solution that can be used to check the solution obtained algebraically.

To find the solution of $4(2x + 1) - 29 = 3(2x - 5)$ on a graphing utility, we use the fact that two expressions with the same value have a difference equal to zero. Use the $\boxed{y(x) =}$ key to enter the following equations:

$y_1 \boxed{=} 4(2x + 1) - 29$ This is the left side of the given equation.

$y_2 \boxed{=} 3(2x - 5)$ This is the right side of the given equation.

$y_3 \boxed{=} y_1 - y_2$ Also enter the difference of the two sides. Your graphing utility manual should explain how to do this.

Now turn off the highlighting on the equals sign for y_1 and y_2. On some utilities, you accomplish this by moving the cursor to y_1 and pressing $\boxed{\text{SELCT}}$, and then do the same for y_2. On others, you'll need to put the cursor on the equal sign and press $\boxed{\text{ENTER}}$. As always, consult your manual.

You will plot the graph of $y_1 - y_2$ and determine where it crosses the x-axis. The solution of $4(2x + 1) - 29 = 3(2x - 5)$ is the x-intercept of the graph of

$$y_3 = \boxed{4(2x + 1) - 29} - \boxed{3(2x - 5)}$$

This is y_1.   This is y_2.

The solution to

$$4(2x + 1) - 29 = 3(2x - 5)$$

is 5, an integer, so it's easy to see this solution using a standard zoom setting on a graphing utility. If the solution is not an integer, $\boxed{\text{TRACE}}$ and $\boxed{\text{ZOOM}}$ features can be used to verify an equation's solution.

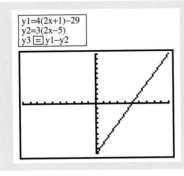

The utility draws only the expression with the highlighting on the equal sign. Use a standard zoom setting to obtain the graph.

The graph of $y_1 - y_2$ crosses the x-axis at 5. The solution set is {5}.

Equations Involving Rational Expressions

2 Solve equations involving rational expressions.

If an equation involves rational expressions, we can clear the equation of all fractions by multiplying both sides by the LCD of the fractions. We then solve for the variable. Examples 2 through 4 illustrate this procedure. Although the original equations are not linear, they become linear equations upon simplification.

EXAMPLE 2 **Solving an Equation with Rational Expressions**

Solve: $\dfrac{2}{3x} + \dfrac{1}{4} = \dfrac{11}{6x} - \dfrac{1}{3}$

Solution

The LCD for the rational expressions is $12x$. Since we must multiply by a nonzero number to obtain an equivalent equation, we multiply both sides by $12x$ with the restriction that $x \neq 0$.

$$\frac{2}{3x} + \frac{1}{4} = \frac{11}{6x} - \frac{1}{3}$$

This is the given equation; each side is undefined if $x = 0$.

$$12x\left(\frac{2}{3x} + \frac{1}{4}\right) = 12x\left(\frac{11}{6x} - \frac{1}{3}\right)$$

Multiply both sides by the LCD. $x \neq 0$

$$12x \cdot \frac{2}{3x} + 12x \cdot \frac{1}{4} = 12x \cdot \frac{11}{6x} - 12x \cdot \frac{1}{3}$$

Apply the distributive property.

$$\overset{4}{\cancel{12x}} \cdot \frac{2}{\underset{1}{\cancel{3x}}} + \overset{3}{\cancel{12x}} \cdot \frac{1}{\underset{1}{4}} = \overset{2}{\cancel{12x}} \cdot \frac{11}{\underset{1}{\cancel{6x}}} - \overset{4}{\cancel{12x}} \cdot \frac{1}{\underset{1}{\cancel{3}}}$$

Simplify. This and the previous step are usually done mentally.

$$8 + 3x = 22 - 4x$$

Multiply. Now solve the resulting equation.

We will collect variable terms on the left and constant terms on the right.

$$8 + 3x + 4x = 22 - 4x + 4x \quad \text{Add } 4x \text{ to both sides.}$$

$$8 + 7x = 22 \quad \text{Simplify.}$$

$$8 + 7x - 8 = 22 - 8 \quad \text{Subtract 8 from both sides.}$$

$$7x = 14 \quad \text{Simplify.}$$

$$\frac{7x}{7} = \frac{14}{7}$$ Divide both sides by 7.

$$x = 2$$ Simplify.

Check

We check our solution by substituting 2 into the original equation or by using a graphing utility. Note that the initial restriction that $x \neq 0$ is met. The solution set is {2}. ∎

Our next example illustrates that multiplying both sides of an equation by an algebraic expression does not necessarily lead to an equivalent equation.

EXAMPLE 3   **An Equation Having No Solution**

Solve: $\dfrac{1}{x - 2} + \dfrac{4}{x + 2} = \dfrac{4}{x^2 - 4}$

Solution

$$\frac{1}{x - 2} + \frac{4}{x + 2} = \frac{4}{x^2 - 4}$$ This is the given equation.

$$\frac{1}{x - 2} + \frac{4}{x + 2} = \frac{4}{(x + 2)(x - 2)}$$ Factor $x^2 - 4$ using $A^2 - B^2 = (A + B)(A - B)$.

$$(x + 2)(x - 2)\left[\frac{1}{x - 2} + \frac{4}{x + 2}\right] = (x + 2)(x - 2)\left[\frac{4}{(x + 2)(x - 2)}\right]$$

Multiply both sides by $(x + 2)(x - 2)$, the LCD. Since we cannot multiply by 0, $x + 2 \neq 0$ and $x - 2 \neq 0$. Equivalently, $x \neq -2$ and $x \neq 2$.

$$(x + 2)(x - 2) \cdot \frac{1}{x - 2} + (x + 2)(x - 2) \cdot \frac{4}{x + 2}$$

$$= (x + 2)(x - 2) \cdot \frac{4}{(x + 2)(x - 2)}$$ Use the distributive property.

$$x + 2 + 4(x - 2) = 4$$ Simplify.

$$x + 2 + 4x - 8 = 4$$ Apply the distributive property.

$$5x - 6 = 4$$ Combine like terms.

$$5x = 10$$ Add 6 to both sides.

$$x = 2$$ Divide both sides by 5.

Check

The proposed solution, 2, is *not* a solution because of the restriction that $x \neq 2$. Let's see what happens when we substitute 2 for x in the original equation.

$$\frac{1}{x - 2} + \frac{1}{x + 2} = \frac{4}{x^2 - 4}$$ This is the original equation.

$$\frac{1}{2-2} + \frac{1}{2+2} \overset{?}{=} \frac{4}{2^2 - 4}$$ Substitute 2 for x.

$$\frac{1}{0} + \frac{1}{4} \overset{?}{=} \frac{4}{0}$$

The expressions $\frac{1}{0}$ and $\frac{4}{0}$ are undefined, so the proposed solution does not check in the original equation. There is *no solution* to this equation. The solution set contains no elements and is called the *null set* (written $\emptyset$), or the *empty set*. ∎

Just as some equations have no solutions, others have infinitely many real numbers in their solution sets. The next example involves such an equation.

EXAMPLE 4   **An Equation Having Infinitely Many Solutions**

Solve: $\dfrac{1}{x-4} - \dfrac{1}{x+4} = \dfrac{8}{x^2 - 16}$

Solution

$$\frac{1}{x-4} - \frac{1}{x+4} = \frac{8}{x^2 - 16}$$ This is the given equation.

$$\frac{1}{x-4} - \frac{1}{x+4} = \frac{8}{(x+4)(x-4)}$$ Factor $x^2 - 16$.

$$(x+4)(x-4)\left[\frac{1}{x-4} - \frac{1}{x+4}\right] = (x+4)(x-4)\left[\frac{8}{(x+4)(x-4)}\right]$$

Multiply by $(x+4)(x-4)$, the LCD. ($x \neq 4$ and $x \neq -4$)

$$x + 4 - (x - 4) = 8$$ Apply the distributive property and simplify.

$$8 = 8$$

We have a trivial statement of equality in the final step, namely, $8 = 8$. The left and right sides of the original equation are equal for all permissible values of the variable. Because of the restriction that $x \neq -4$ and $x \neq 4$ (both -4 and 4 cause division by zero in the original equation), the solution set is $\{x \mid x \neq -4 \text{ and } x \neq 4\}$. Using interval notation, we can express this as

$$(-\infty, -4) \cup (-4, 4) \cup (4, \infty)$$ Recall that the symbol $\cup$ (union) denotes *or*. ∎

3 Solve linear equations involving absolute value.

Linear Equations Involving Absolute Value

We solve linear equations containing absolute value using the fact that the expression inside the absolute value bars can be either positive or negative. For example, the equation

$$|2x - 3| = 11$$

is satisfied if $2x - 3$ is either 11 or -11, resulting in the two equations

$$2x - 3 = 11 \quad \text{and} \quad 2x - 3 = -11.$$

Rewriting an absolute value equation without absolute value bars

If c is positive,

$$|ax + b| = c \quad \text{is equivalent to} \quad ax + b = c \quad \text{or} \quad ax + b = -c$$

EXAMPLE 5 **Solving an Equation Involving Absolute Value**

Solve: $|2x - 3| = 11$

Using technology

(Consult your manual for the location of the $\boxed{\text{ABS}}$, absolute value, key.) For Example 5, enter y_1, y_2, y_3, highlighting only y_3.

$y_1 = \boxed{\text{ABS}}\,(2x - 3)$

$y_2 = 11$

$y_3 \boxed{=} y_1 - y_2$

The graph of y_3 crosses the x-axis at -4 and 7, verifying that $\{-4, 7\}$ is the solution set.

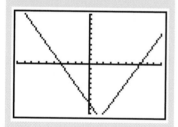

Solution

$\|2x - 3\| = 11$	This is the given equation.
$2x - 3 = 11 \quad \text{or} \quad 2x - 3 = -11$	Rewrite the equation without absolute value bars.
$2x = 14 \qquad\qquad 2x = -8$	Add 3 to both sides of each equation.
$x = 7 \qquad\qquad x = -4$	Divide both sides of each equation by 2.

Check

$\|2x - 3\| = 11$	This is the original equation.
$\|2(7) - 3\| \overset{?}{=} 11 \qquad \|2(-4) - 3\| \overset{?}{=} 11$	Substitute the proposed solutions.
$\|11\| \overset{?}{=} 11 \qquad\qquad \|-11\| \overset{?}{=} 11$	Perform operations inside the absolute value bars.
$11 = 11 \;\checkmark \qquad\qquad 11 = 11 \;\checkmark$	These true statements indicate that 7 and -4 are solutions.

The solution set is $\{-4, 7\}$. ■

Our next equation involves two absolute value expressions. In this case, $|e| = |f|$ *if and only if* the expressions in absolute value are equal to each other ($e = f$) or the expressions in absolute value are negatives of one another ($e = -f$). In terms of linear equations, we can state this observation as follows.

Rewriting an absolute value equation containing two absolute values

The equation $|ax + b| = |cx + d|$ is equivalent to

$$ax + b = cx + d \quad \text{or} \quad ax + b = -(cx + d).$$

EXAMPLE 6 **An Absolute Value Equation with Two Absolute Values**

Solve: $|3x - 1| = |x + 5|$

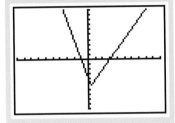

Solution

$\lvert 3x - 1 \rvert = \lvert x + 5 \rvert$		This is the given equation.

$$3x - 1 = x + 5 \quad \text{or} \quad 3x - 1 = -(x + 5)$$

Rewrite without absolute value bars.

$$3x - 1 = x + 5 \qquad\qquad 3x - 1 = -x - 5$$

Use the distributive property in the second equation, thereby removing parentheses.

$$2x - 1 = 5 \qquad\qquad 4x - 1 = -5$$

Subtract x from both sides of the first equation and add x to both sides of the second equation.

$$2x = 6 \qquad\qquad 4x = -4$$

Add 1 to both sides of each equation.

$$x = 3 \qquad\qquad x = -1$$

Divide both sides by 2 and 4, respectively.

Check

$$\lvert 3x - 1 \rvert = \lvert x + 5 \rvert$$

This is the original equation.

$$\lvert 3(3) - 1 \rvert \overset{?}{=} \lvert 3 + 5 \rvert \qquad \lvert 3(-1) - 1 \rvert \overset{?}{=} \lvert -1 + 5 \rvert$$

Substitute the proposed solutions.

$$\lvert 8 \rvert \overset{?}{=} \lvert 8 \rvert \qquad\qquad \lvert -4 \rvert \overset{?}{=} \lvert 4 \rvert$$

Perform operations inside the absolute value bars.

$$8 = 8 \checkmark \qquad\qquad 4 = 4 \checkmark$$

These true statements indicate that 3 and -1 are solutions.

The solution set is $\{-1, 3\}$. ∎

Discover for yourself

Must every absolute value equation have two solutions? Use the technique in Example 6 to solve $\lvert x \rvert = \lvert x - 1 \rvert$. Describe what happens.

4 Solve problems modeled by linear equations.

Mathematical Models

Formulas that describe real world phenomena are called *mathematical models*. Linear models can be written in the form $y = ax + b$. The ability to solve linear equations enables us to solve problems modeled by these equations.

EXAMPLE 7 **Modeling Atmospheric Carbon Dioxide**

According to a 1995 report from the International Panel on Climate Change (a U.N.-sponsored body made up of more than 1500 leading experts from 60 nations) the climatic impact of increased levels of atmospheric carbon dioxide indicates that global warming is already under way. The effects could be catastrophic. The atmospheric concentration of carbon dioxide (CO_2) has been accurately measured over the past 30 years, and the concentration has been rising undeniably. The major source of additional CO_2 is the burning of fossil fuels related to energy consumption.

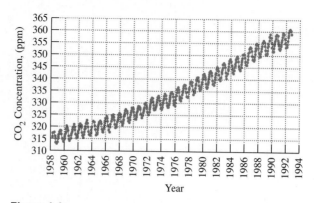

Figure I.I

Atmospheric carbon dioxide has been rising.

Figure 1.1 shows atmospheric CO_2 concentration in parts per million from 1958 through 1994. Although the CO_2 concentration fluctuates between winter and summer, mathematicians have modeled these data points using

$$C = 1.44t + 280$$

where C represents CO_2 concentration in parts per million (ppm) t years after 1939. The preindustrial CO_2 concentration of 280 ppm remained fairly constant until World War II. In what year was the concentration 25% more than the preindustrial level?

Solution

25% more than the preindustrial level of 280 ppm is

$$280 + 25\% \text{ of } 280 = 280 + (0.25)(280) = 350.$$

We can find when concentration was 350 ppm by using the given model, substituting 350 for C and solving for t:

$C = 1.44t + 280$	The given model relates CO_2 concentration to time (t years after 1939).
$350 = 1.44t + 280$	Substitute 350 for C.
$70 = 1.44t$	Subtract 280 from both sides.
$\dfrac{70}{1.44} = t$	Divide both sides by 1.44.
$49 \approx t$	t is approximately equal to ($\approx$) 49.

Since t represents the number of years after 1939, we have

$$1939 + 49 = 1988.$$

Thus, according to the model, CO_2 concentration was 350 ppm in 1988. Figure 1.2 on page 117 indicates that this is not a bad approximation of the actual data, although 350 ppm appears to be a low level in the 1988 seasonal fluctuation.

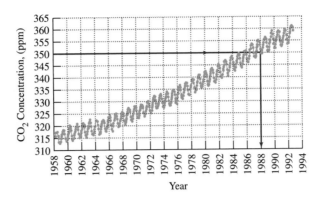

Figure 1.2

CO_2 Concentration: 350 ppm in 1988 ■

5 Solve linear models for a specified variable.

An important skill in mathematics involves solving a formula or a mathematical model for a specified variable. Let's see exactly how this is done.

EXAMPLE 8 **Solving a Mathematical Model for a Specified Variable**

Consider the straight-line depreciation model

$$V = C - \frac{C - S}{L} N$$

where

L = the useful life of an asset (in years)

C = the cost of the asset when it was new

S = the salvage value of the asset at the end of its useful life

V = the value of the asset at the end of year N

a. Solve the formula for C.
b. Use the result of part (a) to answer this question: An automobile has a useful life of six years and has a salvage value of $3000. Its value at the end of the third year of use is $15,000. What was the cost of the automobile when new?

The 1901 Mercedes

Solution

a.
$$V = C - \frac{C - S}{L} N$$ 　This is the given model. We must solve for C.

$$LV = L\left(C - \frac{C - S}{L} N\right)$$ 　Multiply both sides by L, the LCD. $L \neq 0$

$$LV = LC - L \cdot \frac{C - S}{L} N$$ 　Apply the distributive property on the right.

$$LV = LC - (C - S)N$$ 　Simplify.

$$LV = LC - (CN - SN)$$ 　Use the distributive property.

ENRICHMENT ESSAY

The Monsters of Malignancy

In Chapter 2, we will see how mathematicians use data points that appear to lie along a line to write an equation for the line of best fit. Using data from numerous countries that depict daily fat intake (F, in grams) and deaths per 100,000 women (D) from breast cancer, researchers derived the model

$$D = 0.2F - 1.$$

The death rate of U.S. women from breast cancer is 19 per 100,000. Use the model to estimate the daily fat intake in the United States.

Although the linear model provides useful information, it does not convey the way cancer intrudes into the ordinary course of our lives. One woman in ten will be afflicted with breast cancer; 40,000 women in the United States will die of the disease this year.

Nancy Fried "Mourning" 1986, terra cotta, 8 × 5 × 3 1/2 in. Photo courtesy DC Moore Gallery.

$$LV = LC - CN + SN \qquad \text{Distribute } -1 \text{ throughout the parentheses.}$$

$$LV - SN = LC - CN \qquad \text{To solve for } C, \text{ isolate terms with } C \text{ on one side (the right) by subtracting } SN \text{ from both sides.}$$

$$LV - SN = C(L - N) \qquad \text{Since we cannot combine terms on the right, factor out } C \text{ so that it is isolated.}$$

$$\frac{LV - SN}{L - N} = C \qquad \text{Solve for } C \text{ by dividing both sides by } L - N. \ L \neq N$$

When solving a formula or model for a specified variable in terms of other variables appearing in the model, we do not write the solution in set notation. Thus, $C = \dfrac{LV - SN}{L - N}$.

b. $C = \dfrac{LV - SN}{L - N}$ This is the result from part (a).

$$= \frac{6(15,000) - 3000(3)}{6 - 3} \qquad \text{The useful life is six years } (L = 6). \text{ The salvage value is } \$3000 \ (S = 3000). \text{ The value at the end of the third year is } \$15,000 \ (V = 15,000 \text{ when } N = 3). \text{ Substitute these values into the equation.}$$

$$= 27,000 \qquad \text{Use a calculator.}$$

The cost of the automobile when new was \$27,000. ∎

PROBLEM SET 1.1

Practice Problems

Use solution set notation to express all answers in this problem set. Check results algebraically or with a graphing utility. Solve each linear equation in Problems 1–16.

1. $5x - 8 = 72$

2. $6x - 3 = 63$

3. $11x - (6x - 5) = 40$

4. $5x - (2x - 10) = 35$

5. $2x - 7 = 6 + x$

6. $3x + 5 = 2x + 13$

7. $7x + 4 = x + 16$

8. $13x + 14 = 12x - 5$

9. $3(x - 2) + 7 = 2(x + 5)$

10. $2(x - 1) + 3 = x - 3(x + 1)$

11. $3(x - 4) - 4(x - 3) = x + 3 - (x - 2)$

12. $2 - (7x + 5) = 13 - 3x$

13. $16 = 3(x - 1) - (x - 7)$

14. $5x - (2x + 2) = x + (3x - 5)$

15. $25 - [2 + 5y - 3(y + 2)] = -3(2y - 5) - [5(y - 1) - 3y + 3]$

16. $45 - [4 - 2y - 4(y + 7)] = -4(1 + 3y) - [4 - 3(y + 2) - 2(2y - 5)]$

Solve each fractional equation in Problems 17–40 by multiplying both sides by the LCD, thereby clearing fractions.

17. $\dfrac{3x}{5} = \dfrac{2x}{3} + 1$

18. $\dfrac{x}{2} = \dfrac{3x}{4} + 5$

19. $\dfrac{x}{4} = 2 + \dfrac{x - 3}{3}$

20. $5 + \dfrac{x - 2}{3} = \dfrac{x + 3}{8}$

21. $\dfrac{x + 1}{3} = 5 - \dfrac{x + 2}{7}$

22. $\dfrac{3x}{5} - \dfrac{x - 3}{2} = \dfrac{x + 2}{3}$

23. $\dfrac{4}{y} - 3 = \dfrac{5}{2y}$

24. $\dfrac{5}{y} - 4 = \dfrac{10}{3y}$

25. $\dfrac{2}{x} - \dfrac{3}{5} = -\dfrac{1}{2}$

26. $\dfrac{3}{x} - \dfrac{1}{4} = \dfrac{1}{3}$

27. $\dfrac{x - 2}{2x} + 1 = \dfrac{x + 1}{x}$

28. $\dfrac{4}{x} = \dfrac{9}{5} - \dfrac{7x - 4}{5x}$

29. $\dfrac{x}{x + 1} + \dfrac{2}{x} = 1$

30. $\dfrac{x}{x + 5} + \dfrac{3}{x} = 1$

31. $\dfrac{3}{x - 2} + \dfrac{2}{x + 3} = \dfrac{5}{x^2 + x - 6}$

32. $\dfrac{1}{x + 2} + \dfrac{5}{x - 4} = \dfrac{6}{x^2 - 2x - 8}$

33. $\dfrac{6}{y} - \dfrac{3}{y^2 - y} = \dfrac{7}{y - 1}$

34. $\dfrac{4}{x + 5} + \dfrac{2}{x - 5} = \dfrac{32}{x^2 - 25}$

35. $\dfrac{x - 3}{x - 2} + \dfrac{x + 1}{x + 3} = \dfrac{2x^2 - 15}{x^2 + x - 6}$

36. $\dfrac{2y - 14}{y^2 + 3y - 28} + \dfrac{y - 2}{y - 4} = \dfrac{y + 3}{y + 7}$

37. $\dfrac{7}{y + 5} + 2 = \dfrac{2 - y}{y + 5}$

38. $\dfrac{3y}{y - 3} = 1 + \dfrac{9}{y - 3}$

39. $\dfrac{1}{x + 5} - \dfrac{2}{x - 3} = \dfrac{2x + 2}{x^2 + 2x - 15}$

40. $\dfrac{1}{x - 4} - \dfrac{5}{x + 2} = \dfrac{6}{x^2 - 2x - 8}$

Solve each equation in Problems 41–52 by first rewriting each equation as two equations without absolute value bars.

41. $|2x - 5| = 13$

42. $|2x - 1| = 15$

43. $|2y + 3| + 3 = 20$

44. $|4y - 5| - 8 = 3$

45. $\left|-\dfrac{5}{2}y + 4\right| + 3 = 15$

46. $\left|-\dfrac{3}{4}y + 1\right| + 4 = 7$

47. $|2x - 3| = |x + 6|$

48. $|4 - 2x| = |8 - x|$

49. $|5x + 2| = |4x + 7|$

50. $|2x - 5| = |-6x - 5|$

51. $|18x - 16| = |26 - 10x|$

52. $|9x - 12| = |10 - 13x|$

In Problems 53–60, solve each formula for the specified variable.

53. $S = P + Prt$ for P

54. $mv = Ft + mv_o$ for m

55. $I = \dfrac{nE}{R + nr}$ for n

56. $R = \dfrac{R_1 R_2}{R_1 + R_2}$ for R_1

57. $\dfrac{1}{cy} = \dfrac{1}{dy} - \dfrac{1}{e}$ for y

58. $\dfrac{1}{c} - \dfrac{1}{y} = \dfrac{1}{y} - \dfrac{1}{d}$ for y

59. $\dfrac{1}{s} = f + \dfrac{1 - f}{p}$ for f

60. $\dfrac{b}{ay - 1} - \dfrac{a}{by - 1} = 0$ for $y (a \neq b)$

Application Problems

61. The model $C = 1.44t + 280$ describes carbon dioxide concentration in parts per million (ppm) t years after 1939. When will the concentration be 50% greater than that of the preindustrial concentration of 280 ppm?

62. The model $P = -0.5d + 100$ describes the percentage (P) of lost hikers found in search and rescue missions when members of the search team walk parallel to one another separated by a distance of d yards. If a search and rescue team finds 70% of lost hikers, what is the parallel distance of separation between members of the search party?

63. A woman's height (h) is related to the length of the femur (f) (the bone from the knee to the hip socket) by the mathematical model $f = 0.432h - 10.44$. Both h and f are measured in inches. A partial skeleton is found of a woman in which the femur is 16 inches long. Police find the skeleton in an area where a woman slightly over 5 feet tall has been missing for over a year. Can the partial skeleton be that of the missing woman? Explain.

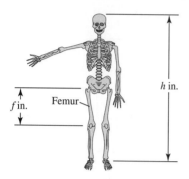

h in.

f in.   Femur

64. The mathematical model $T = 0.143L - 1.18$ relates the total length (L) and the tail length (T) of females of the snake species *Lampropeltis polyzona*, where both variables are measured in millimeters. What is the tail length of such a female snake with a total length of 457 mm?

65. The formula $d = 5000c - 525{,}000$ models the relationship between the annual number of deaths (d) in the United States from heart disease and the average adult cholesterol level (c, in milligrams per deciliter of blood). In 1990, 500,000 Americans died from heart disease. What was the average cholesterol level at that time? If the United States could reduce its average cholesterol level to 180, how many lives could be saved compared to 1990?

66. The mathematical model $y = -0.358709x + 256.835$ is used to project the world record for the mile run (y, in seconds), where x is the last two digits of any year. In what year was the world record for the mile run 224.91 seconds?

True–False Critical Thinking Problems

67. Which one of the following is true?

a. The equation $-7x = x$ has no solution.

b. The equations $\dfrac{x}{x-4} = \dfrac{4}{x-4}$ and $x = 4$ are equivalent.

c. The equations $3y - 1 = 11$ and $3y - 7 = 5$ are equivalent.

d. If a and b are any real numbers, then $ax + b = 0$ always has only one number in its solution set.

68. Which one of the following is true?

a. The equation $\dfrac{1}{x-1} - \dfrac{1}{x+1} = \dfrac{2}{x^2-1}$ is an example of an equation with infinitely many solutions.

b. Solving an equation with a graphing utility is always preferable to using algebraic methods.

c. Some linear equations can only be solved with a graphing utility.

d. If a and b are any negative real numbers, then $ax + b = 0$ has no solution if $|a| = |b|$.

Technology Problems

Estimate the solution of each equation in Problems 69–76 using a graphing utility. If solutions do not appear to be integers, use the TRACE *and* ZOOM *features to estimate solutions to the nearest tenth.*

69. $18 - 45x - 4 = 13x + 24 - 56x$

70. $8x - 3[2 - (x + 4)] = 4(x - 2)$

71. $0.2x + 4.5 = 1.2x$

72. $\dfrac{2x}{3} - \dfrac{3}{5} = -\dfrac{1}{3} - \dfrac{2x}{5}$

73. $|2x - 3| = 7$

74. $\dfrac{2}{3x + 6} = \dfrac{1}{6} - \dfrac{1}{2x + 4}$

75. $\dfrac{x + 6}{x + 3} - 2 = \dfrac{3}{x + 3}$

76. $|3x + 2| = |5x - 2|$

77. Consider the equation $\dfrac{x+3}{6} - \dfrac{2x-3}{9} = \dfrac{5}{6} - \dfrac{x}{18}$.

   a. Substitute each of the following numbers for x: -3, 0, 3, and 9. In each case, compute (by hand or with your calculator) both sides of the equation. What seems to be true about this linear equation?

   b. Solve the equation algebraically. Describe what happens and draw a conclusion.

   c. Use your graphing utility to solve the equation. Describe what appears on the viewing screen.

   d. Change the FORMAT on the viewing screen by deleting the axes Axes off . Press GRAPH . What do you see? Write a description relating what appears on the screen to the solution set of this equation.

78. The method that we discussed for solving linear equations on a graphing utility involves calling the left side of the equation y_1, the right side y_2, and then graphing $y_1 - y_2$. How might you solve the equation using only y_1 and y_2? Try this on Problem 69, graphing both y_1 and y_2. How is the equation's solution determined? (You should already have the solution using the previous method.) Try this method on a few of the exercises in Problems 69–76. Which method do you prefer? Why?

Writing in Mathematics

79. Under what conditions does a rational equation have no solution?

80. Refer to the model described in Problem 62.

   a. The model indicates that the chance of lost hikers being found increases as searchers in any area get closer to one another. If this is the case, why not simply have almost no distance separating members of the search team to obtain near certainty of finding the lost hikers?

   b. The model was determined from actual data collected by search and rescue teams in the American Southwest. How does this limit the usefulness of the model?

81. The optimum heart rate is the rate that a person should achieve during exercise for the exercise to be most beneficial. The formula $r = 0.6(220 - a)$ models optimum heart rate (r, in beats per minute), where a represents age. Write and solve a word problem using this model.

Critical Thinking Problems

In Problems 82–84, solve for x.

82. $\dfrac{x^2 + 2x - 15}{x^2 - 4x + 3} \div \dfrac{x^2 + x - 20}{3x^2 - 3} = -3$

83. $6 + |2 - 4x| = 3$

84. $\dfrac{x - C}{D} + \dfrac{x - D}{C} + \dfrac{x - 1}{CD} = \dfrac{2}{C} + \dfrac{2}{D} + 2$
   $(C + D \neq -1)$

85. The models $J = 30x + 100$ and $A = 4x + 20$ describe the number of robots used in industry by Japan (J) and the United Sates (A) x years after 1985. Both J and A are measured in thousands. In what year will the number of industrial robots in Japan exceed that of the United States by 652,000?

86. The model $G = 0.0193C - 5.4$ describes the average increase in global temperature (G, in degrees Fahrenheit) since 1939, in terms of carbon dioxide concentration (C, in ppm). The model $C = 1.44t + 280$ describes carbon dioxide concentration (C, in ppm) t years after 1939. In 1939, a beachside community was foolishly built right up to the ocean, protected only by a 2-foot seawall. If it is known that a global temperature increase of $1.8°$ Fahrenheit corresponds to a one-foot rise in ocean level, use the given models to determine by what year the beachside community will be flooded.

Global Annual Temperature

Source: NASA

87. Use substitution to check the answer obtained in Example 8 on page 117, substituting the expression for $C\left(C = \dfrac{LV - SN}{L - N}\right)$ into the original equation
   $V = C - \dfrac{C - S}{L} N$.

SECTION 1.2

Solutions
Manual

Tutorial

Video
3

Quadratic Equations

Objectives

1 Solve quadratic equations by factoring.
2 Solve quadratic equations by the square root method.
3 Solve quadratic equations by completing the square.
4 Solve quadratic equations using the quadratic formula.
5 Use the discriminant to determine kinds of solutions.
6 Solve problems modeled by quadratic equations.

In this section, we establish the basic techniques for solving equations containing variables raised to the second power, called *quadratic equations*. (The adjective *quadratic* is derived from the Latin word *quadrus* meaning "square.") We then apply these techniques to answering questions about variables contained in mathematical models that have evolved from real world data.

The Standard Form of a Quadratic Equation

An equation that contains a variable with an exponent of 2, but no higher power, is called a quadratic equation.

> **Definition of a quadratic equation**
>
> A *quadratic equation* in x is an equation that can be written in the standard form
>
> $$ax^2 + bx + c = 0$$
>
> where a, b, and c are real numbers with $a \neq 0$. A quadratic equation in x is also called a *second-degree polynomial equation* in x.

This Babylonian tablet shows a quadratic equation and its solution written sometime between 1900 and 1600 B.C. Yale University Library— Babylonian Collection.

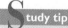 Solve quadratic equations by factoring.

Solving Quadratic Equations by Factoring

If the trinomial $ax^2 + bx + c$ can be factored, then $ax^2 + bx + c = 0$ can be solved by using the *zero product principle*.

In the definition of a quadratic equation, we must state $a \neq 0$. If we allowed a to equal 0 in

$$ax^2 + bx + c = 0$$

the resulting equation would be

$$bx + c = 0$$

which is linear, and not quadratic.

> **The zero product principle**
>
> Let A and B be real numbers, variables, or algebraic expressions. If $AB = 0$, then $A = 0$ or $B = 0$ or A and B are both 0. In words, this says that if a product is zero, then at least one of the factors is equal to zero.

EXAMPLE 1 **Solving Quadratic Equations by Factoring**

Solve by factoring, using the zero product principle:

a. $2x^2 + 7x = 4$ **b.** $4x^2 - 2x = 0$

c. $8x(2x - 1) = -1$ **d.** $\dfrac{4}{x + 1} - 1 = \dfrac{3}{x + 2}$

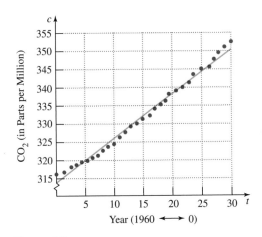

Figure 1.3

Fitting a linear model to data

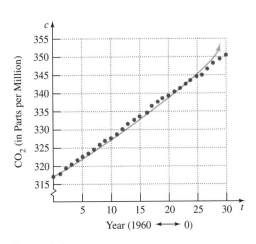

Figure 1.4

Fitting a quadratic model to data

Although linear models are easier to work with than quadratic models, in certain situations they are less accurate. For example, the points shown in Figure 1.3 represent data showing carbon dioxide concentration (C, in ppm) t years after 1960. The linear model $C = 1.24t + 313.6$ has been fitted to the data. Now look at Figure 1.4, in which the quadratic model

$$C = 0.018t^2 + 0.70t + 316.2$$

has been fitted to the data. The quadratic model appears to be a better fit in that its graph passes through more of the data points than does the linear model.

These models form the basis of Example 6.

EXAMPLE 6   Carbon Dioxide Concentration Revisited

Use the linear and quadratic models discussed above to predict in what year carbon dioxide (CO_2) concentration will be 470 ppm.

Solution

$$C = 1.24t + 313.6 \qquad \text{This is the given linear model.}$$

$$470 = 1.24t + 313.6 \qquad \text{Substitute 470 for } C.$$

$$\frac{470 - 313.6}{1.24} = t \qquad \text{Solve for } t.$$

$$t \approx 126 \qquad \text{Use a calculator.}$$

The linear model predicts a CO_2 concentration of 470 ppm 126 years after 1960, or in the year 2086. Now let's see what is predicted by the quadratic model.

$$C = 0.018t^2 + 0.70t + 316.2 \qquad \text{This is the given quadratic model.}$$

$$470 = 0.018t^2 + 0.70t + 316.2 \qquad \text{Substitute 470 for } C.$$

Jordan Massengale "Heaven–Day" 1996, pastel on paper, 16 × 24 in.

$$0 = 0.018t^2 + 0.70t - 153.8$$

Subtract 470 from both sides.

$$a = 0.018 \quad b = 0.70 \quad c = -153.8$$

$$t = \frac{-b \pm \sqrt{b^2 - 4ac}}{2a}$$

Use the quadratic formula.

$$= \frac{-0.70 \pm \sqrt{(0.70)^2 - 4(0.018)(-153.8)}}{2(0.018)}$$

Substitute the appropriate values.

$$= \frac{-0.70 \pm \sqrt{11.5636}}{0.036}$$

Perfom operations under the radical.

$$t \approx -114 \quad \text{or} \quad t \approx 75$$

Use a calculator.

Since the model begins with a value of $t = 0$ corresponding to the year 1960, we reject -114. The quadratic model predicts a CO_2 concentration of 470 ppm 75 years after 1960, or in the year 2035.

Because the quadratic model seems to fit the data better than the linear model, scientists predict that the CO_2 concentration in the Earth's atmosphere in the year 2035 will be 470 parts per million. ∎

PROBLEM SET 1.2

Practice Problems

Solve each equation in Problems 1–14 by factoring.

1. $x^2 - 3x - 10 = 0$

2. $x^2 - 13x + 36 = 0$

3. $x^2 = 8x - 15$

4. $x^2 = -11x - 10$

5. $6x^2 + 11x - 10 = 0$

6. $9x^2 + 9x + 2 = 0$

7. $3x^2 - 2x = 8$

8. $4x^2 - 13x = -3$

9. $3x^2 + 7x = 0$

10. $5x^2 - 9x = 0$

11. $2x(x - 3) = 5x^2 - 7x$

12. $16x(x - 2) = 8x - 25$

13. $7 - 7x = (3x + 2)(x - 1)$

14. $10x - 1 = (2x + 1)^2$

Solve each equation in Problems 15–28 by the square root method.

15. $3x^2 = 27$

16. $5x^2 = 45$

17. $5x^2 + 1 = 51$

18. $3x^2 - 1 = 47$

19. $(x + 2)^2 = 25$

20. $(x - 3)^2 = 36$

21. $(3x + 2)^2 = 9$

22. $(4x - 1)^2 = 16$

23. $(5x - 1)^2 = 7$

24. $(8x - 3)^2 = 5$

25. $(3x - 4)^2 = 8$

26. $(2x + 8)^2 = 27$

27. $(x + 3)^2 = -16$

28. $(x + 5)^2 = -9$

Solve each equation in Problems 29–36 by completing the square.

29. $x^2 - 4x - 11 = 0$

30. $x^2 - 2x - 5 = 0$

31. $2x^2 - 7x + 4 = 0$

32. $9x^2 - 6x - 4 = 0$

33. $4x^2 - 4x - 3 = 0$

34. $2x^2 - x - 6 = 0$

35. $2x^2 - 6x + 5 = 0$

36. $2x^2 + 2x + 5 = 0$

Solve each equation in Problems 37–48 using the quadratic formula.

37. $3x^2 - 3x - 4 = 0$

38. $5x^2 + x - 2 = 0$

39. $4y^2 = 2y + 7$

40. $3y^2 = 6y - 1$

41. $x^2 - 6x + 10 = 0$

42. $x^2 - 2x + 17 = 0$

43. $(w + 2)^2 = 2(5w - 2)$

44. $(w - 12)(w + 7) = (3 - w)(w + 4)$ **45.** $y^2 - 5 = 2(y + 3) - 4$

46. $3y^2 + 11 = 2y(2y - 1)$

47. $1.5x^2 - 7.3 = 10.2$ **48.** $3.2x^2 + 7.6x = 9.1$

Solve each equation in Problems 49–82 by the method of your choice.

49. $(x - 3)(x + 3) = 12$ **50.** $(2x - 3)(3x + 1) = 17$ **51.** $8y^2 - 3 = 0$

52. $12y^2 - 5 = 0$ **53.** $(5z - 1)(2z + 3) = 3z - 3$ **54.** $(2z - 1)(z - 1) = (z - 1)(z + 1)$

55. $2x^2 - 5x - 12 = -5x$ **56.** $5x^2 - 2x + 4 = 8 - 2x$ **57.** $(3x - 4)^2 = 81$

58. $(2x - 3)^2 = 121$ **59.** $2.4y^2 - 12.72y + 3.6 = 0$ **60.** $2.3y^2 - 13.15y + 8.07 = 0$

61. $3w^2 - 4w + 2 = 0$ **62.** $w^2 - 2w + 4 = 0$ **63.** $(y - 3)(y + 4) + 2 = y - 3$

64. $(y - 2)(y - 5) = (2y - 7)y$ **65.** $\dfrac{2}{y + 1} + \dfrac{3y}{2} = 4$ **66.** $\dfrac{3y}{y + 1} + \dfrac{2}{y - 2} = 5$

67. $\dfrac{2}{z + 4} - \dfrac{3}{z + 1} = 4$ **68.** $\dfrac{3}{z + 2} - \dfrac{5}{z - 2} = 2$ **69.** $10^{-4}x^2 + 2(10^{-3})x + 10^{-2} = 0$

70. $10^{-4}x^2 + 3(10^{-3})x + 10^{-2} = 0$ **71.** $\sqrt{2}x^2 + x - 10\sqrt{2} = 0$ **72.** $2\sqrt{5}x^2 - x = 2\sqrt{5}$

73. $(x + 3)^2 = (x - 5)^2$ **74.** $(x + 4)^2 = (x - 1)^2$ **75.** $(x + 1)^2 = 9x^2$

76. $(x - 2)^2 = 16x^2$ **77.** $(2x + 3)^2 - 9 = 0$ **78.** $(3x - 1)^2 - 121 = 0$

79. $(3x - 1)^2 = (x + 5)^2$ **80.** $(5x + 2)^2 = (x - 4)^2$ **81.** $\left| x^2 + 2x - 36 \right| = 12$

82. $\left| x^2 + 6x + 1 \right| = 8$

Application Problems

83. The number of inmates (I, in thousands) in federal and state prisons in the United States is modeled by $I = 2x^2 + 22x + 320$, where x represents the number of years after 1980. In what year does the model predict that the number of inmates will reach 1560 thousand?

84. The average cost of a new car (C, in dollars) t years after 1970 is approximated by the model $C = 30.5t^2 + 4192$. In what year will the average cost of a car reach $25,000?

85. The model

$$D = \frac{n(n - 3)}{2}$$

describes the number of diagonals (D) in an n-sided polygon.

a. Use the model to verify the relationship between the number of sides and diagonals in the figure.

b. Can a polygon have 10 diagonals?

86. The population (P, in millions) of the United States t decades after 1800 is approximated by the model $P = 0.6942t^2 + 6.183$, where $0 \le t \le 9$. Use this model to determine when the population of the United States was 17,290,200. What population is predicted by this model for the present time? How far off is this prediction? What does this tell you about mathematical models?

87. The model $M = 0.0075t^2 - 0.2676t + 14.8$ provides an estimation of fuel efficiency of passenger cars (M, measured in miles per gallon) t years after 1940. Environmentalists are pressuring automobile manufacturers for a fuel efficiency of 45 miles per gallon by the year 2000. In what year does the model predict fuel efficiency will reach 45 miles per gallon?

88. The formula $N = 0.036x^2 - 2.8x + 58.14$ approximately models the number of deaths (N, per year per thousand people) for people who are x years old, where $40 \le x \le 60$. Find, to the nearest whole number, the age at which 12 people per 1000 die annually.

Use the discriminant to answer the questions in Problems 89–91.

89. As shown in the figure, a ball is thrown upward from the top of a 200-foot building with a velocity of 40 feet per second. The height (s, in feet) of the ball above the ground after t seconds is given by the model $s = -16t^2 + 40t + 200$.

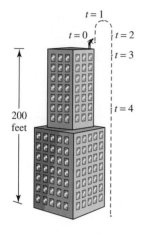

a. Will the ball ever reach a height of 240 feet?

b. Will the ball ever reach a height of 220 feet? How often does this occur? What does this mean in terms of the path that the ball follows?

c. Will the ball ever reach a height of 225 feet? How often does this occur? Explain what this means in terms of the path that the ball follows.

90. The daily profit (y, in dollars) from the sale of x units of a product is given by $y = -x^2 + 180x - 4500$. A newly hired advertising executive has promised the company that a unique advertising campaign will result in daily sales of \$3800. What does the discriminant indicate about this person's future with the company? Explain.

91. The model $P = -5I^2 + 80I$ describes the power (P) of an 80-volt generator subject to a current (I, in amperes) of electricity. Can there ever be enough current to generate 340 volts of power?

True–False Critical Thinking Problems

92. Which one of the following is true?

a. The equation $(2x - 3)^2 = 25$ is equivalent to $2x - 3 = 5$.

b. Every quadratic equation has two distinct numbers in its solution set.

c. A quadratic equation whose coefficents are real numbers can never have a solution set containing one real number and one complex nonreal number.

d. The equation $ax^2 + c = 0$ cannot be solved by the quadratic formula.

93. Which one of the following is true?

a. Some quadratic equations can be solved by factoring but not by the quadratic formula.

b. Some equations in the form $ax^2 + c = 0$ can be solved by factoring.

c. If $(x - 5)(2x + 3) = 0$ then $x = 5$ or $x = \frac{3}{2}$.

d. The quadratic equation whose solution set is $\{-4, -2\}$ has a negative discriminant because both solutions are negative.

Technology Problems

94. Graph the model of Problem 87 ($y = 0.0075x^2 - 0.2676x + 14.8$) using the following range setting:

Xmin = 0, Xmax = 80, Xscl = 20,

Ymin = 0, Ymax = 50, Yscl = 10

Move the cursor along the graph, using the TRACE and ZOOM features to estimate the year in which automobile fuel efficiency was the poorest. What was the gas mileage in that year? Find pictures of the most popular cars for that year and write a sentence relating the most popular cars of the time with the fuel efficiency indicated by the model's graph.

95. Graph the model of Problem 89 ($y = -16x^2 + 40x + 200$) using the following range setting:

Xmin = 0, Xmax = 5, Xscl = 1,

Ymin = 0, Ymax = 240, Yscl = 24

Use the graph with values of time in seconds along the x-axis ($0 \leqslant x \leqslant 5$) and values of the height of the ball along the y-axis to answer each of the three parts of Problem 89.

96. From elementary school through the university level, total school expenditures in the United States y, in millions of dollars, x years after 1975 are approximated by the model

$$y = 459.5x^2 + 9170.3x + 107{,}298.$$

Graph the model using the following range setting:

Xmin = 0, Xmax = 20, Xscl = 2,

Ymin = 0, Ymax = 500,000, Yscl = 50,000

A journalist wrote that total school expenditures in the United States have been increasing *steadily* each year since 1975. Does the graph of the expenditure model seem to support this statement? Explain.

97. In Problems 94–96, you were asked to graph three quadratic models in the form $y = ax^2 + bx + c$. Range settings were given. Try graphing each of the models in the standard range setting and see what happens. How

might you determine the range settings for the models in Problems 94–96 if they were not given? What information might you want to know about the graph of $y = ax^2 + bx + c$ to help determine appropriate range settings?

98. Graphing utilities are capable of providing the solutions to any polynomial equation. A quadratic equation can be thought of as a polynomial equation of degree (or order) 2. If your utility has a key labeled POLY (polynomial equations), try using it to solve $2.7x^2 - 27x - 6 = 0$. As soon as you enter order = 2, a quadratic equation ($a_2 x \wedge 2 + a_1 x + a_0 = 0$) should appear in the viewing screen. Enter the coefficients ($a_2 = 2.7, a_1 = -27, a_0 = -6$) and then press SOLVE. The solutions ($x_1 \approx 10.2174919475, x_2 \approx -0.2174919475$) should appear on the screen. Use the POLY feature to solve some of the quadratic equations in this problem set, including those whose solutions are not real numbers. How does your graphing utility indicate nonreal solutions?

Writing in Mathematics

99. Problem 98 indicates that graphing utilities can instantly provide the solutions to any quadratic equation. Do you think that this eliminates the need for students to learn the four algebraic methods for solving quadratic equations? If you were teaching youngsters, would you use calculators instead of explaining the steps involved in addition, subtraction, multiplication, and division of whole numbers? Are your answers the same to both questions? If not, explain the difference you see between the two situations.

100. Describe the relationship between the discriminant and the graph of $y = ax^2 + bx + c$.

101. If $(x + 2)(x - 4) = 0$ indicates that $x + 2 = 0$ or $x - 4 = 0$, explain why $(x + 2)(x - 4) = 6$ does not mean $x + 2 = 6$ or $x - 4 = 6$. Could we solve the equation using $x + 2 = 3$ and $x - 4 = 2$ since $3 \cdot 2 = 6$?

102. Take any two models presented in this section and for each one describe one unforeseen event that will affect the accuracy of the prediction made by the model.

103. What method would you use to solve each of the following quadratic equations? Explain, in each case, why you would select that method.

a. $x^2 - 5x + 6 = 0$

b. $x^2 - 6x + 2 = 0$

c. $x^2 - 5 = 0$

d. $(x + a)^2 - d^2 = 0$

104. In the first two sections of this chapter, we discussed linear and quadratic equations. Browse through the entire chapter and you'll quickly see that it's almost impossible to randomly select a page that does not contain an equation. In spite of this, Stephen Hawking, talking about his book, *A Brief History of Time*, wrote, "Someone told me that each equation I included in the book would halve the sales. I therefore resolved not to have any equations at all." What do you think Hawking meant by this?

Critical Thinking Problems

105. a. Verify each of the following.

$$\left(\frac{-b + \sqrt{b^2 - 4ac}}{2a}\right)\left(\frac{-b - \sqrt{b^2 - 4ac}}{2a}\right) = \frac{c}{a}$$

$$\frac{-b + \sqrt{b^2 - 4ac}}{2a} + \frac{-b - \sqrt{b^2 - 4ac}}{2a} = -\frac{b}{a}$$

b. Use part (a) to write a statement about the product and sum of the solutions of $ax^2 + bx + c = 0$.

c. Suppose that you solved $x^2 - 7x + 4 = 0$ and found the solution set to be $\left\{\frac{7 + \sqrt{33}}{2}, \frac{7 - \sqrt{33}}{2}\right\}$. You want to check your answers, but do not want to have to substitute each value back into the given equation. Explain how you can use part (a) with your written statement in part (b) to check the solutions. Is the solution set correct?

In Problems 106–107, find the value(s) of k for which each equation will have exactly one solution.

106. $kx^2 + kx + 2 = 0$

107. $3x^2 + (5\sqrt{k})x + 6 = 0$

108. Write a quadratic equation in standard form whose solution set is $\{-3, 5\}$.

109. Verify that $\dfrac{-b + \sqrt{b^2 - 4ac}}{2a}$ is a solution of $ax^2 + bx + c = 0$ by substituting the expression into the quadratic equation.

110. a. Show that

$$ax^2 + bx + c$$

$$= a\left(x - \frac{-b + \sqrt{b^2 - 4ac}}{2a}\right)\left(x - \frac{-b - \sqrt{b^2 - 4ac}}{2a}\right)$$

by multiplying on the right (using the FOIL method) to obtain the trinomial on the left.

b. Use your result from part (a) to derive the quadratic formula.

c. Use your result from part (a) to factor $x^2 + 8x + 144$ and $3x^2 + 10x + 6$.

111. Solve for x in terms of d and e:

$$x^2 - \left(\sqrt{\frac{d}{e}} + \sqrt{\frac{e}{d}}\right)x + 1 = 0$$

112. For what values of b and c will the solution set of $x^2 + bx + c = 0$ be $\{b, c\}$?

113. Consider the quadratic equation $x^2 + bx + c = 0$, where $b \neq 0$ and $c \neq 0$.

a. If one solution is four times the other, show that

$$\frac{b^2}{c} = \frac{25}{4}.$$

b. If one solution is k times the other, show that

$$\frac{b^2}{c} = \frac{(k+1)^2}{k} \quad (k \neq -1 \text{ and } k \neq 0).$$

SECTION 1.3 | Linear and Quadratic Modeling

Solutions Manual

Tutorial

Video 3

Objectives

1 Use linear equations to solve problems.

2 Use quadratic equations to solve problems.

A Problem-Solving Strategy

In the first two sections of this chapter, the models for atmospheric carbon dioxide, depreciation, bacteria concentration, and breast cancer–fat intake correlation were given. Using these models, we were able to solve real world problems. We focus now on how models can be constructed from verbal conditions that are implied in a given situation. Since these problems are a bit more difficult, we offer the following five-step strategy for solving problems.

Strategy for problem solving

Step 1. Read the problem carefully. Attempt to state the problem in your own words and state what the problem is looking for. Let x (or any variable) represent one of the quantities in the problem.

Step 2. If necessary, write expressions for any other unknown quantities in the problem in terms of x.

Step 3. Form a verbal model of the problem's conditions and then write an equation in x that translates the verbal model.

Step 4. Solve the equation written in step 3 and answer the question in the problem.

Step 5. Check your answer against the verbal conditions of the original problem, possibly using a graphing utility to further explore the geometric significance of the answer.

Use linear equations to solve problems.

Wendy Seller "Dissension" 1993, oil on canvas, 34 in. H × 30 in. W. Courtesy of the Pepper Gallery, Boston, MA. In the Collection of Robert and Elayne Simandl. Photo by Clements/Howcroft, Boston.

Constructing Linear Models

Let's see how we can use this five-step strategy by turning to a number of specific examples.

EXAMPLE 1   The Impact of Gender on Education and Income

Numerous variables affect the relationship between education and income. A simplified form of two such models focuses on the effect of gender in these relationships. Yearly income for men increases by $1600 with each year of education; men with no education earn $6300 yearly. For women, yearly income increases by $1200 for each year of education; women with no education earn $2100 yearly. Using these models, how many years of education must a woman have to earn the same yearly salary as a man with 11 years of education?

Discover for yourself

1. Use the fact that men earn $6300 yearly plus $1600 for each year of education to compute the yearly earnings for a man with 11 years of education.
2. Use the fact that women earn $2100 yearly plus $1200 for each year of education to write an algebraic expression for the yearly earnings for a woman with x years of education. Use the same method as in step 1.
3. Read the example again and explain how you can use your work in steps 1 and 2 to solve the problem.

Solution

Steps 1 and 2. Represent unknowns in terms of x.

Let x = the years of education needed by a woman to earn the same yearly salary as at man with 11 years of education.

Step 3. Write an equation that models the verbal conditions.

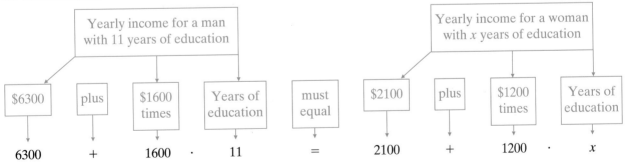

Step 4. Solve the equation and answer the problem's question.

$$6300 + 1600 \cdot 11 = 2100 + 1200x$$ This is the equation that translates the verbal conditions of the models.

$$23{,}900 = 2100 + 1200x$$ Multiply and add on the left.

$$21{,}800 = 1200x$$ Subtract 2100 from both sides.

$$\frac{21,800}{1200} = x$$ Divide both sides by 1200.

$$x \approx 18.2$$ Perform the computation. Remember that $\approx$ means "is approximately equal to."

The models show that a woman must have approximately 18.2 years of education to earn the same salary as a man with 11 years of education.

Step 5. Check the proposed solution in the original wording of the problem.

Discover for yourself

Take a few minutes to check the solution. Explain how the graphs shown in Figure 1.5 approximately illustrate the solution.

Years of Education	Predicted Average Personal Wages for Men
0	$6300
1	$7900
2	$9500
3	$11,100
4	$12,700
5	$14,300
6	$15,900
7	$17,500
8	$19,100
9	$20,700
10	$22,300
11	$23,900
12	$25,500
13	$27,100
14	$28,700
15	$30,300
16	$31,900
17	$33,500
18	$35,100
19	$36,700
20	$38,300

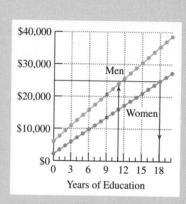

Figure 1.5

Average personal wages for women and men by years of education

Years of Education	Predicted Average Personal Wages for Women
0	$2100
1	$3300
2	$4500
3	$5700
4	$6900
5	$8100
6	$9300
7	$10,500
8	$11,700
9	$12,900
10	$14,100
11	$15,300
12	$16,500
13	$17,700
14	$18,900
15	$20,100
16	$21,300
17	$22,500
18	$23,700
19	$24,900
20	$26,100

EXAMPLE 2   **Selecting a Heating System**

Costs for two different kinds of heating systems for a three-bedroom home are given below.

System	Cost to Install	Operating Cost per Year
Solar	$29,700	$150
Electric	$5000	$1100

After how many years will total costs for solar heating and electric heating be the same? What will be the cost at that time?

Solution

Steps 1 and 2. Represent unknowns in terms of x.

Let x = the number of years after which total costs for the two systems will be the same.

We begin by constructing a model for the total cost for each system.

Step 3. Write an equation that models the verbal conditions.

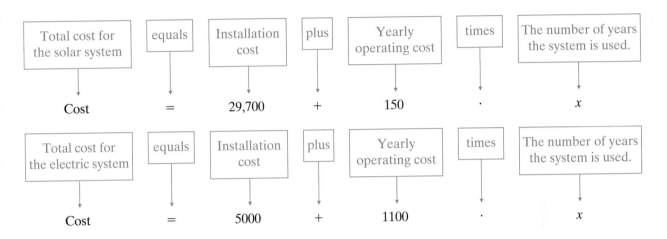

Our total cost models are

$$\text{Solar} = 29{,}700 + 150x$$

$$\text{Electric} = 5000 + 1100x$$

Now that we have modeled the conditions, we model the problem's first question:

After how many years will

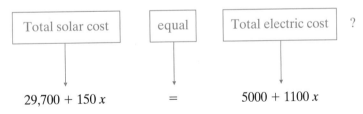

Step 4. Solve the equation and answer the problem's question.

$29{,}700 + 150x = 5000 + 1100x$	This is the equation implied by the problem's question.
$29{,}700 = 5000 + 950x$	Subtract $150x$ from both sides.
$24{,}700 = 950x$	Subtract 5000 from both sides.
$26 = x$	Divide both sides by 950.

Step 5. Check the proposed solution in the original wording of the problem.

After 26 years, the total costs for the two systems will be the same. To answer the problem's second question, we substitute 26 into our total cost models.

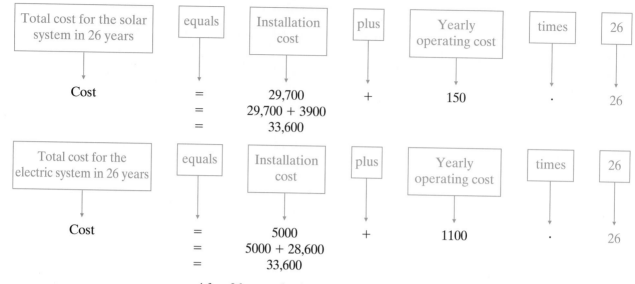

| Total cost for the solar system in 26 years | equals | Installation cost | plus | Yearly operating cost | times | 26 |

Cost = 29,700 + 150 · 26
     = 29,700 + 3900
     = 33,600

| Total cost for the electric system in 26 years | equals | Installation cost | plus | Yearly operating cost | times | 26 |

Cost = 5000 + 1100 · 26
     = 5000 + 28,600
     = 33,600

Figure 1.6

After 26 years, solar and electric systems have the same total costs: $33,600.

After 26 years, both systems will cost $33,600.

We can visualize this solution by graphing the two models in the same rectangular coordinate system. Representing total costs by y, the models are $y = 29,700 + 150x$ and $y = 5000 + 1100x$.

Figure 1.6 shows the graphs obtained on a graphing utility using

$$\text{Xmin} = 0, \text{Xmax} = 40, \text{Xscl} = 2, \text{Ymin} = 5000,$$

$$\text{Ymax} = 50,000, \text{Yscl} = 5000.$$

The graphs intersect at $(26, 33,600)$, verifying that after 26 years total costs for both systems will be $33,600. ∎

EXAMPLE 3   Selecting a Mortgage Plan

Table 1.3 on page 141 gives the monthly mortgage payment for each $1000 of mortgage at various mortgage rates for different periods of time. For example, for a mortgage of $80,000 for 30 years at 8.5%, the monthly payment for principal and interest would be 80 times $7.69 (shown in pink in Table 1.3) or $615.20. The same mortgage payment for 30 years at 7.25% results in monthly payments for principal and interest of 80 times $6.83 (also shown in pink in Table 1.3) or $546.40.

Suppose you are purchasing a home and are considering the following two options for an $80,000 mortgage.

Option 1:
8.5% interest for a 30-year loan, 1 point, (a point is a one-time charge of 1% of the mortgage amount), and a $300 loan application fee

Option 2:
7.25% interest for a 30-year loan, 5 points, and a $1500 loan application fee

Approximately how many months will it take for the total cost of each mortgage option to be the same?

Solution

Steps 1 and 2. Represent unknowns in terms of x.

Let x = the number of months for the total cost for the two mortgage options to be the same.

TABLE 1.3 Any Bank, USA: Equal Monthly Payment to Amortize a Loan of $1000

Rate (%)	Payment for a Mortgage Period (years) of:				Rate (%)	Payment for a Mortgage Period (years) of:			
	15	20	25	30		15	20	25	30
4.500	7.65	6.33	5.56	5.07	8.625	9.93	8.76	8.14	7.78
4.625	7.71	6.39	5.63	5.14	8.750	10.00	8.84	8.23	7.87
4.750	7.78	6.46	5.70	5.22	8.875	10.07	8.92	8.31	7.96
4.875	7.84	6.53	5.77	5.29	9.000	10.15	9.00	8.40	8.05
5.000	7.91	6.60	5.85	5.37	9.125	10.22	9.08	8.48	8.14
5.125	7.97	6.67	5.92	5.44	9.250	10.30	9.16	8.57	8.23
5.250	8.04	6.73	6.00	5.52	9.375	10.37	9.24	8.66	8.32
5.375	8.10	6.81	6.07	5.60	9.500	10.45	9.33	8.74	8.41
5.500	8.17	6.88	6.14	5.68	9.625	10.52	9.41	8.83	8.50
5.625	8.24	6.95	6.22	5.76	9.750	10.60	9.49	8.92	8.60
5.750	8.30	7.02	6.29	5.84	9.875	10.67	9.57	9.00	8.69
5.875	8.37	7.09	6.37	5.92	10.000	10.75	9.66	9.09	8.78
6.000	8.44	7.16	6.44	6.00	10.125	10.83	9.74	9.18	8.87
6.125	8.51	7.24	6.52	6.08	10.250	10.90	9.82	9.27	8.97
6.250	8.57	7.31	6.60	6.16	10.375	10.98	9.90	9.36	9.06
6.375	8.64	7.38	6.67	6.24	10.500	11.06	9.99	9.45	9.15
6.500	8.71	7.46	6.75	6.32	10.625	11.14	10.07	9.54	9.25
6.625	8.78	7.53	6.83	6.40	10.750	11.21	10.16	9.63	9.34
6.750	8.85	7.60	6.91	6.49	10.875	11.29	10.24	9.72	9.43
6.875	8.92	7.68	6.99	6.57	11.000	11.37	10.33	9.81	9.53
7.000	8.99	7.76	7.07	6.66	11.125	11.45	10.41	9.90	9.62
7.125	9.06	7.83	7.15	6.74	11.250	11.53	10.50	9.99	9.72
7.250	9.13	7.91	7.23	6.83	11.375	11.61	10.58	10.08	9.81
7.375	9.20	7.98	7.31	6.91	11.500	11.69	10.67	10.17	9.91
7.500	9.28	8.06	7.39	7.00	11.625	11.77	10.76	10.26	10.00
7.625	9.35	8.14	7.48	7.08	11.750	11.85	10.84	10.35	10.10
7.750	9.42	8.21	7.56	7.17	11.875	11.93	10.93	10.44	10.20
7.875	9.49	8.29	7.64	7.26	12.000	12.01	11.02	10.54	10.29
8.000	9.56	8.37	7.72	7.34	12.125	12.09	11.10	10.63	10.39
8.125	9.63	8.45	7.81	7.43	12.250	12.17	11.19	10.72	10.48
8.250	9.71	8.53	7.89	7.52	12.375	12.25	11.28	10.82	10.58
8.375	9.78	8.60	7.97	7.61	12.500	12.33	11.37	10.91	10.68
8.500	9.85	8.68	8.06	7.69					

Step 3. Write an equation that models the verbal conditions.

As we did in the previous example, we construct models for the total cost for each mortgage option over x months, setting the models equal to each other.

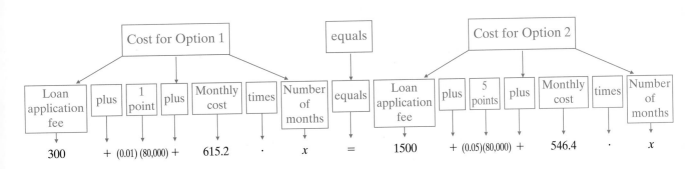

Step 4. Solve the equation and answer the problem's question.

$$300 + (0.01)(80,000) + 615.2x = 1500 + (0.05)(80,000) + 546.4x$$

This is the equation implied by the given conditions .

$$1100 + 615.2x = 5500 + 546.4x$$

Multiply and add as indicated.

$$1100 + 68.8x = 5500$$

Subtract $546.4x$ from both sides.

$$68.8x = 4400$$

Subtract 1100 from both sides.

$$x = \frac{4400}{68.8}$$

Divide both sides by 68.8.

$$\approx 64$$

After approximately 64 months or $\frac{64}{12} = 5\frac{1}{3}$ years, the total cost of both mortgage options will be the same. Notice that option 1 involves less money up front but greater monthly payments. Prior to 64 months, option 1 will result in lower total costs. After that time, option 2 makes more sense. Knowing how long the house will be kept would help you select the loan with the lowest total costs. ■

Step 5. Check the proposed solution in the original wording of the problem.

Take a few minutes to check the solution.

Discover for yourself

Use a graphing utility to visualize the solution to Example 3. Graph $y_1 = 1100 + 615.2x$ and $y_2 = 5500 + 546.4x$ (the simplified models) in the same viewing rectangle. Use a setting such as

Xmin = 0, Xmax = 70, Xscl = 1,

Ymin = 0, Ymax = 45,000, Yscl = 300

Then use the TRACE or ISECT feature to find the point of intersection of the two lines. The x-coordinate of the intersection point should be approximately 64. What is the y-coordinate and what does this represent?

In our next example, we must once again use common sense to write a sentence that will then, phrase by phrase, be translated into an equation.

EXAMPLE 4 **Modeling Implied Conditions**

A two-year union contract guarantees an immediate 6% raise and a 5% raise after one year. How much must an employee be earning weekly at the start of the contract if that employee's weekly salary increases $60 over the two-year life of the contract?

Discover for yourself

One way to familiarize yourself with the problem is to select a particular number and use that number to help understand the problem's conditions. Suppose the worker is making $600 per week at the start of the contract.

1. After the 6% increase, the worker will earn $600 plus 6% of $600. How much is this new salary?

Fernand Léger "Les constructeurs" / Musée Leger, © 1998 Artists Rights Society (ARS), New York / ADAGP, Paris.

2. After the 5% increase, the worker will earn the salary computed in step 1 plus 5% of this salary. How much is this salary with the second increase?
3. What is the increase over the two-year life of the contract? Subtract the original salary ($600) from the salary that you computed in step 2.
4. Read Example 4 again. Based on your answer in step 3, what is a reasonable estimate for the answer to the problem?
5. Rework steps 1 and 2 if the original salary is x dollars rather than $600.

Solution

Steps 1 and 2. Represent unknowns in terms of x.

Let x = the employee's weekly salary at the start of the contract. An implied verbal model in this situation is

Step 3. Write an equation that models the verbal conditions.

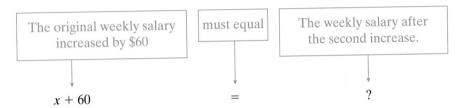

We must find an algebraic expression for the phrase on the right.
  Since there is an immediate 6% raise, the salary after the first raise increases by 6% of what it was originally.

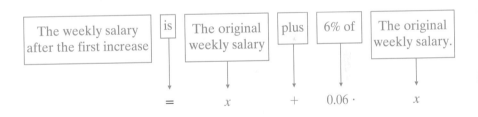

Thus, the weekly salary after the first increase is represented by $x + 0.06x$.
  Since there is a 5% raise after a year, the salary after the second raise increases by 5% of the salary after the first raise.

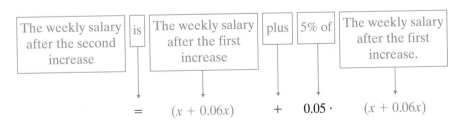

Thus, the weekly salary after the second increase is represented by

$$(x + 0.06x) + 0.05(x + 0.06x).$$

We can now complete the equation implied by our original boxed expression.

The original weekly salary increased by $60	must equal	The weekly salary after the second increase.
$x + 60$	$=$	$(x + 0.06x) + 0.05(x + 0.06x)$

Step 4. Solve the equation and answer the problem's question.

$x + 60 = (x + 0.06x) + 0.05(x + 0.06x)$ This is the equation implied by the problem's conditions.

$x + 60 = x + 0.06x + 0.05x + 0.003x$ Use the distributive property on the right.

$x + 60 = 1.113x$ Combine like terms on the right.

$60 = 0.113x$ Subtract x from both sides.

$x = \dfrac{60}{0.113} \approx 530.97$ Divide both sides by 0.113.

Step 5. Check the proposed solution in the original wording of the problem.

An employee must be earning approximately $530.97 per week for the weekly salary to increase by $60 over the life of the contract. Let's see if this answer makes sense. With the 6% raise, the new weekly salary is

$$530.97 + (0.06)(530.97)$$

or approximately $562.83. With the 5% raise, the new weekly salary is

$$562.83 + (0.05)(562.83)$$

or approximately $590.97. Notice that $590.97 is a $60 increase over the original weekly salary of $530.97. ∎

  Use quadratic equations to solve problems.

Constructing Quadratic Models

We continue using our five-step strategy. The only difference is that the equation that models the verbal conditions will now be quadratic.

EXAMPLE 5 **Constructing a Quadratic Model**

An owner of a large diving boat that can carry as many as 70 people charges $10 per passenger to groups of between 15 and 20 people. If more than 20 divers charter the boat, the fee per passenger is decreased by 10 cents for every person over 20. How many people must there be in a diving group to generate an income of $323.90?

Discover for yourself

Before solving Example 5 using algebra, let's consider a few specific values for the number of people in the group and the resulting income.

Number of People in the Diving Group	Cost per Person	Income = (Number of People) × (Cost per Person)
20	$10.00	$(20)($10.00) = 200
21	$10.00 - $0.10 = $9.90	$(21)($9.90) = 207.90
22	$10.00 - $0.20 = $9.80	$(22)($9.80) = 215.60
23	$10.00 - $0.30 = $9.70	$(23)($9.70) = 223.10

Do you see a pattern forming? If *x* represents the number of people beyond 20 (so there are 20 + *x* people in the diving group), write an algebraic expression for the income.

Take a moment to compute the income if there are 30 people in the group. Repeat this computation for 50 divers. What is a reasonable estimate for the number of divers to generate $323.90?

Solution

Steps 1 and 2. Represent unknowns in terms of *x*.

Since the cost per person is computed differently depending on whether the number of divers is less than or equal to 20 or greater than 20,

let *x* = the number of people beyond 20 to generate $323.90 of income.

Thus,

20 + *x* = the total number of people in the group.

Step 3. Write an equation that models the verbal conditions.

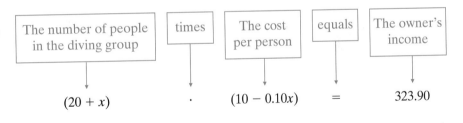

Step 4. Solve the equation and answer the problem's question.

$(20 + x)(10 - 0.10x) = 323.90$ This is the equation implied by the problem's conditions.

$200 + 8x - 0.10x^2 = 323.90$ Multiply using FOIL.

$-0.10x^2 + 8x - 123.9 = 0$ Write the quadratic equation in standard form.

$a = -0.10 \quad b = 8 \quad c = -123.9$

$x = \dfrac{-b \pm \sqrt{b^2 - 4ac}}{2a}$ Write the quadratic formula and then let $a = -0.10$, $b = 8$, and $c = -123.9$.

$= \dfrac{-8 \pm \sqrt{8^2 - 4(-0.10)(-123.9)}}{2(-0.10)}$ Substitute the given numbers.

$= \dfrac{-8 \pm \sqrt{14.44}}{-0.20}$ The positive discriminant (14.44) indicates that the equation will have two real solutions.

$$x = \frac{-8 + 3.8}{-0.20} \quad \text{or} \quad x = \frac{-8 - 3.8}{-0.20} \qquad \sqrt{14.44} = 3.8$$

$$= 21 \qquad\qquad\qquad = 59 \qquad\qquad \text{Simplify.}$$

Since x represents the number of passengers above 20, we see that $41(20 + 21)$ or $79(20 + 59)$ people will generate an income of \$323.90. However, we were told that the boat can carry as many as 70 passengers. Thus, 79 divers are too many, and the required number of people is 41.

Step 5. Check the proposed solution in the original wording of the problem.

With 41 passengers (21 above 20), the cost per person is reduced by $21(0.10)$ or \$2.10. Each person pays \$10.00 $-$ \$2.10 or \$7.90. The income is $41(7.90) =$ \$323.90, which checks with the given conditions. ∎

Using technology

The graph of $y = -0.10x^2 + 8x + 200$, the model for income with $20 + x$ divers in the group, was obtained with a graphing utility using the following range setting:

Xmin = 0, Xmax = 50, Xscl = 5,

Ymin = 0, Ymax = 400, Xscl = 40.

We can use the graph and the ⬛TRACE⬛ feature to find how many divers should be on the boat to maximize income. The graph indicates that income increases up to 40 divers (meaning that $20 + 40$ or 60 passengers will maximize income). After 40, income starts to decrease, as shown in the table.

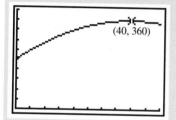
(40, 360)

Number of People in the Diving Group	Cost per Person	Income
59 ($x = 39$)	\$6.10	359.90
60 ($x = 40$)	\$6.00	360.00 (maximum)
61 ($x = 41$)	\$5.90	359.90

Geometric Modeling

Solving geometry problems usually requires a knowledge of basic geometric ideas and formulas. This can range from knowing basic formulas for perimeter, area, and volume to recognizing properties of similar triangles. Often we are asked to use logical reasoning based on a geometric figure.

A knowledge of the formulas in Table 1.4 on page 147 will be useful in solving problems involving perimeter, area, and volume.

Figure 1.7

EXAMPLE 6   Problem Solving Using Geometric Formulas

A path of uniform width is constructed around the outside of a 20 meter by 25 meter rectangular garden (Figure 1.7). Find how wide the path should be if there is enough brick to cover 196 square meters.

TABLE 1.4 Common Formulas for Area, Perimeter, and Volume

Square
$A = s^2$
$P = 4s$

Rectangle
$A = lw$
$P = 2l + 2w$

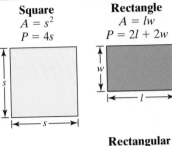

Circle
$A = \pi r^2$
$C = 2\pi r$

Triangle
$A = \frac{1}{2}bh$

Trapezoid
$A = \frac{1}{2}h(a + b)$

Cube
$V = s^3$

Rectangular Solid
$V = lwh$

Circular Cylinder
$V = \pi r^2 h$

Sphere
$V = \frac{4}{3}\pi r^3$

Cone
$V = \frac{1}{3}\pi r^2 h$

ly Kandinsky
ging" (Schaukeln),
Tate Gallery, London.
: John Webb. Art
rce, NY.

Discover for yourself

Suppose that the width of the path in Example 6 is 4 meters.

1. What are the dimensions of the rectangle consisting of the garden and the path combined? What is the area of this rectangle?

2. What is the area of the rectangle consisting of just the garden?

3. Find the area of the path by using the areas you found in steps 1 and 2.

4. Repeat steps 1–3 if the width of the path is x meters rather than 4 meters.

5. Based on your answer in step 3, since the area of the path is 196 square meters, what is a reasonable estimate of its width?

Solution

Steps 1 and 2. Represent unknowns in terms of x.

Let x = the width of the path. The situation is illustrated in Figure 1.8 on page 148. In the Discover for yourself, were you able to observe that although the path is not a rectangle, its area can be determined by subtracting the area of the rectangular garden from the area of the rectangle containing the garden and path combined?

Step 3. Write an equation that models the verbal conditions.

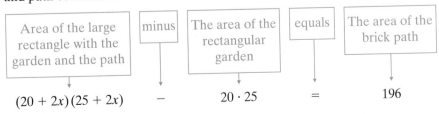

Area of the large rectangle with the garden and the path	minus	The area of the rectangular garden	equals	The area of the brick path
$(20 + 2x)(25 + 2x)$	−	$20 \cdot 25$	=	196

Figure 1.8

Step 4. Solve the equation and answer the problem's question.

Figure 1.9

Step 5. Check the proposed solution in the original wording of the problem.

$$(20 + 2x)(25 + 2x) - 20 \cdot 25 = 196 \qquad \text{This is the equation modeling the path's area.}$$
$$500 + 90x + 4x^2 - 500 = 196 \qquad \text{Multiply using the FOIL method.}$$
$$90x + 4x^2 = 196 \qquad \text{Simplify.}$$
$$4x^2 + 90x - 196 = 0 \qquad \text{Write the quadratic equation in standard form.}$$
$$2x^2 + 45x - 98 = 0 \qquad \text{Divide both sides by 2.}$$
$$(x - 2)(2x + 49) = 0 \qquad \text{Factor.}$$
$$x - 2 = 0 \quad \text{or} \quad 2x + 49 = 0 \qquad \text{Set each factor equal to 0.}$$
$$x = 2 \qquad\qquad x = -\frac{49}{2} \qquad \text{Solve the resulting equations.}$$

Since the path's width must be positive, its width should be 2 meters. The area of the rectangle with the garden and path combined (Figure 1.9) is $24 \cdot 29 = 696$ square meters. The area of the garden is $20 \cdot 25 = 500$ square meters. Thus, the area of the path is $696 - 500 = 196$ square meters, which checks with the problem's conditions. ∎

Using technology

A graphing utility enables us to visualize the solution to Example 6. In graphing the model representing the area of the path, namely,

$$y = (20 + 2x)(25 + 2x) - 20(25),$$

we used the following range setting:

Xmin = 0, Xmax = 3, Xscl = 1,

Ymin = 0, Ymax = 300, Yscl = 4

Using the ⟨TRACE⟩ feature to trace along the graph, we find that when $x = 2$, $y = 196$. This means that when the width of the path is 2 meters, its area is 196 square meters. This serves as another way of checking our solution to the problem.

Figure 1.10

Steps 1 and 2. Represent unknowns in terms of x.

Step 3. Write an equation that models the verbal conditions.

Step 4. Solve the equation and answer the problem's question.

Step 5. Check the proposed solution in the original wording of the problem.

EXAMPLE 7 **Problem Solving Using Geometric Formulas**

A machine produces open boxes using square sheets of metal. Figure 1.10 illustrates that the machine cuts equal-sized squares measuring 2 inches on a side from the corners and then shapes the metal into an open box by turning up the sides. If each box must have a volume of 200 cubic inches, find the size of the length and width of the open box.

Solution

Let $x =$ the length and the width of the open box. The volume of the box is to be 200 cubic inches and can be found by taking the product of its length, width, and height.

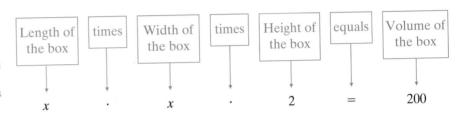

Length of the box	times	Width of the box	times	Height of the box	equals	Volume of the box
x	$\cdot$	x	$\cdot$	2	$=$	200

$2x^2 = 200$ This is the equation modeling the volume of the open box.

$x^2 = 100$ Divide both sides by 2.

$x = \pm\sqrt{100} = \pm 10$ Apply the square root method.

Since the open box must have positive dimensions, it should have a length and width of 10 inches on a side. The volume of the open box is $10(10)(2) = 200$ cubic inches, which checks with the problem's condition. ∎

Our final example has a solution that depends on knowing some basic facts about similar triangles.

EXAMPLE 8   Using Similar Triangles to Solve a Problem

A water tank has the shape of an inverted right circular cone of altitude 12 feet and base radius 6 feet. (Figure 1.11). How much water is in the tank when the water is 8 feet deep?

Figure 1.11

A conical water tank

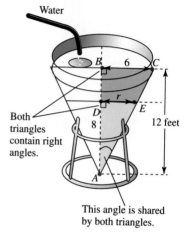

Both triangles contain right angles.

This angle is shared by both triangles.

Figure 1.12

A cross section of the water tank

Solution

The amount of water in the tank can be determined by finding the volume of the cone that is filled with water, shown as the smaller cone on the bottom in Figure 1.11. Since the volume of a cone is $V = \frac{1}{3}\pi r^2 h$ and $h = 8$, we must find r to answer the question.

Let $r =$ the radius of the cone that is filled with water. Figure 1.12 shows a cross section of Figure 1.11. $\triangle ABC$ is similar to $\triangle ADE$ because $\angle B$ has the same measure as $\angle D$ (both measure 90°) and the two triangles share $\angle A$. With two angles of $\triangle ABC$ equal in measure to two angles of $\triangle ADE$, the triangles are similar and the lengths of their corresponding sides are proportional.

$$\frac{BC}{DE} = \frac{AB}{AD}$$ Corresponding sides of similar triangles are proportional.

$$\frac{6}{r} = \frac{12}{8}$$ This is the equation that models the problem's similar triangles.

$$\frac{6}{r} = \frac{3}{2}$$ Simplify.

$$2r \cdot \frac{6}{r} = \frac{3}{2} \cdot 2r$$ Multiply both sides by $2r$, the LCD.

$$12 = 3r$$ Simplify.

$$4 = r$$ Divide both sides by 3.

We have determined that the radius of the cone that is filled with water is 4 feet. We now can determine its volume.

$$v = \frac{1}{3}\pi r^2 h = \frac{1}{3}\pi(4)^2(8) = \frac{128}{3}\pi$$

When the water is 8 feet deep, there are $\frac{128}{3}\pi$ cubic feet of water in the tank, which is approximately 134 cubic feet.   ∎

PROBLEM SET 1.3

Practice and Application Problems

1. In 1990, the average cost of an advertisement during the Super Bowl was $700,000. On the average, this cost has increased by $60,000 each year. Using this model, in what year will the cost of an advertisement during the Super Bowl be $1,480,000? (*Hint*: Let x = the number of years after 1990 when this will occur.)

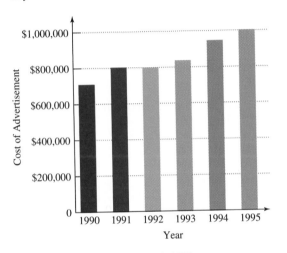

Source: *USA Today,* November 3, 1994

2. The bus fare in a city is $1.25. People who use public transportation have the option of purchasing a monthly coupon book for $21.00. With the coupon book, the fare is reduced to $0.50. How many times in a month must the bus be used so that the total monthly cost without the coupon book is the same as the total monthly cost with the coupon book?

3. A person purchasing a home is considering two options for a $50,000 mortgage.

   Option 1:
   7.5% interest on a 30-year loan and no points

   Option 2:
   7.125% interest on a 30-year loan with 3 points

   Use the table on page 141 to determine how long it will take for the total cost of each mortgage to be the same. How much will be saved by choosing the 7.125% option over 20 years?

4. A person purchasing a home is considering two options for a $60,000 mortgage.

   Option 1:
   9.0% interest on a 30-year loan, no points, and no application fee

   Option 2:
   8.5% interest on a 30-year loan, 2 points, and a $200 application fee

   Use the table on page 141 to determine how long it will take for the total cost of each mortgage to be the same. How much will be saved by choosing the 8.5% option over 20 years?

5. A two-year union contract guarantees an immediate 7% raise and a 3% raise after one year. How much must an employee be earning at the start of the contract if that employee's weekly salary increases by $50 over the two-year life of the contract?

6. A two-year union contract guarantees an immediate 4% raise and a 5% raise after a year. How much must an employee be earning at the start of the contract if that employee's weekly salary increases by $70 over the two-year life of the contract?

7. A grapefruit tree produces approximately 200 grapefruits per year if no more than 16 trees are planted per acre. For each additional tree planted per acre, the yield per tree decreases by 10 grapefruits per year.

   a. If x represents the number of grapefruit trees per acre beyond the basic 16, write a mathematical model for the number of grapefruits produced per year in terms of x.

   b. Approximately how many trees per acre should be planted to generate 3230 grapefruits yearly?

8. Acme Industries can sell 500 radios priced at $60 each. With each $2 reduction in price per radio, an additional 50 radios can be sold.

   a. If x represents the number of $2 reductions, write a mathematical model for the manufacturer's income in terms of x.

   b. How many $2 reductions should be applied to result in an income of $38,250?

9. A job pays an annual salary of $33,150, which includes a holiday bonus of $750. If paychecks are issued twice a month, what is the gross amount for each paycheck?

10. A store is reducing each of its items by 35%. Find the original price of a computer selling for $780.00.

The graph shows differences between the average incomes of full-time workers ages 25 and older. Problems 11–12 are based on this graph.

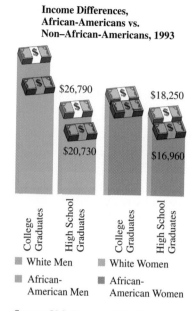

Income Differences, African-Americans vs. Non–African-Americans, 1993

$26,790 $18,250

$20,730 $16,960

■ White Men   ■ White Women

■ African-American Men   ■ African-American Women

College Graduates | High School Graduates | College Graduates | High School Graduates

Source: U.S. Bureau of the Census

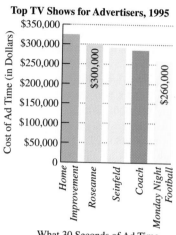

Top TV Shows for Advertisers, 1995

Cost of Ad Time (in Dollars)

$350,000
$300,000
$250,000
$200,000
$150,000
$100,000
$50,000
0

$300,000 $260,000

Home Improvement | Roseanne | Seinfeld | Coach | Monday Night Football

What 30 Seconds of Ad Time Costs on Top-Ranked Programs

Source: Based on statistics from *Advertising Age* magazine

11. Among male college graduates, whites earn $9350 more than blacks. The average annual income for the two groups is $39,015. Find the annual income for white and black male college graduates.

12. Among female college graduates, whites earn $2390 more than blacks. The average annual income for the two groups is $29,325. Find the annual income for white and black female college graduates.

13. An advertiser is considering running 30 seconds of ad time on the top-ranked programs *Home Improvement, Seinfeld,* and *Coach.* As shown in the graph at the top of the next column, a 30-second ad on *Home Improvement* costs $30,000 more than *Seinfeld,* and a 30-second ad on *Seinfeld* costs $5000 more than *Coach.* The total cost to run the 3 ads is three and a half times the cost of running a 30-second ad on *Monday Night Football.* What is the cost of a 30-second ad on each of the three programs?

14. The graph to the right shows the ten major league baseball players with the greatest number of runs as of the end of 1994. Ty Cobb had 71 more runs than Babe Ruth, who tied with Hank Aaron. Pete Rose had 9 fewer runs than both Ruth and Aaron. The four players had a combined total of runs that exceeded four times Frank Robinson's career total by 1442. Find the number of runs for Cobb, Ruth, Aaron, and Rose.

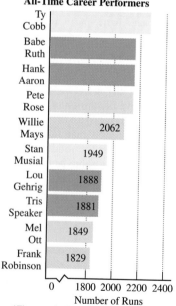

Top 10 Major League Baseball All-Time Career Performers

Ty Cobb
Babe Ruth
Hank Aaron
Pete Rose
Willie Mays   2062
Stan Musial   1949
Lou Gehrig   1888
Tris Speaker   1881
Mel Ott   1849
Frank Robinson   1829

0   1800 2000 2200 2400
Number of Runs
*Figures calculated as of the end of the abortive 1994 baseball season

Source: Based on statistics from Major League Baseball/Adapted from *The Macmillan Visual Almanac,* © 1996, Simon & Schuster

The position model $s = -16t^2 + v_0t + s_0$ describes the height of an object that is falling or is vertically projected into the air. In this formula, s represents the position (in feet) above the ground at time t (in seconds), v_0 represents the original velocity of the object (in feet per second), and s_0 represents the original position above the ground (in feet) of the object. Use this model to answer Problems 15–16.

15. A ball is thrown vertically upward from the top of a 200-foot building with an initial velocity of 40 feet per second. The figure on the right shows that the ball first moves upward, reaches a maximum height above the ground, and then begins to fall.

   a. How long does it take for the ball to pass by the roof of the building?

   b. How long does it take for the ball to hit the ground?

   c. The graph of the position model is shown below. Find the points on the graph corresponding to your solutions in parts (a) and (b).

200 feet

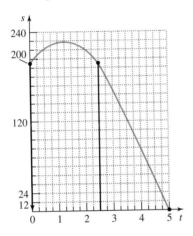

16. A set of car keys is accidentally dropped (not thrown) from the top of a 400-foot skyscraper.

   a. How long does it take for the keys to hit the ground?

   b. Sound travels at approximately 1100 feet per second. The person who dropped the keys shouts "Danger—falling object!" to warn people below. Can a person on the street hear the warning and get out of the way of the falling keys in time to avoid being hit?

Revenue for a company is the money received for the sale of x units of a product, and is found by multiplying the number of units sold by the price per unit. A company's profit is the difference between its revenue and its cost of producing x units of a product. Use these ideas to answer Problems 17–18.

17. Electric Products Incorporated manufactures and sells microwave ovens. They find that they can sell x ovens per hour at a price of $400 - 25x$ per oven, where $0 \leq x \leq 10$. The company expenses amount to $5x^2 + 40x + 600$ dollars per hour. How many ovens should be produced and sold to generate a profit of $450 per hour?

18. Sunshine Energy manufactures and sells solar collector cells. They find that they can sell x cells per day at a price of $100 - 0.05x$ per cell, where $250 \leq x \leq 800$. (Observe how the demand for the product decreases as the price increases. If the price is $100 ($100 = 100 - 0.05x$), then $x = 0$, which means they can't sell any cells at that price. On the other hand, if the price is $20 ($20 = 100 - 0.05x$), then $x = 1600$, which means they can sell 1600 cells at $20 per unit). Company expenses amount to $4000 per day plus $60 - 0.01x$ for each cell manufactured. How many cells should be produced and sold to generate a profit of $6000 per day?

19. The length of a rectangle is 3 feet longer than the width. If the area is 54 square feet, find the rectangle's dimensions.

20. The length of a rectangle is 9 feet longer than 3 times the width. If the area is 210 square feet, find the rectangle's dimensions.

21. A brick path of uniform width is constructed around the outside of a 6- by 10-yard rectangular garden. Find how wide the path should be if there is enough brick to cover 132 square yards.

22. A rectangular garden measuring 80 by 60 feet has its area doubled by a border of uniform width along both shorter sides and one longer side. Find the width of the border.

In Problems 23–26, find the value of x for the given area of the shaded region.

23.

Area of the shaded region is 30 square yards

24.

Area of the shaded region is 790 square yards

25.

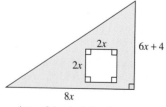

Area of the shaded region is 228 square yards

26.

Area of the shaded region is approximately 72.43 square yards

27. A picture is 20 inches long and 25 inches high. The picture is placed on a mat so that the mat's uniformly wide strip shows as a border for the picture. The perimeter of the mat is 114 inches. Find the width of the mat's strip that surrounds the picture.

28. A gardener has 96 feet of fencing to enclose a rectangular garden and a 2-foot wide surrounding border. If the length of the garden is 3 times its width, what are its dimensions?

29. A machine produces open boxes using rectangular pieces of metal measuring 15 centimeters by 25 centimeters. The machine cuts equal-sized squares from each corner and then shapes the metal into an open box by turning up the sides. If the area of the bottom of the box is 231 square centimeters, find the length of each side of the square that is cut from the four corners.

30. An open box is to be made using a rectangular piece of cardboard whose length is 4 centimeters greater than its width. (See the figure at the top of the next column.) Equal squares measuring 3 centimeters on a side are cut from each corner of the cardboard and the sides that remain are folded up to form the box. If the volume of the resulting box is 180 cubic centimeters, find the dimensions of the original piece of cardboard.

31. A person 5 feet tall is standing 18 feet from the base of a streetlight. If the light is at the top of a 16-foot pole, how long is the person's shadow that is cast from the streetlight?

32. A person 6 feet tall is standing 10 feet from the base of a streetlight. If the light is at the top of an 18-foot pole, how long is the person's shadow that is cast from the streetlight?

33. A water tank has the shape of an inverted right circular cone of altitude 20 feet and base radius 5 feet. How much water is in the tank when the water is 8 feet deep?

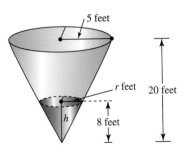

34. A water tank has the shape of an inverted right circular cone of altitude 6 meters and base radius 3 meters. How much water is in the tank when the water is 3 meters deep?

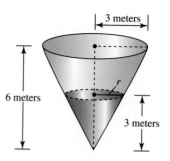

In Problems 35–38, the area of each plane figure is given. Find the value of x.

35.

Area: 48 square meters

36.

Area: 66 square meters

37.

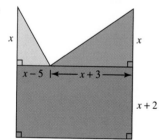

Area: 76 square meters

38.

Area: 159 square meters

39. The Norman window in the figure to the right of Problem 35 has a rectangular base and a semicircular top. If 2500 square centimeters of glass are used in making the window, what is the area of each of the four smaller rectangular regions?

40. The figure shows a rectangle that is 8 meters by 6 meters. If the area of the cross is equal to the sum of the areas of the four smaller rectangles, what is the width of the cross?

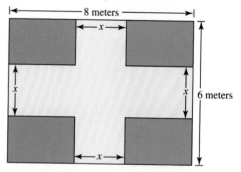

41. A storage bin consists of a cylinder and a roof that is a cone. The height of the roof is half the height of the cylinder, and the total volume of the bin is $11{,}200\,\pi$ cubic feet. Find the height of the cylinder.

42. By how many meters should the radius of a 10-meter circle be increased so that the area increases by 5π square meters?

43. When drawing a rectangle, many artists and architects use a certain ratio of the length to the width to achieve a satisfying visual effect. This ratio, called the golden ratio, can be determined by answering the following question from Euclid's *Elements*:

> Divide a line segment such that the ratio of the larger part to the whole is equal to the ratio of the smaller part to the larger part.

a. Use Euclid's statement and the figure below to set up a proportion. Solve the proportion for x. The exact value of the golden ratio is x to 1.

b. Which part of the figure in the next column do you find most appealing? Explain what this means in terms of the ratio that you determined in part (a).

(a)   (b)

(c)

(d)

44. A long rectangular sheet of metal, 12 centimeters wide, is to be made into a rain gutter by turning up two sides at right angles to the sheet.
  a. If x represents the length of each side that is turned up to form the rain gutter, write a model in terms of x that describes the cross-sectional area of the gutter.
  b. How many centimeters of metal should be turned up to give the gutter a capacity of 16 square centimeters?

Technology Problems

45. A rectangular field is to be fenced on three sides with 1000 meters of fencing. As shown in the figure, the fourth side is a straight river's edge that will not be fenced.

a. Find the dimensions of the field so that the area of the enclosure is 120,000 square meters.

b. Use a graphing utility to graph the area model that you obtained in part (a). Experiment with the range setting until your graph looks like the one shown in the figure on the right. Then trace along the graph and find the point whose coordinates correspond to your algebraic solution in part (a).

c. What is a reasonable estimate of the maximum area that can be enclosed? Trace along the graph and verify this estimate by finding the coordinates of the highest point on the graph. What are the dimensions of the rectangle of maximum area?

d. Does the rectangle enclosed in part (a) make the best use of the 1000 meters of fencing? Explain.

46. Consider the collection of all rectangles whose perimeter is 150 feet, represented by the green rectangle on page 158.
  a. Write a model for the area of all such rectangles.
  b. What values of x are meaningful in this situation? Why?

c. Use a graphing utility to determine the smallest viewing rectangle that will give a relatively complete algebraic picture of the area model and graph the model. (The shape of the graph in Problem 45 should be helpful.)

d. Describe the behavior of the graph that appears in the viewing rectangle, relating this behavior to the area of rectangle.

47. A rock on the moon and a rock on Earth are thrown into the air with an initial velocity of 48 feet per second by a 6-foot person. The position of the rock above the ground (s, in feet) after t seconds is described by

$$s_{\text{Moon}} = -2.7t^2 + 48t + 6$$

$$s_{\text{Earth}} = -16t^2 + 48t + 6$$

a. Graph both position models.

b. Describe differences that you observe in the graphs. How do you account for these differences?

c. Use the graphs to determine how much higher the rock is on the moon than on Earth after 3 seconds. Use the models to verify this observation.

48. The demand for a product tends to decrease as the price increases. A company finds that they can sell x units of a product at a price of $50 - 0.0001x$ dollars per unit.

a. Graph the *demand equation* $y = 50 - 0.0001x$ and describe what the graph indicates in terms of various selling prices and the number of units sold at that price.

b. Graph the revenue model. (Revenue = the number of units sold times the price per unit.)

c. Use the TRACE feature to move the cursor along the graph to approximate the number of units that will maximize revenue. At maximum revenue, what is the price per unit?

d. Use the graph to indicate a revenue amount that will never be obtained.

e. Use the graph to determine the number of units and the corresponding price that yield a revenue of $960,000. If you were to determine the price of this product, what price would you charge and why?

49. Use a graphing utility to graph the model for the cross-sectional area obtained in Problem 44. Does 16 square centimeters give the rain gutter its maximum capacity?

Writing in Mathematics

50. Write and solve an algebraic word problem similar to Problems 11 and 12 on page 152 using the figures for high school graduates shown in the graph.

51. Describe the changes that would take place in solving part (a) of Problem 45 on page 157 if the rectangular field is to be enclosed away from the river with fencing used along all sides of the rectangle.

52. Why should an algebraic word problem be checked using the verbal conditions given in the problem rather than the equation that is modeled from these verbal conditions?

53. Reread the description of the position model that precedes Problem 15 on page 153. Explain the difference between the following situations in terms of writing the appropriate position models.

A set of keys is thrown upward from a 300-foot building with an initial velocity of 20 feet per second.

A set of keys is accidently dropped from a 300-foot building.

Critical Thinking Problems

54. The price of an item is increased by 50%. When the item does not sell, it is reduced by 50% of the increased price. If the final price is $280, what was the original price? When the price is increased by 50% and then reduced by 50%, what percent represents the net reduction in price?

55. Four meters of wire is used to form a circle and a square. Let x represent the amount of wire used to form the square and let $4 - x$ represent the amount of wire used to form the circle.

a. Write a model in terms of x representing the total area enclosed by the square and the circle.

b. A graph of the model in part (a) indicates that the maximum total area that can be enclosed is approximately 1.273 square meters. Find the side of the square and the radius of the circle so that the total area model in part (a) results in 1.273 square meters. Explain what this means about how to use the wire so that a maximum area is enclosed.

56. A Norman window has a rectangular base and a semi-circular top. The perimeter of the Norman window shown in the figure is 16 meters.

a. Write a model for the area of the Norman window using one variable.

b. Find x and y so that the area of the Norman window is 16 square meters.

57. Use the description of the position model that precedes Problem 15 on page 153 to answer this problem:

A ball is dropped from a 576-foot skyscraper. With what initial velocity should a second ball be thrown straight downward 3 seconds later so that the two balls hit the ground at the same time?

Group Activity Problem

58. This problem is intended as a group learning experience and is appropriate for groups of three to five people. Before working on the various parts of the problem, reread the description of the position model that precedes Problem 15 on page 153.

a. Drop a ball from a height of 3 feet, 6 feet, and 12 feet. Record the number of seconds it takes for the ball to hit the ground.

b. For each of the three initial positions, use the position model to determine the time required for the ball to hit the ground.

c. What factors might result in differences between the times that you recorded and the times indicated by the model?

d. What appears to be happening to the time required for a free-falling object to hit the ground as its initial position is doubled? Verify this observation algebraically and with a graphing utility.

e. Repeat part (a) using a sheet of paper rather than a ball. What differences do you observe? What factor seems to be ignored in the mathematical model?

f. What is meant by the acceleration of gravity and how does this number appear in the position model for a free-falling object?

**Solutions
Manual**

Tutorial

**Video
3**

SECTION 1.4 Other Types of Equations

Objectives

1 Solve polynomial equations by factoring.
2 Solve equations that are quadratic in form.
3 Solve radical equations.
4 Solve equations with rational exponents.
5 Solve applied modeling problems.

Our focus in this section is on solving certain kinds of polynomial equations and on equations involving radicals and rational exponents.

| Solve polynomial equations by factoring.

Polynomial Equations

The linear and quadratic equations that we studied in the first two sections of this chapter can be thought of as polynomial equations of degree 1 and 2, respectively. Some polynomial equations of degree greater than 2 can be solved by factoring.

In solving $3x^4 = 27x^2$, be careful not to divide both sides by x^2. If you do, you'll lose 0 as a solution. In general, do not divide both sides of an equation by a variable since that variable might take on the value 0 and you cannot divide by 0.

a. $3x^4 = 27x^2$

Use your graphing utility to graph $y = 3x^4 - 27x^2$ using the following range setting:

Xmin = -6, Xmax = 6,

Xscl = 1, Ymin = -100,

Ymax = 100, Yscl = 50.

The x-intercepts are -3, 0, and 3, corresponding to the equation's solutions.

b. $2x^3 + 3x^2 - 8x - 12 = 0$

Graph

$y = 2x^3 + 3x^2 - 8x - 12$

using the range setting

Xmin = -5, Xmax = 5,

Xscl = 1, Ymin = -20,

Ymax = 5, Yscl = 5

Using the [TRACE] and [ZOOM] features for further clarification, you can see that the x-intercepts are -2, -1.5, and 2, corresponding to the equation's solutions.

(continued)

2 Solve equations that are quadratic in form.

EXAMPLE I   Solving Polynomial Equations by Factoring

Solve by factoring:

a. $3x^4 = 27x^2$ **b.** $2x^3 + 3x^2 - 8x - 12 = 0$ **c.** $x^4 - 8x^2 - 9 = 0$

Solution

a.
$$3x^4 = 27x^2$$ This is the given equation.

$$3x^4 - 27x^2 = 0$$ Set this fourth-degree polynomial equation equal to 0.

$$3x^2(x^2 - 9) = 0$$ Factor $3x^2$ from each term.

$$3x^2 = 0 \quad \text{or} \quad x^2 - 9 = 0$$ Set each factor equal to 0.

$$x^2 = 0 \qquad\qquad x^2 = 9$$ Solve the resulting equations.

$$x = 0 \qquad\qquad x = \pm 3$$ Use the square root method to solve $x^2 = 9$.

The three solutions, 0, -3, and 3, can be checked by substitution into the original equation to verify that the solution set is $\{-3, 0, 3\}$.

b. $2x^3 + 3x^2 - 8x - 12 = 0$ This is the given equation.

$$x^2(2x + 3) - 4(2x + 3) = 0$$ Factor x^2 from the first two terms and -4 from the last two terms.

$$(2x + 3)(x^2 - 4) = 0$$ Factor out $2x + 3$.

$$2x + 3 = 0 \quad \text{or} \quad x^2 - 4 = 0$$ Set each factor equal to 0.

$$2x = -3 \qquad\qquad x^2 = 4$$ Solve for x.

$$x = -\frac{3}{2} \qquad\qquad x = \pm 2$$

The solution set is $\left\{-2, -\frac{3}{2}, 2\right\}$. Observe that the original third-degree (cubic) equation has three solutions. Check these solutions in the original equation.

c. $x^4 - 8x^2 - 9 = 0$ This is the given equation.

$$(x^2 - 9)(x^2 + 1) = 0$$ Factor.

$$x^2 - 9 = 0 \quad \text{or} \quad x^2 + 1 = 0$$ Set each factor equal to 0.

$$x^2 = 9 \qquad\qquad x^2 = -1$$ Solve for x.

$$x = \pm\sqrt{9} \qquad\qquad x = \pm\sqrt{-1}$$ Use the square root method.

$$= \pm 3 \qquad\qquad = \pm i$$

The solution set is $\{-3, 3, -i, i\}$.   ■

Polynomial Equations That Are Quadratic in Form

The equation of Example 1c is *quadratic in form*. Its *structure* is quadratic, which can be seen by replacing x^2 by t.

$$x^4 - 8x^2 - 9 = 0$$ This is the equation of Example 1c.

$$(x^2)^2 - 8x^2 - 9 = 0$$ Replace x^2 with t.

$$t^2 - 8t - 9 = 0$$ This is a quadratic equation in t.

Before we solve a polynomial equation that is quadratic in form, let's consider the following definition.

Using technology (cont.)

c. $x^4 - 8x^2 - 9 = 0$
Graph $y = x^4 - 8x^2 - 9$
using the range setting

Xmin $= -5$, Xmax $= 5$,

Xscl $= 1$, Ymin $= -30$,

Ymax $= 30$, Yscl $= 5$

The real solutions $(-3$
and 3) are the only ones that
appear as x-intercepts.

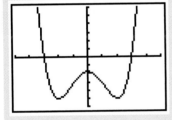

Definition of an equation that is quadratic in form

An equation is *quadratic in form* if it can be written in the form

$$at^2 + bt + c = 0$$

where t is an algebraic expression and $a \neq 0$.

This definition implies that we introduce a substitution so that the quadratic-in-form equation becomes a quadratic equation in t. Let's see how this is done.

EXAMPLE 2 **Solving a Polynomial Equation That Is Quadratic in Form**

Solve: $(x^2 + 3x)^2 - 8(x^2 + 3x) - 20 = 0$

Solution

If we let $t = x^2 + 3x$, the equation can be written as $t^2 - 8t - 20 = 0$ which, in turn, can be solved by factoring or the quadratic formula.

$$(x^2 + 3x)^2 - 8(x^2 + 3x) - 20 = 0 \qquad \text{This is the given equation.}$$
$$\quad t^2 \qquad\quad -8 \quad\; t \qquad\quad -20 = 0 \qquad \text{Let } t = x^2 + 3x.$$

We can solve this quadratic equation in t by factoring.

$$(t - 10)(t + 2) = 0 \qquad\qquad \text{Factor.}$$

$$t - 10 = 0 \quad \text{or} \quad t + 2 = 0 \qquad \text{Set each factor equal to 0.}$$

$$t = 10 \qquad\qquad t = -2 \qquad \text{Solve for } t.$$

The solution process is incomplete because we must solve the original equation for x. However, because we know that $t = x^2 + 3x$, we can replace t with $x^2 + 3x$ in our work up to this point.

$$t = 10 \qquad \text{or} \qquad t = -2 \qquad \text{This was our last step.}$$

$$x^2 + 3x = 10 \qquad \text{or} \quad x^2 + 3x = -2 \qquad \text{Because } t = x^2 + 3x, \text{ replace } t \text{ with } x^2 + 3x.$$

$$x^2 + 3x - 10 = 0 \qquad\quad x^2 + 3x + 2 = 0 \qquad \text{Write each quadratic equation in standard form.}$$

$$(x + 5)(x - 2) = 0 \qquad (x + 2)(x + 1) = 0 \qquad \text{Factor.}$$

$$x + 5 = 0 \quad \text{or} \quad x - 2 = 0 \quad x + 2 = 0 \quad \text{or} \quad x + 1 = 0 \qquad \text{Set each factor equal to 0.}$$

$$x = -5 \qquad\quad x = 2 \qquad\quad x = -2 \qquad\quad x = -1 \qquad \text{Solve for } x.$$

The solution set of the original equation is $\{-5, 2, -2, -1\}$, which can be verified by substitution or with a graphing utility. ∎

> **Solution procedure for equations that are quadratic in form**
>
> ***Solving equations that are quadratic in form***
>
> $$ax^n + bx^{n/2} + c = 0$$
>
> 1. Introduce the substitution $t = x^{n/2}$.
> 2. Use this substitution to express $ax^n + bx^{n/2} + c = 0$ as a quadratic equation in t.
>
> $$a(x^{n/2})^2 + bx^{n/2} + c = 0$$
> $$at^2 + bt + c = 0$$
>
> 3. Solve the quadratic equation for t.
> 4. Solve for x by substituting the value(s) of t into $x^{n/2} = t$.

3 Solve radical equations.

Equations Involving Radicals

Solving equations involving radicals often involves raising both sides of the equation to the same power. All solutions of the original equation are also solutions of the resulting equation. However, the resulting equation may have some extra solutions that do not satisfy the original equation. Because the resulting equation may not be equivalent to the original equation, the solution process always must be completed by substituting all possibilities in the original equation to determine whether they are really solutions. Let's see exactly how this works.

EXAMPLE 3   Solving an Equation Involving a Radical

Solve: $x + \sqrt{26 - 11x} = 4$

Solution

To solve this equation algebraically, we can isolate the radical expression $\sqrt{26 - 11x}$ on one side of the equation. By squaring both sides of the equation, we can then eliminate the square root.

$x + \sqrt{26 - 11x} = 4$	This is the given equation.
$\sqrt{26 - 11x} = 4 - x$	Isolate the radical by subtracting x from both sides.
$(\sqrt{26 - 11x})^2 = (4 - x)^2$	Square both sides.
$26 - 11x = 16 - 8x + x^2$	
$0 = x^2 + 3x - 10$	Write the quadratic equation in standard form.
$0 = (x + 5)(x - 2)$	Factor.
$x + 5 = 0 \quad$ or $\quad x - 2 = 0$	Set each factor equal to 0.
$x = -5 \qquad\qquad x = 2$	Solve for x.

Complete the solution process by checking both proposed solutions.

$$x + \sqrt{26 - 11x} = 4 \qquad \text{This is the original equation.}$$

Using technology

The graph of

$$y = x + \sqrt{26 - 11x} - 4$$

is shown in a $[-10, 3]$ by $[-4, 3]$ viewing rectangle. The x-intercepts are -5 and 2, verifying $\{-5, 2\}$ as the solution set.

Check −5:

$$-5 + \sqrt{26 - 11(-5)} \overset{?}{=} 4$$

$$-5 + \sqrt{81} \overset{?}{=} 4$$

$$-5 + 9 \overset{?}{=} 4$$

$$4 = 4 \checkmark$$

Check 2:

$$2 + \sqrt{26 - 11(2)} \overset{?}{=} 4$$

Substitute −5 and 2, respectively.

$$2 + \sqrt{4} \overset{?}{=} 4$$

Simplify.

$$2 + 2 \overset{?}{=} 4$$

$$4 = 4 \checkmark$$

Both −5 and 2 are solutions.

The solution set is $\{-5, 2\}$.   ∎

The algebraic solution of radical equations with two or more square root expressions involves isolating a radical, squaring both sides, and then repeating this process. Let's consider an example containing two square root expressions.

EXAMPLE 4   **Solving an Equation Involving Two Radicals**

Solve: $\sqrt{3x + 1} - \sqrt{x + 4} = 1$

Solution

$$\sqrt{3x + 1} - \sqrt{x + 4} = 1$$

This is the given equation.

$$\sqrt{3x + 1} = \sqrt{x + 4} + 1$$

Isolate the radicals by adding $\sqrt{x + 4}$ to both sides.

$$(\sqrt{3x + 1})^2 = (\sqrt{x + 4} + 1)^2$$

Square both sides.

$$3x + 1 = x + 4 + 2\sqrt{x + 4} + 1$$

On the right, use $(A + B)^2 = A^2 + 2AB + B^2$.

$$3x + 1 = x + 5 + 2\sqrt{x + 4}$$

Combine numerical terms on the right.

$$2x - 4 = 2\sqrt{x + 4}$$

Isolate $2\sqrt{x + 4}$, the radical term, by subtracting $x + 5$ from both sides.

$$x - 2 = \sqrt{x + 4}$$

Divide both sides by 2.

$$(x - 2)^2 = (\sqrt{x + 4})^2$$

Square both sides.

$$x^2 - 4x + 4 = x + 4$$

Multiply.

$$x^2 - 5x = 0$$

Write the quadratic equation in standard form by subtracting $x + 4$ from both sides.

$$x(x - 5) = 0$$

Factor.

$$x = 0 \quad \text{or} \quad x - 5 = 0$$

Set each factor equal to 0.

$$x = 0 \qquad\qquad x = 5$$

Solve for x.

Complete the solution process by checking both proposed solutions.

Using technology

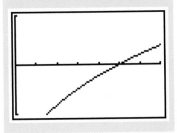

The graph of

$$y = \sqrt{3x + 1} - \sqrt{x + 4} - 1$$

has only one x-intercept at 5. This verifies that the solution set for the given equation is $\{5\}$.

Check 0:

$$\sqrt{3x + 1} - \sqrt{x + 4} = 1$$

Check 5:

$$\sqrt{3x + 1} - \sqrt{x + 4} = 1$$

$$\sqrt{3 \cdot 0 + 1} - \sqrt{0 + 4} \overset{?}{=} 1 \qquad\qquad \sqrt{3 \cdot 5 + 1} - \sqrt{5 + 4} \overset{?}{=} 1$$
$$\sqrt{1} - \sqrt{4} \overset{?}{=} 1 \qquad\qquad \sqrt{16} - \sqrt{9} \overset{?}{=} 1$$
$$1 - 2 \overset{?}{=} 1 \qquad\qquad 4 - 3 \overset{?}{=} 1$$
$$-1 = 1 \text{ False} \qquad\qquad 1 = 1 \checkmark$$

This final step in the solution process indicates that 0 is not a solution. The solution set is {5}.   ∎

4 Solve equations with rational exponents.

Equations with Rational Exponents

We turn now to equations in the form $x^{m/n} = k$ in which m and n are positive integers, $\frac{m}{n}$ is in lowest terms, and k is a real number. To solve such equations, we raise both sides to the $\frac{n}{m}$th power.

If m is even:

$$x^{m/n} = k$$
$$(x^{m/n})^{n/m} = \pm k^{n/m}$$
$$x = \pm k^{n/m}$$

If m is odd:

$$x^{m/n} = k$$
$$(x^{m/n})^{n/m} = k^{n/m}$$
$$x = k^{n/m}$$

| **EXAMPLE 5** | **Solving Equations Involving Rational Exponents** |

Solve:

a. $3x^{3/4} - 6 = 0$ **b.** $x^{2/3} - \dfrac{3}{4} = -\dfrac{1}{2}$ **c.** $(x^2 - 4x + 7)^{3/2} - 2 = 6$

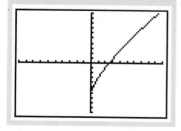
Solution

Our goal in each solution is to isolate the expression with the rational exponent, which is equivalent to isolating the radical expression.

a. $3x^{3/4} - 6 = 0$ This is the given equation; we will isolate $x^{3/4}$.

$\qquad 3x^{3/4} = 6$ Add 6 to both sides.

$\qquad x^{3/4} = 2$ Divide both sides by 3.

$\qquad (x^{3/4})^{4/3} = 2^{4/3}$ Raise both sides to the $\frac{4}{3}$th power. Since $\frac{m}{n} = \frac{3}{4}$ and m is odd, the $\pm$ symbol is not necessary.

$\qquad x = 2^{4/3}$ $(x^{3/4})^{3/4} = x^{3/4 \cdot 4/3} = x^1 = x$

Check

$\qquad 3x^{3/4} - 6 = 0$ This is the original equation.

$\qquad 3(2^{4/3})^{3/4} - 6 \overset{?}{=} 0$ Substitute the proposed solution.

$\qquad 3 \cdot 2 - 6 \overset{?}{=} 0$ $(2^{4/3})^{3/4} = 2^{4/3 \cdot 3/4} = 2^1 = 2$

$\qquad 0 = 0 \checkmark$ Thus, $2^{4/3}$ is a solution.

The solution set is $\{2^{4/3}\}$.

b. $x^{2/3} - \dfrac{3}{4} = -\dfrac{1}{2}$ This is the given equation.

$$x^{2/3} = \frac{1}{4} \qquad \text{Add } \tfrac{3}{4} \text{ to both sides.}$$

$$(x^{2/3})^{3/2} = \pm\left(\frac{1}{4}\right)^{3/2} \qquad \text{Raise both sides to the } \tfrac{3}{2} \text{ power. Since } \frac{m}{n} = \frac{2}{3} \text{ and } m \text{ is even,}$$
the $\pm$ symbol is necessary.

$$x = \pm\frac{1}{8} \qquad (\tfrac{1}{4})^{3/2} = (\sqrt{\tfrac{1}{4}})^3 = (\tfrac{1}{2})^3 = \tfrac{1}{8}$$

Take a moment to verify that the solution set is $\{-\frac{1}{8}, \frac{1}{8}\}$.

c.
$$(x^2 - 4x + 7)^{3/2} - 2 = 6 \qquad \text{This is the given equation.}$$
$$(x^2 - 4x + 7)^{3/2} = 8 \qquad \text{Add 2 to both sides.}$$
$$[(x^2 - 4x + 7)^{3/2}]^{2/3} = 8^{2/3} \qquad \text{Raise both sides to the } \tfrac{2}{3} \text{ power.}$$
$$x^2 - 4x + 7 = 4 \qquad 8^{2/3} = (\sqrt[3]{8})^2 = 2^2 = 4$$
$$x^2 - 4x + 3 = 0 \qquad \text{Write the quadratic equation in standard form.}$$
$$(x - 1)(x - 3) = 0 \qquad \text{Factor.}$$
$$x - 1 = 0 \quad \text{or} \quad x - 3 = 0 \qquad \text{Set each factor equal to 0.}$$
$$x = 1 \qquad\qquad x = 3 \qquad \text{Solve for } x.$$

Both proposed solutions can be shown to satisfy the original equation, indicating that the solution set is $\{1, 3\}$. ■

Some equations involving rational exponents are quadratic in form and can be solved using an appropriate substitution. Example 6 illustrates this.

EXAMPLE 6   **Solving an Equation Containing Rational Exponents That Is Quadratic in Form**

Solve: $5x^{2/3} + 11x^{1/3} + 2 = 0$

Solution

$$5x^{2/3} + 11x^{1/3} + 2 = 0 \qquad \text{This is the given equation.}$$
$$5(x^{1/3})^2 + 11(x^{1/3}) + 2 = 0$$
$$5t^2 + 11t + 2 = 0 \qquad \text{Let } t = x^{1/3}.$$

We can now solve this quadratic equation in t by factoring.

$$(5t + 1)(t + 2) = 0 \qquad \text{Factor.}$$
$$5t + 1 = 0 \quad \text{or} \quad t + 2 = 0 \qquad \text{Set each factor equal to 0.}$$
$$t = -\frac{1}{5} \qquad\qquad t = -2 \qquad \text{Solve for } t.$$
$$x^{1/3} = -\frac{1}{5} \qquad\qquad x^{1/3} = -2 \qquad \text{Replace } t \text{ with } x^{1/3}.$$
$$(x^{1/3})^3 = \left(-\frac{1}{5}\right)^3 \qquad (x^{1/3})^3 = (-2)^3 \qquad \text{Solve for } x \text{ by cubing both sides of each equation.}$$
$$x = -\frac{1}{125} \qquad\qquad x = -8$$

Check these values to verify that the solution set is $\{-\frac{1}{125}, -8\}$. ■

Using technology

We can confirm the solutions to

$(x^2 - 4x + 7)^{3/2} - 2 = 6$

by graphing

$y = (x^2 - 4x + 7)^{3/2} - 8$.

The x-intercepts are 1 and 3, verifying that $\{1, 3\}$ is the solution set.

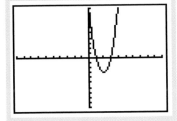

Study tip

It is easy to recognize an equation containing rational exponents that is quadratic in form. When the equation is written in descending powers, the exponent on the middle term is half the exponent on the leading term.

$5x^{2/3} + 11x^{1/3} + 2 = 0 \qquad \frac{1}{3} = \frac{1}{2} \cdot \frac{2}{3}$

5 Solve applied modeling problems.

Rene Magritte, Belgian (1898–1967) "Time Transfixed" 1938, oil on canvas, 147 × 98.7 cm. Joseph Winterbotham Collection, 1970.426. Photograph © 1997, The Art Institute of Chicago, All Rights Reserved. © 1998 C. Herscovici, Brussels / Artists Rights Society (ARS), New York.

Mathematical Models

We have seen a model that describes the position of free-falling objects, derived by Isaac Newton (1642–1727). In Newton's view of the world, mass, length, and time appear identical to every person. By contrast, in Albert Einstein's special theory of relativity, time slows down, mass increases, and length in the direction of motion decreases from the point of view of an observer watching an object moving at a velocity close to the speed of light. Einstein's theory, verified with experiments in atomic physics, forms the basis of Example 7.

EXAMPLE 7　Einstein's Special Relativity Models

Einstein's equations relate the mass, time, and length at rest (M_0, T_0, L_0) to the mass, time, and length (M, T, L) for a velocity v. The speed of light, c, is approximately 186,000 miles per second.

$$M = \frac{M_0}{\sqrt{1 - \dfrac{v^2}{c^2}}} \qquad T = \frac{T_0}{\sqrt{1 - \dfrac{v^2}{c^2}}} \qquad L = L_0 \sqrt{1 - \frac{v^2}{c^2}}$$

How fast would a futuristic starship that is 600 meters tall have to move so that it would measure only 84 meters tall from the perspective of an observer who looks up and sees the ship pass by?

Solution

600 meters

Starship at Rest

84 meters

Change in starship's dimensions when moving at 99% of light's speed when viewed by an observer

Figure 1.13

$$L = L_0 \sqrt{1 - \frac{v^2}{c^2}}$$
This is Einstein's model for length.

$$84 = 600 \sqrt{1 - \frac{v^2}{c^2}}$$
Substitute L_0 (length at rest) = 600 and L (length at the velocity we must determine) = 84.

$$0.14 = \sqrt{1 - \frac{v^2}{c^2}}$$
Divide both sides by 600.

$$0.0196 = 1 - \frac{v^2}{c^2}$$
Square both sides.

$$0.0196c^2 = c^2 - v^2$$
Multiply both sides by c^2. Remember that c, the speed of light, is approximately 186,000 miles per second.

$$v^2 = 0.9804c^2$$
Isolate v^2 on the left.

$$v = \sqrt{0.9804c^2}$$
Assume that the starship is moving upward, so take only the positive root.

$$v \approx 0.99c$$

If the 600-meter tall futuristic starship moves at 99% the speed of light (approximately 184,140 miles per second), it will measure only 84 meters tall from the perspective of our stationary viewer. A before and after picture of the starship is shown in Figure 1.13. Observe that lengths perpendicular to the direction of motion are unchanged by the effect of speed, so the width of the starship remains unchanged. ∎

Figure 1.14

Figure 1.15

Steps 1 and 2. Represent unknowns in terms of x.

Step 3. Write an equation that models the verbal conditions.

Step 4. Solve the equation and answer the problem's question.

In Example 7, we were given the model needed to solve the problem. Often we must create a model based on a problem's conditions, and sometimes these conditions are not given explicitly. Furthermore, in many situations we must bring a knowledge of some basic idea to the problem to obtain a model. This is the situation in Example 8, where modeling depends on the Pythagorean Theorem.

A right triangle like the one in Figure 1.14 will be used to model the problem. We will need to obtain an expression for the hypotenuse in terms of x. We can apply the Pythagorean Theorem:

$$(\text{Hypotenuse})^2 = (\text{Leg})^2 + (\text{Leg})^2$$
$$c^2 = x^2 + 8^2$$

$$c^2 = x^2 + 64$$

Since the length of the hypotenuse must be positive, we take only the positive square root.

$$c = \sqrt{x^2 + 64}$$

EXAMPLE 8 Creating a Mathematical Model

A bird flies from point A on an island that is located 8 miles off shore from point D (see Figure 1.15). Traveling over the water from point A to point B, the bird uses 15 kilocalories (kcal) of energy per mile. The bird then flies from point B to its nest at point C, using 10 kcal of energy per mile over land. Find the location distance from point B to point D so that precisely 240 kcal of energy is used during the entire flight.

Solution

Let

$$x = \text{the distance from point } B \text{ to point } D$$

$$\sqrt{x^2 + 64} = \text{the distance that the bird flies over water}$$
$$\text{(by the Pythagorean Theorem)}$$

$$15 - x = \text{the distance that the bird flies over land}$$

Energy used over water	plus	Energy used over land	must equal	240 Kcal of energy
$15\sqrt{x^2 + 64}$	$+$	$10(15 - x)$	$=$	240

$$15\sqrt{x^2 + 64} + 10(15 - x) = 240 \qquad \text{This is the equation that models the given conditions.}$$

$$15\sqrt{x^2 + 64} = 240 - 10(15 - x) \qquad \text{Isolate the radical.}$$

$$15\sqrt{x^2 + 64} = 90 + 10x \qquad \text{Simplify on the right.}$$

$$3\sqrt{x^2 + 64} = 18 + 2x$$

To keep the numbers smaller, divide both sides by 5.

$$(3\sqrt{x^2 + 64})^2 = (18 + 2x)^2$$

Square both sides.

$$9(x^2 + 64) = 324 + 72x + 4x^2$$

Multiply.

$$9x^2 + 576 = 324 + 72x + 4x^2$$

Use the distributive property on the left.

$$5x^2 - 72x + 252 = 0$$

Write the quadratic equation in standard form.

$$(x - 6)(5x - 42) = 0$$

Factor (or use the quadratic formula.)

$$x - 6 = 0 \qquad \text{or} \qquad 5x - 42 = 0$$

Set each factor equal to 0.

$$x = 6 \qquad \text{or} \qquad x = \tfrac{42}{5} = 8.4$$

Solve the resulting equations.

Step 5. Check the proposed solution in the original wording of the problem.

Look again at Figure 1.15, repeated at the left. The two values for x mean that the bird should reach land and end its flight over water at point B either 6 miles or 8.4 miles from point D so that precisely 240 kcal of energy is used during the entire flight. In other words, the distance from point B to point D is either 6 or 8.4 miles. ■

Discover for yourself

Check these solutions using the given condition of 240 kcal of energy. What is the distance from A to C? (Use the Pythagorean Theorem.) How much energy is needed for that direct water route?

Using technology

The graph of
$$y = 15\sqrt{x^2 + 64} + 10(15 - x)$$
shows that the energy the bird uses in flight depends on how far (x) from point D it reaches land. The graph on the left, obtained using the range setting

Xmin = 0, Xmax = 15, Xscl = 1, Ymin = 0, Ymax = 300, Yscl = 15

and tracing along the curve, shows the energy used if the bird reaches land 15 miles from point D. This means that the entire flight is over water, and 255 kcal of energy must be used. The most efficient path in terms of using the least amount of energy can be determined by finding the lowest point on the curve. Using the minimum value feature of the graphing utility, this point is shown on the right. In practical terms, if the bird comes ashore approximately 7.2 miles from point D, a minimum energy of approximately 239.4 kcal is expended on the entire flight.

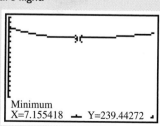

ENRICHMENT ESSAY

Einstein's Model and the Clock Paradox

Einstein's model

$$T = \frac{T_0}{\sqrt{1 - \dfrac{v^2}{c^2}}}$$

relates the passage of time T at a velocity v to the passage of time at rest, T_0. In the model, c is the speed of light, approximately 186,000 miles per second. If a futuristic starship moves at a velocity approaching the speed of light ($v \approx c$), the denominator in the model is close to zero, resulting in very large values for time. This means that time passage for those of us waiting on Earth is much faster than that for the space travelers. The travelers return to Earth in what seems to them to be a few years, though on Earth many centuries have passed. This effect, called the clock paradox, means they return to a futuristic world in which their friends and loved ones would be long dead.

Edward Kienholtz (1927–1994) "The Wait" 1964–65. Tableau: wood, fabric, polyester resin, flock, metal, bones, glass, paper, leather, varnish, b&w photographs, taxidermed cat, live parakeet, wicker and plastic. 13 units, overall: 80 × 160 × 34 in. (203.2 × 406.4 × 213.4 cm). Gift of the Howard and Jean Lipman Foundation, Inc. 66.49a–m. Photograph copyright © 1997: Whitney Museum of American Art, New York. Photography by: Jerry L. Thompson, N.Y. 1994.

PROBLEM SET 1.4

Practice Problems

Find the solution set for each equation in Problems 1–48. Check your proposed solutions by substituting into the original equation or by using a graphing utility.

1. $3x^4 = 48x^2$

2. $5x^4 = 20x^2$

3. $3x^3 + 2x^2 - 12x - 8 = 0$

4. $4x^3 - 12x^2 - 9x + 27 = 0$

5. $2x - 3 = 8x^3 - 12x^2$

6. $x + 1 = 9x^3 + 9x^2$

7. $4y^3 - 2 = y - 8y^2$

8. $9y^2 + 8 = 4y + 18y^2$

9. $x^4 - 10x^2 + 9 = 0$

10. $x^4 - 8x^2 + 15 = 0$

11. $6x^4 - 7x^2 + 2 = 0$

12. $8x^4 - 14x^2 + 3 = 0$

13. $3x^3 - 12x^2 - 15x = 0$

14. $4x^3 - 8x^2 - 12x = 0$

15. $(x^2 - x)^2 - 14(x^2 - x) + 24 = 0$

16. $(x^2 - 2x)^2 - 11(x^2 - 2x) + 24 = 0$

17. $\left(y - \dfrac{8}{y}\right)^2 + 5\left(y - \dfrac{8}{y}\right) - 14 = 0$

18. $\left(y - \dfrac{10}{y}\right)^2 + 6\left(y - \dfrac{10}{y}\right) - 27 = 0$

19. $6\left(\dfrac{2w}{w-3}\right)^2 = 5\left(\dfrac{2w}{w-3}\right) + 6$

20. $4\left(\dfrac{w+1}{w-1}\right)^2 = 8\left(\dfrac{w+1}{w-1}\right) - 3$

21. $\sqrt{3x + 18} = x$

22. $\sqrt{20 - 8x} = x$

23. $x - \sqrt{2x + 5} = 5$

24. $x - \sqrt{x + 11} = 1$

25. $\sqrt{2y - 3} - \sqrt{y - 2} = 1$

26. $\sqrt{2y + 3} + \sqrt{y - 2} = 2$

27. $\sqrt{3\sqrt{x} + 1} = \sqrt{3x - 5}$

28. $\sqrt{1 + 4\sqrt{x}} = 1 + \sqrt{x}$

29. $\sqrt{6x - 2} = \sqrt{2x + 3} - \sqrt{4x - 1}$

30. $\sqrt{x + 4} + \sqrt{x - 1} = \sqrt{x - 4}$

31. $\sqrt{5x + 1} = \sqrt{3x + 4} + \sqrt{x - 6}$

32. $\sqrt{2x - 5} = \sqrt{3x - 5} - \sqrt{x - 6}$

33. $(x - 4)^{3/2} = 8$

34. $(x + 5)^{3/2} = 8$

35. $(x - 4)^{2/3} = 16$

36. $(x + 5)^{2/3} = 4$

37. $(y^2 - y - 4)^{3/4} - 2 = 6$

38. $(y^2 - 3y + 3)^{3/2} - 1 = 0$

39. $(11y^2 - 18)^{1/4} = 14$

40. $(7y^2 - 12)^{1/4} = y$

41. $(-2x + 1)^{-5/3} = -\dfrac{1}{32}$

42. $(3y + 1)^{-3/5} = -\dfrac{1}{8}$

43. $2x^{2/3} + 3x^{1/3} - 2 = 0$

44. $2x^{2/3} + 7x^{1/3} - 15 = 0$

45. $2x - 3x^{1/2} + 1 = 0$

46. $x + 3x^{1/2} - 4 = 0$

47. $(z - 2)^{1/2} = 11(z - 2)^{1/4} - 18$

48. $(z - 1)^{1/2} = 2(z - 1)^{1/4} + 15$

Application Problems

49. The model $v = 2\sqrt{3m}$ gives an approximate relationship between the velocity of a car (v, in miles per hour) that skids to a stop on wet pavement and the length of the resulting skid marks (m, in feet). Approximately how long are the skid marks left by a car traveling 50 miles per hour when the brakes are applied?

50. Shallow-water wave motion can be modeled by $c = \sqrt{gH}$ where c is the wave velocity in feet per second, H is the water depth in feet, and g, the acceleration of gravity, is 32 feet per second squared. If the wave velocity is 24 feet per second, find the water's depth.

Use Einstein's model

$$L = L_0 \sqrt{1 - \frac{v^2}{c^2}}$$

which relates length at rest (L_0) to length (L) at velocity v to answer Problems 51–52. The speed of light, c, is approxmately 186,000 miles per second.

186,000 Miles Per Second
Is Not Just A Good Idea.
It's The Law.

51. How fast would a futuristic starship that is 600 meters tall have to move so that it would measure only half this length from the perspective of an observer who looks up and sees the ship?

52. How fast would a futuristic starship that is 600 meters tall have to move so that its length would be diminished by 75% from the perspective of an observer who looks up and sees the ship?

Use Einstein's models

$$M = \frac{M_0}{\sqrt{1 - \frac{v^2}{c^2}}} \quad \text{and} \quad T = \frac{T_0}{\sqrt{1 - \frac{v^2}{c^2}}}$$

which relate mass and time at rest (M_0, T_0), to mass and time (M, T) at velocity v, to answer Problems 53–54. The speed of light, c, is approximately 186,000 miles per second.

53. How fast would a 120-pound person have to travel for that person's mass to double as perceived by an observer at rest?

54. A clock on board a futuristic starship traveling at $\frac{9}{10}$ of the speed of light measures a 10-second time period. How long is this time period from the perspective of an observer who looks up and sees the ship pass by?

55. Laser Records marketing research department determines that weekly demand for a boxed set of CDs by the Jumping Artichokes depends on the price per set, approximated by the model $p = 30 - \sqrt{0.01x + 1}$, where p represents the price of the set and x represents the number of sets sold each week at price p.

a. At what price will there be no demand for the CD sets?

b. Approximately how many CD sets will sell weekly at a price of $27.76?

The amount of money in an account (A) when interest is compounded n times a year is given by the model

$$A = P\left(1 + \frac{r}{n}\right)^{nt}.$$

In this formula, A is the balance in the account, P is the amount originally deposited, r is the annual interest rate (in decimal form), n is the number of compoundings per year, and t is the time in years. Use this formula to answer Problems 56–57.

56. A total of $12,000 is invested. After five years, the balance in the account is $18,726.11. If the interest is compounded quarterly, what was the annual interest rate for this investment?

57. A total of $2500 is invested. After 10 years, the balance in the account is $8155.09. If the interest is compounded quarterly, what was the annual interest rate for this investment?

58. Two vertical poles of lengths 6 feet and 8 feet stand 10 feet apart (see the figure). A cable reaches from the top of one pole to some point on the ground between the poles and then to the top of the other pole. Where should this point be located to use 18 feet of cable?

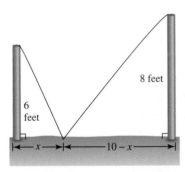

59. Twelve miles separate towns *A* and *B*, located 5 miles and 3 miles, respectively, from a major expressway. Two new roads are to be built from *A* to the expressway and then to *B*. (See the figure.)

a. Find *x* if the length of the new roads is 16 miles.

b. Write a verbal description for the road crew telling them where to position the new roads based on your answer to part (a).

60. A box is in the shape of a cube. If the width is increased by 9 inches and the length is decreased by 4 inches, then the volume of the new box is 180 cubic inches. What are the dimensions of the cubic box?

61. A rectangular box has a volume of 6 cubic feet. Its length is 3 feet greater than its height, and its width is 1 foot less than its height. What are the dimensions of the box?

62. Two spherical paperweights of radius 3 inches and 4 inches are to be melted and reformed into a larger sphere. Find the radius of the larger sphere.

63. A spherical container has a radius of 6 inches. By how much should the radius be increased if the volume of the new container is to be increased by 288π cubic inches?

64. A box with a square base has a height that is 2 inches greater than the length of the base. The box is surrounded by a 1-inch thick layer of packing material. If 130 cubic inches of packing material surrounds the box, what are the dimensions of the box?

65. A power station is located on the shoreline of a 6-mile-wide river. A factory is 12 miles downstream on the other side of the river. It costs $130 thousand per mile to run power lines under water and $80 thousand per mile to run power lines over the land. How far from the factory should the power line come ashore if the cost of the project is $1575 thousand?

True–False Critical Thinking Problems

66. Which one of the following is true?

   a. Squaring both sides of $\sqrt{y + 4} + \sqrt{y - 1} = 5$ leads to $y + 4 + y - 1 = 25$, an equation with no radicals.

   b. The equation $(x^2 - 2x)^9 - 5(x^2 - 2x)^3 + 6 = 0$ is quadratic in form and should be solved by letting $t = x^2 - 2x$.

   c. If a radical equation has two proposed solutions and one of these values is not a solution, the other value is also not a solution.

   d. None of these statements is true.

67. Which one of the following is true?

   a. The polynomial equation $x^{2/3} - 9x^{1/3} + 8 = 0$ can be solved by letting $t = x^{1/3}$, resulting in $t^2 - 9t + 8 = 0$.

   b. If $\left| x^3 - 6x^2 \right| = 5x$, then $x^3 + 6x^2 = 5x$ or $x^3 + 6x^2 = -5x$.

   c. The solution of $2x^{1/4} - 3x^{1/2} + 3 = 0$ can be found by letting $t = x^{1/2}$ and $t^2 = x^{1/4}$.

   d. None of these statements is true.

Technology Problems

In Problems 68–74, use a graphing utility to estimate the real solutions of each equation, accurate to two decimal places.

68. $15x^3 + 14x^2 - 3x - 2 = 0$

69. $x^3 + x^2 - 4x - 4 = 0$

70. $2x^3 - 3x^2 - 11x + 6 = 0$

71. $3x^3 + 7x^2 - 22x - 8 = 0$

72. $x + \sqrt{26 - 11x} = 4$

73. $2x^{\frac{2}{3}} + 4x^{\frac{1}{3}} + 1.8 = 0$

74. $3\sqrt{2} - \dfrac{2}{\sqrt{x}} = 2$

75. a. The model $N = -143x^3 + 1810x^2 - 187x + 2331$ approximates the number of new AIDS cases in the United States x years after 1983, where $0 \leq x \leq 7$. Graph this model using the following range setting:

   Xmin = 0, Xmax = 7, Xscl = 1, Ymin = 0,

   Ymax = 50,000, Yscl = 5000

   b. Describe what the graph of the model visually indicates about the spread of AIDS.

   c. In what year were approximately 40,000 cases reported?

   d. Construct a bar graph based on the graph of the model.

   e. How many new cases does the model indicate there were last year? Look up the actual number of new cases reported for that year. What does this tell you about mathematical models?

76. Use a graphing utility to graph the model that represents the total amount of cable needed for the project in Problem 58. Then use the minimum value feature of the utility to determine approximately where the point should be located to use the least amount of cable.

77. Use a graphing utility to graph the formula that models the total length of the new roads in Problem 59. Then use the minimum value feature of the utility to determine the shortest road that meets the problem's requirements.

78. Use a graphing utility to graph the model that represents the total cost of running the power line under the river and over the land in Problem 65. Then trace along the curve or use the minimum value feature to explain the significance of the cost of the project given in the problem.

79. A person rows in a straight line across a 2-mile wide channel from point A to point D and then walks from point D to a house located at point C. The figure shows that the distance from point B to the house at point C is 6 miles. The rowing rate is 3 miles per hour and the walking rate is 5 miles per hour.

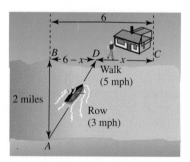

   a. Use the fact that time is distance divided by rate to show that the total time spent rowing and walking, represented by y, is modeled by

$$y = \frac{\sqrt{4 + (6 - x)^2}}{3} + \frac{x}{5}$$

   b. Suppose that the total time spent walking and rowing is 1 hour and 44 minutes, or about $\frac{26}{15}$ hours. Use your graphing utility to graph the model in part (a), using the following range setting:

   Xmin = 0, Xmax = 6, Xscl = 1, Ymin = 1.7,

   Ymax = 2.1, Yscl = 1

Then trace along the curve until $y = \frac{26}{15}$. What is the corresponding value of x? Where, then, should the person come ashore in terms of distance from the house? What is the significance of this rowing–walking path in terms of the time required to reach the house?

c. Verify part (b) algebraically by solving the equation

$$\frac{\sqrt{4 + (6 - x)^2}}{3} + \frac{x}{5} = \frac{26}{15}$$

$$(1 \text{ hour and } 44 \text{ minutes} = 1\frac{44}{60} = 1\frac{11}{15} = \frac{26}{15} \text{ hours})$$

Writing in Mathematics

80. We have seen that squaring both sides of an equation does not always produce an equivalent equation. Is this true when cubing both sides of an equation? Explain.

81. Reread Problem 55 on page 170. Suppose you are writing a report on the relationship between the price of the CDs and the units that will sell. Assume that other than yourself, everyone in the company is innumerate and cannot understand the model $p = 30 - \sqrt{0.01x + 1}$. Consequently, you must describe the relationship between p and x strictly using words. Write such a description, minimizing the use of mathematical terminology.

82. Give an example of an equation that is easier to solve algebraically than with a graphing utility. Give an example of an equation that is easier to solve with a graphing utility than algebraically. What conclusion can you draw?

83. Describe what happens to time and length in Einstein's models (see page 166) as the velocity of futuristic starship approaches the speed of light ($v \approx c$). What does this mean in practical terms for a person returning from a 20-year cruise at nearly the speed of light?

84. Reread Problems 49, 50 and 55. Two of these examples contain models that are the "real thing," and one contains a model that was artificially constructed to provide further practice and drill in solving equations. Which contains the latter? How can you tell?

Critical Thinking Problems

85. Solve for x: $\dfrac{(x - 3)^{1/2}(x - 4)^{1/5}}{(x - 7)^{1/3}} = 0$

86. Solve for x: $x^{5/6} + x^{2/3} - 2x^{1/2} = 0$

Solve each equation in Problems 87–89 for real values of y.

87. $y^{1/3} + 4^{1/4} = \dfrac{2}{2 - \sqrt{2}}$

88. $\sqrt{\dfrac{y - 30}{y}} + 4\sqrt{\dfrac{y}{y - 30}} = 5$

89. $\sqrt{\sqrt{y} + \sqrt{c}} + \sqrt{\sqrt{y} - \sqrt{c}} = \sqrt{2\sqrt{y} + 2\sqrt{d}}$

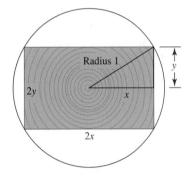

Radius 1

$2y$ x

y

$2x$

90. A beam is to be cut from a circular log of radius 1 foot. Let x and y represent half the length and half the width of a rectangular cross section of the beam.

Rectangular Beam

a. Write an equation in terms of x and y for the area of the beam's cross section.

b. Apply the Pythagorean Theorem to the small right triangle in the figure shown above and write an equation for y in terms of x.

c. Substitute the equation from part (b) into the area model of part (a), representing the area of the beam's cross section in terms of x alone.

d. Use the model from part (c) to determine the value of x that will result in an area of 2 square feet. What are the dimensions of the cross section?

e. Use a graphing utility to graph the area model from part (c) and explain the significance of your answer to part (d).

SECTION I.5

Solutions Manual   **Tutorial**   **Video 3**

Linear Inequalities

Objectives

1 Solve linear inequalities.
2 Solve applied modeling problems.
3 Solve compound inequalities.
4 Solve inequalities involving absolute value.

In this section, we establish the basic techniques for solving inequalities containing variables raised only to the first power, called *linear inequalities*. We also consider the solution of linear inequalities involving absolute value.

Solve linear inequalities.

Linear Inequalities and Their Properties

We know that a linear equation in x can be expressed in the form $ax + b = c$. A similar definition describes a linear inequality in one variable.

> **Definition of a linear inequality**
>
> A *linear inequality* in one variable x is any inequality that can be written in one of the forms
>
> $$ax + b < c \quad ax + b \leq c \quad ax + b > c \quad ax + b \geq c$$
>
> where a, b, and c are real numbers and $a \neq 0$.

An example of a linear inequality in one variable is $2x + 3 < 17$, in which $a = 2$, $b = 3$, and $c = 17$. Because the greatest power on the variable is one, a linear inequality is also called a *first-degree inequality*.

Any value of the variable for which an inequality is true is called a *solution*. The *solution set* of the inequality is the set of all such solutions. The solutions are said to *satisfy* the inequality.

To solve a linear inequality, we use a series of transformations into equivalent inequalities (inequalities that have the same solution set). Our final equivalent inequality should be in the form

$$x > d \quad x < d \quad x \geq d \quad x \leq d.$$

We can use properties of inequalities to isolate the variable. These properties are similar to the properties of equality that we used to solve linear equations. There are, however, two important exceptions. Multiplying or dividing both sides of an inequality by a negative number reverses the sense (or direction) of the inequality. To illustrate, let's take three true inequality statements and multiply both sides by -3.

$$7 < 10 \qquad\qquad -2 < 6 \qquad\qquad -6 < -1$$
$$\downarrow \qquad\qquad\qquad \downarrow \qquad\qquad\qquad \downarrow$$
$$-3(7) > -3(10) \quad -3(-2) > -3(6) \quad -3(-6) > -3(-1)$$
$$-21 > -30 \qquad\quad 6 > -18 \qquad\qquad 18 > 3$$

In each case, the resulting inequality symbol points in the opposite direction from the original one.

When both sides of an inequality are multiplied or divided by a negative number, the direction of the inequality symbol is reversed.

To isolate the variable in a linear inequality, we use the same basic techniques used in solving linear equations. The following properties are used to create equivalent inequalities.

Properties of inequalities

Property	**The Property in Words**	**Example**
Addition and Subtraction Properties If $a < b$, then $a + c < b + c$. If $a < b$, then $a - c < b - c$.	If the same quantity is added to or subtracted from both sides of an inequality, the resulting inequality is equivalent to the original one.	$2x + 3 < 7$ Subtract 3: $2x + 3 - 3 < 7 - 3$ Simplify: $2x < 4$
Positive Multiplication and Division Properties If $a < b$ and c is positive, then $ac < bc$ If $a < b$ and c is positive, then $\dfrac{a}{c} < \dfrac{b}{c}$.	If by the same positive quantity we multiply or divide both sides of an inequality, the resulting inequality is equivalent to the original one.	$2x < 4$ Divide by 2: $\dfrac{2x}{2} < \dfrac{4}{2}$ Simplify: $x < 2$
Negative Multiplication and Division Properties If $a < b$ and c is negative, then $ac > bc$. If $a < b$ and c is negative, then $\dfrac{a}{c} > \dfrac{b}{c}$.	If by the same negative quantity we multiply or divide both sides of an inequality, the result is an equivalent inequality in which the inequality symbol is reversed.	$-4x < 20$ Divide by -4 and reverse the sense of the inequality: $\dfrac{-4x}{-4} > \dfrac{20}{-4}$ Simplify: $x > -5$

Study tip

The properties of inequality are true if $<$ and $>$ are replaced by $\leq$ and $\geq$.

EXAMPLE 1 **Solving a Linear Inequality**

Solve and graph the solution set on a number line: $3 - 2x < 11$

Solution

$3 - 2x < 11$	This is the given inequality.
$3 - 2x - 3 < 11 - 3$	Subtract 3 from both sides.
$-2x < 8$	Simplify.
$\dfrac{-2x}{-2} > \dfrac{8}{-2}$	Divide both sides by -2 and reverse the sense of the inequality.
$x > -4$	Simplify.

Figure 1.16

The graph of $x > -4$

To solve Example 2 on your graphing utility, begin by entering each side of the given inequality:

$y_1 \boxed{=} 7(x + 4) - 13$

$y_2 \boxed{=} 12 + 13(3 + x)$

Now enter y_3, the difference of y_1 and y_2:

$y_3 \boxed{=} y_1 - y_2$

To solve

$7(x + 4) - 13 < 12 + 13(3 + x)$

we must find where $y_1 - y_2 < 0$, or where y_3 lies below the x-axis. Turn off the high-lighting on the equal sign for y_1 and y_2, and graph y_3. The graph of y_3 shows that $y_1 - y_2 < 0$ (lies below the x-axis) if $x > -6$, confirming our algebraic solution.

Figure 1.17

The graph of $x > -6$

The solution set consists of all real numbers that are greater than -4, expressed as $\{x \,|\, x > -4\}$. The interval notation for the solution set is $(-4, \infty)$. The graph is shown on a number line in Figure 1.16. ∎

Discover for yourself

We cannot check all members of an inequality's solution set, but we can take a few values to get an indication of whether it is correct. In Example 1, we found that the solution set to $3 - 2x < 11$ is $(-4, \infty)$. Show that -3 satisfies the given inequality, whereas -5 does not.

EXAMPLE 2   **Solving a Linear Inequality**

Solve and graph the solution set on a number line:

$7(x + 4) - 13 < 12 + 13(3 + x)$

Solution

$7(x + 4) - 13 < 12 + 13(3 + x)$	This is the given inequality.
$7x + 28 - 13 < 12 + 39 + 13x$	Simplify each side and apply the distributive property.
$7x + 15 < 51 + 13x$	Combine numerical terms.

We will collect variable terms on the left and constant terms on the right.

$7x + 15 - 13x < 51 + 13x - 13x$	Subtract $13x$ from both sides.
$-6x + 15 < 51$	Simplify.
$-6x + 15 - 15 < 51 - 15$	Subtract 15 from both sides.
$-6x < 36$	Simplify.
$\dfrac{-6x}{-6} > \dfrac{36}{-6}$	Divide both sides by -6 and reverse the sense of the inequality.
$x > -6$	Simplify.

The solution set consists of all real numbers that are greater than -6. The interval notation for this solution set is $(-6, \infty)$.

The graph of the solution set on a number line is shown in Figure 1.17. ∎

Discover for yourself

The addition and subtraction properties of inequality provide us with the option of collecting all terms with the variable on the right and all numbers on the left. Use this option to solve

$7x + 15 < 51 + 13x$

and compare your solution to that of Example 2.

2 Solve applied modeling problems.

Modeling with Linear Inequalities

Example 3 illustrates how we can apply our five-step strategy for problem solving to an inequality situation. The example involves simple interest. The annual simple interest that an investment earns is given by the formula

$$I = Pr$$

where I is the simple interest, P is the amount invested (called the *principal*), and r is the simple interest rate.

EXAMPLE 3   **An Application: Simple Interest**

A person inherits $16,000 with the stipulation that for the first year the money must be invested in two stocks paying 6% and 8% annual interest, respectively. What is the greatest amount that can be invested at 6% if the total interest earned for the year is to be at least $1180?

Solution

Steps 1 and 2. Represent unknowns in terms of x.

Let

$$x = \text{Amount invested at } 6\%$$

$$16,000 - x = \text{Amount invested at } 8\%$$
$$\text{(since the total amount invested was \$16,000)}$$

The total yearly interest must be at least $1180.

Step 3. Write an inequality that models the verbal conditions.

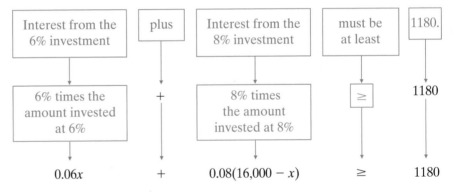

Step 4. Solve the inequality and answer the problem's question.

$$0.06x + 0.08(16,000 - x) \geq 1180 \qquad \text{This is the inequality that models the given conditions.}$$

$$6x + 8(16,000 - x) \geq 118,000 \qquad \text{Multiply by 100 to clear decimals (optional).}$$

$$6x + 128,000 - 8x \geq 118,000 \qquad \text{Use the distributive property.}$$

$$-2x + 128,000 \geq 118,000 \qquad \text{Combine like terms.}$$

$$-2x \geq -10,000 \qquad \text{Subtract 128,000 from both sides.}$$

$$x \leq 5000 \qquad \text{Divide by } -2 \text{ and reverse the sense of the inequality.}$$

Step 5. Check.

Thus, at most $5000 can be invested at 6% if the total yearly interest is to be at least $1180. Suppose that $5000 is invested at 6%. Thus, $16,000 − $5000 or $11,000 is invested at 8%. The interest is

$$0.06(5000) + 0.08(11,000)$$

or $1180. Try this again, with $3000 invested at 6% (at most $5000 can be invested at this rate) and $13,000 invested at 8%. As specified by the problem's conditions, the yearly interest should be at least $1180. ∎

3 Solve compound inequalities.

Solving Compound Inequalities

Two inequalities are often written as a *compound inequality*. For example, consider a hypothetical situation involving the United Cable Television Company. Let x represent the number of customers served by the company. The weekly profit of the company is 50 times the number of customers served less $100. The company has *two* constraints placed upon it:

1. Its weekly profits must be greater than $5000, or the corporation will be sold by the stockholders.
2. Its contract with the local officials restricts weekly profits to less than $30,000.

Since profits are $50x - 100$ (50 times the number of customers minus $100), we have

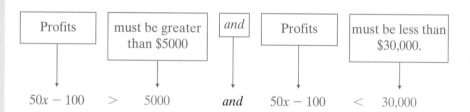

We can express these conditions uslng a compound (or double) inequality as follows:

$$5000 < 50x - 100 < 30,000$$

This form permits us to solve the two inequalities together. Our goal is to isolate x by itself in the middle. Here's how it is done:

$5000 < 50x - 100 < 30,000$	This is the given compound inequality.
$5100 < 50x < 30,100$	Add 100 to all three parts.
$\dfrac{5100}{50} < \dfrac{50x}{50} < \dfrac{30,100}{50}$	Divide all three parts by 50.
$102 < x < 602$	Simplify.

In the context of the original situation, this means that to not be sold or to avoid contract violation, the company must have more than 102 customers *and* fewer than 602 customers.

Our next example involves a compound inequality.

EXAMPLE 4   **Solving a Compound Inequality**

Solve: $\dfrac{2}{3} \le \dfrac{5 - 3x}{2} < \dfrac{3}{4}$

Solution

$$\dfrac{2}{3} \le \dfrac{5 - 3x}{2} < \dfrac{3}{4}$$ This is the given compound inequality; our goal is to isolate x in the middle.

$$12\left(\dfrac{2}{3}\right) \le 12\left(\dfrac{5 - 3x}{2}\right) < 12\left(\dfrac{3}{4}\right)$$ Clear fractions by multiplying each part by 12.

$$8 \le 6(5 - 3x) < 9$$ Multiply.

$$8 \le 30 - 18x < 9$$ Use the distributive property.

$$-22 \le -18x < -21$$ Subtract 30 from each part.

$$\dfrac{-22}{-18} \ge x > \dfrac{-21}{-18}$$ Divide each part by -18 and reverse the sense of the inequality.

$$\dfrac{11}{9} \ge x > \dfrac{7}{6}$$ Simplify the fractions.

This inequality is correct but awkward to interpret. It can be rewritten with the lesser rational number, $\frac{7}{6}$, on the left as

$$\dfrac{7}{6} < x \le \dfrac{11}{9}.$$

The solution set in interval notation is $(\frac{7}{6}, \frac{11}{9}]$. The graph of the solution set is shown on a number line in Figure 1.18. ∎

Figure 1.18

The graph of $\dfrac{7}{6} < x \le \dfrac{11}{9}$

4 Solve inequalities involving absolute value.

Solving Inequalities Involving Absolute Value

In our prerequisites chapter, we interpreted $|x|$ as the distance between x and the origin on a number line. Using this interpretation, Table 1.5 shows how we can rewrite absolute value inequalities without absolute value bars.

TABLE 1.5   Rewriting Absolute Value Inequalities Without Absolute Value Bars

Example	Rewritten Without Absolute Value	Generalization
$|x| < 2$ The distance between x and the origin is less than 2.	All real numbers in $(-2, 2)$ have distances from the origin that are less than 2, so $|x| < 2$ means $-2 < x < 2$.	If c is a positive real number, $|x| < c$ means $-c < x < c$.
$|x| > 3$ The distance between x and the origin is greater than 3.	All real numbers in $(3, \infty)$ or $(-\infty, -3)$ have the distances from the origin that are greater than 3, so $|x| > 3$ means $x > 3$ or $x < -3$.	If c is a positive real number, $|x| > c$ means $x > c$ or $x < -c$.

We can use these relationships to solve inequalities involving absolute value. Both relationships involve rewriting absolute value inequalities as equivalent inequalities without absolute value bars. We can apply these relationships to linear inequalities as follows.

Rewriting absolute value inequalities without absolute value bars

If c is positive,

1. $\left| ax + b \right| < c$ means $-c < ax + b < c.$
2. $\left| ax + b \right| > c$ means $ax + b > c$ or $ax + b < -c.$

These rules are valid if $<$ is replaced by $\leq$ and $>$ is replaced by $\geq$.

Once the absolute value inequality has been rewritten as an equivalent inequality without absolute value bars, the solutions can be found using the methods for solving linear inequalities. This idea is illustrated in our next two examples.

EXAMPLE 5   Solving an Absolute Value Inequality with $<$

Solve: $\left| \dfrac{3x + 3}{5} \right| < 3$

Solution

$\left| \dfrac{3x + 3}{5} \right| < 3$ This is the given inequality.

$-3 < \dfrac{3x + 3}{5} < 3$ Rewrite without absolute value bars. $\left| ax + b \right| < c$ means $-c < ax + b < c.$

$-15 < 3x + 3 < 15$ Multiply each part by 5.

$-18 < 3x < 12$ Subtract 3 from each part.

$-6 < x < 4$ Divide each part by 3.

All real numbers between -6 and 4, excluding -6 and 4, satisfy the original inequality. Using interval notation, the solution set is $(-6, 4)$. The graph of the solution set is shown in Figure 1.19. ∎

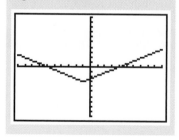
Figure 1.19

The graph of $-6 < x < 4$

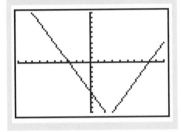

Using technology

You can use a graphing utility to verify the solution to Example 6. Enter

$Y_1 = \boxed{\text{ABS}}\,(-2x + 5)$

$Y_2 = 11$

$Y_3 = Y_1 - Y_2$

and highlight only y_3. The graph of y_3 shows that $y_3 \geq 0$ (lies on or above the x-axis) if $x \leq -3$ or $x \geq 8$, visually confirming our algebraic solution.

Figure 1.20

The graph of $x \leq -3$ or $x \geq 8$

Meret Oppenheim "Object (Le Dejeuner en fourrure)" 1936, fur-covered cup, saucer and spoon; cup 4 3/8 in. diameter; saucer 9 3/8 in. diameter; spoon 8 in. long; overall height 2 7/8 in. The Museum of Modern Art, New York. Purchase. Photograph © 1997 The Museum of Modern Art, New York. © 1998 Artists Rights Society (ARS), New York / Pro Litteris, Zurich.

EXAMPLE 6 **Solving an Absolute Value Inequality with** $\geq$

Solve: $\left|-2x + 5\right| \geq 11$

Solution

$\left|-2x + 5\right| \geq 11$		This is the given inequality.
$-2x + 5 \geq 11$ or	$-2x + 5 \leq -11$	Rewrite without absolute value bars. $\left|ax + b\right| \geq c$ means $ax + b \geq c$ or $ax + b \leq -c$.
$-2x \geq 6$	$-2x \leq -16$	Subtract 5 from both sides of both inequalities.
$x \leq -3$	$x \geq 8$	Divide both sides of both inequalities by -2.

Using interval notation, the solution set is $(-\infty, -3]$ or $[8, \infty)$. This can be expressed as $(-\infty, -3] \cup [8, \infty)$ where the symbol $\cup$ (the union symbol) denotes the set of numbers in $(-\infty, -3]$ *or* in $[8, \infty)$. The graph of the solution set is shown on the number line in Figure 1.20. ∎

Modeling with Absolute Value Inequalities

Example 7 shows how we can apply absolute value inequalities.

EXAMPLE 7 **Modeling Defective Products**

The percentage (p) of defective products manufactured by a company is described by

$$\left|p - 0.35\%\right| \leq 0.16\%$$

or, equivalently

$$\left|p - 0.0035\right| \leq 0.0016\,.$$

If 100,000 products are manufactured and the company offers a $6 refund for each defective product, describe the company's cost of refunds.

Solution

We'll start with what seems most obvious, namely:

The company's cost of refunds	equals	$6 refund for each defective product	times	The number of defective products.
R	$=$	6	$\cdot$	$?$

We now need an expression for the number of defective products.

We can find p by solving the given inequality for this variable.

$|p - 0.0035| \leq 0.0016$ This is the given inequality.

$-0.0016 \leq p - 0.0035 \leq 0.0016$ Rewrite without absolute value bars.

$0.0019 \leq p \leq 0.0051$ Add 0.0035 to each part.

In percent notation, the percentage of defective products ranges from 0.19% to 0.51%. This will give us a range for the number of defective products.

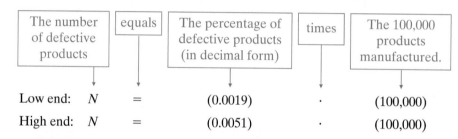

Equivalently,

$(0.0019)(100,000) \leq N \leq (0.0051)(100,000).$

Performing the multiplications, we see that

$190 \leq N \leq 510,$

meaning that the number of defective products is greater than or equal to 190 but less than or equal to 510 for every 100,000 products manufactured. Since the company refunds $6 for each defective product, we can now describe the company's cost of refunds.

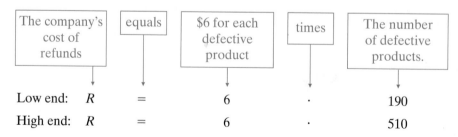

Performing the multiplications, we see that

$1140 \leq R \leq 3060.$

For every 100,000 products manufactured, the cost of refunds ranges from $1140 to $3060.

PROBLEM SET 1.5

Practice Problems

Solve each linear inequality in Problems 1–20 and graph the solution set on a number line.

1. $5x + 11 < 26$

2. $2x + 5 < 17$

3. $3x - 7 \geqslant 13$

4. $8x - 2 \geqslant 14$

5. $-9x \geqslant 36$

6. $-5x \leqslant 30$

7. $8x - 11 \leqslant 3x - 13$

8. $18x + 45 \leqslant 12x - 8$

9. $4(x + 1) + 2 \geqslant 3x + 6$

10. $8x + 3 > 3(2x + 1) + x + 5$

11. $2x - 11 < -3(x + 2)$

12. $-4(x + 2) > 3x + 20$

13. $1 - (x + 3) \geqslant 4 - 2x$

14. $5(3 - x) \leqslant 3x - 1$

15. $\dfrac{x}{4} - \dfrac{3}{5} \leqslant \dfrac{x}{2} + 1$

16. $\dfrac{3x}{10} + 1 \geqslant \dfrac{1}{5} - \dfrac{x}{10}$

17. $1 - \dfrac{x}{2} > 4$

18. $7 - \dfrac{4}{5}x < \dfrac{3}{5}$

19. $4(3y - 2) - 3y < 3(1 + 3y) - 7$

20. $3(y - 8) - 2(10 - y) > 5(y - 1)$

Solve each inequality in Problems 21–38 by isolating the variable by itself in the middle. Graph the solution set on a number line.

21. $6 < x + 3 < 8$

22. $7 < x + 5 < 11$

23. $-3 \leqslant x - 2 < 1$

24. $-6 < x - 4 \leqslant 1$

25. $-9 < 3x \leqslant -6$

26. $-24 \leqslant 4x < -20$

27. $-9 \leqslant -3x \leqslant -6$

28. $-24 \leqslant -4x \leqslant -20$

29. $-11 < 2x - 1 \leqslant -5$

30. $3 \leqslant 4x - 3 < 19$

31. $-3 \leqslant \dfrac{2}{3}x - 5 < -1$

32. $-6 \leqslant \dfrac{1}{2}x - 4 < -3$

33. $-8 < 2 - 3x < 10$

34. $-3 \leqslant 1 - 2x \leqslant 5$

35. $-5 \leqslant 3 - 2x < 18$

36. $0 < 3(-x - 5) - 9 \leqslant 6$

37. $-1 < \dfrac{1 - 4y}{3} \leqslant 1$

38. $\dfrac{2}{3} < \dfrac{5 - 3y}{-2} \leqslant \dfrac{3}{4}$

Solve each inequality in Problems 39–68 by first rewriting each one as an equivalent inequality without absolute value bars. Graph the solution set on a number line.

39. $|x| < 3$

40. $|x| < 5$

41. $|x - 1| \leqslant 2$

42. $|x + 3| \leqslant 4$

43. $|2x - 6| < 8$

44. $|3x + 5| < 17$

45. $|2(x - 1) + 4| \leqslant 8$

46. $|3(x - 1) + 2| \leqslant 20$

47. $\left| \dfrac{2y + 6}{3} \right| < 2$

48. $\left| \dfrac{3(x - 1)}{4} \right| < 6$

49. $|x| > 3$

50. $|x| > 5$

51. $|x - 1| \geqslant 2$

52. $|x + 3| \geqslant 4$

53. $|3x - 8| > 7$

54. $|5x - 2| > 13$

55. $\left| \dfrac{2x + 2}{4} \right| \geqslant 2$

56. $\left| \dfrac{3x - 3}{9} \right| \geqslant 1$

57. $\left| 3 - \dfrac{2}{3}y \right| > 5$

58. $\left| 3 - \dfrac{3}{4}y \right| > 9$

59. $3|y - 1| + 2 \geqslant 8$

60. $-2|4 - x| \geqslant -4$

61. $3 < |2y - 1|$

62. $5 \geqslant |4 - y|$

63. $12 < \left| -2x + \dfrac{6}{7} \right| + \dfrac{3}{7}$

64. $1 < \left| y - \dfrac{11}{3} \right| + \dfrac{7}{3}$

65. $4 + \left| 3 - \dfrac{y}{3} \right| \geqslant 9$

66. $\left| 2 - \dfrac{y}{2} \right| - 1 \leqslant 1$

67. $\left| \dfrac{y + 1}{2} - \dfrac{y - 1}{3} \right| \leq 1$ **68.** $\left| \dfrac{4(y - 1)}{3} + \dfrac{3(y - 2)}{4} \right| \leq 2$

Application Problems

69. A person inherits $25,000 with the stipulation that the first year the money must be invested in two stocks paying 9% and 12% annual interest, respectively. What is the greatest amount that can be invested at 9% if the total interest for the year is to be at least $2250?

70. A person inherits $18,750 with the stipulation that the first year the money must be invested in two stocks paying 10% and 12% annual interest, respectively. What is the greatest amount that can be invested at 10% if the total interest for the year is to be at least $2117?

71. Inclusive of a 6.5% sales tax, the amount a person can spend on a car cannot exceed $17,466. What is the most expensive car that can be purchased?

72. Inclusive of a 6.5% sales tax, the amount a person can spend on a television cannot exceed $788.10. What is the most expensive television that can be purchased?

73. If the cost of producing x units of a commodity is $C = 600(2x + 4) + 600 + 600x$ and the revenue received for the x units is $R = 1850x$, describe the number of units that must be sold to achieve a profit.

74. If the cost of producing x units of a commodity is $C = 400(3x - 1) + 700$ and the revenue received for the x units is $R = 1250x$, describe the number of units that must be sold to achieve a profit.

75. Membership in a fitness club costs $500 yearly plus $1 per hour spent working out. A competing club charges $440 yearly plus $1.74 per hour. How many hours must a person work out yearly to make membership in the first club a better deal?

76. A local bank charges $8 per month plus 5¢ per check. The credit union charges $2 per month plus 8¢ per check. How many checks should be written each month to make the credit union a better deal?

77. A company that manufactures small clocks has fixed costs of $75,000 per month. It costs the company $3 to manufacture each clock. If the clocks sell for $18 each, how many should be manufactured and sold monthly to make a profit?

78. A company that manufactures graphing calculators has fixed costs of $65,000 per month. It costs the company $20 to manufacture each calculator. If the calculators sell for $85 each, how many should be manufactured and sold monthly to make a profit?

79. The figure at the top of the next column shows a square with four identical equilateral triangles attached. If the

perimeter of the figure is at least 24 centimeters and at most 36 centimeters, write an inequality to describe possible values for k.

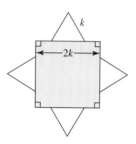

80. The figure below shows a right triangle surmounted by a trapezoid. If the combined area of the triangle and trapezoid is at most 125 square feet and at least 68 square feet, write an inequality to describe possible values for x.

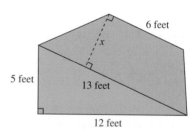

81. The daily production (x) at a refinery is described by $|x - 2,560,00| \leq 135,000$, where x represents the number of barrels of oil produced. Find the high and low production levels.

82. If a coin is tossed 100 times, we would expect approximately 50 of the outcomes to be heads. It can be demonstrated that a coin is unfair if h, the number of outcomes that result in heads, satisfies $\left| \dfrac{h - 50}{5} \right| \geq 1.645$. Describe the number of outcomes that determine an unfair coin that is tossed 100 times.

83. A pool measuring 10 meters by 20 meters is surrounded by a path of uniform width. The perimeter of the rectangle composed of the pool and path combined does not exceed 100 meters and is no less than 76 meters. Write an inequality that describes the width of the path.

84. A rectangle is surmounted by an equilateral triangle in such a way that the rectangle shares its longer side with the triangle. The shorter side of the rectangle is 3 meters less than a side of the triangle. If the perimeter of the figure composed of the rectangle and triangle combined does not exceed 54 meters and is no less than 34 meters, write an inequality that describes the length of a side of the triangle.

85. The bar graph shows the number of people in the United States with various disorders of mental illness. If x represents millions of people, what disorders are described by $11 \leqslant 3x - 4 \leqslant 56$ cases?

Mental Illness in America, by Disorder

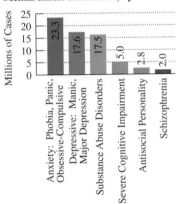

Source: National Institute of Mental Health.

86. The figure in the next column shows a bar graph representing the daily volume of the New York Stock Exchange for five days during a particular week. If x

represents the volume of stock traded, then for how many days is the inequality $|x - 280| > 40$ true, where each side of the inequality is measured in millions?

Volume of Stock Traded on New York Stock Exchange

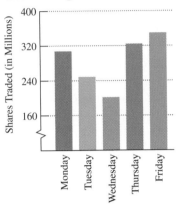

87. The percentage (p) of defective products manufactured by a company is given as $|p - 0.3\%| \leqslant 0.2\%$. If 100,000 products are manufactured and the company offers a $5 refund for each defective product, describe the company's cost of refunds.

88. Brozek's model for calculating the percent of a person's body fat (B) is $B = \dfrac{4.57}{d} - 4.142$, where d is that person's body density. For a particular person, body density is described by $|d - 1.0572| < 0.0061$. Describe the range for the percent of that person's body fat.

True–False Critical Thinking Problems

89. Which one of the following is true?

  a. The first step in solving $|2x - 3| > -7$ is to rewrite the inequality as $2x - 3 > -7$ or $2x - 3 < -7$.

  b. The smallest real number in the solution set of $2x > 6$ is 4.

  c. All irrational numbers satisfy $|x - 4| > 0$.

  d. None of these statements is true.

90. Which one of the following is true?

  a. The first step in solving $|x| + 3 < 7$ is to rewrite the inequality as $-7 < x + 3 < 7$.

  b. The greatest irrational number in the solution set of $-2x \geqslant -8$ is π.

  c. If your age is 32 and the difference between your age and my age (x) is at least 12 years, then $|x - 32| \geqslant 12$ is an accurate model of the given verbal conditions.

  d. None of these statements is true.

Technology Problems

In Problems 91–97, solve each inequality using a graphing utility.

91. $-5(x - 1) > 4x - 13$

92. $2(x + 1) > x - 3$

93. $|3 - 4x| \geqslant 13$

94. $|4(x - 1) - 5x| < 4$

95. $3x - [2 - 2(x - 1)] \leqslant 5 - 2[3x - 2(2x - 3)]$

96. $-2.5 < 0.75x + 1 < 6$

97. $(3x + 8)(9 - 2x) > 1 - 2(x - 8)(3x - 4)$

98. In solving the inequality $7(x + 4) - 13 < 12 + 13(3 + x)$, we used the graph of y_3 in which

$$y_1 = 7(x + 4) - 13$$

$$y_2 = 12 + 13(3 + x)$$

$$y_3 \boxed{=} y_1 - y_2$$

The solution $(-6, \infty)$ is found by determining where the graph of y_3 lies below the x-axis.

Use your graphing utility to devise another method for solving the inequality using only y_1 and y_2. Which method do you prefer?

99. Solve $2(x + 1) \geq 3 + 2x$ using a graphing utility. Then solve the inequality algebraically and explain what's happening.

100. Solve $5(x + 1) \geq 3 + 5x$ using a graphing utility. Then solve the inequality algebraically and explain what's happening.

In Problems 101–102, solve using a graphing utility.

101. The formula for converting Celsius temperature (C) to Fahrenheit (F) is $F = \frac{9}{5}C + 32$. If Fahrenheit temperature exceeds 77°, what does this mean in terms of Celsius temperature?

102. The operating cost for a moving truck is $2300 per year plus 30 cents per mile. What number of miles will result in an annual cost that does not exceed $6800?

Writing in Mathematics

103. Under what conditions does $|ax + b| < c$ have one solution? no solutions? Describe why this is so.

104. Since there are conditions for which $|ax + b| < c$ has no solution, do such conditions exist for $|ax + b| > c$? Explain.

105. Suppose that you are tutoring a student in an introductory algebra course.

a. In solving $|x + 3| > 2$, you write that $x + 3 > 2$ or $x + 3 < -2$. Your student asks, "Where did the absolute value bars go?" What is your response?

b. In solving $|x + 3| > 2$, your student writes $-2 > x + 3 > 2$. If the inequality is then solved for x, how would you explain that the resulting inequality cannot possibly be correct?

Critical Thinking Problems

106. Solve $|x - 3| + |x + 2| < 11$ by considering three cases: $x < -2$, $-2 \leq x < 3$, and $x \geq 3$.

107. a. Why is $-|a| \leq a \leq |a|$?

b. Use the fact that $-|a| \leq a \leq |a|$ and $-|b| \leq b \leq |b|$ adding respective members of both inequalities, to prove that $|a + b| \leq |a| + |b|$. This result is called the *triangle inequality*.

108. If $|x - 1| < 0.2$ and $|y - 2| < 0.02$, show that $|xy - 2| \leq 0.424$. (*Hint:* First verify that $xy - 2 = x(y - 2) + 2(x - 1)$. Then use the triangle inequality proved in Problem 107.)

S E C T I O N   I . 6   # Polynomial and Rational Inequalities

Solutions Manual

Tutorial

Video 3

Objectives

1 Solve quadratic inequalities.

2 Solve higher-order inequalities.

2 Solve applied modeling problems.

3 Solve rational inequalities.

In this section, we establish the basic techniques for solving inequalities containing polynomials and rational expressions.

Solve quadratic inequalities.

Solving Quadratic Inequalities

We know that a quadratic equation can be expressed in the form $ax^2 + bx + c = 0$. A similar definition describes a quadratic inequality in one variable.

> **Definition of a quadratic inequality**
>
> A *quadratic inequality* is any inequality that can be put in one of the forms
>
> $$ax^2 + bx + c < 0 \qquad ax^2 + bx + c > 0$$
>
> $$ax^2 + bx + c \leq 0 \qquad ax^2 + bx + c \geq 0$$
>
> where a, b, and c are real numbers and $a \neq 0$. This is called a *standard form* of a quadratic inequality.

For example, the inequality $x^2 > 10$ becomes $x^2 - 10 > 0$ when written in standard form. Notice that these inequalities are *equivalent*. That is, they have the same set of solutions.

Graphing utilities are extremely useful in terms of estimating solutions of quadratic inequalities. Consider, for example,

$$x^2 - 7x + 10 > 0.$$

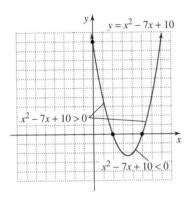

We can analyze this inequality geometrically by graphing $y = x^2 - 7x + 10$. The graph is drawn by hand in Figure 1.21 because we want to emphasize a particular portion of the curve, but you can obtain this graph on a graphing utility using a $[-2, 8]$ by $[-3, 7]$ viewing rectangle.

Because we are interested in the inequality $x^2 - 7x + 10 > 0$, focus on the portion of the graph of $y = x^2 - 7x + 10$ where $y > 0$ (indicated by the blue part of the curve). This occurs where the graph lies above the x-axis, namely, when $x < 2$ or $x > 5$. Thus, the solution set to $x^2 - 7x + 10 > 0$ is $(-\infty, 2) \cup (5, \infty)$.

Notice that Figure 1.21 also gives the solution set for $x^2 - 7x + 10 < 0$, which occurs when the graph lies below the x-axis, between $x = 2$ and $x = 5$. Thus $(2, 5)$, is the solution set for $x^2 - 7x + 10 < 0$.

To solve either $x^2 - 7x + 10 > 0$ or $x^2 - 7x + 10 < 0$ algebraically, we can begin by finding values of x for which $x^2 - 7x + 10 = 0$. These values, 2 and 5, are called the *critical numbers* of the inequality and divide the x-axis into three *test intervals*,

$$(-\infty, 2), (2, 5), \text{ and } (5, \infty).$$

To solve the inequality $x^2 - 7x + 10 > 0$, we need only to test one value from each of these test intervals.

This gives us a procedure for solving quadratic inequalities.

Figure 1.21

The blue portion of

$$y = x^2 - 7x + 10$$

represents

$$x^2 - 7x + 10 > 0$$

> **Procedure for solving quadratic inequalities**
>
> **1.** Express the inequality in *standard* form
>
> $$ax^2 + bx + c > 0 \quad \text{or} \quad ax^2 + bx + c < 0.$$
>
> **2.** Solve the equation $ax^2 + bx + c = 0$. The real solutions are the *critical numbers*.

3. Locate these critical numbers on a number line, thereby dividing the number line into *test intervals*.

4. Choose one representative number for each test interval. If substituting that value into the equivalent inequality from step 1 produces a true statement, then all real numbers in the test interval belong to the solution set. The solution set is the union of all such test intervals.

5. The graph of the solution set on a number line usually appears as

or

This procedure is valid if $<$ is replaced by $\leq$ and $>$ is replaced by $\geq$.

EXAMPLE I   Solving a Quadratic Inequality

Solve and graph the solution set on a real number line: $2x^2 + x < 15$

Solution

$2x^2 + x < 15$	This is the given inequality.
$2x^2 + x - 15 < 0$	Write the inequality in standard form.
$2x^2 + x - 15 = 0$	Solve the related quadratic equation.
$(2x - 5)(x + 3) = 0$	Factor.
$2x - 5 = 0$ or $x + 3 = 0$	Set each factor equal to 0.
$x = \frac{5}{2}$ $x = -3$	Solve for x. The critical numbers -3 and $\frac{5}{2}$. These values are located on a number line. The intervals are $(-\infty, -3), (-3, \frac{5}{2})$, and $(\frac{5}{2}, \infty)$.

Now we will take one representative number from each test interval and substitute that number into the inequality in standard form.

Test Interval	Representative Number	Substitute into $2x^2 + x - 15 < 0$	Conclusion
$(-\infty, -3)$	-4	$2(-4)^2 + (-4) - 15 \overset{?}{<} 0$ $13 < 0$ False	$(-\infty, -3)$ does not belong to the solution set.
$\left(-3, \frac{5}{2}\right)$	0	$2 \cdot 0^2 + 0 - 15 \overset{?}{<} 0$ $-15 < 0$ True	$\left(-3, \frac{5}{2}\right)$ belongs to the solution set.
$\left(\frac{5}{2}, \infty\right)$	3	$2 \cdot 3^2 + 3 - 15 \overset{?}{<} 0$ $6 < 0$ False	$\left(\frac{5}{2}, \infty\right)$ does not belong to the solution set.

Figure 1.22

Our analysis shows that the solution set is $(-3, \frac{5}{2})$, represented on a number line in Figure 1.22.

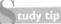tudy tip

In solving $2x^2 + x - 15 < 0$, or, equivalently, $(2x - 5)(x + 3) < 0$, an option to the use of test points is to use *sign analysis* on the product $(2x - 5)(x + 3)$.

$(2x - 5) < 0$	$(2x - 5) < 0$	$(2x - 5) > 0$	If $x < -3 : (2x - 5) < 0$ and $(x + 3) < 0$
$(x + 3) < 0$	$(x + 3) > 0$	$(x + 3) > 0$	If $-3 < x < \frac{5}{2} : (2x - 5) < 0$ and $(x + 3) > 0$

$$\xrightarrow{\qquad\qquad -3 \qquad\qquad \frac{5}{2} \qquad\qquad}$$

If $x > \frac{5}{2} : (2x - 5) > 0$ and $(x + 3) > 0$

This analysis indicates that $(2x - 5)(x + 3)$ is negative in the interval $\left(-3, \frac{5}{2}\right)$, confirming our previous solution.

EXAMPLE 2 Solving A Quadratic Inequality

Solve and graph the solution set on a real number line: $x^2 \geq 4x - 2$

Solution

$$x^2 \geq 4x - 2$$

This is the given inequality.

$$x^2 - 4x + 2 \geq 0$$

Write the inequality in standard form.

$$\underset{\underset{a = 1}{\uparrow}}{x^2} \underset{\underset{b = -4}{\uparrow}}{- 4x} \underset{\underset{c = 2}{\uparrow}}{+ 2} = 0$$

Solve the related quadratic equation.

$$x = \frac{-b \pm \sqrt{b^2 - 4ac}}{2a}$$

Use the quadratic formula with $a = 1, b = -4$, and $c = 2$.

$$= \frac{-(-4) \pm \sqrt{(-4)^2 - 4(1)(2)}}{2(1)}$$

Substitute the given numbers.

$$= \frac{4 \pm \sqrt{8}}{2}$$

Simplify under the radical sign.

$$= \frac{4 \pm 2\sqrt{2}}{2}$$

$\sqrt{8} = \sqrt{4}\sqrt{2} = 2\sqrt{2}$

$$= 2 \pm \sqrt{2}$$

Divide numerator and denominator by 2. The critical numbers are $2 - \sqrt{2} \approx 0.6$ and $2 + \sqrt{2} \approx 3.4$.

Approximately 0.6   Approximately 3.4

$$\xrightarrow{\qquad 2 - \sqrt{2} \qquad\qquad 2 + \sqrt{2} \qquad}$$

Locate these values on a number line.

The intervals are $(-\infty, 2 - \sqrt{2})$, $(2 - \sqrt{2}, 2 + \sqrt{2})$, and $(2 + \sqrt{2}, \infty)$. Now we will take one representative number from each test interval and substitute that number into the original inequality.

Test Interval	Representative Number	Substitute into $x^2 \geq 4x - 2$	Conclusion
$(-\infty, 2 - \sqrt{2})$	0	$0^2 \overset{?}{\geq} 4 \cdot 0 - 2$ $0 \geq -2$ True	$(-\infty, 2 - \sqrt{2})$ belongs to the solution set.
$(2 - \sqrt{2}, 2 + \sqrt{2})$	1	$1^2 \overset{?}{\geq} 4 \cdot 1 - 2$ $1 \geq 2$ False	$(2 - \sqrt{2}, 2 + \sqrt{2})$ does not belong to the solution set.
$(2 + \sqrt{2}, \infty)$	4	$4^2 \overset{?}{\geq} 4 \cdot 4 - 2$ $16 \geq 14$ True	$(2 + \sqrt{2}, \infty)$ belongs to the solution set.

Our analysis shows that $(-\infty, 2 - \sqrt{2})$ and $(2 + \sqrt{2}, \infty)$ belong to the solution set. Because we were given that $x^2 \geq 4x - 2$, the values of x satisfying $x^2 = 4x - 2$ (equivalently, $x^2 - 4x + 2 = 0$) are also included in the solution. Thus, the solution set is $(-\infty, 2 - \sqrt{2}] \cup [2 + \sqrt{2}, \infty)$, shown on a number line in Figure 1.23.

Figure 1.23

The graph of $x \leq 2 - \sqrt{2}$ or $x \geq 2 + \sqrt{2}$ ∎

Discover for yourself

The quadratic inequalities in Examples 1 and 2 had solution sets consisting of a single interval and the union of two intervals. However, other possibilities can occur.

The graph of $y = 4x^2 - 8x + 7$ is shown in Figure 1.24. Use the graph to solve $4x^2 - 8x + 7 > 0$ and $4x^2 - 8x + 7 < 0$.

The graph of $y = x^2 - 4x + 4$ is shown in Figure 1.25. Use the graph to solve $x^2 - 4x + 4 > 0$ and $x^2 - 4x + 4 \leq 0$.

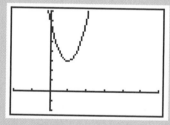

Figure 1.24

The graph of $y = 4x^2 - 8x + 7$

Figure 1.25

The graph of $y = x^2 - 4x + 4$

Discover for yourself

Try solving $4x^2 - 8x + 7 > 0$ and $4x^2 - 8x + 7 < 0$ algebraically. First solve

$$4x^2 - 8x + 7 = 0.$$

There should be no real solutions, so the test interval is the entire number line because there are no critical numbers.

Now see what happens if you solve $x^2 - 4x + 4 > 0$ and $x^2 - 4x + 4 \leq 0$ algebraically. First solve

$$x^2 - 4x + 4 = 0.$$

There should be only one solution, so the number line is divided into two test intervals.

How can the discriminant be useful in this exercise?

In the Discover for yourself, did you observe that some quadratic inequalities are satisfied by all real numbers, some are satisfied by no real numbers, and some are satisfied by only a single number?

For example, the graph of $y = 4x^2 - 8x + 7$ (Figure 1.24) lies above the x-axis (is positive) everywhere, so the solution set of $4x^2 - 8x + 7 > 0$ consists of the entire set of real numbers, $(-\infty, \infty)$. The graph of $y = 4x^2 - 8x + 7$ is not less than zero (does not lie below the x-axis) for any value of x, so the solution set of $4x^2 - 8x + 7 < 0$ is the empty set, $\emptyset$.

Now look at the graph of $y = x^2 - 4x + 4$ in Figure 1.25. The graph lies above the x-axis for all values of x except at $x = 2$. Thus, the solution set for $x^2 - 4x + 4 > 0$ is $(-\infty, 2) \cup (2, \infty)$. The graph of $y = x^2 - 4x + 4$ is never less than 0 and is equal to 0 only if $x = 2$. Thus, the solution set of $x^2 - 4x + 4 \leq 0$ consists of the single real number $\{2\}$.

Our next example involves anticipating what will appear in the viewing rectangle of a graphing utility for a given equation.

EXAMPLE 3 **Anticipating the Graph of an Equation**

Suppose that you decide to graph $y = \sqrt{27 - 3x^2}$ using a graphing utility. For what values of x would you anticipate seeing the graph?

Solution

We anticipate seeing the graph for all x-values that cause $\sqrt{27 - 3x^2}$ to be a real number. Because $\sqrt{27 - 3x^2}$ is a real number only if $27 - 3x^2$ is nonnegative, the graph will appear if $27 - 3x^2 \geq 0$.

$27 - 3x^2 \geq 0$ This is the inequality that answers the given question.

$27 - 3x^2 = 0$ Solve the related quadratic equation.

$27 = 3x^2$ Add $3x^2$ to both sides.

$9 = x^2$ Divide both sides by 3.

$\pm 3 = x$ Apply the square root method. Critical numbers are -3 and 3.

Locate these values on a number line.

The intervals are $(-\infty, -3)$, $(-3, 3)$, and $(3, \infty)$. We will take a representative number from each test interval and substitute that number into the original inequality.

Test Interval	Representative Number	Substitute into $27 - 3x^2 \geq 0$	Conclusion
$(-\infty, -3)$	-4	$27 - 3(-4)^2 \overset{?}{\geq} 0$ $-21 \geq 0$ False	$(-\infty, -3)$ does not belong to the solution set.
$(-3, 3)$	0	$27 - 3 \cdot 0^2 \overset{?}{\geq} 0$ $27 \geq 0$ True	$(-3, 3)$ belongs to the solution set.
$(3, \infty)$	4	$27 - 3 \cdot 4^2 \overset{?}{\geq} 0$ $-21 \geq 0$ False	$(3, \infty)$ does not belong to the solution set.

Figure 1.26

The graph of $y = \sqrt{27 - 3x^2}$ appears for $-3 \leq x \leq 3$.

Because we were given that $27 - 3x^2 \geq 0$, values of x satisfying $27 - 3x^2 = 0$ are also included in the solution. Thus, the solution set is the *closed interval* $[-3, 3]$. The graph of $y = \sqrt{27 - 3x^2}$ shown in Figure 1.26 confirms our anticipation of seeing a graph appear for $-3 \leq x \leq 3$. (The graphing utility shows gaps when the graph appears nearly vertical.) ■

2 Solve higher-order inequalities.

Solving Polynomial Inequalities of Degree Greater Than 2

Methods for solving quadratic inequalities may be applied to some higher-order polynomial inequalities.

EXAMPLE 4   Solving a Third-Degree Polynomial Inequality

Solve: $x^3 + x^2 - 4x - 4 > 0$

Solution

$x^3 + x^2 - 4x - 4 > 0$	This is the given inequality.
$x^3 + x^2 - 4x - 4 = 0$	Solve the related polynomial equation.
$x^2(x + 1) - 4(x + 1) = 0$	Factor by grouping.
$(x + 1)(x^2 - 4) = 0$	Complete the factoring.
$x + 1 = 0$ or $x^2 - 4 = 0$	Set each factor equal to 0.
$x = -1$ $x^2 = 4$	Solve for x.
$x = \pm 2$	The critical numbers are -2, -1, and 2.

Locate the critical numbers on a number line.

The intervals are $(-\infty, -2)$, $(-2, -1)$, $(-1, 2)$, and $(2, \infty)$. Once again we will take a representative number from each test interval and substitute that number into the original inequality.

Test Interval	Representative Number	Substitute into $x^3 + x^2 - 4x - 4 > 0$	Conclusion
$(-\infty, -2)$	-3	$(-3)^3 + (-3)^2 - 4(-3) - 4 \overset{?}{>} 0$ $-10 > 0$ False	$(-\infty, -2)$ does not belong to the solution set.
$(-2, -1)$	-1.5	$(-1.5)^3 + (-1.5)^2 - 4(-1.5) - 4 \overset{?}{>} 0$ $0.875 > 0$ True	$(-2, -1)$ belongs to the solution set.
$(-1, 2)$	0	$0^3 + 0^2 - 4 \cdot 0 - 4 \overset{?}{>} 0$ $-4 > 0$ False	$(-1, 2)$ does not belong to the solution set.
$(2, \infty)$	3	$3^3 + 3^2 - 4 \cdot 3 - 4 \overset{?}{>} 0$ $20 > 0$ True	$(2, \infty)$ belongs to the solution set.

Our analysis shows that the solution set is $(-2, -1) \cup (2, \infty)$, represented on a number line in Figure 1.27.

Figure 1.27

Some polynomial inequalities cannot be easily solved by algebraic techniques but can be handled with a graphing utility.

> **EXAMPLE 5**   **Estimating the Solution of a Polynomial Inequality with a Graphing Utility**

Solve: $x^3 - 3x - 1 > 0$

Solution

We begin by graphing $y = x^3 - 3x - 1$, as shown in Figure 1.28. We need to find values of x where the graph is positive (lies above the x-axis). Using ‾TRACE‾ and ‾ZOOM‾ features (shown partly for one of the three critical numbers in Figure 1.29), we see that the solution set is approximately

$$(-1.53, -0.35) \cup (1.88, \infty).$$

Figure 1.28
The graph of $y = x^3 - 3x - 1$

X=-.3571428571 Y=.02587463546

Figure 1.29
The graph of $y = x^3 - 3x - 1$ using the ‾TRACE‾ and ‾ZOOM‾ features

3 Solve applied modeling problems.

Modeling with Polynomial Inequalities

In Problem Set 1.3 you worked with the following position model for a falling object.

> **Position model for a free-falling object near earth's surface**
>
> An object that is falling or vertically projected into the air has its height in feet above the ground modeled by
>
> $$s = -16t^2 + v_0 t + s_0$$
>
> where s is the height (in feet), v_0 is the original velocity (initial velocity) of the object (in feet per second), t is the time that the object is in motion (in seconds), and s_0 is the original height (initial height) of the object (in feet).

In Example 6 we apply the solution process for a quadratic inequality to solve a problem about the position of a free-falling object.

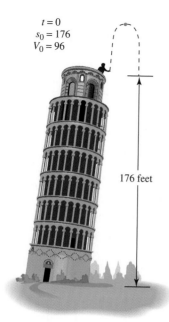

$t = 0$
$s_0 = 176$
$V_0 = 96$

176 feet

Figure 1.30

Throwing a ball from 176 feet with a velocity of 96 feet per second

The graphs of

$$y_1 = -16x^2 + 96x + 176$$

and

$$y_2 = 176$$

were obtained with a graphing utility using the following range setting:

Xmin = 0, Xmax = 8, Xscl = 1,

Ymin = 0, Ymax = 320, Yscl = 32
The graph shows that $y_1 > y_2$ (height exceeds that of the tower) for $0 < x < 6$.

$y_1 = -16x^2 + 96x + 176$

$y_2 = 176$

4 Solve rational inequalities.

EXAMPLE 6   **Using the Position Model**

A ball is thrown vertically upward from the top of the Leaning Tower of Pisa (176 feet high) with an initial velocity of 96 feet per second (Figure 1.30). During what time period will the ball's height exceed that of the tower?

Solution

$$s = -16t^2 + v_0t + s_0 \qquad \text{This is the position model for a free-falling object.}$$

$$s = -16t^2 + 96t + 176 \qquad \text{Since } v_0 \text{ (initial velocity)} = 96 \text{ and } s_0 \text{ (initial position)} = 176, \text{ substitute these values into the model.}$$

When will the ball's height exceed that of the tower?

$$-16t^2 + 96t + 176 \qquad > \qquad 176$$

$$-16t^2 + 96t + 176 > 176 \qquad \text{This is the inequality implied by the problem's question. We must find } t.$$

$$-16t^2 + 96t > 0 \qquad \text{Subtract 176 from both sides.}$$

$$-16t^2 + 96t = 0 \qquad \text{Solve the related quadratic equation.}$$

$$-16t(t - 6) = 0 \qquad \text{Factor.}$$

$$-16t = 0 \quad \text{or} \quad t - 6 = 0 \qquad \text{Set each factor equal to 0.}$$

$$t = 0 \qquad\qquad t = 6 \qquad \text{Solve for } t. \text{ The critical numbers are 0 and 6.}$$

0   6

Locate these values on a number line, with $t \geqslant 0$.

The intervals are $(0, 6)$ and $(6, \infty)$, although the time interval should not extend to infinity but rather to the value of t when the ball hits the ground. (By setting $-16t^2 + 96t + 176$ equal to zero, we find $t \approx 7.47$; the ball hits the ground after approximately 7.47 seconds.)

At this point, with intervals of $(0, 6)$ and $(6, 7.47)$, it seems geometrically obvious that the ball's height exceeds that of the tower during its first 6 seconds. We verify this in the usual manner.

Test Interval	Representative Number	Substitute into $-16t^2 + 96t > 0$	Conclusion
$(0, 6)$	1	$-16 \cdot 1^2 + 96 \cdot 1 \overset{?}{>} 0$ $80 > 0$ True	$(0, 6)$ belongs to the solution set.
$(6, 7.47)$	7	$-16 \cdot 7^2 + 96 \cdot 7 \overset{?}{>} 0$ $-112 > 0$ False	$(6, 7.47)$ does not belong to the solution set.

The ball's height exceeds that of the tower between 0 and 6 seconds, excluding $t = 0$ and $t = 6$. ■

Solving Rational Inequalities

Inequalities that involve quotients can be solved in the same manner as polynomial inequalities. For example, the inequalities

$$(x + 3)(x - 7) > 0 \quad \text{and} \quad \frac{x + 3}{x - 7} > 0$$

are very similar in that both are positive under the same conditions. Each of these inequalities must have two positive factors

$$x + 3 > 0 \quad \text{and} \quad x - 7 > 0$$

or two negative factors

$$x + 3 < 0 \quad \text{and} \quad x - 7 < 0.$$

Consequently, we can once again use critical numbers to divide the number line into test intervals and select one representative number in each interval to determine whether that interval belongs to the solution set.

EXAMPLE 7 Solving a Rational Inequality

Solve: $\dfrac{x + 1}{x + 3} < 2$

Solution

Our first step is to obtain 0 on one side of the inequality.

$\dfrac{x + 1}{x + 3} < 2$	This is the given inequality.
$\dfrac{x + 1}{x + 3} - 2 < 0$	Subtract 2 from both sides, obtaining 0 on the right.
$\dfrac{x + 1}{x + 3} - \dfrac{2(x + 3)}{x + 3} < 0$	Prepare to subtract fractions, writing the 2 as an equivalent fraction with $x + 3$ as the denominator.
$\dfrac{x + 1 - 2(x + 3)}{x + 3} < 0$	Subtract rational expressions.
$\dfrac{-x - 5}{x + 3} < 0$	Simplify the numerator.
$-x - 5 = 0 \qquad x + 3 = 0$	Set the numerator and denominator equal to 0. These are the values that make the previous quotient zero or undefined.
$x = -5 \qquad\qquad x = -3$	Solve for x. The critical numbers are -5 and -3.

Locate these values on a number line.

We've used open dots because -5 cannot be a solution (it makes $\dfrac{-x - 5}{x + 3}$ equal zero and we want solutions that make the fraction less than zero) and -3 cannot be a solution (it makes the denominator zero).

The intervals are $(-\infty, -5)$, $(-5, -3)$, and $(-3, \infty)$. Now we will take one representative number from each test interval and substitute that number into the original inequality.

PROBLEM SET 1.6

Practice Problems

Solve each inequality in Problems 1–48 and graph the solution set on a real number line. Express each solution set in interval notation.

1. $x^2 - 8x > -15$

2. $x^2 - 3x > 10$

3. $2x^2 + 5x \leqslant 3$

4. $2x^2 - 7x \leqslant -5$

5. $x^2 + 8x + 13 \geqslant 0$

6. $x^2 - 2x - 17 \geqslant 0$

7. $2x^2 - 7x + 4 < x - 1$

8. $2x^2 - 5x + 4 < x + 1$

9. $2x^2 - 7x - 3 \leqslant 9 - 7x$

10. $(x - 3)(x + 1) \leqslant 1$

11. $x^2 + 2x + 5 > 0$

12. $x^2 - 8x + 19 > 0$

13. $2x^2 + 3x + 4 \leqslant 0$

14. $3x^2 + 4x + 3 \leqslant 0$

15. $2(x - 1) + 8 < 2(x + 3)(x - 5)$

16. $(x - 2)(x + 3) - 2 < 2(x + 2)(x - 2)$

17. $x^2 - 4x + 4 \geqslant 0$

18. $x^2 - 6x + 9 \geqslant 0$

19. $x^3 + 2x^2 - x - 2 \geqslant 0$

20. $x^3 + 2x^2 - 4x - 8 \geqslant 0$

21. $x^3 - 3x^2 - 9x + 27 < 0$

22. $x^3 + 7x^2 - x - 7 < 0$

23. $9x^3 + 8 > 4x + 18x^2$

24. $4x^3 - 2 > x - 8x^2$

25. $x^3 + x^2 + 4x + 4 > 0$

26. $x^3 - x^2 + 9x - 9 > 0$

27. $(x - 2)^3 > 0$

28. $(x - 3)^3 > 0$

29. $\dfrac{x + 3}{x - 7} > 0$

30. $\dfrac{x - 4}{x + 3} > 0$

31. $\dfrac{x + 3}{x + 4} < 0$

32. $\dfrac{x + 5}{x + 2} < 0$

33. $\dfrac{x + 3}{x - 2} \leqslant 2$

34. $\dfrac{x - 2}{x + 2} \leqslant 2$

35. $\dfrac{x + 4}{2x - 1} \geqslant 3$

36. $\dfrac{4x + 2}{2x - 3} \geqslant 2$

37. $\dfrac{3}{x + 3} > \dfrac{3}{x - 2}$

38. $\dfrac{1}{x + 1} > \dfrac{2}{x - 1}$

39. $\dfrac{3}{x - 1} - \dfrac{x}{x + 1} > 1$

40. $\dfrac{2}{x} - \dfrac{2}{x + 1} > 1$

41. $\dfrac{2x + 1}{x - 1} < 1 + \dfrac{2}{x - 3}$

42. $\dfrac{2x}{x + 5} < \dfrac{1}{5} - \dfrac{x - 1}{x - 5}$

43. $\dfrac{x}{x - 2} \geqslant 2 + \dfrac{3}{x + 1}$

44. $x \geqslant 4 + \dfrac{10}{x - 1}$

45. $\dfrac{x^2 - x - 2}{x^2 - 4x + 3} > 0$

46. $\dfrac{x^2 - 3x + 2}{x^2 - 2x - 3} > 0$

47. $\left| x^2 + 2x - 36 \right| > 12$

48. $\left| x^2 + 6x + 1 \right| > 8$

Application Problems

Use the position model

$$s = -16t^2 + v_0 t + s_0 \ (v_0 = \text{initial velocity}, s_0 = \text{initial position}, t = \text{time})$$

to answer Problems 49–52.

49. A projectile is fired straight upward from ground level with an initial velocity of 80 feet per second. During what interval of time will the projectile's height exceed 96 feet?

50. A projectile is fired straight upward from ground level with an initial velocity of 128 feet per second. During what interval of time will the projectile's height exceed 128 feet?

51. A ball is thrown upward with a velocity of 64 feet per second from the top edge of a building 80 feet high. For how long is the ball higher than 96 feet?

52. A diver leaps into the air at 20 feet per second from a diving board that is 10 feet above the water. For how

many seconds is the diver at least 12 feet above the water?

53. The sum of the first *n* natural numbers is given by

$$1 + 2 + 3 + \cdots + n = \frac{n^2 + n}{2}.$$

What values of *n* will produce a sum that is less than 66?

54. The total cost of producing *x* radios per hour is $C = \frac{1}{4}x^2 + 35x + 25$, and the price at which each radio can be sold is given by $50 - \dfrac{x}{2}$. What should be the hourly output to obtain a profit that exceeds $47 per radio?

55. The cost of removing $p\%$ of the bacteria from a river is given by the model

$$C = \frac{4p}{100 - p}$$

where C is measured in hundreds of thousands of dollars. If less than $600,000 is spent, what percentage of the bacteria can be removed?

56. The average cost per unit $(\overline{C})$ of producing x units of a product is modeled by

$$\overline{C} = \frac{150,000 + 0.25x}{x}.$$

How many units must be produced so that the average cost of producing each unit does not exceed $1.75?

57. A pool measuring 30 feet by 20 feet is to have a brick path of uniform width placed completely around it. If no more than 336 square feet of brick are to be used, describe possibilities for the path's width.

58. Identical squares are removed from the four corners of an 8-by-11-centimeter rectangular sheet of cardboard. The sides are turned up to form a box with no lid. Find the possible lengths of the sides of the removed squares

if the area of the bottom does not exceed 50 square centimeters.

True–False Critical Thinking Problems

59. Which one of the following is true?

a. The solution set to $x^2 > 25$ is $(5, \infty)$.

b. The inequality $\dfrac{x - 2}{x + 3} < 2$ can be solved by multiplying both sides by $x + 3$, resulting in the equivalent inequality $x - 2 < 2(x + 3)$.

c. $(x + 3)(x - 1) > 0$ and $\dfrac{x + 3}{x - 1} > 0$ have the same solution set.

d. None of these statements is true.

60. Which one of the following is true?

a. The solution set to $(2x - 3)(x + 2) < 0$ is $(-\infty, -2)$ $\cup (1.5, \infty)$.

b. Every quadratic inequality contains at least one real number in its solution set.

c. The solution set to $\dfrac{x - 3}{(x + 4)^2} > 0$ is $(3, \infty)$.

d. None of these statements is true.

Technology Problems

Use a graphing utility to estimate the solution of each inequality in Problems 61–66.

61. $12x^3 - 6x^2 - 24x + 18 > 0$

62. $x^4 - 5x^3 + 6x^2 + 4x - 8 \leqslant 0$

63. $\dfrac{x}{x + 3} > 4$

64. $\dfrac{4}{x} \leqslant x$

65. $\dfrac{x^2 - 1}{x^2 + 1} \geqslant 0$

66. $\dfrac{6}{x - 1} - \dfrac{6}{x} \geqslant 1$

67. The cost (y) of removing $x\%$ of pollutants in a lake is given by the mathematical model

$$y = \frac{80,000x}{100 - x}.$$

a. If less than $320,000 is spent, what percent of the lake's pollutants can be removed? (Solve algebraically.)

b. Verify your algebraic solution by graphing the model on your graphing utility using the following range setting:

Xmin = 0, Xmax = 100, Xscl = 10, Ymin = 0,

Ymax = 1,000,000, Yscl = 100,000

c. What does the graph indicate about removing all of the lake's pollutants?

68. In a study of the winter moth in Nova Scotia, the number of eggs (N) in a female moth depended on her abdominal width (W, in millimeters), approximated by $N = 14W^3 - 17W^2 - 6W + 34$, where $1.5 \leqslant W \leqslant 3.5$. Graph the model on your graphing utility and use the ⬚TRACE⬚ and ⬚ZOOM⬚ features to describe the abdominal width of a moth with more than 46 eggs.

69. The concentration of a particular drug in the bloodstream is approximated by the model

$$C = \frac{3t}{t^2 + t + 1}$$

where C is the concentration in milligrams per liter t hours after the drug is orally administered.

a. Graph the model on your graphing utility using the following range setting:

$$\text{Xmin} = 0, \text{Xmax} = 10, \text{Xscl} = 1,$$

$$\text{Ymin} = 0, \text{Ymax} = 1, \text{Yscl} = 0.1$$

b. If the concentration exceeds 0.6 milligram per liter, the drug is effective. Use the graph to determine the time interval in which this occurs.

c. Experiment with the range settings for Xmax and Xscl, describing what happens to the concentration with increased time. From the behavior of the graph, when, if ever, is the concentration zero?

Suppose that you decide to graph each equation in Problems 70–81 using a graphing utility. For what values of x would you anticipate seeing the graph? After finding each interval algebraically, verify your result by using a utility to graph the equation.

70. $y = \sqrt{x^2 - x - 2}$

71. $y = \sqrt{x^2 - 7x + 10}$

72. $y = \dfrac{1}{\sqrt{x^2 - x - 2}}$

73. $y = \dfrac{1}{\sqrt{x^2 - 7x + 10}}$

74. $y = \sqrt[3]{x^2 - x - 2}$

75. $y = \sqrt[3]{x^2 - 7x + 10}$

76. $y = \sqrt{\dfrac{x + 1}{x - 3}}$

77. $y = \sqrt{\dfrac{x + 2}{x - 5}}$

78. $y = \dfrac{1}{\sqrt{3x^3 + 3x^2}}$

79. $y = \dfrac{1}{\sqrt{2x^4 + 6x^3}}$

80. $y = \sqrt{x^2 - x + 15}$

81. $y = \dfrac{1}{\sqrt{16x^2 + 24x + 9}}$

Writing in Mathematics

In Problems 82–85, describe how to solve each inequality by inspection. What is the solution set for each?

82. $(x - 2)^2 > 0$?

83. $\dfrac{1}{(x - 2)^2} > 0$

84. $-\dfrac{1}{(x - 2)^2} > 0$

85. $(x - 2)^2 \geqslant 0$

86. Suppose you are a math tutor and your student brings you the following problem. First solve the problem and then describe how you would explain the solution to your student.

A piece of wire 6 decimeters long is cut into two pieces and each piece is then bent to form a square. If the length of one piece is represented by x, describe the values of x that will result in the two squares having a combined area that exceeds 20 square decimeters.

Critical Thinking Problems

87. For what values of c is $x = 1$ a solution of $\dfrac{c + 2x}{c + 5x} \leqslant 1$?

88. For what values of k will $x^2 + kx + k = 0$ have two real numbers in its solution set?

89. Write a quadratic inequality whose solution set is $[-3, 5]$.

90. Write a rational inequality whose solution set is $(-\infty, -4) \cup [3, \infty)$.

91. Solve $(x - 1)^{-2} + 2(x - 1)^{-1} + 3 \geqslant 0$ by letting $t = (x - 1)^{-1}$.

92. Solve for x: $b^2x^{-2} - 2bx^{-1} + 1 > 0$.

CHAPTER PROJECT

Space-time and the Fourth Dimension

In Section 1.4, we introduced Einstein's equations relating mass, time, and length from his theory of special relativity, and looked at some interesting problems in space and time. The theory of special relativity is concerned with the motions of objects in space.

1. In your mind, create a three-dimensional coordinate system by looking at a corner of the room. Let the xy-plane be the floor beneath your feet, and another axis, the z-axis, extend up from the floor to the ceiling. Think of the positive x-axis as running along the bottom of the left-hand wall, the positive y-axis as running along the bottom of the right-hand wall and the positive z-axis as running up and down where the two walls meet. The origin of our coordinate system is the corner at the bottom where the walls meet the floor. Sit quietly for a few seconds. Relative to this coordinate system, did you move? Picture a coordinate system centered on the sun. Sit quietly for a few seconds. Did you move with respect to the sun-centered coordinate system? In general, when sitting perfectly still, how could you answer the question, "Are you moving?"

Einstein's theory of general relativity is concerned with the structure, or the geometry, of the universe as a whole. In order to describe the universe, Einstein discovered that he needed four variables: three variables to locate an object in space and a fourth variable describing time. This system is known as *space-time*.

2. In a random pattern, wave a pencil in the air. Try this same motion with a small flashlight in a darkened room. Concentrate on the trail in space created by the motion. How could you describe the existence of the trail you follow with your eyes? To help answer that question, move the pencil or light in a repeating figure eight pattern. Why doesn't the pencil or light ever hit itself as it moves through the pattern? To see the world in terms of space-time, walk through a mall and try to picture people walking as trails in space-time.

3. If we attempt to view the universe as points in space-time, we may ask the question, "What causes the illusion of time passing?" Some philosophers have argued that the passage of time is a myth, that each moment of our lives exists already and we are, in fact, existing in each moment simultaneously. They state it is only our memories keeping an "order" to time. There is no such thing as free will because each moment in space-time already exists and has always existed. On the other hand, every possible choice may also exist. We exist as many different "selves," each of them following a different choice. This is called the *branching universe model*.

To view a point in Einstein's space-time, we would need four coordinates to plot, three coordinates for space and one for time. Since we are three-dimensional beings, how can we imagine a four-dimensional graph? One interesting approach to visualizing four dimensions is to consider an analogy of a two-dimensional being struggling to understand three dimensions. This approach first appeared in a book called *Flatland* by Edwin Abbott written around 1884.

Flatland is a world existing on a flat, two-dimensional plane. The beings in Flatland are geometric objects such as squares and triangles. A house in Flatland would look like a blueprint or a line drawing to us. If we were to draw a closed circle around a being in Flatland, they would be imprisoned in a cell with no way to see out or escape because there is no way to move up and over the line. For a two-dimensional being moving only on a plane, the idea of up would be incomprehensible. We could explain that up means moving in a new direction, perpendicular to the two dimensions they know, but it would be similar to someone telling us we can move in the fourth dimension by traveling perpendicular to our three dimensions.

Obtain a copy of *Flatland* from your library and read this early science fiction story.

4. Imagine a Flatland square sitting in its house in a closed room. You begin speaking to the square. How would the square describe where the voice was coming from? You try to show the square the existence

of the third dimension by pushing a ball through the plane where the square sits. What would the square see as the ball is being pushed through its plane? If you pushed your hand through the plane, what would the square see? You look down from above, and tell the square what is happening in the next room. In fact, you can tell the square what is happening inside its body. There is no place in Flatland closed to you. How would you interpret this analogy with a four-dimensional being intruding in our world?

5. Using resources on the Worldwide Web or your library, discover a representation of the four-dimensional version of a cube called a hypercube or tesseract. Does this representation help to visualize the fourth dimension? Would it help to make a three-dimensional model of the hypercube to study? Share your findings with the class.

6. Imagine pushing a three-dimensional cube through a plane. Can you sketch what you would see if you could only look in two dimensions? Change the orientation of the cube slightly and repeat the push through a plane. How do your new sketches differ from the first set? Would a two-dimensional being understand a cube by looking at the different sets of sketches? Contrast this exercise using a cube with one using a sphere.

These two different approaches to understanding the fourth dimension, one where it is time, the other where it is another spatial dimension, are not incompatible. Time may always be viewed as one more dimension added on, no matter how many spatial dimensions exist. In fact, some modern theories now use as many as ten dimensions to explain the structure of the universe.

Worldwide Web Resources

Go to the Prentice Hall website (http://www.prenhall.com/blitzer) to access other locations on the Internet that will allow you to further explore the concepts presented in this project.

Chapter Review

SUMMARY

1. **Solving Linear Equations**

   a. If necessary, clear fractions, multiplying both sides by the LCD.

   b. Simplify each side.

   c. Add (or subtract) the same real number or variable expression on both sides to collect all terms with the variable on one side and all other terms on the other side.

   d. Multiply (or divide) both sides of the equation by the same nonzero quantity and solve for the variable.

   e. Check the proposed solution by substituting or with a graphing utility.

2. **Solving Linear Equations Involving Absolute Value**

   a. If c is positive, rewrite $|ax + b| = c$ as $ax + b = c$ or $ax + b = -c$ and solve each of the resulting equations for x.

   b. If $|ax + b| = |cx + d|$, rewrite as $ax + b = cx + d$ or $ax + b = -(cx + d)$ and solve each of the resulting equations for x.

3. **Solving Formulas and Linear Mathematical Models for a Specified Variable**

   These equations often contain more than one variable. Follow the procedure for solving linear equations. If the terms containing the specified variable cannot be combined as like terms, factor the variable from these terms. Then solve for the specified variable by dividing both sides of the equation by the factor that appears with the specified variable.

4. **Solving Quadratic Equations by Factoring**

   a. The standard form of a quadratic equation is

   $$ax^2 + bx + c = 0 \qquad (a \neq 0).$$

   b. Some quadratic equations can be solved by factoring.

1. Write the equation in standard form.
2. Factor $ax^2 + bx + c$.
3. Apply the zero product principle, setting each factor equal to 0.
4. Solve the equations in step 3.
5. Check proposed solutions by substitution or with a graphing utility.

5. **Solving Quadratic Equations by the Square Root Method**
   a. The square root method states that if $u^2 = d$, then $u = \pm \sqrt{d}$, where u is an algebraic expression.
   b. The square root method works well on quadratic equations in the form $ax^2 + c = 0$. Solve for x^2 and then apply the method.
   c. The method works well on equations of the form $(ax + b)^2 = d$, resulting in $ax + b = \pm \sqrt{d}$.

6. **Solving Quadratic Equations by Completing the Square**
   a. Write the equation in the form $ax^2 + bx = c$.
   b. If $a \neq 1$, divide both sides by a.
   c. Complete the square by adding the square of half the coefficient of the x-term to both sides.
   d. Factor the left side and simplify the right side, if possible.
   e. Apply the square root method and solve.

7. **Solving Quadratic Equations by the Quadratic Formula**
   The formula is derived by completing the square.

   If $ax^2 + bx + c = 0$, then $x = \dfrac{-b \pm \sqrt{b^2 - 4ac}}{2a}$.

8. **The Discriminant**
   The discriminant, $b^2 - 4ac$, determines the nature of the solutions to a quadratic equation.
   a. If $b^2 - 4ac$ positive, the equation has two real solutions.
   b. If $b^2 - 4ac = 0$, the equation has one rational solution.
   c. If $b^2 - 4ac < 0$, the solutions are not real numbers. There are two nonreal complex solutions.

9. **A Problem-Solving Strategy**
   1. Read the problem and let x represent one unknown quantity.
   2. If necessary, represent other unknowns in terms of x.
   3. Form a verbal model of the problem's conditions and then write an equation in x that translates the verbal model.
   4. Solve the equation and answer the problem's question.
   5. Check the answer using the verbal conditions given in the problem.

10. **Polynomial Equations**
    a. Some polynomial equations of degree greater than 2 can be solved by factoring.
    b. Real solutions to an nth-degree polynomial equation can be found (or approximated) by using a graphing utility. The solutions correspond to the x-intercepts.
    c. Some polynomial equations are quadratic in form in that they can be written in the form $at^2 + bt + c = 0$ where t is a polynomial and $a \neq 0$.

11. **Solving Equations That Are Quadratic in Form**
    Introduce the substitution $t = x^{\frac{n}{2}}$ in the equation $ax^n + bx^{\frac{n}{2}} + c = 0$. Solve $at^2 + bt + c = 0$ for t. Find x by substituting the value(s) of t into $x^{\frac{n}{2}} = t$.

12. **Solving Equations Involving Radicals**
    a. Isolate one of the radical terms on one side of the equation.
    b. Raise both sides of the equation to a power that is the same number as the index of the radical.
    c. Solve the resulting equation.
    d. Substitute all proposed solutions in the original radical equation, eliminating solutions that do not check.

13. **Solving Equations in the Form $x^{\frac{m}{n}} = k$**
    a. Raise both sides to the $\dfrac{n}{m}$ power.
    b. If m is even: $x = \pm k^{\frac{n}{m}}$
       If m is odd: $x = k^{\frac{n}{m}}$

14. **Solving Linear Inequalities**
    Use the procedure for solving linear equations. However, when multiplying or dividing by a negative number, reverse the sense of the inequality.

15. **Solving Linear Inequalities Involving Absolute Value**
    If c is positive:
    a. $|ax + b| < c$ means $-c < ax + b < c$.
    b. $|ax + b| > c$ means $ax + b > c$ or $ax + b < -c$.
    These rules are valid if $<$ is replaced by $\leq$ and $>$ is replaced by $\geq$.

16. **Solving Quadratic Inequalities**
    a. Express the inequality in the form $ax^2 + bx + c > 0$ or $ax^2 + bx + c < 0$
    b. Solve the equation $ax^2 + bx + c = 0$. The real solutions are *critical numbers*.
    c. Locate these critical numbers on a number line, thereby dividing the number line into test intervals.
    d. Choose one representative number for each test interval. If substituting that value into the original inequality produces a true statement, then all real numbers in the test interval belong to the solution set.
    e. The solution set is the union of all such test intervals.

17. Solving Rational Inequalities

a. Write the inequality so that one side is 0.

b. If necessary, combine terms on the other side into a single quotient.

c. Locate points on a number line for which the quotient is zero (numbers making the numerator zero) or undefined (numbers making the denominator

zero). These critical numbers will divide the number line into test intervals.

d. Choose one representative number for each test interval. If substituting that value into the original inequality produces a true statement, then all real numbers in the test interval belong to the solution set. The solution set is the union of all such test intervals.

REVIEW PROBLEMS

Find the solution set for each equation in Problems 1–31. Check your answer by substitution or with a graphing utility.

1. $x - 4(2x - 7) = 3(x + 6)$

2. $\frac{1}{2}(3x + 1) = \frac{1}{3}(3 - x) + \frac{1}{6}(7x + 3)$

3. $3 - [2x - (2x - 1)] = 5x - [6x + 4(5 - x)]$

4. $\frac{9}{4} - \frac{1}{2x} = \frac{4}{x}$

5. $\frac{7}{x - 5} + 2 = \frac{x + 2}{x - 5}$

6. $\frac{1}{x - 1} - \frac{1}{x + 1} = \frac{2}{x^2 - 1}$

7. $\frac{1}{x^2 - x - 2} = \frac{1}{x^2 - 3x + 2} - \frac{2}{x^2 - 1}$

8. $|3x - 2| = 4$

9. $\left|1 - \frac{3}{4}x\right| + 4 = 7$

10. $|3x - 5| = |5x + 3|$

11. $x(x - 3) - 12 = 2x(x + 2)$

12. $\frac{12}{x} + 1 = \frac{12}{x - 1}$

13. $3x^2 - 6x = 0$

14. $6x^2 - 5 = 0$

15. $(3x - 6)^2 = 27$

16. $2x^2 - 2x + 2 = 7$

17. $\frac{2x}{x + 2} = 1 - \frac{3}{x + 4}$

18. $\frac{x}{2} + \frac{x^2}{2} = \frac{-3}{4}$

19. $2x^4 = 50x^2$

20. $2x^3 - x^2 - 18x + 9 = 0$

21. $x^4 - 5x^2 + 4 = 0$

22. $(x^2 + 2x)^2 = 5(x^2 + 2x) - 6$

23. $5 + \sqrt{5x - 1} = x$

24. $\sqrt{5x} - \sqrt{2x - 1} = 2$

25. $\sqrt{x + 9} - \sqrt{x + 16} + \sqrt{x + 1} = 0$

26. $x^{\frac{2}{3}} - 1 = 8$

27. $3x^{\frac{3}{4}} - 24 = 0$

28. $(x^2 - x - 4)^{\frac{3}{4}} - 2 = 6$

29. $x^{\frac{1}{2}} + 3x^{\frac{1}{4}} - 10 = 0$

30. $3x^{\frac{4}{3}} - 5x^{\frac{2}{3}} + 2 = 0$

31. $\left(x + \frac{12}{x}\right)^2 - 15\left(x + \frac{12}{x}\right) + 56 = 0$

Solve each inequality in Problems 32–47, expressing the solution set in interval notation. Graph the solution set on a real number line. Verify your solution sets with a graphing utility.

32. $3 - (4 - x) \geq 3x - (x + 5)$

33. $4(x - 2)(x + 3) < (2x + 3)(2x - 3)$

34. $\frac{x}{3} - \frac{3}{4} - 1 > \frac{x}{2}$

35. $7 < 2x + 3 \leq 9$

36. $1 \leq 1 - (5x - 2) < 11$

37. $|3(x - 1) + 2| < 20$

38. $\left|1 - \frac{4x}{3}\right| \geq 5$

39. $|3 - 2x| - 8 < 4$

40. $2x^2 + 7x \leq 4$

41. $2x^2 > 6x - 3$

42. $x^2 + 3x + 8 \leq 0$

43. $x^2 + 2x > -6$

44. $x^3 + 2x^2 - 9x - 18 > 0$

45. $x^4 + 4x^3 + 3x^2 < 0$

46. $\frac{x + 3}{x - 4} < 5$

47. $\frac{x}{x + 1} - \frac{2}{x + 3} \leq 1$

In Problems 48–49, solve each formula for the specified variable.

48. $A = 2LW + 2WH + 2LH$, for H

49. $R_T = \frac{R_1 R_2}{R_1 + R_2}$, for R_1

50. Chamberlain's model describes the number of years (N) that you should drive your car before purchasing a new one. The formula states

$$N = \frac{GMC}{(G - M)DP}$$

where G = new car's gas mileage, M = your present car's gas mileage, C = the cost of the new car, D = number of miles driven yearly, and P = price of gasoline per gallon.

   a. Solve the formula for G.

   b. Use part (a) to write and solve a problem involving gas mileage that should be expected from a new car. You'll need to provide values for each variable, except G, in the model.

51. The models $C = 1.24t + 313.6$ and $C = 0.018t^2 + 0.70t + 316.2$ both describe carbon dioxide concentration (C, in ppm) t years after 1960. Use each model to predict in what year carbon dioxide concentration will be 400 ppm.

52. The model

$$d = x + \frac{x^2}{20}$$

describes the distance (d, in feet) that it takes for a car to come to a complete stop once the brakes are applied, where x is the car's speed in miles per hour. If a car travels 175 feet once the brakes are suddenly applied, what was its speed prior to the brakes being hit?

Use the position model $s = -16t^2 + v_0t + s_0$, where v_0 represents initial velocity, s_0 represents initial position, and t represents time to answer Problems 53–54.

53. A diver jumps directly upward from a diving board that is 32 feet above the water with an initial velocity of 16 feet per second. How long does it take for the diver to hit the water?

54. A person standing close to the edge of an 80-foot cliff throws a rock directly upward with an initial velocity of 64 feet per second.

   a. Write the formula that models the position of the rock above the ground at any time t.

   b. Use the discriminant to determine if the rock will ever reach a height of 150 feet.

   c. Verify part (b) using a graphing utility.

55. Costs for two different kinds of heating systems for a three-bedroom house are given below.

System	Cost to Install	Operating Cost per Year
Electric	$5000	$1100
Gas	$12,000	$700

After how long will total costs for electric heating and gas heating be the same? What will be the cost at that time?

56. A person purchasing a house is considering two options for a $40,000 mortgage:

Option 1:
8.5% interest on a 30-year loan with no points

Option 2:
8% interest on a 30-year loan with 3 points

Use the table on page 141 to determine how long it will take for the total cost of each mortgage to be the same.

57. A two-year union contract guarantees an immediate 4% raise and a 7% raise after a year. How much must an employee be earning at the start of the contract if that employee's weekly salary increases by $45.12 over the two-year life of the contract?

58. An owner of a large diving boat that can carry as many as 50 people charges $8 per passenger to groups of between 5 and 10 people. If more than 10 divers charter the boat, the fee per passenger is decreased by 20 cents times the number of people over 10. How many people must there be in a diving group to generate an income of $117.80?

59. a. In 1993, there were 42.3 million Americans who were never married. This is a 98% increase over the number for 1970. How many Americans in 1970 were never married?

   b. The number of married Americans in 1993 is 170% greater than the number of never-married Americans for the same year. How many married Americans were there in 1993?

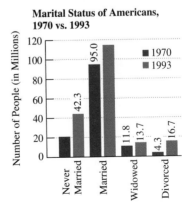

Marital Status of Americans, 1970 vs. 1993

Source: U.S. Bureau of the Census

Revenue for a company is the money received for the sale of x units of a product, and is found by multiplying the number of units sold by the price per unit. A company's profit is the difference between its revenue and its cost of producing x units of a product. Use these ideas to answer Problem 60.

60. A publishing company spends $10,000 to set up the press for publishing a book that costs the company $8 for each book printed. They find that they can sell x books at a price of $20 - \dfrac{x}{1000}$ dollars per book. How many books should be printed and sold to generate a profit of $26,000?

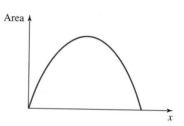

61. A billboard is 15 feet longer than it is high and has space for 324 square feet of advertising. What are the billboard's dimensions?

62. A swimming pool has a length that is $2\frac{1}{2}$ times longer than its width. The pool is surrounded by a brick path that has a uniform width of 5 feet. The path requires 1150 square feet of brick. Determine the pool's dimensions.

63. A rectangular field is to be fenced on three sides with 2400 feet of fencing. As shown in the figure, the fourth side is a straight river's edge that will not be fenced.

a. If the area of the enclosure is 720,000 square feet, find the field's dimensions.

b. Use a graphing utility to graph the area model obtained in part (a). Experiment with the range setting until your graph resembles the one shown in the figure at the top of the next column. Does the rectangle enclosed in part (a) make the best use of the 2400 feet of fencing? Explain.

64. An open box is made from a square piece of cardboard by cutting 3-inch squares from each corner and turning up the sides. If the volume of the box is 108 cubic inches, what are the dimensions of the original piece of cardboard?

65. The figure shows a triangle drawn inside a square. If the area of the shaded region is 368.5 square centimeters, find the dimensions of the square. Be sure to check your value of x with the given condition about the area of the shaded region.

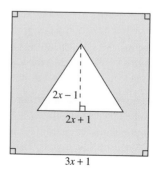

66. If the area of the rectangular base of the solid shown in the figure is 40 square inches, find the volume of the solid.

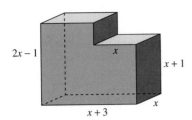

67. A water tank has the shape of an inverted right circular cone of altitude 8 feet and base radius 4 feet. How much water is in the tank when the water is 6 feet deep?

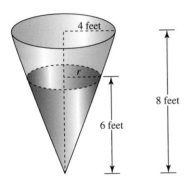

68. Use Einstein's model

$$L = L_0 \sqrt{1 - \frac{v^2}{c^2}}$$

which relates length at rest (L_0) to length (L) at velocity v, to answer this question. (The speed of light, c, is approximately 186,000 miles per second.) How fast would a futuristic starship that is 500 meters tall have to move so that its length would be diminished by 80% from the perspective of a stationary observer who looks up and sees the ship?

69. Use Einstein's model

$$T = \frac{T_0}{\sqrt{1 - \frac{v^2}{c^2}}}$$

which relates time at rest (T_0) to time (T) at velocity v, to answer this question. A clock on board a futuristic starship traveling at 80% of the speed of light measures a 20-second time period. How long is this time period from the perspective of a stationary observer who looks up and sees the ship?

70. The demand equation for a product is $p = 60 - \sqrt{0.01x + 1}$, where x is the number of units demanded per day and p is the price per unit. Find the demand if the price is set at $57.00.

71. A person rows in a straight line across a 5-mile wide channel from point P to point C, and then walks from point C to point B, as shown in the figure. The distance from A to B is 6 miles. The rowing rate is 2 miles per hour, and the walking rate is 6 miles per hour.

a. Since

$$\text{Time} = \frac{\text{Distance}}{\text{Rate}}$$

we can use the figure and the given information to set up a model for the total time spent rowing and walking. Refer to the figure and fill in the missing portions in the modeling process shown below.

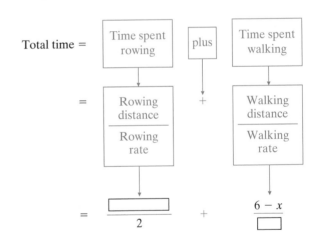

b. If the total time spent rowing and walking is $\frac{11}{3}$ hours (3 hours and 40 minutes), use your total time model from part (a) to find x. How far from point B does this person come ashore?

72. The remaining life expectancies shown in the graph on page 208 indicate that a male child born in 1993 could expect to live to age 72.1; a female to age 78.9. A 70-year old male in 1993 could expect to live another 12.4 years; a female, another 15.5 years. The formula $E = \sqrt{0.66A^2 - 110.55A + 4680.24}$ is an approximate model for some of the data in the graph, where A represents current age and E stands for remaining life expectancy (in years).

a. Is the formula a better model for males or for females?

b. If $E = 10$, find A and describe what your result means in terms of the variables modeled by the formula.

Remaining Life Expectancies in the United States

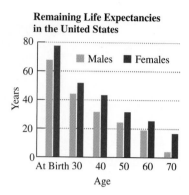

Source: Department of Health and Human Services, 1993

73. A person inherits $10,000 with the stipulation that for the first year the money must be invested in two stocks paying 8% and 12% annual interest, respectively. What is the greatest amount that can be invested at 8% if the total interest for the year is to be at least $950?

74. In 1984, approximately 1644 thousand turntables were sold in the United States. This number has decreased by around 82 thousand each year since then. On the other hand, annual sales of compact disc players has increased by 496 thousand each year, with approximately 284 thousand units sold in 1984. What was the first year in which the sales of compact disc players exceeded those of turntables?

75. A projectile is fired vertically upward from ground level with an initial velocity of 48 feet per second. During what time period will the projectile's height exceed 32 feet? (Use the position model described prior to Problem 53 on page 205.)

76. Suppose that you decide to graph $y = \sqrt{x^2 + 7x + 10}$ using a graphing utility. For what values of x would you anticipate seeing the graph? Verify this algebraic analysis by graphing the equation.

The graph indicates that the U.S. has the world's highest incarceration rate. If x represents the incarceration rate per 100,000 population, list the country or countries that satisfy each inequality in Problems 77–78.

77. $437 \leq 4x - 7 \leq 1229$

78. $|x - 320| > 80$

Countries with the Highest Incarceration Rate

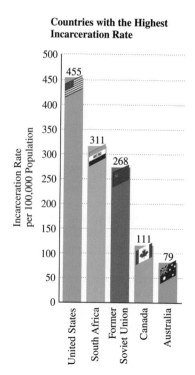

Source: FBI Uniform Crime Report

CHAPTER 1 TEST

In Problems 1–12, find each solution set and check by substitution or with a graphing utility.

1. $7(x - 2) = 4(x + 1) - 21$

2. $|2x + 1| = |x + 3|$

3. $2x^2 - 3x - 2 = 0$

4. $(3x - 1)^2 = 75$

5. $x(x - 2) = 4$

6. $\dfrac{x - 1}{2} + \dfrac{2x}{x + 1} = 0$

7. $4x^2 = 8x - 5$

8. $x^3 - 4x^2 - x + 4 = 0$

9. $(x^2 - 3x)^2 - 2(x^2 - 3x) - 8 = 0$

10. $2\sqrt{x + 2} - \sqrt{2x + 3} = 3$

11. $x^{1/3} - 9x^{1/6} + 8 = 0$

12. $5x^{3/2} - 10 = 0$

Solve each inequality in Problems 13–17. Express the answer in interval notation and graph the solution on a real number line.

13. $x - 4[1 - (2x + 1)] \le 3x - 2$

14. $-3 \le \dfrac{2x + 5}{3} < 6$

15. $|3x + 2| \ge 3$

16. $x^2 < x + 12$

17. $\dfrac{2x + 1}{x - 3} > 3$

18. The monthly benefit (B) of a retirement plan is given by

$$B = \frac{2}{5}w + \frac{1}{125}n$$

where

$w = $ an employee's average monthly salary

$n = $ the number of years an employee worked for the company

a. Solve the formula for n.

b. Find the number of years an employee whose average monthly salary is $800 must work to receive a monthly benefit of $512.

19. The life expectancy for a person born in the United States in 1950 is 65 years for a man and 71 years for a woman. This has increased by approximately 0.16 year for each year of birth after 1950 for a man and by 0.2 year for a woman. In what year of birth will a woman's life expectancy exceed a man's by 10 years?

20. A computer online service charges a flat monthly rate of $25 or a rate of $10 plus 25 cents for each hour spent online. How many hours online each month will result in the same charge for the two billing options?

21. With a 9% raise, a physical therapist will earn $34,880 annually. What is the therapist's salary prior to this raise?

22. An open-top box is made from a square piece of cardboard by cutting 3-inch squares from each corner and then folding up the sides. (See the figure at the top of the next column.) If the box is to hold 243 cubic inches, what size cardboard should be used?

23. An L-shaped sidewalk connects two apartment buildings. The path connecting the buildings is 340 meters, although most residents cut diagonally across the lawn, a distance of 260 meters. How long are the lengths of the two legs of the existing path?

24. A water tank has the shape of an inverted right circular cone of altitude 8 feet and base radius 4 feet. How much water is in the tank when the water is 3 feet deep?

25. The floor plan shown is to have an area of at least 1000 square feet and at most 1160 square feet. Solve for x and then write a sentence that describes possible lengths x of the two rooms on the upper left shown in the figure.

Using technology (cont.)

values that make the denominator 0. These values occur when the graph crosses the x-axis, at −5 and 3. Although the graph is partly cut off, we can see that the domain of g is the set of all real numbers excluding −5 and 3.

c. $h(x) = \dfrac{1}{\sqrt{2x^2 + 7x - 4}}$

Once again, the graph of h is difficult to see, so we instead graph $y = 2x^2 + 7x - 4$. Since $2x^2 + 7x - 4$ must be greater than 0, the graph lies above the x-axis for $x < -4$ or $x > \frac{1}{2}$, which also describes the domain.

a. $f(x) = \sqrt{3x + 12}$ This is the given function.

$3x + 12 \geqslant 0$ Since we want $\sqrt{3x + 12}$ to equal a real number, the quantity under the radical sign must be nonnegative.

$3x \geqslant -12$ Because the domain is the set of values taken on by x, we now solve for x.

$x \geqslant -4$ Divide both sides by 3.

The domain of $f(x) = \sqrt{3x + 12}$ is the set of all real numbers greater than or equal to −4, represented by $[-4, \infty)$.

b. $g(x) = \dfrac{3}{x^2 + 2x - 15}$ This is the given function.

$g(x) = \dfrac{3}{(x + 5)(x - 3)}$ We must exclude x-values that yield zero in the denominator. Factoring the denominator, we find that we must exclude $x = -5$, and $x = 3$.

The domain of $g(x) = \dfrac{3}{x^2 + 2x - 15}$ is the set of all real numbers excluding −5 and 3. This can be represented as $(-\infty, -5) \cup (-5, 3) \cup (3, \infty)$.

c. $h(x) = \dfrac{1}{\sqrt{2x^2 + 7x - 4}}$ This is the given function.

$2x^2 + 7x - 4 > 0$ We want $\sqrt{2x^2 + 7x - 4}$ to equal a *positive* real number. (Why can't $2x^2 + 7x - 4$ equal 0?)

At this point we must solve the resulting quadratic inequality using methods of Section 1.6. Solve $2x^2 + 7x - 4 = 0$ using factoring:

$(x + 4)(2x - 1) = 0$

$x = -4$ or $x = \frac{1}{2}$

The test intervals are $(-\infty, -4)$, $\left(-4, \frac{1}{2}\right)$, and $\left(\frac{1}{2}, \infty\right)$. Using a representative number from each test interval, we find that the solution is $(-\infty, -4) \cup \left(\frac{1}{2}, \infty\right)$.

The domain of $h(x) = \dfrac{1}{\sqrt{2x^2 + 7x - 4}}$ is $(-\infty, -4) \cup \left(\frac{1}{2}, \infty\right)$.

d. The area of a circle, given by $A = \pi r^2$, is a function of the radius. We can equivalently write $A(r) = \pi r^2$, choosing positive values for the radius r. The domain of the function is the set of all real numbers r such that $r > 0$, represented by $(0, \infty)$. ∎

PROBLEM SET 2.1

Practice Problems

Determine which of the relations in Problems 1–8 are not functions. Give the domain and range for each relation.

1. $\{(1, 2), (3, 4), (5, 5)\}$

2. $\{(4, 5), (6, 7), (8, 8)\}$

3. $\{(3, 4), (3, 5), (4, 4), (4, 5)\}$

4. $\{(5, 6), (5, 7), (6, 6), (6, 7)\}$

5. $\{(-3, -3), (-2, -2), (-1, -1), (0, 0)\}$

6. $\{(-7, -7), (-5, -5), (-3, -3), (0, 0)\}$

7. $\{(1, 4), (1, 5), (1, 6)\}$

8. $\{(4, 1), (5, 1), (6, 1)\}$

Find the function values in Problems 9–14.

9. $f(x) = 4x - 6$

   a. $f(0)$ **b.** $f(-2)$ **c.** $f(\frac{1}{2})$ **d.** $f(a)$ **e.** $f(-a)$ **f.** $f(2a)$

10. $f(x) = 3x - 5$

   a. $f(0)$ **b.** $f(-4)$ **c.** $f(-\frac{2}{3})$ **d.** $f(a)$ **e.** $f(-a)$ **f.** $f(2a)$

11. $f(x) = x^2 - 3x + 7$

   a. $f(0)$ **b.** $f(4)$ **c.** $f(-4)$ **d.** $f(-x)$ **e.** $f(a + h)$

12. $f(x) = 4x^2 - 2x + 6$

   a. $f(0)$ **b.** $f(-3)$ **c.** $f(3)$ **d.** $f(-x)$ **e.** $f(a + h)$

13. $g(x) = x^2 + \dfrac{1}{x^2}$

   a. $g(1)$ **b.** $g(-\frac{1}{2})$ **c.** $g(a)$ **d.** $g(-a)$

14. $g(x) = x^3 + \dfrac{1}{x^3}$

   a. $g(1)$ **b.** $g(-\frac{1}{2})$ **c.** $g(a)$ **d.** $g(-a)$

In Problems 15–22, find: **a.** $f(a)$ **b.** $f(a + h)$ **c.** $\dfrac{f(a + h) - f(a)}{h}$ **d.** $f(a) + f(h)$

15. $f(x) = 4x + 2$ **16.** $f(x) = 3x - 1$ **17.** $f(x) = 2x^2 - 3x + 5$ **18.** $f(x) = 3x^2 - 7x - 2$

19. $f(x) = 6$ **20.** $f(x) = 7$ **21.** $f(x) = \dfrac{1}{x}$ **22.** $f(x) = \dfrac{1}{x + 1}$

In Problems 23–26, find: **a.** $f(-x)$ **b.** $f(x + h)$ **c.** $\dfrac{f(x + h) - f(x)}{h}$

23. $f(x) = 6x - 5$ **24.** $f(x) = -4x + 3$ **25.** $f(x) = 2x^2 - 4x - 1$ **26.** $f(x) = -3x^2 + 2x + 8$

Find the function values in Problems 27–28.

27. $f(x) = \begin{cases} x + 3 & \text{if } x \geqslant -3 \\ -(x + 3) & \text{if } x < -3 \end{cases}$

   a. $f(0)$ **b.** $f(-6)$ **c.** $f(-3)$ **d.** $f(-\pi)$

28. $f(x) = \begin{cases} x + 5 & \text{if } x \geqslant -5 \\ -(x + 5) & \text{if } x < -5 \end{cases}$

   a. $f(0)$ **b.** $f(-6)$ **c.** $f(-5)$ **d.** $f(-\sqrt{10})$

In Problems 29–50, find the domain of each function.

29. $f(x) = 4x^2 - 3x + 1$ **30.** $f(x) = 8x^2 - 5x + 2$ **31.** $g(x) = \dfrac{3}{x - 4}$

32. $g(x) = \dfrac{2}{x + 5}$ **33.** $h(x) = \dfrac{4}{x^2 + 11x + 24}$ **34.** $h(x) = \dfrac{5}{6x^2 + x - 2}$

35. $f(t) = \dfrac{3}{t^2 + 4}$ **36.** $f(t) = \dfrac{5}{t^2 + 9}$ **37.** $f(x) = \sqrt{x - 3}$

38. $f(x) = \sqrt{x + 2}$ **39.** $f(x) = \sqrt[3]{x - 3}$ **40.** $f(x) = \sqrt[3]{x + 2}$

41. $g(t) = \dfrac{1}{\sqrt[4]{t - 3}}$ **42.** $g(t) = \dfrac{1}{\sqrt[4]{t + 2}}$ **43.** $g(x) = \sqrt{x^2 + 2x - 8}$

44. $g(x) = \sqrt{6x^2 + 13x - 5}$ **45.** $h(r) = \dfrac{\sqrt{r - 1}}{r - 3}$ **46.** $h(r) = \dfrac{\sqrt{r - 2}}{r - 5}$

47. $f(x) = \dfrac{3}{\sqrt{3x^2 - 7x + 2}}$

48. $f(x) = \dfrac{5}{\sqrt{6x^2 - x - 2}}$

49. $r(v) = \sqrt[4]{1 - v^2}$

50. $r(v) = \sqrt[4]{16 - v^2}$

Application Problems

51. The function $N(x) = -143x^3 + 1810x^2 - 187x + 2331$ describes the number of new AIDS cases in the United States x years after 1983, where $0 \leqslant x \leqslant 7$. Find and interpret $N(5)$.

52. The function $C(t) = 0.018t^2 + 0.70t + 316.2$ describes carbon dioxide concentration (in ppm) t years after 1960. Find and interpret $C(30)$.

53. The function $I(x) = (30 + x)(20 - 0.05x)$ describes income (in dollars) for a diving boat where x represents the number of passengers above 30 on the boat. Find and interpret $I(20) - I(10)$.

54. The function $s(t) = -16t^2 + 96t + 176$ describes the position of a free-falling body above the ground (in feet) t seconds after being thrown upward from the top of a 176-foot tall building. Find and interpret $s(5) - s(4)$.

55. The function $L(v) = 400\sqrt{1 - \dfrac{v^2}{c^2}}$ describes the length of a 400-meter tall starship moving at velocity v from the perspective of an observer at rest. (c, the speed of light, is approximately 186,000 miles per second.) Find and interpret $L(148,800)$.

56. The function $L(v) = 800\sqrt{1 - \dfrac{v^2}{c^2}}$ describes the length of a 800-meter tall starship moving at velocity v from the perspective of an observer at rest. (c, the speed of light, is approximately 186,000 miles per second.) Find and interpret $L(93,000)$.

57. A particle is moving along a horizontal number line. Its position on the number line at any time t (in seconds) is

given by the function $s(t) = t^3 + t^2 - t - 1$. If average velocity is defined as change in position divided by change in time, find $\dfrac{s(4) - s(2)}{4 - 2}$ and interpret the result in terms of average velocity.

58. A particle is moving along a horizontal number line. Its position on the number line at any time t (in seconds) is given by the function $s(t) = t^3 - 3t^2 + 5$. If average velocity is defined as change in position divided by change in time, find $\dfrac{s(5) - s(2)}{5 - 2}$ and interpret the result in terms of average velocity.

59. The average price of a mobile home in the United States t years after 1984 is modeled by the piecewise function

$$p(t) = \begin{cases} 1753.6t + 19,503.6 & \text{if } 0 \leqslant t \leqslant 5 \\ 81.11t^2 + 19,838.8 & \text{if } 6 \leqslant t \leqslant 14 \end{cases}$$

Find and interpret $p(12) - p(2)$.

60. During a particular year, the taxes owed by a married person filing separately with an adjusted gross income of x dollars is given by the piecewise function

$$T(x) = \begin{cases} 0.15x & \text{if } 0 \leqslant x < 17,900 \\ 0.28(x - 17,900) + 2685 & \text{if } 17,900 \leqslant x < 43,250 \\ 0.31(x - 43,250) + 9783 & \text{if } x \geqslant 43,250 \end{cases}$$

Find and interpret $T(70,000) - T(40,000)$.

True–False Critical Thinking Problems

61. Which one of the following is true?

a. Any set of only two ordered pairs must be a function.

b. If $f = \{(1, 1), (2, 2), (3, 4)\}$, then $f(6) = 7$.

c. If $f(x) = x^2$, then $f(x + h) = x^2 + h$.

d. For people filing a single return, federal income tax is a function of adjusted gross income.

62. Which one of the following is true?

a. If $f = \{(1, 1), (2, 4), (3, 9), (5, 25)\}$, and $g(x) = x^2$, then f and g represent the same function.

b. If $f(x) = x^2$, then $f(a + h) = a^2 + h$.

c. If $f = \{(1, 1), (2, 2), (3, 4)\}$, then $f(1) = 2$.

d. If a set of ordered pairs that represents a function has all of its components reversed, the new set might not be a function.

63. Which one of the following is true?

a. If $f(t) = \dfrac{t - 3}{t + 3}$, then $f(0) = -3$.

b. If $f(x) = 2x + 1$, then $f(1 + 3) = f(1) + f(3)$.

c. If $f(x) = 4x^2$, then $f(2x) \neq 2f(x) \neq f(x^2) \neq [f(x)]^2$.

d. If $f(x) = \dfrac{x - b}{x + b}$, then $f(5b) \neq 2f(2b)$.

64. Which one of the following is true?

a. If $f(x) = 2x - 3$, then $f(x^2) = [f(x)]^2$.

b. If $f(x) = \sqrt{x}$, then $f(1 + 3) = f(1) + f(3)$.

c. If $f(x) = 3x^2$, then $f\left(\dfrac{x}{2}\right) \neq \dfrac{f(x)}{2} \neq 2f(x) \neq f(2x)$.

d. If $f(x) = 2x^2 - x$ and $g(x) = 3$, then there are no real numbers x_0 such that $f(x_0) = g(x_0)$.

65. Which one of the following is true?

a. There are no integers m and n such that $y^m = x^n$ defines y as a function of x.

b. If $f(1) = 1, f(2) = 1 - 2, f(3) = 1 - 2 + 3, f(4) = 1 - 2 + 3 - 4$, and so on, then $f(20) + f(40) - f(65) = 3$.

c. If $f(x) = $ the digit in the 10^{-4} place when x is expressed in decimal notation, then $f\left(\frac{18}{19}\right) < f(\sqrt{17})$.

d. None of the above is true.

Technology Problems

Use a graphing utility to find the domain of each function in Problems 66–73.

66. $f(x) = \dfrac{2}{x^2 - 8x + 15}$

67. $f(x) = \dfrac{4}{x^2 - 8x + 12}$

68. $g(x) = \sqrt{6 - 2x}$

69. $g(x) = \sqrt{15 - 3x}$

70. $h(x) = \dfrac{4}{\sqrt{x^2 - 7x + 10}}$

71. $h(x) = \dfrac{3}{\sqrt{x^2 + 5x + 4}}$

72. $\phi(x) = \sqrt{4x^2 - 8x + 7}$

73. $\phi(x) = \dfrac{3}{\sqrt{x^2 - 4x + 4}}$

74. Consider the function $L(x) = $ the exponent to which 10 must be raised to obtain x.

   a. Fill in the table in the next column.

x	$\frac{1}{100}$	$\frac{1}{10}$	1	$\sqrt{10}$	10	100
$L(x)$						

b. Use a graphing utility to graph $y = \log x$. Use the following range setting:

   Xmin = 0, Xmax = 10, Xscl = 1,

   Ymin = -3, Ymax = 3, Yscl = 1

Use the TRACE feature and experiment with the range setting to show the ordered pairs in the previous table as points on the graph of $y = \log x$. Convince yourself that $y = \log x$ is the same function as the one defined by $L(x)$.

c. Use your conclusion in part (b) to write an equation in x and y that expresses the verbal rule used to define $L(x)$.

75. The sum of two numbers is 6. One of the numbers is represented by x.

   a. Express the product P as a function of x.

   b. Graph the function by replacing $P(x)$ by y.

   c. Describe one bit of useful information revealed by the graph of $P(x)$ that is not obvious by looking at its equation.

Writing in Mathematics

In Problems 76–79, determine whether the correspondence is a function. Explain your answer.

Domain	Correspondence	Range
76. The set of houses in a town	Each house's area	A set of positive numbers
77. The air temperature each day at noon at an ocean beach over a one-week period	The number of people at the beach each day at noon over the one-week period	A set of positive numbers
78. The set of numbers representing the weight of each person in a town	The number of years of education for each person in the town	A set of nonnegative numbers
79. The set of real numbers	The square of each number	A set of nonnegative numbers

80. For people filing a single return, federal income tax is a function of adjusted gross income because for each value of adjusted gross income there is a unique tax to be paid. On the other hand, the price of a house is not a function of the lot size on which the house sits because houses on same-sized lots can sell for many different prices.

a. Describe two everyday situations between variables that are functions.

b. Describe two everyday situations between variables that are not functions.

Critical Thinking Problems

81. Suppose that a relation assigns to every natural number the prime number that is nearest to it on a number line.

   a. Is the relation a function? Explain your answer.

   b. If the relation is not a function, how might the assignment be changed slightly so that it becomes a function?

82. Give an example of an equation that does not define y as a function of x but that does define x as a function of y.

83. Give an example of a function f defined by an equation in x

   a. Whose domain is $[-3, \infty)$.

   b. Whose domain is $(-\infty, -3) \cup (-3, 5) \cup (5, \infty)$.

c. Describe the process that you used to determine the function in parts (a) and (b).

84. If $f(x) = ax^2 + bx + c$ and $r_1 = \dfrac{-b + \sqrt{b^2 - 4ac}}{2a}$, find $f(r_1)$ without doing any algebra and explain how you arrived at your result.

85. If $f(x) = \dfrac{cx + d}{ax - c}$, find $f\left(\dfrac{cx + d}{ax - c}\right)$ and simplify.

86. If $f(x) = $ the number of prime numbers $\leq x$, where x is a positive integer, find two numbers a and b such that $f(a) = 2f(b)$.

87. Find a function $g(t)$ such that $g(x)\,g(y) - g(xy) = x + y$.

SECTION 2.2

Solutions Manual   **Tutorial**   **Video 4**

Linear Functions and Slope

Objectives

1 Compute a line's slope.

2 Interpret slope as average rate of change.

3 Write the point-slope form of a line.

4 Write the slope-intercept form of a line.

5 Write the general form of a line.

6 Recognize equations for horizontal and vertical lines.

7 Write equations for lines parallel and perpendicular to a given line.

8 Model data with linear functions.

9 Model using direct variation.

When we attempt to fit a curve to a set of data, our goal is to find a function whose graph fits the data well. In this section, we consider data that fall along a straight line, using linear functions to model the data and make predictions.

An Introduction to Linear Functions

Now that we have introduced functions and their notation, we turn to a special class of functions called *linear functions*.

> **Definition of a linear function**
>
> A function that can be expressed in the form
>
> $$f(x) = mx + b$$
>
> is called a *linear function*.

The graph of a linear function is a line. The value b is related to an important point on the line and the value m is significant in terms of the line's steepness.

Discover for yourself

Use a graphing utility to graph the linear functions in each column in the same viewing rectangle. Use the $\boxed{\text{ZOOM SQUARE}}$ feature to avoid possible distortions. In what way are the graphs the same? How does the value of m (the coefficient of x) affect the graphs? What affect does b (the constant term) have on the graphs?

$f(x) = x + 2$	$f(x) = -x + 2$
$g(x) = 2x + 2$	$g(x) = -2x + 2$
$h(x) = 3x + 2$	$h(x) = -3x + 2$

In the Discover for yourself, did you observe that the graph of $f(x) = mx + b$ passes through the point $(0, b)$ and that b is the line's y-intercept? Did you also observe that the value m is responsible for the steepness or slant of the line? For the lines in which m is positive, there is an upward slant from left to right and for the lines in which m is negative there is a downward slant from left to right. This is illustrated in Figure 2.4.

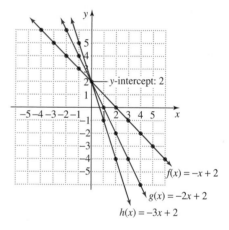

Figure 2.4

When m is positive, the lines slant upward
When m is negative, the lines slant downward

Figure 2.5

Lines with various steepnesses

The Slope of a Line

An important characteristic of a line is the angle that the line makes with the x-axis (see Figure 2.5). Some lines are quite steep, forming an angle close to 90°. Other lines rise quite slowly, forming an angle close to 0°.

Mathematicians have developed a useful measure of the steepness of a line, called the *slope* of the line. Slope compares the vertical change (the *rise*) to the horizontal change (the *run*) encountered when moving from one fixed point to another along the line. To calculate the slope of a line, mathematicians use a ratio comparing the change in y (the rise) to the change in x (the run).

Compute a line's slope.

Definition of slope

The *slope* of the line through the distinct points (x_1, y_1) and (x_2, y_2) is

$$\frac{\text{Change in } y}{\text{Change in } x} = \frac{\text{Rise}}{\text{Run}} = \frac{y_2 - y_1}{x_2 - x_1}$$

where $x_2 - x_1 \neq 0$.

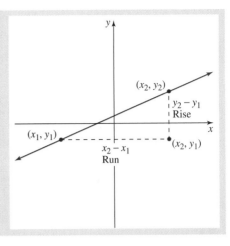

The letter m—the first letter in the French verb *monter*, meaning to go up or to climb—is used to denote slope.

The quantity $x_2 - x_1$ in the definition of slope represents the amount by which x changes in moving from (x_1, y_1) to (x_2, y_2) along the line. This *change in x* is represented by the symbol Δx (read *delta x*). Similarly, the change in y, namely, $y_2 - y_1$, is represented by Δy. Using these ideas (see Figure 2.6), we can represent slope by

$$m = \frac{y_2 - y_1}{x_2 - x_1} = \frac{\Delta y}{\Delta x}.$$

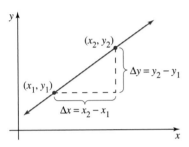

Figure 2.6

Slope as Δy divided by Δx

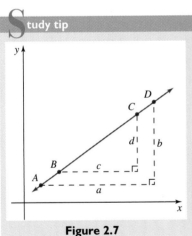

The slope of a line does not depend on which two points on the line are used in the computation. This is shown in Figure 2.7, in which the two right triangles are similar. Because corresponding sides of similar triangles are proportional,

$$\frac{b}{a} = \frac{d}{c}.$$

Since $\dfrac{b}{a}$ is slope calculated using points A and D, and $\dfrac{d}{c}$ is slope calculated using points B and C, the values obtained for slope are equal regardless of what two points are used on the line.

Figure 2.7

EXAMPLE 1   Using the Definition of Slope

Calculate and compare the slopes of the four lines shown in Figure 2.8.

Solution

L_1: **Line L_1 passes through $(-3, -1)$ and $(-2, 4)$.**
Let $(x_1, y_1) = (-3, -1)$ and $(x_2, y_2) = (-2, 4)$. By definition, the slope is

$$m = \frac{y_2 - y_1}{x_2 - x_1} = \frac{4 - (-1)}{-2 - (-3)} = \frac{5}{1} = 5.$$

Figure 2.8

Four lines and their slopes

Figure 2.8 (repeated)

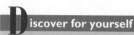iscover for yourself

In Example 1, let (x_1, y_1) represent the point that we called (x_2, y_2) and let (x_2, y_2) represent the point that we called (x_1, y_1). Find the slope for lines L_1, L_2, and L_3. What can you conclude? What happens if you call one point (x_1, y_2) and the other (x_2, y_1) subtract in one order in the numerator and then in the opposite order in the denominator?

This means that for line L_1, for every 1 unit we move to the right (the change in x) the line rises 5 units (the change in y).

L_2: Line L_2 passes through ($1, -1$) and ($0, 5$).
Let $(x_1, y_1) = (1, -1)$ and $(x_2, y_2) = (0, 5)$.

$$m = \frac{y_2 - y_1}{x_2 - x_1} = \frac{5 - (-1)}{0 - 1} = \frac{6}{-1} = -6$$ Slope is the difference in y-values divided by the difference in x-values.

L_3: Line L_3, a horizontal line, passes through ($-4, 2$) and ($3, 2$).

$$m = \frac{2 - 2}{3 - (-4)} = \frac{0}{7} = 0$$

A horizontal line is neither increasing nor decreasing from left to right, and its slope is 0.

L_4: Line L_4, a vertical line, passes through ($5, -1$) and ($5, 3$).

$$m = \frac{3 - (-1)}{5 - 5} = \frac{4}{0}$$

which is undefined. The slope of a vertical line is not defined.   ∎

Example 1 contains the four basic situations that can be encountered about the slope of a line. These situations can be generalized as follows.

The slope of a line

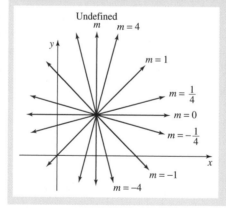

1. Lines with positive slope ($m > 0$) rise (increase) from left to right.
2. Lines with negative slope ($m < 0$) fall (decrease) from left to right.
3. Lines with zero slope ($m = 0$) are horizontal.
4. Lines with undefined slope are vertical.

2 Interpret slope as average rate of change.

Modeling with Slope

Slope is defined as $\frac{\Delta y}{\Delta x}$, the ratio of a change in y to a corresponding change in x. Consequently, in applied situations slope can be thought of as the *average change in y per unit of change in x*, where y is a function of x. This idea is illustrated in Example 2.

EXAMPLE 2   **Slope as the Average Rate of Change**

World population started a rapid growth phase in the early 1800s and has grown sixfold in the last 200 years (see Figure 2.9 on the next page).

ENRICHMENT ESSAY

Slope and the Streets of San Francisco

San Francisco's Filbert Street has a slope of 0.613, meaning that for every horizontal change of 100 feet, the street ascends 61.3 feet vertically. The street is too steep to pave and is only accessible by wooden stairs. Legend has it that the cottages along this street with its 31.5° angle of inclination were once used to "shanghai" sailors. "To shanghai" was a verb coined in early San Francisco. (Look up "shanghai" in a dictionary if you are not sure of its meaning.)

Carol Simowitz / San Francisco Convention and Visitors Bureau.

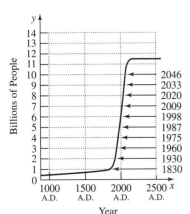

Figure 2.9

World population

Source: Population Reference Bureau

a. Compute the slope of the line drawn through the years 1830 and 1930. Interpret this value in terms of average rate of change.

b. Repeat part (a) for the years 1987 and 1998.

Solution

a. For 1830 and 1930, we use the values from the graph, namely, $(1830, 1)$ and $(1930, 2)$. (The y-coordinate) represents the world population in billions for each of these years.) We then apply the definition of slope.

$$m = \frac{2 - 1}{1930 - 1830} = \frac{1}{100} = 0.01$$

Between 1830 and 1930, the average world population grew at a rate of 0.01 billion people (or 10 million people) each year.

b. For 1987 and 1998, we again use the values from the graph, namely, $(1987, 5)$ and $(1998, 6)$. We then apply the definition of slope.

$$m = \frac{6 - 5}{1998 - 1987} = \frac{1}{11} \approx 0.09$$

Between 1987 and 1930, the average world population grew at a rate of 0.09 billion people (or approximately 90 million people) each year. ∎

3 Write the point-slope form of a line.

The Point-Slope Form of a Line

If a particular point on a line and the slope of a line are known, we can write an equation that describes the line. Let (x_1, y_1) represent a fixed point on the line. Let m represent the slope of the line. Let (x, y) stand for all ordered

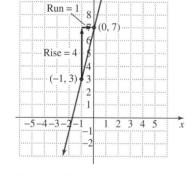

Figure 2.10

A line passing through (x_1, y_1) with slope m

pairs corresponding to points along the line other than (x_1, y_1). The situation is illustrated in Figure 2.10. By definition,

$$\frac{y - y_1}{x - x_1} = m.$$

If we multiply both sides by $x - x_1$, we obtain

$$y - y_1 = m(x - x_1).$$

This discussion leads to the following statement.

Point-slope form of the equation of a line

The point-slope equation of the line that passes through the point (x_1, y_2) and has slope m is

$$y - y_1 = m(x - x_1).$$

EXAMPLE 3   **Writing the Point-Slope Equation of a Line**

Write the point-slope equation of the line passing through $(-1, 3)$ with slope 4. Solve the equation for y and sketch the line.

Solution

We use the point-slope equation of a line with $m = 4$, $x_1 = -1$, and $y_1 = 3$.

$y - y_1 = m(x - x_1)$	This is the point-slope equation.
$y - 3 = 4[x - (-1)]$	Substitute the given values.
$y - 3 = 4(x + 1)$	We now have the point-slope equation for the given line.
$y - 3 = 4x + 4$	Solve for y; apply the distributive property on the right.
$y = 4x + 7$	Add 3 to both sides.

Figure 2.11

The line passing through $(-1, 3)$ with slope 4

Graph the line by first plotting the point $(-1, 3)$. Since the slope is 4, this means that a rise of 4 units corresponds to a run of 1 unit. (Equivalently, when we move 1 unit to the right, the line rises 4 units.) This enables us to sketch the line shown in Figure 2.11.   ■

Using technology

Use a graphing utility to graph $y = 4x + 7$ and obtain a graph similar to the one shown in Figure 2.11. If you use the $\boxed{\text{ZOOM SQUARE}}$ feature, horizontal and vertical tick marks will have equal spacing, and the slope should visually appear to equal 4.

4 Write the slope-intercept form of a line.

The Slope-Intercept Form of a Line

We have seen that linear functions can be expressed in the form

$$f(x) = mx + b.$$

Now it's time to verify that m, the coefficient of x, is the slope of the line, and the constant term b is the y-intercept. We can do this by writing an equation of the line having slope m and y-intercept b.

EXAMPLE 4   Deriving the Slope-Intercept Equation of a Line

Write an equation of the nonvertical line that has slope m and y-intercept b.

Solution

As shown in Figure 2.12, since the y-intercept is b, the line intersects the y-axis at $(0, b)$. We use the point-slope equation of a line with $x_1 = 0$ and $y_1 = b$.

$y - y_1 = m(x - x_1)$ This is the point-slope equation.

$y - b = m(x - 0)$ Since $(x_1, y_1) = (0, b)$, we let $x_1 = 0$ and $y_1 = b$. The slope is m.

$y - b = mx$ Multiply on the right.

$y = mx + b$ Solve for y.

$\underset{\text{Slope}}{\nearrow}\quad\underset{\text{y-intercept}}{\downarrow}$

■

The last equation in Example 4 is called the *slope-intercept form* of the equation of a line.

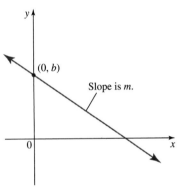

Figure 2.12

A line with slope m and y-intercept b

Slope-intercept form of the equation of a line

The slope-intercept equation of the line that has slope m and y-intercept b is

$$y = mx + b.$$

The slope-intercept equation, $y = mx + b$, can be expressed in function notation, replacing y with $f(x)$.

$$f(x) = mx + b$$

EXAMPLE 5   Using the Slope-Intercept Equation

Find the slope and y-intercept of each line. Then graph the line.

a. $4x + y = 2$ **b.** $2x - 3y + 6 = 0$

Solution

We solve each equation for y. In the form $y = mx + b$, the coefficient of x is the slope of the line, and the constant term is its y-intercept.

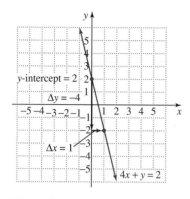

Figure 2.13

The line with y-intercept 2 and slope −4

a. Solving $4x + y = 2$ for y, we obtain $y = -4x + 2$. Thus, the slope is −4 and the y-intercept is 2. Since the line's y-intercept is 2, the line intersects the y-axis at $(0, 2)$. We plot this point. We graph the slope, −4, using

$$m = \frac{\Delta y}{\Delta x} = \frac{-4}{1}.$$

The graph of $4x + y = 2$ or, equivalently, $y = -4x + 2$, is shown in Figure 2.13.

b. We begin by writing the equation in the form $y = mx + b$.

$2x - 3y + 6 = 0$ This is the given equation.

$2x + 6 = 3y$ To isolate the y-term, add 3y on both sides.

$3y = 2x + 6$ Reverse the two sides. (This step is optional.)

$y = \frac{2}{3}x + 2$ Divide both sides by 3.

From the slope-intercept form of the line's equation, we see that the slope is $m = \frac{2}{3}$ and the y-intercept is $b = 2$. Starting at $(0, 2)$ and using

$$m = \frac{\Delta y}{\Delta x} = \frac{2}{3}$$

we graph the line in Figure 2.14.

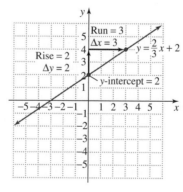

Figure 2.14

The line with y-intercept 2 and slope $\frac{2}{3}$ ∎

5 Write the general form of a line.

Other Forms of a Line's Equation

In Example 5b, we wrote the slope-intercept form of a line whose equation was given as

$2x - 3y + 6 = 0$.

This form of the line is called its *general equation*.

6 Recognize equations for horizontal and vertical lines.

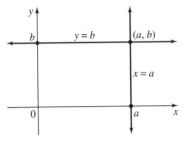

Figure 2.15

Equations of horizontal and vertical lines

Study tip

Straight-line graphs, with the exception of vertical lines, are graphs of linear functions.

7 Write equations for lines parallel and perpendicular to a given line.

Discover for yourself

Use a graphing utility to graph the following equations in the same viewing rectangle.

$$y_1 = \frac{2}{3}x + 2$$

$$y_2 = \frac{2}{3}x$$

$$y_3 = \frac{2}{3}x - 1$$

What is true about the slopes of the three lines? What do you observe about their graphs? In general, what appears to be true about the graphs of lines with equal slopes?

General form of the equation of a line

Every line has an equation that can be written in the *general form*

$$Ax + By + C = 0$$

where A and B are not both zero.

Finally, let's consider horizontal and vertical lines. If a line is horizontal, its slope is zero ($m = 0$), so the equation $y = mx + b$ becomes $y = b$, where b is the y-intercept. This is illustrated in Figure 2.15.

A vertical line has slope that is undefined. However, Figure 2.15 illustrates that the x-coordinate of every point on the vertical line is a. Thus we can write its equation as $x = a$, where a is the x-intercept.

Vertical and horizontal lines

The equation of a horizontal line through (a, b) is $y = b$. The line's y-intercept is b.
        The equation of a vertical line through (a, b) is $x = a$. The line's x-intercept is a.

Parallel and Perpendicular Lines

Two nonintersecting lines that lie in the same plane are parallel. If two lines do not intersect, the ratio of the vertical change to the horizontal change is the same for each line. Because two parallel lines have the same "steepness," they must have the same slope.

Slope and parallel lines

1. If two nonvertical lines are parallel, then they have the same slope.
2. If two distinct nonvertical lines have the same slope, then they are parallel.
3. Two vertical lines, both with undefined slopes, are parallel.

EXAMPLE 6 **Writing Equations of a Line Parallel to a Given Line**

Write an equation of the line passing through $(-3, 2)$ and parallel to the line whose equation is $y = 2x + 1$. Express the equation in point-slope form, slope-intercept form, and general form.

Solution

Figure 2.16 on page 232 should help us to analyze the problem. We begin with the point-slope form. We see that $(x_1, y_1) = (-3, 2)$ since this is a point on the

Figure 2.16

Writing equations of a line parallel to a given line

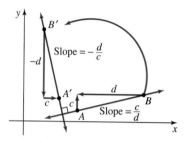

Figure 2.17

Slopes of perpendicular lines

line. Since the slope of the line whose equation is given is 2, then $m = 2$ for the line whose equation we must write. Parallel lines have the same slope.

$$y - y_1 = m(x - x_1)$$ This is the point-slope equation.

$$y - 2 = 2[x - (-3)]$$ $(x_1, y_1) = (-3, 2)$ and $m = 2$.

$$y - 2 = 2(x + 3)$$ This is the point-slope form of our problem's equation.

$$y - 2 = 2x + 6$$ Apply the distributive property. By solving for y we will obtain the slope-intercept form.

$$y = 2x + 8$$ Add 2 to both sides. This is the slope-intercept form $(y = mx + b)$.

$$2x - y + 8 = 0$$ Subtract y from both sides. This is the general form $(Ax + By + C = 0)$.   ∎

The relationship between the slopes of perpendicular lines is not as obvious as that between parallel lines. Figure 2.17 shows line AB, with a slope of $\frac{c}{d}$. Rotate line AB 90° to the left to obtain line $A'B'$ perpendicular to line AB. The figure indicates that the rise and the run of the new line are reversed from the original line, but the rise is now negative. This means that the slope of the new line is $-\frac{d}{c}$. Notice that the product of the slopes of the two perpendicular lines is -1:

$$\left(\frac{c}{d}\right)\left(-\frac{d}{c}\right) = -1.$$

This relationship holds for all perpendicular lines and is summarized below.

Slope and perpendicular lines

1. If two nonvertical lines are perpendicular, then the product of their slopes is -1.
2. If the product of the slopes of two lines is -1, then the lines are perpendicular.
3. A horizontal line having zero slope is perpendicular to a vertical line having undefined slope.

An equivalent way of stating this relationship is to say that one line is perpendicular to another line if its slope is the *negative reciprocal* of the slope of the other.

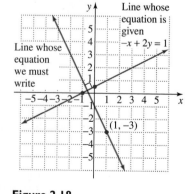

Figure 2.18

Writing equations of a line perpendicular to a given line

EXAMPLE 7   **Writing Equations of a Line Perpendicular to a Given Line**

Write an equation of the line passing through $(1, -3)$ and perpendicular to the line whose equation is $-x + 2y = 1$. Again, express the equation in point-slope form, slope-intercept form, and general form.

Solution

The situation is illustrated in Figure 2.18. We begin with the point-slope equation. We must find two things: a point on the line [which, again, we have:

Use a graphing utility to graph

$$y_1 = \frac{1}{2}x + \frac{1}{2}$$

and

$$y_2 = -2x - 1$$

in the same viewing rectangle. Do the lines appear to be perpendicular? Now use the ZOOM SQUARE setting. What do you observe?

$(1, -3)]$ and its slope. Because the line through $(1, -3)$ is to be perpendicular to the line whose equation is $-x + 2y = 1$, its slope is the negative reciprocal of the slope of the given equation. We can find the slope of $-x + 2y = 1$ by using slope-intercept form. We solve the equation for y.

$$-x + 2y = 1 \qquad \text{This is the given equation.}$$

$$2y = x + 1 \qquad \text{Add } x \text{ to both sides.}$$

$$y = \frac{1}{2}x + \frac{1}{2} \qquad \text{Obtain slope-intercept form by dividing both sides by 2.}$$

Slope y-intercept

The slope of the line whose equation we must write is -2, the negative reciprocal of $\frac{1}{2}$. With $(x_1, y_1) = (1, -3)$ and $m = -2$, we obtain

$$y - y_1 = m(x - x_1)$$

$$y - (-3) = -2(x - 1) \qquad (x_1, y_1) = (1, -3) \text{ and } m = -2.$$

$$y + 3 = -2(x - 1) \qquad \text{This is the point-slope form.}$$

Solving for y, we obtain

$$y + 3 = -2x + 2$$

$$y = -2x - 1 \qquad \text{This is the slope-intercept form.}$$

Since general form $(Ax + By + C = 0)$ is usually written with $A > 0$, we add $2x + 1$ to both sides, obtaining

$$2x + y + 1 = 0 \qquad \text{This is the general form.} \qquad ∎$$

8 Model data with linear functions.

Linear Modeling

Our next example illustrates how we can use real world data to develop a mathematical model. Once the model is developed, we can *interpolate* and *extrapolate* from the data. *Interpolation* refers to finding numerical values *between* actual data measurements. *Extrapolation* refers to finding numerical values *outside* the actual data measurements.

Average and Minimum Salaries for Major League Baseball Players

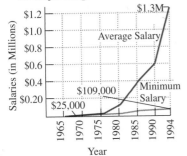

Figure 2.19

Source: Based on statistics from the National Baseball League Players Association

EXAMPLE 8   Modeling Average Baseball Salaries

The graph in Figure 2.19 shows average and minimum salaries for major league baseball players. Write the equation that models the data for the line representing average salaries from 1990 through 1994. Then extrapolate from the data and predict the average salary for a major league baseball player in the year 2000.

Solution

The graph indicates that the average salary in 1990 was $0.6 million, so we will use the data points $(1990, 0.6)$ and $(1994, 1.3)$. To write the point-slope equation of the line, we need (x_1, y_1), a fixed point, and m, the slope. *Either* ordered pair can be taken as (x_1, y_1). Using the smaller numbers, we have

$$x_1 = 1990 \quad \text{and} \quad y_1 = 0.6.$$

Now we must calculate the slope.

$$m = \frac{y_2 - y_1}{x_2 - x_1} = \frac{1.3 - 0.6}{1994 - 1990} = \frac{0.7}{4} = 0.175$$

This indicates that average salaries between 1990 and 1994 increased at a rate of $0.175 million, or $175,000 each year.

Now we are ready to use the point-slope form of a line to model the data.

$y - y_1 = m(x - x_1)$	This is the point-slope equation.
$y - 0.6 = 0.175(x - 1990)$	Use the values from above: $x_1 = 1990$, $y_1 = 0.6$, $m = 0.175$
$y - 0.6 = 0.175x - 348.25$	Multiply on the right.
$y = 0.175x - 347.65$	Solve for y. This is the slope-intercept form of the line's equation.

This is the equation that models the data from 1990 through 1994. We now extrapolate from the data. We predict the average salary for the year 2000 by substituting 2000 for x and solving for y.

$$y = 0.175(2000) - 347.65 = 2.35$$

The model predicts that the average salary for a major league baseball player in the year 2000 will be $2.35 million. ■

Scatter Plots and Regression Lines

Mathematical models can be obtained for a set of data points that appear to fall nearly on a straight line. For example, Figure 2.20 shows a collection of points representing men's and women's winning times (in seconds) in the Olympic 100-meter freestyle swimming race. This collection of points is called a *scatter plot*. The line that best fits the data is called the *regression line*, and a regression line is shown for both the women and the men.

A graphing utility will give you the equation of a line that best fits a set of data. Details for this type of linear modeling are discussed under Technology Problems in Problem Set 2.2.

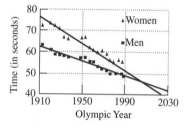

Figure 2.20

9 Model using direct variation.

Modeling Using Direct Variation

The linear model $y = mx$ that has a y-intercept of zero is useful in modeling situations described by the language of *variation*. If $y = mx$, we say that y *varies directly* as x, or that y is *proportional* to x.

Direct variation

y *varies directly* as x if there exists some nonzero constant m such that

$$y = mx.$$

We also say that y is *proportional* to x. The number m is called the *constant of variation* or the *constant of proportionality*.

EXAMPLE 9   **Modeling Using Direct Variation**

The volume of gas (V) at constant pressure is directly proportional to the temperature (T). A certain gas has a volume of 250 cubic meters at a temperature of 30 Kelvin.

a. Find a model that gives volume in terms of pressure.
b. Use this model to find the volume of the gas at a temperature of 90 Kelvin.

Solution

a. $V = mT$ Translate "volume is directly proportional to temperature" into a linear model. (Equivalently: Volume *varies directly* as temperature.)

$250 = m \cdot 30$ Find m. We are given that when $V = 250$, $T = 30$.

$\dfrac{25}{3} = m$ Solve for m.

$V = \dfrac{25}{3}T$ Substitute the value of m into the original equation.

The model that gives volume in terms of pressure is $V = \dfrac{25}{3}T$.

b. $V = \dfrac{25}{3}T$ We now want the value for V if $T = 90$.

$V = \dfrac{25}{3}(90)$ Substitute 90 for T into the model.

$= 750$

At a temperature of 90 Kelvin, the volume of the gas is 750 cubic meters. ■

PROBLEM SET 2.2

Practice Problems

In Problems 1–6, find the slope of the line that passes through the given pair of points.

1. $(7, 3)$ and $(6, 9)$

2. $(8, 5)$ and $(5, 2)$

3. $(-3, 2)$ and $(-7, -6)$

4. $(2, -4)$ and $(-3, 2)$

5. $(-12, -2)$ and $(7, -2)$

6. $(-4, -3)$ and $(2, -3)$

7. Compute the slopes of the three lines shown in the figure.

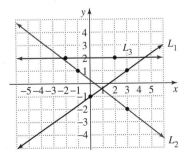

8. Compute the slopes of the three lines shown in the figure.

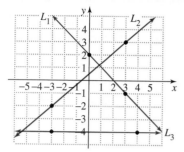

9. Use the figure to make the following lists.

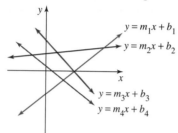

a. List the slopes m_1, m_2, m_3, and m_4 in order of decreasing size.

b. List the number b_1, b_2, b_3, and b_4 in order of decreasing size.

10. Use the figure to make the following lists.

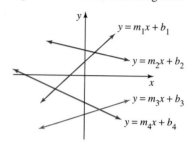

a. List the slopes m_1, m_2, m_3, and m_4 in order of decreasing size.

b. List the number b_1, b_2, b_3, and b_4 in order of decreasing size.

For Problems 11–22, use the given conditions to write an equation for each line in point-slope form, slope-intercept form, and general form.

11. Passing through $(-5, 6)$ with slope 5

12. Passing through $(3, -4)$ with slope -2

13. Passing through $(6, -1)$ and $(3, 2)$

14. Passing through $(3, -8)$ and $(5, 0)$

15. Passing through $(-1, -3)$ and $(7, -2)$

16. Passing through $(1, 4)$ and $(-2, 3)$

17. Passing through $(-8, -10)$ and parallel to the line whose equation is $y = -4x + 3$

18. Passing through $(-2, -7)$ and parallel to the line whose equation is $y = -5x + 4$

19. Passing through $(4, -7)$ and perpendicular to the line whose equation is $x - 2y - 3 = 0$

20. Passing through $(5, -9)$ and perpendicular to the line whose equation is $x + 7y - 12 = 0$

21. Having an x-intercept of -3 and perpendicular to the line passing through $(0, 0)$ and $(6, -2)$

22. Perpendicular to the line whose equation is $3x - 2y = 4$ with the same y-intercept

Find the slope and y-intercept of each line in Problems 23–40. Then graph the line.

23. $y = 2x + 1$

24. $y = 3x + 2$

25. $y = -2x + 1$

26. $y = -3x + 2$

27. $y = \frac{3}{4}x - 2$

28. $y = \frac{3}{4}x - 3$

29. $3x + y = 2$

30. $4x + y = 3$

31. $f(x) = -\frac{3}{2}x$

32. $f(x) = -\frac{4}{3}x$

33. $3x - y + 2 = 0$

34. $4x - y + 3 = 0$

35. $3x - 4 = 5$

36. $5x - 2 = 0$

37. $3y + 6 = 0$

38. $4y + 12 = 0$

39. $y + \sqrt{7} = \sqrt{7}$

40. $y + \pi = \pi$

Application Problems

41. As shown in the graph at the top of the next page, from 1975 through 1990 U.S. health-care costs increased from $132 billion to $671 billion.

a. Compute the slope of the line drawn through 1975 and 1980. Interpret this value in terms of average rate of change.

b. Repeat part (a) for the line drawn through 1985 and 1990.

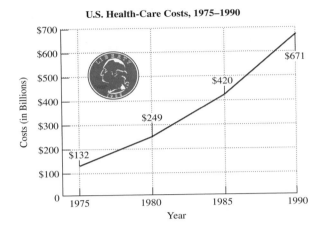

U.S. Health-Care Costs, 1975–1990

Source: U.S. Health Care Financing Administration

42. The graph below shows violent crime arrests per 100,000 U.S. juveniles ages 10–17 from 1965 through 1990.

a. Find a reasonable estimate for the number of arrests per 100,000 juveniles in 1970. Then use this estimate to compute the slope of the line drawn through 1965 and 1970. Interpret this value in terms of average rate of change.

b. Find a reasonable estimate for the number of arrests per 100,000 juveniles in 1980 and 1985. Then use these estimates to compute the slope of the line drawn through 1980 and 1985. Interpret this value in terms of average rate of change.

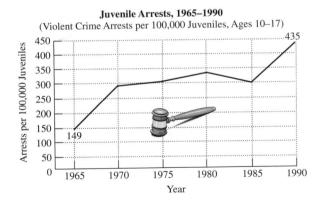

Juvenile Arrests, 1965–1990
(Violent Crime Arrests per 100,000 Juveniles, Ages 10–17)

Source: U.S. Department of Justice; Federal Bureau of Investigation

43. The first graph in the next column shows the number of motor-vehicle deaths in the United States from 1975 through 1993.

a. Through which two years specified on the horizontal axis can a line be drawn with the greatest slope? What is a reasonable estimate for the slope of this line? Interpret this value in terms of average rate of change.

b. Through which two years specified on the horizontal axis can a line be drawn with a slope that is negative and greatest in absolute value? What is a reasonable estimate for the slope of this line? Interpret this value in terms of average rate of change.

c. What is misleading about the scale on the horizontal axis?

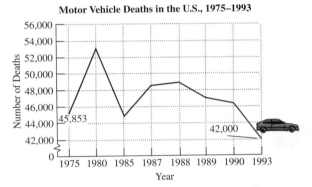

Motor Vehicle Deaths in the U.S., 1975–1993

Source: National Safety Council

44. Graphs of linear functions show the number of women and the number of men in the United States projected to live alone through 2010.

a. In 1995, 14 million U.S. women lived alone. In 2010, this number is projected to be 17 million. Find the slope of the line containing (1995,14) and (2010,17). What does this mean in terms of the yearly increase for women?

b. In 1995, 10 million U.S. men lived alone. In 2010, this number is projected to be 12 million. Find the slope of the line containing (1995,10) and (2010,12). What does this mean in terms of the yearly increase for men?

45. The graph in the top left column on page 238 indicates the number of U.S. companies on the Internet from 1991 through 1994. Write the equation that models the data for a line drawn through 1991 and 1994. Then extrapolate from the data and predict the number of U.S. companies on the Internet for the year 2000.

Number of U.S. Companies on the Internet, 1991–1994

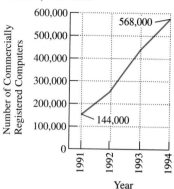

Year

Source: Statistics based on IBM user survey;
USA Today research

46. The graph below indicates the number of accidental deaths in the U.S. at work and at home from 1930 through 1993. Write the equation that models the data for a line drawn through 1930 and 1993 for the number of accidental deaths at work. Then use this equation to predict the year in which work-related accidental deaths will reach zero.

Accidental Deaths in the United States

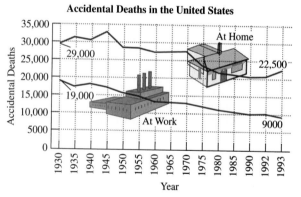

Year

Source: National Safety Council

47. Spending on drug control has skyrocketed in the United States, as shown in the graph at the top of the next column. Draw a line through the years 1981 and 1994 and write the equation of the line through these two data points. Then extrapolate from the data and predict the amount that the government will spend on its drug-control interception budget in the year 2000. Interpolate from the data and use your model to predict drug-control spending for 1988. How close does this come to the number shown in the graph?

U.S. Government Spending on Drug Interceptions and Seizures

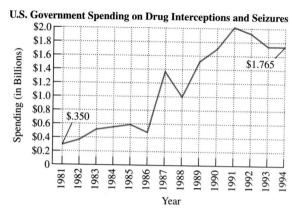

Year

Source: Office of Management and Budget

48. The number of women on active duty in the U.S. military is shown in the graph. Draw a line through the years 1981 and 1994 and write the equation of the line through these two data points. Then extrapolate from the data and predict the number of women on active duty in the year 2000. Interpolate from the data and use the model to predict the number of women on duty for 1992. How close does this come to the number shown in the graph?

Military Women on Active Duty, 1981–1994

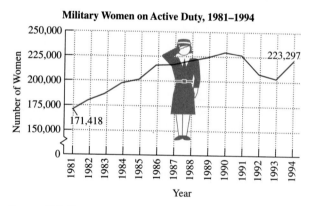

Year

Source: U.S. Department of Defense

49. A person's starting salary in 1995 was $26,500 with yearly increases of $2500. Write a linear model for salary (y) x years after 1995.

50. A company purchases an office machine for $9300 in 1995. The machine is expected to last for 6 years with a yearly loss in value of $1200. Write a linear model for the value of the machine (V) t years after 1995.

51. The cost (C) of an airplane trip is directly proportional to the number of miles in the trip (M). A 3000-mile trip costs $400.

   a. Find a model that gives cost in terms of mileage.

b. Use this model to determine the number of miles that can be covered at a cost of $20.

52. The state of Pennsylvania has a state income tax that is directly proportional to a resident's gross income. A person working in Pennsylvania with a gross yearly income of $21,000 paid $441 in state taxes.

  a. Find a model that gives state income tax as a function of gross income.

  b. Use the model to determine state taxes for a yearly income of $36,000.

53. Running at a constant speed, a runner's distance varies directly as time. If a runner covers 1 mile in 6 minutes, what distance will be covered in 45 minutes?

54. The distance that a spring is stretched varies directly as the force pulling on the spring. For a particular spring, a pull of 4 pounds results in a stretch of 5 inches. How far will a pull of 13 pounds stretch the spring?

True–False Critical Thinking Problems

55. Which one of the following is true?

  a. The slope of the line through $(5, 5)$ and $(7, 7)$ is $\frac{7}{5}$.

  b. The graph of $y = 5$ in the Cartesian coordinate plane is the single point $(0, 5)$.

  c. Every line in the Cartesian coordinate plane has an equation in point-slope form.

  d. The line whose equation is $x - 3y + 10 = 0$ passes through the point $(-1, 3)$ and has slope $\frac{1}{3}$.

56. Which one of the following is true?

  a. A linear function with nonnegative slope has a graph that rises from left to right.

  b. The equations $y = 4x$ and $y = -4x$ have graphs that are perpendicular lines.

  c. The line whose equation is $5x + 6y - 30 = 0$ passes through the point $(6, 0)$ and has slope $-\frac{5}{6}$.

  d. The graph of $y = 7$ in the Cartesian coordinate plane is the single point $(7, 0)$.

Technology Problems

Use a graphing utility to graph the three equations in Problems 57–60 on the same viewing rectangle.

57. $y = 3x, y = -3x, y = \frac{1}{3}x$

58. $y = \frac{3}{4}x, y = -\frac{3}{4}x, y = \frac{3}{4}x + 1$

59. $y = -\frac{1}{3}x, y = -\frac{1}{3}x + 2, y = 3x - 4$

60. $y = x - 5, y = x + 2, y = -x + 4$

61. In parts (a) through (d), solve each equation for y and use a graphing utility to graph the line. For each of the original equations, write down the x- and y-intercepts determined from the graph.

  a. $\frac{x}{3} + \frac{y}{2} = 1$

  b. $\frac{x}{-3} + \frac{y}{-2} = 1$

  c. $\frac{x}{4} + \frac{y}{7} = 1$

  d. $\frac{x}{-4} + \frac{y}{-7} = 1$

  e. Based on parts (a)–(d), describe the graph of $\frac{x}{a} + \frac{y}{b} = 1$.

Your graphing utility will give you the equation of a line that best fits a set of data. The line of best fit is the one in which the sum of the squares of the vertical distances from each point to the line are at a minimum. The line is called the regression line. Problems 62–64 involve regression lines.

62. The data below is from an article in the *Journal of Environmental Health*, May–June 1965, Volume 27, Number 6, pages 883–897. Radioactive wastes seeping into the Columbia River have exposed citizens of eight Oregon counties and the city of Portland to radioactive contamination. The table lists the number of cancer deaths per 10,000 people for the eight Oregon counties and the city of Portland.

County	Index x	Cancer Deaths per 100,000 Residents y
Sherman	1.3	114
Wasco	1.6	138
Umatilla	2.5	147
Morrow	2.6	130
Gilliam	3.4	130
Hood River	3.8	162
Columbia	6.4	178
Clatsop	8.3	210
City of Portland	11.6	208

a. Use the statistical menu of your graphing utility to enter the nine data points ($(1.3, 114)$ through $(11.6, 208)$).

b. Use the draw menu and the scatter plot capability to draw a scatter plot of the data points.

c. Select the linear regression option. Your utility should give you the regression coefficients, a and b, for the regression equation (usually in the form $y = ax + bx$). You may also be given a correlation coefficient, r. Values of r close to 1 indicate that the points can be described by a linear relationship and the regression line has a positive slope. Values of r close to -1 indicate that the points can be described by a linear relationship and the regression line has a negative slope. Values of r close to 0 indicate no linear relationship between the variables.

d. Use the appropriate sequence (consult your manual) to graph the regression equation on top of the points in the scatter plot.

63. The National Center for Health Statistics issued the following data for years of life expected at birth for American women and men.

Year	Years of Life Expected at Birth
1950	68.2
1960	69.7
1965	70.2
1970	70.8
1975	72.6
1980	73.7
1985	74.7
1990	75.4

a. Let x = the number of years after 1950 and y = years of life expected at birth. Use the statistical menu of your graphing utility to enter the eight (x, y) data points.

b. Use the draw menu and the scatter plot capability to draw a scatter plot of the data points.

c. Select the linear regression option and find the equation of the regression line, as well as the correlation coefficient.

d. Use the appropriate sequence to graph the regression equation on top of the points in the scatter plot.

e. Use the regression line's equation to predict years of life expected at birth for the year 2010.

f. In what year will Americans be expected to live 90 years from the time of their birth?

64. The following table presents the men's and women's winning times (in seconds) in the Olympic 100-meter freestyle swimming race from 1912 to 1988.

Year	Men's	Women's
1912	63.2	72.2
1920	61.4	73.6
1924	59.0	72.4
1928	58.6	71.0
1932	58.2	66.8
1936	57.6	65.9
1948	57.3	66.3
1952	57.4	66.8
1956	55.4	62.0
1960	55.2	61.2
1964	53.4	59.5
1968	52.2	60.0
1972	51.22	58.59
1976	49.99	55.65
1980	50.40	54.79
1984	49.80	55.92
1988	48.63	54.93

Figure 2.20 on page 234 shows the graphs of the best-fitting lines (the regression lines) through the points representing the data values for the men and women.

a. Use the statistical menu of your graphing utility to enter the data values in the table for the men's winning times.

b. Select the linear regression option. Your utility should give you the regression coefficients, a and b, for the regression equation (usually in the form $y = ax + b$) and the correlation coefficient r. What is the value of r? Can you explain what this value means?

c. Repeat parts (a) and (b) for the data values in the table for the women's winning times.

d. Graph the equations of both regression lines using your graphing utility. Graph the equations in the same viewing rectangle. Use the ISECT or the TRACE feature to find the coordinates of the intersection point.

e. What does the intersection point mean in terms of the women's time and the men's time? What predic-

tions could be made about the swimming race in the Olympic years to the right of the intersection point?

Writing in Mathematics

65. What is a reasonable estimate for the slope of each of the six lines designated by L_1 through L_6 in the figure? Describe how you determined a value for the slope of each line.

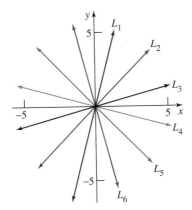

66. Which of the following variables will have a linear relationship over time? Which will not? Explain how you arrived at your answers.

a. U.S. health-care expenditure

b. The number of people with AIDS in the world

c. The price for admission to a movie

d. Population of Canada

e. Population of third-world countries

f. Cost of a computer

g. Position of a free-falling body thrown vertically upward

h. Value of an original painting by Salvador Dali

i. Value of an office copying machine

67. A grasshopper that is $1\frac{1}{4}$-inches long can jump 28 inches. Could this information be used to create a linear model based on the idea that jumping ability is directly proportional to body length? Could this linear model be used to predict how high a person who is 5′10″ can jump? Explain.

Critical Thinking Problems

68. Use the figure to answer the following.

a. Find the equation of the line from C to the midpoint of $\overline{AB}$, called the *median*.

b. Find the equation of the line from C that is perpendicular to $\overline{AB}$, called the *altitude*.

c. Find the equation of the line passing through the midpoint of $\overline{AB}$ and perpendicular to $\overline{AB}$, called the *perpendicular bisector* of $\overline{AB}$.

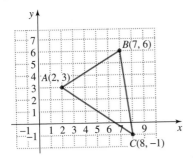

d. Repeat part (a) for the other two medians of the triangle.

e. Repeat part (b) for the other two altitudes of the triangle.

f. Repeat part (c) for the other two perpendicular bisectors of the triangle's sides.

69. Repeat all parts of Problem 68 for the triangle shown below.

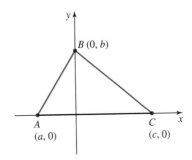

70. Find all points P on the graph of $y = x^2 + 4$ so that the line between P and $(0, 1)$ is perpendicular to the line whose equation is $y = -\frac{1}{4}x + 2$.

71. A line with negative slope has a y-intercept of 5. The area of the triangle in the first quadrant formed by the line and the two coordinate axes is 15 square units. Write the point-slope and slope-intercept equations of the line.

72. Prove that the equation of a line passing through $(a, 0)$ and $(0, b)$ $(a \neq 0, b \neq 0)$ can be written in the form $\dfrac{x}{a} + \dfrac{y}{b} = 1$. Why is this called the *intercept form* of a line?

Group Activity Problem

73. This problem is a "contest" problem. Work on the problem in groups of 3 to 5 people. Use as many suggestions as possible from group members to solve the problem.

A line with negative slope passes through the point $\left(2, \frac{6}{5}\right)$. The area of the triangle in the first quadrant formed by the line and the two coordinates axes is 5 square units. Write the general form of the line's equation.

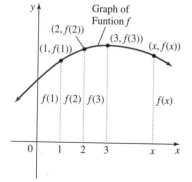

Solutions Manual   Tutorial   Video 4

S E C T I O N 2 . 3 # Graphs of Relations and Functions

Objectives

1 Graph functions and relations.
2 Use the vertical line test to identify functions.
3 Graph circles and write their equations.
4 Graph piecewise functions.

René Descartes' rectangular coordinate system made it possible to construct graphs for relationships between interconnected variables, usually designated by x and y. In this section, we apply Descartes' ideas to generate relatively accurate pictures of relations and functions.

 Graph functions and relations.

Figure 2.21

The graph of a function

Graphs of Relations and Functions

A useful method for visualizing a function's behavior is from its graph.

> **Graphs of relations and functions**
>
> The graph of a relation is the graph of its ordered pairs. The graph of a function f is the set of points $(x, f(x))$ such that x is in the domain of f.

The graph of function f is shown in Figure 2.21. The y-coordinate of any point (x, y) on the graph is $y = f(x)$. This means that the value of $f(x)$ is the height of

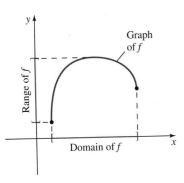

Figure 2.22

A function's domain and range

the graph above the value x. Figure 2.22 illustrates that we can picture a function's domain on the x-axis and its range on the y-axis.

One way to graph a relation or a function is by plotting ordered pairs.

EXAMPLE 1   Graphing Functions by Plotting Ordered Pairs

Graph each function and use the graph to specify the function's domain and range.

a. $f(x) = x^2 + 1$ **b.** $f(x) = \sqrt{x}$

Solution

a. The graph of $f(x) = x^2 + 1$ is, by definition, the graph of $y = x^2 + 1$. We begin by setting up a table of coordinates.

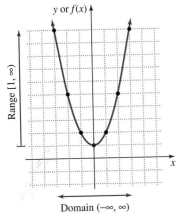

Figure 2.23

The graph of $f(x) = x^2 + 1$

x	$f(x) = x^2 + 1$	(x, y) or $(x, f(x))$
-3	$f(-3) = (-3)^2 + 1 = 10$	$(-3, 10)$
-2	$f(-2) = (-2)^2 + 1 = 5$	$(-2, 5)$
-1	$f(-1) = (-1)^2 + 1 = 2$	$(-1, 2)$
0	$f(0) = 0^2 + 1 = 1$	$(0, 1)$
1	$f(1) = 1^2 + 1 = 2$	$(1, 2)$
2	$f(2) = 2^2 + 1 = 5$	$(2, 5)$
3	$f(3) = 3^2 + 1 = 10$	$(3, 10)$

Now we plot the seven points and draw a smooth curve through them, as shown in Figure 2.23. Notice that the vertical axis can be labeled y or $f(x)$. The graph of f has a cuplike shape, with a domain consisting of all real numbers, represented by $(-\infty, \infty)$. The range consists of real numbers greater than or equal to 1, represented by $[1, \infty)$.

b. The graph of $f(x) = \sqrt{x}$ is, by definition, the graph of $y = \sqrt{x}$. We construct a table of coordinates, plot the resulting points, and draw a smooth curve through them to obtain the graph of f shown in Figure 2.24.

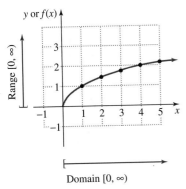

Figure 2.24

The graph of $f(x) = \sqrt{x}$

x	$f(x) = \sqrt{x}$	(x, y) or $(x, f(x))$
0	$f(0) = \sqrt{0} = 0$	$(0, 0)$
1	$f(1) = \sqrt{1} = 1$	$(1, 1)$
2	$f(2) = \sqrt{2} \approx 1.4$	$(2, \sqrt{2}) \approx (2, 1.4)$
3	$f(3) = \sqrt{3} \approx 1.7$	$(3, \sqrt{3}) \approx (3, 1.7)$
4	$f(4) = \sqrt{4} = 2$	$(4, 2)$
5	$f(5) = \sqrt{5} \approx 2.2$	$(5, \sqrt{5}) \approx (5, 2.2)$

The graph indicates that both the domain and the range of $f(x) = \sqrt{x}$ consist of 0 and all positive real numbers, represented by $[0, \infty)$. ■

The functions in Example 2 can be graphed by either plotting points or by using our knowledge of graphing linear functions.

EXAMPLE 2 **Graphing Functions Using y-Intercepts and Slopes**

Graph each function and use the graph to specify the function's domain and range.

a. $f(x) = |x|$ **b.** $f(x) = \dfrac{x^2 - 9}{x - 3}$

Solution

a. The graph of $f(x) = |x|$ is, by definition, the graph of the equation $y = |x|$. We can construct a table of coordinates that satisfy $y = |x|$ or we can use the definition of absolute value.

Using coordinates:

x	$f(x) = |x|$	(x, y) or $(x, f(x))$
-3	$f(-3) = |-3| = 3$	$(-3, 3)$
-2	$f(-2) = |-2| = 2$	$(-2, 2)$
-1	$f(-1) = |-1| = 1$	$(-1, 1)$
0	$f(0) = |0| = 0$	$(0, 0)$
1	$f(1) = |1| = 1$	$(1, 1)$
2	$f(2) = |2| = 2$	$(2, 2)$
3	$f(3) = |3| = 3$	$(3, 3)$

Using absolute value:

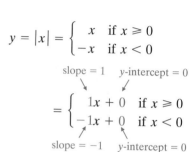

$$y = |x| = \begin{cases} x & \text{if } x \geq 0 \\ -x & \text{if } x < 0 \end{cases}$$

slope = 1   y-intercept = 0

$$= \begin{cases} 1x + 0 & \text{if } x \geq 0 \\ -1x + 0 & \text{if } x < 0 \end{cases}$$

slope = -1 y-intercept = 0

We can either plot the ordered pairs or graph the two lines whose equations are

$y = x$ (graphed for $x \geq 0$, on and to the right of the y-axis)

and

$y = -x$ (graphed for $x < 0$, to the left of the y-axis).

The graph of $f(x) = |x|$ has a V-shape, shown in Figure 2.25. The domain of f consists of all real numbers, represented by $(-\infty, \infty)$. The range consists only of nonnegative real numbers, represented by $[0, \infty)$.

b. We can obtain the graph of $f(x) = \dfrac{x^2 - 9}{x - 3}$ by first simplifying the expression that defines the function. The exclusion of x-values that yield zero in the denominator means that 3 must be excluded from the domain of f.

$$f(x) = \frac{x^2 - 9}{x - 3} = \frac{(x + 3)(x - 3)}{x - 3} = x + 3 \quad (\text{where } x \neq 3)$$

Thus we graph f by graphing the equation $y = x + 3$ with $x \neq 3$. We can plot points or we can use the fact that $y = x + 3$ has a y-intercept of 3 and slope 1. The graph of f is shown in Figure 2.26. The open dot above 3 excludes this value from the graph, indicating that $(3, 6)$ does not belong to the graph of f. The domain of f is the set of all real numbers excluding 3, represented by $(-\infty, 3) \cup (3, \infty)$. The range of f is the set of all real numbers excluding 6, represented by $(-\infty, 6) \cup (6, \infty)$. ∎

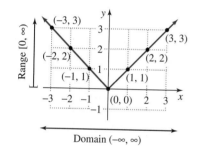

Range $[0, \infty)$

Domain $(-\infty, \infty)$

Figure 2.25

The graph of $f(x) = |x|$

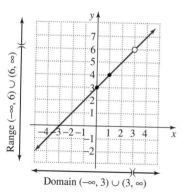

Range $(-\infty, 6) \cup (6, \infty)$

Domain $(-\infty, 3) \cup (3, \infty)$

Figure 2.26

The graph of $f(x) = \dfrac{x^2 - 9}{x - 3}$

Graphing Relations That Are Not Functions: The Vertical Line Test

In Section 2.1, we saw that not every equation in x and y defines y as a function of x. Relations that are not functions can still be graphed by plotting points.

EXAMPLE 3 Graphing a Relation That Is Not a Function

Graph the relation given by $x = y^2$ and use the graph to specify the relation's domain and range.

Solution

We can obtain the graph of $x = y^2$ by using the square root method and solving the equation for y.

$$y = \pm\sqrt{x}$$

Notice that $\pm$ indicates that corresponding to every nonzero value of x there are two values of y. Therefore, the relation does not define y as a function of x. However, we can still begin by setting up a table of coordinates.

x	$y = \pm\sqrt{x}$	(x, y)
0	$y = \pm\sqrt{0} = 0$	$(0, 0)$
1	$y = \pm\sqrt{1} = \pm1$	$(1, 1)$ and $(1, -1)$
2	$y = \pm\sqrt{2} \approx \pm1.4$	$(2, \sqrt{2}) \approx (2, 1.4)$ and $(2, -\sqrt{2}) \approx (2, -1.4)$
3	$y = \pm\sqrt{3} \approx 1.7$	$(3, \sqrt{3}) \approx (3, 1.7)$ and $(3, -\sqrt{3}) \approx (3, -1.7)$
4	$y = \pm\sqrt{4} = \pm2$	$(4, 2)$ and $(4, -2)$
5	$y = \pm\sqrt{5} \approx \pm2.2$	$(5, \sqrt{5}) \approx (5, 2.2)$ and $(5, -\sqrt{5}) \approx (5, -2.2)$

By plottings points and drawing a smooth curve through them, we obtain the graph of $x = y^2$ shown in Figure 2.27. The domain is $[0, \infty)$ and the range is the set of all real numbers, $(-\infty, \infty)$. ∎

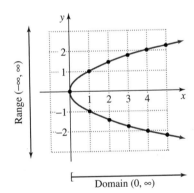

Figure 2.27

The graph of $x = y^2$

2 Use the vertical line test to identify functions.

Discover for yourself

Look at the graphs in Examples 1–3 (Figure 2.23 through Figure 2.26). How is the graph of $x = y^2$ in Figure 2.27 different from the other graphs? How can this difference be illustrated using vertical lines that intersect each graph?

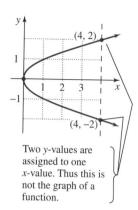

Two *y*-values are
assigned to one
x-value. Thus this is
not the graph of a
function.

Figure 2.28

The graph of a relation that is
not a function

In the Discover for yourself, did you observe that you can draw a vertical line
that intersects the graph of $x = y^2$ in two points? You could not do this with
any of the graphs in Examples 1 and 2. The vertical line drawn through the two
points (4, 2) and (4, −2) on the graph of $x = y^2$ (Figure 2.28) indicates that the
same *x*-value, 4, is assigned two different *y*-values, 2 and −2. Recall that if *y* is
a function of *x*, then at most one *y*-value corresponds to a given *x*-value. For
each *a* in the domain of a function there should be *only one* point $(a, f(a))$ on
the graph. Equivalently, each vertical line drawn through the graph of the
function must intersect the graph in *at most* one point. We can use this *vertical
line test* to determine if a graph defines *y* as a function of *x*.

The vertical line test for functions

If any vertical line intersects the graph of a relation in more than one
point, the relation does not define *y* as a function of *x*.

The vertical line test is illustrated in the following box.

Using the vertical line test

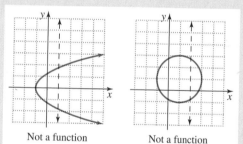

Function	Function	Function	Not a function	Not a function

No vertical line intersects the graph more than
once, so *y* is a function of *x*.

At least one vertical line intersects
the graph more than once,
so *y* is not a function of *x*.

Using technology

The function $N(x) = 0.036x^2 - 2.8x + 58.14$ approximates the number of deaths per
year per thousand people (N) for people who are *x* years old, where $40 \leq x \leq 60$. Use
a graphing utility to graph the function. Points along the graph can be described in
practical terms:

$N(40) \approx 4$ Approximately 4 people per 1000 who are 40 years old die annually.

$N(60) \approx 20$ Approximately 20 people per 1000 who are 60 years old die annually.

Change range settings to extend the graph to $x = 100$. Why isn't the function a good
model for $60 \leq x \leq 100$? Draw a graph by hand that models death rate in a more
accurate manner for $60 \leq x \leq 100$.

Paul Thek "Dust" 1988, acrylic/gesso on newspaper,
21 1/4 × 27 1/2 in. Photo courtesy Alexander and Bonin.

3 Graph circles and write their equations.

Circles

The vertical line test for functions, shown in the preceding box, reveals that the graph of a circle in the Cartesian coordinate plane does not define y as a function of x. However, we can still use the coordinate system to translate the definition of a circle into an algebraic equation involving x and y.

A circle is the set of all points in a plane that are equidistant from a fixed point, called the *center*. The fixed distance from the circle's center to any point on the circle is called the *radius*. Figure 2.29 illustrates a circle with radius of length r and center (h, k) in the Cartesian coordinate plane. The point (x, y) is on this circle if and only if its distance from the center is r. Using the distance formula, we have

$$\sqrt{(x - h)^2 + (y - k)^2} = r.$$

Figure 2.29

A circle centered at (h, k) with radius of length r

Squaring both sides of this equation yields the *standard form of the equation of a circle*.

Standard form of the equation of a circle

The equation of the circle with the center at (h, k) and radius of length r is

$$(x - h)^2 + (y - k)^2 = r^2.$$

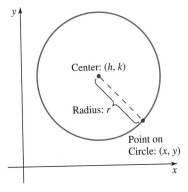

Keith Haring "Monkey Puzzle" 1988, acrylic on canvas, 120 in. diameter. ©The Estate of Keith Haring.

EXAMPLE 4	**Finding the Equation of a Circle and Graphing the Circle**

Find the equation of the circle with a radius of length 2 and the center at $(0, 0)$. Graph the circle.

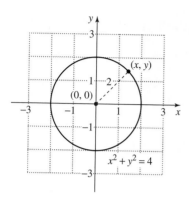

Figure 2.30

The graph of $x^2 + y^2 = 4$

Solution

Because $(h, k) = (0, 0)$ and $r = 2$, we have

$$(x - h)^2 + (y - k)^2 = r^2 \qquad \text{This is the equation of a circle.}$$

$$(x - 0)^2 + (y - 0)^2 = 2^2 \qquad \text{Substitute 0 for } h, 0 \text{ for } k, \text{ and 2 for } r.$$

$$x^2 + y^2 = 4 \qquad \text{Simplify.}$$

The equation of the circle is $x^2 + y^2 = 4$. Figure 2.30 shows the graph.   ∎

Observe from Example 4 that the equation of any circle with the center at the origin $(0, 0)$, and radius r is $x^2 + y^2 = r^2$. The equation $x^2 + y^2 = 4$, graphed in Figure 2.30, does not define y as a function of x. Vertical lines drawn between -2 and 2 intersect the graph more than once.

Example 5 involves finding the equation of a circle whose center is not at the origin.

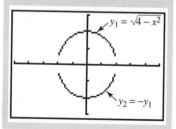
EXAMPLE 5   **Writing the Equation of a Circle**

Find the equation of the circle with the center at $(-2, 3)$ and a radius of length 4.

Solution

We have $(h, k) = (-2, 3)$ and $r = 4$. Thus,

$$(x - h)^2 + (y - k)^2 = r^2 \qquad \text{This is the equation of a circle.}$$

$$[x - (-2)]^2 + (y - 3)^2 = 4^2 \qquad \text{Substitute } -2 \text{ for } h, 3 \text{ for } k, \text{ and 4 for } r.$$

$$(x + 2)^2 + (y - 3)^2 = 16 \qquad \text{Simplify.}$$

The equation of the circle is $(x + 2)^2 + (y - 3)^2 = 16$.   ∎

EXAMPLE 6   **Using the Equation of a Circle to Graph It**

Find the center and radius of the circle whose equation is

$$(x - 2)^2 + (y + 4)^2 = 9$$

and sketch the graph.

Solution

Because $(x - h)^2 + (y - k)^2 = r^2$ and we have $(x - 2)^2 + [(y - (-4)]^2 = 3^2$, the center is at $(2, -4)$ and the radius is 3. Figure 2.31 on page 249 shows the graph.   ∎

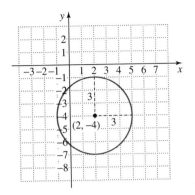

Figure 2.31

The graph of the relation
$(x - 2)^2 + (y + 4)^2 = 9$

If we square $x - 2$ and $y + 4$ in the equation of Example 6, we obtain

$$(x - 2)^2 + (y + 4)^2 = 9 \qquad \text{This is the equation from Example 6.}$$

$$x^2 - 4x + 4 + y^2 + 8y + 16 = 9 \qquad \text{Square } x - 2 \text{ and } y + 4.$$

$$x^2 + y^2 - 4x + 8y + 20 = 9 \qquad \text{Combine numerical terms.}$$

$$x^2 + y^2 - 4x + 8y + 11 = 0 \qquad \text{Subtract 9 from both sides.}$$

This result suggests that an equation in the form $x^2 + y^2 + Dx + Ey + F = 0$ represents a circle. We can return to the familiar form $(x - h)^2 + (y - k)^2 = r^2$ by completing the square on x and y. Let's see how this is done.

EXAMPLE 7   **Completing the Square to Find a Circle's Center and Radius**

Graph: $x^2 + y^2 + 4x - 6y - 23 = 0$

Solution

Because we plan to complete the square on both x and y, let's rearrange terms so that x-terms are arranged in descending order, y-terms are arranged in descending order, and the constant term appears on the right.

$$x^2 + y^2 + 4x - 6y - 23 = 0$$

$$(x^2 + 4x \quad) + (y^2 - 6y \quad) = 23 \qquad \begin{array}{l}\text{Rewrite in anticipation of} \\ \text{completing the square.}\end{array}$$

$$(x^2 + 4x + 4) + (y^2 - 6y + 9) = 23 + 4 + 9 \qquad \begin{array}{l}\text{Complete the square on } x\text{:} \\ \frac{1}{2} \cdot 4 = 2 \text{ and } 2^2 = 4, \text{ so add 4} \\ \text{to both sides. Complete the} \\ \text{square on } y\text{: } \frac{1}{2}(-6) = -3 \text{ and} \\ (-3)^2 = 9, \text{ so add 9 to both} \\ \text{sides.}\end{array}$$

$$(x + 2)^2 + (y - 3)^2 = 36 \qquad \begin{array}{l}\text{Factor on the left and add on} \\ \text{the right.}\end{array}$$

$$(x + 2)^2 + (y - 3)^2 = 6^2 \qquad \begin{array}{l}\text{This equation is in the form} \\ (x - h)^2 + (y - k)^2 = r^2, \text{ with} \\ \text{the center at } (h, k) \text{ and radius } r.\end{array}$$

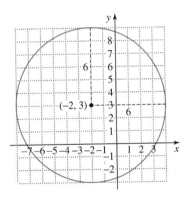

Figure 2.32

The graph of the relation
$(x + 2)^2 + (y - 3)^2 = 36$

Thus, the center is at $(-2, 3)$, and the radius 6. Figure 2.32 shows the graph. ∎

Using technology

To graph $x^2 + y^2 + 4x - 6y - 23 = 0$, rewrite the equation as a quadratic equation in y.

$$y^2 - 6y + (x^2 + 4x - 23) = 0$$

Now solve for y using the quadratic formula, with $a = 1$, $b = -6$, and $c = x^2 + 4x - 23$.

$$y = \frac{-b \pm \sqrt{b^2 - 4ac}}{2a} = \frac{-(-6) \pm \sqrt{(-6)^2 - 4 \cdot 1(x^2 + 4x - 23)}}{2 \cdot 1} = \frac{6 \pm \sqrt{36 - 4(x^2 + 4x - 23)}}{2}$$

Since we will enter these equations, there is no need to simplify. Enter

$$y_1 = \frac{6 + \sqrt{36 - 4(x^2 + 4x - 23)}}{2}$$

and

$$y_2 = \frac{6 - \sqrt{36 - 4(x^2 + 4x - 23)}}{2}.$$

Use a ZOOM SQUARE setting. The graph is shown on the right.

4 Graph piecewise functions.

Modeling with Piecewise Functions

Because conditions frequently change over time, functions that model real world phenomena over time must frequently be defined by two or more equations. Therefore, descriptions of the physical world often require piecewise functions. Graphing utilities are helpful in drawing these functions.

EXAMPLE 8 Modeling the Average Miles Driven

The piecewise function

$$f(x) = \begin{cases} 0.0005x^2 + 0.025x + 8.8 & \text{if } 0 \le x \le 30 \\ 0.0202x^2 - 1.58x + 39.22 & \text{if } x > 30 \end{cases}$$

models the average number of miles driven in thousands per car in the United States x years after 1940. Use a graphing utility to draw the graph of the function.

Solution

We will use our graphing utility to graph the functions

$$y_1 = 0.0005x^2 + 0.025x + 8.8$$

and

$$y_2 = 0.0202x^2 - 1.58x + 39.22$$

If we project the model up to the year 2000, a reasonable range setting for x is

Xmin = 0, Xmax = 60, and Xscl = 2.

Since $f(x)$ represents the average number of miles driven in thousands per car per year, we will use

Ymin = 0, Ymax = 25, and Yscl = 1.

Figure 2.33

We used the ISECT feature to obtain Figure 2.33, which shows that the graphs intersect at (30, 10). The graph of the first function ends up at the same point where the second one begins. In practical terms, this means that 30 years after 1940, or in 1970, cars in the United States were driven (on the average) 10 thousand miles.

Now we can draw f (by hand) by taking the part of the graph of y_1 to the left of $x = 30$ and combining it with the part of the graph of y_2 to the right of $x = 30$. The resulting graph is shown in Figure 2.34. ∎

Figure 2.34

A graph showing average miles driven per car in the U.S.

Using technology

The hand-drawn graph in Figure 2.34 can be obtained with a graphing utility. An equation similar to

$$y_1 = (x \le 30)(0.0005x^2 + 0.025x + 8.8) + (x > 30)(0.0202x^2 - 1.58x + 39.22)$$

should give the graph. Consult your manual for the location of the $\boxed{\le}$ and $\boxed{>}$ keys.

A piecewise function can also be drawn by hand by plotting ordered pairs and using techniques for graphing linear functions.

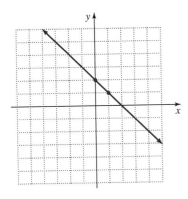

Figure 2.35

The graph of $y = -x + 2$

EXAMPLE 9 **Graphing a Piecewise Function**

Sketch by hand the graph of the function f defined by

$$f(x) = \begin{cases} -x + 2 & \text{if } x \le 2 \\ x^2 & \text{if } x > 2 \end{cases}$$

Solution

The graph of $y = -x + 2$ is a line with slope -1 and y-intercept 2, as shown in Figure 2.35.

We can graph $y = x^2$ by constructing a table of coordinates. The graph is shown in Figure 2.36.

x	-2	-1	0	1	2	3
$y = x^2$	4	1	0	1	4	9

To graph f (Figure 2.37), we graph the part of the line that lies to the left of $x = 2$. The solid dot at $(2, 0)$ shows that this point is included on the graph. The graph of $y = x^2$ is shown only for $x > 2$; the open dot at $(2, 4)$ indicates that this point is not part of the graph. ∎

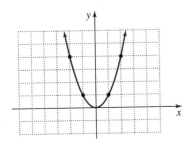

Figure 2.36

The graph of $y = x^2$

Some piecewise functions have graphs that consist of a collection of horizontal line segments, or *steps,* with a jump occurring at each integer.

EXAMPLE 10 **Modeling the Cost of a Long Distance Phone Call**

The cost of a daytime long distance phone call from Miami to Talahassee is $0.50 for the first minute and $0.25 for each additional minute (or portion of a minute). Draw a graph of the cost (C, in dollars) of the phone call as a function of time (t, in minutes).

Figure 2.37

The graph of $y = -x + 2$ for $x \le 2$ and $y = x^2$ for $x > 2$

Solution

Let $C(t)$ be the cost for t minutes. For calls up to 1 minute, the cost is $0.50. For calls between 1 and 2 minutes, the cost is $0.75; between 2 and 3 minutes, the cost is $1.00, and so on.

Figure 2.38

Cost of a long distance call

t: Length of call	$0 < t \leq 1$	$1 < t \leq 2$	$2 < t \leq 3$	$3 < t \leq 4$
C(t): Cost of call	0.50	0.75	1.00	1.25

Using these values, we obtain the graph of the cost function shown in Figure 2.38. Since $C(t)$ is constant in each interval, the graph consists of a different horizontal line in each interval. ■

A general step function, called the *greatest integer function*, is denoted by $[[x]]$.

Definition of the greatest integer function

$f(x) = [[x]] =$ the greatest integer less than or equal to x.

Some values of the greatest integer function are as follows:

If $-1 \leq x < 0$,

$$[[-1]] = -1, \quad [[-0.9]] = -1, \quad [[-0.5]] = -1, \quad [[-0.001]] = -1$$

Greatest integer less than or equal to -1

Greater integer less than or equal to -0.9

Greater integer less than or equal to -0.5

Greater integer less than or equal to -0.001

Thus, if $-1 \leq x < 0$, then $[[x]] = -1$.

If $0 \leq x < 1$,

$$[[0]] = 0, \quad [[0.3]] = 0, \quad [[\tfrac{1}{2}]] = 0, \quad [[0.9]] = 0.$$

The greatest integer less than or equal to $0, 0.3, \tfrac{1}{2}$, and 0.9 is 0.

Thus, if $0 \leq x < 1$, then $[[x]] = 0$.

If $1 \leq x < 2$,

$$[[1]] = 1, \quad [[1.3]] = 1, \quad [[1\tfrac{1}{2}]] = 1, \quad [[1.9]] = 1.$$

The greatest integer less than or equal to $1, 1.3, 1\tfrac{1}{2}$, and 1.9 is 1.

Thus, if $1 \leq x < 2$ then $[[x]] = 1$.

In general:

If $n \leq x < n + 1$, where n is an integer, then $[[x]] = n$.

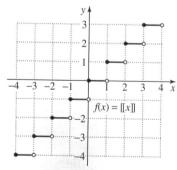

Figure 2.39

The graph of the greatest integer function

The graph of $f(x) = [[x]]$ is shown in Figure 2.39 for x in the interval $[-4, 4)$. The graph of f consists of a collection of horizontal line segments, or steps, with a jump occurring at each integer. The domain is $(-\infty, \infty)$ and the range is the set of integers.

U sing technology

You can use a graphing utility to graph the greatest integer function. The function's equation is entered as

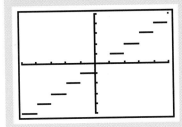

$$Y_1 = \boxed{\text{INT}}\ X$$

Consult your manual for the location of the $\boxed{\text{INT}}$ (greatest integer) key. Without tracing along the graph, it is impossible to tell by looking at the graph that for each step the point on the left is included and the point on the right is not.

PROBLEM SET 2.3

Practice Problems _____

Graph the relations in Problems 1–30 by either plotting points or, if applicable, using your knowledge about slope and y-intercept for graphing linear functions. Specify the relation's domain and range from the graph.

1. $f(x) = x^2 - 2$ **2.** $f(x) = x^2 - 1$ **3.** $f(x) = x^2 + 2x + 1$ **4.** $f(x) = x^2 - 4x + 4$

5. $f(x) = x^3$ **6.** $f(x) = x^3 + 1$ **7.** $f(x) = x^3 - 2x$ **8.** $f(x) = x^3 - 3x$

9. $f(x) = \sqrt{x} + 1$ **10.** $f(x) = \sqrt{x} + 2$ **11.** $f(x) = \sqrt{x + 1}$ **12.** $f(x) = \sqrt{x + 2}$

13. $f(x) = 2|x|$ **14.** $f(x) = 3|x|$ **15.** $f(x) = |x| - 1$ **16.** $f(x) = |x| - 2$

17. $f(x) = |x - 1|$ **18.** $f(x) = |x - 2|$ **19.** $f(x) = |x| + x$ **20.** $f(x) = |x| - x$

21. $f(x) = \dfrac{x^2 - 4}{x - 2}$ **22.** $f(x) = \dfrac{x^2 - 16}{x - 4}$ **23.** $f(x) = \dfrac{x^2 - 1}{x + 1}$ **24.** $f(x) = \dfrac{x^2 - 25}{x + 5}$

25. $x = 4y^2$ **26.** $x = 8y^2$ **27.** $x = -y^2$ **28.** $x = -4y^2$

29. $G(x) = \dfrac{x}{|x|}$ **30.** $H(x) = \dfrac{|x|}{x}$

For Problems 31–42, use the vertical line test to identify graphs in which y is a function of x. Use the graph to give the domain and range of each relation.

31.

32.

33.

34.

35.

36.

37.

38.

39.

40.

41.

42.

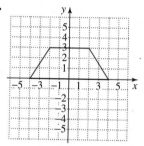

In Problems 43–52, write the standard form of the equation of the circle with the given center and radius.

43. Center $(0, 0)$, $r = 7$

44. Center $(0, 0)$, $r = 8$

45. Center $(3, 2)$, $r = 5$

46. Center $(2, -1)$, $r = 4$

47. Center $(-1, 4)$, $r = 2$

48. Center $(-3, 5)$, $r = 3$

49. Center $(-3, -1)$, $r = \sqrt{3}$

50. Center $(-5, -3)$, $r = \sqrt{5}$

51. Center $(-4, 0)$, $r = 0$

52. Center $(-2, 0)$, $r = 6$

In Problems 53–60, give the center and radius of the circle described by the equation and graph each equation.

53. $x^2 + y^2 = 16$

54. $x^2 + y^2 = 49$

55. $(x - 3)^2 + (y - 1)^2 = 36$

56. $(x - 2)^2 + (y - 3)^2 = 16$

57. $(x + 3)^2 + (y - 2)^2 = 4$

58. $(x + 1)^2 + (y - 4)^2 = 25$

59. $(x + 2)^2 + (y + 2)^2 = 4$

60. $(x + 4)^2 + (y + 5)^2 = 36$

In Problems 61–68, complete the square and then give the center and radius of each circle. Then graph each equation.

61. $x^2 + y^2 + 6x + 2y + 6 = 0$

62. $x^2 + y^2 + 8x + 4y + 16 = 0$

63. $x^2 + y^2 - 10x - 6y - 30 = 0$

64. $x^2 + y^2 - 4x - 12y - 9 = 0$

65. $x^2 + y^2 + 8x - 2y - 8 = 0$

66. $x^2 + y^2 + 12x - 6y - 4 = 0$

67. $x^2 - 2x + y^2 - 15 = 0$

68. $x^2 + y^2 - 6y - 7 = 0$

Graph each piecewise function in Problems 69–78.

69. $f(x) = \begin{cases} 2x + 3 & \text{if } x \le 0 \\ x + 3 & \text{if } x > 0 \end{cases}$

70. $f(x) = \begin{cases} x + 4 & \text{if } x \le 0 \\ 2x + 4 & \text{if } x > 0 \end{cases}$

71. $f(x) = \begin{cases} -x + 1 & \text{if } x \le 1 \\ 2x - 2 & \text{if } x > 1 \end{cases}$

72. $f(x) = \begin{cases} -x + 2 & \text{if } x \le 2 \\ 3x - 6 & \text{if } x > 2 \end{cases}$

73. $f(x) = \begin{cases} 3 - x & \text{if } x < 3 \\ \sqrt{x - 3} & \text{if } x \ge 3 \end{cases}$

74. $f(x) = \begin{cases} -x - 2 & \text{if } x < -2 \\ \sqrt{x + 2} & \text{if } x \ge -2 \end{cases}$

75. $f(x) = \begin{cases} 2 & \text{if } x \le 0 \\ x^2 & \text{if } x > 0 \end{cases}$

76. $f(x) = \begin{cases} 3 & \text{if } x \le -1 \\ x^2 + 1 & \text{if } x > -1 \end{cases}$

77. $g(x) = \begin{cases} x^2 + 1 & \text{if } x \ne 0 \\ 4 & \text{if } x = 0 \end{cases}$

78. $g(x) = \begin{cases} x^2 - 1 & \text{if } x \ne 0 \\ 2 & \text{if } x = 0 \end{cases}$

Application Problems

79. The concentration of a drug (in parts per million) in a patient's bloodstream t hours after the drug is administered is given by the function $f(t) = -t^4 + 12t^3 - 58t^2 + 132t$. Fill in the following table of coordinates and graph the function. What does the shape of the graph indicate about the drug's concentration over time? After how many hours will the drug be totally eliminated from the bloodstream? How is this indicated by the graph?

t	$f(t) = -t^4 + 12t^3 - 58t^2 + 132t$
0	
1	
2	
3	
4	
5	
6	

80. A cargo service charges a flat fee of $4 plus $1 for each pound or fraction of a pound to mail a package. Let $C(x)$ represent the cost to mail a package that weighs x pounds. Graph the cost function in the interval $(0, 5]$.

81. The cost of a telephone call between two cities is $1 for the first minute and $0.50 for each additional minute or portion of a minute. Draw a graph of the cost (C, in dollars) of the phone call as a function of time (t, in minutes) in the interval $(0, 5]$.

True–False Critical Thinking Problems

82. Which one of the following is true based on the graph of f in the figure?

a. The domain of f is $[-4, 1) \cup (1, 4]$.

b. The range of f is $[-2, 2]$.

c. $f(-1) - f(4) = 2$

d. $f(0) = 2.1$

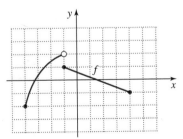

a. There is precisely one value of x for which $g(x) = f(1)$.

b. $f(2) - g(2) > f(1) - g(1)$

c. The sum of $\dfrac{f(x) - f(2)}{x - 2}$ when $x = 3$ and

$\dfrac{g(x) - g(-2)}{x + 2}$ when $x = -3$ is 1.

d. None of these statements is true.

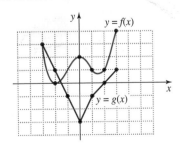

83. Which one of the following is true based on the graphs of f and g in the figure shown at the right?

84. Which one of the following is true?

    a. The equation of the circle whose center is at the origin with radius of length 16 is $x^2 + y^2 = 16$.

    b. The graph of $(x - 3)^2 + (y + 5)^2 = 36$ is a circle with a radius of 6 centered at $(-3, 5)$.

    c. The graph of $(x - 4) + (y + 6) = 25$ is a circle with a radius of 5 centered at $(4, -6)$.

    d. None of the above is true.

85. Which one of the following is true?

    a. The coordinates of a circle's center satisfy the circle's equation.

    b. The radius of the circle whose equation is given by $x^2 - 6x + y^2 = 25$ is 5.

    c. If the center of a circle is at $(-1, -2)$ and the circle passes through the origin, then not enough information is provided to write the circle's equation.

    d. None of the above is true.

Technology Problems

86. The function

$$C(x) = \begin{cases} -0.35x + 220 & \text{for } 0 \le x \le 20 \\ -0.80x + 229 & \text{for } x > 20 \end{cases}$$

describes the number of milligrams of cholesterol per deciliter of blood for American adults x years after 1960.

    a. Graph the function using a graphing utility.

    b. What does the graph indicate about cholesterol level from 1960 to the present?

    c. Will the goal of lowering cholesterol to a level under 200 be reached by the turn of the century?

Use a graphing utility to graph each relation and function in Problems 87–92.

87. $f(x) = 2[[x+1]]$

88. $g(x) = 4 - [[x]]$

89. $y^2 = x^4 + 3x^2$

90. $f(x) = x^2 + x - 2$ and $g(x) = |x^2 + x - 2|$ (In what ways are these graphs similar and different?)

91. $f(x) = \begin{cases} 3x - x^2 & \text{if } x > 1 \\ (x - 1)^2 & \text{if } x \le 1 \end{cases}$

92. $f(x) = \begin{cases} \sqrt{-x} & \text{if } x < 0 \\ x^2 & \text{if } 0 \le x < 3 \\ \sqrt{x - 3} & \text{if } x \ge 3 \end{cases}$

Use a graphing utility to graph each circle whose equation is given in Problems 93–95.

93. $x^2 + y^2 = 25$

94. $(y + 1)^2 = 36 - (x - 3)^2$

95. $x^2 + 10x + y^2 - 4y - 20 = 0$

Writing in Mathematics

96. Discuss one disadvantage to using point plotting as a method for graphing functions.

97. The equation $x^2 + y^2 = 25$ does not define y as a function of x. However, the semicircles whose equations are $y = \sqrt{25 - x^2}$ and $y = -\sqrt{25 - x^2}$ do represent y as a function of x. Does every semicircle formed by $x^2 + y^2 = 25$ define y as a function of x? Explain, illustrating with graphs and equations.

98. Does $(x - 3)^2 + (y - 5)^2 = 0$ represent the equation of a circle? If not, describe the graph of this equation.

99. Does $(x - 3)^2 + (y - 5)^2 = -25$ represent the equation of a circle? What sort of set is the graph of this equation?

Critical Thinking Problems

For Problems 100–103, select the graph from (a)–(h) shown below that best models the given verbal conditions.

(a)

(b)

(c)

(d)

(e)

(f)

(g)

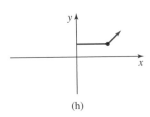

(h)

100. A utility charges a flat fee of $14 for the first 35 kilo-watt-hours or less, and $0.13 more for each kilowatt-hour above 35. Select the graph that models the relationship between the amount of an electric bill (y) and the total number of kilowatt-hours (x) used by a customer each month.

101. A person walks from home at 1:00 P.M., walking westward at a constant speed of 3 miles per hour for 30 minutes. After 30 minutes, that person meets a friend and stops to talk for 10 minutes. Select the graph that models the relationship between distance from home (y) and time (x).

102. A car travels 60 miles per hour for 2 hours, then slows down to 40 miles per hour for the next 3 hours. Select the graph that models the relationship between the distance that the car travels (y) in x hours.

103. A company cannot sell any radios if the price is $600. However, each price decrease of $45 per radio is accompanied by one additional radio being sold. Select the graph that models the relationship between the price per radio (y) and the number of radios that can be sold (x).

104. Find the area of the region bounded by the graphs of $(x - 2)^2 + (y + 3)^2 = 25$ and $(x - 2)^2 + (y + 3)^2 = 36$.

S E C T I O N   2 . 4

Solutions Manual

Tutorial

Video 4

Increasing and Decreasing Functions; Extreme Values

Objectives

1 Identify intervals in which a function increases or decreases.

2 Use a verbal model to sketch a function.

3 Find relative extrema.

The graph of a function provides a visual way of showing the relationship between the independent and the dependent variable. Knowing where the graph of a function rises and where it falls provides useful information. Also useful is the ability to identify lowest and highest points on the graph.

Identify intervals in which a function increases or decreases.

EXAMPLE 1   **Summer's Air Pollution as a Function of the Time of the Day**

Although the level of air pollution varies from day to day and from hour to hour, during the summer the level of air pollution is generally a function of the time of the day. The function

$$f(x) = 0.1x^2 - 0.4x + 0.6, \; 0 \leqslant x \leqslant 5$$

describes the level of air pollution (in parts per million, ppm), where x corresponds to the number of hours after 9 A.M. The graph of this function is shown in Figure 2.40.

a. Verify the point $(1, 0.3)$ and describe what this means in practical terms.
b. For what values of x is the graph of the function falling? What does this mean?
c. For what values of x is the graph of the function rising? What does this mean?
d. For what value of x does the lowest point on the graph of f occur? What is the minimum value of y? Describe the practical significance of this minimum value.
e. Researchers have determined that a level of 0.3 ppm of pollutants in the air can be hazardous to your health. Based on the graph, at what time of day should runners exercise to be at a safe level?

Solution

a. We can verify the point $(1, 0.3)$ by evaluating the function at $x = 1$.

$$f(x) = 0.1x^2 - 0.4x + 0.6 \qquad \text{This is the given function.}$$
$$f(1) = 0.1(1)^2 - 0.4(1) + 0.6 \qquad \text{Find } f \text{ at } 1.$$
$$= 0.3$$

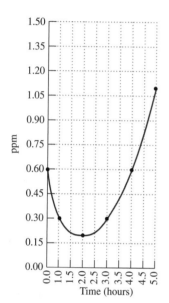

Figure 2.40

Air pollution as a function of time

This means that one hour after 9 A.M., or at 10 A.M., the level of air pollution is 0.3 ppm.

b. The graph in Figure 2.40 falls and then rises as we move from left to right. It is falling between $x = 0$ and $x = 2$. We can say that the function f is *decreasing* on the interval $(0, 2)$. This means that between 0 and 2 hours after 9 A.M., or between 9 A.M. and 11 A.M., the level of air pollution is decreasing.

c. The graph of the function f is rising between $x = 2$ and $x = 5$. We can say that the function f is *increasing* on the interval $(2, 5)$. This means that between 2 and 5 hours after 9 A.M., or between 11 A.M. and 2 P.M., the level of air pollution is increasing.

d. The lowest point on the graph of f occurs when $x = 2$. The minimum value of y can be found by evaluating the function at $x = 2$.

$$f(x) = 0.1x^2 - 0.4x + 0.6 \qquad \text{This is the given function.}$$
$$f(2) = 0.1(2)^2 - 0.4(2) + 0.6 \qquad \text{Find } f \text{ at } 2.$$
$$= 0.2$$

This means that air pollution reaches its lowest level 2 hours after 9 A.M., or at 11 A.M., and that the minimum level is 0.2 ppm.

e. The graph in Figure 2.41 indicates that the level of air pollution decreases to a minimum at 11 A.M. and then increases above safe levels. A runner should

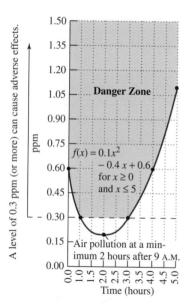

Figure 2.41

Air pollution as a function of time

exercise sometime between 1 and 3 hours after 9 A.M. (between 10 A.M. and noon), with 11 A.M. being the ideal time of day.   ■

Example 1 illustrates that a function f is increasing when its graph rises and decreasing when its graph falls. It is also possible for a function to remain constant, neither rising nor falling. We provide a formal definition of these concepts as follows.

Discover for yourself

The lowest point on the graph of

$$f(x) = 0.1x^2 - 0.4x + 0.6$$

is $(2, 0.2)$. Provide numerical support to this statement by evaluating $f(1.9)$ and $f(2.1)$.

Increasing, decreasing, and constant functions

1. A function is *increasing* on an interval if for any x_1 and x_2 in the interval, where $x_1 < x_2$, then $f(x_1) < f(x_2)$.
2. A function is *decreasing* on an interval if for any x_1 and x_2 in the interval, where $x_1 < x_2$, then $f(x_1) > f(x_2)$.
3. A function is *constant* on an interval if for any x_1 and x_2 in the interval, where $x_1 < x_2$, then $f(x_1) = f(x_2)$.

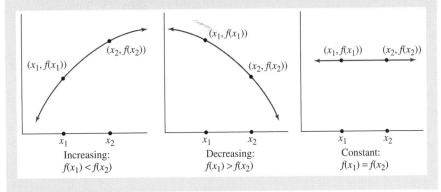

Increasing: $f(x_1) < f(x_2)$ | Decreasing: $f(x_1) > f(x_2)$ | Constant: $f(x_1) = f(x_2)$

EXAMPLE 2   **Intervals on Which a Function Increases or Decreases**

When a person receives a drug injected into a muscle, the concentration of the drug in the blood (measured in milligrams per 100 milliliters) is a function of the time elapsed since the injection (measured in hours). Figure 2.42 shows the graph of such a function, where

x = hours since the injection

and

$f(x)$ = drug concentration at time x.

State the intervals on which the function is increasing and decreasing and describe what this means in terms of the variables modeled in the graph.

Solution

The function is increasing on the interval $(0, 3)$, that is, between $x = 0$ and $x = 3$. It is decreasing on the interval $(3, 13)$, or between $x = 3$ and $x = 13$. This means that once the drug is injected into the muscle, the drug spreads into the blood and its concentration increases up to 3 hours after the injection. (A maximum concentration of 0.05 milligram per 100 milliliters is reached after 3

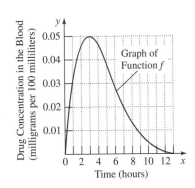

Figure 2.42

Concentration of a drug as a function of time

hours.) Between 3 and 13 hours after the injection, the drug concentration in the blood decreases. Since $f(13) = 0$, at the end of 13 hours there is no longer any drug in the blood. ∎

2 Use a verbal model to sketch a function.

Hannah Wilke "Why Not Sneeze" 1992, wire bird cage, plastic medicine bottles and syringes, $7 \times 9 \times 6\ 7/8$ in. Courtesy Ronald Feldman Fine Arts, NY. Photo by Dennis Cowley.

EXAMPLE 3 **Sketching a Function Using Given Conditions**

A person who is ill with the flu discovers that body temperature, $f(x)$, is a function of time x, where x represents the number of hours after 8 A.M. Sketch the function based on the following properties.

a. $f(0) = 101$ (Temperature at 8 A.M. is 101°.)
b. Temperature decreases on the interval $(0, 3)$, reaching normal (98.6°) by 11 A.M.
c. Temperature increases on the interval $(3, 5)$.
d. $f(5) = 100$ (Temperature at 1 P.M. is 100°.)
e. Temperature remains constant at 100° on the interval $(5, 7)$. (The last time temperature is taken is at 3 P.M., where $f(7) = 100$.)

Solution

Figure 2.43 shows the graph of body temperature as a function of time.

(a) $f(0) = 101$

(b) Temperature decreases in $(0, 3)$, reaching 98.6° by 11 A.M.

(c) Temperature increases in $(3, 5)$.

(d) $f(5) = 100$

(e) Temperature remains constant at 100° in $(5, 7)$.

Figure 2.43

Body temperature as a function of time ∎

Verbal descriptions can often be translated into graphs, allowing us to visualize a given situation.

EXAMPLE 4 **A Graph That Models a Verbal Description**

Represent the following description by a possible graph that models distance from home as a function of time.

I left home for school driving at a constant rate. I briefly stopped at a friend's house when I remembered I had forgotten my homework. I returned home, still driving at a constant rate, although faster than I had originally driven. At that point, I left home again and continued to speed up as I became concerned about being late for my first class.

Solution

Figure 2.44 shows a possible graph.

Distance from Home

Time

Figure 2.44

Modeling a verbal description with a graph

1. This piece of the graph shows the distance from home increasing at a constant rate, since the narrator drove at a constant speed.
2. This piece of the graph shows the narrator's stop at a friend's house. During the duration of the stop, the distance from home remains constant.
3. This piece of the graph represents the return home, steadily decreasing until the distance from home is 0. Notice that (3) falls more rapidly than (1) rises because the return home was at a faster rate than originally driven.
4. A brief period of time is spent at home to find the forgotten homework. The distance from home remains constant at 0.
5. The increasing steepness of this part of the graph shows distance from home increasing at a faster and faster rate as the narrator continued to speed up. The y-coordinate of the point on the right represents the distance from home to school. ∎

If a function's equation is known, a graphing utility can be used to determine intervals on which the function increases and decreases.

Figure 2.45

The graph of $y = x^{2/3} + 1$

Study tip

Some graphing utilities do not evaluate $x^{2/3}$ (entered as x ⌃ (2/3)) when x is negative. If you do not obtain the graph in Figure 2.45, enter the function's equation as

$$y_1 = (x \;⌃\; (1/3)) \;⌃\; 2 + 1.$$

EXAMPLE 5 **Using a Graphing Utility**

a. Use a graphing utility to graph the function $f(x) = x^{2/3} + 1$.
b. Find the domain and range of the function.
c. State the intervals on which f increases and decreases.

Solution

a. Using a graphing utility, we graph $f(x) = x^{2/3} + 1$ as shown in Figure 2.45.
b. From the graph, we can see that the domain of f is $(-\infty, \infty)$ and the range is $[1, \infty)$.
c. The graph indicates that f is decreasing on the interval $(-\infty, 0)$ and increasing on the interval $(0, \infty)$. ∎

Look again at the graph of the function in Figure 2.45. The function is decreasing on the interval $(-\infty, 0)$ and increasing on the interval $(0, \infty)$. At the point $(0, 1)$, the function changes from decreasing to increasing, and 1 is a *minimum* value of the function, with this minimum occurring at $x = 0$.

Lowest and highest points on functions are extremely important in applications. These extreme values of a function are the lowest and largest value of the function on some interval and can be formally defined as follows.

3 Find relative extrema.

Definitions of relative maximum and relative minimum

1. A function value $f(a)$ is a *relative maximum* of f if there exists an open interval about a such that $f(a) \geq f(x)$ for all x in the open interval.
2. A function value $f(b)$ is a *relative minimum* of f if there exists an open interval about b such that $f(b) \leq f(x)$ for all x in the open interval.

Average Number of Children Born to Each U.S. Woman

Figure 2.46

Source: U.S. Bureau of the Census

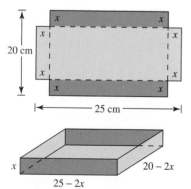

Figure 2.47

Constructing an open-top box

EXAMPLE 6   **U.S. Women and Childbearing**

The average number of children born to each U.S. woman from 1920 to 1990 is shown in Figure 2.46. Approximate the maximum number of children born per woman. When did this occur?

Solution

From the graph, we can see that the maximum number of children born per woman is approximately 4. This occurred in 1960.   ∎

Techniques for finding *relative extrema* (relative maximum and/or relative minimum) are studied extensively in calculus. However, a graphing utility with FMIN (function minimum) and FMAX (function maximum), or similar command, will approximate relative extrema in an interval.

EXAMPLE 7   **An Application of Extrema**

From each of the four corners of a rectangular piece of cardboard measuring 20 by 25 centimeters, a square piece x centimeters on a side is cut out. The flaps are then turned up to form an open-top box (Figure 2.47)

a. Express the volume V of the open-top box as a function of x.
b. Use a graphing utility to graph the function, drawing a relatively complete graph for meaningful values of x.
c. Use the graph and the utility's maximum function FMAX feature to determine x so that the resulting box has maximum possible volume. What is the maximum possible volume?

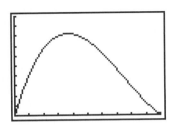

Figure 2.48

The graph of volume as a function of the size of squares cut from corners

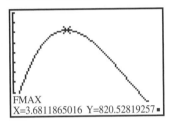

Figure 2.49

Squares whose sides measure 3.68 centimeters give a maximum volume of 820.5 cubic centimeters.

Solution

a. We begin with the volume of the open-top box, or the volume of a rectangular solid.

Volume	=	Length	times	Width	times	Height

$$V = (25 - 2x) \cdot (20 - 2x) \cdot x$$

$$V(x) = (25 - x)(20 - 2x)x \qquad \text{This is the volume } V \text{ of the box as a function of } x.$$

b. The width of the cardboard is 20 centimeters. At most, 10 centimeters can be cut from each end of this line segment and at least, 0 centimeters can be cut (no cutting). This suggests the range setting Xmin = 0, Xmax = 10, and Xscl = 1. Volume must be positive, so we can begin with Ymin = 0. Substituting a few values of x into $V(x)$ suggests a fairly large setting for Ymax. We've used Ymax = 1000 and Yscl = 100 to graph the volume function as shown in Figure 2.48.

c. We now use the maximum function feature of our graphing utility. Although we can also use the [TRACE] and [ZOOM] capabilities to identify coordinates of the graph's peak, we chose the [FMAX] feature, as shown in Figure 2.49. The maximum possible volume results when the square cut from each corner measures 3.68 centimeters. The maximum volume of the box is 820.5 cubic centimeters. ∎

PROBLEM SET 2.4

Practice Problems

1. The graph of a function f is shown in the figure.

   a. State the values of $f(-6)$, $f(0)$, and $f(3)$.

   b. State the intervals on which f is increasing and on which f is decreasing.

   c. State the minimum value of f. At what value of x does this occur?

   d. If the domain of f is $(-\infty, \infty)$, what is the function's range?

   a. State the values of $g(0)$ and $g(1)$.

   b. State the intervals on which g is increasing and on which g is decreasing.

   c. State the minimum value of g. At what value of x does this occur?

   d. State the maximum value of g. At what value of x does this occur?

   e. If the domain of g is $[-4, 4]$, what is the function's range?

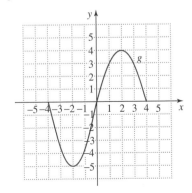

2. The graph of a function g is shown in the figure on the right.

3. The graph of a function f is shown in the figure.

  a. State the values of $f(-2), f(-1)$, and $f(5)$.

  b. State the intervals on which f is increasing, decreasing, and constant.

  c. If the domain of f is $[-5, 6]$, what is the function's range?

4. The graph of a function g is shown in the figure.

  a. State the values of $g(-1)$ and $g(2)$.

  b. State the intervals on which g is increasing and decreasing.

  c. If the domain of g is $[-6, 6]$, what is the function's range?

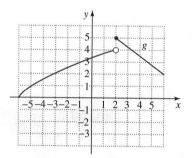

Sketch each function in Problems 5–14 using the given properties. (More than one correct graph is possible.)

5. The domain of f is $[0, 4]$ and the range of f is $[-1, 1]$. $f(0) = 0, f(1) = 1, f(2) = 0, f(3) = -1$, and $f(4) = 0$.

6. The domain of f is $[0, 4]$ and the range of f is $[0, -3]$. -3 is a relative minimum and occurs at $x = 2$.

7. The domain of f is $[-3, \infty)$. $f(-3) = 2, f(0) = 5$, and f is increasing on the interval $(-3, \infty)$.

8. f is increasing on the intervals $(-\infty, 0)$ and $(4, \infty)$, decreasing on the interval $(0, 4), f(-3) = f(3) = 0$, and $f(0) = 4$.

9. f is a piecewise function that is linear and decreasing on $(-\infty, 2), f(2) = 0, f$ is nonlinear and increasing on $(2, \infty)$, and the range of f is $[0, \infty)$.

10. f is a piecewise function that is linear and decreasing on $(-\infty, 4), f(4) = 0, f$ is nonlinear and increasing on $(4, \infty)$, and the range of f is $[0, \infty)$.

11. The domain of f is $(-\infty, \infty), f(8) = 6, -\frac{1}{2}$ is a relative minimum that occurs at $x = \frac{1}{2}$ and $f(0) = 0$.

12. The domain of f is $(-\infty, \infty), f(0) = 0$, and -3 is a relative minimum that occurs at $x = 1$.

13. The domain of f is $(-\infty, \infty)$, 2 is a relative maximum that occurs at $x = 0$, and -1 is a relative minimum that occurs at $x = 3.5$.

14. f is increasing on $(-\infty, 0)$, constant on $(0, 2)$, and decreasing on $(2, \infty); f(-1) = f(3) = 0$; and $f(1.7) = 1$.

Application Problems _____

15. The graph in the top left column on page 265 shows the percent of females and males who have dropped out of high school in the United States from 1965 through 1990.

  a. During what time intervals is the dropout rate for U.S. males decreasing?

  b. During what time interval is the dropout rate for U.S. males increasing?

  c. For what year is the dropout rate for males at a minimum? What percent of males dropped out of high school in that year? (You'll need to approximate your answers in this part.)

  d. In approximately what year did males and females have the same dropout rate? Approximately what percent of the females and males dropped out of high school in that year?

High School Dropout Rates, by Gender, 1965–1990

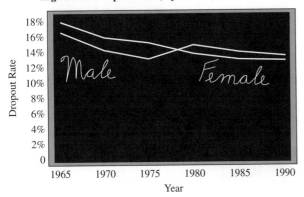

Source: U.S. Department of Education

16. The graph below shows the number of fires in the United States from 1985 through 1994.

   a. During what time periods is the number of fires on the increase?

   b. During what time periods is the number of fires on the decrease?

   c. Between what two consecutive years did the number of fires remain constant?

   d. In what year is the number of fires at a minimum? Approximately how many fires were there in that year?

   e. In what year is the number of fires at a maximum? Approximately how many fires were there in that year?

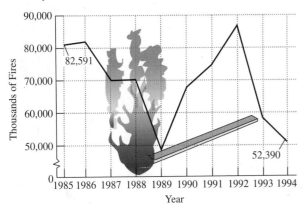

Source: National Interagency Fire Center, National Oceanic and Atmospheric Administration

17. The function $f(x) = 0.4x^2 - 36x + 1000$ describes the number of accidents per 50 million miles driven as a function of age (x, in years), where $16 \leq x \leq 74$. The graph of f is shown in the figure at the top of the next column.

a. State the intervals on which the function is increasing and decreasing and describe what this means in terms of the variables modeled by the function.

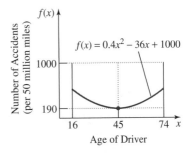

b. For what value of x does the function have a relative minimum? What is the minimum value of y? Describe the practical significance of this minimum value.

c. The domain of f is [16, 74]. Use the function's equation to determine the range of f. What is the practical significance of this range in terms of the meaning of $f(x)$ in the given model?

18. Based on a study by Vance Tucker (*Scientific American*, May 1969) the power expenditure of migratory birds in flight is a function of their flying speed (x, in miles per hour), approximated by $f(x) = 0.67x^2 - 27.74x + 387$. Power expenditure, $f(x)$, is measured in calories, and migratory birds generally fly between 12 and 30 miles per hour. The graph of f is shown in the figure, with a domain of [12, 30].

a. State the approximate intervals on which the function is increasing and decreasing and describe what this means in terms of the variables modeled by the function.

b. For what approximate value of x does the function have a relative minimum? What is the minimum value of y? Describe the practical significance of this minimum value.

c. The domain of f is [12, 30]. Use the function's equation to find the range of f. What is the practical significance of this range in terms of the meaning of $f(x)$ in the given model?

In Problems 19–20, use the given description to sketch each function.

19. According to the U.S. Center for Disease Control, in 1960 there were approximately 50,000 cases of tuberculosis in the United States. For the function that models these variables, let x represent the number of years after 1960 and let $f(x)$ represent the number of tuberculosis cases. The number of cases steadily increased, reaching a maximum of 60,000 in 1965. Then there was a decrease, with 21,000 cases reported in 1987. From 1987 to 1991, the number of cases continued to increase, reaching 25,500 in 1991. This number remained relatively constant until 1995.

20. According to the College Board, in 1967 the average math SAT score was 490. For the function that models these variables, let x represent the number of years after 1967 and let $f(x)$ represent the average SAT score. Scores decreased, reaching a minimum of 465 in 1981. Scores generally increased from 1981 through 1993, although there was a slight bit of fluctuation, reaching an average of 478 in 1993.

For Problems 21–22, select the graph from (a)–(e) that best models the given situation.

(a)

(b)

21. The perimeter of a rectangle is 100 feet. Express the area A of the rectangle as a function of x, one of the rectangle's dimensions. Then select the graph that most closely represents the graph of the area function.

(c)

(d)

22. A small cruising ship that has a capacity of 50 passengers provides two-day excursions to groups of 35 or more. The cost is $60 per person for groups of 35 people, $59 per person for groups of 36 people, $58 per person for groups of 37 people, with everyone's cost reduced by $1 for each person in excess of 35. If x represents the number of people in excess of 35 who take the cruise, express the ship's revenue R as a function of x. Then select the graph that most closely represents the graph of the revenue function.

(e)

True–False Critical Thinking Problems

23. Which one of the following is true based on the graph of f in the figure shown?

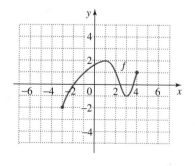

a. The domain of f is $[-2, 2]$.

b. The function has a relative maximum of 2 that occurs at $x = 2$.

c. f is decreasing on the interval $(-1, 2)$.

d. $f(3) - f(-3) = 1$

24. Which one of the following is true based on the graph of f in the figure shown?

a. The domain and range of f is $(-\infty, \infty)$.

b. This piecewise function can be defined by three different equations, all in the form $y = mx + b$.

c. f is decreasing on the interval $(-\infty, -2)$.

d. The function has a minimum value of -2 that occurs at $x = -3$.

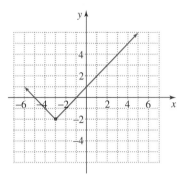

Technology Problems

In Problems 25–32, use a graphing utility to graph each function. Approximate the intervals over which the function is increasing, decreasing, or constant. Also approximate (to two decimal places) any relative maximum or minimum values of the function.

25. $f(x) = x^3 - 6x^2 + 9x + 1$

26. $f(x) = x\sqrt{4 - x}$

27. $g(x) = |4 - x^2|$

28. $g(x) = |x - 2| + |x + 2|$

29. $h(x) = x^{1/3}(x - 4)$

30. $h(x) = \begin{cases} 3 & \text{if } x < 0 \\ \sqrt{x} + 3 & \text{if } x \geqslant 0 \end{cases}$

31. $f(x) = x^{2/3}$

32. $f(x) = 2 - x^{2/5}$

33. a. Graph the functions $f(x) = x^n$ for $n = 2, 4$, and 6 in the viewing rectangle $[-2, 2]$ by $[-1, 3]$.

b. Graph the functions $f(x) = x^n$ for $n = 1, 3$, and 5 in the viewing rectangle $[-2, 2]$ by $[-2, 2]$.

c. If n is even, where is the graph of $f(x) = x^n$ increasing and where is it decreasing?

d. If n is odd, what can you conclude about the graph of $f(x) = x^n$ in terms of increasing or decreasing behavior?

e. Graph all six functions in a $[-1, 3]$ by $[-1, 3]$ viewing rectangle. What do you observe about the graphs in terms of how flat or how steep they are?

34. a. Use a graphing utility to graph both $f(x) = x^3 - 3x^2 - 9x + 1$ and $f'(x) = 3x^2 - 6x - 9$. (We read $f'(x)$ as "f prime of x.")

b. Use the graphs to describe the relationship between intervals where f is increasing and those in which f' is positive.

c. Use the graphs to describe the relationship between intervals where f is decreasing and those in which f' is negative.

d. Describe what happens to the graph of f' when f has a relative maximum or minimum.

Problems 35–37 involve relative extrema. Use a graphing utility to graph all functions.

35. Two positive numbers have a sum of 9. One of the numbers is represented by x.

a. Express the product (P) of the numbers as a function of x.

b. Graph the function, drawing a relatively complete graph for meaningful values of x.

c. Use the graph to determine x so that the two numbers have a maximum product. What is the maximum product possible?

36. From each of the four corners of a rectangular piece of cardboard measuring 5 by 8 inches, a square piece x inches on a side is cut out. The flaps are then turned up to form an open-top box.

a. Express the volume V of the open-top box as a function of x.

b. Graph the function, using an appropriate range setting to draw a relatively complete graph for meaningful values of x.

c. Use the graph to determine x so that the resulting box has a maximum possible volume. What is the maximum possible volume?

37. A manufacturer can produce and sell x items a week for a revenue r given by $r(x) = 200x - 0.01x^2$ cents. The manufacturer has fixed weekly costs of $200 and variable costs of 50¢ to produce each item.

a. Express the weekly profit (P) as a function of x.

b. Graph the function, using an appropriate range setting to draw a relatively complete graph for meaningful values of x.

c. Use the graph to determine the number of items that should be produced and sold to maximize weekly profit. What is the maximum weekly profit?

Writing in Mathematics

For Problems 38–41, create a verbal problem or situation that can be modeled by the graph of each function shown.

38.

39.

40.

41.

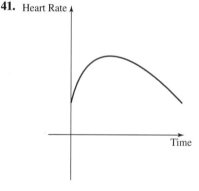

Critical Thinking Problem

42. Define a piecewise function on the intervals $(-\infty, 2]$, $(2, 5)$, and $[5, \infty)$ that does not "jump" at 2 or 5 such that one piece is a constant function, another piece is a linear function that is increasing, and another piece is a nonlinear function that is decreasing.

Group Activity Problem

43. Group members should consult almanacs and appropriate references to find examples of variables that increased, decreased, and remained constant from 1985 through 1995. Once each member finds an example of each, these examples should be presented to other people in the group. Group members should identify increasing or decreasing phenomena whose data points appear to lie on a line. Use a graphing utility with a linear regression option to model the data. Try using this option to model data that clearly do not represent linear growth or decline. What value of the correlation coefficient does the graphing utility give? What does this mean?

| Solutions Manual | Tutorial | Video 5 |

SECTION 2.5

Transformations of Functions

Objectives

1 Use vertical and horizontal shifts to graph functions.
2 Use reflections to graph functions.
3 Use stretching and shrinking to graph functions.
4 Graph functions involving a sequence of transformations.
5 Identify even and odd functions.

Hans Bellmer "Peg-Top" c. 1937–52, oil on canvas, 648 × 648 mm. Tate Gallery, London. Photo: John Webb. Art Resource, NY.

In Section 2.3, we focused on the graphs of relations and functions. In this section, we continue our study of graphing techniques by using graphs of basic functions and transforming them into the graphs of new functions.

Algebra's Common Graphs

Figure 2.50 shows the graphs of six commonly used functions in algebra. You should become familiar with these graphs for your work in this section.

Identity Function $f(x) = x$

Standard Quadratic Function $f(x) = x^2$

Standard Cubic Function $f(x) = x^3$

Absolute Value Function $f(x) = |x|$

Square Root Function $f(x) = \sqrt{x}$

Cube Root Function $f(x) = \sqrt[3]{x}$

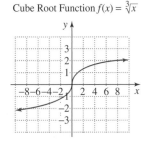

Figure 2.50
Algebra's common graphs

Discover for yourself

Use a graphing utility to verify the six graphs shown in Figure 2.50.

1 Use vertical and horizontal shifts to graph functions.

Vertical and Horizontal Shifts

The study of how transformations of a function can affect its graph can be previewed and explored with a graphing utility. Use your graphing utility and work the Discover for yourself exercises as you read this section.

Study tip

To work the first three parts of the Discover for yourself exercise without a graphing utility, begin by filling in this table of coordinates. Then graph f, g, and h in the same rectangular coordinate system.

x	$f(x)=x^2$	$g(x) = x^2 + 2$	$h(x) = x^2 - 3$
-2			
-1			
0			
1			
2			

iscover for yourself

1. Use your graphing utility to graph the functions $f(x) = x^2$, $g(x) = x^2 + 2$, and $h(x) = x^2 - 3$ in the same viewing rectangle.

2. Describe the relationship among the graphs of f, g, and h.

3. Generalize by describing the relationship among the graphs of f, g, and h, if $g(x) = f(x) + c$ and $h(x) = f(x) - c$, with c a positive constant.

4. Reinforce the generalization in part 3 by using a graphing utility, determining a particular function f and a particular value for c. Graph $f(x)$ and $g(x) = f(x) + c$.

In the Discover for yourself, did you observe that the graph of $g(x) = x^2 + 2$ shifts the graph of $f(x) = x^2$ two units upward? Similarly, the graph of $g(x) = x^2 - 3$ shifts the graph of $f(x) = x^2$ three units downward. These relationships are shown in Figure 2.51 at the top of page 271. In general, if c is positive, $y = f(x) + c$ shifts the graph of f upward c units and $y = f(x) - c$ shifts the graph of f downward c units. These are called *vertical shifts* of the graph of f.

Variations in the equation of a function also enable us to shift the function's graph horizontally.

Study tip

To work the first three parts of the Discover for yourself exercise without a graphing utility, begin by filling in these tables of coordinates. Then graph f, g, and h in the same rectangular coordinate system.

x	$f(x)=x^2$	x	$g(x)=(x-5)^2$	x	$h(x)=(x+5)^2$
-2		3		-7	
-1		4		-6	
0		5		-5	
1		6		-4	
2		7		-3	

iscover for yourself

1. Use your graphing utility to graph the functions $f(x) = x^2$, $g(x) = (x - 5)^2$, and $h(x) = (x + 5)^2$ in the same viewing rectangle.

2. Describe the relationship among the graphs of f, g, and h.

3. Generalize by describing the relationship among the graphs of f, g, and h if $g(x) = f(x - c)$ and $h(x) = f(x + c)$, with c a positive real number.

4. Reinforce the generalization in part 3 by using a graphing utility, determining a particular function f and a particular value for c. Graph $f(x)$ and $g(x) = f(x + c)$.

In the Discover for yourself, did you observe that the graph of $g(x) = (x - 5)^2$ shifts the graph of $f(x) = x^2$ five units to the right? Similarly, the graph of $h(x) = (x + 5)^2$ shifts the graph of $f(x) = x^2$ five units to the left. These relationships are shown in Figure 2.52 on page 271. In general, if c is positive, $y = f(x - c)$ shifts the graph of f to the right c units and $y = f(x + c)$ shifts the graph of f to the left c units. These are called *horizontal shifts* of the graph of f.

Vertical and horizontal shifts, also called *translations*, are summarized in the box on page 271.

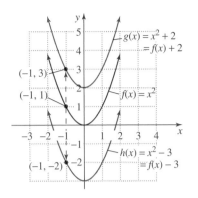

Figure 2.51

Shifting $f(x) = x^2$ two units upward and three units downward

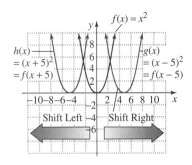

Figure 2.52

Shifting $f(x) = x^2$ five units to the right and five units to the left

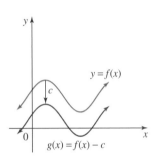

Figure 2.53

Upward and downward shifts

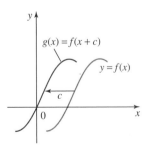

Figure 2.54

Shifting to the right and the left

Vertical and horizontal shifts

Let c represent a positive real number. *Vertical* and *horizontal shifts* in the graph of $y = f(x)$ can be obtained as follows.

Function	How to Obtain the Graph of g from the Graph of f
$g(x) = f(x) + c$	Shift f *upward* c units.
$g(x) = f(x) - c$	Shift f *downward* c units.

These shifts are illustrated in Figure 2.53.

$g(x) = f(x - c)$	Shift f horizontally to the *right* c units.
$g(x) = f(x + c)$	Shift f horizontally to the *left* c units.

These shifts are illustrated in Figure 2.54.

EXAMPLE 1   **Graphing Translated Functions**

Use the graph of $f(x) = \sqrt{x}$ to sketch the graph of:

a. $g(x) = \sqrt{x} - 5$ **b.** $g(x) = \sqrt{x + 5}$ **c.** $g(x) = \sqrt{x - 1} - 2$

Solution

(The three graphs described below appear on page 272, so be sure to turn the page and look at the graphs as you read each part of the solution.)

a. We obtain the graph of $g(x) = \sqrt{x} - 5$ by shifting the graph of $f(x) = \sqrt{x}$ downward five units. As shown in Figure 2.55, every point in the graph of g is exactly five units below the corresponding point on the graph of f.

b. We obtain the graph of $g(x) = \sqrt{x + 5}$ by shifting the graph of $f(x) = \sqrt{x}$ horizontally to the left five units. As shown in Figure 2.56, every point in the graph of g is exactly five units to the left of a corresponding point on the graph of f.

c. The graph of $g(x) = \sqrt{x - 1} - 2$ involves two shifts in terms of the graph of $f(x) = \sqrt{x}$. First we shift f one unit to the right $(\sqrt{x - 1})$ and then shift the resulting graph two units downward $(\sqrt{x - 1} - 2)$. The graph of g is shown in Figure 2.57. ∎

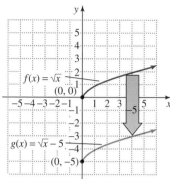

Figure 2.55

Shifting $f(x) = \sqrt{x}$ five units downward

Figure 2.56

Shifting $f(x) = \sqrt{x}$ five units left

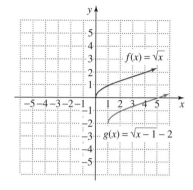

Figure 2.57

Shifting $f(x) = \sqrt{x}$ one unit to the right and two units downward

Figure 2.58

EXAMPLE 2   **Finding Equations from Graphs**

Find an equation for each function shown in Figure 2.58.

Solution

a. The graph of g is both a horizontal shift of five units to the right of the graph of f ($y = (x - 5)^2$) and a vertical shift of three units upward of the graph of f. Thus, the equation of g is $g(x) = (x - 5)^2 + 3$.

b. The graph of h is both a horizontal shift of four units to the left of the graph of f ($y = (x + 4)^2$) and a vertical shift of one unit downward of the graph of f. Thus, the equation of h is $h(x) = (x + 4)^2 - 1$. ∎

Reflections

2 Use reflections to graph functions.

A second type of transformation is called a *reflection*. Once again, a graphing utility is an ideal tool for exploring this transformation.

Study tip

To work the first three parts of the Discover for yourself exercise without a graphing utility, begin by filling in these tables of coordinates. Then graph f, g, and h in the same rectangular coordinate system.

x	$f(x) = \sqrt{x}$	x	$g(x) = -\sqrt{x}$	x	$h(x) = \sqrt{-x}$
0		0		0	
1		1		-1	
4		4		-4	
9		9		-9	

Discover for yourself

1. Use your graphing utility to graph the functions $f(x) = \sqrt{x}$, $g(x) = -\sqrt{x}$, and $h(x) = \sqrt{-x}$ in the same viewing rectangle.
2. Describe the relationship among the graphs of f, g, and h.
3. Generalize by describing the relationship among the graphs of f, g, and h if $g(x) = -f(x)$ and $h(x) = f(-x)$.
4. Reinforce the generalization in part 3 by using a graphing utility and determining a particular function f. Graph $f(x)$, $-f(x)$, and $f(-x)$.

Figure 2.59

Reflecting $f(x) = \sqrt{x}$

In the Discover for yourself, did you observe that the graph of $g(x) = -\sqrt{x}$ reflects the graph of $f(x) = \sqrt{x}$ in the x-axis? Similarly, the graph of $h(x) = \sqrt{-x}$ reflects the graph of $f(x) = \sqrt{x}$ in the y-axis. These relationships are shown in Figure 2.59. In general, the graph of $y = -f(x)$ reflects the graph of f in the x-axis and the graph of $y = f(-x)$ reflects the graph of f in the y-axis.

These observations can be summarized as follows.

Reflections in the rectangular coordinate system

Reflections of the graph of $y = f(x)$ can be obtained as follows.

Function	How to Obtain the Graph of g from the Graph of f
$g(x) = -f(x)$	Reflect f in the x-axis (Figure 2.60)
$g(x) = f(-x)$	Reflect f in the y-axis (Figure 2.61)

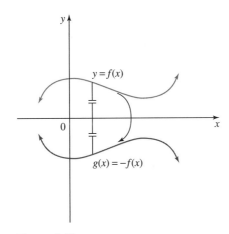

Figure 2.60

Reflecting f in the x-axis

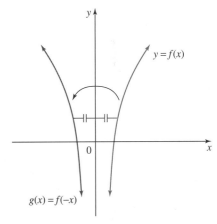

Figure 2.61

Reflecting f in the y-axis

Figure 2.62 illustrates reflections of $f(x) = x^2 - 2x$ in the x-axis and the y-axis.

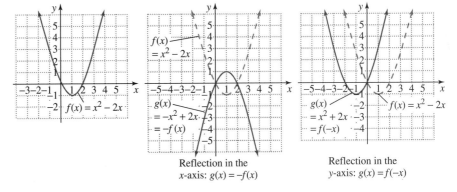

Reflection in the
x-axis: $g(x) = -f(x)$

Reflection in the
y-axis: $g(x) = f(-x)$

Figure 2.62

EXAMPLE 3   Graphing Reflected Functions

As shown in Figure 2.63, the graph of f is a line segment joining the points $(-3, 2)$ and $(4, 5)$. Use the graph of f to graph:

a. $y = -f(x)$ **b.** $y = f(-x)$ **c.** $y = -f(-x)$

Figure 2.63

Figure 2.64

Figure 2.65

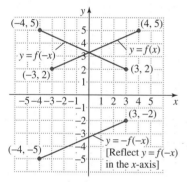

Figure 2.66

Solution

a. Figure 2.64 shows the graph of $y = -f(x)$, obtained by reflecting the graph of f in the x-axis. Observe that points on the reflected function have the same x-coordinates as corresponding points on the given function and opposite y-coordinates.

b. Figure 2.65 shows the graph of $y = f(-x)$, obtained by reflecting the graph of f in the y-axis. In this situation, points on the reflected function have opposite x-coordinates as corresponding points on the given function and the same y-coordinates.

c. Figure 2.66 shows the graph of $y = -f(-x)$, obtained by reflecting the graph of $y = f(-x)$ in the x-axis. ∎

Discover for yourself

Describe how the graph of $y = -f(-x)$ can be obtained from the graph of $y = -f(x)$.

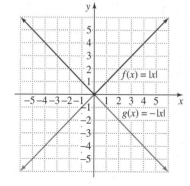

Figure 2.67

EXAMPLE 4   Reflections and Shifts

Compare the graph of each function with the graph $f(x) = |x|$:

a. $g(x) = -|x|$ **b.** $h(x) = -|x - 2|$ **c.** $k(x) = -|x - 2| + 3$

Solution

a. The graph of g is a reflection of the graph of $f(x) = |x|$ in the x-axis because

$$g(x) = -|x| = -f(x).$$

(Figure 2.67)

b. From the equation

$$h(x) = -|x - 2| = -f(x - 2)$$

we see that the graph of h is a right shift of the graph of f two units ($f(x - 2)$), followed by a reflection in the x-axis ($-f(x - 2)$). (Figure 2.68)

c. From the equation

$$k(x) = -|x - 2| + 3 = -f(x - 2) + 3$$

we see that the graph of k is a right shift of the graph of f two units ($f(x - 2)$), followed by a reflection in the x-axis ($-f(x - 2)$), followed by an upward shift of three units ($-f(x - 2) + 3$). (Figure 2.69) We also could obtain the graph of k by taking the graph of h in Figure 2.68 and shifting it upward three units. ∎

Figure 2.68

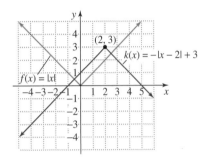

Figure 2.69

3 Use stretching and shrinking to graph functions.

Nonrigid Transformations: Stretching and Shrinking

Up to this point, we have studied horizontal shifts, vertical shifts, and reflections. These transformations are called *rigid* because they do not change the basic shape of the graph.

Let's contrast these rigid transformations with transformations that cause a distortion or a change in shape in a function's graph. These distortions involve stretching or shrinking the graph.

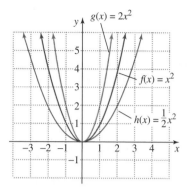

Figure 2.70

Stretching and shrinking
$f(x) = x^2$

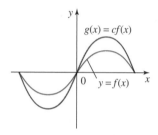

Figure 2.71

$c > 1$: Stretching

Figure 2.72

$0 < c < 1$: Shrinking

4 Graph functions involving a sequence of transformations.

In the Discover for yourself, did you observe that the graph of $g(x) = 2x^2$ or $g(x) = 2f(x)$, has y-coordinates that are twice as large as the corresponding y-coordinates on f? Figure 2.70 shows that the graph of g is obtained by *stretching* the graph of f. The result is a narrower graph. On the other hand, the graph of $h(x) = \frac{1}{2}x^2$, or $h(x) = \frac{1}{2}f(x)$, has y-coordinates that are one-half as large as the corresponding y-coordinates on f. We say that the graph of h is obtained by *shrinking* the graph of f. The result is a wider graph.

These observations can be summarized as follows.

Nonrigid transformations: stretching and shrinking

Let c represent a positive real number. Stretching and shrinking the graph of $y = f(x)$ can be obtained as follows.

Function	How to Obtain the Graph of g from the Graph of f
$g(x) = cf(x)$, where $c > 1$	Stretch the graph of f, multiplying each of its y-coordinates by c. (Figure 2.71)
$g(x) = cf(x)$, where $0 < c < 1$	Shrink the graph of f, multiplying each of its y-coordinates by c. (Figure 2.72)

EXAMPLE 5   **Nonrigid Transformations**

Compare the graph of each function in Figure 2.73 at the bottom of this page with the graph of $f(x) = \sqrt{x}$.

Solution

a. Relative to the graph $f(x) = \sqrt{x}$, the graph of

$$g(x) = 2\sqrt{x} = 2f(x)$$

is a vertical stretch (multiply each y-value by 2) of the graph of f.

b. Relative to the graph $f(x) = \sqrt{x}$, the graph of

$$h(x) = \frac{1}{2}\sqrt{x} = \frac{1}{2}f(x)$$

is a vertical shrink (multiply each y-value by $\frac{1}{2}$) of the graph of f. ∎

Sequences of Transformations

If a function involves more than one transformation and is to be graphed without a graphing utility, use the following procedure.

Graphing involving a sequence of transformations

A function involving more than one transformation can be graphed in the following order:

1. Horizontal translation
2. Stretching or shrinking
3. Reflecting
4. Vertical translation

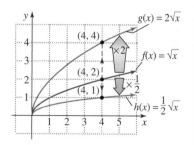

Figure 2.73

EXAMPLE 6 **Graphing Using a Sequence of Transformations**

Use the graph of $f(x) = \sqrt{x}$ to graph $g(x) = 5 - 2\sqrt{x + 1}$.

Solution

The following sequence of steps is illustrated below in Figure 2.74. We begin with the graph of $f(x) = \sqrt{x}$.

1. *Horizontal translation:* The graph of $y = \sqrt{x + 1} = f(x + 1)$ is obtained from the graph of f by shifting the graph of f horizontally one unit to the left.
2. *Stretching:* The graph of $y = 2\sqrt{x + 1}$ is obtained from $y = \sqrt{x + 1}$ by stretching the graph by a factor of 2. Each y-coordinate is multiplied by 2.
3. *Reflecting:* The graph of $y = -2\sqrt{x + 1}$ is obtained by reflecting the graph of $y = 2\sqrt{x + 1}$ in the x-axis.
4. *Vertical translation:* The graph of $g(x) = 5 - 2\sqrt{x + 1}$ is obtained from the graph of $y = -2\sqrt{x + 1}$ by shifting the graph five units upward.

Begin with the graph of $f(x) = \sqrt{x}$

1. Translate 1 Unit Left

2. Stretch by a Factor of 2

3. Reflect in the x-axis

4. Translate 5 Units Up

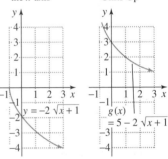

Figure 2.74

Transformations of $f(x) = \sqrt{x}$ ∎

EXAMPLE 7 **Graphing Using a Sequence of Transformations**

Use the graph of f shown in Figure 2.75 to graph $g(x) = -3 - \frac{1}{2}f(x - 2)$.

Solution

The following sequence of steps is illustrated in Figure 2.76 on page 278. We begin with the graph of f.

1. *Horizontal translation:* Shift f two units to the right. $(f(x - 2))$
2. *Shrinking:* Shrink the graph in step 2 by a factor of $\frac{1}{2}$

$$\left(\tfrac{1}{2}f(x - 2)\right)$$

3. *Reflecting:* Reflect the graph in step 3 in the x-axis.

$$\left(y = -\tfrac{1}{2}f(x - 2)\right)$$

4. *Vertical translation:* Shift the graph in step 4 three units downward.

$$\left(g(x) = -3 - \tfrac{1}{2}f(x - 2)\right)$$ ∎

Figure 2.75

Begin with the graph of f

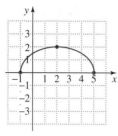

1. $y = f(x - 2)$
Translate 2
Units Right

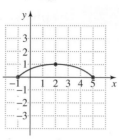

2. $y = \frac{1}{2}f(x - 2)$
Shrink by a
Factor of $\frac{1}{2}$

3. $y = -\frac{1}{2}f(x - 2)$
Reflect in
x-axis

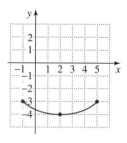

4. $g(x) = -3 - \frac{1}{2}f(x - 2)$
Translate 3
Units Down

Figure 2.76

Transformations of f described in Example 7

EXAMPLE 8 Describing a Sequence of Transformations

Use a graphing utility to graph the two functions $f(x) = x^3$ and $g(x) = 4 - 3(x - 2)^3$ on the same screen. Describe how the graph of g is obtained from the graph of f as a sequence of transformations.

Figure 2.77

The graphs of $y_1 = x^3$ and $y_2 = 4 - 3(x - 2)^3$

Use your graphing utility to graph the functions given in each of the four steps on the right. The resulting graphs visually show each of the transformations.

5 Identify even and odd functions.

Solution

Enter

$\quad$ Y₁ $\boxed{=}$ X $\boxed{\wedge}$ 3 and Y₂ $\boxed{=}$ 4 $-$ 3(X $-$ 2) $\boxed{\wedge}$ 3

with the following range setting

$\quad$ Xmin $= -5$, Xmax $= 5$, Xscl $= 1$,

$\quad$ Ymin $= -10$, Ymax $= 10$, Yscl $= 1$

The graphs are shown in Figure 2.77. The graph of g can be obtained from the graph of f through the following transformations:

1. *Horizontal translation:* Shift the graph of $f(x) = x^3$ two units to the right.

$\quad (y = (x - 2)^3)$

2. *Stretching:* Stretch the graph of $y = (x - 2)^3$ by a factor of 3.

$\quad (y = 3(x - 2)^3)$

3. *Reflecting:* Reflect the graph of $y = 3(x - 2)^3$ in the x-axis.

$\quad (y = -3(x - 2)^3)$

4. *Vertical translation:* Shift the graph of $y = -3(x - 2)^3$ four units upward.

$\quad (g(x) = 4 - 3(x - 2)^3)$ $\quad\blacksquare$

Even and Odd Functions

We know that $y = f(-x)$ reflects the graph of $y = f(x)$ in the y-axis. For some functions, $f(-x) = f(x)$ for every number x in its domain. Under these conditions, we say that f is an *even function.* For example, the function $f(x) = x^2 - 4$ is even because

$f(-x) = x^2 - 4$

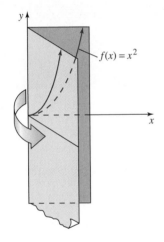

Figure 2.78

y-axis symmetry with
$f(-x) = f(x)$

$$f(-x) = (-x)^2 - 4 = x^2 - 4 = f(x).$$

The graph of $f(x) = x^2 - 4$ is shown in Figure 2.78.

Since $f(-x) = f(x)$, this causes the graph to be *symmetric with respect to the y-axis*. Each half of the curve is a mirror image of the other half about the y-axis. If we were to fold the paper along the y-axis, the two halves of the graph would coincide.

y-Axis symmetry and even functions

The graph of f is *symmetric with respect to the y-axis* if $f(-x) = f(x)$. The graph of this *even function* can be obtained by graphing f for $x \geq 0$ and then reflecting this portion in the y-axis.

Some functions satisfy $f(-x) = -f(x)$ for all numbers x in their domains. Under these conditions, we say that f is an *odd function*. For example, the function $f(x) = x^3$ is odd because

$$f(-x) = (-x)^3 = -x^3 = -f(x).$$

The graph of $f(x) = x^3$ is shown in Figure 2.79 at the bottom of the page.

Since $f(-x) = -f(x)$, this causes the graph to be *symmetric with respect to the origin*. Points such as $(2, 8)$ and $(-2, -8)$ are reflections of one another through the origin, meaning that they are the same distance from the origin and lie on a line through the origin. For each point (x, y) on the graph, the point $(-x, -y)$ is also on the graph, causing the first- and third-quadrant portions of $f(x) = x^3$ to be reflections of each other about the origin.

Origin symmetry and odd functions

The graph of f is *symmetric with respect to the origin* if $f(-x) = -f(x)$. The graph of this *odd function* can be obtained by graphing f for $x \geq 0$ and then rotating this portion through $180°$ about the origin.

Figure 2.79

Origin symmetry with
$f(-x) = -f(x)$

EXAMPLE 9   Determining Even and Odd Functions

Determine whether the following functions are even, odd, or neither.

a. $f(x) = x^3 - x$ **b.** $f(x) = x^4 - 4x^2$ **c.** $f(x) = x^4 - 6x^3 + 8x^2$

Solution

In each case, we must find $f(-x)$. If $f(-x) = f(x)$, then f is even and its graph has y-axis symmetry. If $f(-x) = -f(x)$, then f is odd and its graph has origin symmetry. If neither of these things occurs, the graph has neither kind of symmetry and f is neither even nor odd.

a. $f(x) = x^3 - x$ This is the given polynomial function.

     $f(-x) = (-x)^3 - (-x)$ Replace x with $-x$.

          $= -x^3 + x$ Simplify.

ENRICHMENT ESSAY

Shape and Symmetry

Origin symmetry and y-axis symmetry are just two examples of a powerful concept whose workings appear in art, nature, the sciences, poetry, and architecture. The two halves of a bridge span, the wings of a bird or an aircraft, the blades of a propeller—all have symmetry. Although we take symmetry for granted, a form's lack of symmetry may be the quality that makes it interesting and appealing.

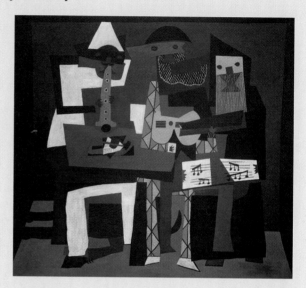

Pablo Picasso "Three Musicians," Fontainebleau, Summer 1921, oil on canvas, 6 ft. 7 in. × 7 ft. 3 3/4 in. The Museum of Modern Art, New York. Mrs. Simon Guggenheim Fund. Photograph © 1997 The Museum of Modern Art, New York. © 1998 Estate of Pablo Picasso / Artists Rights Society (ARS), New York.

Figure 2.80

An odd function with origin symmetry

Because $f(-x) = -f(x)$, the graph of f is symmetric with respect to the origin (Figure 2.80) and f is an odd function.

b. $f(x) = x^4 - 4x^2$ This is the given polynomial function.

$f(-x) = (-x)^4 - 4(-x)^2$ Replace x with $-x$.

$\quad\quad = x^4 - 4x^2$ Simplify.

Because $f(-x) = f(x)$, the graph of f is symmetric with respect to the y-axis (Figure 2.81 on page 281) and f is an even function.

c. $f(x) = x^4 - 6x^3 + 8x^2$ This is the given polynomial function.

$f(-x) = (-x)^4 - 6(-x)^3 + 8(-x)^2$ Replace x with $-x$.

$\quad\quad = x^4 - 6(-x^3) + 8x^2$ Simplify.

$\quad\quad = x^4 + 6x^3 + 8x^2$

Because $f(-x) \neq f(x)$ and $f(-x) \neq -f(x)$, the graph has neither y-axis nor origin symmetry (Figure 2.82 on page 281) and f is neither even nor odd. ∎

Discover for yourself

How can you tell whether a polynomial function is even, odd, or neither simply by looking at its equation?

In the Discover for yourself, did you observe that polynomial functions with only even powers are even functions and those with only odd powers are odd functions? If the function's equation contains both even and odd powers, it is neither even nor odd.

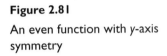

Figure 2.81

An even function with y-axis symmetry

Figure 2.82

Neither y-axis nor origin symmetry

PROBLEM SET 2.5

Practice Problems

In Problems 1–26, sketch the graphs of the three given functions by hand on the same Cartesian coordinate plane. Verify the result with a graphing utility.

1. $f(x) = x^2$
$g(x) = x^2 - 3$
$h(x) = x^2 + 2$

2. $f(x) = x^2$
$g(x) = x^2 - 2$
$h(x) = x^2 + 3$

3. $f(x) = x^2$
$g(x) = (x - 3)^2$
$h(x) = (x + 2)^2$

4. $f(x) = x^2$
$g(x) = (x - 2)^2$
$h(x) = (x + 3)^2$

5. $f(x) = \sqrt{x}$
$g(x) = \sqrt{x} - 3$
$h(x) = \sqrt{x} + 2$

6. $f(x) = \sqrt{x}$
$g(x) = \sqrt{x} - 2$
$h(x) = \sqrt{x} + 3$

7. $f(x) = \sqrt{x}$
$g(x) = \sqrt{x - 3}$
$h(x) = \sqrt{x + 2}$

8. $f(x) = \sqrt{x}$
$g(x) = \sqrt{x - 2}$
$h(x) = \sqrt{x + 3}$

9. $f(x) = \sqrt{x}$
$g(x) = \sqrt{x - 3} + 2$
$h(x) = \sqrt{x + 2} - 4$

10. $f(x) = \sqrt{x}$
$g(x) = \sqrt{x - 2} + 3$
$h(x) = \sqrt{x + 3} - 5$

11. $f(x) = |x|$
$g(x) = |x - 2| + 3$
$h(x) = -|x - 2|$

12. $f(x) = |x|$
$g(x) = |x - 3| + 2$
$h(x) = -|x - 3|$

13. $f(x) = |x|$
$g(x) = 2|x - 3|$
$h(x) = -2|x - 3|$

14. $f(x) = |x|$
$g(x) = \frac{1}{2}|x - 4|$
$h(x) = -\frac{1}{2}|x - 4|$

15. $f(x) = x^2$
$g(x) = (x - 2)^2 + 1$
$h(x) = (x + 2)^2 - 1$

16. $f(x) = x^2$
$g(x) = (x - 1)^2 + 2$
$h(x) = (x + 1)^2 - 2$

17. $f(x) = x^3$
$g(x) = (x - 2)^3 + 1$
$h(x) = -x^3$

18. $f(x) = x^3$
$g(x) = (x - 1)^3 + 2$
$h(x) = -x^3$

19. $f(x) = |x|$
$g(x) = |x - 4|$
$h(x) = -|x - 4| + 2$

20. $f(x) = |x|$
$g(x) = |x - 3|$
$h(x) = -|x + 3| + 4$

21. $f(x) = \sqrt[3]{x}$
$g(x) = \sqrt[3]{x + 1}$
$h(x) = -2 + \sqrt[3]{x + 1}$

22. $f(x) = \sqrt[3]{x}$
$g(x) = \sqrt[3]{x + 2}$
$h(x) = -3 + \sqrt[3]{x + 2}$

23. $f(x) = \sqrt[3]{x}$
$g(x) = -\sqrt[3]{x + 1}$
$h(x) = \frac{1}{2}\sqrt[3]{x}$

24. $f(x) = \sqrt[3]{x}$
$g(x) = -\sqrt[3]{x + 2}$
$h(x) = 2\sqrt[3]{x}$

25. $f(x) = |x|$
$g(x) = -\frac{1}{2}|x| + 4$
$h(x) = -\frac{1}{2}(|x| + 4)$

26. $f(x) = |x|$
$g(x) = 3|x| - 2$
$h(x) = 3(|x| - 2)$

In Problems 27–34, functions f and g are graphed on the same Cartesian coordinate plane. If g is obtained from f through a sequence of transformations, find an equation for g.

27.

28.

29.

30.

31.

32.

33.

34.

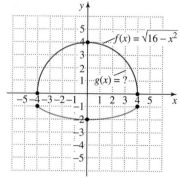

35. Use the graph of $f(x) = \sqrt{x}$ to graph
$g(x) = 4 - 2\sqrt{x-1}$.

36. Use the graph of $f(x) = \sqrt{x}$ to graph
$g(x) = 3 - \frac{1}{2}\sqrt{x+2}$.

37. Use the graph of $f(x) = x^2$ to graph
$g(x) = -\frac{1}{2}(x+2)^2 + 3$.

38. Use the graph of $f(x) = x^2$ to graph $g(x) = -2(x-1)^2 + 3$.

39. Use the graph of $f(x) = |x|$ to graph
$g(x) = -2|x+3| - 4$.

40. Use the graph of $f(x) = |x|$ to graph
$g(x) = -\frac{1}{2}|x-2| - 3$.

41. Use the graph of $f(x) = \sqrt[3]{x}$ to graph
$g(x) = 3 - 4\sqrt[3]{x-1}$.

42. Use the graph of $f(x) = \sqrt[3]{x}$ to graph
$g(x) = 2 - 2\sqrt[3]{x-2}$.

43. Use the graph of $f(x) = [[x]]$ to graph $g(x) = f(x) - 4$.

44. Use the graph of $f(x) = [[x]]$ to graph $g(x) = f(x+2)$.

In Problems 45–52, use the graph of the function f to sketch the graph of the function g.

45.

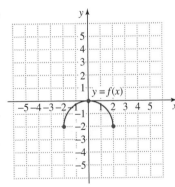

a. $g(x) = f(x-3)$
b. $g(x) = f(x) + 2$
c. $g(x) = f(x+1) - 2$
d. $g(x) = f(-x)$
e. $g(x) = -f(x) + 3$
f. $g(x) = -f(x-1)$

46.

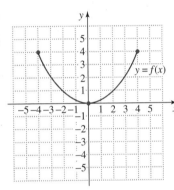

a. $g(x) = f(x-2)$
b. $g(x) = f(x+2) - 3$
c. $g(x) = f(-x)$
d. $g(x) = -f(x) + 4$
e. $g(x) = -f(x-1)$
f. $g(x) = -1 - f(x+1)$

47.

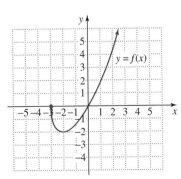

a. $g(x) = f(x-1)$
b. $g(x) = -f(x+1)$
c. $g(x) = f(-x) - 2$
d. $g(x) = f(x-2) + 3$

48.

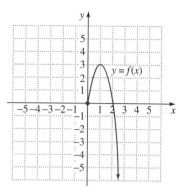

a. $g(x) = f(x - 1)$
c. $g(x) = f(-x) - 2$

b. $g(x) = -f(x + 1)$
d. $g(x) = f(x - 2) + 3$

49.

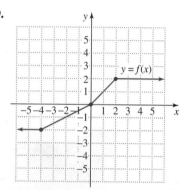

a. $g(x) = f(x - 2)$
c. $g(x) = -f(x)$
e. $g(x) = 2f(x)$

b. $g(x) = f(x) + 2$
d. $g(x) = f(-x)$
f. $g(x) = \frac{1}{2}f(x)$

50.

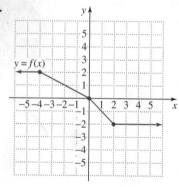

a. $g(x) = f(x - 2)$
c. $g(x) = -f(x)$
e. $g(x) = 3f(x)$

b. $g(x) = f(x) + 2$
d. $g(x) = f(-x)$
f. $g(x) = \frac{1}{2}f(x)$

51.

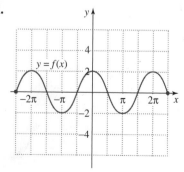

a. $g(x) = 2f(x)$
c. $g(x) = f(x + \pi)$

b. $g(x) = \frac{1}{2}f(x)$
d. $g(x) = -f(x)$

52.

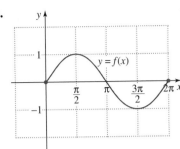

a. $g(x) = 2f(x)$
c. $g(x) = f(x + \frac{\pi}{2})$

b. $g(x) = \frac{1}{2}f(x)$
d. $g(x) = -f(x - \pi) + 1$

In Problems 53–62, determine whether each function is even, odd, or neither.

53. $f(x) = \frac{1}{5}x^6 - 3x^2$

54. $f(x) = x^3 - 6x$

55. $f(x) = x\sqrt{1 - x^2}$

56. $f(x) = x^2\sqrt{1 - x^2}$

57. $f(x) = x^4 + 3x - 5$

58. $f(x) = x^2 + 5x - 2$

59. $f(x) = 3x^{2/3}$

60. $f(x) = 5x^{2/5}$

61. $f(x) = 4x^{2n} + 6x^{2n-2} + 5$; n represents an integer.

62. $f(x) = 5x^{2n+1} + 3x^{2n-1} + 7$; n represents an integer.

Graph each function in Problems 63–67 using the given properties. (More than one correct graph is possible.)

63. The domain of f is $(-\infty, \infty)$, $f(4) = 5$, -1 is a relative minimum that occurs at $x = 1$, $f(0) = 0$, and f is an odd function.

64. The domain of f is $(-\infty, \infty)$, $f(0) = 0$, -3 is a relative minimum that occurs at $x = 1$, and f is an even function.

65. The domain of f is $(-\infty, \infty)$, $f(0) = 1$, 0 is a relative minimum that occurs at $x = 1$, and f is an even function.

66. The domain of f is $(-\infty, \infty)$, 2 is a relative maximum that occurs at $x = 0$, -1 is a relative minimum that occurs at $x = 3.5$, and f is neither even nor odd.

67. The domain of f is $(-\infty, \infty)$, 4 is a relative maximum that occurs at $x = 0$, -2 is a relative minimum that occurs at $x = 3.5$, and f is neither even nor odd.

True–False Critical Thinking Problems

68. Which one of the following is true?

a. If $f(x) = |x|$ and $g(x) = |x + 3| + 3$, then the graph of g is a translation of three units to the right and three units upward of the graph of f.

b. If $f(x) = -\sqrt{x}$ and $g(x) = \sqrt{-x}$, then f and g have identical graphs.

c. If $f(x) = x^2$ and $g(x) = 5(x^2 - 2)$, then the graph of g can be obtained from the graph of f by stretching f five units followed by a downward shift of two units.

d. If $f(x) = x^3$ and $g(x) = -(x - 3)^3 - 4$, then the graph of g can be obtained from the graph of f by moving f three units to the right, reflecting in the x-axis, and then moving the resulting graph down four units.

69. Which one of the following is true?

a. If $f(x) = |x|$ and $g(x) = |x - 3| - 3$, then the graph of g is a translation of three units to the left and three units downward of the graph of f.

b. If $f(x) = x^2$ and $g(x) = -(x - 2)^2 - 4$, then the graph of g can be obtained from the graph of f by moving f two units to the right and four units downward, and then reflecting in the x-axis.

c. If $f(x) = x^2$ and $g(x) = 5x^2 - 2$, then the graph of g is a vertical stretch of five units and a downward shift of two units of the graph of f.

d. If $f(x) = \sqrt{x}$ and $g(x) = -\sqrt{-x}$, then f and g have identical graphs.

Technology Problems

In Problems 70–75, use a graphing utility to graph the three given functions on the same Cartesian coordinate plane. Describe the graphs of g and h relative to the graph of f.

70. $f(x) = x^2 - 2x$
$g(x) = f(x - 1)$
$h(x) = -f(x)$

71. $f(x) = x^2 - 3x - 4$
$g(x) = f(x - 1)$
$h(x) = -f(x)$

72. $f(x) = x^3 - 2x^2$
$g(x) = -\frac{1}{2}f(x)$
$h(x) = f(-x)$

73. $f(x) = x^3 - 3x^2$
$g(x) = -\frac{1}{2}f(x)$
$h(x) = f(-x)$

74. $f(x) = \sqrt{x}$ (Xmin = −6, Xmax = 6, Xscl = 1, Ymin = −4, Ymax = 4, Yscl = 1)

$g(x) = f(x + 3)$ $\qquad$ $h(x) = f(x + 3) - 3$

75. $f(x) = \sqrt{2x - x^2}$ (Xmin = −5, Xmax = 5, Xscl = 1, Ymin = −4, Ymax = 4, Yscl = 1)

$g(x) = 2f(x - 1)$ $\qquad$ $h(x) = -2f(-x)$

76. a. Use a graphing utility to graph $f(x) = x^2 + 1$.

b. Graph $f(x) = x^2 + 1$, $g(x) = f(2x)$, $h(x) = f(3x)$, and $k(x) = f(4x)$ on the same viewing rectangle.

c. Describe the relationship among the graphs of f, g, h, and k with emphasis on different values of x for points on all four graphs that give the same y-coordinate.

d. Generalize by describing the relationship between the graph of f and the graph of g, where $g(x) = f(cx)$ for $c > 1$.

e. Try out your generalization by sketching the graphs of $f(cx)$ for $c = 1$, $c = 2$, $c = 3$, and $c = 4$ for a function of your choice.

77. a. Use a graphing utility to graph $f(x) = x^2 + 1$.

b. Graph $f(x) = x^2 + 1$, and $g(x) = f(\frac{1}{2}x)$, and $h(x) = f(\frac{1}{4}x)$ on the same viewing rectangle.

c. Describe the relationship among the graphs of f, g, and h with emphasis on different values of x for points on all three graphs that give the same y-coordinate.

d. Generalize by describing the relationship between the graph of f and the graph of g, where $g(x) = f(cx)$ for $0 < c < 1$.

e. Try out your generalization by sketching the graphs of $f(cx)$ for $c = 1$, and $c = \frac{1}{2}$, and $c = \frac{1}{4}$ for a function of your choice.

78. a. Use a graphing utility to graph f and g on the same viewing rectangle, where $f(x) = x^2$ and $g(x) = f(x - 1) - 4$.

b. Use the graph of g to find all x such that $g(x) < 0$.

c. What inequality did you solve in part (c)?

Writing in Mathematics

79. Describe the sequence of transformations that yield the graph of $g(x) = 4(x^2 - 3)$ and $h(x) = 4x^2 - 3$ from the graph of $f(x) = x^2$. Contrast the order of applying transformations to obtain the graphs of g and h.

80. A company's profit is given by the function $y = P(x)$, where x represents the amount spent on advertising and P represents weekly profits, both expressed in hundreds of dollars.

a. Describe a situation that might occur in the company that would result in the graph of its profit function undergoing a vertical shift.

b. Now consider the function $y = D(x)$, where x represents the amount spent on advertising and D represents weekly profits, both expressed in dollars rather than hundreds of dollars. If D and P are both graphed on the same axes, describe the relationship between the two graphs.

81. Many people now study college algebra assisted by a graphing utility. With the use of a graphing utility, what purpose, if any, is there in studying translations, reflections, stretching, and shrinking?

82. Excluding $f(x) = 0$, can the graph of a function be symmetric with respect to the x-axis? Explain.

83. Excluding $f(x) = 0$, can a function be both even and odd? Explain.

Critical Thinking Problems

For Problems 84–90, assume that (a, b) is a point on the graph of f. What is the corresponding point on the graph of each of the following functions?

84. $y = f(-x)$ $\qquad$ **85.** $y = 2f(x)$ $\qquad$ **86.** $y = f(x - 3)$ $\qquad$ **87.** $y = f(x) - 3$

88. $y = f(x + 2) - 4$ $\qquad$ **89.** $y = -f(x - 5)$ $\qquad$ **90.** $y = -f(x + 3) + 2$

For Problems 91–93, assume that f is decreasing on the interval $(-\infty, 1)$, increasing on the interval $(1, 6)$, and decreasing on the interval $(6, \infty)$. Describe the interval(s) on which each function is increasing and decreasing.

91. $y = f(-x)$ $\qquad$ **92.** $y = -f(x)$

93. $y = -f(-x)$

94. Suppose that $h(x) = \dfrac{f(x)}{g(x)}$. The function f can be even, odd, or neither. The same is true for the function g.

a. Under what conditions is h definitely an even function?

b. Under what conditions is h definitely an odd function?

95. A line whose equation is $y = mx + b$ is shifted vertically so that it passes through, (x_1, y_1). What is the general form of the transformed line's equation?

SECTION 2.6

Solutions Manual

Tutorial

Video 5

Combinations of Functions

Objectives

1 Combine functions arithmetically, specifying domains.

2 Form composite functions.

3 Write functions as compositions.

4 Model with combinations of functions.

5 Find the iterates of a function.

6 Determine whether a number belongs to the Mandelbrot set.

In this section, we study ways of combining functions to form new functions. One such combination leads to a discussion of continuously inputting a function back into itself, hinting at a new branch of mathematics called chaos.

⎸ Combine functions arithmetically, specifying domains.

Arithmetic Operations with Functions

Functions can be combined using addition, subtraction, multiplication, and division to create new functions. For example, the functions

$$f(x) = 2x + 1 \quad \text{and} \quad g(x) = x^2 - 4$$

can be combined to form the sum, difference, product, and quotient of f and g. Here's how it's done.

$$f(x) + g(x) = (2x + 1) + (x^2 - 4) = x^2 + 2x - 3 \qquad \text{Sum: } f + g$$

$$f(x) - g(x) = (2x + 1) - (x^2 - 4) = -x^2 + 2x + 5 \qquad \text{Difference: } f - g$$

$$f(x)g(x) = (2x + 1)(x^2 - 4) = 2x^3 + x^2 - 8x - 4 \qquad \text{Product: } fg$$

$$\frac{f(x)}{g(x)} = \frac{2x + 1}{x^2 - 4}, \qquad x \neq \pm 2 \qquad \text{Quotient: } \frac{f}{g}$$

The domain of an arithmetic combination of functions f and g consists of all real numbers that are common to the domains of f and g. In the case of the quotient function $\dfrac{f(x)}{g(x)}$, we must remember not to divide by 0, so we add the further restriction that $g(x) \neq 0$.

We define arithmetic operations with functions using these ideas.

Definitions: sum, difference, product, and quotient of functions

Let f and g be two functions. The *sum $f + g$*, the *difference $f - g$*, the *product fg*, and the *quotient $\dfrac{f}{g}$* are functions whose domains are the set of all real numbers common to the domains of f and g, defined as follows:

1. Sum: $\qquad\qquad\qquad (f + g)(x) = f(x) + g(x)$

2. Difference: $\qquad\qquad (f - g)(x) = f(x) - g(x)$

3. Product: $\qquad\qquad (fg)(x) = f(x) \cdot g(x)$

4. Quotient: $\qquad\qquad \left(\dfrac{f}{g}\right)(x) = \dfrac{f(x)}{g(x)}$, provided $g(x) \neq 0$

ENRICHMENT ESSAY

Graphs and the Sum of Functions

Graphs that appear in magazines and newspapers are often based on the sum of functions. Shown here is

$$F(x) = f(x) + g(x)$$

where $F(x)$ denotes total world population over time, x.

Source: Population Reference Bureau

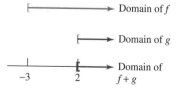
EXAMPLE I   Combining Functions

Let $f(x) = \sqrt{x + 3}$ and $g(x) = \sqrt{x - 2}$. Find the following functions, and the domain of each function.

a. $(f + g)(x)$ **b.** $(f - g)(x)$ **c.** $(fg)(x)$ **d.** $\left(\dfrac{f}{g}\right)(x)$

Solution

a. $(f + g)(x) = f(x) + g(x)$ This is the definition $(f + g)(x)$.

$\qquad\qquad\quad\; = \sqrt{x + 3} + \sqrt{x - 2}$ Substitute the given functions.

The domain of $f + g$ is all x common to the domains of f and g. Since $f(x) = \sqrt{x + 3}$, the domain of f is all x such that $x + 3 \geq 0$ or, equivalently, $x \geq -3$. The domain of f is $[-3, \infty)$. Similarly, since $g(x) = \sqrt{x - 2}$, its domain is all x such that $x - 2 \geq 0$ or, equivalently, $x \geq 2$. The domain of g is $[2, \infty)$. Figure 2.83 shows the set of all real numbers common to the domains of f and g. Shown on a number line, we see that the numbers in the two domains intersect at $x \geq 2$. Thus, the domain of $f + g$ is $[2, \infty)$.

b. $(f - g)(x) = f(x) - g(x)$ This is the definition of $(f - g)(x)$.

$\qquad\qquad\quad\; = \sqrt{x + 3} - \sqrt{x - 2}$ Substitute the given functions.

The domain of $f - g$ is all x common to the domains of f and g, so $(f - g)(x) = \sqrt{x + 3} - \sqrt{x - 2}$ has a domain of $[2, \infty)$, the same as the domain of $f + g$.

c. $(fg)(x) = f(x)g(x)$ This is the definition of $(fg)(x)$.

$\qquad\quad\; = \sqrt{x + 3} \sqrt{x - 2}$ Substitute the given functions.

We see that $(fg)(x) = \sqrt{x+3}\,\sqrt{x-2}$ or, equivalently, $(fg)(x) = \sqrt{x^2 + x - 6}$. The domain of fg is the same as the domains of $f + g$ and $f - g$, namely, $[2, \infty)$.

d. $\left(\dfrac{f}{g}\right)(x) = \dfrac{f(x)}{g(x)}$ This is the definition of $\left(\dfrac{f}{g}\right)(x)$.

$\qquad\qquad = \dfrac{\sqrt{x+3}}{\sqrt{x-2}}$ Substitute the given functions.

We see that $\left(\dfrac{f}{g}\right)(x) = \dfrac{\sqrt{x+3}}{\sqrt{x-2}}$ or, equivalently, $\left(\dfrac{f}{g}\right)(x) = \sqrt{\dfrac{x+3}{x-2}}$. Since

the denominator of $\dfrac{f}{g}$ cannot equal zero, we must exclude 2 from the

domain. Unlike $f + g, f - g$, and fg, whose domain was $[2, \infty)$, the domain of

$\dfrac{f}{g}$ is $(2, \infty)$. ∎

Composition of Functions

Another method for combining functions is to form the *composition* of one with the other. For example, if $f(x) = x^3$ and $g(x) = x + 5$, then we can form the composition of f with g by taking the output of g, namely, $g(x) = x + 5$, and using it as the input of f.

$f(g(x))$ We must substitute $g(x)$ for x in function f.

$\quad = [g(x)]^3$ Use $f(x)$ and replace x by $g(x)$.

$\quad = (x + 5)^3$ Replace $g(x)$ by $x + 5$.

Thus, $f(g(x)) = (x + 5)^3$. Observe how this composition, represented by $f \circ g$, is illustrated in Figure 2.84.

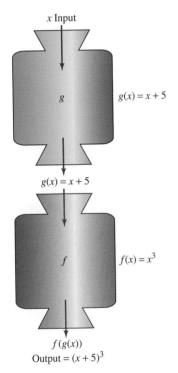

x Input

$g(x) = x + 5$

g $g(x) = x + 5$

f $f(x) = x^3$

$f(g(x))$
Output $= (x + 5)^3$

Figure 2.84

Inputting one function into a second function

Definition: composition function $f \circ g$

Given two functions f and g, the *composition* of f and g, denoted by $f \circ g$, is defined by

$$(f \circ g)(x) = f(g(x)).$$ We read $f(g(x))$ as "f of g of x."

The domain of $f \circ g$ is the set of all x in the domain of g such that $g(x)$ is in the domain of f.

The composition of f and g, $f \circ g$, is pictured with the arrow diagram in Figure 2.85. The diagram indicates that the output of g, or $g(x)$, becomes the input for "machine" f. If $g(x)$ is not in the domain of f, it cannot be inputted into machine f, and so $g(x)$ must be discarded.

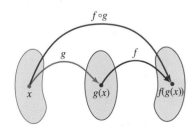

$f \circ g$

g f

x $g(x)$ $f(g(x))$

Figure 2.85

The composition of f and g: Inputting $g(x)$ into f

EXAMPLE 2   **Forming the Composition of f with g**

Let $f(x) = \sqrt{x}$ and $g(x) = 2x - 1$. Find:

a. $(f \circ g)(x)$ **b.** The domain of $f \circ g$ **c.** $(f \circ g)(5)$ and $(f \circ g)(0)$

The graphs of f, g, and $f \circ g$ can be obtained on a graphing utility by entering

$$y_1 = \sqrt{x}$$

$$y_2 = 2x - 1$$

$$y_3 = \sqrt{y_2}$$

Using a $[-2, 8]$ by $[-1, 6]$ viewing rectangle, the graph indicates that the domain of $f \circ g$ is $[\frac{1}{2}, \infty)$.

Using technology

The graphs of $f \circ g$ and $g \circ f$ can be obtained on a graphing utility by entering

$$Y_1 = \boxed{\sqrt{}} X$$

$$Y_2 = 2X - 1$$

$$Y_3 = \boxed{} \boxed{\sqrt{}} Y_2 \qquad \text{This is } f \circ g.$$

$$Y_4 = \boxed{} 2Y_1 - 1 \qquad \text{This is } g \circ f.$$

Deselect y_1 and y_2 and use

Xmin = -2, Xmax = 4,

Xscl = 1, Ymin = -1,

Ymax = 3, Yscl = 1

The graph of y_3 ($f \circ g$) has a domain of $[\frac{1}{2}, \infty)$ and the graph of y_4 ($g \circ f$) has a domain of $[0, \infty)$.

Solution

a. $(f \circ g)(x) = f(g(x))$ This is the definition of $f \circ g$.

$\qquad\qquad\quad = \sqrt{g(x)}$ Use f and replace x with $g(x)$.

$\qquad\qquad\quad = \sqrt{2x - 1}$ Replace $g(x)$ with $2x - 1$.

b. The domain of f is $[0, \infty)$. For $\sqrt{2x - 1}$ to be defined, we must have $2x - 1 \geq 0$, so $x \geq \frac{1}{2}$. The domain of $f \circ g$ is $[\frac{1}{2}, \infty)$.

c. $(f \circ g)(x) = \sqrt{2x - 1}$ This is the function from part (a).

$(f \circ g)(5) = \sqrt{2(5) - 1}$ To find $(f \circ g)(5)$, replace x with 5.

$\qquad\qquad\quad = 3$ An x-value of 5 in $f \circ g$ has a corresponding y-value of 3.

We can find $(f \circ g)(5)$ because 5 is in the domain of $f \circ g$, namely, $[\frac{1}{2}, \infty)$. However, $(f \circ g)(0)$ is undefined because 0 is not in the domain. ∎

An alternative method for Example 2c is to use the given functions

$$f(x) = \sqrt{x} \qquad \text{and} \qquad g(x) = 2x - 1.$$

We have

$$(f \circ g)(5) = f(g(5)) = f(9) = \sqrt{9} = 3 \qquad \text{Note that } g(5) = 2 \cdot 5 - 1 = 9.$$

$$(f \circ g)(0) = f(g(0)) = f(-1) = \sqrt{-1} \qquad \sqrt{-1} \text{ is not a real number.}$$

The composition of f with g, $f \circ g$, is generally not the same function as the composition of g with f, $g \circ f$. Furthermore, the functions may not have the same domain.

EXAMPLE 3   **Forming the Composition of g with f**

Let $f(x) = \sqrt{x}$ and $g(x) = 2x - 1$. Find:

a. $(g \circ f)(x)$ **b.** The domain of $g \circ f$

Solution

a. $(g \circ f)(x) = g(f(x))$ This is the definition of $g \circ f$.

$\qquad\qquad\quad = 2f(x) - 1$ Use g and replace x with $f(x)$.

$\qquad\qquad\quad = 2\sqrt{x} - 1$ Replace $f(x)$ with $\sqrt{x}$.

b. The domain of g is $(-\infty, \infty)$. Since $f(x)$ must be in this interval, then $\sqrt{x}$ must be a real number, so $x \geq 0$. The domain of $g \circ f$ is $[0, \infty)$. ∎

The graphs in the Using Technology box show that in general, $f \circ g \neq g \circ f$. It is helpful to remember that the notation $f \circ g$ means that the function g is applied first and then f is applied second.

We need to be careful in describing the domain of a composite function, as we will see in the next example.

sing technology

We can use a graphing utility to find the domain of $f \circ g$. Enter

$Y_1 \; \boxed{=} \; X \; \boxed{\wedge} \; 2 - 4$

              This is f.

$Y_2 \; \boxed{=} \; \boxed{\sqrt{}} \; (4 - X \; \boxed{\wedge} \; 2)$

              This is g.

$Y_3 \; \boxed{=} \; Y_2 \; \boxed{\wedge} \; 2 - 4$

              This f(g(x)).

Use a $[-4, 4]$ by $[-8, 2]$ viewing rectangle. The graph of $f \circ g$ does not extend to the left of $x = -2$ or to the right of $x = 2$, reinforcing the fact that the domain of $f \circ g$ is $[-2, 2]$.

3 Write functions as compositions.

iscover for yourself

Consider

$h(x) = \sqrt[3]{x^2 + 1}$

the function in Example 5. Let

$f(x) = \sqrt[3]{x + 1}$

and

$g(x) = x^2$.

Show that

$f(g(x)) = h(x)$.

What can you conclude about writing a function as a composition?

EXAMPLE 4   **Finding the Domain of a Composite Function**

If $f(x) = x^2 - 4$ and $g(x) = \sqrt{4 - x^2}$ find:

a. $(f \circ g)(x)$ and   **b.** The domain of $f \circ g$

Solution

a. $(f \circ g)(x) = f(g(x))$ This is the definition of $f \circ g$.

            $= [g(x)]^2 - 4$ Use f and replace x by $g(x)$.

            $= (\sqrt{4 - x^2})^2 - 4$ Replace $g(x)$ by $\sqrt{4 - x^2}$

            $= 4 - x^2 - 4$

            $= -x^2$ Simplify.

b. We see that $(f \circ g)(x) = -x^2$. You may initially think that the domain of $f \circ g$ is the set of all real numbers, since any real number can be used as an input in the expression $-x^2$. However, the expression $(\sqrt{4 - x^2})^2 - 4$, which simplifies to $-x^2$, is defined when $4 - x^2 \geq 0$.

$$4 - x^2 \geq 0$$

$$x^2 \leq 4$$

$$-2 \leq x \leq 2$$

Thus, the domain of $f \circ g$ is $[-2, 2]$.   ∎

Up to this point, our examples have called for the formation of the composition of two functions. Often it is useful to recognize the two (or more) simpler functions that make up a given complicated composite function. For example, the function h defined by

$$h(x) = (3x^2 - 4x + 1)^5$$

is the composition of f with g, where $f(x) = x^5$ and $g(x) = 3x^2 - 4x + 1$. That is,

$$h(x) = (3x^2 - 4x + 1)^5 = (g(x))^5 = f(g(x)).$$

Note that in expressing h as $f \circ g$, we choose g to be the "inner" function, that is, the expression inside parentheses: $g(x) = 3x^2 - 4x + 1$. Similarly, $f(x) = x^5$ is the "outer" function.

EXAMPLE 5   **Writing a Function as a Composition**

Express as a composition of two functions: $h(x) = \sqrt[3]{x^2 + 1}$.

Solution

We let g be the inner function; that is, let $g(x)$ be the binomial under the radical.

$$g(x) = x^2 + 1$$

Then we let f be the outer function.

$$f(x) = \sqrt[3]{x}$$

Check

These choices for f and g are appropriate if $f(g(x)) = h(x)$.

$$f(g(x))$$
We chose $f(x) = \sqrt[3]{x}$ and $g(x) = x^2 + 1$

$$= \sqrt[3]{g(x)}$$
Replace x in f with $g(x)$.

$$= \sqrt[3]{x^2 + 1}$$
Replace $g(x)$ with $x^2 + 1$.

$$= h(x)$$
This is the definition of the given function h. ∎

S tudy tip

If $h(x) = (\text{polynomial in } x)^p$, where p represents a real number, then one way to express h as a composition of two functions is to select

$$g(x) = \text{polynomial in } x$$

and

$$f(x) = x^p.$$

With these choices,

$$f(g(x)) = h(x).$$

Math SAT Scores, 1967–1993

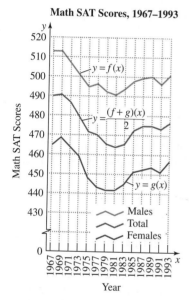

Figure 2.86

Source: The College Board

April Gornick "Two Fires" 1983, oil on canvas, 74 × 96 in. Courtesy Edward Thorp Gallery, New York.

Modeling with Combinations of Functions

Combinations of functions can be used to describe the physical world. For example, Figure 2.86 indicates that math SAT scores for males and females are a function of time. The function f represents the scores for males over time and the function g the scores of females over time. Total scores over time can be obtained by taking the average of the scores for males and females, represented by the function

$$y = \frac{(f + g)(x)}{2}.$$

The graph of $\dfrac{f + g}{2}$ can be obtained by adding the corresponding y-coordinates of f and g and dividing this sum by 2.

Composite functions often model real world phenomena, as illustrated in Example 6.

4 Model with combinations of functions

EXAMPLE 6   An Environmental Application

The relationship between average global temperature increase (G, in degrees Fahrenheit) and carbon dioxide (CO_2) concentration (C, in parts per million, ppm) is modeled by the function

$$G(C) = 0.0193C - 5.4.$$

One possible model for CO_2 concentration (C, in parts per million) t years after 1939 is

$$C(t) = 1.44t + 280.$$

Find the following:

a. The composite function $G(C(t))$. What does this function represent? What information is conveyed by its slope?

b. $G(C(61))$. What information is conveyed by the resulting function value?

Solution

Take a moment to examine the significance of the slope of the given functions.

$$G(C) = 0.0193C - 5.4$$

There is a 0.0193°F increase in global temperature for each ppm increase in CO_2 concentration.

Slope = 0.0193

$$C(t) = 1.44t + 280$$

There is an increase in CO_2 concentration of 1.44 ppm each year.

Slope = 1.44

a. $G(C(t)) = 0.0193C(t) - 5.4$ Use G and replace C with $C(t)$.

$= 0.0193(1.44t + 280) - 5.4$ Replace $C(t)$ with $1.44t + 280$.

$= 0.027792t + 5.404 - 5.4$ Apply the distributive property.

$= 0.027792t + 0.004$ Simplify.

Slope = 0.027792

This composite function represents average global temperature increase as a function of time. The slope, 0.027792, indicates that average global temperature will increase 0.027792°F each year.

b. $G(C(t)) = 0.027792t + 0.004$ This is the composite function derived in part (a).

$G(C(61)) = 0.027792(61) + 0.004$ Replace t with 61.

$= 1.695712$

This result indicates that we can expect average global temperature increase of approximately 1.7°F 61 years after 1939, in the year 2000. ∎

Modeling the Mandelbrot Set

By opening up our discussion to include the complex plane and by composing a function with itself, we can construct dramatic visual images.

Recall from our prerequisites chapter that the complex number $a + bi$ can be represented as a point in the complex plane. In this plane, the horizontal axis represents the real part of the complex number and the vertical axis the imaginary part. Figure 2.87 shows the graph of the two points corresponding to $3 + 2i$ and $-2 - 4i$.

Now let's see what is meant by composing a function with itself.

The iterates of a function

$$f^2(x) = f(f(x))$$
$$f^3(x) = f(f(f(x))) = f(f^2(x))$$
$$\vdots$$

$f^n(x)$, called the nth iterate of a function, is found by composing f with itself n times.

For example, consider a function that adds a constant c to the square of each input: $f(x) = x^2 + c$. The second and third iterates of this function are:

Discover for yourself

Environmentalists have found that a temperature increase of 1.8°F corresponds to a one-foot rise in ocean level. Use the result of part (a) to find by how much the oceans will rise each year.

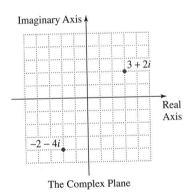

Figure 2.87

Plotting complex numbers

5 Find the iterates of a function.

$$f^2(x) = f(f(x)) = (f(x))^2 + c = (x^2 + c)^2 + c$$

$$f^3(x) = f(f^2(x)) = (f^2(x))^2 + c = [(x^2 + c)^2 + c]^2 + c$$

If we evaluate the given function and its first two iterates at 0, we obtain

$$f(0) = 0^2 + c = c$$

$$f^2(0) = (0^2 + c)^2 + c = c^2 + c$$

$$f^3(0) = [(0^2 + c)^2 + c]^2 + c = (c^2 + c)^2 + c.$$

Since each successive iterate is obtained by adding c to the square of the previous result, the next iterate is

$$[(c^2 + c)^2 + c]^2 + c$$

6 Determine whether a number belongs to the Mandelbrot set.

This sequence of iterates remains small for some values of c and is said to be *bounded*. For other values of c, the successive numbers in the sequence become larger and larger, and the sequence is *unbounded*. The set of all complex numbers for which the sequence is bounded is called the *Mandelbrot set*.

EXAMPLE 7 The Mandelbrot Set

Determine which of the following numbers belong to the Mandelbrot set: $1, -1, i, 1 + i$.

Solution

Complex Number c	c	$(c^2 + c)$	$(c^2 + c)^2 + c$	$[(c^2 + c)^2 + c]^2 + c$	Keep squaring the previous result and add c
$c = 1$	1	$1^2 + 1 = 2$	$2^2 + 1 = 5$	$5^2 + 1 = 26$	$26^2 + 1 = 677$
		The numbers 1, 2, 5, 26, 677, ... are getting larger and larger. Thus, 1 is not a member of the Mandelbrot set.			
$c = -1$	-1	$(-1)^2 + (-1) = 0$	$0^2 + (-1) = -1$	$(-1)^2 + (-1) = 0$	$0^2 + (-1) = -1$
		The sequence of numbers $-1, 0, -1, 0, -1, \ldots$ remains small. Thus, -1 is a member of the Mandelbrot set.			
$c = i$	i	$i^2 + i$ $= -1 + i$	$(-1 + i)^2 + i$ $= 1 - 2i + i^2 + i$ $= -i$	$(-i)^2 + i$ $= -1 + i$	$(-1 + i)^2 + i$ $= -i$
		The next number in the sequence is $-1 + i$, and the sequence $i, -1 + i, -i, -1 + i, -i, -1 + i, \ldots$ is bounded. Thus, i is a member of the Mandelbrot set.			
$c = 1 + i$	$1 + i$	$(1 + i)^2 + 1 + i$ $= 1 + 3i$	$(1 + 3i)^2 + 1 + i$ $= -7 + 7i$	$(-7 + 7i)^2 + 1 + i$ $= 1 - 97i$	$(1 - 97i)^2 + 1 + i$ $= -9407 - 193i$
		The sequence of numbers $1 + i, 1 + 3i, -7 + 7i, 1 - 97i, -9407 - 193i \ldots$ does not remain small and is not bounded. Thus, $1 + i$ is not a member of the Mandelbrot set.			

The numbers -1 and i are members of the Mandelbrot set. ∎

A black-and-white rendering of the Mandelbrot set is shown in Figure 2.88 on page 295. Points that are in the set consist of the number for which the sequence of iterates is bounded. The resulting graph assumes an image that is "buglike" in shape.

Mathematicians and computer artists have added colors to the graph of the boundary of the Mandelbrot set (see the image in the chapter introduction).

ENRICHMENT ESSAY

Recursive Processes; The Sierpinski Gasket

So Nat'ralists observe, A Flea
Hath Smaller Fleas that on him prey
and these have smaller Fleas to bite'em
And so proceed, ad infinitum
—Jonathan Swift

A specified sequence of computational steps is called an algorithm. If an algorithm proceeds by repeating a sequence of steps, using the result from the previous step as the input for the next step, it is called *recursive*. Each repetition is an iteration.

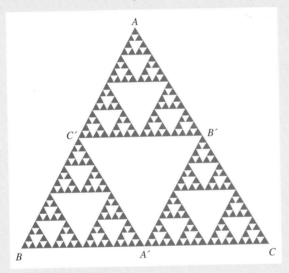

Shown here is an iteration where triangles are repeatedly subtracted from within triangles. From the midpoints of the sides of $\triangle ABC$, remove

$\triangle A'B'C'$. Repeat the process for the three remaining triangles, then with each of the triangles left after that, and so on ad infinitum.

After infinitely many steps of this recursive process, an unusual "Swiss cheese"-like triangle called the Sierpinski gasket, named after mathematician Waclaw Sierpinski (1822–1910), emerges. The Sierpinski iteration, shown below, was generated on a computer by scientists at the University of Regina in Canada by subtracting pyramids from within pyramids.

The word *fractal* (from the Latin word *fractus,* meaning "broken up, fragmented") was first used by mathematician Benoit Mandelbrot to describe objects like the Sierpinski gasket.

Daryl H. Hepting and Allan N. Snider "Desktop Tetrahedron" 1990. Computer generated at the University of Regina in Canada.

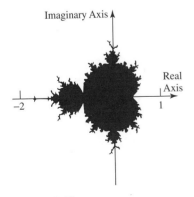

Figure 2.88
The Mandelbrot set

Color choices depend on how quickly the numbers in the boundary approach infinity. The magnified boundary yields repetition of the original overall bug-like structure as well as new and interesting patterns. With each new level of magnification, repetition and unpredictable formations interact to create what has been called the most complicated mathematical object ever known.

The Mandelbrot set is a mathematical *fractal*, a set of points that exhibits increasing detail with increasing magnification. Fractals are as complex in their details as in their overall form. The blending of infinite repetition and infinite variety is one of the hallmarks of the Mandelbrot set in particular and mathematics in general.

PROBLEM SET 2.6

Practice Problems

In Problems 1–8, find $f + g, f - g, fg,$ and $\dfrac{f}{g}$ and their domains.

1. $f(x) = 2x^2 - x - 3, \quad g(x) = x + 1$
3. $f(x) = \sqrt{x + 4}, g(x) = \sqrt{x - 1}$
5. $f(x) = \dfrac{1}{x}, g(x) = \dfrac{1}{x^3}$
7. $f(x) = \sqrt{2x - 6}, g(x) = \dfrac{1}{x}$

2. $f(x) = 6x^2 - x - 1, \quad g(x) = 2x - 1$
4. $f(x) = \sqrt{x + 6}, g(x) = \sqrt{x - 3}$
6. $f(x) = \dfrac{1}{x - 2}, g(x) = \dfrac{1}{(x - 2)^2}$
8. $f(x) = \sqrt{3x - 12}, g(x) = \dfrac{1}{x}$

In Problems 9–12, graph the functions $f, g,$ and $f + g$ on the same set of coordinate axes.

9. $f(x) = 3x, g(x) = 2x - 4$
11. $f(x) = 2x, g(x) = -2x + 3$

10. $f(x) = 2x, g(x) = x + 5$
12. $f(x) = 4x, g(x) = -4x + 1$

13. If $f(x) = 2x^2 - x - 10$ and $g(x) = x + 2$, find $\left(\dfrac{f}{g}\right)(x)$, simplify and graph the function.

14. If $f(x) = x^2 + 8x + 15$ and $g(x) = x + 3$, find $\left(\dfrac{f}{g}\right)(x)$, simplify and graph the function.

In Problems 15–20, find **a.** $f \circ g$, **b.** $g \circ f$, and **c.** $f \circ f$.

15. $f(x) = x^2, g(x) = x + 2$
17. $f(x) = 2x + 3, g(x) = 4 - x$
19. $f(x) = 4x^3 - 1, g(x) = \sqrt[3]{\dfrac{x + 1}{4}}$

16. $f(x) = x^2, g(x) = x - 3$
18. $f(x) = 4x - 1, g(x) = 3 - x$
20. $f(x) = x^3 - 2, g(x) = \sqrt[3]{x + 2}$

In Problems 21–34, find **a.** $f \circ g$ and **b.** $g \circ f$. Also give the domain for each function.

21. $f(x) = \sqrt{x}, g(x) = 2x + 1$
23. $f(x) = \dfrac{1}{x}, g(x) = \dfrac{1}{2x}$
25. $f(x) = x^2 - 9, g(x) = \sqrt{9 - x^2}$
27. $f(x) = x^{1/3}, g(x) = x^6$
29. $f(x) = |x|, g(x) = 3x - 1$
31. $f(x) = \dfrac{3x + 1}{x - 1}, g(x) = \dfrac{x + 1}{x - 3}$
33. $f(x) = \sqrt[5]{\dfrac{x^3 + 1}{2}}, g(x) = \sqrt[3]{2x^5 - 1}$

22. $f(x) = \sqrt{x}, g(x) = 3x - 1$
24. $f(x) = \dfrac{1}{x}, g(x) = \dfrac{1}{3x}$
26. $f(x) = x^2 - 1, g(x) = \sqrt{1 - x^2}$
28. $f(x) = x^{2/3}, g(x) = x^3$
30. $f(x) = |x|, g(x) = 2x + 3$
32. $f(x) = \dfrac{x + 1}{1 - x}, g(x) = \dfrac{x - 1}{x + 1}$
34. $f(x) = (x + 4)^{5/3}, g(x) = x^{3/5} - 4$

In Problems 35–44, use the graphs of f and g to evaluate the expression.

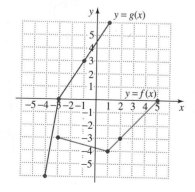

35. $(f \circ g)(1)$
37. $(g \circ g)(-3)$
39. $(g \circ f)(5)$
41. $(f + g)(1)$
43. $(f - g)(-3)$

36. $(g \circ f)(1)$
38. $(f \circ f)(1)$
40. $(f \circ g)(-1)$
42. $(f + g)(-3)$
44. $(f - g)(1)$

In Problems 45–56, find two functions f and g so that $h(x) = (f \circ g)(x)$. *(More than one correct answer is possible for each problem.)*

45. $h(x) = (3x - 1)^4$

46. $h(x) = (2x - 5)^3$

47. $h(x) = \sqrt[3]{x^2 - 9}$

48. $h(x) = \sqrt{5x^2 + 3}$

49. $h(x) = |2x - 5|$

50. $h(x) = |3x - 4|$

51. $h(x) = \dfrac{1}{2x - 3}$

52. $h(x) = \dfrac{3}{(5x - 1)^2}$

53. $h(x) = (2x^2 - 5x + 1)^{2/3}$

54. $h(x) = (3x^2 - 7x + 4)^{3/4}$

55. $h(x) = 3(x - 1)^2 + 5(x - 1)$

56. $h(x) = 4(x - 3)^2 + 6(x - 3)$

In Problems 57–62, let $f(x) = 3x - 1, g(x) = x^2$, *and* $h(x) = |x|$. *Write each function as a composition of functions chosen from f, g, and h.*

57. $k(x) = (3x - 1)^2$

58. $k(x) = 3x^2 - 1$

59. $k(x) = 3|x| - 1$

60. $k(x) = |3x - 1|$

61. $k(x) = (3|x| - 1)^2$

62. $k(x) = |3x - 1|^2$

In Problems 63–68, find $f^3(x)$, *the third iterate of the given function f.*

63. $f(x) = 2x - 3$

64. $f(x) = 3x + 2$

65. $f(x) = x^2 + 1$

66. $f(x) = 2x^2 - 1$

67. $f(x) = x^3$

68. $f(x) = -2x^3$

69. If $f(x) = 1 + \dfrac{1}{x}$, find $f^4(x)$ and predict the result for $f^n(x)$ as n continues to get larger.

Application Problems

70. Consider two functions M and F that represent the number of male and female members of the House of Representatives for the years 1977, 1981, 1991, and 1994. Sketch the graphs of M and F in the same Cartesian coordinate plane, using the data in the graphs. Each graph should consist of four points whose first coordinates are the years and second coordinates are the numbers of representatives, male or female. Now add to the graphs in your coordinate plane the graph of $M + F$. What constant function do you obtain? What is the significance of this constant?

Gender Breakdown of the House of Representatives for Four Selected Years

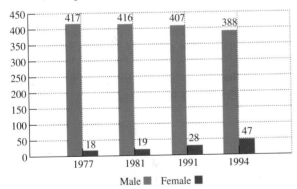

Male ■ Female ■

71. A department store has two locations in a city. From 1994 through 1998, the profits for each of the store's two branches are modeled by the functions $f(x) = -0.44x + 13.62$ and $g(x) = 0.51x + 11.14$. In each model, x represents the number of years after 1994 and f and g represent the profit in millions of dollars.

a. What is the slope for f? Describe what this means.

b. What is the slope for g? Describe what this means.

c. Find $f + g$. What is the slope for this function? What does this mean?

72. Skin temperature (T, in degrees Celsius) is a function of the Celsius temperature C of the environment, modeled by $T(C) = 0.27C + 27.4$. Celsius temperature C is a function of Fahrenheit temperature F, described by $C(F) = \frac{5}{9}(F - 32)$.

a. Find and interpret $T(C(F))$.

b. Find and interpret $T(C(41))$.

73. A stone is dropped into a calm lake, creating a circular ripple that travels outward at a speed of 0.4 feet per second. Thus, $r(t) = 0.4t$, where t represents time in seconds. If the area of the circle is described by $A(r) = \pi r^2$, find $(A \circ r)(t)$ and interpret the resulting composite function.

Solution

To show that f and g are inverses of each other, we must show that $f(g(x)) = x$ and $g(f(x)) = x$.

$$f(g(x)) = 3[g(x)] + 2$$

Put $g(x)$ into f.
$$= 3\left(\frac{x-2}{3}\right) + 2$$

$$= x - 2 + 2$$

$$= x$$

$$g(f(x)) = \frac{f(x) - 2}{3}$$

Put $f(x)$ into g.
$$= \frac{3x + 2 - 2}{3}$$

$$= \frac{3x}{3}$$

$$= x$$

Because g is the inverse of f (and vice versa), we can use the notation

$$f(x) = 3x + 2 \quad \text{and} \quad f^{-1}(x) = \frac{x-2}{3}.$$

Notice how f^{-1} undoes the changes produced by f. f changes x by *multiplying* by 3 and *adding* 2. f^{-1} undoes this by *substracting* 2 and *dividing* by 3. This "undoing" process is illustrated in Figure 2.96.

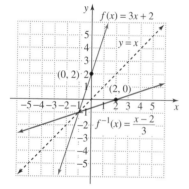

Figure 2.97

Symmetry about $y = x$

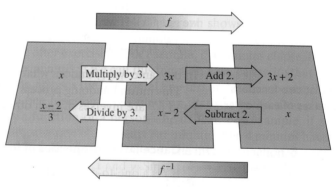

Figure 2.96

f^{-1} undoes the changes produced by f.

■

Graphs of f and f^{-1}

Figure 2.97 shows the graphs of $f(x) = 3x + 2$ and $f^{-1}(x) = \dfrac{x-2}{3}$. The graphs are mirror images of each other with respect to the line $y = x$.

In general, if f is a one-to-one function and $f(a) = b$, then $f^{-1}(b) = a$, because the inverse function reverses the coordinates of the function. This means that the point (a, b) belongs the the graph of f, and the point (b, a) belongs to the graph of f^{-1}. Since the points (a, b) and (b, a) are symmetric with respect to the line $y = x$, the graph of f^{-1} is reflection of the graph of f with respect to the line $y = x$. This is illustrated in Figure 2.98.

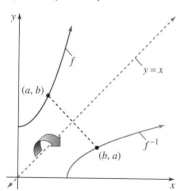

Figure 2.98

The graph of f^{-1} as a reflection of f in $y = x$

4 Find the equation of the inverse.

Finding Formulas for Inverses

If a function is one-to-one, its inverse function may be obtained by reversing the first and second coordinates in each ordered pair of the function. In this reversal, the domain of the function becomes the range of the inverse function, and the range of the function becomes the domain of the inverse function. This means that for each ordered pair (x, y) in the function, the ordered pair (y, x) will be in the inverse function.

In short, if a one-to-one function is defined by an equation, we can obtain the equation for f^{-1}, the inverse of f, by interchanging the role of x and y in the equation for f.

Finding the inverse of a one-to-one function

The formula for the inverse of a one-to-one function f can be found as follows.

1. Replace $f(x)$ by y in the equation for $f(x)$.
2. Interchange x and y.
3. Solve for y.
4. Replace y by $f^{-1}(x)$.

This process can be checked by showing that $f(f^{-1}(x)) = x$ and $f^{-1}(f(x)) = x$.

$\mathcal{ZOLUTLON}$
$\mathcal{PROBLEM}$

$\mathcal{PROBLEM}$
$\mathcal{SOLUTLON}$

© Scott Kim. From Inversions (W. H. Freeman, 1989).

EXAMPLE 4 **Finding the Inverse of a Function**

Find the inverse of $f(x) = 7x - 5$.

Solution

Since the graph of $f(x) = 7x - 5$ is a non-horizontal line, this function is one-to-one.

Step 1. Replace $f(x)$ by y:

$y = 7x - 5$

Step 2. Interchange x and y:

$x = 7y - 5$ This is the inverse function.

Step 3. Solve for y:

$x + 5 = 7y$ Add 5 to both sides.

$\dfrac{x + 5}{7} = y$ Divide both sides by 7.

Step 4. Replace y by $f^{-1}(x)$:

$f^{-1}(x) = \dfrac{x + 5}{7}$ The equation is written with f^{-1} on the left.

Thus, $f(x) = 7x - 5$ and $f^{-1}(x) = \dfrac{x + 5}{7}$.

Once again, f^{-1} undoes the changes produced by f. f changes x by multiplying by 7 and subtracting 5. f^{-1} undoes this by adding 5 and dividing by 7. ■

Discover for yourself

In Example 4, we found that if $f(x) = 7x - 5$, then

$f^{-1}(x) = \dfrac{x + 5}{7}$.

1. Verify this result by showing that

$f(f^{-1}(x)) = x$

and

$f^{-1}(f(x)) = x$.

2. Find $f(0), f^{-1}(-5), f(1), f^{-1}(2), f(3)$, and $f^{-1}(16)$. What is f^{-1} doing to the ordered pairs of f?

EXAMPLE 5 **Finding the Equation of the Inverse**

a. Find the inverse of $f(x) = 4x^3 - 1$.
b. Verify that $f(f^{-1}(x)) = x$ and $f^{-1}(f(x)) = x$.

Solution

The graph of $f(x) = 4x^3 - 1$, shown in the Using Technology, passes the horizontal line test and is one-to-one.

a. ***Step 1.*** Replace $f(x)$ by y: $\qquad\qquad y = 4x^3 - 1$

     Step 2. Interchange x and y: $\qquad\quad x = 4y^3 - 1$

     Step 3. Solve for y: $\qquad\qquad\quad x + 1 = 4y^3$

$$\frac{x+1}{4} = y^3$$

$$\sqrt[3]{\frac{x+1}{4}} = y$$

Step 4. Replace y by $f^{-1}(x)$: $\qquad f^{-1}(x) = \sqrt[3]{\frac{x+1}{4}}$

Thus, the inverse of $f(x) = 4x^3 - 1$ is

$$f^{-1}(x) = \sqrt[3]{\frac{x+1}{4}}.$$

b. To verify algebraically that $f(x) = 4x^3 - 1$ and $f^{-1}(x) = \sqrt[3]{\frac{x+1}{4}}$ are inverses of each other, we must show that

$$f(f^{-1}(x)) = x \qquad\qquad \text{and} \qquad f^{-1}(f(x)) = x.$$

$$f(f^{-1}(x)) = 4[f^{-1}(x)]^3 - 1 \qquad\qquad f^{-1}(f(x)) = \sqrt[3]{\frac{f(x)+1}{4}}$$

$$\text{Put } f^{-1}(x) \text{ into } f. \quad = 4\left(\sqrt[3]{\frac{x+1}{4}}\right)^3 - 1 \qquad\qquad \text{Put } f(x) \text{ into } f^{-1}. \quad = \sqrt[3]{\frac{4x^3 - 1 + 1}{4}}$$

$$= 4\left(\frac{x+1}{4}\right) - 1 \qquad\qquad = \sqrt[3]{\frac{4x^3}{4}}$$

$$= x + 1 - 1 \qquad\qquad = \sqrt[3]{x^3}$$

$$= x \qquad\qquad = x \qquad\qquad ■$$

Using technology

The graphs of

$$y_1 = 4x^3 - 1$$

$$y_2 = \sqrt[3]{\frac{x+1}{4}}$$

and

$$y_3 = x$$

were obtained with a graphing utility. The graphs of f and f^{-1} indicate that the graph of f^{-1} is the reflection of the graph of f in the line $y = x$.

5 Verify inverses with a graphing utility.

EXAMPLE 6 **Using a Graphing Utility to Verify Inverse Functions**

Use a graphing utility to determine whether $f(x) = x^3 + 2$ and $g(x) = \sqrt[3]{x} - 2$ are inverse functions.

Solution

Enter y_1 through y_4 as follows:

    $\text{Y}_1 \boxed{=} \text{X} \boxed{\wedge} 3 + 2$ This is f.

    $\text{Y}_2 \boxed{=} \boxed{\sqrt[3]{}} (\text{X} - 2)$ This is g.

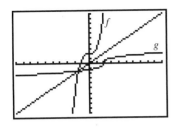

Figure 2.99

The graphs of the inverse functions $f(x) = x^3 + 2$ and $g(x) = \sqrt[3]{x - 2}$

 Solve applied modeling problems using inverses.

Giacomo Balla "Abstract Speed, The Car Has Passed" 1913. Tate Gallery, London. Photo: John Webb. Art Resource, NY.

$Y_3 \boxed{=} Y_2 \boxed{\wedge} 3 + 2$ This is $f \circ g$.

$Y_4 \boxed{=} \boxed{\sqrt[3]{}} (Y_1 - 2)$ This is $g \circ f$.

Figure 2.99 shows the resulting graphs. The functions f and g are inverses if $f(g(x)) = x$ and $g(f(x)) = x$, so that the graphs of y_3 and y_4 should be the line $y = x$. This is indeed the case, verified using the $\boxed{\text{TRACE}}$ feature along the line and observing that the x- and y-coordinates are equal. Notice the symmetry of the graphs of f and g about the line $y = x$. ■

Modeling with Inverses

We began our discussion of inverse functions with a graph that described heart rate as a function of time after exercising. We then considered time after exercising as a function of heart rate. We now do the same thing—that is, switch the roles of independent and dependent variables—with a mathematical model for speed and stopping distance.

EXAMPLE 7   **Speed and Stopping Distance**

The function $d = f(v) = 0.06v^2 + 0.8v$ expresses the stopping distance of a car (d, in feet) as a function of the car's speed (v, in miles per hour). Find a formula for the function giving the car's speed as a function of its stopping distance.

Solution

We are given that $d = 0.06v^2 + 0.8v$, a model expressing d in terms of v. We want v in terms of d, so we must solve for v.

$d = 0.06v^2 + 0.8v$ This is the given function.

$0 = 0.06v^2 + 0.8v - d$ To solve for v, set the quadratic equation equal to 0.

$v = \dfrac{-b \pm \sqrt{b^2 - 4ac}}{2a}$ Use the quadratic formula.

$= \dfrac{-0.8 \pm \sqrt{(0.8)^2 - 4(0.06)(-d)}}{2(0.06)}$ Substitute $a = 0.06$, $b = 0.8$, and $c = -d$.

$= \dfrac{-0.8 \pm \sqrt{0.64 + 0.24d}}{0.12}$ Perform the indicated operations.

$= \dfrac{-0.8 \pm \sqrt{0.04(16 + 6d)}}{0.12}$ Simplify.

$= \dfrac{-0.8 \pm 0.2\sqrt{16 + 6d}}{0.12}$

$= \dfrac{-20 \pm 5\sqrt{16 + 6d}}{3}$ Divide the numerator and denominator by 0.04.

$v = \dfrac{-20 + 5\sqrt{16 + 6d}}{3}$ Reject $\dfrac{-20 - 5\sqrt{16 + 6d}}{3}$ because v, the car's speed, must be positive.

Andy Warhol "White Car Crash 19 Times" 1963, synthetic polymer paint and silkscreen ink on canvas, 145 × 83 1/4 in. © The Andy Warhol Foundation for the Visual Arts/ARS, New York. Art Resource, NY.

We now have the car's speed in terms of its stopping distance. Since we called the given function f and reversed the roles of the variables, we can use f^{-1} to represent speed as a function of stopping distance:

$$f^{-1}(d) = \frac{-20 + 5\sqrt{16 + 6d}}{3}.$$

Let's find just one function value for f^{-1}, say, $f^{-1}(40)$.

$$f^{-1}(40) = \frac{-20 + 5\sqrt{16 + 6(40)}}{3} = \frac{-20 + 5(16)}{3} = 20$$

With $f^{-1}(40) = 20$, a police officer investigating an accident in which skid marks measured 40 feet can determine that the car in question was traveling at 20 miles per hour at the moment the brakes were applied. ∎

PROBLEM SET 2.7

Practice Problems

Problems 1–10 show graphs of relations. Which of these relations are functions? Which of these functions are one-to-one?

1.

2.

3.

4.

5.

6.

7.

8.

9.

10.

Explain why the functions whose graphs are shown in Problems 11–14 are not one-to-one. Then suggest a restriction on each function's domain so that the resulting function is one-to-one. More than one restriction is possible.

expression, the implied domain is the set of all real numbers excluding those that cause division by zero and those that result in an even root of a negative number.

d. The range of a function is the set of all values taken on by the dependent variable.

2. Slope

a. The slope m of the line through (x_1, y_1) and (x_2, y_2) is $m = \dfrac{y_2 - y_1}{x_2 - x_1} = \dfrac{\Delta y}{\Delta x}$, $\Delta x \neq 0$.

b. Lines with positive slope rise and those with negative slope fall from left to right. Lines with zero slope are horizontal and those with undefined slope are vertical.

c. If y is a function of x, slope is the average change in y per unit of change in x.

d. Two nonvertical lines are parallel if and only if their slopes are equal. Two nonvertical lines are perpendicular if and only if their slopes are negative reciprocals.

3. Equations of Lines

a. General Form: $Ax + By + C = 0$

b. Vertical line: $x = a$

c. Horizontal line: $y = b$

d. Point-slope form: $y - y_1 = m(x - x_1)$

e. Slope-intercept form: $y = mx + b$

f. Linear Function: $f(x) = mx + b$

4. Graphs of Relations and Functions

a. The graph of a relation is the graph of its ordered pairs. The graph of a function f is the set of points $(x, f(x))$ such that x is in the domain of f.

b. The Vertical Line Test for Functions: If any vertical line intercepts the graph of a relation in more than one point, the relation does not define y as a function of x.

5. The Circle

a. A circle is the set of all points in a plane that are equidistant from a fixed point called the center. The fixed distance from the circle's center to any point on the circle is called the radius.

b. The equation of the circle with center at (h, k) and radius r is given by $(x - h)^2 + (y - k)^2 = r^2$.

6. Increasing and Decreasing Functions, Extreme Values

a. *Increasing, Decreasing, Constant Functions*

If x_1 and x_2 are any values for x in an interval, where $x_1 < x_2$, then:

  1. f is increasing on the interval if $f(x_1) < f(x_2)$.

  2. f is decreasing on the interval if $f(x_1) > f(x_2)$.

  3. f is constant on the interval if $f(x_1) = f(x_2)$.

b. *Relative Extrema*

  1. A function value $f(a)$ is a relative maximum of f if there exists an open interval about a such that $f(a) \geq f(x)$ for all x in the open interval.

  2. A function value $f(b)$ is a relative minimum of f if there exists an open interval about b such that $f(b) \leq f(x)$ for all x in the open interval.

7. Algebra's Common Graphs

Identity Function $f(x) = x$

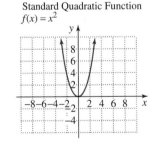

Standard Quadratic Function $f(x) = x^2$

Standard Cubic Function $f(x) = x^3$

Absolute Value Function $f(x) = |x|$

Square Root Function $f(x) = \sqrt{x}$

Cube Root Function $f(x) = \sqrt[3]{x}$

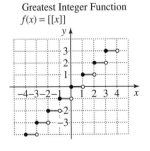

Greatest Integer Function $f(x) = [[x]]$

8. Techniques in Graphing; Transforming the Graph of $y = f(x)$

a. In each case, c represents a positive real number.

Function		How to obtain the graph of g
Vertical translations	$\begin{cases} g(x) = f(x) + c \\ g(x) = f(x) - c \end{cases}$	Shift f upward c units. Shift f downward c units.
Horizontal translations	$\begin{cases} g(x) = f(x - c) \\ g(x) = f(x + c) \end{cases}$	Shift f to the right c units. Shift f to the left c units.
Reflections	$\begin{cases} g(x) = -f(x) \\ g(x) = f(-x) \end{cases}$	Reflect f in the x-axis. Reflect f in the y-axis.
Stretching or Shrinking	$\begin{cases} g(x) = cf(x); c > 1 \\ g(x) = cf(x); 0 < x < 1 \end{cases}$	Stretch f, multiplying each of its y-values by c. Shrink f, multiplying each of its y-values by c.

b. *Order of Transformations:*
   1. Horizontal translation
   2. Stretching or shrinking
   3. Reflecting
   4. Vertical translation

c. *Symmetry; Even and Odd Functions*
   Find $f(-x)$ and test for symmetry. If $f(-x) = f(x)$, then f is an even function and its graph has y-axis symmetry. If $f(-x) = -f(x)$, then f is an odd function and its graph has origin symmetry.

9. Operations with Functions

a. *Sum:* $(f + g)(x) = f(x) + g(x)$

b. *Difference:* $(f - g)(x) = f(x) - g(x)$

c. *Product:* $(fg)(x) = f(x) \cdot g(x)$

d. *Quotient:* $\left(\dfrac{f}{g}\right) = \dfrac{f(x)}{g(x)}$, provided $g(x) \neq 0$

The domains are the set of all real numbers common to the domains of f and g.

10. Composition Functions

a. $(f \circ g)(x) = f(g(x))$; $f \circ g$ is the composition of f and g. We read $(f \circ g)(x)$ as "f of g of x."

b. The domain of $f \circ g$ is the set of all x in the domain of g such that $g(x)$ is in the domain of f.

c. Iterates of f: $f^2(x) = f(f(x)), f^3(x) = f(f^2(x))$, etc.

11. Inverse Functions

a. A function is one-to-one if $f(x_1) \neq f(x_2)$ whenever $x_1 \neq x_2$.

b. *The Horizontal Line Test:* If no horizontal line intersects the graph of a function more than once, then the function is one-to-one.

c. *Increasing and Decreasing Functions*
   1. If f is increasing on its entire domain, then f is one-to-one.
   2. If f is decreasing on its entire domain, then f is one-to-one.

d. If f is one-to-one such that $f(x) = y$, then its inverse function reverses this direction so that $f^{-1}(y) = x$.

e. *Cancellation Properties:* $f^{-1}(f(x)) = x$ and $f(f^{-1}(x)) = x$.

f. The graphs of f and f^{-1} are symmetric with respect to the line $y = x$.

g. If f is one-to-one, the formula for f^{-1} is found by:
   1. Replacing $f(x)$ by y in the equation for $f(x)$.
   2. Interchanging x and y.
   3. Solving for y.
   4. Replacing y by $f^{-1}(x)$.

REVIEW PROBLEMS

1. The function $L(v) = 900 \sqrt{1 - \left(\dfrac{v}{186,000}\right)^2}$ describes the length of a 900-meter tall starship moving at velocity v (in miles per second) from the perspective of an observer at rest. Find $L(74,400)$ and describe in practical terms what the function value means.

2. The function
$$f(x) = \begin{cases} 0.0005x^2 + 0.025x + 8.8 & \text{if } 0 \leq x < 30 \\ 0.0202x^2 - 1.58x + 39.2 & \text{if } x \geq 30 \end{cases}$$
describes the average number of miles (in thousands) that each automobile in the United States was driven x years after 1940. Find and interpret $f(45) - f(10)$.

In Problems 3–4, find: **a.** $f(0)$ **b.** $f(-2)$ **c.** $f(a)$ **d.** $f(a + h)$

e. $\dfrac{f(a + h) - f(a)}{h}$ **f.** $f(a) + f(h)$ **g.** $f(2a)$

3. $f(x) = 7x - 3$

4. $f(x) = 4x^2 - 5x + 11$

In Problems 5–10, find the domain of each function. Check your result with a graphing utility.

5. $f(x) = \sqrt{8 - 2x}$

6. $f(x) = \sqrt[3]{8 - 2x}$

7. $f(x) = \sqrt{x^2 - 5x + 4}$

8. $f(x) = \dfrac{2}{\sqrt{x^2 - 5x + 4}}$

9. $f(x) = \sqrt{4 - x^2}$

10. $f(x) = \dfrac{\sqrt{x - 2}}{x - 5}$

In Problems 11–14, use the given conditions to write the equation of each line in point-slope form, slope-intercept form, and general form.

11. Passing through $(-3, 2)$ with a slope of -6

12. Passing through $(1, 6)$ and $(-1, 2)$

13. Passing through $(4, -7)$ and parallel to the line whose equation is $3x + y - 9 = 0$

14. Passing through $(-3, 6)$ and perpendicular to the line whose equation is $x - 3y - 5 = 0$

15. The graph below shows the number of victims of violent crime in the United States for the period 1975 through 1990.

    a. Find a reasonable estimate for the number of victims (in millions) for 1980. Then use this estimate to compute the slope of the line drawn through 1975 and 1980. Interpret this value in terms of average rate of change.

    b. Find an estimate for the slope of the line drawn through 1980 and 1985. Interpret this value in terms of average rate of change.

Violent Crime in the United States, 1975–1990

Source: Bureau of Justice Statistics

16. The graph in the next column shows the number of registered nurses in the United States per 100,000 population. Find a reasonable estimate for the number of nurses per 100,000 population for the years 1983 and 1993. Write the equation that models the data for the line drawn through these years. Then extrapolate from the data and predict the number of nurses per 100,000 population for the year 2000.

Number of Registered Nurses
(per 100,000 Population)

Source: American Hospital Association

17. The data points $(3, 546)$ and $(5, 666.2)$ shown in the table fall on a straight line.

x (Number of Years after 1985)	y (Total of All Health-Care Expenditures in the United States, in Billions of Dollars)
3	546.0
5	666.2

    a. Write the equation of the line on which these measurements fall in point-slope form and slope-intercept form.

    b. Extrapolate from the data to find U.S. health-care expenditures for 1987.

    c. Extrapolate from the data to find U.S. health-care expenditures for the year 2000.

18. Sketch the graphs of $y = \frac{3}{4}x - 2$, $y = -\frac{4}{3}x + 3$, $y = 2x + 1$, and $4x - 2y - 8 = 0$ on the same set of coordinates axes. What two ideas about slope are illustrated?

19. The graph on page 318 shows the relationship between the volume of a room and the power needed to achieve a peak volume level of 106 decibels for a pair of acoustic loudspeakers. Three different kinds of rooms—dead, average, and live—require different power to achieve loud peak volume levels. Find the slope for each kind of room (you'll need to approximate) and interpret the slope for each room in terms of power and volume.

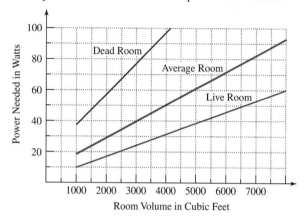

Room Volume in Cubic Feet

20. Drive-On Rental Company offers cars for $30 a day and 15¢ a mile. Hit the Road Rental charges $40 a day and 10¢ a mile.

   a. Write equations for each company that model daily cost of renting as a function of miles traveled.

   b. Graph both linear functions on the same set of coordinate axes.

   c. What do the graphs indicate in terms of which company has the better offer?

21. A state has an income tax that is directly proportional to a resident's gross income. A person working in that state with a gross yearly income of $23,000 paid $400 in state taxes.

   a. Write an equation that models income tax as a function of gross income.

   b. Use the model to determine state taxes for a yearly gross income of $35,000.

Graph each relation in Problems 22–29 by plotting ordered pairs or, if applicable, using your knowledge about slope and y-intercept for graphing linear functions. Specify the relation's domain and range from the graph. Verify your hand-drawn graph with a graphing utility.

22. $f(x) = x^2 - 5x + 6$

23. $f(x) = x^3 - 5x$

24. $f(x) = \dfrac{x^2 - 25}{x - 5}$

25. $g(x) = |2 - x|$

26. $H(x) = \sqrt{x + 3}$

27. $x = -y^2$

28. $g(x) = \begin{cases} 2 - x & \text{if } x < 0 \\ x^2 & \text{if } x \geq 0 \end{cases}$

29. $f(x) = \begin{cases} \sqrt{x - 4} & \text{if } x \geq 4 \\ 4 - x & \text{if } x < 4 \end{cases}$

30. The graph of function f is shown in the figure.

   a. What is the domain of f?

   b. What is the range of f?

   c. Find $|f(3) - f(0)|$.

In Problems 31–32, give the center and radius of the circle described by each equation and then graph the equation.

31. $(x - 2)^2 + (y + 1)^2 = 9$

32. $x^2 + 2x + y^2 - 4y - 4 = 0$

33. The graph of a function f is shown in the figure.

   a. State the values of $f(-6), f(-2),$ and $f(6)$.

   b. State the intervals on which f is increasing and on which f is decreasing.

   c. State the relative maximum and minimum values of the function and the values of x at which they occur.

   d. Is f a one-to-one function? If not, suggest a restriction on its domain so that the resulting function is one-to-one.

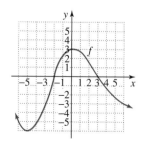

34. The graph shows the height (in meters) of a vulture as a function of its time (in seconds) in flight.

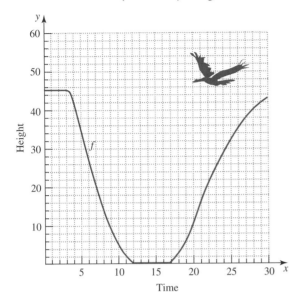

a. How does the graph indicate that height is a function of time?

b. In what interval is the function decreasing? Describe what this means in practical terms.

c. In what intervals is the function constant? What does this mean for each of these intervals?

d. In what interval is the function increasing? What does this mean?

e. Is the function one-to-one? Why is it incorrect to write $f^{-1}(30)$?

35. The model $f(x) = -0.02x^2 + x + 1$ describes the number of inches $f(x)$ that a young redwood tree grows per year as a function of annual rainfall (x, in inches).

a. For what value of x does the function have a maximum value? What is the maximum value of y? Describe the practical significance of this maximum value.

b. The domain of f is [0, 50]. Use the function's equation to find the range of f. What is the practical significance of this range in terms of the meaning of $f(x)$ in the given model?

Sketch each function in Problems 36–37 using the given properties. (More than one graph is possible.)

36. f is constant on the interval $(-\infty, -1)$, increasing on the intervals $(-1, 0)$ and $(1, \infty)$, and decreasing on the interval $(0, 1)$. f has a y-intercept equal to 2.

37. The domain of f is $[-2\pi, 2\pi]$ and its range is $[-1, 1]$. f, an even function, is decreasing on $(0, \pi)$ and increasing on $(\pi, 2\pi)$.

38. For a function g, 2 and 3 are the only relative maxima, occurring at -2 and 3.5, respectively. Furthermore, -1 is the only relative minimum occurring at 2.

a. Sketch g. (More than one graph is possible.)

b. How many x-intercepts does g have?

c. Where is g increasing?

d. Where is g decreasing?

39. Model the following narrative by a possible graph that shows distance from home as a function of time.

I left for school concerned about being late, so I drove quite rapidly at first but then slowed down. Realizing that I felt sluggish, I stopped briefly at a diner for a cup of coffee. I then continued my drive to school at a constant rate of travel.

40. Model the following narrative by a possible graph that shows income as a function of rooms rented.

A hotel gives special rates to groups that reserve between 30 and 60 rooms, decreasing the charge per room by a fixed amount times the number of rooms over 30.

41. A cargo service charges a flat fee of $5 plus $1.50 for each pound or fraction of a pound. Graph shipping cost (in dollars) as a function of weight (x, in pounds) for $0 < x \leq 5$.

Write a narrative that can be modeled by each graph shown in Problems 42–43.

42.

43.

*In Problems 44–47, use a graphing utility to graph the function and use the graph to **a.** determine (to two decimals places where an approximation is needed) intervals in which the function is increasing, decreasing, or constant; **b.** determine any relative maximum or minimum values of the function (use an approximation if necessary); and **c.** state whether the function is even, odd, or neither.*

44. $f(x) = |x + 1| - |x - 1|$

45. $f(x) = 2x^3 - x^2$

46. $g(x) = (x^2 + 1)^2$

47. $h(x) = \sqrt[3]{x(x - 2)^2}$

48. From each of the four corners of a square piece of cardboard measuring 18 inches on a side, a square piece x inches on a side is cut out. The flaps are then turned up to form an open-top box.

   a. Express the volume of the box as a function of x.

   b. Use a graphing utility to graph the function, drawing a relatively complete graph for meaningful values of x.

   c. Use the graph to determine x so that the resulting box has maximum possible volume. What is the maximum volume?

49. A tour operator uses a 400-seat airplane for trips to London. If the plane is full, the airfare is $200 per passenger. If the group has fewer than 400 people, the airfare rises $25 per person for each unoccupied seat.

   a. If x represents the number of passengers under 400, write a model expressing airfare income as a function of x.

   b. Use a graphing utility to graph the function, drawing a relatively complete graph for meaningful values of x.

   c. Use the graph to determine the number of people on the airplane that will generate maximum airfare income. What is the maximum income?

50. A child's playpen can be attached to a wall and opened as shown in the figure. Each side of the playpen is 4 feet in length.

   a. Write a formula in terms of x that models the rectangular area of the playpen.

   b. Write a formula in terms of x that models the triangular area of the playpen.

   c. Add the formulas from parts (a) and (b) and write a function f that models the total area enclosed by the playpen.

   d. Use a graphing utility to graph the area function and determine an approximate value for x that will maximize the playpen's area. Approximately what is the maximum area that can be enclosed?

51. Suppose that the graph of f is given. Describe how the graph of each of the following functions can be obtained using the graph of f.

   a. $y = f(x) + 3$ **b.** $y = f(x + 3)$

   c. $y = 2f(x)$ **d.** $y = f(x - 1) - 3$

   e. $y = f(-x)$ **f.** $y = -f(x)$

   g. $y = -f(-x)$ **h.** $y = f^{-1}(x)$

In Problems 52–58, sketch the graphs of the three given functions by hand on the same set of coordinate axes. Verify the result with a graphing utility.

52. $f(x) = \sqrt{x}$
$g(x) = \sqrt{x} - 2$
$h(x) = \sqrt{x - 2}$

53. $f(x) = \sqrt{x}$
$g(x) = \sqrt{x - 3} + 1$
$h(x) = \sqrt{x + 2} - 1$

54. $f(x) = |x|$
$g(x) = |x - 1| + 2$
$h(x) = -2|x - 1|$

55. $f(x) = x^2$
$g(x) = (x - 3)^2 + 1$
$h(x) = -2x^2 - 1$

56. $f(x) = x^3$
$g(x) = (x - 2)^3 - 1$
$h(x) = -x^3$

57. $f(x) = \sqrt[3]{x}$
$g(x) = \sqrt[3]{x + 2}$
$h(x) = -1 + \sqrt[3]{x + 2}$

58. $f(x) = \sqrt[3]{x}$
$g(x) = -\frac{1}{2}\sqrt[3]{x}$
$h(x) = -\sqrt[3]{x - 1}$

59. The graphs in the figure were obtained by transformations of the graph of $f(x) = |x|$. Write equations for g and h and state the domain and range for g and h.

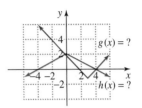

In Problems 60–66, use the graph of f shown below to sketch the graph of each function.

60. $f(x - 1)$

61. $f(x) - 1$

62. $2f(x)$

63. $\frac{1}{2}f(x)$

64. $f(-x)$

65. $-f(x)$

66. $-f(-x)$

67. Use the graph of f to graph $g(x) = -2 - \frac{1}{2}f(x + 2)$.

68. The graph of g in the figure shown was obtained from the graph of f through a sequence of transformations. Find an equation for g.

In Problems 69–71, use algebraic methods to determine whether each function is even, odd, or neither. State each function's symmetry. Verify your results by using a graphing utility to graph each function.

69. $f(x) = x^3 - 5x$

70. $f(x) = x^4 - 2x^2 + 1$

71. $f(x) = 2x\sqrt{1 - x^2}$

72. If $f(x) = x^2 - 7x + 8$ and $g(x) = 5 - 2x$, find each of the following functions.

a. $f + g$ **b.** $f - g$
c. fg **d.** $\frac{f}{g}$
e. $f \circ g$ **f.** $g \circ f$

73. Let $f(x) = \sqrt{x + 4}$ and $g(x) = \sqrt{x - 1}$. Find each function and state its domain.

a. $f + g$ **b.** $f - g$

c. fg **d.** $\frac{f}{g}$

Verify the domains by graphing $f + g, f - g, fg$, and $\frac{f}{g}$ with a graphing utility.

74. If $f(x) = \sqrt{x}$ and $g(x) = 2x + 1$, find:

    a. $f \circ g$ **b.** $g \circ f$

    c. $(f \circ g)(4)$ **d.** $(g \circ f)(25)$

    e. State the domain for each composite function in parts (a) and (b).

75. If $f(x) = x^2 - 25$ and $g(x) = \sqrt{25 - x^2}$, find $(f \circ g)(x)$ and the domain of $f \circ g$. Check your result with a graphing utility.

76. The function $L(p) = 0.7\sqrt{p^2 + 3}$ models the level L of carbon monoxide in the air (in ppm) as a function of population (p, in hundred-thousands). The population p of a hypothetical city is described by $p(t) = 1 + 0.01t^3$, where t is time from 1990 and p is population in hundred-thousands.

    a. Find $L \circ p$ and describe in practical terms what the function models.

    b. Find $(L \circ p)(10)$. What information is conveyed by 10 and the resulting function value?

In Problems 77–79, find two functions f and g so that $h(x) = (f \circ g)(x)$. (More than one correct answer is possible for each problem.)

77. $h(x) = (2x + 7)^4$ **78.** $h(x) = \sqrt{3x^2 - 7}$ **79.** $h(x) = 3(x - 4)^2 + 5(x - 4)$

In Problems 80–81, find $f^3(x)$, the third iterate of the given function f.

80. $f(x) = 3x - 2$
81. $f(x) = x^2 - 1$
82. Suppose that deforestation of a rain forest occurs at a rate of 5% per year. If x represents the area of the rain

forest at the start of 1997, then $f(x) = 0.95x$ models the area of the rain forest at the start of 1998. Find $f^3(x)$ and interpret the third iterate in practical terms.

Problems 83–86 show graphs of relations. Which of these relations are functions? Which of these functions are one-to-one?

83.

84.

85.

86.

In Problems 87–92, **a.** *find $f^{-1}(x)$;* **b.** *verify algebraically that $f(f^{-1}(x)) = x$ and $f^{-1}(f(x)) = x$;* **c.** *use a graphing utility to verify part (b).*

87. $f(x) = \frac{1}{2}x - 4$ **88.** $f(x) = 4x - 3$

89. $f(x) = \sqrt{x + 2}$ **90.** $f(x) = 8x^3 + 1$

91. $f(x) = x^2 - 4, x \geq 0$ **92.** $f(x) = \sqrt[3]{2x - 1}$

93. If \$10,000 is invested in an account paying 12% yearly with compounding N times a year, then the balance in the account at the end of the year is a function of N, the number of compounding periods. The graph of this function f is shown in the figure. The figure indicates that the graph approaches but never reaches the constant function $g(x) = 11,274.97$.

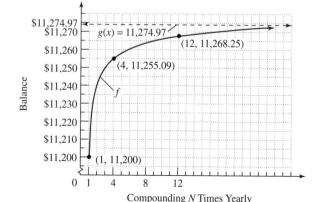

Compounding N Times Yearly

a. Is f a one-to-one function? Explain.

b. What is the practical meaning of $f^{-1}(11, 250)$?

c. An investor stated that by investing $10,000 with more and more compounding periods, there would

be no limit to the balance in the account at the end of the year. Critique this statement using the graph of f. In your critique, describe the practical meaning of the range of f.

For Problems 94–96:

a. *Use a graphing utility to graph f.*

b. *Use the graph of f to restrict its domain to an interval where f is increasing.*

c. *Use algebraic methods to find f^{-1} on the restricted domain.*

d. *Use the graphing utility to graph f^{-1} in the same viewing rectangle as f.*

94. $f(x) = (x - 2)^2$

95. $f(x) = |x + 3|$

96. $f(x) = \sqrt{x^2 - 9}$

In Problems 97–100, use the graph of f to sketch the graph of each function.

97. $f^{-1}(x)$

98. $f^{-1}(x + 1)$

99. $f^{-1}(x) + 1$

100. $-f^{-1}(x)$

101. The snow cricket chirps in such a way that the chirp rate is a linear function of temperature. At a temperature of 50°F, the cricket chirps 40 times per minute and at a temperature of 70°F, the cricket chirps 120 times per minute.

a. Model this situation with a linear function expressing chirp rate (C) as a function of Fahrenheit temperature (T) $(C = f(T))$.

b. Find $f(90)$ and describe what this means in practical terms.

c. The domain of the model consists of all temperatures for which the predicted chirp rate is positive, up to 136°F. What is the domain of f?

d. What is the range of f?

e. Find a formula expressing temperature as a function of chirp rate.

102. Complete the table so that:

a. f has origin symmetry.   **b.** g has y-axis symmetry.

c. $h = f \circ g$

x	$f(x)$	$g(x)$	$h(x)$
-3	0	0	
-2	5	5	
-1	5	5	
0	0	0	
1			
2			
3			

C H A P T E R 2 T E S T

1. The function $f(x) = 0.002x^2 + 0.41x + 7.34$ models the percent of the population in the United States $(f(x))$ that graduated from college x years after 1960. Find and interpret $f(10)$.

2. If $f(x) = 7x^2 - 9x + 13$, find $\dfrac{f(a + h) - f(a)}{h}$.

3. If $f(x) = \sqrt{12 - 3x}$, find the domain of f.

Use the conditions given in Problems 4–5 to write the equation of each line in point-slope form, slope-intercept form, and general form.

4. Passing through $(2, 1)$ and $(-1, -8)$

5. Passing through $(-4, 6)$ and perpendicular to the line whose equation is $y = -\frac{1}{4}x + 5$

6. The data points $(4, 401.1)$ and $(9, 475.6)$, shown and described in the table, fall on a straight line.

x (Number of Years after 1985)	y (Average Weekly Earnings of U.S. Workers)
4	401.1
9	475.6

a. Write the equation of the line on which these measurements fall in point-slope form and slope-intercept form.

b. Extrapolate from the data to predict the average weekly earnings for U.S. workers for the year 2005.

Graph each function in Problems 7–8

7. $f(x) = \dfrac{x^2 - 36}{x - 6}$

8. $f(x) = \begin{cases} \sqrt{x - 3} & \text{if } x \geq 3 \\ 3 - x & \text{if } x < 3 \end{cases}$

9. Use the graph of the function f shown below to answer the following questions.

a. What is $f(4) - f(-3)$?

b. On what interval or intervals is f increasing?

c. On what interval or intervals is f decreasing?

d. What is the relative maximum value of the function and where does this occur?

e. What is the relative minimum value of the function and where does this occur?

10. From each of the four corners of a square piece of cardboard 12 inches on a side, a square piece x inches on a side is cut out and the flaps are turned up to form an open-top box. The volume of the box, $f(x)$ in cubic inches, is a function of the size of the square cut from each corner, given by $f(x) = 4x^3 - 48x^2 + 144x$. Use the graph of f in the figure shown to find the maximum possible volume of the box.

Length of Square Cut Out

11. Sketch the graph of a function f using the following properties: f is decreasing on $(-\infty, -2)$, increasing on $(-2, \infty)$, has a y-intercept of 3, and a minimum y-value of -1. (More than one correct graph is possible.)

12. The graph of g shown in the figure below is a transformation of the graph of $f(x) = x^3$. Write an equation for g.

13. The figure shows how the graph of $h(x) = -2(x - 3)^2$ is obtained from the graph of $f(x) = x^2$. Describe this process, using the graph of g in your description.

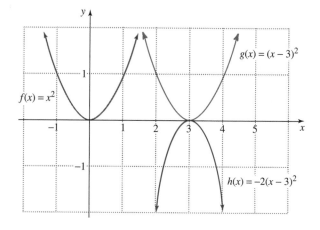

14. Determine whether $f(x) = x^4 - x^2$ even or odd. Then use your answer to explain why the graph in the figure shown cannot be the graph of f.

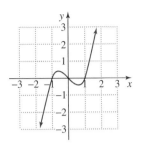

If $f(x) = x^2 + 3x - 4$ and $g(x) = 5x - 2$, find each function or function value in Problems 15–19.

15. $f - g$

16. $f \circ g$

17. $g \circ f$

18. $f(g(2))$

19. $g(f(2))$

20. If $f(x) = \sqrt{x - 2}$, find $f^{-1}(x)$. Then verify either algebraically or graphically that the two functions are inverses.

21. A function f defines a man's recommended weight (in pounds) as a function of his height (in inches). The graph of f is shown in the figure.

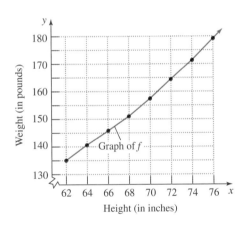

Height (in inches)

a. Can we also say that a man's height is a function of his recommended weight? Explain your answer using the graph of f and the horizontal line test.

b. Describe in practical terms the meaning of $f^{-1}(170)$.

22. Use a graphing utility to graph $f(x) = x^4 - 6x^3 + 8x^2$ in a $[-3, 5]$ by $[-10, 6]$ viewing rectangle. Now use the graph to answer the following.

a. Is f one-to-one? Explain.

b. Is f even, odd, or neither? Explain.

c. Find the relative maximum and minimum values of f and the values of x at which they occur.

d. What is the range of f?

e. Find the interval or intervals on which f is increasing.

f. Find the interval or intervals on which f is decreasing.

CUMULATIVE REVIEW PROBLEMS (CHAPTERS P–2)

Simplify Problems 1–2.

1. $\left(\dfrac{4x^2 y}{2x^5 y^{-3}} \right)^{-3}$

2. $-6\sqrt{32y} + 10\sqrt{2y}$

3. Factor: $x^2 - 2x + 1 - y^2$.

In Problems 4–5, perform the operations and simplify.

4. $\dfrac{x^2 - 2x}{x^2 - 9} \div \dfrac{x^4 - 4x^3 + 4x^2}{x^2 + 3x}$

5. $\dfrac{x - 1}{\sqrt{x + 1} - \sqrt{2}}$

Solve Problems 6–10.

6. $(12x - 5)(x - 1) = 10$

7. $\dfrac{2x}{x - 1} - \dfrac{4}{x^2 - x} = \dfrac{x - 1}{x}$

8. $\sqrt{x + 12} - \sqrt{x} = 2$

9. $x^{2/3} - x^{1/3} - 6 = 0$

10. $-5 < 8 - 2(x + 3) \leqslant 13$

11. Write the point-slope form, the slope-intercept form, and the general form of the line passing through $(-2, 5)$ and perpendicular to the line whose equation is $x - 2y - 3 = 0$.

12. Graph $f(x) = \sqrt{x}$ and then use horizontal and vertical shifts to graph $g(x) = \sqrt{x - 3} + 4$ on the same rectangular coordinate system.

13. Find the inverse function of $f(x) = \dfrac{x^5 - 3}{2}$.

14. The graph of $f(x) = x^2 - 2x - 3$ is shown in the figure. Describe one way the domain of f can be restricted so that the resulting function is one-to-one.

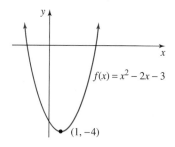

$f(x) = x^2 - 2x - 3$

$(1, -4)$

15. If $f(x) = mx + b$, find $\dfrac{f(a + h) - f(a)}{h}$ and describe what this represents in terms of the given function f.

16. Solve for r: $G = \dfrac{a}{1 - r}$.

17. The number of diagonals D of a polygon of n sides is given by

$$D = \dfrac{n^2 - 3n}{2}.$$

How many sides does a polygon with 90 diagonals have?

18. In 1970, the U.S. gross federal debt was approximately $380 billion, increasing at about $43 billion each year. In what year was the gross federal debt $1369 billion?

19. The length of a rectangular garden is 2 feet more than twice its width. If 22 feet of planking is needed to enclose the garden, what are its dimensions?

20. A bridge toll currently charges $2.50 per car. The average number of cars crossing per day is 200. However, this number is expected to decrease by one car per day for every 5¢ increase over $2.50. If the bridge needs to bring in an income of $630 per day, what should the toll be?

3

Modeling with Polynomial and Rational Functions

Henry Small "Friends in the Florida Keys," acrylic on wood, 3 ft. × 4 ft., 1985.

In this century, human impacts on populations and ecosystems have caused hundreds of species of plants and animals to become extinct each year. If present trends continue, we may destroy thousands of species in the next few decades.

Large-scale public projects aimed at reversing this trend and reducing environmental pollution are subject to cost-benefit analyses. The costs of a project must be compared with the benefits that will be achieved. One type of function we will be studying in this chapter is used to model the costs of a given project, illustrating how algebra contributes to decision making on environmental policies.

S E C T I O N   3 . 1

Solutions
Manual

Tutorial

Video
6

Quadratic Functions

Objectives

1 Graph quadratic functions.
2 Solve optimization problems using given models.
3 Solve optimization problems by modeling verbal conditions.

In the prerequisites chapter, we encountered the graph of $y = ax^2 + bx + c$ and called it a *parabola*. We have seen that the real solutions of $ax^2 + bx + c = 0$ can be found by determining where the parabola crosses the x-axis. The quadratic models in Chapter 1 ($y = ax^2 + bx + c$) were viewed as quadratic functions ($f(x) = ax^2 + bx + c$) in Chapter 2. In this section, we continue our ongoing study of quadratic functions.

1 Graph quadratic functions.

Quadratic Functions as Second-Degree Polynomial Functions

An important class of functions in algebra is defined using polynomials; such functions are called *polynomial functions*.

> ### Definition of a polynomial function
>
> Let n be a nonnegative integer and let $a_n, a_{n-1}, \ldots, a_2, a_1, a_0$, be real numbers with $a_n \neq 0$. The function defined by
>
> $$f(x) = a_n x^n + a_{n-1} x^{n-1} + \cdots + a_2 x^2 + a_1 x + a_0$$
>
> is called a *polynomial function of x of degree n*. The number a_n, the coefficient of the highest power, is called the *leading coefficient*. A polynomial written as shown is said to be in *general form*.

A constant function $f(x) = a$, where $a \neq 0$, is a polynomial function of degree 0. A linear function $f(x) = ax + b$, where $a \neq 0$, is a polynomial function of degree 1. Our focus in this section is on second-degree polynomial functions, or *quadratic functions*.

> ### Definition of a quadratic function
>
> A *quadratic function* is any function of the form
>
> $$f(x) = ax^2 + bx + c$$
>
> where a, b, and c are real numbers and $a \neq 0$. The graph of a quadratic function is called a *parabola*.

Characteristics of Parabolas

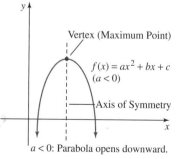

Figure 3.1

Characteristics of parabolas

As shown in Figure 3.1, parabolas are symmetric to a line called the *axis of symmetry*. The turning point on the parabola, the point where the axis of symmetry intersects the parabola, is called the *vertex*. If $a > 0$, the graph of $f(x) = ax^2 + bx + c$ opens upward and the vertex is the *minimum point* on the graph. If $a < 0$, then the parabola opens downward and the vertex is the *maximum point* on the graph.

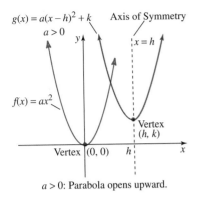

$g(x) = a(x - h)^2 + k$ Axis of Symmetry

$a > 0$

$x = h$

$f(x) = ax^2$

Vertex (h, k)

Vertex $(0, 0)$ h

$a > 0$: Parabola opens upward.

Axis of Symmetry

$x = h$

$g(x) = a(x - h)^2 + k$

$a < 0$

Vertex (h, k)

Vertex $(0, 0)$

h

$f(x) = ax^2$

$a < 0$: Parabola opens downward.

Figure 3.2

Transformations of $f(x) = ax^2$

Using Transformations to Graph Parabolas

In Section 2.5, we applied a series of transformations to the graph of the quadratic function $f(x) = x^2$. Figure 3.2 compares the graphs of $f(x) = ax^2$ and $g(x) = a(x - h)^2 + k$. Observe that h determines the horizontal shift and k determines the vertical shift of the graph of $f(x) = ax^2$. Consequently, the vertex $(0, 0)$ on the graph of $f(x) = ax^2$ moves to the point (h, k) on the graph of $g(x) = a(x - h)^2 + k$. The axis of symmetry is the vertical line whose equation is $x = h$.

The form of the expression for g is convenient since it immediately identifies the vertex of the parabola as (h, k). This is the *standard form* of a quadratic function.

The standard form of a quadratic function

The quadratic function

$$f(x) = a(x - h)^2 + k, \qquad a \neq 0$$

is in *standard form*. The graph of f is a parabola whose vertex is the point (h, k). The parabola is symmetric to the line $x = h$. If $a > 0$, the parabola opens upward; if $a < 0$, the parabola opens downward.

EXAMPLE 1   **Graphing a Parabola**

Use the vertex and intercepts to sketch the graph of:

a. $f(x) = -2(x - 3)^2 + 2$ **b.** $g(x) = (x + 3)^2 + 1$

Solution

a. The equation for f is expressed in standard form.

$f(x) = -2(x - 3)^2 + 2$ The parabola has a vertex at $(h, k) = (3, 2)$.

$f(x) = a(x - h)^2 + k$ Because $a = -2$, $a < 0$ and the parabola opens downward.

Let's find the x-intercepts by replacing $f(x)$ in the given equation by 0.

$0 = -2(x - 3)^2 + 2$ Find x-intercepts, letting $f(x)$ (or y) equal 0.

$2(x - 3)^2 = 2$ Solve for x. Add $2(x - 3)^2$ to both sides of the equation.

$(x - 3)^2 = 1$ Divide both sides by 2.

$(x - 3) = \pm 1$ Apply the square root principle. If $(x - c)^2 = d$, then $x - c = \pm\sqrt{d}$.

$x = 2$ or $x = 4$ The x-intercepts are 2 and 4.

Finally, we find the y-intercept by replacing x in the given equation with 0.

$f(0) = -2(0 - 3)^2 + 2$ $f(0)$ is the value that gives the y-intercept.

$f(0) = -16$ The y-intercept is -16.

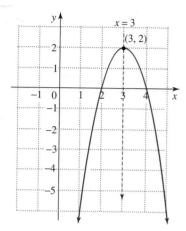

Figure 3.3

The graph of $f(x) = -2(x-3)^2 + 2$

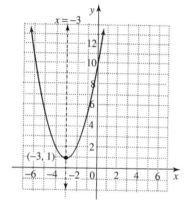

Figure 3.4

The graph of $g(x) = (x+3)^2 + 1$

iscover for yourself

Use a graphing utility to verify the hand-drawn graphs in Figures 3.3 and 3.4. Trace along each graph and verify the vertex.

With a vertex at $(3, 2)$, x-intercepts at 2 and 4, and a y-intercept at -16, the graph of f is shown in Figure 3.3. (Because of the scale chosen on the axes, the y-intercept is not shown.) The axis of symmetry is the vertical line whose equation is $x = 3$.

b. The equation for g is also expressed in standard form.

$$g(x) = (x+3)^2 + 1$$

$$g(x) = 1[x - (-3)]^2 + 1 \qquad \text{The parabola has a vertex at } (h, k) = (-3, 1).$$
$$\qquad\qquad\qquad\qquad\qquad\qquad \text{Because } a = 1, a > 0 \text{ and the parabola opens upward.}$$
$$g(x) = a(x-h)^2 + k$$

With a vertex at $(-3, 1)$ and opening upward, the parabola appears to have no x-intercepts (see Figure 3.4). We can verify this observation algebraically.

$$0 = (x+3)^2 + 1 \qquad \text{Find possible } x\text{-intercepts letting } g(x) \text{ (or } y\text{) equal 0.}$$

$$-1 = (x+3)^2 \qquad \text{Solve for } x. \text{ Subtract 1 from both sides.}$$

$$x + 3 = \pm\sqrt{-1} \qquad \text{Apply the square root principle.}$$

$$x + 3 = \pm i \qquad \text{Recall that } \sqrt{-1} = i, \text{ an imaginary number.}$$

$$x = -3 \pm i \qquad \text{The equation has no real solution, so there are no } x\text{-intercepts.}$$

The y-intercept is found by replacing x in the given equation with 0.

$$g(0) = (0+3)^2 + 1 \qquad \text{The } y\text{-intercept is } g(0).$$

$$g(0) = 10 \qquad \text{The } y\text{-intercept is 10.}$$

With a vertex at $(-3, 1)$, no x-intercepts, and a y-intercept at 10, the graph of g is shown in Figure 3.4. The axis of symmetry is the vertical line whose equation is $x = -3$. ∎

Quadratic Functions in the Form $f(x) = ax^2 + bx + c$

Quadratic functions are frequently expressed in the form

$$f(x) = ax^2 + bx + c.$$

We can complete the square to express the function's equation in standard form. Let's see how this is done.

EXAMPLE 2 Writing a Quadratic Function in Standard Form

Rewrite in standard form and sketch the graph: $f(x) = -2x^2 + 4x - 5$

Solution

We begin by completing the square. The first step is to factor out any coefficient of x^2 from the x-terms that differs from 1.

$$f(x) = -2x^2 + 4x - 5 \qquad \text{This is the given function.}$$

$$= -2(x^2 - 2x) - 5 \qquad \text{Factor } -2 \text{ out of the } x\text{-terms.}$$

$$= -2(x^2 - 2x + 1 - 1) - 5$$

$$\tfrac{1}{2}(-2) = -1$$
and
$$(-1)^2 = 1$$

Complete the square for $x^2 - 2x$ by taking half the x-coefficient and squaring. The resulting number (1) is added and subtracted within the parentheses.

$$= -2(x^2 - 2x + 1) + (-2)(-1) - 5$$

Regroup terms by removing the -1 from the parentheses.

$$= -2(x - 1)^2 - 3$$

Factor $x^2 - 2x + 1$ using $A^2 - 2AB + B^2 = (A - B)^2$. Simplify numerical terms.

The function is now expressed in standard form.

$$f(x) = -2(x - 1)^2 - 3$$
$$f(x) = a(x - h)^2 + k$$

The parabola has a vertex at $(h, k) = (1, -3)$ and opens downward.

The parabola has no x-intercepts. By letting $x = 0$ in either the given form of the function or the standard form, we find that the y-intercept is -5. The graph of f is shown in Figure 3.5.   ∎

Because quadratic functions are frequently given in the form $f(x) = ax^2 + bx + c$, we would like to immediately recognize the parabola's vertex when its equation is in this form. To do this, let's complete the square on the general quadratic function $f(x) = ax^2 + bx + c$ to obtain its standard form.

$$f(x) = ax^2 + bx + c$$

This is the given function.

$$= a\left(x^2 + \frac{b}{a}x\right) + c$$

Factor a out of the x-terms.

$$= a\left(x^2 + \frac{b}{a}x + \frac{b^2}{4a^2} - \frac{b^2}{4a^2}\right) + c$$

$$\frac{1}{2}\left(\frac{b}{a}\right) = \frac{b}{2a}$$
and
$$\left(\frac{b}{2a}\right)^2 = \frac{b^2}{4a^2}$$

Complete the square for $x^2 + \frac{b}{a}x$ by taking half the x-coefficient and squaring. The resulting number, $\frac{b^2}{4a^2}$, is added and subtracted within the parentheses.

$$= a\left(x^2 + \frac{b}{a}x + \frac{b^2}{4a^2}\right) + a\left(-\frac{b^2}{4a^2}\right) + c$$

Regroup terms by removing $\frac{-b^2}{4a^2}$ from the parentheses.

$$= a\left(x + \frac{b}{2a}\right)^2 + \left(c - \frac{b^2}{4a}\right)$$

Factor $x^2 + \frac{b}{a}x + \frac{b^2}{4a^2}$

$$= x^2 + 2 \cdot \frac{b}{2a}x + \left(\frac{b}{2a}\right)^2 \text{ using}$$
$$A^2 + 2AB + B^2 = (A + B)^2.$$
Simplify constant terms.

By writing $f(x) = ax^2 + bx + c$ in standard form,

$$f(x) = a\left(x + \frac{b}{2a}\right)^2 + \left(c - \frac{b^2}{4a}\right)$$

Figure 3.5

The graph of $f(x) = -2x^2 + 4x - 5$

we see that $h = -\dfrac{b}{2a}$ and $k = c - \dfrac{b^2}{4a}$. The important part of this result is that

the x-coordinate of the vertex is $-\dfrac{b}{2a}$. The y-coordinate can be found by eval-

uating the function at $-\dfrac{b}{2a}$.

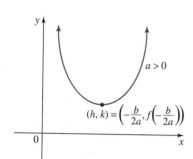

> **The vertex of a parabola (see Figure 3.6)**
>
> 1. Standard form: $f(x) = a(x - h)^2 + k$
>   *Vertex of the parabola:* (h, k)
>   If $a > 0$, then the minimum value of f occurs at $x = h$ and this value
>   is $f(h) = k$.
>   If $a < 0$, then the maximum value of f occurs at $x = h$ and this value
>   is $f(h) = k$.
> 2. The form $f(x) = ax^2 + bx + c$
>   *Vertex of the parabola:* $\left(-\dfrac{b}{2a}, f\left(-\dfrac{b}{2a} \right) \right)$
>
>   If $a > 0$, then the minimum value of f occurs at $x = -\dfrac{b}{2a}$ and this
>   value is $f\left(-\dfrac{b}{2a} \right)$.
>
>   If $a < 0$, then the maximum value of f occurs at $x = -\dfrac{b}{2a}$ and this
>   value is $f\left(-\dfrac{b}{2a} \right)$.

Figure 3.6

Graphs of $f(x) = a(x - h)^2 + k$
or $f(x) = ax^2 + bx + c$

EXAMPLE 3   Graphing a Parabola

Use the vertex and intercepts to sketch the graph of: $f(x) = -2x^2 - x + 5$

Solution

We begin with the vertex. Its x-coordinate is $-\dfrac{b}{2a}$.

$$x = -\frac{b}{2a}$$

$$= \frac{-(-1)}{2(-2)} \qquad \text{We are given } f(x) = -2x^2 - x + 5, \text{ so } a = -2 \text{ and } b = -1.$$

$$= -\frac{1}{4} \qquad \text{The } x\text{-coordinate of the vertex is } -\tfrac{1}{4}.$$

The y-coordinate of the vertex is

$$f\left(-\frac{1}{4} \right) = -2\left(-\frac{1}{4} \right)^2 - \left(-\frac{1}{4} \right) + 5 \qquad \text{Substitute } -\tfrac{1}{4} \text{ for } x \text{ in } -2x^2 - x + 5.$$

$$= 5.125$$

The parabola has a vertex at $(-\tfrac{1}{4}, 5.125)$. Because $a = -2$, the parabola opens downward. With a vertex in quadrant II, the parabola will have x-intercepts. We can find them by setting $f(x) = 0$.

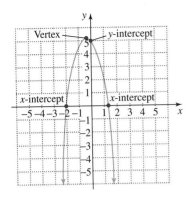

Figure 3.7

The graph of $f(x) = -2x^2 - x + 5$

2 Solve optimization problems using given models.

$$0 = -2x^2 - x + 5 \qquad \text{Set } f(x) \text{ (or } y\text{) equal to 0.}$$

$$x = \frac{-b \pm \sqrt{b^2 - 4ac}}{2a} = \frac{-(-1) \pm \sqrt{(-1)^2 - 4(-2)(5)}}{2(-2)} = \frac{1 \pm \sqrt{41}}{-4}$$

Use the quadratic formula with $a = -2$, $b = -1$, and $c = 5$.

With $\sqrt{41} \approx 6.4$, the x-intercepts are approximately -1.9 and 1.4. We find the y-intercept by setting $x = 0$.

$$f(0) = -2 \cdot 0^2 - 0 + 5 \qquad \text{Use the given function } f(x) = -2x^2 - x + 5 \text{ and let } x = 0.$$

$$f(0) = 5 \qquad \text{The } y\text{-intercept is 5.}$$

Summary:
Vertex: $\left(-\frac{1}{4}, 5.125\right)$
x-intercepts: approximately -1.9 and 1.4
y-intercept: 5

The parabola is shown in Figure 3.7.   ■

Optimization: Using Given Mathematical Models

In Section 2.3, we used a graphing utility to find optimum (maximum and minimum) values of a function. In the case of a quadratic function

$$f(x) = ax^2 + bx + c$$

we know that the lowest point on the parabola is the vertex when it opens upward (if $a > 0$) and the highest point on the parabola is the vertex when it opens downward (if $a < 0$) Because the x-coordinate of the vertex is $-\dfrac{b}{2a}$, in either case we can find the minimum or maximum value of f by evaluating the quadratic function at $x = -\dfrac{b}{2a}$.

Minimum and maximum: quadratic functions

Consider $f(x) = ax^2 + bx + c$.

1. If $a > 0$, then f has a minimum that occurs at $x = -\dfrac{b}{2a}$.

2. If $a < 0$, then f has a maximum that occurs at $x = -\dfrac{b}{2a}$.

EXAMPLE 4   **An Application: Alcohol Consumption**

Based on data provided by the U.S. Department of Agriculture, the model

$$f(x) = -0.053x^2 + 1.17x + 35.6$$

describes the average number of gallons of alcohol consumed by each adult in the United States as a function of time, where x represents the number of years after 1970. In what year was alcohol consumption at a maximum? What was the average consumption for that year?

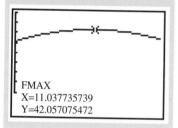
3 Solve optimization problems by modeling verbal conditions.

Solution

For this quadratic function we have

$$f(x) = -0.053x^2 + 1.17x + 35.6$$
$$f(x) = \quad ax^2 + \quad bx + \quad c$$

which means that $a = -0.053$ and $b = 1.17$. With $a < 0$, the function has a maximum when $x = -\dfrac{b}{2a}$.

$$x = -\frac{b}{2a} = -\frac{1.17}{2(-0.053)} \approx 11.04$$

This means that alcohol consumption was at a maximum approximately 11 years after 1970, or in 1981. The average consumption for that year was

$$f(11) = -0.053(11)^2 + 1.17(11) + 35.6 \approx 42.06$$

or approximately 42 gallons of alcohol by each adult. ∎

Optimization: Creating Mathematical Models

Verbal problems involving optimization require us to model functions based on given or implied conditions. If the resulting function is quadratic, we can then use the x-coordinate of the vertex to determine the maximum or minimum value of the function. Here's the general strategy that we will follow in the remainder of our examples.

> **Strategy for solving optimization problems involving quadratic functions**
>
> 1. Read the problem carefully and decide which quantity is to be maximized or minimized.
> 2. Use the conditions of the problem to express the quantity as a function in one variable.
> 3. Rewrite the function in the form $f(x) = ax^2 + bx + c$.
> 4. If $a > 0$, f has a minimum at $x = -\dfrac{b}{2a}$. If $a < 0$, f has a maximum at $x = -\dfrac{b}{2a}$.
> 5. Answer the question posed in the problem.

EXAMPLE 5   **Solving a Number Problem**

Among all pairs of numbers whose sum is 40, find a pair whose product is as large as possible. What is the maximum product?

Solution

Step 1. Decide what must be maximized or minimized. We must maximize the product of two numbers. Calling the numbers x and y, and calling the product P, we must maximize

$$P = xy.$$

Step 2. Express this quantity as a function in one variable.
Right now, P is expressed in terms of two variables, x and y. However, since the sum of the numbers is 40, we can write

$$x + y = 40.$$

We can solve this equation for y in a terms of x (or vice versa), substitute the result into $P = xy$, and obtain P as a function of one variable. Solving for y, we get

$$y = 40 - x.$$

Now we substitute $40 - x$ for y in $P = xy$.

$$P = xy = x(40 - x).$$

Since P is now a function of x, we can write

$$P(x) = x(40 - x).$$

Step 3. Write the function in the form $f(x) = ax^2 + bx + c$. We apply the distributive property to obtain

$$P(x) = x(40 - x) = 40x - x^2$$

which can be expressed as

$$P(x) = -x^2 + 40x.$$

Step 4. If $a < 0$, the function has a maximum at $x = -\dfrac{b}{2a}$.

Since $P(x) = -x^2 + 40x$, we see that $a = -1$ and $b = 40$. The function P has a maximum at $x = -\dfrac{b}{2a}$.

$$x = -\frac{b}{2a}$$ Remember that x represents one of the numbers.

$$= -\frac{40}{2(-1)}$$ Since $P(x) = -x^2 + 40x$, substitute -1 for a and 40 for b.

$$= 20$$ Simplify.

Step 5. Answer the question posed in the problem. The numbers are $x = 20$ and $y = 40 - x = 40 - 20 = 20$. The number pair whose sum is 40 and whose product is as large as possible is 20, 20. The maximum product is $20(20)$, or 400. ∎

EXAMPLE 6   **Maximizing Income**

A small cruising ship that can hold up to 50 people provides two-day excursions to groups of 34 or more. If the group contains 34 people, each person pays $60. The cost per person is reduced by $1 for each person in excess of 34. Find the size of the group that will maximize income for the owners of the ship and determine this maximum income.

Solution

Step 1. Decide what must be maximized or minimized. We must maximize income. What we do not know is how many people in excess of 34 we should have on board to generate maximum income.

Step 2. Express this quantity as a function in one variable.

Let x = the number of people in the group in excess of 34. We write our function based on the verbal model that income equals the number of people in the group times the cost per person.

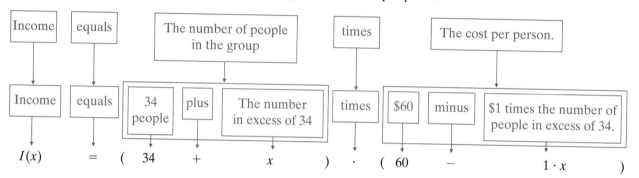

The income function that we must maximize is

$$I(x) = (34 + x)(60 - x).$$

Step 3. Write the function in the form $f(x) = ax^2 + bx + c$.

$I(x) = (34 + x)(60 - x)$ This is the function from step 2.

$\quad = 2040 + 26x - x^2$ Multiply using the FOIL method.

$\quad = -x^2 + 26x + 2040$ Write the function's equation in descending powers of x.

Step 4. Since $a < 0$, the function has a maximum at $x = -\dfrac{b}{2a}$. Using the formula for $I(x)$, we see that $a = -1$ and $b = 26$.

$$x = -\frac{b}{2a} = -\frac{26}{2(-1)} = 13$$ Remember that x represents the number of people in excess of 34.

Step 5. Answer the problem's question. The size of the group that will maximize income for the owners of the ship is $34 + x = 34 + 13$, or 47 people. The maximum income is $I(13)$.

$$I(13) = (34 + 13)(60 - 13) = 2209$$ Substitute 13 for x in $I(x) = (34 + x)(60 - x)$.

The maximum income is $2209.   ∎

Study tip

In Example 6, the graph of the income function should actually be a collection of discrete points corresponding to the integer values of x, as shown in Figure 3.8. Because

Income

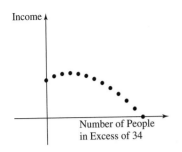

Number of People in Excess of 34

Figure 3.8

Income Function as a collection of points

Figure 3.9

Using 1000 feet of fencing to construct six corrals

x represents the number of people in excess of 34, we cannot permit values of x such as $x = 12.57$. The function $I(x) = -x^2 + 26x + 2040$ is a continuous model whose graph connects the points in Figure 3.8. In Example 6, the solution to the continuous function also gave the solution for the discrete function.

In our next problem, although the function we need to maximize is continuous, the challenge will be to represent this function in one variable.

EXAMPLE 7 **Maximizing Area**

A rancher has 1000 feet of fencing to construct six corrals, as shown in Figure 3.9. Find the dimensions that maximize the enclosed area. What is the maximum area?

Solution

Step 1. Decide what must be maximized or minimized. We must maximize area. What we do not know are the rectangle's dimensions, x and y.

Step 2. Express this quantity as a function in one variable. Since we must maximize area, we have

$$A = xy.$$

Once again, A is represented in terms of two variables. However, we are given that the rancher has 1000 feet of fencing. Referring to Figure 3.9, this means that

$$3x + 4y = 1000 \qquad \text{Fencing is placed along three lengths, each of dimension } x, \text{ and four widths, each of dimension } y.$$

$$y = \frac{1000 - 3x}{4} \qquad \text{Solve for } y.$$

$$A = xy \qquad \text{This is our expression for the area.}$$

$$A(x) = x\left(\frac{1000 - 3x}{4}\right) \qquad \text{Substitute } \frac{1000 - 3x}{4} \text{ for } y. \text{ This is the function implied by the problem's conditions.}$$

Step 3. Write the function in the form $f(x) = ax^2 + bx + c$. We apply the distributive property.

$$A(x) = x\left(\frac{1000 - 3x}{4}\right) = \frac{1000x - 3x^2}{4} = -\frac{3}{4}x^2 + 250x$$

Step 4. Since $a < 0$ the function has a maximum at $x = -\dfrac{b}{2a}$. With $A(x) = -\dfrac{3}{4}x^2 + 250x$, we see that $a = -\dfrac{3}{4}$ and $b = 250$.

$$x = -\frac{b}{2a} \qquad \text{Remember that } x \text{ represents the length of the structure.}$$

ENRICHMENT ESSAY

The Road to Nowhere

The polynomial function $M(t) = 0.0075t^2 - 0.2676t + 14.8$ models fuel efficiency of passenger cars (M, measured in miles per gallon) t years after 1940. The vertex of the graph is approximately (18, 12.4), indicating that fuel efficiency was poorest in 1958 (1940 + 18), a dismal 12.4 miles per gallon. Huge cars with hanging dice and big fins dominated the roadways in the late 1950s.

By 1989, the miles-per-gallon average for American cars had increased to 20.5. However, with increasingly efficient automobile engines, Americans collectively logged more highway miles in the 1990s (62% more miles in 1992 than in 1978) and purchased 75% more vehicles. In spite of appeals to save gasoline, the falling cost of driving a mile has encouraged more driving. The plan for increased gas savings due to the increased fuel efficiency predicted by the quadratic model backfired; increased consumption was instead the result.

Alexis Smith "Pair O'Dice" 1990, mixed media collage, 85 1/2 × 67 × 3 in. Photo: Douglas M. Parker Studio, Los Angeles. Courtesy of Margo Leavin Gallery, Los Angeles.

Using technology

The graph of the area function

$$A(x) = -0.75x^2 + 250x$$

was obtained with a graphing utility using

[0, 250] × [0, 22,000]

Xscl = 25, Yscl = 1200

Using the trace or maximum function feature, the graph verifies a maximum area of $20,833\frac{1}{3}$ square feet when one dimension is $166\frac{2}{3}$ feet.

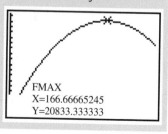

FMAX
X=166.66665245
Y=20833.333333

$$= -\frac{250}{2\left(-\dfrac{3}{4}\right)}$$ Since $A(x) = -\frac{3}{4}x^2 + 250x$, $a = -\frac{3}{4}$ and $b = 250$.

$$= 166\frac{2}{3}$$ This is the length of the divided structure that maximizes its area.

Step 5. Answer the problem's question. To find the width, we substitute $166\frac{2}{3}$ into the equation for y.

$$y = \frac{1000 - 3x}{4} = \frac{1000 - 3(166\frac{2}{3})}{4} = 125$$ y represents the structure's width.

The dimensions that maximize area are $166\frac{2}{3}$ feet by 125 feet. The maximum area is $(166\frac{2}{3})(125)$, or $20,833\frac{1}{3}$ square feet. ∎

Let's conclude with an example that calls for finding a minimum value.

EXAMPLE 8   Minimizing Distance

Find a point on the graph of $y = \sqrt{x - 2} + 1$ that is closest to the point (4, 1).

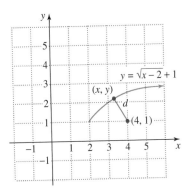

Figure 3.10

Minimizing the distance d from a point on $y = \sqrt{x-2} + 1$ to $(4, 1)$

Solution

Step 1. Decide what must be maximized or minimized.
The situation is illustrated in Figure 3.10. We must find (x, y) on $y = \sqrt{x-2} + 1$ that minimizes the distance d to $(4, 1)$.

Step 2. Express this quantity as a function in one variable.
We'll use the distance formula to write the distance between the point (x, y) on the graph and the point $(4, 1)$. We must find x and y.

$$d = \sqrt{(x-4)^2 + (y-1)^2} \qquad \text{The distance between } (x_1, y_1) \text{ and } (x_2, y_2) \text{ is } \sqrt{(x_2 - x_1)^2 + (y_2 - y_1)^2}.$$

This expresses distance in terms of two variables. To express d in terms of x alone, we use the given equation $y = \sqrt{x-2} + 1$ and substitute $\sqrt{x-2} + 1$ for y in the formula for d.
We obtain

$$
\begin{aligned}
d(x) &= \sqrt{(x-4)^2 + (\sqrt{x-2} + 1 - 1)^2} \\
&= \sqrt{(x-4)^2 + x - 2} \qquad \scriptstyle (\sqrt{x-2} + 1 - 1)^2 = (\sqrt{x-2})^2 \text{ and } (\sqrt{x-2})^2 = x - 2. \\
&= \sqrt{x^2 - 7x + 14} \qquad \scriptstyle \text{Square } x - 4 \text{ and combine like terms.}
\end{aligned}
$$

Step 3. Write the function in the form $f(x) = ax^2 + bx + c$. At this point, the problem is that $d(x)$ is not a quadratic function. However, we can minimize $d(x)$ finding the x-value that minimizes the algebraic expression under the square root, namely, $x^2 - 7x + 14$. Let's call this expression $f(x)$.

$$f(x) = x^2 - 7x + 14 \qquad \scriptstyle \text{Minimize } \sqrt{x^2 - 7x + 14} \text{ by minimizing } x^2 - 7x + 14.$$

Step 4. Since $a > 0$, the function $f(x)$ has a minimum at $x = -\dfrac{b}{2a}$. We are working with $f(x) = x^2 - 7x + 14$, so $a = 1$ and $b = -7$.

$$x = -\frac{b}{2a} = -\frac{(-7)}{2 \cdot 1} = \frac{7}{2}$$

Step 5. Answer the problem's question.
We now have the x-coordinate of the point on $y = \sqrt{x-2} + 1$ closest to $(4, 1)$. We are ready to find the y-coordinate.

$$
\begin{aligned}
y &= \sqrt{x-2} + 1 \qquad \scriptstyle \text{The point is on this function.} \\
&= \sqrt{\frac{7}{2} - 2} + 1 \qquad \scriptstyle \text{Substitute } \frac{7}{2} \text{ for } x. \\
&= \sqrt{\frac{3}{2}} + 1 \\
&= \frac{\sqrt{6}}{2} + \frac{2}{2} \qquad \scriptstyle \frac{\sqrt{3}}{\sqrt{2}} = \frac{\sqrt{3}}{\sqrt{2}} \cdot \frac{\sqrt{2}}{\sqrt{2}} = \frac{\sqrt{6}}{2} \\
&= \frac{2 + \sqrt{6}}{2}
\end{aligned}
$$

The point on the graph of $y = \sqrt{x-2} + 1$ that is closest to $(4, 1)$ is $\left(\dfrac{7}{2}, \dfrac{2 + \sqrt{6}}{2}\right)$. ∎

Discover for yourself

Use a graphing utility to verify the result of Example 8. Is it easier to graph $y = \sqrt{x^2 - 7x + 14}$ or $y = x^2 - 7x + 14$? Which one of these functions will give the minimum distance (a value that we did not compute in the solution process)?

PROBLEM SET 3.1

Practice Problems

In Problems 1–18, use the vertex and intercepts to sketch the graph of each quadratic function by hand. Give the equation for the parabola's axis of symmetry. Then use a graphing utility to verify that your graph is correct.

1. $f(x) = (x - 4)^2 - 1$

2. $f(x) = (x - 1)^2 - 2$

3. $f(x) = (x - 1)^2 - 2$

4. $f(x) = (x - 3)^2 + 2$

5. $y - 1 = (x - 3)^2$

6. $y - 3 = (x - 1)^2$

7. $y = 2(x + 2)^2 - 1$

8. $y = \frac{5}{4} - (x - \frac{1}{2})^2$

9. $f(x) = 4 - (x - 1)^2$

10. $f(x) = 1 - (x - 3)^2$

11. $f(x) = x^2 - 2x - 3$

12. $f(x) = x^2 - 2x - 15$

13. $f(x) = x^2 + 3x - 10$

14. $f(x) = 2x^2 - 7x - 4$

15. $y = 2x - x^2 + 3$

16. $y = 5 - 4x - x^2$

17. $y = 2x - x^2 - 2$

18. $y = 6 - 4x + x^2$

Application Problems

19. The U.S. Center for Disease Control modeled the average annual per capita consumption C of cigarettes by Americans 18 and older as a function of time. The function is $C(t) = -3.1t^2 + 51.4t + 4024.5$, where t represents years after 1960. According to this model, in what year did cigarette consumption per capita reach a maximum?

20. The function $R(x) = -0.0065x^2 + 0.23x + 8.47$ models the American marriage rate R (the number of marriages per 1000 population) x years after 1960. According to this model, in what year was the marriage rate the highest?

Johnson Antonio "Smoking Break" 1986, 28 1/2 × 5 × 6 in. Collection of Chuck and Jan Rosenak. Photo Credit: Lynn Lown.

Solve Problems 21–35, which involve optimization of quadratic functions, without the use of a graphing utility. Then use a graphing utility to verify your result.

21. Among all pairs of numbers whose sum is 16, find a pair whose product is as large as possible. What is the maximum product?

22. Among all pairs of numbers whose sum is 9, find a pair whose product is large as possible. What is the maximum product?

23. Among all rectangles that have a perimeter of 20 yards, find the dimensions of the one with the largest area.

24. Among all rectangles that have a perimeter of 80 feet, find the dimensions of the one with the largest area.

25. A rancher has 1000 feet of fencing to put around a rectangular field and then subdivide the field into three identical smaller rectangular plots by placing two fences parallel to one of the field's shorter sides. Find the dimensions that maximize the enclosed area. What is the maximum area?

26. A rancher has 600 yards of fencing to put around a rectangular field and then subdivide the field into two identical plots by placing a fence parallel to one of the field's shorter sides. Find the dimensions that maximize the enclosed area. What is the maximum area?

27. Find the point on the graph of $y = \sqrt{x}$ that is closest to the point $(1, 0)$.

28. Find the point on the graph of $2x + y = 6$ that is closest to the origin.

29. Find the number that exceeds its square by the greatest amount.

30. Find two numbers whose difference is 50 with the smallest possible product.

31. Find two positive numbers whose sum is 40 and the sum of whose squares is as small as possible.

32. Use the position function $s(t) = -16t^2 + v_0t + s_0$, in which s_0 is the initial height of an object that is thrown directly upward and v_0 is the initial velocity with which the object is thrown to answer this problem. The bridge over the Royal Gorge in Colorado is the highest bridge in the world, and is 1053 feet above the Arkansas River. A rock is thrown vertically upward from the bridge with an initial velocity of 64 feet per second.

   a. Write a function that models the height of the rock above the water as a function of time.

   b. After how many seconds does the rock reach its maximum height? What is the maximum height?

33. A theater that has 300 seats presents revivals of classic American musicals to groups of 100 people or more. The theater charges $6 per person to groups of 100, reducing the price by 20¢ per ticket for each 10 people in excess of 100. What size group will maximize the theater's income? What is the maximum income?

34. A watermelon grower can now ship 6 tons at a profit of $2 per ton. For each week that the grower waits, 3 tons can be added to the shipment, but the profit will be reduced by $\frac{1}{3}$ dollar per ton per week. How many weeks should the grower wait to maximize profit? What is the maximum profit?

35. A rain gutter is made from sheets of aluminum that are 20 inches wide. As shown in the figure at the top of the next column, the edges are turned up to form right angles. Determine the depth of the gutter that will maximize its cross-sectional area and allow the greatest amount of water to flow.

36. The figure shows a Norman window that has the shape of a rectangle with a semicircle attached at the top. The diameter of the circle is equal to the width of the rectangle. If the window has a perimeter of 12 feet, find the dimensions of h and r that allow the maximum amount of light to enter. (*Hint:* Maximize the window's area. You'll need to use the formulas for a circle's circumference and area: Circumference $= 2\pi r$; Area $= \pi r^2$).

37. An outdoor athletic field is to be constructed in the shape of a rectangle with semicircles at each end. The perimeter of the entire field is to be 440 yards. Find the dimensions of x and r that maximize the area of the rectangular portion of the field.

True–False Critical Thinking Problems

38. Which one of the following is true?

    a. No quadratic functions have a range of $(-\infty, \infty)$.

    b. The vertex of the parabola described by $f(x) = 2(x - 5)^2 - 1$ is at $(5, 1)$.

    c. The graph of $f(x) = -2(x + 4)^2 - 8$ has one y-intercept and two x-intercepts.

    d. The maximum value of y for the quadratic function $f(x) = -x^2 + x + 1$ is 1.

39. Which one of the following is true?

    a. The minimum value of y in the function $f(x) = 3(x + 2)^2 - 5$ is -2.

    b. The graphs of some quadratic functions have two y-intercepts.

    c. The function $f(x) = -2(x + \frac{5}{4})^2 + \frac{33}{8}$ is increasing on the interval $(-\infty, -\frac{5}{4})$.

    d. Some quadratic functions have a range of $(-\infty, \infty)$.

Technology Problems

In this section we've focused on quadratic functions. In the next section we'll be studying polynomial functions of higher degree. Problems 40–46 will give you the opportunity to explore the ideas that will be discussed in Section 3.2.

40. Graph $y = 2x^2$, $y = x^4$, and $y = 0.5x^6$ using a graphing utility. Which one of the following seems to be true about the graph of $y = a_n x^n$ if n is even and $a_n > 0$?

    a. The graph rises to the left and falls to the right.

    b. The graph rises to the left and right.

    c. The graph falls to the left and rises to the right.

    d. The graph falls to the left and right.

41. Use a graphing utility to graph $y = -2x^2$, $y = -x^4$, and $y = -0.5x^6$. Which statement listed in Problem 40 seems to be true about the graph of $y = a_n x^n$ if n is even and $a_n < 0$?

42. Use a graphing utility to graph $y = 2x^3$, $y = x^5$, and $y = 0.5x^7$. Which statement in Problem 40 seems to be true about the graph of $y = a_n x^n$ if n is odd and $a_n > 0$?

43. Use a graphing utility to graph $y = -2x^3$, $y = -x^5$, and $y = -0.5x^7$. Which statement listed in Problem 40 appears to be true about the graph of $y = a_n x^n$ if n is odd and $a_n < 0$?

44. Graph both $f(x) = 2x^3 - 7x^2 - 8x + 16$ and $g(x) = 2x^3$ using the following range setting

    Xmin = -8, Xmax = 8, Xscl = 1,

    Ymin = -100, Ymax = 100, Yscl = 10.

    Then zoom out using the following range setting:

    Xmin = -40, Xmax = 40, Xscl = 10,

    Ymin = $-10,000$, Ymax = 10,000, Yscl = 1000.

    Notice that $2x^3$ models the function $f(x) = 2x^3 - 7x^2 - 8x + 16$ when $|x|$ is large.

45. Repeat Problem 44 for each of the following functions, showing that the behavior of f is the same as that of g when $|x|$ is large.

    a. $f(x) = x^4 - 3x^2 + 5x^2 - 6x + 4$; $g(x) = x^4$

    b. $f(x) = -2x^3 + 7x^2 + 8x - 16$; $g(x) = -2x^3$

    c. $f(x) = -2x^4 - x^3 + 6x^2 - x - 2$; $g(x) = -2x^4$

46. Use your observations in Problems 44–45 to select the statement listed in Problem 40 that applies to the graph of

$$f(x) = a_n x^n + a_{n-1}x^{n-1} + \cdots + a_1 x + a_0$$

    for each of the following cases.

    a. n is odd; $a_n > 0$

    b. n is odd; $a_n < 0$

    c. n is even; $a_n > 0$

    d. n is even; $a_n < 0$

    e. Experiment with additional polynomial functions and their graphs to reinforce the results obtained in parts (a–d).

47. The number of AIDS cases reported from 1983 through 1990 can be modeled by $f(x) = -143x^3 + 1810x^2 - 187x + 2331$, where x represents the number of years after 1983. Graph the polynomial function using the following range setting:

    Xmin = 0, Xmax = 15, Xscl = 1,

    Ymin = 0, Ymax = 50,000, Yscl = 5000.

    How does the graph indicate that the polynomial model does not describe the spread of AIDS over an extended period of time? Is this true in general for polynomial functions modeling nonnegative phenomena over time?

Writing in Mathematics

48. What explanations can you offer for your answer to Problem 19? Use a graphing utility to graph C. Do you agree with the long-term predictions made by the graph? Explain.

49. Discuss the relationship between the midpoint of the two x-intercepts for $f(x) = ax^2 + bx + c$ and the x-coordinate of the vertex. Assume that $b^2 - 4ac$ is positive. Why is this assumption necessary?

Critical Thinking Problems

In Problems 50–51, find the axis of symmetry for each parabola whose equation is given. Use the axis of symmetry to find a second point on the parabola whose y-coordinate is the same as the given point.

50. $f(x) = 3(x + 2)^2 - 5$; $(-1, -2)$

51. $f(x) = (x - 3)^2 + 2$; $(6, 11)$

In Problems 52–53, write an equation of the quadratic function whose graph satisfies the given conditions. Check your result with a graphing utility.

52. Vertex: $(-1, 5)$; point on graph: $(-2, 3)$

53. Vertex: $(3, 1)$; x-intercept: 2

54. If $f(x) = x - 2$ and $g(x) = x^2 - 3x + 1$, find the absolute value of the sum of the minimum values for $f \circ g$ and $g \circ f$.

55. Prove that of all rectangles with a given perimeter P, the square has a maximum area.

56. Prove that of all rectangles with a given perimeter P, the one with the shortest possible diagonal is a square.

57. A right triangle has legs of lengths 3 and 4 feet. What is the area of the largest rectangle that can be inscribed in the right triangle?

58. For what value of c will the minimum of the function $f(x) = 3x^2 - 2x + c$ be $-\frac{19}{2}$?

59. Find the vertex of the quadratic function $f(x) = x^2 + 2(d + e)x + 2(d^2 + e^2)$. Can the graph of f have two x-intercepts? Explain.

60. Find the equation of the circle that passes through the origin and whose center is at the vertex of the parabola described by $y - 2 = (x - 3)^2$.

61. A quadratic function is described by $f(x) = dx^2 + dx + e$.

   a. Prove that if the vertex of the parabola whose equation is f lies on the x-axis, then $d = 4e$.

   b. Prove the converse of part (a). (The converse of "if p then q" is "if q then p.")

62. If $f(x) = x^2 + kx + 1$, find k that minimizes the distance from the parabola's vertex to the origin.

Solutions Manual   **Tutorial**   **Video 6**

Determine the end behavior of a polynomial function.

Discover for yourself

You can use your graphing utility to discover all aspects of this discussion on end behavior and the Leading Coefficient Test by working Problems 40–46 in Problem Set 3.1.

SECTION 3.2

Polynomial Functions of Higher Degree and Polynomial Variation

Objectives

1 Determine the end behavior of a polynomial function.
2 Use factoring to find zeros of polynomial functions.
3 Model using polynomial functions.
4 Model using polynomial variation.

Now that we've studied polynomial functions of degree 2, we turn our attention to those of degree 3 or higher. The graphs of these functions exhibit the same kinds of behavior that we found in parabolas.

End Behavior and the Leading Coefficient Test

Polynomial functions of degree 2 or less have graphs that are either parabolas or lines and can be graphed by plotting points. Although polynomial functions of degree 3 or higher also can be graphed by plotting numerous points, the process is rather tedious. Thus, recognizing some of the basic features of the

Bridget Riley "Drift No. 2" 1966, acrylic on canvas, p 1 1/2 × 89 1/2 in. Albright-Knox Art Gallery, Gift of Seymour H. Knox, 1967.

graphs of polynomial functions is important for graphing by hand and in choosing an appropriate viewing rectangle for a graphing utility.

Like quadratic functions, all polynomial functions have graphs that are continuous curves with no breaks (such as those found in the graph of the greatest integer function). Polynomial functions have graphs with smooth, rounded turns (unlike the graph of $f(x) = |x|$, which has a sharp corner at $(0, 0)$).

The behavior of the graph of a function to the far right (as $x \to \infty$; that is, as x goes to infinity) and to the far left (as $x \to -\infty$; that is, as x goes to negative infinity) is called the *end behavior* of a function. All polynomial functions have graphs that eventually rise or fall without bound as $x \to \infty$ or $x \to -\infty$. We can express this symbolically in a number of ways.

The symbolism of end behavior

Symbolic Statement	What It Means	Example
$f(x) \to \infty$ as $x \to \infty$	$f(x)$ increases without bound as x moves to the right without bound.	(graph of $f(x) = x^3 - 3x + 2$)
$f(x) \to -\infty$ as $x \to -\infty$	$f(x)$ decreases without bound as x moves to the left without bound.	
$f(x) \to \infty$ as $x \to -\infty$	$f(x)$ increases without bound as x moves to the left without bound.	(graph of $f(x) = -x^3 + 4x$)
$f(x) \to -\infty$ as $x \to \infty$	$f(x)$ decreases without bound as x moves to the right without bound.	

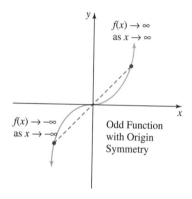

Figure 3.11

If *n* is odd and $a_n > 0$, the graph of $y = a_n x^n$ falls to the left and rises to the right

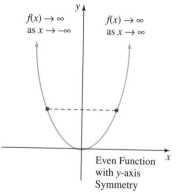

Figure 3.12

If *n* is even and $a_n > 0$, the graph of $y = a_n x^n$ rises to the left and to the right

There is a relationship between a polynomial function's end behavior and its term of highest degree. The end behavior is actually the same as that of $y = a_n x^n$, the term of highest degree, so let's take a moment to examine the end behavior of this term.

If a_n is positive and n is odd, the function $y = a_n x^n$ is an odd function with origin symmetry. Figure 3.11 shows that its graph falls to the left and rises to the right. On the other hand, if a_n is positive and n is even, the function $y = a_n x^n$ is an even function with y-axis symmetry. Figure 3.12 shows that its graph rises to the left and to the right.

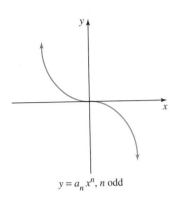

$y = a_n x^n$, n odd

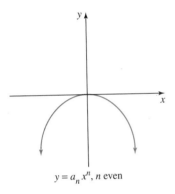

$y = a_n x^n$, n even

Figure 3.13

If a_n is negative, the end behavior shown in Figures 3.11 and 3.12 is reversed.

If a_n is negative, the graphs in Figures 3.11 and 3.12 are reflected in the x-axis. Figure 3.13 illustrates how this reflection reverses the end behavior.

As we noted on the previous page, the end behavior of

$$f(x) = a_n x^n + a_{n-1}x^{n-1} + \cdots + a_1 x + a_0$$

is the same as that of $y = a_n x^n$. In terms of end behavior, only the term of highest degree counts. This observation is summarized by the *Leading Coefficient Test*.

The Leading Coefficient Test

As x increases ($x \to \infty$) or decreases ($x \to -\infty$) without bound, the graph of the polynomial function $f(x) = a_n x^n + a_{n-1}x^{n-1} + \cdots + a_1 x + a_0$ eventually rises ($f(x) \to \infty$) or falls ($f(x) \to -\infty$). In particular:

1. For n odd and $a_n > 0$:

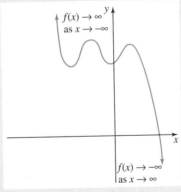

The graph falls to the left and rises to the right.

2. For n odd and $a_n < 0$:

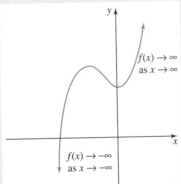

The graph rises to the left and falls to the right.

3. For n even and $a_n > 0$:

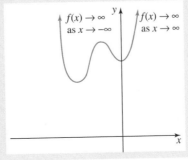

The graph rises to the left and to the right.

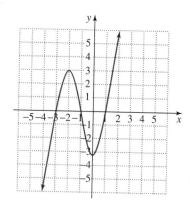

Figure 3.14

The graph of $f(x) = x^3 + 3x^2 - x - 3$, rising to the right and falling to the left

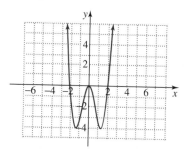

Figure 3.15

The graph of $f(x) = x^4 - 4x^2$, rising to the left and right

2 Use factoring to find zeros of polynomial functions.

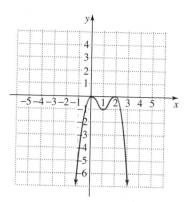

Figure 3.16

The graph of $f(x) = -x^4 + 4x^3 - 4x^2$, falling to the left and right

4. For n even and $a_n < 0$:

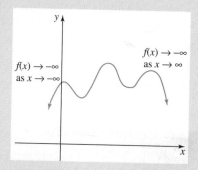

The graph falls to the left and to the right.

EXAMPLE I   Using the Leading Coefficient Test

Use the Leading Coefficient Test to determine the end behavior of the graph of:

a. $f(x) = x^3 + 3x^2 - x - 3$ **b.** $f(x) = x^4 - 4x^2$ **c.** $f(x) = -x^4 + 4x^3 - 4x^2$

Solution

a. $f(x) = x^3 + 3x^2 - x - 3$

Because the degree is odd ($n = 3$) and the leading coefficient is positive, the graph rises to the right and falls to the left, as shown in Figure 3.14.

b. $f(x) = x^4 - 4x^2$

Because the degree is even ($n = 4$) and the leading coefficient is positive, the graph rises to the left and right, as shown in Figure 3.15.

c. $f(x) = -x^4 + 4x^3 - 4x^2$

Because the degree is even ($n = 4$) and the leading coefficient is negative, the graph falls to the left and right, as shown in Figure 3.16.   ∎

Zeros of Polynomial Functions

There is an important relationship between the graph of $f(x) = a_n x^n + a_{n-1} x^{n-1} + \cdots + a_1 x + a_0$ and the real solutions to the polynomial equation $a_n x^n + a_{n-1} x^{n-1} + \cdots + a_1 x + a_0 = 0$. Let's explore this relationship for the three polynomial functions in Example 1.

EXAMPLE 2   Solving a Polynomial Equation

Solve: $x^3 + 3x^2 - x - 3 = 0$

Solution

$$x^3 + 3x^2 - x - 3 = 0$$

This is the given polynomial equation.

$$x^2(x + 3) - 1(x + 3) = 0$$

Factor x^2 from the first two terms and -1 from the last two terms.

$$(x + 3)(x^2 - 1) = 0$$

A common factor of $x + 3$ is factored from the expression on the left.

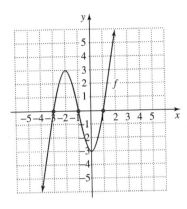

Figure 3.17
The solutions of $x^3 + 3x^2 - x - 3 = 0$ are the x-intercepts for $f(x) = x^3 + 3x^2 - x - 3$.

tudy tip

Like end behavior, zeros of a polynomial function are another important property that determines the shape of the graph.

$$x + 3 = 0 \quad \text{or} \quad x^2 - 1 = 0 \qquad \text{Set each factor equal to 0.}$$

$$x = -3 \qquad\qquad x^2 = 1 \qquad \text{Solve for } x.$$

$$x = \pm 1 \qquad \text{Remember that if } x^2 = d, \text{ then } x = \pm\sqrt{d}.$$

The solution set is $\{-3, -1, 1\}$. Look at Figure 3.17 and observe that the graph crosses the x-axis at -3, -1, and 1 Because $f(-3) = 0, f(-1) = 0$, and $f(1) = 0$, we call the solutions, or roots, of the polynomial equation (that is, -3, -1, and 1) the *zeros* of the polynomial function. ∎

Example 2 demonstrates the interrelationship among solving polynomial equations, finding zeros of polynomial functions, and finding x-intercepts. These relationships are summarized as follows.

Real zeros of polynomial functions

If $f(x) = a_n x^n + a_{n-1} x^{n-1} + \cdots + a_1 x + a_0$ and $f(a) = 0$ for any real number a,

1. a is *zero* of the function f.
2. a is a *solution* or *root* of the polynomial equation $f(x) = 0$.
3. a is an *x-intercept* of the graph f.
4. $x - a$ is a *factor* of the polynomial $f(x)$.

EXAMPLE 3   **Finding Zeros of a Fourth-Degree Polynomial Function**

Find all real zeros of: $f(x) = x^4 - 4x^2$

Solution

To find the zeros of the function, we solve the equation $f(x) = 0$.

$$x^4 - 4x^2 = 0 \qquad\qquad \text{Set } f(x) \text{ equal to 0.}$$

$$x^2(x^2 - 4) = 0 \qquad\qquad \text{Factor.}$$

$$x^2 = 0 \quad \text{or} \quad x^2 - 4 = 0 \qquad \text{Set each factor equal to 0.}$$

$$x = 0 \qquad\qquad x^2 = 4 \qquad \text{Solve for } x.$$

$$x = \pm 2$$

The real zeros of $f(x) = x^2 - 4x^2$ are $-2, 0$, and 2. The graph of f, shown in Figure 3.18, has x-intercepts at $-2, 0$, and 2. ∎

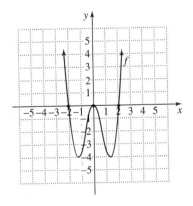

Figure 3.18
The real zeros of $f(x) = x^4 - 4x^2$ are the x-intercepts for the graph of f.

EXAMPLE 4   **Finding Zeros of a Polynomial Function**

Find all real zeros of: $f(x) = -x^4 + 4x^3 - 4x^2$

Figure 3.19

The real zeros of $f(x) = -x^4 + 4x^3 - 4x^2$, namely 0 and 2, are the x-intercepts for the graph of f.

Solution

We find the zeros of f by setting $f(x)$ equal to 0.

$$-x^4 + 4x^3 - 4x^2 = 0 \qquad \text{We now have a polynomial equation.}$$

$$x^4 - 4x^3 + 4x^2 = 0 \qquad \text{Multiply both sides by } -1. \text{ This step is optional.}$$

$$x^2(x^2 - 4x + 4) = 0 \qquad \text{Factor out } x^2.$$

$$x^2(x - 2)^2 = 0 \qquad \text{Factor completely.}$$

$$x^2 = 0 \quad \text{or} \quad (x - 2)^2 = 0 \qquad \text{Set each factor equal to 0.}$$

$$x = 0 \qquad\qquad x = 2 \qquad \text{Solve for } x.$$

The real zeros of $f(x) = -x^4 + 4x^3 - 4x^2$ are 0 and 2. The graph of f, shown in Figure 3.19 has x-intercepts at 0 and 2. ∎

Multiple Roots and x-Intercepts

In Example 3, the real zero arising from $x^2 = 0$ is a repeated zero. In Example 4, both real zeros arising from $x^2 = 0$ and $(x - 2)^2 = 0$ are repeated zeros. The graph in Example 4 touched, but did not cross, the x-axis at 0 and 2. In general, a factor of $(x - a)^k$ yields the repeated zero a of *multiplicity k*.

Multiplicity and x-intercepts

1. If the factor $x - a$ occurs k times ($k \geqslant 2$) in the complete factorization of the polynomial $f(x)$, then a is called a repeated zero with multiplicity k.
2. If k is even, then the graph touches but does not cross the x-axis at $x = a$.
3. If k is odd, the graph crosses the x-axis at $x = a$.
4. Regardless of whether k is even or odd, if a is a repeated zero, the graph flattens out at $(a, 0)$.

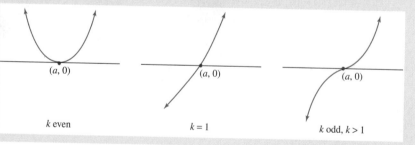

There is a relationship between the degree of a polynomial and the number of real zeros. Another relationship exists between the polynomial's degree and the number of turning points on its graph. Study the results of Examples 2–4, summarized below, and see if you can state these relationships for an nth-degree polynomial.

Polynomial Function	Degree	Real Zeros	Number of Real Zeros	Number of Turning Points on the Graph
$f(x) = x^3 + 3x^2 - x - 3$	3	$-3, -1, 1$	Three	Two
$f(x) = x^4 - 4x^2$	4	$-2, 0, 2$	Three	Three
$f(x) = -x^4 + 4x^3 - 4x^2$	4	$0, 2$	Two	Three

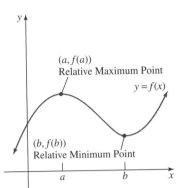

In the Discover for yourself, did you observe the following relationships?

Degrees, real zeros, and turning points

1. An nth-degree polynomial function can have *at most n* real zeros.
2. An nth-degree polynomial function has a graph with *at most $n - 1$* turning points. Equivalently, the graph has at most $n - 1$ relative extrema (relative minimums or maximums).

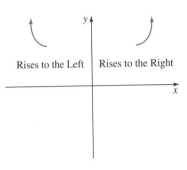

Rises to the Left   Rises to the Right

EXAMPLE 5   Sketching the Graph of a Polynomial Function

Sketch the graph of $f(x) = 2x^4 - 4x^3$ without the use of a graphing utility.

Solution

The end behavior of f is the same as that of $y = 2x^4$. Because the leading coefficient is positive and the degree is even, the graph rises to the left and right, as shown in Figure 3.20.

Let's find the zeros of f, thereby determining the graph's x-intercepts.

$2x^4 - 4x^3 = 0$	Set $f(x)$ equal to 0.
$2x^3(x - 2) = 0$	Factor.
$2x^3 = 0$ or $x - 2 = 0$	Set each factor equal to 0.
$x = 0$ $x = 2$	Solve for x.

Since 0 and 2 are of odd multiplicity, the graph of f crosses the x-axis at both of these intercepts. At $x = 0$, because the multiplicity is 3, the graph will flatten out. We'll plot a few additional points as shown in the accompanying table.

x	-1	0.5	1	1.5
$f(x) = 2x^4 - 4x^3$	6	-0.375	-2	-3.375

Figure 3.20

End behavior of the graph of $f(x) = 2x^4 - 4x^3$

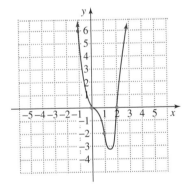

Figure 3.21

The graph of $f(x) = 2x^4 - 4x^3$

The graph of $f(x) = 2x^4 - 4x^3$ appears in Figure 3.21. ∎

A Strategy for Graphing Polynomial Functions

Here's a general strategy for graphing a polynomial function. A graphing utility is a valuable complement to this strategy. Some of the steps listed below will help you to select a viewing rectangle that shows the important parts of the graph.

Graphing a polynomial function

$$f(x) = a_nx^n + a_{n-1}x^{n-1} + a_{n-2}x^{n-2} + \cdots + a_1x + a_0$$

1. Use the Leading Coefficient Test to determine the graph's end behavior.

2. Find *x*-intercepts by setting $f(x) = 0$ and solving the resulting polynomial equation. If there is an *x*-intercept at *a* as a result of $(x - a)^k$ in the complete factorization of $f(x)$, then:
   a. If *k* is even, the graph touches the *x*-axis at *a*, but does not cross the *x*-axis.
   b. If *k* is odd, the graph crosses the *x*-axis at *a*.
   c. If $k > 1$, the graph flattens out at $(a, 0)$.
3. Find the *y*-intercept by setting *x* equal to 0 and computing $f(0)$.
4. Use symmetry, if applicable, to help draw the graph:
   a. *y*-axis symmetry: $f(-x) = f(x)$
   b. Origin symmetry: $f(-x) = -f(x)$
5. Use the fact that the maximum number of turning points of the graph is $n - 1$ to check whether it is drawn correctly.

3 Model using polynomial functions.

Modeling with Polynomial Functions

Polynomial models are often useful for describing nonnegative real world phenomena over short periods of time. However, based on end behavior, accurate modeling for extended time periods is a problem. Let's see why.

EXAMPLE 6   AIDS Cases

The number of AIDS cases for the years 1983 through 1991 is approximated by the polynomial function

$$f(x) = -143x^3 + 1810x^2 - 187x + 2331$$

where *x* represents years after 1983. Use end behavior to explain why the model is only valid for a limited time period.

Solution

Because the leading coefficient (-143) is negative and the degree (3) is odd, the graph falls to the right. This indicates at some point the number of AIDS cases will be negative, an impossibility. No function with a graph that decreases without bound as *x* (time) increases can model nonnegative real world phenomena over a long period.

Figure 3.22 shows the graph of *f* from 1983 through 1991 using the range setting:

$$\text{Xmin} = 0, \text{Xmax} = 8, \text{Xscl} = 1,$$

$$\text{Ymin} = 0, \text{Ymax} = 50{,}000, \text{and Yscl} = 5000.$$

Look what happens to the graph when we change the range setting to

$$\text{Xmin} = 0, \text{Xmax} = 15, \text{Xscl} = 1,$$

$$\text{Ymin} = -5000, \text{Ymax} = 50{,}000, \text{and Yscl} = 5000.$$

(Figure 3.23). By year 13 (1996), the values of *y* are negative and the function no longer models AIDS cases.

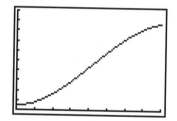

Figure 3.22

The graph of a function modeling the number of AIDS cases from 1983 through 1991

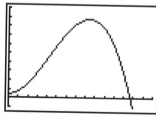

Figure 3.23

By extending the range setting, *y* is negative and the function no longer models the number of AIDS cases.

ENRICHMENT ESSAY

The Hot Zone

As the tropical forests of the world are destroyed, viruses that have lived undetected in the wilderness are entering human populations. The appearance of AIDS is part of a pattern that, according to author Richard Preston (*The Hot Zone*) involves viruses of extraordinary virulence capable of being spread by airborne mucus or casual contact, bringing grotesque, agonizing, and near-certain death within weeks after infection. The ongoing tragedy of AIDS and the outbreak of the Ebola virus in Zaire in 1995 confirm the reality of modern-day plagues reminiscent of the black death of times gone by.

Juan Gonzalez "Mar de Lagrimas" 1987–88, w/c and gouache on paper, 27 1/2 × 43 1/4 in. Courtesy Nancy Hoffman Gallery.

Polynomial models are often useful for describing real-world phenomena over short periods of time. They also model many geometric situations, as illustrated in Example 7.

EXAMPLE 7 A Geometric Application

A rectangular piece of cardboard measures 12 inches by 20 inches. A box with an open top is formed by cutting identical squares that measure x by x from each corner and then folding up the sides, as shown in Figure 3.24.

a. Express the volume V of the box as a polynomial function of x.
b. Graph the function.

Figure 3.24

Solution

a. The lengths of the sides of the open-top box are x, $12 - 2x$, and $20 - 2x$ (see Figure 3.24). The volume of the box is the product of its length, width, and height, and is given by

$$V(x) = x(12 - 2x)(20 - 2x).$$

By multiplying on the right, we can express the volume as

$$V(x) = 4x^3 - 64x^2 + 240x.$$

Rises to the Right

Falls to the Left

Figure 3.25

b. Now we are ready to graph the function that models the volume of the box.
  1. Determine end behavior. Since n is odd and the leading coefficient (4) is positive, the graph falls to the left and rises to the right (see Figure 3.25).
  2. Find x-intercepts by setting $V(x) = 0$.

$$4x^3 - 64x^2 + 240x = 0$$

$$x(12 - 2x)(20 - 2x) = 0$$ Use the factored form of the function.

Figure 3.26

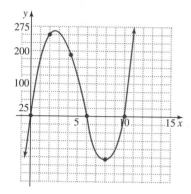

Figure 3.27

The graph of $V(x) = 4x^3 - 64x^2 + 240x$, with uncertainty as to the coordinates of the turning points

FMAX
X=2.4274017016
                    Y=262.68226353

Figure 3.28

Cutting 2.4-inch squares gives a maximum volume of 263 cubic inches.

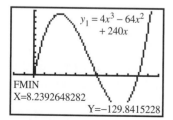

FMIN
X=8.2392648282
                    Y=−129.8415228

Figure 3.29

Coordinates of the second turning point

$$x = 0 \quad \text{or} \quad 12 - 2x = 0 \quad \text{or} \quad 20 - 2x = 0 \qquad \text{Set each factor equal to 0.}$$

$$x = 0 \qquad\qquad x = 6 \qquad\qquad x = 10 \qquad \text{Solve for } x.$$

The multiplicity of each factor is 1, so the graph crosses the x-axis (and does not flatten out) at 0, 6, and 10 (see Figure 3.26).

3. Since the graph passes through $(0, 0)$, we have also found the y-intercept.

4. It seems unlikely that the graph has either y-axis symmetry or origin symmetry. We confirm this by finding $V(-x)$:

$$V(-x) = 4(-x)^3 - 64(-x)^2 + 240(-x) \qquad \text{Replace } x \text{ with } -x \text{ in the formula for } V(x).$$

$$= -4x^3 - 64x^2 - 240x$$

Because $V(-x) \neq V(x)$ and $V(-x) \neq -V(x)$, the graph has neither y-axis nor origin symmetry.

5. Plot a few additional points as shown in the table.

x	2	4	8
$V(x) = 4x^3 - 64x^2 + 240x$	256	192	−128

Figure 3.27 shows the graph of $V(x) = 4x^3 - 64x^2 + 240x$. The maximum number of turning points is $n - 1$ or $3 - 1 = 2$. Since we have 2 turning points, this does not violate the maximum number possible. Although we do not know the precise coordinates of these turning points, we can use point plotting to further refine the graph. ∎

D iscover for yourself

Since the original piece of cardboard measured 12 inches by 20 inches, what is the largest possible square that can be cut from each corner? How much "volume" would be attained by cutting a square this large? Trace over the part of the graph in Figure 3.27 that is significant in terms of serving as a realistic model for the volume for the open-top box. For what values of x does the function model the problem?

U sing technology

We can use a graphing utility to refine the hand-drawn graph in Figure 3.27 and determine the coordinates of the two turning points. Figure 3.28 was obtained using the FMAX feature. We can see that one turning point for the function occurs at approximately $(2.4, 263)$. This indicates that a box of maximum volume (263 cubic inches) can be obtained by cutting squares that measure 2.4 inches from each corner. Figure 3.29 was obtained using the FMIN feature. Here we see that the other turning point for the function occurs at approximately $(8.2, -130)$.

4 Model using polynomial variation.

Modeling Using Polynomial Variation

In Section 2.2, we modeled the statement "y varies directly as x" with the linear equation $y = mx$. Variation can also be modeled by higher-order polynomial equations.

Direct variation with powers

y *varies directly as the nth power of x* (or y *is proportional to the nth power of x*) if there exists some nonzero constant k such that

$$y = kx^n.$$

The number k is called the *constant of variation* or the *constant of proportionality*.

H. C. Westermann "High Swan Dive: The Sea of Cortez" 1973. Courtesy of Allan Franklin, NY. © Estate of H. C. Westermann / Licensed by VAGA, New York, 1998.

EXAMPLE 8   Solving a Direct Variation Problem

The distance (d) that a body falls from rest varies directly as the square of the time (t) of the fall. If a body falls 64 feet in 2 seconds, how far will it fall in 4.5 seconds?

Solution

$d = kt^2$	Translate "Distance (d) varies directly as the square of time (t)."
$64 = k \cdot 2^2$	Find k. Because a body falls 64 feet in 2 seconds, when $t = 2$, $d = 64$.
$64 = 4k$	
$16 = k$	Solve for k, dividing both sides by 4.
$d = 16t^2$	Substitute the value for k into the original equation.
$\quad = 16(4.5)^2$	Find d when $t = 4.5$.
$\quad = 16(20.25)$	
$\quad = 324$	

Thus, in 4.5 seconds, a body will fall 324 feet. ∎

It is easy to determine whether a data set can be modeled by polynomial variation.

$y = kx^n$	This is the polynomial model.
$\dfrac{y}{x^n} = k$	Solve for k.

This last form of the variation model tells us that if a data set is to be modeled by polynomial variation, the ratio $\dfrac{y}{x^n}$ must remain constant.

Let's apply this idea to the model in Example 8. Expressing the model as

$$y = 16x^2$$

we obtain the data points for the function shown in the margin. The graph of $f(x) = 16x^2$ appears below the data points on page 354 (Figure 3.30).

Given only the data points (the ordered pairs in the third column of the table of coordinates), the ratio $\dfrac{y}{x^2}$ remains constant.

x	$y = 16x^2$	Ordered Pair
0	$16 \cdot 0^2 = 0$	$(0, 0)$
1	$16 \cdot 1^2 = 16$	$(1, 16)$
2	$16 \cdot 2^2 = 64$	$(2, 64)$
3	$16 \cdot 3^2 = 144$	$(3, 144)$
4	$16 \cdot 4^2 = 256$	$(4, 256)$
5	$16 \cdot 5^2 = 400$	$(5, 400)$

$(1, 16)$: $\dfrac{y}{x^2} = \dfrac{16}{1^2} = 16$

$(2, 64)$: $\dfrac{y}{x^2} = \dfrac{64}{2^2} = 16$

$(3, 144)$: $\dfrac{y}{x^2} = \dfrac{144}{3^2} = 16$

$(4, 256)$: $\dfrac{y}{x^2} = \dfrac{256}{4^2} = 16$

$(5, 400)$: $\dfrac{y}{x^2} = \dfrac{400}{5^2} = 16$

Discover for yourself

Why isn't the ordered pair $(0, 0)$ considered in these ratios?

Figure 3.30

The graph of $f(x) = 16x^2$

Determining whether data can be modeled by polynomial variation

A data set with ordered pairs in the form (x, y) can be modeled by polynomial variation if the ratio

$$\frac{y}{x^n}$$

remains constant for some positive integer n.

PROBLEM SET 3.2

Practice Problems

In Problems 1–6, use end behavior to match each polynomial function with its graph (The graphs are labeled (a) through (f).)

1. $f(x) = x^3 - 4x^2$ **2.** $f(x) = -x^4 + x^2$ **3.** $f(x) = -x^3 - x^2 + 5x - 3$ **4.** $f(x) = (x - 3)^2$

5. $f(x) = (x + 1)^2(x - 1)^2$ **6.** $f(x) = x - 3$

a.

b.

c.

d.

e.

f.

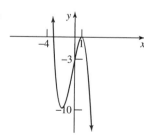

In Problems 7–22:

a. *Use the Leading Coefficient Test to determine the right-hand ($x \to \infty$) and left-hand ($x \to -\infty$) end behavior of the polynomial function.*

b. *Find all real zeros of the polynomial function.*

c. *Graph the function without the use of a graphing utility.*

d. *Verify your hand-drawn graph with a graphing utility.*

7. $f(x) = x^3 + x^2 - 4x - 4$

8. $f(x) = x^3 + 2x^2 - x - 2$

9. $f(x) = x^4 - x^2$

10. $f(x) = x^4 - 9x^2$

11. $f(x) = -x^4 + 4x^2$

12. $f(x) = -x^4 + 16x^2$

13. $f(x) = x^4 - 6x^3 + 9x^2$

14. $f(x) = x^4 - 2x^3 + x^2$

15. $f(x) = -2x^4 + 2x^3$

16. $f(x) = -2x^4 + 4x^3$

17. $f(x) = 6x - x^3 - x^5$

18. $f(x) = 6x^3 - 9x - x^5$

19. $f(x) = \frac{1}{2} - \frac{1}{2}x^4$

20. $f(x) = 3x^2 - x^3$

21. $f(x) = -2(x - 4)^2(x^2 - 25)$

22. $f(x) = -3(x - 1)^2(x^2 - 4)$

Application Problems

23. The table below shows the accumulated total number of AIDS cases in the United States from 1983 through 1995.

Year	1983	1984	1985	1986	1987	1988	1989	1990	1991	1992	1993	1994	1995
Number of AIDS Cases	4589	10,750	22,399	41,256	69,592	104,644	146,574	193,878	251,638	326,648	399,613	457,280	496,896

Source: Center for Disease Control

This data can be modeled by the cubic polynomial function

$$f(x) = -68.8x^3 + 4781.7x^2 - 2666.2x + 7094.5$$

where $f(x)$ is the number of AIDS cases and x is the number of years after 1983. The graph of this function is shown in the figure superimposed over actual data points.

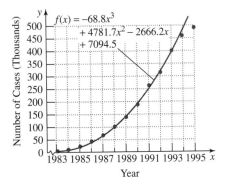

Year

a. How well does the graph indicate that the cubic polynomial models the data?

b. Select a year where the polynomial gives nearly the exact number of AIDS cases. Verify this observation by evaluating the polynomial function for this year and comparing your answer to the number of AIDS cases in the table.

c. Select a year where the polynomial either underestimates or overestimates the actual number of AIDS cases. Verify this observation by evaluating the polynomial function and comparing your answer to the number of AIDS cases given in the table.

d. Why will this cubic polynomial function not model the number of AIDS cases over an extended period of time?

24. A herd of 100 elk is introduced to a small island. The number of elk $N(t)$ after t years is described by the polynomial function $N(t) = -t^4 + 21t^2 + 100$.

a. Use the Leading Coefficient Test to determine the graph's end behavior to the right. What does this mean about what will eventually happen to the elk population?

b. Graph the function.

c. Graph only the portion of the function that serves as a realistic model for the elk population over time. When does the population die off?

25. A rectangular piece of cardboard measures 12 inches by 18 inches. A box with an open top is formed by cutting identical squares that measure x by x from each corner and then folding up the sides.

  a. Express the volume (V) of the box as a polynomial function of x.

  b. Graph the function.

12 inches

18 inches

26. The distance required to stop a car varies directly as the square of its speed. If 200 feet are required to stop a car traveling 60 miles per hour, how many feet are required to stop a car traveling 100 miles per hour.

27. The distance that a body falls varies directly as the square of time in which it falls. A body falls 64 feet in 2 seconds. Predict the distance the same body will fall in 10 seconds.

In Problems 28–29, show that each data set can be modeled by polynomial variation for the given value of n. Then write a polynomial function that models the data.

28.

x	$y\,(n = 3)$
2	$\dfrac{32\pi}{3}$
3	36π
5	$\dfrac{500\pi}{3}$
9	972π

(What familiar formula do you obtain? What do x and y represent?)

29.

x	$y\,(n = 5)$
1	0.1
2	3.2
3	24.3
5	312.5

True–False Critical Thinking Problems

30. Which one of the following is true?

  a. If $f(x) = -x^3 + 4x$, then the graph of f falls to the left and to the right.

  b. If $f(x) = x^4 - 5x^2 + 3$, then $f(x) \to \infty$ as $x \to -\infty$.

  c. A mathematical model that is a polynomial of degree n whose leading term is $a_n x^n$, n odd and $a_n < 0$, is ideally suited to describe nonnegative phenomena over long periods of time.

  d. There is only one fourth-degree polynomial with four known x-intercepts.

31. Which one of the following is true?

  a. If $f(x) = x^5 - 3x$, the graph of f falls to the left and to the right.

  b. If $f(x) = -3x^4 + 3x^2$, then $f(x) \to -\infty$ as $x \to \infty$.

  c. There is only one third-degree polynomial with three known x-intercepts.

  d. The graph of a function with origin symmetry can rise to the left and to the right.

Technology Problems

Write a polynomial function that imitates the end behavior of each graph in Problems 32–35. Then use your graphing utility to graph the polynomial function and verify your result.

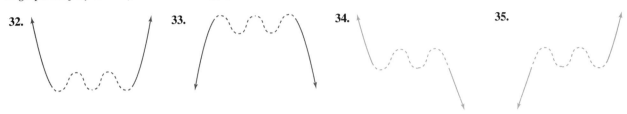

32.   **33.**   **34.**   **35.**

For Problems 36–39, describe the end behavior of the graph of each polynomial function using the Leading Coefficient Test. After describing what happens as $x \to \infty$ and $x \to -\infty$, use a graphing utility to obtain a complete graph of the function to verify your description.

36. $f(x) = -2x^3 + 6x^2 + 3x - 1$

37. $g(x) = -\frac{1}{2}(3x^4 - 2x + 5)$

38. $h(x) = 10^4 + x^3$

39. $h(t) = -3t^2 + 4t^4$

For Problems 40–43:

  a. *Use a graphing utility to graph each function in a standard viewing rectangle.*

  b. *Based on what you know about the end behavior of the graph, explain why the graph is not complete.*

  c. *Modify the range setting to obtain a complete graph of the function showing its end behavior.*

40. $f(x) = x^3 + 13x^2 + 10x - 4$

41. $f(x) = -x^4 + 8x^3 + 4x^2 + 2$

42. $f(x) = (x + 2)(x + 1)(x - 1)(x - 3)(x - 5)$

43. $f(x) = -x^5 + 5x^4 - 6x^3 + 2x + 20$

For Problems 44–47, use a graphing utility to graph f and g in the same viewing rectangle. Then use the ⬛ZOOM OUT⬛ *feature to show that the end behavior of f and g (as $x \to \infty$ and $x \to -\infty$) is identical.*

44. $f(x) = x^3 - 6x + 1, g(x) = x^3$

45. $f(x) = 2x^4 - 3x^2, g(x) = 2x^4$

46. $f(x) = -\frac{1}{2}x^3 + x - 4, g(x) = -\frac{1}{2}x^3$

47. $f(x) = -x^4 + 2x^3 - 6x, g(x) = -x^4$

48. Is $|a - b - c| = |a| - |b| - |c|$? Answer the question by graphing $f(x) = |x^3 - 4x^2 - x|$ and $g(x) = |x^3| - |4x^2| - |x|$ in the same viewing rectangle.

49. In South America and Africa, trees are being cut at the rate of 30 acres a minute, day and night. An area of forest nearly twice as large as the state of New York is destroyed every year. This alarming rate of destruction of tropical rainforests is a major factor in the overall increase of atmospheric CO_2 concentration. A short-term polynomial model for the years 1980 through 1982 is $f(x) = 36x^4 - 142x^3 + 175x^2 - 67x + 340$, where x denotes the year ($x = 0$ represents April 1980) and $f(x)$ approximates CO_2 concentration (in ppm). Use your graphing utility to graph the function. What do you observe about the CO_2 concentration during the course of each year?

Fanny Brennan "Forest" 1987, 2 1/8 × 3 in. Courtesy of Salander–O'Reilly Galleries.

Writing in Mathematics

50. Explain how you can determine whether the graph shown below represents $f(x) = (x - 2)^2$, $f(x) = (x - 2)^3$, or $f(x) = (x - 2)^4$.

51. Explain why the graph at the top of the next column cannot represent a fifth-degree polynomial function.

52. What is the smallest possible degree of the polynomial function in the graph? How do you know?

Group Activity Problems

Explore the capability of a graphing utility to fit a polynomial function to a data set. This is usually found in the statistics menu. Look for the polynomial regression feature. There are characteristics of a data set that indicate it can be modeled by a polynomial function. For example, take the function $f(x) = x^3$ and consider first-, second-, and third-order differences:

x	$f(x) = x^3$	First-order Differences	Second-order Differences	Third-order Differences
−3	−27			
		−8 − (−27) 19		
−2	−8		7 − 19 −12	
		−1 − (−8) 7		−6 − (−12) 6
−1	−1		1 − 7 −6	
		0 − (−1) 1		0 − (−6) 6
0	0		1 − 1 0	
		1 − 0 1		6 − 0 6
1	1		7 − 1 6	
		8 − 1 7		
2	8			

Observe that for equally spaced x-values the third-order differences are constant. This observation can be generalized as follows:

> *If the nth-order differences of y-values of a data set are constant for equally spaced x-values, the data can be modeled by a polynomial function of degree n.*

53. Once members of the group have learned to use technology to model data, work with the data given on the next page related to the common cold. The common cold is caused by a rhinovirus. The virus enters our bodies, multiplies, and although there is no cure, the virus begins to die at a certain point. After t days there are N billion viral particles in our bodies, as shown in the table.

t (Days)	N (Viral Particles, in billions)
0	5
1	7.25
2	17
3	22.25
4	5

a. Model the data with a fourth-degree polynomial that describes the number of viral particles as a function of time.

b. Use a graphing utility to draw a complete graph of the function. When (to the nearest hour) does the model indicate that we feel sickest, that is, when is the number of particles at a maximum?

54. Consult the Internet or the research department of your library to find data of interest to the group. Look for data that can be modeled by a polynomial function—that is, data with relatively constant nth-order differences. Use the computer or a graphing calculator to fit a polynomial function to the data, and then describe how well the function predicts the actual data values.

SECTION 3.3 — Zeros of Polynomial Functions

Solutions Manual   **Tutorial**   **Video 6**

Objectives

1 Use long division to divide polynomials.
2 Use synthetic division to divide polynomials.
3 Evaluate a polynomial using the Remainder Theorem.
4 Use the Factor Theorem to solve a polynomial equation.
5 Use the Rational Zero Theorem to find possible rational zeros.
6 Use technology to eliminate possible rational zeros.
7 Use Descartes' Rule of Signs.
8 Find bounds for the roots of a polynomial equation.
9 Use a strategy to solve polynomial equations.

We have seen that the zeros of the polynomial function

$$f(x) = a_n x^n + a_{n-1} x^{n-1} + \cdots + a_1 x + a_0$$

are the solutions of the polynomial equation

$$a_n x^n + a_{n-1} x^{n-1} + \cdots + a_1 x + a_0 = 0.$$

Furthermore, if a is a real zero, then a is an x-intercept of the graph of f. In this section, we focus in greater detail on these ideas.

The Division Algorithm: Long Division and Synthetic Division

Consider the polynomial function

$$f(x) = 15x^3 + 14x^2 - 3x - 2.$$

Suppose we know that a zero of f occurs at -1. This means that $x + 1$ is a factor of $f(x)$ and that $f(x)$ can be expressed as

$$f(x) = (x + 1)q(x)$$

where $q(x)$ is a second-degree polynomial. We find $q(x)$ using long division of polynomials.

Use long division to divide polynomials.

EXAMPLE 1 **Reviewing Long Division of Polynomials**

Divide $f(x) = 15x^3 + 14x^2 - 3x - 2$ by $x + 1$. Use the result to find all real zeros of f.

Solution

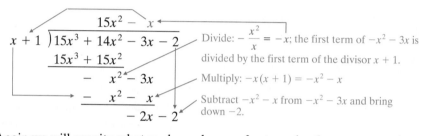

Although the process of division, multiplication, subtraction, and bringing down terms is continued without interruption, we'll rewrite what we have done so far to make the algorithm easier to follow.

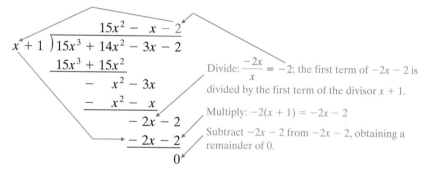

Again we will rewrite what we have done so far to make the process easier to follow.

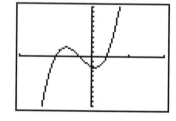

The completed division shows that

$$f(x) = 15x^3 + 14x^2 - 3x - 2 = (x + 1)(15x^2 - x - 2).$$

We can use this result to find all zeros of f.

$15x^3 + 14x^2 - 3x - 2 = 0$ Set $f(x)$ equal to 0.

$(x + 1)(15x^2 - x - 2) = 0$ Factor using the result from the division.

$(x + 1)(5x - 2)(3x + 1) = 0$ Factor the trinomial.

$3x + 1 = 0 \quad x + 1 = 0$ or $5x - 2 = 0$ or   Set each factor equal to 0.

$x = -\dfrac{1}{3} \quad x = -1 \qquad\qquad x = \dfrac{2}{5}$ Solve for x.

The real zeros of $f(x) = 15x^3 + 14x^2 - 3x - 2$ are -1, $-\frac{1}{3}$, and $\frac{2}{5}$. This can be seen from the graph of f (Figure 3.31), where the x-intercepts occur at -1, $-\frac{1}{3}$, and $\frac{2}{5}$. ∎

Figure 3.31

The graph of $f(x) = 15x^3 + 14x^2 - 3x - 2$ with zeros of -1, $-\frac{1}{3}$, and $\frac{2}{5}$.

2 Use synthetic division to divide polynomials.

There is a faster method, called *synthetic division,* for long division by polynomials of the form $x - c$. Compare the two methods showing $15x^3 + 14x^2 - 3x - 2$ divided by $x + 1$.

Long Division of Polynomials

$$
\begin{array}{r}
15x^2 - x - 2 \quad \leftarrow \text{Quotient} \\
\text{Divisor} \rightarrow x + 1 \overline{\smash{)}15x^3 + 14x^2 - 3x - 2} \quad \leftarrow \text{Dividend} \\
\underline{15x^3 + 15x^2} \\
-\ x^2 - 3x \\
\underline{-\ x^2 - x} \\
-2x - 2 \\
\underline{-2x - 2} \\
0 \quad \leftarrow \text{Remainder}
\end{array}
$$

Synthetic Division

$$
\begin{array}{r|rrrr}
-1 & 15 & 14 & -3 & -2 \\
 & \downarrow & -15 & 1 & 2 \\
\hline
 & 15 & -1 & -2 & 0
\end{array}
$$

Discover for yourself

Study the two methods and answer these questions.

1. How is the dividend represented in the synthetic division process?
2. How is the divisor represented in the synthetic division process? If the divisor is $x + c$, what number would appear to the left of the coefficients of the dividend?
3. How is the quotient represented in the synthetic division process?
4. Where is the remainder in the synthetic division process?
5. The red arrow indicates that the 15 is brought down to the last row. Describe how you might obtain the other three numbers in this row (-1, -2, and 0) using a series of multiplications and additions.

Synthetic division works only for divisors of the form $x - c$. The process of synthetic division is a series of multiplications and additions, shown in the following pattern. How many questions in the Discover for yourself were you able to answer?

Details Behind the Synthetic Division

Divisor:
$x - (-1)$

These are the coefficients of $15x^3 + 14x^2 - 3x - 2$.

The vertical pattern is to add the two numbers in the column. The diagonal pattern is to multiply the resulting sum by -1.

Using long division, we found that

$$
\frac{15x^3 + 14x^2 - 3x - 2}{x + 1} = 15x^2 - x - 2.
$$

The first three numbers in the bottom row of the synthetic division, 15, -1, and -2, are the coefficients of the quotient $15x^2 - x - 2$. The last number, 0, is the remainder.

EXAMPLE 2 **Using Synthetic Division**

Use synthetic division to divide: $x^4 - 6x^3 + 2$ by $x + 4$

Solution

Synthetic Division
To divide a polynomial by $x - c$:

1. Arrange polynomials in descending powers, with a 0 coefficient for any missing term.

$$x - (-4) \overline{) x^4 - 6x^3 + 0x^2 + 0x + 2}$$

2. Write c for the divisor, $x - c$. To the right, write the coefficients of the dividend.

$$-4 \mid \;\; 1 \;\; -6 \;\; 0 \;\; 0 \;\; 2$$

3. Write the leading coefficient of the dividend on the bottom row.

$$-4 \mid \;\; 1 \;\; -6 \;\; 0 \;\; 0 \;\; 2$$
$$\downarrow$$
$$1$$

4. Multiply c (in this case, -4) times the value just written on the bottom row. Write the product in the next column in the second row.

$$-4 \mid \;\; 1 \;\; -6 \;\; 0 \;\; 0 \;\; 2$$
multiply $\quad -4$
$$1$$

5. Add the values in this new column, writing the sum in the bottom row.

$$-4 \mid \;\; 1 \;\; -6 \;\; 0 \;\; 0 \;\; 2$$
$$\underline{\qquad -4 \; \text{Add.}}$$
$$1 \;\; -10$$

6. Repeat this series of multiplications and additions until all columns are filled in.

$$-4 \mid \;\; 1 \;\; -6 \;\; 0 \;\; 0 \;\; 2$$
multiply $\quad -4 \;\; 40 \; \text{Add.}$
$$1 \;\; -10 \;\; 40$$

$$-4 \mid \;\; 1 \;\; -6 \;\; 0 \;\;\;\;\; 0 \;\;\;\; 2$$
$$\downarrow \;\;\;\; -4 \;\; 40 \;\; -160 \;\; 640$$
$$1 \;\; -10 \;\; 40 \;\; -160 \;\; 642$$

7. Use the last row to write the quotient. The final value in this row is the remainder.

$$\frac{x^4 - 6x^3 + 2}{x + 4} = x^3 - 10x^2 + 40x - 160 + \frac{642}{x + 4}$$

The degree of the first term of the quotient is one less than the degree of the first term of the dividend. ∎

The result of Example 2 can be interpreted in two ways:

Dividend: $f(x)$ Quotient: $q(x)$ Remainder: $r(x)$

$$\frac{x^4 - 6x^3 + 2}{x + 4} = x^3 - 10x^2 + 40x - 160 + \frac{642}{x + 4}$$

Divisor: $d(x)$ Divisor: $d(x)$

or

$$x^4 - 6x^3 + 2 = (x + 4)(x^3 - 10x^2 + 40x - 160) + 642$$

Dividend: $f(x)$ Divisor: $d(x)$ Quotient: $q(x)$ Remainder: $r(x)$

Paul Klee (1879–1940) "Woman in Peasant Dress" (Frau in Tracht) 1940.254, paste colour on paper, 48 × 31.3 cm. Kunstmuseum Bern, Paul–Klee–Stiftung, Bern. © ARS, New York.

Notice that the remainder must be a constant when the divisor is in the form $x - c$. We can generalize the last line of this result and write

$$f(x) = d(x)q(x) + r.$$

Dividend Divisor Quotient Remainder

This is known as the *Division Algorithm*.

The Division Algorithm

If $f(x)$ and $d(x)$ are polynomials, with $d(x) \neq 0$, and the degree of $d(x)$ is less than or equal to the degree of $f(x)$, then there exist unique polynomials $q(x)$ and $r(x)$ such that

$$f(x) \quad = \quad d(x) \cdot q(x) + r(x).$$

Dividend   Divisor · Quotient + Remainder

The remainder $r(x)$ equals 0 or it is of degree less than the degree of $d(x)$. If $r(x) = 0$, we say that $d(x)$ *divides evenly* into $f(x)$ and that $d(x)$ and $q(x)$ are *factors* of $f(x)$.

The Remainder and Factor Theorems

If the divisor in the Division Algorithm is of the form $x - c$, then the remainder must be a constant because its degree is less than one, the degree of $x - c$.

$$f(x) = d(x)q(x) + r(x) \qquad \text{This is the Division Algorithm.}$$

Dividend Divisor Quotient Remainder

$$f(x) = (x - c)q(x) + r \qquad \text{The divisor is } x - c. \text{ Call the constant remainder } r.$$

$$f(c) = (c - c)q(c) + r \qquad \text{Find } f(c), \text{ setting } x = c. \text{ This will give an expression for } r.$$

$$f(c) = 0 \cdot q(c) + r \qquad c - c = 0 \text{ and } 0 \cdot q(c) = 0.$$

$$f(c) = r \qquad \text{This final result gives the remainder when } f(x) \text{ is divided by } x - c.$$

This result is called the *Remainder Theorem*.

3 Evaluate a polynomial using the Remainder Theorem.

The Remainder Theorem

If the polynomial $f(x)$ is divided by $x - c$, then the remainder is $f(c)$.

Example 3 shows how we can use the Remainder Theorem to evaluate a polynomial.

EXAMPLE 3   **Using the Remainder Theorem to Evaluate a Polynomial Function**

Given $f(x) = x^3 - 4x^2 + 5x + 3$, use the Remainder Theorem to find $f(2)$.

Since $f(2) = 5$, this means $(2, 5)$ is a point on the graph of $f(x) = x^3 - 4x^2 + 5x + 3$. You can check by substituting 2 for x in $f(x)$.

X=2   Y=5

Solution

By the Remainder Theorem, if $f(x)$ is divided by $x - 2$, then the remainder is $f(2)$. We'll use synthetic division to divide.

$$\begin{array}{r|rrrr} 2 & 1 & -4 & 5 & 3 \\ & & 2 & -4 & 2 \\ \hline & 1 & -2 & 1 & 5 \end{array}$$

Remainder

$$x - 2 \overline{\smash{\big)}\, x^3 - 4x^2 + 5x + 3} \qquad x^2 - 2x + 1 + \dfrac{5}{x - 2}$$

The remainder, 5, is the value of $f(2)$. Thus, $f(2) = 5$.   ∎

Let's look again at the Division Algorithm when the divisor is of the form $x - c$.

$$f(x) = (x - c)q(x) + r$$

↑ Dividend ↑ Divisor ↑ Quotient ↑ Constant remainder

By the Remainder Theorem, the remainder r is $f(c)$, so we can substitute $f(c)$ for r:

$$f(x) = (x - c)q(x) + f(c).$$

Notice that if $f(c) = 0$, then

$$f(x) = (x - c)q(x)$$

so that $x - c$ is a factor of $f(x)$. This means that for the polynomial function $f(x)$, if $f(c) = 0$ then $x - c$ is a factor of $f(x)$.

Let's reverse directions and see what happens if $x - c$ is a factor of $f(x)$. This means that

$$f(x) = (x - c)q(x).$$

If we replace x with c we obtain

$$f(c) = (c - c)q(c) = 0.$$

Thus, if $x - c$ is a factor of $f(x)$, then $f(c) = 0$.

We have proved a result known as the *Factor Theorem.*

The Factor Theorem

Let $f(x)$ be a polynomial.

a. If $f(c) = 0$, then $x - c$ is a factor of $f(x)$.
b. If $x - c$ is a factor of $f(x)$, then $f(c) = 0$.

4 Use the Factor Theorem to solve a polynomial equation.

The examples that follow show how the Factor Theorem can be used to solve polynomial equations.

EXAMPLE 4   Using the Factor Theorem

Solve the equation $2x^3 - 3x^2 - 11x + 6 = 0$ given that 3 is a zero of $f(x) = 2x^3 - 3x^2 - 11x + 6$.

Solution

Since $f(3) = 0$, the Factor Theorem tells us that $x - 3$ is a factor of $f(x)$. We'll use the synthetic division to divide $f(x)$ by $x - 3$.

$$\begin{array}{r|rrrr} 3 & 2 & -3 & -11 & 6 \\ & & 6 & 9 & -6 \\ \hline & 2 & 3 & -2 & 0 \end{array}$$

$$\begin{array}{r} 2x^2 + 3x - 2 \\ x - 3 \overline{\smash{)}\, 2x^3 - 3x^2 - 11x + 6} \end{array}$$

Equivalently:

$$2x^3 - 3x^2 - 11x + 6 = (x - 3)(2x^2 + 3x - 2)$$

Now we can solve the polynomial equation.

$2x^3 - 3x^2 - 11x + 6 = 0$	This is the given equation.
$(x - 3)(2x^2 + 3x - 2) = 0$	Factor using the result from the synthetic division.
$(x - 3)(2x - 1)(x + 2) = 0$	Factor the trinomial.
$x - 3 = 0$ or $2x - 1 = 0$ or $x + 2 = 0$	Set each factor equal to 0.
$x = 3 \qquad x = \frac{1}{2} \qquad x = -2$	Solve for x.

The solution set is $\{-2, \frac{1}{2}, 3\}$. ∎

Using technology

Since the solution set of

$$2x^3 - 3x^2 - 11x + 6 = 0$$

is $\{-2, \frac{1}{2}, 3\}$, this implies that the polynomial function

$$f(x) = 2x^3 - 3x^2 - 11x + 6$$

has x-intercepts (or zeros) at $-2, \frac{1}{2}$, and 3. This is verified by the graph of f.

$f(x) = 2x^3 - 3x^2 - 11x + 6$; x-intercept: $\frac{1}{2}$; x-intercept: -2; x-intercept: 3

Study tip

Synthetic Division and Remainders of Zero

In Example 4 we used synthetic division to divide $f(x) = 2x^3 - 3x^2 - 11x + 6$ by $x - 3$. We obtained a remainder of 0. This indicated that 3 was a solution of the polynomial equation $f(x) = 0$, namely, $2x^3 - 3x^2 - 11x + 6 = 0$. By the Factor Theorem, the following statements are useful in solving polynomial equations.

1. If $f(x)$ is divided by $x - c$ and the remainder is zero, then c is a zero of f and c is a solution of the polynomial equation $f(x) = 0$.
2. If $f(x)$ is divided by $x - c$ and the remainder is 0, then $x - c$ is a factor of $f(x)$.

EXAMPLE 5 Solving a Polynomial Equation

Solve the equation $3x^4 - 11x^3 - x^2 + 19x + 6 = 0$ given that -1 and 2 are roots.

Solution

Related to the given equation is the polynomial function

$$f(x) = 3x^4 - 11x^3 - x^2 + 19x + 6.$$

Since -1 is given to be a root, then $f(-1) = 0$. The Factor Theorem tells us that $x - (-1)$, or $x + 1$, is a factor of $f(x)$. We'll use synthetic division to divide $f(x)$ by $x + 1$.

$$\begin{array}{r|rrrrr} -1 & 3 & -11 & -1 & 19 & 6 \\ & & -3 & 14 & -13 & -6 \\ \hline & 3 & -14 & 13 & 6 & 0 \end{array}$$

$$x + 1 \overline{\smash{)}\, 3x^4 - 11x^3 - x^2 + 19x + 6} \quad \overset{3x^3 - 14x^2 + 13x + 6}{}$$

Equivalently:

$$3x^4 - 11x^3 - x^2 + 19x + 6 = (x + 1)(3x^3 - 14x^2 + 13x + 6)$$

Let's see what we have so far.

$$3x^4 - 11x^3 - x^2 + 19x + 6 = 0 \qquad \text{This is the given equation.}$$

$$(x + 1)(3x^3 - 14x^2 + 13x + 6) = 0 \qquad \text{Factor using the result from the synthetic division.}$$

We were also told that 2 is a root of this equation. Since 2 is not a root of $x + 1 = 0$, it must be a solution of the *reduced equation* $3x^3 - 14x^2 + 13x + 6 = 0$. By the Factor Theorem, $x - 2$ must be a factor of $3x^3 - 14x^2 + 13x + 6$. Now we can use synthetic division to find the other factor.

$$\begin{array}{r|rrrr} 2 & 3 & -14 & 13 & 6 \\ & & 6 & -16 & -6 \\ \hline & 3 & -8 & -3 & 0 \end{array}$$

$$x - 2 \overline{\smash{)}\, 3x^3 - 14x^2 + 13x + 6} \quad \overset{3x^2 - 8x - 3}{}$$

Equivalently:

$$3x^3 - 14x^2 + 13x + 6 = (x - 2)(3x^2 - 8x - 3)$$

Let's put this all together and see what we have.

$$3x^4 - 11x^3 - x^2 + 19x + 6 = 0 \qquad \text{Once again, this is the given equation.}$$

$$(x + 1)(3x^3 - 14x^2 + 13x + 6) = 0 \qquad \text{This was the result of the first synthetic division.}$$

$$(x + 1)(x - 2)(3x^2 - 8x - 3) = 0 \qquad \text{Factor the cubic factor, using the result from the second synthetic division.}$$

$$(x + 1)(x - 2)(3x + 1)(x - 3) = 0 \qquad \text{Factor the trinomial.}$$

$$x + 1 = 0 \text{ or } x - 2 = 0 \text{ or } 3x + 1 = 0 \text{ or } x - 3 = 0 \qquad \text{Set each factor equal to 0.}$$

$$x = -1 \qquad x = 2 \qquad x = -\tfrac{1}{3} \qquad x = 3 \qquad \text{Solve for } x.$$

Thus, the solution set of $3x^4 - 11x^3 - x^2 + 19x + 6 = 0$ is $\{-1, -\tfrac{1}{3}, 2, 3\}$. ∎

Using technology

Since the solution set of

$$3x^4 - 11x^3 - x^2 + 19x + 6 = 0$$

is $\{-1, -\tfrac{1}{3}, 2, 3\}$, this implies that the polynomial function

$$f(x) = 3x^4 - 11x^3 - x^2 + 19x + 6$$

has x-intercepts (or zeros) at $-1, -\tfrac{1}{3}, 2$, and 3. This is verified by the graph of f.

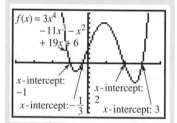

$[-4, 4] \times [-20, 20]$ Yscl $= 2$

---

5 Use the Rational Zero Theorem to find possible rational zeros.

The Rational Zero Theorem

In Examples 4 and 5, we were given a root of the polynomial equation $f(x) = 0$. We used the fact that if c is a root of $f(x) = 0$, then $x - c$ is a factor of $f(x)$. But how do we find c? Once we obtain this first zero, the search for roots is simplified by working with the lower-degree polynomial factor obtained by synthetic division.

The best that mathematicians can provide is a theorem that gives a list of *possible* rational roots of the polynomial equation $f(x) = 0$. Not every number in the list will be a zero, but every rational zero of the polynomial equation will appear somewhere in the list.

The Rational Zero Theorem

If $f(x) = a_n x^n + a_{n-1} x^{n-1} + \cdots + a_1 x + a_0$ has *integer* coefficients and $\dfrac{p}{q}$ (where $\dfrac{p}{q}$ is reduced) is a rational zero, then p is a factor of the constant term a_0 and q is a factor of the leading coefficient a_n.

The "why" behind the Rational Zero Theorem is discussed in Problem 64 of Problem Set 3.3. For now, let's see how we can use this theorem to find possible rational zeros.

EXAMPLE 6 **Using the Rational Zero Theorem**

List all possible rational zeros of $f(x) = 15x^3 + 14x^2 - 3x - 2$.

Solution

$$\text{Possible rational zeros} = \frac{\text{Factors of the constant term}}{\text{Factors of the leading coefficient}}$$

p (factors of the constant term, -2): $\pm 1, \pm 2$
q (factors of the leading coefficient, 15): $\pm 1, \pm 3, \pm 5, \pm 15$

Possible rational zeros are in the form $\dfrac{p}{q}$:

$\pm 1, \pm 2$	Divide each p by $q = \pm 1$.
$\pm\frac{1}{3}, \pm\frac{2}{3},$	Divide each p by $q = \pm 3$.
$\pm\frac{1}{5}, \pm\frac{2}{5}$	Divide each p by $q = \pm 5$.
$\pm\frac{1}{15}, \pm\frac{2}{15},$	Divide each p by $q = \pm 15$.

There are 16 possible rational zeros. The actual solution set to $15x^3 + 14x^2 - 3x - 2 = 0$ is $\{-1, -\frac{1}{3}, \frac{2}{5}\}$, which contains 3 of the 16 possible roots. ∎

The Rational Zero Theorem (Special Case)

Let f be a polynomial of degree $n \geq 1$ with **integer** coefficients and leading coefficient equal to 1. That is, let

$$f(x) = x^n + a_{n-1} x^{n-1} + \cdots + a_1 x + a_0$$

with integer coefficients and $n > 0$. If p is an integer and $f(p) = 0$ (that is, p is a zero of $f(x)$), then p is a factor of a_0.

We will often use this theorem to limit the *possible* integer roots of a given polynomial. The following example is a good illustration.

Let $f(x) = x^3 + 15x^2 - 3x - 45$. We note the following:

(a) 5 is a *possible* integer root of $f(x)$ since it is a factor 45.

(b) We can list all of the possible integer roots:

$$\pm \{1, 3, 5, 15, 45\}$$

The convention used above is a notational convenience. It is simply an abbreviation for

$$\pm 1, \pm 3, \pm 5, \pm 15, \pm 45$$

(c) It is easy to see that $f(x)$ has 3 real roots. Why? It is also easy to check that $f(15) = 0$. What are the other two real roots?

6 Use technology to eliminate possible rational zeros.

Using Technology to Narrow Down the List of Possible Rational Zeros

Example 6 illustrates that a list of possible rational zeros may be quite large. Although we can use synthetic division to check some of the easier values, such as 1, -1, 2, and -2, there are ways of ruling out many of the possible rational roots generated by the Rational Zero Theorem.

A graphing utility can help guide us in determining which possible rational zeros to test. Let's see how this works.

EXAMPLE 7   **Eliminating Possible Rational Zeros with a Graphing Utility**

Find all real zeros of $f(x) = 4x^3 + x^2 - 20x - 5$.

Solution

We begin by listing all possible rational zeros.

p (factors of the constant term, -5): $\pm 1, \pm 5$
q (factors of the leading coefficient, 4): $\pm 1, \pm 2, \pm 4$

Possible rational zeros $\left(\dfrac{p}{q}\right)$: $\pm 1, \pm 5, \pm \dfrac{1}{2}, \pm \dfrac{5}{2}, \pm \dfrac{1}{4}, \pm \dfrac{5}{4}$

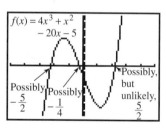

Figure 3.32

The graph of $f(x) = 4x^3 + x^2 - 20x - 5$

With 12 possible rational zeros, we'll graph f using a graphing utility. From Figure 3.32, it looks like possible choices occur at $-\frac{5}{2}$, $-\frac{1}{4}$, and $\frac{5}{2}$. The most reasonable of these options seems to be at $-\frac{1}{4}$, so let's test this value by synthetic division.

$$
\begin{array}{r|rrrr}
-\frac{1}{4} & 4 & 1 & -20 & -5 \\
 & & -1 & 0 & 5 \\
\hline
 & 4 & 0 & -20 & 0
\end{array}
$$

$$
\begin{array}{r}
4x^2 \qquad\quad -20 \\
x + \frac{1}{4} \;\overline{\big)\; 4x^3 + x^2 - 20x - 5}
\end{array}
$$

Equivalently:

$$4x^3 + x^2 - 20x - 5 = (x + \tfrac{1}{4})(4x^2 - 20)$$

The zero remainder tells us that $-\frac{1}{4}$ is a solution of $4x^3 + x^2 - 20x - 5 = 0$, so $x + \frac{1}{4}$ is a factor of the polynomial.

$$4x^3 + x^2 - 20x - 5 = 0$$

Finding zeros of $f(x) = 4x^3 + x^2 - 20x - 5$ is the same as finding solutions of this polynomial equation.

$$(x + \tfrac{1}{4})(4x^2 - 20) = 0$$

Factor using the result from the synthetic division.

$$x + \frac{1}{4} = 0 \quad \text{or} \quad 4x^2 - 20 = 0 \qquad \text{Set each factor equal to 0.}$$
$$x = -\frac{1}{4} \qquad\qquad 4x^2 = 20 \qquad \text{Solve for } x.$$
$$x^2 = 5$$
$$x = \pm\sqrt{5}$$

The solution set is: $\{-\sqrt{5}, -\frac{1}{4}, \sqrt{5}\}$. The real zeros of f are $-\sqrt{5}$, $-\frac{1}{4}$, and $\sqrt{5}$, and these are the x-intercepts shown in Figure 3.32. ∎

Using Algebraic Methods to Narrow Down the List of Possible Rational Zeros

In addition to the graphing utility method, there are two algebraic methods that are useful for eliminating possible rational zeros. One is *Descartes' Rule of Signs* and the other is the *Upper and Lower Bound Theorem*.

7 Use Descartes' Rule of Signs.

Descartes' Rule of Signs

In Section 3.2, we noted that an nth-degree polynomial function can have at most n real zeros. *Descartes' Rule of Signs* provides even more specific information about the number of real zeros that a polynomial can have. The rule is based on considering *variations in sign* between consecutive coefficients. For example, the function

$$f(x) = 3x^7 - 2x^5 - x^4 + 7x^2 + x - 3$$

has three sign changes.

An equation can have as many true [positive] roots as it contains changes of sign, from plus to minus or from minus to plus. ... René Descartes (1596–1650) in *La Géométrie* (1637)
Library of Congress

> #### Descartes' Rule of Signs
>
> Let $f(x) = a_n x^n + a_{n-1} x^{n-1} + \cdots + a_2 x^2 + a_1 x + a_0$ be a polynomial with real coefficients and $a_0 \neq 0$.
> 1. The number of *positive real zeros* of f is either equal to the number of sign changes of $f(x)$ or is less than that number by an even integer. If there is only one variation in sign, there is exactly one positive real zero.
> 2. The number of *negative real zeros* of f is either equal to the number of sign changes of $f(-x)$ or is less than that number by an even integer. If $f(-x)$ has only one variation in sign, then f has exactly one negative real zero.

EXAMPLE 8 **Eliminating Possible Rational Zeros Using Descartes' Rule of Signs**

Solve: $\dfrac{1}{12}x^4 - \dfrac{7}{6}x^3 + \dfrac{71}{12}x^2 - \dfrac{77}{6}x + 10 = 0$

Solution

$$\frac{1}{12}x^4 - \frac{7}{6}x^3 + \frac{71}{12}x^2 - \frac{77}{6}x + 10 = 0 \qquad \text{This is the given equation.}$$

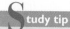
$$12\left(\frac{1}{12}x^4 - \frac{7}{6}x^3 + \frac{71}{12}x^2 - \frac{77}{6}x + 10\right) = 12(0)$$

both sides by 12.

$$x^4 - 14x^3 + 71x^2 - 154x + 120 = 0$$

Simplify. With integer coefficients, we can apply the Rational Zero Theorem.

We begin by listing possible rational roots dividing factors of the constant term by factors of the leading coefficient.

$$\frac{\text{Factors of 120 (the constant term)}}{\text{Factors of 1 (the leading coefficient)}}$$

$$= \pm 1, \pm 2, \pm 3, \pm 4, \pm 5, \pm 6, \pm 8, \pm 10, \pm 12, \pm 15, \pm 20,$$

$$\pm 24, \pm 30, \pm 40, \pm 60, \pm 120$$

Now let's apply Descartes' Rule of Signs to determine the possible number of positive and negative real roots of $x^4 - 14x^3 + 71x^2 - 154x + 120 = 0$.

$$f(x) = x^4 - 14x^3 + 71x^2 - 154x + 120$$

There are four variations in sign.

$$\quad\quad\quad\quad\quad 1 \quad\quad 2 \quad\quad\quad 3 \quad\quad\quad 4$$

This means that the equation has either four, two, or zero positive real roots.

To find possibilities for negative roots, replace x with $-x$ in the polynomial function $f(x) = x^4 - 14x^3 + 71x^2 - 154x + 120$.

$$f(-x) = (-x)^4 - 14(-x)^3 + 71(-x)^2 - 154(-x) + 120$$ Replace x with $-x$.

$$= x^4 + 14x^3 + 71x^2 + 154x + 120$$

There are no variations of sign.

This means that the equation has no negative real roots.

At this point, we have the possible rational roots:

$$1, 2, 3, 4, 5, 6, 8, 10, 12, 15, 20, 24, 30, 40, 60, 120$$

Let's test the two smallest using synthetic division.

Test 1:

$$\begin{array}{r|rrrrr} 1 & 1 & -14 & 71 & -154 & 120 \\ & & 1 & -13 & 58 & -96 \\ \hline & 1 & -13 & 58 & -96 & 24 \end{array}$$

Is 1 a solution of $x^4 - 14x^3 + 71x^2 - 154x + 120$?

← The remainder is not 0, so 1 is not a solution.

Test 2:

$$\begin{array}{r|rrrrr} 2 & 1 & -14 & 71 & -154 & 120 \\ & & 2 & -24 & 94 & -120 \\ \hline & 1 & -12 & 47 & -60 & 0 \end{array}$$

Is 2 a solution of $x^4 - 14x^3 + 71x^2 - 154x + 120$?

← The remainder is 0, so 2 is a solution.

$$x^4 - 14x^3 + 71x^2 - 154x + 120 = 0$$ This is the simplified equation.

$$(x - 2)(x^3 - 12x^2 + 47x - 60) = 0$$ Factor using the result from the second synthetic division.

$$x - 2 = 0 \quad \text{or} \quad x^3 - 12x^2 + 47x - 60 = 0$$ Set each factor equal to 0.

31. $3x^4 + 5x^3 - x^2 - 5x - 2 = 0$

32. $3x^4 + 10x^3 - 14x^2 - 20x + 16 = 0$

33. $5x^5 - x^4 - 25x^3 + 5x^2 + 20x - 4 = 0$

34. $8x^5 - 44x^4 + 86x^3 - 73x^2 + 28x - 4 = 0$

Use the same general strategy as above to find all real zeros of each function in Problems 35–40.

35. $f(x) = 3x^4 + 5x^3 - 11x^2 - 15x + 6$

36. $f(x) = 2x^4 - 5x^3 - 14x^2 + 5x + 12$

37. $f(x) = 4x^5 - 24x^4 + 25x^3 + 39x^2 - 38x - 24$

38. $f(x) = 3x^5 - 9x^4 - 28x^3 + 84x^2 + 9x - 27$

39. $f(x) = x^3 - \frac{5}{2}x^2 - 23x + 12$

40. $f(x) = x^3 + 2x^2 + \frac{11}{9}x + \frac{2}{9}$

Application Problems

41. A box with an open top is to be formed by cutting squares out of the corners of a rectangular piece of cardboard 10 inches by 5 inches and then folding up the sides. What size square must be cut from each corner if the volume of the box is to be 24 cubic inches?

42. An open-top box is to have a square base and a volume of 10 cubic feet. If the material for the bottom costs 15 cents per square foot and that for the sides cost 6 cents per square foot, what dimensions will result in a cost of three dollars?

43. If the volume of the solid shown in the figure is 208 cubic inches, find the value of x.

44. An automobile manufacturer can produce x cars per hour. Hourly costs are $5200, plus $2000 per car. The manufacturer can sell x cars per hour at a price of $7070 - 0.4x^2$ per car. How many cars should be produced and sold per hour to generate a profit of $214,500?

45. The common cold is caused by a rhinovirus. The number of viral invaders present on a given day is estimated by the function $N(t) = -\frac{3}{4}t^4 + 3t^3 + 5$, where N is in billions. What is the fewest number of days such that there are 17 billion viral particles present?

46. The function $S_n(n) = \dfrac{n(n + 1)(2n + 1)}{6}$ describes the sum of the squares of the first n natural numbers. How many natural numbers must be added to produce a sum of 1015?

True–False Critical Thinking Problems

47. Which one of the following is true?

a. The equation $x^3 + 5x^2 + 6x + 1 = 0$ has one positive real solution.

b. Descartes' Rule of Signs gives the exact number of positive and negative roots for a polynomial equation.

c. If $x^3 - 5x^2 + 3x - 2 = 0$, we must replace x with $-x$ to find possibilities for negative real solutions, obtaining $-x^3 + 5x^2 - 3x - 2 = 0$.

d. All real roots of the equation $x^4 - 3x^2 + 2x - 5 = 0$ must lie between -3 and 2.

48. Which one of the following is true?

a. Descartes' Rule of Signs never gives the exact number of positive real roots to a polynomial equation.

b. All real roots of the equation $x^4 - 2x^3 - 9x^2 + 2x + 8 = 0$ must lie between -3 and 5.

c. The equation $x^3 + 8x - 30 = 0$ cannot have a solution between 2 and 3.

d. By graphing $f(x) = 3x^4 + 4x^3 - 7x^2 - 2x - 3$ in a $[-3, 2]$ by $[-20, 20]$ viewing rectangle, it is obvious that the real zeros are rational.

Technology Problems

The equations in Problems 49–52 have real solutions that are rational. Use the Rational Zero Theorem to list all possible rational roots. Then graph the polynomial in the given viewing rectangle to determine which possible rational roots are actual solutions of the equation.

49. $2x^3 - 15x^2 + 22x + 15 = 0$; $[-1, 6]$ by $[-50, 50]$
50. $6x^3 - 19x^2 + 16x - 4 = 0$; $[0, 2]$ by $[-3, 2]$
51. $2x^4 + 7x^3 - 4x^2 - 27x - 18 = 0$; $[-4, 3]$ by $[-45, 45]$
52. $4x^4 + 4x^3 + 7x^2 - x - 2 = 0$; $[-2, 2]$ by $[-5, -5]$
53. Use Descartes' Rule of Signs to determine the possible number of positive and negative real zeros of $f(x) = 3x^4 + 5x^2 + 2$. What does this mean in terms of the graph of f? Verify your result by using a graphing utility to graph f.
54. Use Descartes' Rule of Signs to determine the possible number of positive and negative real zeros of $f(x) = x^5$

$- x^4 + x^3 - x^2 + x - 8$. Verify your result by using a graphing utility to graph f.

55. Make up a number of polynomial functions of odd degree and graph each function. Is it possible for the graph to have no real zeros? Explain. Try doing the same thing for polynomial functions of even degree. Now is it possible to have no real zeros?

56. Show that -1 is a lower bound of $f(x) = x^3 - 53x^2 + 103x - 51$. Show that 60 is an upper bound. Use this information and a graphing utility to draw a relatively complete graph of f.

For Problems 57–58, use a graphing utility to determine upper and lower bounds for the zeros of f. Verify your observations using synthetic division.

57. $f(x) = 2x^3 + x^2 - 14x - 7$

58. $f(x) = 2x^4 - 7x^3 - 5x^2 + 28x - 12$

Writing in Mathematics

59. Give an example of a polynomial function for which Descartes' Rule of Signs eliminates all possible negative rational zeros but retains the possibility of positive rational zeros. Describe the process by which you generated the function.

60. Describe the relationship between the zeros of $f(x) = \frac{1}{4}x^3 + x^2 + 2x - 3$ and $g(x) = x^3 + 4x^2 + 8x - 12$. Are f and g the same function? Explain.

61. How many real solutions does $x^5 + x + 1 = 0$ have? How do you know?

62. Give an example of a polynomial equation that has no real solutions. Describe how you obtained the equation.

63. Most graphing utilities have the ability to find solutions to polynomial equations. The polynomial root-finding

capabilities are accessed using a sequence similar to
2nd POLY . Once the POLY order screen appears, enter an integer representing the order of the equation and then enter its coefficients. Try doing this for the following polynomial equations whose solution sets are given.

$$2x^4 + 7x^3 - 4x^2 - 27x - 18 = 0 \qquad \{-3, -\tfrac{3}{2}, -1, 2\}$$

$$6x^4 - 19x^3 + 21x^2 - 19x + 15 = 0 \qquad \{\tfrac{3}{2}, \tfrac{5}{3}, \pm i\}$$

Describe what happens. Should the techniques for solving polynomial equations discussed in this section be eliminated, using only calculator key sequences to obtain zeros? Defend your position on this issue.

Critical Thinking Problems

64. In this problem, we lead you through the steps involved in the proof of the Rational Zero Theorem. Consider the polynomial equation

$$a_n x^n + a_{n-1} x^{n-1} + a_{n-2} x^{n-2} + \cdots + a_1 x + a_0 = 0$$

where $\frac{p}{q}$ is a rational solution reduced to lowest terms.

a. Substitute $\frac{p}{q}$ for x in the equation and show that the

equation can be written as

$$a_n p^n + a_{n-1} p^{n-1} q + a_{n-2} p^{n-2} q^2 + \cdots + a_1 p q^{n-1} = -a_0 q^n$$

b. Why is p a factor of the left side of the equation?
c. Because p divides the left side, it must also divide

the right side. However, because $\frac{p}{q}$ is reduced to

lowest terms, p cannot divide q. Thus, p and q have no common factors other than -1 and 1. Because p does divide the right side and it is not a factor of q^n, what can you conclude?

d. Rewrite the equation from part (a) with all terms containing q on the left and the term that does not have a factor of q on the right. Use an argument that parallels parts (b) and (c) to conclude that q is a factor of a_n.

65. Consider the polynomial equation $x^2 - 3 = 0$. Use the Rational Root Theorem to show that $\sqrt{3}$ is not a rational number.

66. Suppose the equation $x^3 + x^2 + x - p = 0$ (p is a prime number) has one rational root. Find value(s) of p. For each value of p, find the solution set of the equation.

SECTION 3.4

Solutions Manual   Tutorial   Video 6

More on Zeros of Polynomial Functions

Objectives

1 Approximate irrational zeros.
2 Factor polynomials over the complex nonreals.
3 Find polynomials with given zeros.
4 Solve a polynomial equation with a given nonreal complex root.

In this section, we continue our study of zeros of polynomial functions. We'll be focusing more closely on both irrational and nonreal complex zeros.

1 Approximating irrational zeros.

Approximating Irrational Zeros

A graphing utility provides an effective method for finding decimal approximations to irrational roots of polynomial equations. There is also an effective numerical method for obtaining these approximations.

Let's consider a specific example. The graph of $f(x) = x^3 + x - 1$, shown in Figure 3.38, was obtained with a graphing utility using a standard range setting. It appears that f has a real zero somewhere between 0.5 and 1. This seems plausible because the graph of f lies below the x-axis to the left of this zero and above the x-axis to the right of this zero.

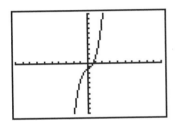

Figure 3.38

The graph of $f(x) = x^3 + x - 1$ with a real zero between 0.5 and 1

We can provide numerical support for our observation that there may be a real zero between 0.5 and 1 by evaluating the function at these values:

$$f(0.5) = -0.375 < 0 \quad \text{and} \quad f(1) = 1 > 0.$$

Since the function value is negative at 0.5 and positive at 1, its graph will have to cross the x-axis somewhere between 0.5 and 1.

Figure 3.39 once again shows the graph of f, but this time in a $[-1, 1]$ by $[-2, 2]$ viewing rectangle. It now appears that there is a real zero somewhere between 0.6 and 0.8. Once again, the graph lies below the x-axis prior to this value and above the x-axis after this value. This is reinforced by evaluating the function at each value:

$$f(0.6) = -0.184 < 0 \quad \text{and} \quad f(0.8) = 0.312 > 0.$$

Figure 3.40 shows an approximation for the function's zero. Correct to the nearest hundredth, the zero is 0.68.

Discover for yourself

Prove that the real zero for $f(x) = x^3 + x - 1$, shown in Figure 3.38, is not rational. Use the Rational Zero Theorem and show that the function does not have any possible rational zeros between 0 and 1.

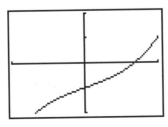

Figure 3.39

The graph of $f(x) = x^3 + x - 1$

X=.68232780383   Y=0

Figure 3.40

The zero is approximately 0.68.

Using technology

The graph in Figure 3.40 was obtained by entering

$$y_1 = x^3 + x - 1$$

and

$$y_2 = 0$$

and then using the $\boxed{\text{ISECT}}$ feature. Another option is to enter only y_1, changing the scale on the x-axis to, say, 0.001, and zooming in several times.

A nonvisual approach is to use the utility's polynomial equation-solving feature as shown in the figures. To solve $x^3 + 0x^2 + x - 1 = 0$, enter the order (3), followed by the coefficients (1, 0, 1, and -1). Then press $\boxed{\text{SOLVE}}$. The third screen on the right verifies that the real zero (x_3) is approximately 0.68.

The order (degree) of
$x^3 + x - 1 = 0$ is 3.

The coefficients of
$x^3 + 0x^2 + x - 1 = 0$
are 1, 0, 1, -1.

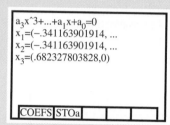

The real zero (x_3) is
approximately 0.68.

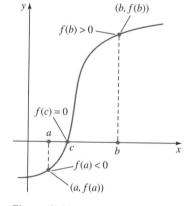

Figure 3.41

The graph must cross the x-axis
at some value between a and b.

The numerical support that we provided in narrowing down the location of a real zero is generalized in Figure 3.41. The figure shows that if $(a, f(a))$ lies below the x-axis and $(b, f(b))$ lies above the x-axis, the smooth, continuous graph of a polynomial function f must cross the x-axis at some value c between a and b. This value is a real zero for the function.

These observations are summarized in the *Intermediate Value Theorem*.

The Intermediate Value Theorem for polynomials

Let $f(x)$ be a polynomial with real coefficients. If $f(a)$ and $f(b)$ have opposite signs, then there is at least one value of c between a and b for which $f(c) = 0$. Equivalently, the equation $f(x) = 0$ has at least one real root between a and b.

Discover for yourself

Use the Rational Zero Theorem
to show that

$$f(x) = x^3 - 2x - 5$$

does not have any possible
rational zeros between 2 and 3.
Thus, the zero between 2 and 3
must be irrational.

EXAMPLE 1   Approximating a Real Zero

a. Show that the polynomial $f(x) = x^3 - 2x - 5$ has a zero between 2 and 3.
b. Use the Intermediate Value Theorem to find an approximation for this zero to the nearest tenth.
c. Use a graphing utility to verify part (b) and find the function's real zero correct to the nearest thousandth.

Solution

a. Since $f(2) = -1 < 0$ and $f(3) = 16 > 0$, the Intermediate Value Theorem states that there is a number c between 2 and 3 for which $f(c) = 0$. In other words, the polynomial has a zero between 2 and 3.

b. A numerical approach is to evaluate f at successive tenths between 2 and 3, looking for a sign change. This sign change will place the real zero between the successive tenths.

x	$f(x) = x^3 - 2x - 5$	
2	$f(2) = 2^3 - 2(2) - 5 =$	-1 ⎤ sign
2.1	$f(2.1) = (2.1)^3 - 2(2.1) - 5 = 0.061$	⎦ change ←

The sign change indicates that f has a real zero between 2 and 2.1. We now follow a similar procedure to locate the real zero between successive hundredths. We divide the interval $[2, 2.1]$ into ten equal subintervals, evaluate f at each endpoint, and look for a sign change.

$f(2.00) = -1$ $f(2.06) = -0.378184$

$f(2.01) = -0.899399$ $f(2.07) = -0.270257$

$f(2.02) = -0.797592$ $f(2.08) = -0.161088$

$f(2.03) = -0.694573$ $f(2.09) = -0.050671$ ⎤ sign

$f(2.04) = -0.590336$ $f(2.1) = 0.061$ ⎦ change ←

$f(2.05) = -0.484875$

The sign change indicates that f has a real zero between 2.09 and 2.1. Correct to the nearest tenth, the zero is 2.1.

c. The graph in Figure 3.42 was obtained by entering $Y_1 = X \boxed{\wedge} 3 - 2X - 5$ and $Y_2 = 0$ and using the $\boxed{\text{ISECT}}$ feature in a $[-3, 3]$ by $[-10, 10]$ viewing rectangle. You can also change the scale on the x-axis to 0.001 and zoom in several times. Correct to the nearest thousandth, the function's real zero is 2.095. ∎

Nonreal Complex Zeros

Up to this point, our focus has been on real zeros of polynomials. Let's now look at an example of a polynomial equation that has two roots that are complex and nonreal.

Discover for yourself

Spreadsheet programs or the table function can be used to make tables and perform calculations on a graphing utility. Use these features to find the values for

$f(x) = x^3 - 2x - 5$

for values of the domain shown on the right. You can use the values of $f(x)$ to determine where zeros occur. Now modify this procedure to get closer approximations of the zero.

X=2.0945514815   Y=0

Figure 3.42

The real zero for $f(x) = x^3 - 2x - 5$ is approximately 2.095.

EXAMPLE 2   **Solving a Polynomial Equation**

Solve: $x^4 - 6x^2 - 8x + 24 = 0$

Solution

First we list all possible rational solutions.

p (factors of the constant term, 24): $\pm1, \pm2, \pm3, \pm4, \pm6, \pm8, \pm12, \pm24$

q (factors of the leading coefficient, 1): ±1

Possible rational $(\frac{p}{q})$ solutions are $\pm1, \pm2, \pm3, \pm4, \pm6, \pm8, \pm12, \pm24$.

Using synthetic division, we can show that 2 is a solution.

$$\begin{array}{r|rrrrr} 2 & 1 & 0 & -6 & -8 & 24 \\ & & 2 & 4 & -4 & -24 \\ \hline & 1 & 2 & -2 & -12 & 0 \end{array}$$ ← Coefficients of $x^4 + 0x^3 - 6x^2 - 8x + 24$

← The zero remainder indicates that 2 is a solution.

Now we can rewrite the given equation in factored form.

$x^4 - 6x^2 - 8x + 24 = 0$ This is the given equation.

$(x - 2)(x^3 + 2x^2 - 2x - 12) = 0$ This is the result obtained from the synthetic division.

$(x - 2)(x - 2)(x^2 + 4x + 6) = 0$ Reapply the Rational Zero Theorem and synthetic division to
$(x - 2)^2(x^2 + 4x + 6) = 0$ $x^3 + 2x^2 - 2x - 12 = 0$.
2 is a root:

$$\begin{array}{r|rrrr} 2 & 1 & 2 & -2 & -12 \\ & & 2 & 8 & 12 \\ \hline & 1 & 4 & 6 & 0 \end{array}$$

$(x - 2)^2 = 0$ or $x^2 + 4x + 6 = 0$ Set each factor equal to 0.

$x = 2$ Solve for x.

We can use the quadratic formula to solve $x^2 + 4x + 6 = 0$.

$$x = \frac{-4 \pm \sqrt{4^2 - 4(1)(6)}}{2(1)} = \frac{-4 \pm \sqrt{-8}}{2}$$ $a = 1$, $b = 4$, and $c = 6$. Substitute in $\dfrac{-b \pm \sqrt{b^2 - 4ac}}{2a}$.

$$= \frac{-4 \pm 2i\sqrt{2}}{2}$$ $\sqrt{-8} = \sqrt{4 \cdot 2}\, i = 2i\sqrt{2}$

$$= -2 \pm i\sqrt{2}$$ Divide numerator and denominator by 2.

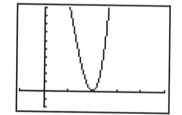

Figure 3.43

The graph of $f(x) = x^4 - 6x^2 - 8x + 24$ in a $[-1, 5]$ by $[-2, 10]$ viewing rectangle

The solution set of $x^4 - 6x^2 - 8x + 24 = 0$ is $\{2, -2 - i\sqrt{2}, -2 + i\sqrt{2}\}$. ■

In Example 2, the factor $x - 2$ occurred twice in the factorization. The factor $(x - 2)^2$ yielded the repeated root 2 of multiplicity 2. Notice how the graph of $f(x) = x^4 - 6x^2 - 8x + 24 = 0$ in Figure 3.43 flattens out at $(2, 0)$. The end behavior (rising to the left and to the right) suggests that we have a relatively complete picture of the function. The graph illustrates that nonreal complex zeros do not appear as x-intercepts.

We can generalize our work in Example 2 and discover two useful properties of polynomial equations.

Discover for yourself

Shown on page 383 are four polynomial equations and their solutions. Study the given information and:

1. Write a statement about the number of solutions for a polynomial equation of degree n if multiplicities are counted.
2. Write a statement about the relationship between the two nonreal complex solutions.

Equation	Degree	Solutions	Number of Solutions (Counting Multiplicities)
$x^4 - 6x^2 - 8x + 24 = 0$ (Example 2)	4	2(Multiplicity two) $-2 + i\sqrt{2}$ $-2 - i\sqrt{2}$	Four
$2x^4 - 3x^3 + 12x^2 + 22x - 60 = 0$	4	$-2, \dfrac{3}{2},$ $1 + 3i, 1 - 3i$	Four
$x^5 - 5x^4 + 12x^3 - 24x^2 + 32x - 16 = 0$	5	1, 2, (Multiplicity two), $2i$ (or $0 + 2i$), $-2i$ (or $0 - 2i$)	Five
$3x^3 + 13x^2 - 16 = 0$	3	$-4, -\frac{4}{3}, 1$	Three

In the Discover for yourself, were you able to write the following relationships?

Properties of polynomial equations

1. If a polynomial equation is of degree n, then counting multiplicities, the equation has exactly n solutions.
2. If $a + bi$ is a solution of a polynomial equation ($b \neq 0$), then the nonreal complex number $a - bi$ is also a solution. Nonreal complex roots, if they exist, occur in conjugate pairs.

Let's develop these ideas in more detail.

The Fundamental Theorem of Algebra

In 1799, a 22-year-old student named Carl Friedrich Gauss proved in his doctoral dissertation that every polynomial equation of degree n, where $n \geq 1$, has at least one complex solution. His result is called the *Fundamental Theorem of Algebra*.

The Fundamental Theorem of Algebra

If $f(x)$ is a polynomial of degree n, where $n \geq 1$, then the equation $f(x) = 0$ has at least one complex root.

As an immediate consequence of the Fundamental Theorem, we can prove the following theorem.

The Linear Factorization Theorem

If $f(x) = a_n x^n + a_{n-1} x^{n-1} + \cdots + a_1 x + a_0$, where $n \geq 1$ and $a_n \neq 0$, then

$$f(x) = a_n(x - c_1)(x - c_2) \cdots (x - c_n)$$

2 Factor polynomials over the complex nonreals.

where $c_1, c_2, \ldots, c_n$ are complex numbers (possibly real and not necessarily distinct).

In words: An nth-degree polynomial can be expressed as the product of n linear factors.

Proof of the Linear Factorizaton Theorem

To prove the Linear Factorization Theorem, we'll begin with a polynomial equation of degree n:

$$f(x) = 0.$$

By the Fundamental Theorem of Algebra, we know that this equation has at least one complex root; we'll call it c_1. By the Factor Theorem, we know that $x - c_1$ is a factor of $f(x)$. Therefore, we obtain

$$(x - c_1)q_1(x) = 0$$ The degree of the polynomial $q_1(x)$ is $n - 1$. (Since we divided by $x - c_1$, $q_1(x)$ has a_n as its leading coefficient).

$$x - c_1 = 0 \quad \text{or} \quad q_1(x) = 0$$ Set each factor equal to 0.

If the degree of $q_1(x)$ is at least 1, by the Fundamental Theorem the equation $q_1(x) = 0$ has at least one complex root. We'll call it c_2. The Factor Theorem gives us

$$q_1(x) = 0$$ The degree of $q_1(x)$ is $n - 1$.

$$(x - c_2)q_2(x) = 0$$ The degree of $q_2(x)$ is $n - 2$.

$$x - c_2 = 0 \quad \text{or} \quad q_2(x) = 0$$ Set each factor equal to 0.

Let's see what we have up to this point, and then continue the process.

$$f(x) = 0$$ This is the original polynomial equation of degree n.

$$(x - c_1)q_1(x) = 0$$ This is the result from our first application of the Fundamental Theorem.

$$(x - c_1)(x - c_2)q_2(x) = 0$$ This is the result from our second application of the Fundamental Theorem.

$$\vdots$$

$$(x - c_1)(x - c_2)(x - c_3) \cdots (x - c_n)a_n = 0$$ Continue the process n times until obtaining the quotient $q_n(x) = a_n$.

Equating the first and last expressions that are both equal to 0, we obtain

$$f(x) = a_n(x - c_1)(x - c_2) \cdots (x - c_n)$$

as we wished to show.

In Example 2, we found that $x^4 - 6x^2 - 8x + 24 = 0$ has $\{2, -2 - i\sqrt{2}, -2 + i\sqrt{2}\}$ as a solution set, where 2 is a root of multiplicity 2. With these zeros, we can write the polynomial $f(x) = x^4 - 6x^2 - 8x + 24$ as a product of linear factors.

$$x^4 - 6x^2 - 8x + 24 = (x - 2)(x - 2)[x - (-2 - i\sqrt{2})][x - (-2 + i\sqrt{2})]$$
$$= (x - 2)^2(x + 2 + i\sqrt{2})(x + 2 - i\sqrt{2})$$

> **Study tip**
>
> The Linear Factorization Theorem tells us that an nth-degree polynomial can be expressed as the product of n linear factors. However, it does not tell us how to find the factors. Finding the factors involves the techniques for solving polynomial equations illustrated in Example 2.

Notice that the Linear Factorization Theorem tells us that an nth-degree polynomial has n linear factors. Equivalently, an nth-degree polynomial equation has precisely n solutions. Keep in mind that these solutions can be real or nonreal complex, and they may be repeated.

The Numbers of Roots Theorem

If $f(x)$ is a polynomial of degree at least 1, then $f(x) = 0$ has exactly n roots, where roots are counted according to their multiplicity.

The Linear Factorization Theorem involves factors somewhat different than you are used to seeing. For example, the polynomial $x^2 - 3$, although irreducible over the rational numbers, can be factored over the reals as follows:

$$x^2 - 3 = (x + \sqrt{3})(x - \sqrt{3}).$$ Use $a^2 - b^2 = (a + b)(a - b)$ with $a = x$ and $b = \sqrt{3}$.

However, the polynomial $x^2 + 1$ is irreducible over the reals, but reducible over the complex nonreals.

$$x^2 + 1 = (x + i)(x - i)$$

Study tip

The sum of squares, irreducible over the reals, can be factored over the complex nonreals as

$$a^2 + b^2 = (a + bi)(a - bi)$$

EXAMPLE 3   Factoring a Polynomial

Factor $x^4 - 3x^2 - 28$:

a. As the product of factors that are irreducible over the rationals.
b. As the product of factors that are irreducible over the reals.
c. In completely factored form involving complex nonreals.

Solution

a. $x^4 - 3x^2 - 28 = (x^2 - 7)(x^2 + 4)$ Both quadratic factors are irreducible over the rationals.

b. $\qquad = (x + \sqrt{7})(x - \sqrt{7})(x^2 + 4)$ The third factor is still irreducible over the reals.

c. $\qquad = (x + \sqrt{7})(x - \sqrt{7})(x + 2i)(x - 2i)$ This is the completely factored form using complex nonreals. ∎

Barry Flanagan "Large Mirror Nijinski" 1992, bronze, 121 3/4 × 89 × 36 in. (309.2 × 226 × 91.4 cm). © Barry Flanagan, courtesy Waddington Galleries, London.

Conjugate Pairs

Another result that is sometimes helpful in finding roots and in understanding graphing patterns for polynomial functions is the Conjugate Roots Theorem.

The Conjugate Roots Theorem

Let $f(x)$ be a polynomial with real coefficients. If the complex number $a + bi$ is a root of $f(x) = 0$, then $a - bi$ is also a root (a and b are real numbers).
In words: Complex nonreal zeros occur in conjugate pairs.

3 Find polynomials with given zeros.

| **EXAMPLE 4** | **Finding a Polynomial Satisfying a Given Description** |

Find a fourth-degree polynomial function $f(x)$ with real coefficients that has $-2, 2,$ and i as zeros and such that $f(3) = -150$.

Solution

Because i is a zero and the polynomial has real coefficients, the conjugate $-i$ must also be a zero. We can now use the Linear Factorization Theorem.

$$f(x) = a_n(x - c_1)(x - c_2)(x - c_3)(x - c_4)$$
This is the linear factorization for a fourth-degree polynomial.

$$= a_n(x + 2)(x - 2)(x - i)(x + i)$$
Use the given zeros: $c_1 = -2, c_2 = 2, c_3 = i,$ and, from above, $c_4 = -i$.

$$= a_n(x^2 - 4)(x^2 + 1)$$
Multiply.

$$= a_n(x^4 - 3x^2 - 4)$$
Complete the multiplication.

$$f(3) = a_n(3^4 - 3 \cdot 3^2 - 4) = -150$$
To find a_n, use the fact that $f(3) = -150$.

$$50a_n = -150$$
Solve for a_n.

$$a_n = -3$$

Substituting -3 for a_n in the formula for $f(x)$, we obtain

$$f(x) = -3(x^4 - 3x^2 - 4).$$

Equivalently,

$$f(x) = -3x^4 + 9x^2 + 12.$$ ∎

Using technology

In Example 4, we found that

$$f(x) = -3x^4 + 9x^2 + 12$$

is the function that has $-2, 2,$ and i as zeros and such that $f(3) = -150$. Now let's use a graphing utility to check that this function really does satisfy the four given conditions. Since we are checking real zeros of -2 and 2, a reasonable range setting for x is

Xmin $= -3$, Xmax $= 3$, Xscl $= 1$.

To establish a range setting for y, notice that the leading coefficient (-3) is negative and the degree (4) is even, so the graph falls to the left and to the right. The y-intercept is

$$f(0) = -3(0)^4 + 9(0)^2 + 12, \text{ or } 12$$

and we also know that $f(3) = -150$. Using this information, we've chosen a range setting for y as

Ymin $= -200$, Ymax $= 20$, Yscl $= 20$.

Figure 3.44

The graph of $f(x) = -3x^4 + 9x^2 + 12$, verifying real zeros of -2 and 2

The graph of $f(x) = -3x^4 + 9x^2 + 12$ is shown in Figure 3.44, verifying real zeros of -2 and 2. The graph crosses the x-axis at each zero without flattening out, a convincing visual representation that each zero has multiplicity 1. Trace along the curve and verify that $f(3) = -150$.

EXAMPLE 5 **Finding a Polynomial with Given Zeros**

Find a third-degree polynomial function $f(x)$ with real coefficients that has 3 and $1 - 2i$ as zeros and such that $f(2) = 20$.

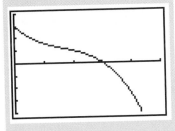

Using technology

The graph of
$f(x) = -4x^3 + 20x^2 - 44x + 60$
was obtained using
Xmin = 0, Xmax = 5, Xscl = 1,
Ymin = -80, Ymax = 80,
Yscl = 20

The graph verifies a real zero at 3, and even without using the TRACE feature, we can see that $f(2) = 20$ since $(2, 20)$ appears to be a point on the graph.

Solution

Because $1 - 2i$ is a zero of f, so is $1 + 2i$.

$$f(x) = a_n(x - c_1)(x - c_2)(x - c_3)$$

This is the linear factorization for a cubic (third-degree) polynomial.

$$= a_n(x - 3)[x - (1 - 2i)][x - (1 + 2i)]$$

Use the zeros:
$c_1 = 3, c_2 = 1 - 2i,$
and $c_3 = 1 + 2i$.

$$\overset{F}{} \quad \overset{O}{} \quad \overset{I}{} \quad \overset{L}{}$$
$$= a_n(x - 3)[x^2 - x(1 + 2i) - x(1 - 2i) + (1 - 4i^2)]$$

Multiply the last two factors using the FOIL pattern for binomial multiplication.

$$= a_n(x - 3)(x^2 - 2x + 5)$$

Simplify. Use the fact that $i^2 = -1$.

$$= a_n(x^3 - 5x^2 + 11x - 15)$$

Complete the multiplication.

$$f(2) = a_n(2^3 - 5 \cdot 2^2 + 11 \cdot 2 - 15) = 20$$

Use the fact that $f(2) = 20$ to find the value of a_n.

$$-5a_n = 20$$

$$a_n = -4$$

Substituting -4 for a_n in the formula for $f(x)$, we obtain

$$f(x) = -4(x^3 - 5x^2 + 11x - 15) = -4x^3 + 20x^2 - 44x + 60 \qquad ∎$$

4 Solve a polynomial equation with a given nonreal complex root.

EXAMPLE 6 **Using the Conjugate Roots Theorem to Solve a Polynomial Equation**

Solve $x^4 - 4x^3 + 3x^2 + 8x - 10 = 0$ given that $2 + i$ is a root.

Solution

Because complex nonreal roots come in conjugate pairs, we know that $2 - i$ is also a root. By the Factor Theorem, both

$$[x - (2 + i)] \text{ and } [x - (2 - i)]$$

are factors of the given polynomial. We multiply these known factors.

$$[x - (2 + i)][x - (2 - i)]$$

$$\overset{F}{} \quad \overset{O}{} \quad \overset{I}{} \quad \overset{L}{}$$
$$= x^2 - x(2 - i) - x(2 + i) + (2 + i)(2 - i)$$

Multiply using the FOIL method.

$$= x^2 - 2x + ix - 2x - ix + (4 - i^2)$$

Continue multiplying.

$$= x^2 - 4x + 5$$

Simplify, using $i^2 = -1$.

We can find the other factor(s) by dividing $x^2 - 4x + 5$ into the polynomial on the left side of the given equation.

$$
\begin{array}{r}
x^2 \qquad\quad - 2 \\
x^2 - 4x + 5 \overline{\smash{\big)}\, x^4 - 4x^3 + 3x^2 + 8x - 10} \\
\underline{x^4 - 4x^3 + 5x^2} \\
-2x^2 + 8x - 10 \\
\underline{-2x^2 + 8x - 10} \\
0
\end{array}
$$

We can now solve the given equation.

$$x^4 - 4x^3 + 3x^2 + 8x - 10 = 0 \qquad \text{This is the original equation.}$$

$$(x^2 - 4x + 5)(x^2 - 2) = 0 \qquad \text{Factor using the result of the polynomial long division.}$$

$$x^2 - 4x + 5 = 0 \quad \text{or} \quad x^2 - 2 = 0 \qquad \text{Set each factor equal to 0.}$$

$$x = 2 \pm i \qquad\quad x = \pm\sqrt{2} \qquad \text{Solve for } x. \text{ We know the roots for the first equation by our previous analysis.}$$

The solution set is $\{2 \pm i, \pm\sqrt{2}\}$. ∎

Using technology

Figure 3.45

The graph of $f(x) = x^4 - 4x^3 + 3x^2 + 8x - 10$ with real zeros approximately equal to -1.4 and 1.4

We can use the results of Example 6 to obtain a relatively complete graph of

$$f(x) = x^4 - 4x^3 + 3x^2 + 8x - 10.$$

The real zeros $\pm\sqrt{2}$ correspond to x-intercepts at approximately ± 1.4, so we'll set Xmin = -4 and Xmax = 4, with Xscl = 1. Since $n = 4$ and $a_n = 1 > 0$, the graph rises to the left and right.

The graph of f shown in Figure 3.45 was obtained using the following range setting:

Xmin = -4, Xmax = 4, Xscl = 1, Ymin = -15, Ymax = 5, Yscl = 1

The graph confirms that the real zeros of f are $\pm\sqrt{2}$, or approximately ± 1.4.

Study tip

You can use the graph of a polynomial function to convince yourself that a polynomial of degree n has n roots, and that nonreal complex zeros come in pairs. Let's do this for the third-degree polynomial function

$$f(x) = a_3 x^3 + a_2 x^2 + a_1 x + a_0.$$

If $a_3 > 0$, we know that the graph of f falls to the left and rises to the right. As we see in Figure 3.46 on page 388, the first graph of f has three distinct real zeros, with each real zero corresponding to an x-intercept. By sliding the graph up and down, nonreal complex zeros are gained in pairs.

This also occurs in the case of multiple zeros, shown in Figure 3.47 on page 388. (Remember that a graph crosses the x-axis at a zero of odd multiplicity.)

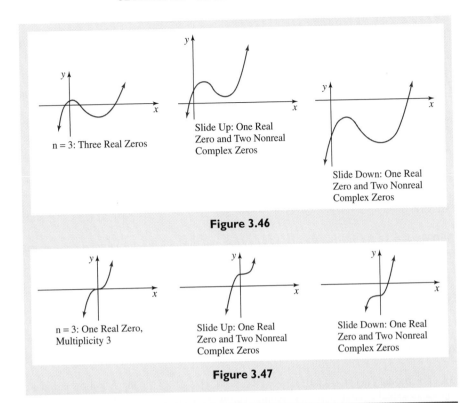

Figure 3.46

Figure 3.47

PROBLEM SET 3.4

Practice Problems

In Problems 1–8, show that each polynomial has a zero between the given integers. Then use the Intermediate Value Theorem to find an approximation for this zero to the nearest tenth. Use a graphing utility to verify your result.

1. $f(x) = x^3 - x - 1$; between 1 and 2

2. $f(x) = x^3 - 4x^2 + 2$; between 0 and 1

3. $f(x) = 2x^4 - 4x^2 + 1$; between -1 and 0

4. $f(x) = x^4 + 6x^3 - 18x^2$; between 2 and 3

5. $f(x) = x^3 + x^2 - 2x + 1$; between -3 and -2

6. $f(x) = x^5 - x^3 - 1$; between 1 and 2

7. $f(x) = 3x^3 - 10x + 9$; between -3 and -2

8. $f(x) = 3x^3 - 8x^2 + x + 2$; between 2 and 3

In Problems 9–12, find an nth-degree polynominal function with real coefficients satisfying the given conditions. Use a graphing utility to graph the function and verify your answers.

9. $n = 3$; -5 and $4 + 3i$ are zeros; $f(2) = 91$

10. $n = 3$; $-\frac{3}{4}$ and $1 + \frac{1}{2}i$ are zeros; $f(1) = 7$

11. $n = 4$; i and $3i$ are zeros; $f(-1) = 20$

12. $n = 4$; -2, $-\frac{1}{2}$, and i are zeros; $f(1) = 18$

In Problems 13–24, use the given root to find the solution set of the polynomial equation.

13. $x^3 - 2x^2 + 4x - 8 = 0$; $-2i$

14. $x^4 + 13x^2 + 36 = 0$; $3i$

15. $3x^3 - 7x^2 + 8x - 2 = 0$; $1 + i$

16. $x^3 - 7x^2 + 16x - 10 = 0$; $3 + i$

17. $x^4 - 6x^2 + 25 = 0$; $2 - i$

18. $x^4 - x^3 - 9x^2 + 29x - 60 = 0$; $1 + 2i$

19. $3x^4 + 2x^3 + 13x^2 + 22x - 6 = 0$; $1 - i$

20. $4x^4 - 28x^3 + 129x^2 - 130x + 125 = 0$; $3 - 4i$

21. $x^4 - 12x^3 + 56x^2 - 120x + 96 = 0;\ 3 - i\sqrt{3}$

22. $9x^4 + 18x^3 + 20x^2 - 32x - 64 = 0;\ -1 - i\sqrt{3}$

23. $x^5 - 2x^4 + 6x^3 + 24x^2 + 5x + 26 = 0;\ 2 - 3i$

24. $x^5 + x^4 + 7x^3 - x^2 + 12x - 20 = 0;\ -1 + 2i$

In Problems 25–32, find all the zeros of the function and write the polynomial as a product of linear factors.

25. $f(x) = x^3 - x^2 + 25x - 25$

26. $g(x) = x^3 - 10x^2 + 33x - 34$

27. $p(x) = x^4 + 37x^2 + 36$

28. $p(x) = x^4 + 8x^3 + 9x^2 - 10x + 100$

29. $p(x) = 16x^4 + 36x^3 + 16x^2 + x - 30$

30. $p(x) = 2x^4 - x^3 + 7x^2 - 4x - 4$

31. $g(r) = 3r^6 + 5r^5 + r^4 + 5r^3 + r^2 + 5r - 2$

32. $g(x) = x^5 + x^4 - 14x^3 - 14x^2 + 49x + 49$

In Problems 33–34, use the Rational Zero Theorem to show that the equation has no rational roots. Approximate any irrational root to the nearest tenth, checking your answer using the polynomial root-finding capability of your graphing utility.

33. $x^3 - x^2 - 2 = 0$

34. $x^4 + 2x - 2 = 0$

Application Problems

35. The model $f(x) = -0.0013x^3 + 0.078x^2 - 1.43x + 18.1$ describes the percent of U.S. families below the poverty level x years after 1960, where $0 \leqslant x \leqslant 30$.

  a. What percent of U.S. families were below the poverty level in 1970?

  b. In what other years were the percent of U.S. families below the poverty level the same as that of 1970?

36. One of Egypt's largest pyramids was built by Khufu, a king of the fourth dynasty. The pyramid has a square base and a height that is 8 dekameters less than the length of a side of the square base. If the pyramid's volume is 2645 cubic dekameters, what are its dimensions? (The volume of a pyramid is the product of $\frac{1}{3}$, the area of the base, and the height.)

Romilly Lockyer / The Image Bank

37. A slice 2 centimeters thick is cut from one face of a cube. If the volume of the resulting solid is 567 cubic centimeters, find the dimensions of the cube.

38. A hollow cubical box has a uniform thickness of 1 inch. The space inside the box is $\frac{1}{8}$ the volume of the material used in its construction. Find the dimensions of the box to the nearest tenth of an inch.

39. A person standing on the roof of a hotel 30 feet above the ground observes a bungee jumper leaping from a platform 70 feet above the roof. The bungee jumper passes the roof level after 3 seconds, again after 7 seconds on the way back up, and after 10 seconds on the way back down. Find a cubic polynomial function that models the height of the bungee jumper relative to the hotel's roof level.

True–False Critical Thinking Problems

40. Which one of the following is true?

    a. Some polynomials of odd degree have no x-intercepts.

    b. The graph of $f(x) = x^5 + 2x^4 - 6x^3 + 2x - 3$ shown in the figure is drawn completely.

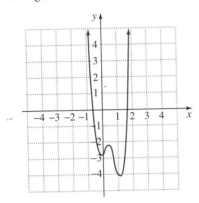

    c. If $c > 0$, $d > 0$, and $e > 0$, then the solution set of $x^4 + cx^2 + dx - e = 0$ contains one positive number, one negative number, and two nonreal complex numbers.

    d. Fourth-degree polynomial functions have graphs with at least one x-intercept.

41. Which one of the following is true?

    a. The function whose graph is shown in the figure at the top of the next column cannot be a fourth-degree polynomial.

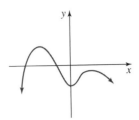

    b. The equation $x^n - 1 = 0$ has $n - 2$ nonreal complex roots if n is even. $(n \neq 0)$

    c. The graph of $f(x) = (x - 2)^3(x + 1)^2$ shown in the figure below is not drawn completely.

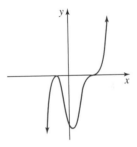

    d. A polynomial function of degree n has a graph with precisely $n - 1$ turning points.

Technology Problems

42. The function $f(x) = -0.00002x^3 + 0.008x^2 - 0.3x + 6.95$ models the number of annual physician visits f by a person of age x.

    a. Graph the function for meaningful values of x and discuss what the graph reveals in terms of the variables described by the model.

    b. Use the polynomial root-finding capability of your graphing utility to find the age (to the nearest year) for the group that averages 13.43 annual physician visits.

    c. Verify part (b) using the graph of f.

43. Graph the model in Problem 39 and determine the relative minimum and maximum height of the bungee jumper relative to the hotel's roof level.

Use a graphing utility to obtain a complete graph for each polynomial function in Problems 44–51. Then determine the number of real zeros and the number of nonreal complex zeros for each function.

44. $f(x) = x^3 - 6x - 9$

46. $f(x) = 3x^5 - 2x^4 + 6x^3 - 4x^2 - 24x + 16$

48. $f(x) = x^6 - 64$

50. $f(x) = x^4 - 3x^3 - 4x^2$

45. $f(x) = x^5 + x^3 + 2x^2 - 12x + 8$

47. $f(x) = 3x^4 + 4x^3 - 7x^2 - 2x - 3$

49. $f(x) = 3x^5 + 24x^3 + 48x$

51. $f(x) = x^5 - 1.5x^4 - 3.2x^3 + 1.3x^2 + 1.5x - 0.6$

Writing in Mathematics

In Problems 52–55, what is the smallest degree that each polynomial could have? Explain how you arrived at your answer.

52.

53.

54.

55.

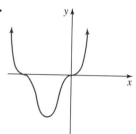

56. Explain why nonreal complex zeros are gained or lost in pairs in terms of graphs of polynomial functions.

57. Explain why a polynomial function of degree 20 cannot cross the *x*-axis exactly once.

58. Explain how you can find a polynomial of least degree with real coefficients that has zeros of 3, $-1 + 2i$, and $1 - 2i$.

59. Is it possible for a third-degree polynomial function to have exactly one relative maximum? Explain.

Critical Thinking Problems

60. Draw a polynomial function with a positive leading coefficient whose degree is 4 and with four distinct real zeros. Then use the shape of this graph and slide it upward (or downward) to graph a fourth-degree polynomial function having:

  a. Three distinct real zeros, one with multiplicity 2
  b. Two distinct real zeros
  c. One real zero of multiplicity 2
  d. No real zeros

61. Draw a polynomial function with a positive leading coefficient whose degree is 5 and with five distinct real

zeros. Then use the shape of this graph and slide it upward (or downward) to graph a fifth-degree polynomial function having:

  a. Four distinct real zeros, one with multiplicity 2
  b. Three distinct real zeros
  c. Two distinct real zeros, one with multiplicity 2
  d. One real zero
  e. Is it possible to have no real zeros? Explain.

Solve each polynomial inequality in Problems 62–64.

62. $x^5 - x^3 \geq 0$
63. $x^3 - 4x^2 - x + 4 \leq 0$
64. $x^3 - 4x + 1 < 0$
65. **a.** Show that $2i$ is a solution of $x^3 - 2ix^2 - 4x + 8i = 0$.
  b. Show that $-2i$ is *not* a solution of the equation in part (a).

  c. Since $0 + 2i$ is a solution of the given equation, shouldn't $0 - 2i$ also be a solution? Explain why this is *not* a contradiction of the Conjugate Roots Theorem.

66. Give an example of a function that is not subject to the Intermediate Value Theorem.

Group Activity Problem

67. Use the Intermediate Value Theorem to write a computer or graphing calculator program for estimating a positive irrational zero of a polynomial function to any specified degree of accuracy.

SECTION 3.5 ## Graphing Rational Functions

Objectives

Solutions   Tutorial   Video
Manual   7

1 Graph the reciprocal function.
2 Graph transformations of the reciprocal function.
3 Give the equation of a rational function's horizontal asymptote.
4 Determine symmetry for a rational function's graph.
5 Graph rational functions.
6 Graph rational functions with slant asymptotes.

Rational functions such as

$$f(x) = \frac{x}{x^2 - 16} \quad \text{and} \quad g(x) = \frac{2x^2 + 3x - 5}{x - 2}$$

consist of the quotient of two polynomial functions. Unlike polynomial functions, many rational functions have graphs wtith breaks in their curves (see Figure 3.48). Asymptotes—lines that curves approach—are helpful in graphing rational functions.

Rational Functions

Rational functions are quotients of polynomial functions.

Figure 3.48

The graph of $f(x) = \dfrac{x}{x^2 - 16}$ has breaks at -4 and 4 but approaches $x = -4$ and $x = 4$.

> **Rational functions and their domains**
>
> A *rational function* is one that can be written in the form
>
> $$f(x) = \frac{p(x)}{q(x)}$$
>
> where $p(x)$ and $q(x)$ are polynomial functions and $q(x) \neq 0$. The *domain* of a rational function is the set of all real numbers except the x-values that make the denominator $q(x)$ equal zero.

	Graph the reciprocal function.

The most basic rational function is the *reciprocal function*, defined by

$$f(x) = \frac{1}{x}.$$

EXAMPLE 1 **The Reciprocal Function**

Find the domain of $f(x) = \dfrac{1}{x}$ and graph the function.

Solution

The denominator of the reciprocal function is zero when $x = 0$, so the domain of f is the set of all real numbers except for 0.

To examine the behavior of f near the excluded value 0, we evaluate $f(x)$ to the left and right of 0.

		x approaches 0 from the left.			
x	-1	-0.5	-0.1	-0.01	-0.001
$f(x) = \dfrac{1}{x}$	-1	-2	-10	-100	-1000

	x approaches 0 from the right.				
x	0.001	0.01	0.1	0.5	1
$f(x) = \dfrac{1}{x}$	1000	100	10	2	1

Figure 3.49 illustrates the behavior of $f(x) = \dfrac{1}{x}$ near 0, decreasing without bound as x approaches 0 from the left and increasing without bound as x approaches 0 from the right. We use our special arrow notation to describe this situation symbolically:

$$f(x) \to -\infty \quad \text{as} \quad x \to 0^- \qquad \text{and} \qquad f(x) \to \infty \quad \text{as} \quad x \to 0^+$$

$f(x)$ approaches negative infinity (that is, the graph falls) as x approaches 0 from the left.

$f(x)$ approaches infinity (that is, the graph rises) as x approaches 0 from the right.

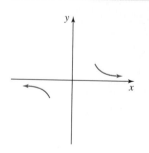

Figure 3.49

Figure 3.49 illustrates that the function is getting closer and closer to the y-axis. A line that the graph of a function gets closer and closer to is called an *asymptote*. Thus, the line whose equation is $x = 0$ (that is, the y-axis) is a *vertical asymptote* of the graph of $f(x) = \dfrac{1}{x}$.

Now let's see what happens for values of x that get farther away from the origin. We create tables for x as $|x|$ increases without bound.

Study tip

The minus $(-)$ superscript on the 0 $(x \to 0^-)$ is read "from the left;" the plus $(+)$ superscript $(x \to 0^+)$ is read "from the right."

x increases without bound:

x	1	10	100	1000
$f(x) = \dfrac{1}{x}$	1	0.1	0.01	0.001

x decreases without bound:

x	-1	-10	-100	-1000
$f(x) = \dfrac{1}{x}$	-1	-0.1	-0.01	-0.001

Figure 3.50 illustrates the behavior of $f(x) = \dfrac{1}{x}$ as x increases or decreases without bound. The values of y are getting progressively closer to 0. This means that the graph of f is approaching the horizontal line $y = 0$ (that is, the x-axis) as x increases or decreases without bound. We use the arrow notation to describe this situation.

Figure 3.50

$f(x)$ approaches 0 as x increases or decreases without bound.

$$f(x) \to 0 \quad \text{as} \quad x \to \infty \qquad \text{and} \qquad f(x) \to 0 \quad \text{as} \quad x \to -\infty$$

$f(x)$ approaches 0 as x increases without bound.

$f(x)$ approaches 0 as x decreases without bound.

Figure 3.51

The graph of $f(x) = \dfrac{1}{x}$

Since the graph of f is approaching the horizontal line $y = 0$ as $x \to \infty$ and as $x \to -\infty$, the line whose equation is $y = 0$ (the x-axis) is a *horizontal asymptote* of the graph of $f(x) = \dfrac{1}{x}$. The completed graph of f is shown in Figure 3.51. ■

The arrow notation used throughout Example 1 is summarized in the following box.

Arrow notation

Symbol	Meaning
$x \to a^+$	x approaches a from the right.
$x \to a^-$	x approaches a from the left.
$x \to \infty$	x approaches infinity; that is, x increases without bound.
$x \to -\infty$	x approaches negative infinity; that is, x decreases without bound.

Horizontal and Vertical Asymptotes

The graph of the rational function $f(x) = \dfrac{1}{x}$ differs from the graph of a polynomial function in two ways. First, the graph has a break in it and is composed of two distinct branches. Second, the curve has *linear asymptotes*, lines that the graph approaches arbitrarily closely. Many, but not all, rational functions have vertical and horizontal asymptotes.

Vertical and horizontal asymptotes

1. The line $x = a$ is a *vertical asymptote* of a function f if $f(x)$ increases or decreases without bound as x approaches a.

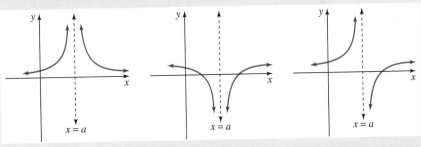

Thus, $x = a$ is a vertical asymptote of f if $f(x) \to \infty$ or $f(x) \to -\infty$ as $x \to a^+$ or $x \to a^-$.

2. The line $y = b$ is a *horizontal asymptote* of a function f if $f(x)$ approaches b as x increases or decreases without bound.

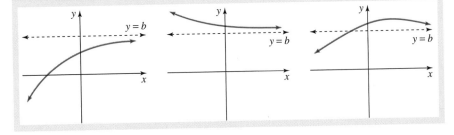

Study tip

The zeros of the denominator of a rational function will often give the vertical asymptotes.

Study tip

A curve can never cross a vertical asymptote. However, it can intersect a horizontal asymptote.

Thus, $y = b$ is a horizontal asymptote of f if $f(x) \to b$ as $x \to \infty$ or $x \to -\infty$.

2 Graph transformations of the reciprocal function.

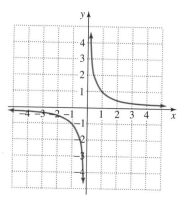

Figure 3.52

The graph of the reciprocal function $f(x) = \dfrac{1}{x}$

Some rational functions can be graphed using transformations of the graph of $f(x) = \dfrac{1}{x}$.

EXAMPLE 2   **Transformations of the Reciprocal Function**

Use the graph of the reciprocal function $f(x) = \dfrac{1}{x}$, shown again in Figure 3.52, to graph each function. Give equations for the vertical and horizontal asymptotes of each function.

a. $y = \dfrac{1}{x - 3}$ **b.** $y = \dfrac{1}{x} - 2$ **c.** $y = \dfrac{2}{x}$

d. $y = -\dfrac{1}{x}$ **e.** $y = -\dfrac{3}{x - 2} - 1$

Solution

Equation and Transformation	Graph	Vertical Asymptote	Horizontal Asymptote
a. $y = \dfrac{1}{x - 3}$ Shift the graph of $y = \dfrac{1}{x}$ to the right three units.	Shift right 3 units. 	$x = 3$ $y \to -\infty$ as $x \to 3^-$ and $y \to \infty$ as $x \to 3^+$	$y = 0$ (x-axis) $y \to 0$ as $x \to -\infty$ and $y \to 0$ as $x \to \infty$
b. $y = \dfrac{1}{x} - 2$ Shift the graph of $y = \dfrac{1}{x}$ downward two units.		$x = 0$ (y-axis) $y \to -\infty$ as $x \to 0^-$ and $y \to \infty$ as $x \to 0^+$	$y = -2$ $y \to -2$ as $x \to -\infty$ and $y \to -2$ as $x \to \infty$
c. $y = \dfrac{2}{x}$ Multiply each y-value of $y = \dfrac{1}{x}$ by 2. Each point on the graph is twice as far from the x-axis.		$x = 0$ (y-axis) $y \to -\infty$ as $x \to 0^-$ and $y \to \infty$ as $x \to 0^+$	$y = 0$ (x-axis) $y \to 0$ as $x \to -\infty$ and $y \to 0$ as $x \to \infty$

Equation and Transformation	Graph	Vertical Asymptote	Horizontal Asymptote
d. $y = -\dfrac{1}{x}$ Reflect the graph of $y = \dfrac{1}{x}$ in the x-axis.		$x = 0$ (y-axis) $y \to \infty$ as $x \to 0^-$ and $y \to -\infty$ as $x \to 0^+$	$y = 0$ (x-axis) $y \to 0$ as $x \to -\infty$ and $y \to 0$ as $x \to \infty$

e. $y = -\dfrac{3}{x-2} - 1$
1. Shift the graph of
   $y = \dfrac{1}{x}$ to the right two
   units. $\left(y = \dfrac{1}{x-2}\right)$
2. Stretch, multiplying
   y-values by 3. $\left(y = \dfrac{3}{x-2}\right)$
3. Reflect in the
   x-axis. $\left(y = -\dfrac{3}{x-2}\right)$
4. Shift downword one unit.
   $\left(y = -\dfrac{3}{x-2} - 1\right)$
		$x = 2$
		$y \to \infty$ as $x \to 2^-$
		and
		$y \to -\infty$ as $x \to 2^+$
			$y = -1$
			$y \to -1$ as $x \to -\infty$
			and
			$y \to -1$ as $x \to \infty$

∎

In Example 2, we can obtain the equation for each rational function's vertical asymptote by setting the denominator equal to 0. For example, the rational function in part (a)

$$y = \frac{1}{x - 3}$$

has a vertical asymptote when $x - 3 = 0$. The equation of the vertical asymptote is $x = 3$. The zeros of the denominator of a rational function will often give the vertical asymptotes.

There is also a rapid way to determine the horizontal asymptotes, if there are any. Before we state this procedure, take a few minutes to discover it for yourself with the aid of your graphing utility. (Use the Study tip on page 398 to work the Discover for yourself without a graphing utility.)

M. C. Escher (1898–1972) "Bond of Union" © 1997 Cordon Art – Baarn – Holland. All rights reserved.

Discover for yourself

1. Use a graphing utility to graph f and g in the same viewing rectangle. Begin with a standard viewing rectangle. Then zoom out to a viewing rectangle such as $[-100, 100]$ by $[-1000, 1000]$. In each case, show that g is a horizontal asymptote for f.

$$f(x) = \frac{4x}{2x^2 + 1} \quad \text{and} \quad g(x) = 0$$

$$f(x) = \frac{-6x}{2x^2 + 1} \quad \text{and} \quad g(x) = 0$$

If the highest power in the numerator of a rational function's equation is less than the highest power in the denominator, generalize from these examples and write the

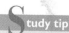

S tudy tip

You can work the first two parts of the Discover for yourself without a graphing utility. Simply generalize from the equation of the function and the horizontal asymptote, using the pattern to write the horizontal asymptote's equation based on the highest powers in the numerator and denominator of the given rational function.

equation of the function's horizontal asymptote. Use your graphing utility to verify this observation for a rational function of your choice.

2. Now repeat the exercise with your graphing utility, again showing that g is a horizontal asymptote for f in the following cases:

$$f(x) = \frac{4x^2}{2x^2 + 1} \quad \text{and} \quad g(x) = 2$$

$$f(x) = \frac{-6x^2}{2x^2 + 1} \quad \text{and} \quad g(x) = -3$$

If a rational function has the same highest power in the numerator and denominator, generalize from these examples and describe how you can use the leading coefficients to write the equation of the function's horizontal asymptote. Use your graphing utility to verify this observation for a function of your choice.

3. Now graph the rational functions

$$f(x) = \frac{4x^3}{2x^2 + 1} \quad \text{and} \quad f(x) = \frac{4x^2}{2x + 1}$$

where the highest power in the numerator is greater than the highest power in the denominator. Begin with a standard viewing rectangle, zooming out to $[-100, 100]$ by $[-1000, 1000]$. What can you conclude about horizontal asymptotes when the highest power in the numerator is greater than the highest power in the denominator? Use your graphing utility to verify this observation for a function of your choice.

In the Discover for yourself, did you observe that the equation for the horizontal asymptote, if there is one, depends on the highest power in the numerator and denominator of the rational function's equation? In particular, were you able to discover the following rules for obtaining horizontal asymptotes for rational functions?

3 Give the equation of a rational function's horizontal asymptote.

S tudy tip

For the rational function whose equation appears in the box on the right, recall that n, the highest power in the numerator, is called the *degree* of the numerator. Similarly, m, the highest power in the denominator, is called the *degree* of the denominator.

Horizontal asymptote of a rational function

Let f be the rational function given by

$$f(x) = \frac{a_n x^n + a_{n-1} x^{n-1} + \cdots + a_1 x + a_0}{b_m x^m + b_{m-1} x^{m-1} + \cdots + b_1 x + b_0}, \quad a_n \neq 0, b_m \neq 0.$$

1. If $n < m$, the x-axis is a horizontal asymptote.

2. If $n = m$, the line $y = \dfrac{a_n}{b_m}$ is a horizontal asymptote.

3. If $n > m$, there is no horizontal asymptote.

EXAMPLE 3 **Horizontal Asymptotes of Rational Functions**

Give the equation for the horizontal asymptote, if there is one, for each rational function:

a. $f(x) = \dfrac{4x}{2x^2 + 1}$ **b.** $g(x) = \dfrac{4x^2}{2x^2 + 1}$ **c.** $h(x) = \dfrac{4x^3}{2x^2 + 1}$

(a)

(b)

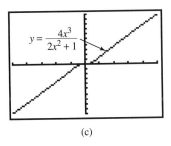

(c)

Figure 3.53

4 Determine symmetry for a rational function's graph.

Solution

a. $f(x) = \dfrac{4x}{2x^2 + 1}$

The degree of the numerator, 1, is less than the degree of the denominator, 2. Thus, the graph of f has the x-axis as a horizontal asymptote (see Figure 3.53(a)). The equation of the horizontal asymptote is $y = 0$.

b. $g(x) = \dfrac{4x^2}{2x^2 + 1}$

The degree of the numerator, 2, is equal to the degree of the denominator, 2. The leading coefficients of the numerator and denominator, 4 and 2, are used to obtain the equation of the horizontal asymptote. The equation of the horizontal asymptote is $y = \frac{4}{2}$ or $y = 2$ (see Figure 3.53(b)).

c. $h(x) = \dfrac{4x^3}{2x^2 + 1}$

The degree of the numerator, 3, is greater than the degree of the denominator, 2. Thus, the graph of h has no horizontal asymptote (see Figure 3.53(c)). ∎

Symmetry

The presence of symmetry is helpful in graphing rational functions. The tests of symmetry are the same as those used for polynomial functions and are restated below.

> **y-axis and origin symmetry**
>
> The graph of a rational function f is symmetric with respect to the y-axis if $f(-x) = f(x)$. The graph is symmetric with respect to the origin if $f(-x) = -f(x)$.

> **EXAMPLE 4**   **Determining Symmetry for Graphs of Rational Functions**

Discuss the symmetry of the graph of each rational function.

a. $f(x) = \dfrac{4x}{2x^2 + 1}$ **b.** $g(x) = \dfrac{4x^2}{2x^2 + 1}$

Solution

In each case, replace x with $-x$.

a. $f(x) = \dfrac{4x}{2x^2 + 1}$

$f(-x) = \dfrac{4(-x)}{2(-x)^2 + 1} = \dfrac{-4x}{2x^2 + 1} = -f(x)$

Since $f(-x) = -f(x)$, the graph is symmetric with respect to the origin (see Figure 3.54(a)).

b. $g(x) = \dfrac{4x^2}{2x^2 + 1}$

(a)

Figure 3.54(a)

(b)

Figure 3.54(b)

$$g(-x) = \frac{4(-x)^2}{2(-x)^2 + 1} = \frac{4x^2}{2x^2 + 1} = g(x)$$

Since $g(-x) = g(x)$, the graph is symmetric with respect to the y-axis (see Figure 3.54 (b)). ∎

Discover for yourself

Give an example of a rational function that has neither y-axis nor origin symmetry. Then verify this fact by graphing the function with a graphing utility.

5 Graph rational functions.

Graphing Rational Functions

Here are some suggestions for graphing rational functions.

Strategy for graphing a rational function

Suppose that

$$f(x) = \frac{p(x)}{q(x)}$$

where $p(x)$ and $q(x)$ are polynomial functions with no common factors.
1. Determine whether the graph of f has symmetry.

   $f(-x) = f(x)$: y-axis symmetry

   $f(-x) = -f(x)$: origin symmetry

2. Find and plot the y-intercept (if there is one) by evaluating $f(0)$.
3. Find and plot the x-intercepts (if there are any) by solving the equation $p(x) = 0$.
4. Find any vertical asymptote(s) by solving the equation $q(x) = 0$. Sketch the vertical asymptotes.
5. Find and sketch the horizontal asymptote (if there is one) using the rule for determining the horizontal asymptote of a rational function.
6. Plot at least one point between and beyond each x-intercept and vertical asymptote.
7. Use smooth curves to graph the function between and beyond the vertical asymptotes.
8. Use a graphing utility in the DOT mode to verify that the graph has been drawn correctly.

Study tip

Values where the denominator of a rational function are zero do not necessarily result in vertical asymptotes. There is a hole and not a vertical asymptote in the graph if there is a reduced form of the function's equation that does not make the denominator zero. Here's an example that we graphed in Chapter 2:

$$f(x) = \frac{x^2 - 9}{x - 3}$$

$$= \frac{(x + 3)(x - 3)}{x - 3}$$

$$= x + 3 \quad (x \neq 3)$$

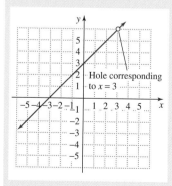

EXAMPLE 5 **Graphing a Rational Function**

Graph: $f(x) = \dfrac{2x}{x - 1}$

Solution

Step 1. Determine symmetry.

$$f(-x) = \frac{2(-x)}{-x - 1} = \frac{-2x}{-x - 1} = \frac{2x}{x + 1}$$

Figure 3.55

The y-intercept is 0.

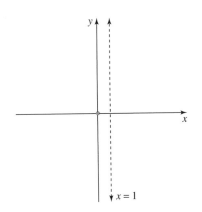

Figure 3.56

The vertical asymptote is $x = 1$.

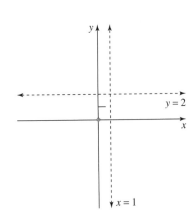

Figure 3.57

The horizontal asymptote is $y = 2$.

Since $f(-x)$ does not equal $f(x)$ or $-f(x)$, the graph has neither y-axis nor origin symmetry.

Step 2. Find the y-intercept by evaluating $f(0)$.

$$f(0) = \frac{2 \cdot 0}{0 - 1} = \frac{0}{-1} = 0$$

The y-intercept is 0, and so the graph passes through the origin (Figure 3.55).

Step 3. Find x-intercept(s) by solving $p(x) = 0$.

$2x = 0$ Set the numerator equal to 0.

$x = 0$

There is only one x-intercept. Again, the graph passes through the origin.

Step 4. Find the vertical asymptote(s) by solving $q(x) = 0$.

$x - 1 = 0$ Set the denominator equal to 0.

$x = 1$

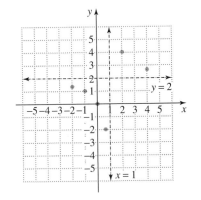

Figure 3.58

The equation of the vertical asymptote is $x = 1$ (Figure 3.56).

Step 5. Find the horizontal asymptote. Since the numerator and denominator have the same degree, the equation of the horizontal asymptote is

$$y = \frac{2}{1} = 2.$$

The graph of $y = 2$ is shown in Figure 3.57.

Step 6. Plot points between and beyond each x-intercept and vertical asymptote.

x	-2	-1	$\frac{1}{2}$	2	4
$f(x) = \dfrac{2x}{x - 1}$	$\dfrac{4}{3}$	1	-2	4	$\dfrac{8}{3}$

Figure 3.58 shows these points, the y-intercept, and the asymptotes.

Step 7. Use a smooth curve to graph the function. The graph of $f(x) = \dfrac{2x}{x - 1}$ is shown in Figure 3.59.

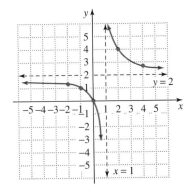

Figure 3.59

The graph of $f(x) = \dfrac{2x}{x - 1}$

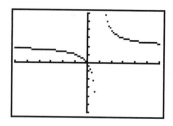

Figure 3.60

The graph of $y = \dfrac{2x}{x-1}$ generated by a graphing utility

Step 8. Although most graphing utilities do not produce good graphs of rational functions, the graph obtained in Figure 3.60 (using the DOT mode) verifies that our hand-drawn graph is correct. ∎

EXAMPLE 6 Graphing a Rational Function

Graph: $f(x) = \dfrac{3x}{x^2 - 1}$

Solution

Step 1. Determine symmetry.

$$f(-x) = \frac{3(-x)}{(-x)^2 - 1} = \frac{-3x}{x^2 - 1} = -f(x)$$

The graph is symmetric with respect to the origin. This should become more obvious as we continue with our graphing strategy.

Step 2. Find the y-intercept by evaluating $f(0)$.

$$f(0) = \frac{3 \cdot 0}{0^2 - 1} = \frac{0}{-1} = 0$$

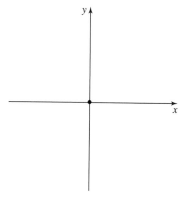

Figure 3.61

The y-intercept is 0.

The y-intercept is 0, and so the graph passes through the origin (Figure 3.61).

Step 3. Find the x-intercept(s) by solving $p(x) = 0$.

$3x = 0$ Set the numerator equal to 0.

$x = 0$

There is only one x-intercept. Again, the graph passes through the origin.

Step 4. Find the vertical asymptote(s) by solving $q(x) = 0$.

$x^2 - 1 = 0$ Set the denominator equal to 0.

$x^2 = 1$

$x = \pm 1$

The equations of the vertical asymptotes are $x = -1$ and $x = 1$.

Step 5. Find the horizontal asymptote. Since the degree of the numerator, 1, is less than the degree of the denominator, 2, the x-axis is a horizontal asymptote. The equation of the horizontal asymptote is $y = 0$. Figure 3.62 shows the intercept and the asymptotes.

Step 6. Plot points between and beyond the x-intercept and the vertical asymptotes.

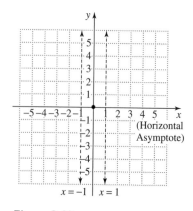

Figure 3.62

The function's intercept and asymptotes

x	-3	-2	-0.5	0.5	2	3
$f(x) = \dfrac{3x}{x^2 - 1}$	$-\dfrac{9}{8}$	-2	2	-2	2	$\dfrac{9}{8}$

Figure 3.63 on page 402 shows these points, the y-intercept, and the asymptotes.

Step 7. Use a smooth curve to graph the function. The graph of $f(x) = \dfrac{3x}{x^2 - 1}$ is shown on page 402 in Figure 3.64. The origin symmetry is now obvious.

Figure 3.63

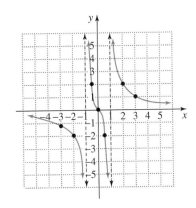

Figure 3.64

The graph of $f(x) = \dfrac{3x}{x^2 - 1}$

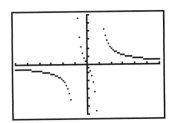

Figure 3.65

The graph of $y = \dfrac{3x}{x^2 - 1}$

generated by a graphing utility

Step 8. The graph shown in Figure 3.65, obtained with a graphing utility, verifies that our hand-drawn graph is correct. ∎

EXAMPLE 7   **Graphing a Rational Function**

Graph: $f(x) = \dfrac{3x^2}{x^2 - 4}$

Solution

Step 1. Symmetry: $f(-x) = \dfrac{3(-x)^2}{(-x)^2 - 4} = \dfrac{3x^2}{x^2 + 4} = f(x)$: Symmetric with respect to the y-axis.

Step 2. y-intercept: $f(0) = \dfrac{3 \cdot 0^2}{0^2 - 4} = \dfrac{0}{-4} = 0$: y-intercept is 0.

Step 3. x-intercept: $3x^2 = 0$, so $x = 0$: x-intercept is 0.

Step 4. Vertical asymptotes: Set $q(x) = 0$.

$\quad x^2 - 4 = 0 \qquad$ Set the denominator equal to 0.

$\qquad\quad x^2 = 4$

$\qquad\quad x = \pm 2$

Vertical asymtotes: $x = -2$ and $x = 2$

Step 5. Horizontal asymptote: $y = \dfrac{3}{1} = 3$

Step 6. Additional points:

x	-3	-1	1	3	4
$f(x) = \dfrac{3x^2}{x^2 - 4}$	$\dfrac{27}{5}$	-1	-1	$\dfrac{27}{5}$	4

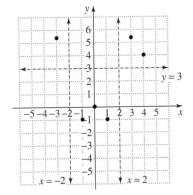

Figure 3.66

Figure 3.66 shows these points, the y-intercept, and the asymptotes.

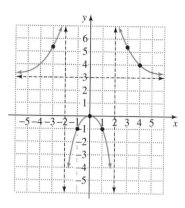

Figure 3.67

The graph of $f(x) = \dfrac{3x^2}{x^2 - 4}$

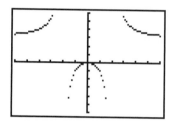

Figure 3.68

The graph of $y = \dfrac{3x^2}{x^2 - 4}$

generated by a graphing utility

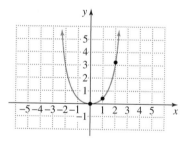

Figure 3.69

The graph of $f(x) = \dfrac{x^4}{x^2 + 1}$

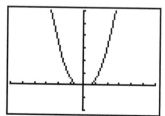

Figure 3.70

The graph of $y = \dfrac{x^4}{x^2 + 1}$,

generated by a graphing utility

Step 7. Use a smooth curve to graph the function. The graph of $f(x) = \dfrac{3x^2}{x^2 - 4}$ is shown in Figure 3.67. The y-axis symmetry is now obvious.

Step 8. The graph shown in Figure 3.68, obtained with a graphing utility, verifies that our hand-drawn graph is correct.   ∎

Example 8 illustrates that not every rational function has vertical and horizontal asymptotes.

EXAMPLE 8 **Graphing a Rational Function**

Graph: $f(x) = \dfrac{x^4}{x^2 + 1}$

Solution

Step 1. Symmetry: $f(-x) = \dfrac{(-x)^4}{(-x)^2 + 1} = \dfrac{x^4}{x^2 + 1}$: Symmetric with respect to the y-axis

Step 2. y-intercept: $f(0) = \dfrac{0^4}{0^2 + 1} = \dfrac{0}{1} = 0$: y-intercept is 0.

Step 3. x-intercept: also 0

Step 4. Vertical asymptote: Set $q(x) = 0$.

$x^2 + 1 = 0$ Set the denominator equal to 0.

$x^2 = -1$

Although this equation has imaginary solutions ($x = \pm i$), there are no real solutions. Thus, there is no vertical asymptote.

Step 5. Horizontal asymptote: Since the degree of the numerator, 4, is greater than the degree of the denominator, 2, there is no horizontal asymptote.

Step 6. Additional points:

x	0	1	2	3
$f(x) = \dfrac{x^4}{x^2 + 1}$	0	$\dfrac{1}{2}$	$\dfrac{16}{5}$	$\dfrac{81}{10}$

Step 7. Figure 3.69 shows the graph of f, using three points obtained from the table and y-axis symmetry. Notice that as x gets infinitely large or infinitely small, the function is getting larger without bound.

Step 8. The graph shown in Figure 3.70, obtained with a graphing utility, verifies that our hand-drawn graph is correct. The graph has no asymptotes, so we did not use the DOT mode.   ∎

6 Graph rational functions with slant asymptotes.

Slant Asymptotes

The graph of

$$f(x) = \frac{x^2 + 1}{x - 1}$$

Degree = 2
Degree = 1

has no horizontal asymptote because the degree of the numerator is greater than the degree of the denominator. However, in this situation, there is a *slant asymptote,* as shown in Figure 3.71.

The equation of the slant asymptote can be found by division.

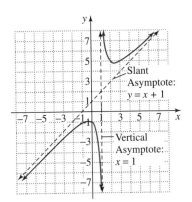

Figure 3.71

The graph of $f(x) = \dfrac{x^2 + 1}{x - 1}$

with a slant asymptote

$$\begin{array}{r|rrr} 1 & 1 & 0 & 1 \\ & & 1 & 1 \\ \hline & 1 & 1 & 2 \end{array}$$

$$x + 1 + \frac{2}{x + 1}$$

$$x - 1 \overline{\smash{\big)}\, x^2 + 0x + 1}$$

Since $f(x) = \dfrac{x^2 + 1}{x - 1}$, divide $x - 1$ into $x^2 + 1$.

Observe that

$$f(x) = \frac{x^2 + 1}{x - 1} = \underbrace{x + 1}_{\substack{\text{Slant asymptote:} \\ y = x + 1}} + \frac{2}{x - 1}$$

If $|x| \to \infty$, the value of $\dfrac{2}{x - 1}$ is approximately 0. Thus, when $|x|$ is large, the function is very close to $y = x + 1 + 0$. This means that as $x \to \infty$ or as $x \to -\infty$, the graph of f gets closer and closer to the line whose equation is $y = x + 1$. The line is a slant asymptote of the graph.

We can generalize from these observations and obtain a procedure for finding slant asymptotes, sometimes called *oblique asymptotes.*

Finding slant (or oblique) asymptotes

If $f(x) = \dfrac{p(x)}{q(x)}$ and the degree of p is one greater than the degree of q, the graph of f has a slant asymptote. Find the slant asymptote by dividing $q(x)$ into $p(x)$. The division will take the form

$$\frac{p(x)}{q(x)} = \underbrace{mx + b}_{\substack{\text{Slant asymptote:} \\ y = mx + b}} + \frac{R(x)}{q(x)}$$

As $|x| \to \infty$, the term $\dfrac{R(x)}{q(x)}$ is close to 0. Consequently, $y = mx + b$ is the equation of the slant or oblique asymptote.

EXAMPLE 9 **A Rational Function with a Slant Asymptote**

Graph the function: $f(x) = \dfrac{x^2 - 4x - 5}{x - 3}$

Solution

Notice that the degree of the numerator is one more than the degree of the denominator, so the function will have a slant asymptote. We can express the function in two ways:

$$f(x) = \frac{x^2 - 4x - 5}{x - 3} = \frac{(x-5)(x+1)}{x-3}$$

In this form, we see that there are x-intercepts at 5 and -1, the values of x where the numerator is 0.

$$f(x) = \frac{x^2 - 4x - 5}{x - 3} = \underbrace{x - 1}_{} - \frac{8}{x - 3}$$

Using this form, $y = x - 1$ is a slant asymptote.

Use synthetic division.

$$\begin{array}{r|rrr} 3 & 1 & -4 & -5 \\ & & 3 & -3 \\ \hline & 1 & -1 & -8 \end{array}$$

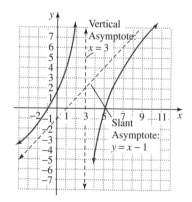

Study tip

The equation of the slant asymptote is obtained by setting y equal to the partial quotient without the remainder.

Now we continue by using our strategy for graphing rational functions.

Step 1. Symmetry: $f(-x) = \dfrac{(-x)^2 - 4(-x) - 5}{-x - 3} = \dfrac{x^2 + 4x - 5}{-x - 3}$

Since $f(-x)$ is not equal to $f(x)$ or $-f(x)$, we do not have symmetry with respect to the y-axis or the origin.

Step 2. y-intercept: $f(0) = \dfrac{0^2 - 4 \cdot 0 - 5}{0 - 3} = \dfrac{5}{3}$: y-intercept is $1\dfrac{2}{3}$.

Step 3. x-intercepts: Set the numerator equal to 0.

$$(x - 5)(x + 1) = 0$$

$$x = 5 \quad \text{or} \quad x = -1 \qquad \text{There are } x\text{-intercepts at 5 and } -1.$$

Step 4. Vertical asymptote: Set $q(x) = 0$.

$$x - 3 = 0 \qquad \text{Set the denominator equal to 0.}$$

$$x = 3 \qquad \text{The equation of the vertical asymptote is } x = 3.$$

Step 5. Horizontal asymptote: Since the degree of the numerator is greater than the degree of the denominator, there are no horizontal asymptotes.

Step 6. Additional points:

x	-3	1	4	7
$f(x) = \dfrac{x^2 - 4x - 5}{x - 3}$	$-2\dfrac{2}{3}$	4	-5	4

Figure 3.72

The graph of

$$f(x) = \frac{x^2 - 4x - 5}{x - 3}$$

Step 7. Remembering that the equation of the slant asymptote is $y = x - 1$, we draw the graph of f shown in Figure 3.72.

Step 8. See the Discover for yourself that follows. ∎

Discover for yourself

Use a graphing utility to graph

$$f(x) = \frac{x^2 - 4x - 5}{x - 3}$$

and $y = x - 1$ in the same viewing rectangle. Use the $\boxed{\text{ZOOM OUT}}$ feature to verify that $y = x - 1$ is indeed a slant asymptote.

PROBLEM SET 3.5

Practice Problems

In Problems 1–18, use the graph of $f(x) = \dfrac{1}{x}$ to graph each function. Graph f and g on the same axes. Identify the horizontal and vertical asymptotes of g.

1. $g(x) = \dfrac{1}{x - 2}$

2. $g(x) = \dfrac{1}{x - 1}$

3. $g(x) = \dfrac{1}{x + 2}$

4. $g(x) = \dfrac{1}{x + 1}$

5. $g(x) = \dfrac{1}{x} - 1$

6. $g(x) = \dfrac{1}{x} - 3$

7. $g(x) = \dfrac{1}{x} + 2$

8. $g(x) = \dfrac{1}{x} + 1$

9. $g(x) = \dfrac{0.5}{x}$

10. $g(x) = \dfrac{0.25}{x}$

11. $g(x) = -\dfrac{2}{x}$

12. $g(x) = -\dfrac{3}{x}$

13. $g(x) = \dfrac{1}{x + 2} - 1$

14. $g(x) = \dfrac{1}{x + 1} - 2$

15. $g(x) = -\dfrac{2}{x + 2} - 1$

16. $g(x) = -\dfrac{2}{x + 1} - 2$

17. $g(x) = \dfrac{2}{x - 2} + 1$

18. $g(x) = \dfrac{2}{x - 1} + 2$

In Problems 19–50, use the strategy for graphing rational functions outlined on page 399 to graph each function. Do not use a graphing utility until your hand-drawn graph is complete. Then verify your graph with a graphing utility.

19. $f(x) = \dfrac{2x}{x^2 - 4}$

20. $f(x) = \dfrac{3x}{x^2 - 9}$

21. $g(x) = \dfrac{3x - 6}{x + 4}$

22. $g(x) = \dfrac{4x - 8}{x + 2}$

23. $h(x) = \dfrac{2x^2}{x^2 - 1}$

24. $h(x) = \dfrac{4x^2}{x^2 - 9}$

25. $r(x) = \dfrac{-x}{x + 1}$

26. $r(x) = \dfrac{-3x}{x + 2}$

27. $f(x) = -\dfrac{1}{x^2 - 4}$

28. $f(x) = -\dfrac{2}{x^2 - 1}$

29. $g(x) = \dfrac{4x}{x^2 - 2x + 1}$

30. $g(x) = \dfrac{2x}{x^2 + 6x + 9}$

31. $h(x) = \dfrac{x - 1}{x^2 - x - 6}$

32. $h(x) = \dfrac{x + 1}{x^2 - x - 6}$

33. $r(x) = \dfrac{3x^2 + x - 4}{2x^2 - 5x}$

34. $r(x) = \dfrac{x^2 - 4x + 3}{x^2 - 2x}$

35. $f(t) = \dfrac{t^2 - 2t - 8}{t^2 - 4t + 3}$

36. $f(t) = \dfrac{t^2 - 4t + 3}{(t + 1)^2}$

37. $h(v) = \dfrac{2 - v}{3 - v}$

38. $h(v) = \dfrac{3 + v}{1 - v}$

39. $f(x) = \dfrac{x^2 - 1}{x}$

40. $f(x) = \dfrac{x^2 - 4}{x}$

41. $f(x) = \dfrac{x^2 + 1}{x}$

42. $f(x) = \dfrac{x^2 + 4}{x}$

43. $g(x) = \dfrac{x^2 + x - 6}{x - 3}$

44. $g(x) = \dfrac{x^2 - x + 1}{x - 1}$

45. $r(x) = \dfrac{6x^2 - 6x - 12}{3x^2 + 4x + 5}$

46. $r(x) = \dfrac{4x^2 + 8x - 12}{2x^2 + 3x + 5}$

47. $h(v) = \dfrac{3v^3 - 2v^2 + 3v - 2}{v^2 + 3}$

48. $h(v) = \dfrac{v^3 + v^2 + 2v + 2}{v^2 + 9}$

49. $f(x) = \dfrac{x^2 - 4}{x^2 + 1}$

50. $f(x) = \dfrac{x^2 - 1}{x^2 + 4}$

True–False Critical Thinking Problems

51. Which one of the following is true?

   a. The function $f(x) = \dfrac{1}{\sqrt{x - 3}}$ is a rational function.

   b. The domain of $f(x) = \dfrac{x + 5}{x - 5}$ is $(-\infty, -5) \cup (-5, 5)$
   $\cup (5, \infty)$.

   c. The graph of a rational function cannot intersect any of its asymptotes.

   d. None of the above is true.

52. Which one of the following is true?

   a. The x-axis is a horizontal asymptote for the graph of $f(x) = \dfrac{4x - 1}{x + 3}$.

   b. The graph shown in the figure on the right cannot possibly represent the rational function $f(x) = \dfrac{-x^3 + 1}{x^2}$.

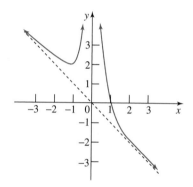

   c. The graph of $f(x) = \dfrac{2x + 4}{x^2 - 4}$ has only one vertical asymptote.

   d. The line whose equation is $y = x - 1$ is an asymptote for the graph of $f(x) = x - 4 + \dfrac{1}{x - 1}$.

Technology Problems

53. Use a graphing utility to graph $y = \dfrac{1}{x}$, $y = \dfrac{1}{x^3}$, and $\dfrac{1}{x^5}$ in the same viewing rectangle. For odd values of n, how does changing n affect the graph?

54. Use a graphing utility to graph $y = \dfrac{1}{x^2}$, $y = \dfrac{1}{x^4}$, and $y = \dfrac{1}{x^6}$ in the same viewing rectangle. For even values of n, how does changing n affect the graph?

55. The model $f(x) = \dfrac{72{,}900}{100x^2 + 729}$ describes the 1992

unemployment rate (as a percent) in the United States as a function of years of education (x).

   a. Use a graphing utility to graph the model for $x \geqslant 0$.

   b. What does the shape of the graph indicate about increasing levels of education?

   c. Explain why f is one-to-one. What is $f^{-1}(3.6)$ and what practical information does this provide?

   d. Is there an education level that leads to guaranteed employment? How is your answer indicated on the graph?

Throughout Section 3.5 we assumed that the rational function $f(x) = \dfrac{p(x)}{q(x)}$ *was written so that* $p(x)$ *and* $q(x)$ *contained no common factors. Problems 56–59 explore the possibility of p and q sharing common factors.*

56. Use a graphing utility to graph $f(x) = \dfrac{x^2 - 4}{x - 2}$. Does your graphing utility show that f has a "hole" at $x = 2$?

(Note: $f(x) = \dfrac{(x + 2)(x - 2)}{x - 2} = x + 2; x \neq 2$.)

57. Use a graphing utility to graph $f(x) = \dfrac{x^2 - 2x}{x}$. Does your graphing utility show that f has a "hole" at $x = 0$?

(Note: $f(x) = \dfrac{x^2 - 2x}{x} = \dfrac{x(x - 2)}{x} = x - 2; x \neq 0$.)

What does your graphing utility indicate about the domain of f?

58. a. Use a graphing utility to graph $f(x) = \dfrac{x^3 + 4x^2 + 7x + 6}{x + 2}$. Does your graphing utility show that f has an asymptote, a "hole," or neither at $x = -2$?

    b. Divide $x^3 + 4x^2 + 7x + 6$ by $x + 2$. What is the relationship between the quotient and the graph of f in part (a)?

59. If $f(x) = \dfrac{p(x)}{q(x)}$ and $q(a) = 0$, use Problems 57 and 58 to generalize when the graph of f has a "hole" at $x = a$ and when the graph of f has a vertical asymptote whose equation is $x = a$.

60. Use a graphing utility to graph $f(x) = \dfrac{2|x - 1|}{x + 2}$. How does the situation with horizontal asymptotes differ from the other functions graphed throughout this section?

61. Use a graphing utility to graph $f(x) = \dfrac{x^2 - 4x + 3}{x - 2}$ and $g(x) = \dfrac{x^2 - 5x + 6}{x - 2}$. What differences do you observe between the graphs of f and g? How do you account for these differences?

62. a. Graph $f(x) = \dfrac{2x^4 + 7x^3 + 7x^2 + 2x}{x^3 - x + 50}$ using the following range setting:

Xmin = -20, Xmax = 20, Xscl = 10,

Ymin = -20, Ymax = 20, Yscl = 10

    b. Now change the range setting to

Xmin = -2.1, Xmax = 1.1, Xscl = 0.1,

Ymin = -0.04, Ymax = 0.04, Yscl = 0.01

What behavior do you now observe that was not obvious from the graph in part (a)?

    c. What theory would you need to know to predict the hidden behavior that becomes more obvious in the graph of part (b)? (This theory is studied in calculus.)

63. Some rational functions have parabolic asymptotes. For example, if $f(x) = \dfrac{x^3 + 4}{x}$, using the technique to find slant asymptotes, we can divide and obtain

$$f(x) = \frac{x^3 + 4}{x} = x^2 + \frac{4}{x}$$

$y = x^2$ is a parabolic asymptote.

    a. Use a graphing utility to graph f and $y = x^2$ in the same viewing rectangle. Use the $\boxed{\text{ZOOM OUT}}$ feature to convince yourself that $y = x^2$ is a parabolic asymptote.

    b. In general, if $f(x) = \dfrac{p(x)}{q(x)}$, under what conditions will f have a parabolic asymptote?

    c. Give an example of another rational function with a parabolic asymptote, where the equation of the asymptote must be found by long division of polynomials. Verify your result with a graphing utility.

64. Explain how you can use a graphing utility to solve $\dfrac{2x^2 + 6x - 8}{2x^2 + 5x - 3} - 1 < 0$. Then use your graphing utility to show that the solution set is $(-\infty, -3) \cup (\frac{1}{2}, 5)$.

Writing in Mathematics _____

65. The figure on page 409 shows the graphs of $f(x) = \dfrac{1}{x - 1}$ and $g(x) = \dfrac{1}{(x - 1)^2}$, but not necessarily in that order. The graphs are only shown for $x > 1$. Describe how you can determine which is the graph of f and which is the graph of g.

66. Explain why $f(x) = \dfrac{x^6 + 1}{x^4 + 8x^2 + 12}$ has no vertical, horizontal, or slant asymptotes, and no x-intercepts. Verify by graphing f using a graphing utility.

67. Is every rational function a polynomial function? Why or why not? Does a true statement result if the two adjectives *rational* and *polynomial* are reversed? Explain.

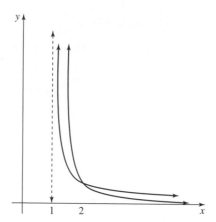

Critical Thinking Problems

68. If $c \neq 0$ and $d \neq 0$, describe the domain and range of $f(x) = \dfrac{ax + b}{cx + d}$.

In Problems 69–72, write the equation of a rational function $f(x) = \dfrac{p(x)}{q(x)}$ having the indicated properties, in which the degrees of p and q are as small as possible. More than one correct function may be possible. Graph your function using a graphing utility to verify that it has the required properties.

69. f has a vertical asymptote given by $x = 3$, a horizontal asymptote $y = 0$, y-intercept $= -1$, and no x-intercept.

70. f has vertical asymptotes given by $x = -2$ and $x = 2$, a horizontal asymptote $y = 2$, y-intercept $= \dfrac{9}{2}$, x-intercepts of -3 and 3, and y-axis symmetry.

71. f has a vertical asymptote given by $x = 1$, a slant asymptote whose equation is $y = x$, y-intercept $= 2$, and x-intercepts of -1 and 2.

72. f has no vertical, horizontal, or slant asymptotes, and no x-intercepts.

SECTION 3.6   Modeling with Rational Functions and Inverse Variation

Solutions Manual   Tutorial   Video 7

Objectives
1 Solve problems using given rational functions.
2 Solve problems by creating rational models.
3 Model data using inverse variation.

There are numerous examples of asymptotic behavior in functions that model real world phenomena.

Solve problems using given rational functions.

EXAMPLE I   Modeling Average Cost of Producing a Product

A company that manufactures running shoes has costs given by the function

$$C(x) = 40x + 50{,}000$$

where x is the number of pairs of shoes produced per week and $C(x)$ is measured in dollars. The average cost per pair for the company is given by

$$\overline{C}(x) = \frac{40x + 50{,}000}{x}.$$

a. Find and interpret $\overline{C}(1000)$, $\overline{C}(10{,}000)$, and $\overline{C}(100{,}000)$.

b. What is the horizontal asymptote for this function? Describe what this represents for the company.

Study tip

The cost function

$$C(x) = 40x + 50{,}000$$

implies that the company has fixed costs of $50,000 and variable costs of $40 for each pair of running shoes manufactured.

Solution

a. $\overline{C}(1000) = \dfrac{40(1000) + 50{,}000}{1000} = 90$

The average cost per pair of shoes of producing 1000 pairs per week is $90.00.

$$\overline{C}(10{,}000) = \frac{40(10{,}000) + 50{,}000}{10{,}000} = 45$$

The average cost per pair of shoes of producing 10,000 pairs per week is $45.00.

$$\overline{C}(100{,}000) = \frac{40(100{,}000) + 50{,}000}{100{,}000} = 40.5$$

The average cost per pair of shoes of producing 100,000 pairs per week is $40.50. Notice that with higher production levels, the cost of producing each unit of the product decreases.

b. We are given the average cost function

$$\overline{C}(x) = \frac{40x + 50{,}000}{x}$$

in which the degree of the numerator, 1, is equal to the degree of the denominator, 1. The leading coefficients of the numerator and denominator, 40 and 1, are used to obtain the equation of the horizontal asymptote. The equation of the horizontal asymptote is

$$y = \frac{40}{1} \quad \text{or} \quad y = 40.$$

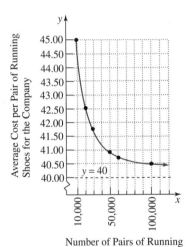

Figure 3.73

As production level increases, the average cost per unit approaches $40.00.

The horizontal asymptote is shown in Figure 3.73. This means that the more pairs of running shoes produced per week, the closer the average cost per pair for the company comes to $40. The least possible cost per pair is approaching $40.00. Competitively low prices take place with high production levels, posing a major problem for small businesses. ∎

An economic tool involving a *cost-benefit model* is often applied when making decisions on public policies dealing with the environment. For example, a graph of reducing air pollution in Tarnobrzeg, Poland, is shown in Figure 3.74. The graph indicates that removing the highest 40 to 50 percent of particles of pollution costs far less than removing 70 percent. Costs seem to be spiraling upward as the percent of removed pollutants increases. There is also a vertical asymptote associated with the graph of the cost function. Example 2 shows how these ideas can be expressed using a rational function.

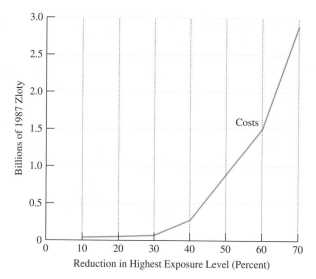

Figure 3.74

Source: J. Cofala, T. Lis, and H. Balandynowicz, *Cost-Benefit Analysis of Regional Air Pollution Control: Case Study for Tarnobrzeg,* 1991, Polish Academy of Sciences, Warsaw.

Jim Richardson / Richardson Photography

EXAMPLE 2 A Cost-Benefit Model

Cost-benefit models involving environmental pollution express cost as a function of the percentage of pollutants removed from the environment. For example, the rational function

$$C(x) = \frac{250x}{100 - x}$$

models the cost ($C(x)$, in millions of dollars) to remove x percent of the pollutants that are discharged into a river.

a. Find and interpret $C(90) - C(40)$.
b. What is the equation of the vertical asymptote for the cost-benefit model? What does this mean in terms of cleaning up the river?

Solution

a. First we will find and interpret $C(40)$ and $C(90)$.

$$C(40) = \frac{250(40)}{100 - 40} \approx 166.67$$

The cost to remove 40% of the river's pollutants is approximately $166.67 million.

$$C(90) = \frac{250(90)}{100 - 90} = 2250$$

The cost to remove 90% of the river's pollutants is $2250 million. Thus,

$$C(90) - C(40) \approx 2250 - 166.67 = 2083.33 .$$

The difference in cost between removing 90% of the river's pollutants and 40% of its pollutants is approximately $2083.33 million.

b. The vertical asymptote for

$$C(x) = \frac{250x}{100 - x}$$

is $x = 100$, the zero of the denominator. As x approaches 100, $C(x)$ increases without bound (see Figure 3.75). This means that no amount of money can possibly clean up 100% of the river's pollutants. How much would it cost to remove 99% of the pollutants?

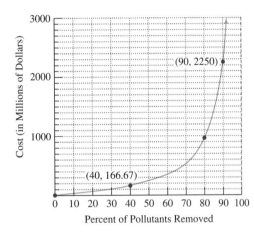

Figure 3.75

The graph of $C(x) = \dfrac{250x}{100 - x}$

2 Solve problems by creating rational models.

In Example 3, we use a rational function to model uniform motion. The example is based on the formula

$$RT = D$$

which states that the product of rate and time equals distance. Equivalently,

$$T = \frac{D}{R}$$

so that time is the quotient of distance and rate.

EXAMPLE 3 Modeling Involving Uniform Motion

Two commuters drove to work a distance of 40 miles and then returned again on the same route. The average rate on the return trip was 30 miles per hour faster than the average rate on the outgoing trip.

a. Find a rational function that models the total time T required to complete the round trip as a function of the rate x on the outgoing trip.

b. Use a graphing utility to graph the function for meaningful values of x.

c. If the commuters would like to complete the round trip in 2 hours, use the graph to determine what the average rate on the outgoing trip should be.

Solution

Roy Lichtenstein "In the Car" 1963. The Scottish National Gallery of Modern Art. © Roy Lichtenstein.

a. Let

$$x = \text{average rate on the outgoing trip}$$

$$x + 30 = \text{average rate on the return trip}$$

The critical sentence that we must model is:

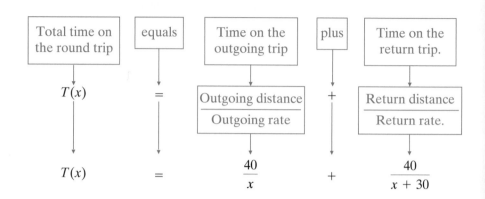

$$T(x) = \frac{40}{x} + \frac{40}{x + 30}. \quad \text{This is the function that models total time } T.$$

Figure 3.76

The graph of

$T(x) = \dfrac{40}{x} + \dfrac{40}{x + 30}.$ As the

rate increases, time decreases.

b. Let's graph the function for $0 \leq x \leq 60$, since it seem unlikely that an average outgoing rate exceeds 60 miles per hour with a return rate that is 30 miles per hour faster.

Figure 3.76 shows the graph of $T(x) = \dfrac{40}{x} + \dfrac{40}{x + 30}$, obtained on a graphing utility using the following range setting:

Xmin = 0, Xmax = 60, Xscl = 3,

Ymin = 0, Ymax = 10, Yscl = 1.

The graph shows decreasing times with increasing rates. The vertical asymptote, $x = 0$, indicates that close to an outgoing rate of zero miles per hour, the round trip will take nearly forever.

c. The commuters have 2 hours, so we trace along the curve until $y = 2$, remembering that y represents total time. Figure 3.77 shows that $x = 30$, meaning that the commuters must average 30 miles per hour on the outgoing trip to complete the round trip in 2 hours. For this one-to-one function, $T^{-1}(2) = 30$. ∎

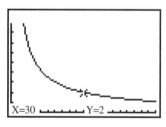

Figure 3.77

An average speed of 30 miles per hour on the outgoing trip results in 2 hours for the round trip.

3 Model data using inverse variation.

Modeling Using Inverse Variation

It is possible to look at a data set and notice patterns to suggest modeling with rational functions in the form

$$y = \frac{k}{x^n}, \quad \text{where } n \geq 1.$$

If x and y are related by this equation, we say that y *varies inversely as the nth power of x.*

> **Inverse variation**
>
> *y varies inversely as the nth power of x* (or *y is inversely proportional to the nth power of x*) if there exists some nonzero constant *k* such that
>
> $$y = \frac{k}{x^n}.$$
>
> *k* is called the *constant of variation* or the *constant of proportionality.*

EXAMPLE 4 **Solving an Inverse Variation Problem**

The number of pens sold varies inversely as the price per pen. If 4000 pens are sold at a price of $1.50 per pen, write a function *f* that models the number of pens sold and the price per pen. Then graph the function. Is the function one-to-one? What is the practical meaning of $f^{-1}(2000)$?

Solution

$$y = \frac{k}{x}$$ Translate "Number sold (*y*) varies inversely as price per pen (*x*)."

$$4000 = \frac{k}{1.5}$$ Find *k*. Because 4000 pens are sold at $1.50 per pen, when *x* = 1.5, then *y* = 4000.

$$6000 = k$$ Multiply both sides of the equation by 1.5 and solve for *k*.

$$y = \frac{6000}{x}$$ Substitute the value for *k* into the original equation.

The function that models the number of pens sold and the price per pen is

$$y = \frac{6000}{x} \quad \text{or} \quad f(x) = \frac{6000}{x}.$$

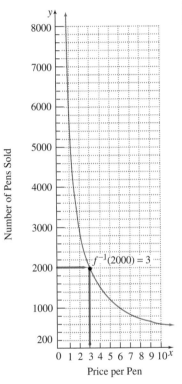

Figure 3.78

The graph of $f(x) = \dfrac{6000}{x}$

We can graph the function by multiplying each *y*-value of the graph of $y = \dfrac{1}{x}$ by 6000. The graph of $f(x) = \dfrac{6000}{x}$ appears in Figure 3.78. The graph is drawn only for meaningful values of *x*, namely, *x* > 0. The curve indicates that as the price per pen increases, the number of pens sold decreases quite rapidly. Since every horizontal line that can be drawn intersects the graph no more than once, the function is one-to-one—that is, its inverse is a function. The graph indicates the practical meaning of $f^{-1}(2000)$: If 2000 pens are sold, then the price per pen is $3.00. ■

Because $y = \dfrac{k}{x^n}$ means *y* varies inversely as the *n*th power of *x*, we can tell if a given data set is consistent with an inverse *n*th power variation by multiplying both sides of the equation by x^n. We obtain

$$yx^n = k$$

indicating that the product of x^n and *y* remains constant.

Modeling with inverse variation

If a data set is given such that the product $x^n y$ remains constant (k), then the data can be modeled by the function $y = \dfrac{k}{x^n}$.

EXAMPLE 5   **Modeling Gravitational Force**

Use the data shown below to write a rational function that models gravitational force and distance.

x (Distance of Object from Earth's Center)	y (Gravitational Force with which Earth Attracts the Object)
1000 miles	2560 pounds
2000 miles	640 pounds
4000 miles	160 pounds
10,000 miles	25.6 pounds

Solution

If we are to model the data using inverse variation, then $x^n y = k$.

x	y	If $n = 1$	If $n = 2$
1000	2560	$xy = 2{,}560{,}000$	$x^2 y = (1000)^2 (2560) = 2{,}560{,}000{,}000$
2000	640	$xy = 1{,}280{,}000$	$x^2 y = (2000)^2 (640) = 2{,}560{,}000{,}000$
4000	160	Products are not constant.	$x^2 y = (4000)^2 (160) = 2{,}560{,}000{,}000$
10,000	25.6	$y = \dfrac{k}{x}$ does not model the data.	$x^2 y = (10{,}000)^2 (25.6) = 2{,}560{,}000{,}000$

Since the products in the last column are constant, $x^2 y = 2{,}560{,}000{,}000$. Equivalently, the rational function that models the data is

$$y = \frac{2{,}560{,}000{,}000}{x^2} \quad \text{or} \quad f(x) = \frac{2{,}560{,}000{,}000}{x^2}.$$

In practical terms, the model states: The gravitational force with which Earth attracts an object varies inversely with the square of the distance the object is from the center of Earth. Thus, the force of gravity falls off rapidly as an object gets farther from Earth's center.   ∎

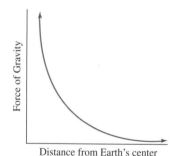

Force of Gravity

Distance from Earth's center

The force of gravity falls off rapidly as objects get farther apart from Earth's center.

Isaac Newton's model for gravitation involves *combined variation*, where gravitational force depends on several other variables.

Basic variation models

y varies directly as x^n: $y = kx^n$

y varies inversely as x^n: $y = \dfrac{k}{x^n}$

z varies jointly as x^n and y^m: $z = kx^n y^m$

Jane Lewis "The Illusionist" 1995, oil on canvas. Original paintings available: Portal Gallery, London, England.

Newton's theory of gravitation is modeled by

$$F = G\,\frac{m_1 m_2}{d^2}$$

which states that the force of gravitation (F) between two bodies varies jointly as the product of their masses (m_1 and m_2) and inversely as the square of the distance between them (d^2). (G is the gravitational constant.) The formula indicates that gravitational force exists between any two objects in the universe, increasing as the distance between the bodies decreases. One practical result is that the pull of the moon on the oceans is greater on the side of Earth closer to the moon. This gravitational imbalance is what produces tides.

EXAMPLE 6 **Combined Variation: Modeling Centrifugal Force**

The centrifugal force (C) of a body moving in a circle varies jointly with the radius of the circular path (r) and the body's mass (m), and inversely with the square of the time (t) it takes to move about one full circle. A 6-gram body moving in a circle with radius 100 centimeters at a rate of 1 revolution in 2 seconds has a centrifugal force of 6000 dynes. Find the centrifugal force of an 18-gram body moving in a circle with radius 100 centimeters at a rate of 1 revolution in 3 seconds.

Solution

$C = \dfrac{krm}{t^2}$ Translate "Centrifugal force (C) varies jointly with radius (r) and mass (m) and inversely with the square of time (t)."

$6000 = \dfrac{k(100)(6)}{2^2}$ If $r = 100$, $m = 6$, and $t = 2$, then $C = 6000$.

$40 = k$ Solve for k.

$C = \dfrac{40rm}{t^2}$ Substitute 40 for k in the model for centrifugal force.

$= \dfrac{40(100)(18)}{3^2}$ Find C when $r = 100$, $m = 18$, and $t = 3$.

$= 8000$

David Madison / Duomo Photography

The centrifugal force is 8000 dynes.   ∎

ENRICHMENT ESSAY

Atonal Music for the Planetary Spheres

Chloe: The future is all programmed like a computer—that's a proper theory, isn't it?
Valentine: The deterministic universe, yes ... There was someone, forgot his name, 1820s, who pointed out that from Newton's laws you could predict everything to come...
Chloe: But it doesn't work, does it?
Valentine: No. It turns out the mathematics is different.

Tom Stoppard, *Arcadia*

Kingsley Parker "Primitive Orrery #1"
1993. Courtesy of Kingsley Parker.

PROBLEM SET 3.6

Practice and Application Problems

1. A company that manufactures small canoes has costs given by the function $C(x) = 20x + 20,000$, where x is the number of canoes manufactured and $C(x)$ is measured in dollars. The average cost to manufacture each canoe is given by

$$\overline{C}(x) = \frac{20x + 20,000}{x}.$$

   a. Find the average cost per canoe when $x = 100, 1000, 10,000$, and $100,000$.

   b. What is the horizontal asymptote for this function, and what does it represent?

2. A bicycle manufacturing business has fixed costs of $100,000 and variable costs of $100 per bicycle.

   a. Find a function $\overline{C}$ that models the average cost per bicycle for x bicycles. (*Hint:* Costs, $C(x)$, are given by 100 times the number of bicycles manufactured plus fixed costs. The average cost to manufacture each bicycle is the quotient of $C(x)$ and the number of bicycles manufactured.)

   b. Find and interpret $\overline{C}(500), \overline{C}(1000), \overline{C}(2000)$, and $\overline{C}(4000)$.

   c. What is the horizontal asymptote for the function $\overline{C}$? Describe what this means in practical terms.

3. The cost in dollars of removing p percent of the air pollutants in the stack emission of a utility company that burns coal to generate electricity is given by

$$C(p) = \frac{60,000p}{100 - p}.$$

   a. Current law requires that the company remove 80% of the pollutants from their smokestack emissions. A new law before the legislature would require increasing this amount by 5%. How much will it cost to remove another 5% of the pollutants?

   b. Does this model indicate the possibility of removing 100% of the pollutants? Explain.

4. The rational function

$$C(x) = \frac{130x}{100 - x} \quad 0 \leq x < 100,$$

   models the cost (C, in millions of dollars) to inoculate $x\%$ of the population against a particular strain of flu.

   a. Find and interpret $C(80) - C(40)$.

   b. Graph the function.

   c. Describe the practical meaning of the observation that $x = 100$ is an asymptote.

5. The temperature (F, in degrees Fahrenheit) of a dessert placed in an icebox for t hours is modeled by

$$f(t) = \frac{80}{t^2 + 4t + 1}.$$

   a. Find and interpret $F(0)$.

   b. Find the temperature of the dessert after 1 hour, 2 hours, 3 hours, 4 hours, and 5 hours.

   c. What is the equation of the horizontal asymptote associated with this function? Describe what this means in terms of the dessert's temperature over time.

   d. Graph the function.

6. The electrical resistance of a wire varies directly as its length and inversely as the square of its diameter. A wire of 720 feet with a $\frac{1}{4}$-inch diameter has a resistance of 1.5 ohms. Predict the resistance for 960 feet of the same kind of wire if its diameter is doubled.

7. The force of attraction between two bodies varies jointly as the product of their masses and inversely as the square of the distance between them. Two 1-kilogram masses separated by 1 meter exert a force of attraction of 6.67×10^{-11} newton. What is the gravitational force exerted by Earth on a 1000-kilogram satellite orbiting at an altitude of 300 kilometers? (The mass of Earth is 5.98×10^{24} kilograms and its radius is 6400 kilometers.)

8. Use the results of Example 5 on page 416 to answer this question: If a person weighs 160 pounds on Earth's surface and if Earth's radius is 6370 kilometers, how much does that person weigh on a jet that is flying at an altitude of 8 kilometers above the surface?

9. Use the data shown below to write a rational function of the form $y = \dfrac{k}{x^n}$ that models intensity of illumination on a surface (y) and the distance of the light source from the surface (x). Describe what the model states in practical terms.

x (in feet)	y (in foot-candles)
2	100
4	25
10	4
20	1

In Problems 10–12, determine whether the data can be modeled by the rational function $y = \dfrac{k}{x^n}$ for the given value of n. If it can, write the function.

10.

x	y ($n = 2$)
4	100
5	64
8	25
10	16

11.

x	y ($n = 3$)
3	8000
4	3375
5	1728
10	216

12.

x	y ($n = 3$)
2	25
4	$3\frac{1}{8}$
5	$1\frac{3}{5}$
10	$\frac{1}{5}$

Technology Problems

13. A person drove from home to a vacation resort 600 miles away. The return trip was on the same highway. The average rate on the return trip was 10 miles per hour slower than the average rate on the outgoing trip.

   a. Find a rational function that models the total time T required to complete the round trip as a function of the rate x on the outgoing trip.

   b. Use a graphing utility to graph the function for meaningful values of x.

   c. Use the graph to find $T^{-1}(22)$ and describe what this means in practical terms.

   d. Modify the given word problem by writing a problem whose solution can be found by graphing $y = 20$ in the same viewing rectangle as the graph of T, and then finding positive values of x for which the graph for T lies below the graph of $y = 20$.

14. A contractor is constructing the house shown in the figure on page 419. The cross section up to the roof is in the shape of a rectangle with an area of 2500 square feet. The width of the rectangle is represented by x.

   a. Write a rational function that models the perimeter of the rectangle.

   b. A minimum perimeter will reduce construction costs for the house. Use a graphing utility to graph the perimeter function and find the dimensions of the rectangle with the least possible perimeter.

Width: x Length

15. A grocery store sells 4000 cases of canned soup per year. By averaging costs and storage costs, the owner has

determined that if x cases are ordered at a time, the inventory cost will be

$$C(x) = \frac{10,000}{x} + 3x.$$

a. Use a graphing utility to graph the inventory function.

b. Use the $\boxed{\text{ZOOM}}$ and $\boxed{\text{TRACE}}$ features or the minimum function feature of your graphing utility to approximate the number of cases that should be ordered to minimize inventory cost. What is the minimum cost?

Writing in Mathematics

16. You have been hired as vice-president in charge of advertising for the Worldwide Widget Corporation. You were told that the demand for widgets varies directly as the amount spent on advertising and inversely as the price of the product. However, as more money is spent on advertising, the price of a widget rises. Under what conditions would you recommend an increased expense in advertising? Once you've determined what a "widget" is, write mathematical models for the given conditions and experiment with hypothetical numbers. What other factors might you take into consideration in terms of your recommendation?

17. Suppose you are a sales analyst for a home video game company. It has been determined that the rational function

$$f(x) = \frac{200x}{x^2 + 100}$$

models the monthly sales (in thousands of games) of a new video game as a function of the number of months (x) after the game is introduced. Use a graphing utility to graph the function. What are your recommendations to the company in terms of how long the video game should be on the market before another new video game is introduced? What other factors might you want to take into account in terms of your recommendations? What will eventually happen to sales, and how is this indicated by the graph? What does this have to do with a horizontal asymptote? What could the company do to change the behavior of this function and continue generating sales? Would this be cost effective?

Critical Thinking Problems

18. The heat generated by a stove element varies directly as the square of the voltage and inversely as the resistance. If the voltage remains constant, what needs to be done to triple the amount of heat generated?

19. Galileo's telescope brought about revolutionary changes in astronomy. A comparable leap in our ability to observe the universe is now taking place as a result of

the Hubble Space Telescope. The space telescope can see stars and galaxies whose brightness is $\frac{1}{50}$ of the faintest objects now observable using ground-based telescopes. Use the fact that the brightness of a point source, such as a star, varies inversely as the square of its distance from an observer to show that the space telescope can see about seven times farther than a ground-based telescope.

Group Activity Problem

20. A cost-benefit analysis compares the estimated costs of a project with the benefits that will be achieved. Costs and benefits are given monetary values and compared by using a benefit-cost ratio. As shown in the figure on

page 421, a favorable ratio for a project means that the benefits outweigh the costs, and the project is cost-effective. As a group, select an environmental project that has been implemented in your area of the country.

Research the cost and benefit graphs that resulted in the implementation of this project. How were the benefits converted into monetary terms? Is there an equation for either the cost model or the benefit model? Group members may need to interview members of environmental groups and businesses that were part of the project. You may also wish to consult an environmental science textbook to find out more about cost-benefit analyses. After doing your research, the group should write or present a report explaining why the cost-benefit analysis resulted in the project's implementation.

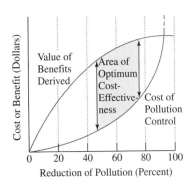

CHAPTER PROJECT

Women in Mathematics

Glancing at most mathematics textbooks, it is obvious that the majority of people mentioned are men. For example, look at the essay on page 374 entitled "A Brief History of Polynomial Equations" and read the list of names contributing to the study of polynomials. No women appear on the list which covers almost 2000 years. If we looked through a similar list of notable names for the same time period, roughly 200 B.C. to the mid 1800s, in almost any area of science and mathematics, we would see very few women mentioned.

1. People have argued that the absence of women in mathematics for the time period discussed above "proves" women cannot do math. Compare the following two arguments and discuss their validity:
   • Before the mid 1900s, there were no African-Americans playing major league baseball. Therefore, African-Americans do not play baseball very well.
   • Before the mid 1800s, there were almost no women working in mathematics. Therefore, women do not do mathematics very well.
   Consider as part of your argument the fact that in 1991, 47 percent of the Bachelor's degrees in mathematics from American schools went to women.

As the above problem illustrates, if we are looking for the contributions of women in mathematics, we must keep in mind the historical period we are studying. Historically, how did women obtain an education? For many years women were denied a formal education, precisely the kind of education required for work in advanced mathematics. While men worked with mentors or tutors, and subsequently may have progressed on to universities, women had virtually no contact with this style of learning. In addition, most advanced learning in the sciences or mathematics required a high standard of living. In many cases, only the affluent would have the large blocks of time needed to devote to study. Some women, who did contribute to mathematics in the 1800s, had access to learning because they came from wealthy families and were able to use private libraries.

2. Working with a group, select a woman mathematician from the list below. Prepare a report about women and learning in the time period in which she lived. Please note, this is not necessarily a report on the mathematics, it is a discussion of how any subject in general was available for study to women. As we move closer to our time period, the mathematics discussed may be beyond the scope of this course, but the human aspect of learning remains.

   Theano (wife of Pythagoras, around
       5th Century B.C.)
   Hypatia (3__?–415)
   Elena Lucrezia Cornaro Piscopia (first woman
       to receive a doctoral degree, 1646–1684)

   Emilie du Chatelet (1706–1749)
   Maria Gaetana Agnesi (1718–1799)
   Caroline Herschel (1750–1848)
   Sophie Germain (1776–1831)
   Mary Fairfax Somerville (1780–1872)

3. The first PhD in mathematics was awarded to Winifred Edgerton Merrill (1862–1951) by Columbia University in 1886. Her son later wrote that she "said that a condition of her admission was to dust the astro-

nomical [instruments] and so comport herself as not to disturb the male students." The separate treatment of men and women, even when allowing women access to the same universities, was not unusual. In a small group, use resources in your library or on the Worldwide Web to find a man in the sciences or mathematics who lived and worked in approximately the same time frame as one of the women below. Compare and contrast the opportunities given for education and the lifestyles of each. Share your results with the class.

Ada Byron Lovelace (1815–1852)
Florence Nightingale (1820–1910)
Mary Everest Boole (1832–1916)
Christine Ladd-Franklin (1847–1930)
Sonya Kovalevskaya (1850–1891)
Charlotte Angas Scott (1858–1931)
Charlotte Barnum (1860–1934)
Winifred Edgerton Merrill (1862–1951)

Clara Eliza Smith (1865–1943)
Grace Chisholm Young (1868–1944)
Ada Isabel Maddison (1869–1950)
Mary Frances Winston Newson (1869–1959)
Agnes Baxter (1870–1917)
Emmy Noether (1882–1935)
Anna Pell Wheeler (1883–1966)

Worldwide Web Resources

Go to the Prentice Hall website (http://www.prenhall.com/blitzer) to access other locations on the Internet that will allow you to further explore the concepts presented in this project.

Chapter Review

SUMMARY

1. Quadratic Functions

a. Standard form: $f(x) = a(x - h)^2 + k$
Vertex of the graph, which is a parabola: (h, k)

b. The form $f(x) = ax^2 + bx + c$
Vertex of the parabola: $\left(-\dfrac{b}{2a}, f\left(-\dfrac{b}{2a}\right)\right)$

c. Optimization

1. If $a > 0$, the minimum value of f occurs at $x = h$ or $x = -\dfrac{b}{2a}$. This minimum value is $f(h) = k$ or $f\left(-\dfrac{b}{2a}\right)$.

2. If $a < 0$, the maximum value of f occurs at $x = h$ or $x = -\dfrac{b}{2a}$. This maximum value is $f(h) = k$ or $f\left(-\dfrac{b}{2a}\right)$.

2. Graphing a Polynomial Function
$f(x) = a_n x^n + a_{n-1} x^{n-1} + a_{n-2} x^{n-2} + \cdots + a_1 x + a_0$

a. Use the Leading Coefficient Test to determine the graph's end behavior.

1. If n is odd and $a_n > 0$, the graph falls to the left and rises to the right.

2. If n is odd and $a_n < 0$, the graph rises to the left and falls to the right.

3. If n is even and $a_n > 0$, the graph rises to the left and to the right.

4. If n is even and $a_n < 0$, the graph falls to the left and to the right.

b. Find x-intercepts by setting $f(x) = 0$ and solving the resulting polynomial equation. If there is an x-intercept at a as a result of $(x - a)^k$ in the complete factorization of $f(x)$, then:

1. If k is even, the graph touches the x-axis at a but does not cross the x-axis.

2. If k is odd, the graph crosses the x-axis at a.

3. If $k > 1$, the graph flattens out at $(a, 0)$.

c. Find the y-intercept by setting x equal to 0 and calculating $f(0)$.

d. Use symmetry, if applicable, to help draw the graph:

1. y-axis symmetry: $f(-x) = f(x)$

2. Origin symmetry: $f(-x) = -f(x)$

e. Use the fact that the maximum number of turning points of the graph is $n - 1$ to check whether the graph is drawn correctly.

3. **Real Zeros of Polynomial Functions**
   If f is a polynomial function and $f(a) = 0$ for any real number a:
   a. a is a zero of f.
   b. a is a solution or root of $f(x) = 0$.
   c. a is an x-intercept of the graph of f.
   d. $x - a$ is a factor of the polynomial f.

4. **Solving Polynomial Equations; Finding Zeros of Polynomial Functions**
   $$a_n x^n + a_{n-1} x^{n-1} + a_{n-2} x^{n-2} + \cdots + a_1 x + a_0 = 0$$
   a. Use the Rational Zero Theorem to list all possible rational roots, $\dfrac{p}{q}$. p is a factor of the constant term, a_0, and q is a factor of the leading coefficient, a_n.
   b. Use Descartes' Rule of Signs to determine the possibilities for positive and negative roots. The number of positive roots is equal to the number of variations in sign in the equation or less than the number of variations by a positive even integer. The number of negative real roots applies to a similar statement when x is replaced by $-x$ in the given equation.
   c. Use synthetic division to check the positive and negative candidates for rational zeros listed in step (a). A graphing utility, showing the graph of the polynomial function and its zeros, might be helpful. Stop when you find a root (remainder $= 0$).
   d. If step (c) indicates that c is a root, then one factor is $x - c$. The second factor is the quotient obtained from the synthetic division.
   e. Set each factor equal to zero.
   f. 1. Solve the equation obtained by setting the linear factor equal to zero.
      2. If the second factor is quadratic, solve the resulting quadratic equation by factoring (if possible), by the quadratic formula, or by the square root method.
      3. If the second factor is of degree 3 or greater, repeat steps (a) through (e) on the resulting polynomial equation.

5. **Theorems that Help to Find Zeros of Polynomial Functions**
   a. *The Factor Theorem:* If $f(c) = 0$, then $x - c$ is a factor of $f(x)$. If $x - c$ is a factor of $f(x)$, then $f(c) = 0$.
   b. *The Rational Zero Theorem:* If $f(x) = a_n x^n + a_{n-1} x^{n-1} + \cdots + a_1 x + a_0$ has integer coefficients and $\dfrac{p}{q}$ (where $\dfrac{p}{q}$ is reduced) is a rational zero, then p divides a_0 and q divides a_n.
   c. *Descartes' Rule of Signs:* The number of positive real zeros of f equals the sign changes of $f(x)$ or is less than that number by an even integer. The number of negative real zeros of f applies a similar statement to $f(-x)$.
   d. *The Upper and Lower Bound Theorem:* The number $b > 0$ is an upper bound for the real roots of $f(x) =$ 0 if synthetic division of $f(x)$ by $x - b$ results in no negative numbers. The number a ($a < 0$) is a lower bound if similar synthetic division results in numbers that alternate in sign, counting zero entries as positive or negative.
   e. *The Linear Factorization Theorem:* If
   $$f(x) = a_n x^n + a_{n-1} x^{n-1} + \cdots + a_1 x + a_0$$
   $$(n \geqslant 1, a_n \neq 0),$$
   then
   $$f(x) = a_n (x - c_1)(x - c_2) \cdots (x - c_n)$$
   where $c_1, c_2, \ldots, c_n$ are complex numbers (possibly real and not necessarily distinct).
   f. *The Number of Roots Theorem:* If $f(x)$ is a polynomial of degree $n \geqslant 1$, then $f(x) = 0$ has exactly n roots, where roots are counted according to their multiplicity.
   g. *The Conjugate Roots Theorem:* If $a + bi$ is a root of $f(x) = 0$, then $a - bi$ is also a root.
   h. *The Intermediate Value Theorem:* If $f(a)$ and $f(b)$ have opposite signs, there is at least one value of c between a and b for which $f(c) = 0$.

6. **Rational Functions**
   a. A rational function is one that can be written in the form $f(x) = \dfrac{p(x)}{q(x)}$, where $p(x)$ and $q(x)$ are polynomial functions, and $q(x) \neq 0$.
   b. The domain of a rational function is the set of all real numbers except those for which $q(x) = 0$.
   c. *Vertical Asymptotes:* The line $x = a$ is a vertical asymptote of f if $f(x) \to \infty$ or $f(x) \to -\infty$ as $x \to a^+$ or $x \to a^-$.
   d. *Horizontal Asymptotes:* The line $y = b$ is a horizontal asymptote of f if $f(x) \to b$ as $x \to \infty$ or $x \to -\infty$.
   e. *The Reciprocal Function:* $f(x) = \dfrac{1}{x}$

   Horizontal asymptote: $y = 0$ (the x-axis)

   Vertical asymptote: $x = 0$ (the y-axis)

   Some rational functions can be graphed using transformations of the reciprocal function.

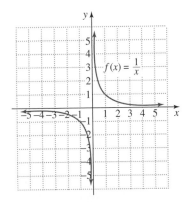

7. Graphing Rational Functions

$f(x) = \dfrac{p(x)}{q(x)}$: $p(x)$ and $q(x)$ are polynomial functions with no common factors.

a. Determine whether the graph of f has symmetry. (See 2(d).)

b. Find and plot the y-intercept (if there is one) by evaluating $f(0)$.

c. Find and plot the x-intercepts (if there are any) by solving the equation $p(x) = 0$.

d. Find any vertical asymptote(s) by solving the equation $q(x) = 0$. Sketch the vertical asymptotes.

e. Find and sketch the horizontal asymptote (if there is one).

   1. If the degree of p is less than the degree of q, then $y = 0$ (the x-axis) is a horizontal asymptote.

   2. If the degree of p is equal to the degree of q, the horizontal asymptote is found by taking the quotient of the leading coefficient of p and q. Setting y equal to this quotient gives the equation of the horizontal asymptote.

   3. If the degree of p is greater than the degree of q, there is no horizontal asymptote.

f. Find and sketch the slant asymptote (if there is one). If the degree of p is one greater than the degree of q, divide $q(x)$ into $p(x)$. If $\dfrac{p(x)}{q(x)} = mx + b + \dfrac{R(x)}{q(x)}$, then $y = mx + b$ describes the slant asymptote.

g. Plot at least one point between and beyond each x-intercept and vertical asymptote or between and beyond each x-intercept and slant asymptote.

h. Use smooth curves to graph the function by having the curve pass through the indicated points and then having it approach but never touch the indicated asymptotes.

i. Use a graping utility in the DOT mode to verity that the graph has been drawn correctly.

8. Modeling with Variation

a. *Direct Variation:* y varies directly as the nth power of x (or y is proportional to the nth power of x) if there exists $k > 0$ such that $y = kx^n$. A data set in the form (x, y) can be modeled by direct variation if the ratio $\dfrac{y}{x^n}$ remains constant for some positive integer n.

b. *Joint Variation:* z varies jointly as x^n and y^m is modeled by $z = kx^n y^m$.

c. *Inverse Variation:* y varies inversely as the nth power of x (or y is inversely proportional to the nth power of x) if there exists $k > 0$ such that $y = \dfrac{k}{x^n}$. A data set in the form (x, y) can be modeled by inverse variation if the product $x^n y$ remains constant for some positive integer n.

REVIEW PROBLEMS

In Problems 1–4, use the vertex and the intercepts to sketch the graph of each quadratic function by hand. Give the equation for the parabola's axis of symmetry. Use a graphing utility to verify that your graph is correct.

1. $f(x) = -2(x - 1)^2 + 3$

2. $g(x) = (x + 4)^2 - 2$

3. $r(x) = -x^2 + 2x + 3$

4. $h(x) = 2x^2 - 4x - 6$

5. The function $p(x) = 0.0014x^2 - 0.1529x + 5.855$ models the percent (p) of income that Americans contribute to charities in terms of annual household income (x), where x is expressed in thousands of dollars, where $5 \leqslant x \leqslant 100$. What income level corresponds to the minimum percentage given to charities?

6. The function $M(t) = 0.0075t^2 - 0.2676t + 14.8$ describes the fuel efficiency of passengers cars (M, measured in miles per gallon) t years after 1940. What is the vertex for the graph of this quadratic function? Describe the significance of the vertex in practical terms.

7. A person standing close to the edge on the top of an 80-foot building throws a ball vertically upward with an initial velocity of 64 feet per second.

   a. Use the position function $s(t) = -16t^2 + v_0 t + s_0$, in which v_0 represents initial velocity and s_0 represents initial position to write the function modeling the height of the ball above the ground as a function of time.

   b. After how many seconds does the ball reach its maximum height? What is the maximum height?

   c. Sketch the graph of the function in part (a) by hand, verifying your result with a graphing utility.

8. A field bordering a straight stream is to be enclosed. The side bordering the stream is not to be fenced. If 1000 yards of fencing material are to be used, what are the dimensions of the largest rectangular field that can be fenced? What is the maximum area?

9. An owner of a large diving boat that can hold as many as 70 people charges $10 per passenger to groups between 15 and 20 people. If more than 20 divers charter the boat, the fee per passenger is decreased by 10¢ times the number of people in excess of 20. Find the size of the group that will maximize the boat owner's income. What is the maximum income?

10. Find the point on the line whose equation is $2x + y = 2$ that is closest to the origin.

In Problems 11–14:

a. *Use the Leading Coefficient Test to determine the right-hand $(x \to \infty)$ and left-hand $(x \to -\infty)$ end behavior of the polynomial function.*

b. *Use factoring to find all zeros of the polynomial function.*

c. *Graph the function by hand.*

d. *Use a graphing utility to verify that your graph is correct.*

11. $f(x) = x^3 - 5x^2 - x + 5$

12. $g(x) = -x^4 + 25x^2$

13. $h(x) = -x^4 + 6x^3 - 9x^2$

14. $r(x) = 3x^4 - 15x^3$

15. The function $f(x) = -0.0013x^3 + 0.078x^2 - 1.43x + 18.1$ describes the percentage of U.S. families below the poverty level x years after 1960. Use end behavior to explain why the model is valid only for a limited period of time.

In Problems 16–19, use end behavior and, if necessary, zeros to match each polynomial function with its graph.

a.

b.

c.

d.

16. $f(x) = -x^3 + 12x^2 - x$

17. $g(x) = x^6 - 6x^4 + 9x^2$

18. $h(x) = x^5 - 5x^3 + 4x$

19. $r(x) = x^3 + 1$

20. Can the data shown on the right be modeled by a direct variation equation in which $n = 4$? If so, write a polynomial function that models the data.

x	y
0.2	48
0.3	243
0.5	1875
0.8	12,288
1.0	30,000

In Problems 21–22, use Descartes' Rule of Signs to determine the possible number of positive and negative solutions of the polynomial equation.

21. $3x^4 - 2x^3 - 8x + 5 = 0$

22. $2x^5 - 3x^3 - 5x^2 + 3x - 1 = 0$

23. Explain why $2x^4 + 6x^2 + 8 = 0$ has no real roots.

For Problems 24–28:

a. *List all possible rational solutions.*

b. *Use Descartes' Rule of Signs to determine the possible number of positive and negative real solutions.*

c. *(Optional) If there is a fairly long list of possible rational zeros for f (where $f(x) = 0$), use a graphing utility to graph f and eliminate some of the possible rational zeros.*

d. *Find the solution set.*

24. $8x^3 - 36x^2 + 46x - 15 = 0$

25. $x^4 - x^3 - 7x^2 + x + 6 = 0$

26. $2x^4 - 5x^3 - 8x^2 + 25x - 10 = 0$

27. $4x^4 - 8x^3 - 43x^2 + 29x + 60 = 0$

28. $3x^5 - 2x^4 - 15x^3 + 10x^2 + 12x - 8 = 0$

For Problems 29–31:

a. *List all possible rational zeros.*

b. *Use Descartes' Rule of Signs to determine the possible number of positive and negative real zeros.*

c. *(Optional) If there is a fairly long list of possible rational zeros, use a graphing utility to graph the function and eliminate some of the possible rational zeros.*

d. *Find all zeros of the function.*

29. $f(x) = 6x^3 + x^2 - 4x + 1$

30. $g(x) = 2x^4 + x^3 - 2x^2 - 4x - 3$

31. $h(x) = 3x^4 - 7x^3 + 6x^2 - 28x - 24$

32. Consider the equation $2x^4 - x^3 - 5x^2 + 10x + 12 = 0$.

   a. List all possible rational roots.

   b. Determine whether 2 is a root using synthetic division. In terms of bounds, what can you conclude?

   c. Determine whether -2 is a root using synthetic division. In terms of bounds, what can you conclude?

   d. Use the results of parts (b) and (c) to discard some of the possible rational roots from part (a). Now what are the possible rational roots?

33. Show that all real solutions of the equation $2x^4 - 7x^3 - 5x^2 + 28x - 12 = 0$ lie between -2 and 6. Use this result to list all possible rational roots.

34. The function

$$S_n(n) = \frac{n(n + 1)(2n + 1)}{6}$$

describes the sum of the squares of the first n natural numbers. How many natural numbers must be added to produce a sum of 140?

35. The number of eggs (N) in a female moth is a function of her abdominal width (W, in millimeters), modeled by $N = 14W^3 - 17W^2 - 16W + 34$, for $1.5 \leqslant W \leqslant 3.5$. What is the abdominal width when there are 211 eggs?

36. If the volume of the solid shown in the figure is 164 cubic centimeters, find the value of x.

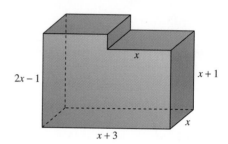

In Problems 37–38, show that the polynomial has a zero between the given integers. Then use the Intermediate Value Theorem to find an approximation for this zero to the nearest tenth. Use a graphing utility to verify your result.

37. $f(x) = x^3 - 2x - 1$; between 1 and 2

38. $f(x) = 3x^3 + 2x^2 - 8x + 7$; between -3 and -2

In Problems 39–41, find an nth-degree polynomial function with real coefficients satisfying the given conditions. Use a graphing utility to graph the function and check your answer.

39. $n = 3$; 2 and $2 - 3i$ are zeros; $f(1) = -10$

40. $n = 4$; i is a zero; -3 is a zero of multiplicity 2; $f(-1) = 16$

41. $n = 4$; $-2, 3$, and $1 + 3i$ are zeros; $f(2) = -40$

In Problems 42–45, use the given root to find the solution set of each polynomial equation.

42. $4x^3 - 47x^2 + 232x + 61 = 0$; $6 + 5i$

43. $x^4 - 4x^3 + 16x^2 - 24x + 20 = 0$: $1 - 3i$

44. $2x^4 - 17x^3 + 137x^2 - 57x - 65 = 0$; $4 + 7i$

45. $x^5 + 3x^4 + 2x^3 + 14x^2 + 29x + 15 = 0$; $1 + 2i$

In Problems 46–47, find all the zeros of each polynomial function and write the polynomial as a product of linear factors.

46. $f(x) = 2x^4 + 3x^3 + 3x - 2$

47. $g(x) = x^4 - 6x^3 + x^2 + 24x + 16$

In Problems 48–51, graphs of fifth-degree polynomial functions are shown. In each case, specify the number of real zeros and the number of nonreal complex zeros. Indicate whether there are any real zeros with multiplicity other than 1.

48.

49.

50.

51.

52. Show that $x^4 + 2x - 1 = 0$ has no rational roots. Use a graphing utility to graph $f(x) = x^4 + 2x - 1$. Use the

$\boxed{\text{ZOOM}}$ and $\boxed{\text{TRACE}}$ features to approximate the irrational roots of $x^4 + 2x - 1 = 0$ to two decimal places.

53. A one-inch thick slice is cut from the edge of a cube. The volume of the remaining solid is 448 cubic inches. Model these conditions with a polynomial equation. Solve the equation with a graphing utility and determine the original length of the cube.

Slice to Be Removed

1 inch

In Problems 54–58, use the graph of $f(x) = \dfrac{1}{x}$ to graph each function. Graph f and g on the same axes. Identify the horizontal and vertical asymptotes of g.

54. $g(x) = \dfrac{1}{x - 4}$

55. $g(x) = \dfrac{1}{x} - 4$

56. $g(x) = \dfrac{1}{x + 3} - 1$

57. $g(x) = -\dfrac{1}{x + 3}$

58. $g(x) = -\dfrac{2}{x - 1} + 1$

In Problems 59–66, use the strategy for graphing rational functions outlined in the chapter summary (item 7) to graph each function. Do not use a graphing utility until your hand-drawn graph is complete. Then verify your graph with a graphing utility.

59. $f(x) = \dfrac{2x}{x^2 - 9}$

60. $g(x) = \dfrac{2x - 4}{x + 3}$

61. $h(x) = \dfrac{x^2 - 3x - 4}{x^2 - x - 6}$

62. $r(x) = \dfrac{x^2 + 4x + 3}{(x + 2)^2}$

63. $y = \dfrac{x^2}{x + 1}$

64. $y = \dfrac{x^2 + 2x - 3}{x - 3}$

65. $f(x) = \dfrac{-2x^3}{x^2 + 1}$

66. $g(x) = \dfrac{4x^2 - 16x + 16}{2x - 3}$

Problems 67–69 involve rational functions that model the given situations. In each case, find the horizontal asymptote as $x \to \infty$ and then describe what this means in practical terms.

67. $N(x) = \dfrac{60(x - 2)}{x}$; the number of words that a person can type per minute (N) after x weeks of practice.

68. $F(x) = \dfrac{30(4 + 5x)}{1 + 0.05x}$; the number of fish $(F$, in thousands) after x weeks in a lake that was stocked with 120,000 fish.

69. $P(x) = \dfrac{72{,}900}{100x^2 + 729}$; the percentage rate (P) of U.S. unemployment for groups with x years of education.

70. A company that manufactures graphing calculators has fixed costs of \$80,000 and variable costs of \$20 per calculator. The company's total costs are modeled by $C(x)$

$= 20x + 80,000$. The average cost to manufacture each calculator is given by

$$\overline{C}(x) = \frac{20x + 80,000}{x}.$$

a. Find and interpret $\overline{C}(50), \overline{C}(100), \overline{C}(1000)$, and $\overline{C}(100,000)$.

b. What is the horizontal asymptote? Describe what this means in practical terms.

c. Graph $\overline{C}$.

71. In Silicon Valley, California, a government agency ordered computer-related companies to contribute to a monetary pool to clean up underground water supplies. (The companies had stored toxic chemicals in leaking underground containers.) The rational function

$$C(x) = \frac{200x}{100 - x}$$

models the cost (C, in tens of thousands of dollars) for removing $x\%$ of the contaminants.

a. Find and interpret $C(90) - C(50)$.

b. Graph the function.

c. Describe the practical meaning of the observation that $x = 100$ is an asymptote.

72. In a get-tough drug policy, a politician promises to spend whatever it takes to seize all illegal drugs as they enter the country. If the cost of this venture is

$$C(p) = \frac{Ap}{100 - p}$$

where A is a positive constant, C is expressed in millions of dollars, and p is the percent of illegal drugs seized, use this model to critique the politician's promise.

73. The force of attraction between two bodies varies jointly as the product of their masses and inversely as the square of the distance between them. Two 1-kilogram masses separated by 1 meter exert a force of attraction of 6.67×10^{-11} newton. Earth has a mass of 5.98×10^{24} kilograms and the moon has a mass of 6.7×10^{22} kilograms. If the moon is 385,000 kilometers from Earth, what is the gravitational attraction between the two bodies?

74. Use the data shown below to write a rational function of the form $y = \dfrac{k}{x^n}$ that models intensity of light on a surface (y) and the distance from the light source to the surface (x).

x (in meters)	y (in lumens)
2	300
4	75
10	12
20	3

Describe what the model states in practical terms. Predict the light intensity at a distance of 30 meters. What is the effect on light intensity as the distance increases without limit?

75. A commuter drove to work a distance of 60 miles and then returned again on the same highway. The average rate on the return trip was 30 miles per hour faster than the average rate on the outgoing trip.

a. Find a rational function that models the total time (T) required to complete the round trip as a function of the rate (x) on the outgoing trip.

b. Use a graphing utility to graph the function for meaningful values of x.

c. If the commuter would like to complete the round trip in 3 hours, use the graph to determine what the average rate on the outgoing trip should be.

76. Suppose that x ounces of pure acid is added to a ounces of a $p\%$ acid solution. The concentration of the mixture is given by

$$C = \frac{100x + pa}{x + a}$$

where the mixture is $C\%$ acid.

Pure Acid: x ounces

Mixture

a. Take the particular case in which x ounces of pure acid is added to 50 ounces of a 35% acid solution. Write the function C for this case. Then graph C using a graphing utility for meaningful values of x.

b. What do you observe about the graph of C in terms of its domain, intercepts, asymptotes, and general shape?

c. Use the graph to determine the amount of pure acid that must be added to produce a 75% acid mixture.

CHAPTER 3 TEST

In Problems 1–2, use the vertex and intercepts to graph each quadratic function. Give the equation of the axis of symmetry.

1. $f(x) = (x - 1)^2 - 4$

2. $f(x) = 2x^2 - 4x - 6$

3. The function $f(x) = -x^2 + 46x - 360$ models the daily profit ($f(x)$, in hundreds of dollars) for a company that manufactures x VCRs daily. How many VCRs should be manufactured each day to maximize profit? What is the maximum daily profit?

4. A rectangular plot of land along a river is to be fenced along 3 sides using 600 feet of fencing. No fencing is to be placed along the river's edge. Find the dimensions that maximize the enclosed area. What is the maximum area?

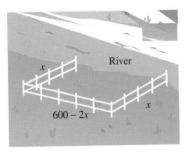

5. Consider the function $f(x) = x^3 - 5x^2 - 4x + 20$.

a. Use factoring to find all zeros of f.

b. Use the Leading Coefficient Test and the zeros of f to graph the function.

6. Use end behavior to explain why the graph at the top of the next column cannot be the graph of $f(x) = x^5 - x$. Then use intercepts to explain why the graph cannot represent $f(x) = x^5 - x$.

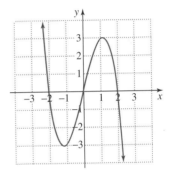

7. The graph of $f(x) = 6x^3 - 19x^2 + 16x - 4$ is shown in the figure.

a. Based on the graph of f, find the integral root of the equation $6x^3 - 19x^2 + 16x - 4 = 0$.

b. Use synthetic division to find the other two roots of $6x^3 - 19x^2 + 16x - 4 = 0$.

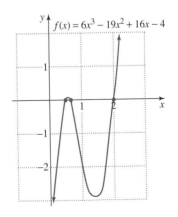

$f(x) = 6x^3 - 19x^2 + 16x - 4$

8. List all possible rational solutions to $2x^3 + 11x^2 - 7x - 6 = 0$.

9. Use Descartes' Rule of Signs to determine the possible number of positive and negative solutions to $3x^5 - 2x^4 - 2x^2 + x - 1 = 0$.

10. Solve: $x^3 + 6x^2 - x - 30 = 0$.

11. Consider the function whose equation is given by $f(x) = 2x^4 - x^3 - 13x^2 + 5x + 15$.

    a. List all possible rational zeros.

    b. Use the graph of f in the figure shown and synthetic division to find all zeros of the function.

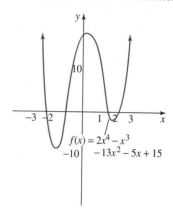

12. Use the graph of $f(x) = 3x^4 + 4x^3 - 7x^2 - 2x - 3$ in the figure at the top of the next column to find the smallest positive integer that is an upper bound and the largest

negative integer that is a lower bound for the real roots of $3x^4 + 4x^3 - 7x^2 - 2x - 3 = 0$. Then use synthetic division to show that all the real roots of the equation lie between these integers.

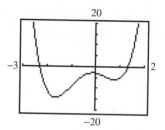

13. Solve $x^4 - 7x^3 + 18x^2 - 22x + 12 = 0$ given that $1 - i$ is a root.

14. Use the graph of $f(x) = x^3 + 3x^2 - 4$ in the figure shown to factor $x^3 + 3x^2 - 4$.

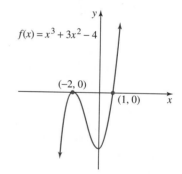

Graph each rational function in Problems 15–18.

15. $f(x) = \dfrac{x}{x^2 - 16}$ **16.** $f(x) = \dfrac{x^2 - 9}{x - 2}$

17. $f(x) = \dfrac{x + 1}{x^2 + 2x - 3}$ **18.** $f(x) = \dfrac{4x^2}{x^2 + 3}$

19. The average cost per manual for a company to produce x graphing utility manuals is given by

$$\overline{C}(x) = \frac{6x + 3000}{x}.$$

    a. How many manuals must be produced so that the average cost per manual is $10?

    b. What is the horizontal asymptote for what this function? Describe what this means for the company.

20. The horsepower required to move a ship varies directly as the cube of its speed. The horsepower required for a speed of 15 knots is 10,125. Find the horsepower required for double this speed.

21. Use a graphing utility to obtain a relatively complete graph of $f(x) = 8x^4 - 8x^2 + 1$. Now use the graph to determine each of the following.

    a. Find all real zeros to two decimal places.

    b. Find the relative maximum and minimum values of f and the values of x at which they occur. Express all answers to two decimal places.

CUMULATIVE REVIEW PROBLEMS (CHAPTERS P–3)

In Problems 1–2, simplify.

1. $\dfrac{1}{2 - \sqrt{3}}$

2. $2\sqrt[3]{54} + 4\sqrt[3]{250}$

3. Factor: $x^3 + x^2y - xy^2 - y^3$.

Solve Problems 4–7.

4. $|x^2 - 1| = 3$

5. $(x^2 + 5x)^2 + 10(x^2 + 5x) + 24 = 0$

6. $3x^2 > 2x + 5$

7. $x^3 + 2x^2 - 5x - 6 = 0$

8. Solve for t: $V = C\left(1 - \dfrac{t}{15}\right)$.

9. If $f(x) = \sqrt{45 - 9x}$, find the domain of f.

10. The graph of g shown in the figure was obtained by a transformation of the graph of $f(x) = \sqrt{x}$. Write an equation for g.

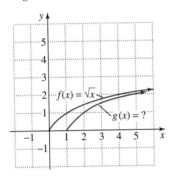

11. If $f(x) = x^3 + 4$, find $f^{-1}(x)$.

12. If $f(x) = x^2 - 5x + 6$ and $g(x) = 7x - 4$, find $f \circ g$ and $g \circ f$.

13. Sketch the graph of a function f having the following properties: f is increasing on $(-\infty, -2)$, decreasing on $(-2, \infty)$, has a y-intercept of -5, and a maximum y-value of 2. (More than one correct graph is possible.)

14. Use the vertex and intercepts to graph the quadratic function whose equation is $f(x) = 4x^2 - 16x + 7$.

15. Consider the function $f(x) = x^3 - 4x^2 - x + 4$.

   a. Use factoring to find all zeros of f.

   b. Use the Leading Coefficient Test and the zeros of f to graph the function.

16. Graph: $f(x) = (x - 1)(x - 2)^2(x - 3)^3$.

17. Graph: $f(x) = \dfrac{x - 1}{x - 2}$.

18. A brick path of uniform width is constructed around the outside of a 20-foot by 30-foot rectangular pool. Find how wide the path should be if there is enough brick to cover 336 square feet.

19. An orchard contains 30 apple trees, each of which yields approximately 400 apples over the growing season. For each new tree added to the orchard, crowding will result in a reduction of 10 apples per tree for all trees in the orchard. How many trees should be added to maximize the total yield of apples? What is the maximum yield?

20. The intensity of illumination on a surface varies inversely as the square of the distance of the light source from the surface. If the illumination from a source is 25 foot-candles when the distance is 4 feet, find the illumination when the distance is 6 feet.

Exponential and Logarithmic Functions

René Magritte "Golconde" 1953. Menil Collection, Houston, TX, USA / Giraudon / Art Resource, NY. © 1998 C. Herscovici, Brussels / Artists Rights Society (ARS), New York.

In a report entitled *Resources and Man,* the U.S. National Academy of Sciences concluded that a world population of 10 billion "is close to (if not above) the maximum that an intensely managed world might hope to support with some degree of comfort and individual choice." For this reason, 10 billion is called the carrying capacity of Earth. How long will it take for this carrying capacity to be reached? Expo-nential and logarithmic functions provide a frightening answer to this question (see Problem 39 in Problem Set 4.1), raising serious concerns about the kind of world we are leaving for our children. Modeling with these remark-able functions helps us to both predict the future and redis-cover the past.

Solutions Manual   Tutorial   Video 8

Exponential Functions

Objectives

1 Evaluate exponential functions.
2 Graph exponential functions.
3 Use compound interest formulas.
4 Solve applied problems using exponential functions.

Throughout this book, we have seen examples of polynomial functions such as $f(x) = x^2$ and $g(x) = x^3$. These functions involve a variable raised to a constant power. We will now interchange the variable and the constant, obtaining functions such as $F(x) = 2^x$ and $G(x) = 3^x$. These functions, with constant bases and variable exponents, are called *exponential functions*.

Exponential functions are used to model many situations. For example, we can use an exponential function to model the accumulated total number of AIDS cases in the United States. Table 4.1 shows the accumulated number of cases from 1983 through 1995.

TABLE 4.1   Accumulated Number of AIDS Cases in the United States

Year	1983	1984	1985	1986	1987	1988	1989	1990	1991	1992	1993	1994	1995
Number of AIDS Cases	4589	10,750	22,399	41,256	69,592	104,644	146,574	193,878	251,638	326,648	399,613	457,280	496,896

Source: Center for Disease Control

This data can be modeled by the function

$$f(t) = 9420.9(1.492)^t$$

where $f(t)$ is the number of AIDS cases and t is the number of years after 1983. Notice that the variable, t, is in the exponent, making this an example of an exponential function with base 1.492. All exponential functions contain a constant base and a variable exponent.

Definition of the exponential function

The exponential function f with base b is defined by

$$f(x) = b^x \quad \text{or} \quad y = b^x$$

where b is a positive constant other than 1 ($b > 0$ and $b \neq 1$) and x is any real number.

S tudy tip

Notice the difference between polynomial and exponential functions.

Polynomial Functions   **Exponential Functions**

Constant exponent   Variable exponent

$y = x^2, y = x^{10}$ $y = 2^x, y = 10^x$

Variable base   Constant base

Evaluate exponential functions.

Pablo Picasso "Weeping Woman," 1937. Tate Gallery, London / Art Resource, NY. © 1998 Estate of Pablo Picasso / Artists Rights Society (ARS), New York.

EXAMPLE 1 **Evaluating an Exponential Model**

The exponential function $f(t) = 9420.9(1.492)^t$ describes the accumulated total number of AIDS cases in the United States t years after 1983.

a. According to the model, how many cases were there in 1983? How does this compare with the actual number?
b. How well does the function describe the actual number of AIDS cases for the years 1985, 1989, and 1992?

Solution

a. Since 1983 is zero years after 1983, we substitute 0 for t.

$f(t) = 9420.9(1.492)^t$ This is the given function.

$f(0) = 9420.9(1.492)^0$ Substitute 0 for t.

$\quad\ = 9420.9(1)$ $b^0 = 1$. A calculator is not necessary.

$\quad\ = 9420.9$

According to the model, there were approximately 9421 cases, which overestimates the actual number of cases (4589) given in Table 4.1.

b. We'll begin with the year 1985. Since 1985 is 2 years after 1983, we substitute 2 for t.

$f(t) = 9420.9(1.492)^t$ This is the given function.

$f(2) = 9420.9(1.492)^2$ Substitute 2 for t.

$\quad\ \approx 20,972$ Use a calculator: 9420.9 ✕ 1.492 ^ 2 ENTER

The model predicts 20,972 cases, and the actual number from Table 4.1 is 22,399. The function slightly underestimates the actual number.
We now follow the same procedure for the years 1989 and 1992.

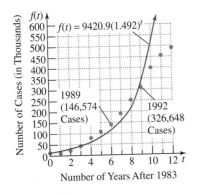

Figure 4.1

Comparing a model for the number of AIDS cases in the United States with the actual numbers

1989:	**1992:**
6 years after 1983	**9 years after 1983**
$f(6) = 9420.9(1.492)^6$	$f(9) = 9420.9(1.492)^9$
$\approx 103,921$	$\approx 345,153$
Actual number = 146,574	Actual number = 326,648
The model underestimates	The model overestimates
the actual number.	the actual number.

The graph of the exponential function is superimposed over the actual data points in Figure 4.1. Notice how the curve lies below the data point for 1989, underestimating the actual number, and above the data point for 1992, overestimating the actual number. The function does not appear to fit the data too well beyond 1992. ■

2 Graph exponential functions.

Graphing Exponential Functions

We are familiar with expressions involving b^x where x is a rational number. For example:

$$b^{1.7} = b^{17/10} = \sqrt[10]{b^{17}} \quad \text{and} \quad b^{1.73} = b^{173/100} = \sqrt[100]{b^{173}}.$$

However, because the definition $f(x) = b^x$ includes all real numbers for x, you may wonder what b^x means when x is an irrational number, such as $b^{\sqrt{3}}$ or b^π. A precise definition for $b^{\sqrt{3}}$ is really impossible without a background in calculus. However, using the nonrepeating and nonterminating approximation 1.73205 for $\sqrt{3}$ we can think of $b^{\sqrt{3}}$ as the value that has the successively closer approximations

$$b^{1.7}, b^{1.73}, b^{1.732}, b^{1.73205}, \ldots .$$

In this way, we will be able to graph the exponential function with no holes or points of discontinuity at the irrational domain values. Let's consider the graphs of some exponential functions.

EXAMPLE 2 **Graphing an Exponential Function**

Graph: $f(x) = 2^x$

Solution

We begin by setting up a table of coordinates.

x	$f(x) = 2^x$
-3	$f(-3) = 2^{-3} = \frac{1}{8}$
-2	$f(-2) = 2^{-2} = \frac{1}{4}$
-1	$f(-1) = 2^{-1} = \frac{1}{2}$
0	$f(0) = 2^0 = 1$
1	$f(1) = 2^1 = 2$
2	$f(2) = 2^2 = 4$
3	$f(3) = 2^3 = 8$

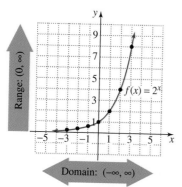

Figure 4.2

The graph of $f(x) = 2^x$

We plot these points, connecting them with a continuous curve. Figure 4.2 shows the graph of $f(x) = 2^x$. Observe that the graph approaches but never touches the negative portion of the x-axis, indicating a range of all positive real numbers. There are no values of x that will result in 0 or negative numbers in the range of $f(x) = 2^x$. Furthermore, we chose integers for x in our table of coordinates. However, you can use a calculator to find additional coordinates. For example, $f(0.3) = 2^{0.3} \approx 1.231$, $f(0.95) = 2^{0.95} \approx 1.932$, and the points $(0.3, 1.231)$ and $(0.95, 1.932)$ really do fit the graph. ∎

EXAMPLE 3 **Graphing an Exponential Function**

Graph: $f(x) = \left(\dfrac{1}{3}\right)^x$

Solution

We again begin with a table of coordinates.

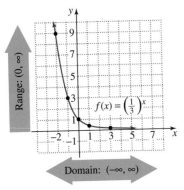

Figure 4.3

The graph of $f(x) = \left(\frac{1}{3}\right)^x$

Figure 4.4

Graphs of four exponential functions

x	$f(x) = \left(\dfrac{1}{3}\right)^x$
-2	$f(-2) = \left(\dfrac{1}{3}\right)^{-2} = \dfrac{1}{\left(\dfrac{1}{3}\right)^2} = \dfrac{1}{\dfrac{1}{9}} = 9$
-1	$f(-1) = \left(\dfrac{1}{3}\right)^{-1} = \dfrac{1}{\left(\dfrac{1}{3}\right)} = 3$
0	$f(0) = \left(\dfrac{1}{3}\right)^0 = 1$
1	$f(1) = \left(\dfrac{1}{3}\right)^1 = \dfrac{1}{3}$
1.2	$f(1.2) = \left(\dfrac{1}{3}\right)^{1.2} \approx 0.268$ ← Using a calculator: $(\ 1\ \div\ 3\ )\ ^\wedge\ 1.2\ \boxed{\text{ENTER}}$
2	$f(2) = \left(\dfrac{1}{3}\right)^2 = \dfrac{1}{9}$

We plot these points and connect them with a smooth continuous curve. Figure 4.3 shows the graph. ■

Four exponential functions have been graphed in Figure 4.4. Compare the graphs of functions where $b > 1$ to those where $b < 1$. When $b > 1$, the value of y increases as the value of x increases. When $b < 1$, the value of y decreases as the value of x-increases.

These graphs illustrate the following general characteristics of exponential functions.

Characteristics of exponential functions

1. The domain of $f(x) = b^x$ consists of all real numbers. The range of $f(x) = b^x$ consists of all positive real numbers.
2. The graphs of all exponential functions pass through the point $(0, 1)$ because $f(0) = b^0 = 1$ $(b \neq 0)$.
3. If $b > 1$, $f(x) = b^x$ has a graph that goes up to the right and is an increasing function.
4. If $0 < b < 1$, $f(x) = b^x$ has a graph that goes down to the right and is a decreasing function.
5. $f(x) = b^x$ is one-to-one and has an inverse that is a function.
6. The graph of $f(x) = b^x$ approaches but does not cross the x-axis. The x-axis is a horizontal asymptote.

Red Grooms "Subway" (detail) from Ruckus Manhattan, 1976. Mixed media, 9 ft. × 18 ft. 7 in. × 37 ft. 2 in. Photo courtesy Marlborough Gallery, New York. © 1998 Red Grooms / Artists Rights Society (ARS), New York.

The graphs of exponential functions can be translated vertically or horizontally, reflected, stretched, or shrunk using the ideas of Section 2.5, as summarized in Table 4.2.

TABLE 4.2   Transformations Involving Exponential Functions

Transformation	Equation	Description
Horizontal translation	$y = b^{x+c}$	Shifts the graph of $y = b^x$ to the left c units if $c > 0$ and to the right c units if $c < 0$.
Stretching or shrinking	$y = cb^x$	Stretches the graph of $y = b^x$ for $c > 1$ and shrinks the graph of $y = b^x$ for $0 < c < 1$, multiplying y-coordinates of $y = b^x$ by c.
Reflecting	$y = -b^x$	Reflects the graph of $y = b^x$ in the x-axis.
	$y = b^{-x}$	Reflects the graph of $y = b^x$ in the y-axis.
Vertical translation	$y = b^x + c$	Shifts the graph of $y = b^x$ upward c units if $c > 0$ and downward c units if $c < 0$.

By realizing that a function is a transformation of the graph of $f(x) = b^x$, you should have a good idea of what its graph looks like. Using this information and a table of coordinates will result in relatively accurate graphs that can be verified using a graphing utility. This idea is illustrated in the next example.

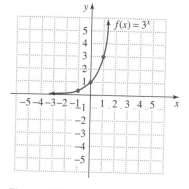

Figure 4.5

The graph of $f(x) = 3^x$

EXAMPLE 4   Transformations Involving Exponential Functions

Sketch the graph of each function by using transformations of the graph of $f(x) = 3^x$. State each function's domain and range.

a. $g(x) = 3^{x+1}$ **b.** $h(x) = 3^{x+2} - 4$
c. $k(x) = 2 \cdot 3^{x+1} - 5$ **d.** $r(x) = -3^{-x} + 1$

Solution

We begin with the graph of $f(x) = 3^x$. Using a table of coordinates, we obtain the graph shown in Figure 4.5.

x	$f(x) = 3^x$
-2	$f(-2) = 3^{-2} = \frac{1}{9}$
-1	$f(-1) = 3^{-1} = \frac{1}{3}$
0	$f(0) = 3^0 = 1$
1	$f(1) = 3^1 = 3$
2	$f(2) = 3^2 = 9$

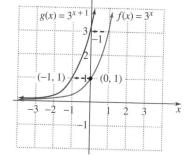

Figure 4.6

The graph of $g(x) = 3^{x+1}$ shifts the graph of $f(x) = 3^x$ to the left one unit.

a. To graph $g(x) = 3^{x+1}$, we shift the graph of $f(x) = 3^x$ one unit to the left, as shown in Figure 4.6. This is the case because $g(x) = 3^{x+1} = f(x + 1)$. As a check, we can find a few ordered pairs satisfying $g(x) = 3^{x+1}$.

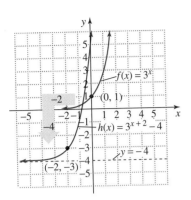

x	-3	-2	-1	0
$g(x) = 3^{x+1}$	$3^{-2} = \frac{1}{9}$	$3^{-1} = \frac{1}{3}$	$3^0 = 1$	$3^1 = 3$

The domain of $g(x) = 3^{x+1}$ is $(-\infty, \infty)$, and the range is $(0, \infty)$.

b. To graph $h(x) = 3^{x+2} - 4$, we first shift the graph of $f(x) = 3^x$ to the left two units ($y = 3^{x+2}$) and then shift the graph of $y = 3^{x+2}$ downward four units, as shown in Figure 4.7. This graph can be verified with a graphing utility or with a few ordered pairs.

x	-2	-1	0
$h(x) = 3^{x+2} - 4$	$3^0 - 4 = -3$	$3^1 - 4 = -1$	$3^2 - 4 = 5$

Figure 4.7

The graph of $h(x) = 3^{x+2} - 4$ shifts the graph of $f(x) = 3^x$ to the left two units and downward four units.

The domain of $h(x) = 3^{x+2} - 4$ is $(-\infty, \infty)$, and the range is $(-4, \infty)$.

Study tip

If an exponential function is translated upward or downward, the horizontal asymptote is shifted by the amount of the vertical shift. This is illustrated in Figure 4.7.

c. We obtain the graph of $k(x) = 2 \cdot 3^{x+1} - 5$ from the graph of $f(x) = 3^x$ using the following transformations.
  1. Translate to the left one unit, obtaining $y = 3^{x+1}$.
  2. Stretch by a factor of 2, obtaining $y = 2 \cdot 3^{x+1}$.
  3. Translate downward five units, obtaining $y = 2 \cdot 3^{x+1} - 5$.
The graph of $k(x) = 2 \cdot 3^{x+1} - 5$ is shown in Figure 4.8. Once again, we can verify the graph with a graphing utility or with a few ordered pairs.

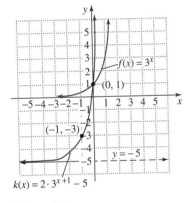

x	-2	-1	0
$k(x) = 2 \cdot 3^{x+1} - 5$	$2 \cdot 3^{-1} - 5 = -4\frac{1}{3}$	$2 \cdot 3^0 - 5 = -3$	$2 \cdot 3 - 5 = 1$

Figure 4.8

The graph of $k(x) = 2 \cdot 3^{x+1} - 5$ translates and stretches the graph of $f(x) = 3^x$.

The domain of $k(x) = 2 \cdot 3^{x+1} - 5$ is $(-\infty, \infty)$, and the range is $(-5, \infty)$.

d. We obtain the graph of $r(x) = -3^{-x} + 1$ from the graph of $f(x) = 3^x$ using three transformations at the top of the next page (see Figure 4.9).

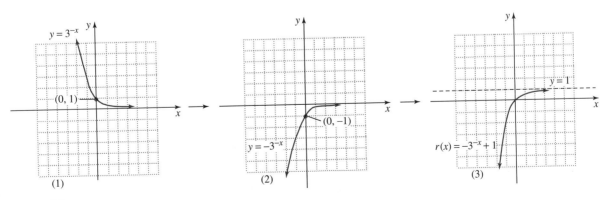

Figure 4.9

Using transformations to graph $r(x) = -3^{-x} + 1$

1. Reflect f in the y-axis, obtaining $y = 3^{-x}$.
2. Reflect $y = 3^{-x}$ in the x-axis, obtaining $y = -3^{-x}$.
3. Translate $y = -3^{-x}$ upward one unit, obtaining $r(x) = -3^{-x} + 1$. The domain of $r(x) = -3^{-x} + 1$ is $(-\infty, \infty)$, and the range is $(-\infty, 1)$.   ■

3 Use compound interest formulas.

Compound Interest and the Irrational Number e

Compound interest is another situation that can be modeled by exponential functions. Suppose a sum of money P (called the principal) is invested at an annual percentage rate r (in decimal form), compounded once a year. Because the interest is added to the principal at year's end, the accumulated value (A) is

$$A = P + Pr = P(1 + r).$$

The accumulated amount of money follows this pattern of multiplying the previous principal by $(1 + r)$ for each successive year, as indicated in Table 4.3.

TABLE 4.3

Time in Years	Accumulated Value after Each Compounding
0	$A = P$
1	$A = P(1 + r)$
2	$A = P(1 + r)(1 + r) = P(1 + r)^2$
3	$A = P(1 + r)^2(1 + r) = P(1 + r)^3$
4	$A = P(1 + r)^3(1 + r) = P(1 + r)^4$
⋮	⋮
t	$A = P(1 + r)^t$

If money invested at a specified rate of interest is compounded more than once a year, then the model $A = P(1 + r)^t$ can be adjusted to take into account the number of compounding periods in a year. If n represents the number of compounding periods in a year, the mathematical model becomes

$$A = P\left(1 + \frac{r}{n}\right)^{nt}.$$

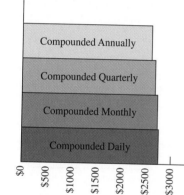

Future value of $1000 invested at 10% interest in 10 years; the increasing bar lengths show greater accumulated values as the number of compounding periods in a year increases.

EXAMPLE 5   Using the Compound Interest Model

A sum of $10,000 is invested at an annual interest rate of 8%, compounded quarterly. Find the balance in the account after 5 years.

Solution

$$A = P\left(1 + \frac{r}{n}\right)^{nt} \qquad \text{Use the compound interest model.}$$

We are given that P (the principal) = $10,000, r (the interest rate) = 8% = 0.08, n (the number of compounding periods with quarterly compounding) = 4, and t (the time, in years) = 5. We substitute these values into the model.

$$A = 10,000\left(1 + \frac{0.08}{4}\right)^{4\cdot5} \approx 14,859.47$$

After 5 years, the balance in the account is $14,859.47.   ■

Barton Lidice Benes "Dustpan" 1990,
mixed media with currency,
12 × 14 1/2 × 2 in.

Figure 4.10

As x increases to the right,
$(1 + \frac{1}{x})^x$ gets closer to e.

The Irrational Number e

Suppose that $1 is invested at an interest rate of 100% for 1 year, and the compounding periods increase infinitely (compounding interest every trillionth of a second, every quadrillionth of a second, etc.). As the compounding periods increase, the amount you would receive at the end of the year gets closer and closer to $2.718281828459045…. Mathematicians represent this irrational number by the symbol e, where e is approximately equal to 2.72 ($e \approx 2.72$).

Let's rewrite our compound interest model so that we can visualize what all this means.

$$A = P\left(1 + \frac{r}{n}\right)^{nt}$$ This is the compound interest model.

$$= 1\left(1 + \frac{1}{n}\right)^{n \cdot 1}$$ P (the principal) = $1, r (the interest rate) = 100% = 1, and t (time) = 1 year.

$$= \left(1 + \frac{1}{n}\right)^{n}$$ Simplify.

Remembering that A represents the balance in the account, we've used a graphing utility to graph $A = (1 + \frac{1}{n})^n$ and $A = e$ (approximately 2.72) in the same viewing rectangle. Figure 4.10 illustrates that as n (the number of compounding periods) increases, the balance in the account gets closer and closer to e, or approximately $2.72.

The irrational number e is the base for the *natural exponential function*.

The natural exponential function

The function

$$f(x) = e^x$$

is called the *natural exponential function*. The irrational number e is called the *natural base*, where $e \approx 2.7183$.

You will need to use a calculator to evaluate the natural exponential function. Here are some examples obtained using the natural exponential key $\boxed{e^x}$.

Study tip

Remember that e is the constant
number 2.71828... and x is a
variable.

Function Value	$f(x) = e^x$ Keystrokes	Approximate Display
$f(2) = e^2$	$\boxed{e^x}$ 2 $\boxed{\text{ENTER}}$	7.389056
$f(-3) = e^{-3}$	$\boxed{e^x}$ $\boxed{(-)}$ 3 $\boxed{\text{ENTER}}$	0.049787
$f(4.6) = e^{4.6}$	$\boxed{e^x}$ 4.6 $\boxed{\text{ENTER}}$	99.4843156

Because $2 < e < 3$, the graph of $y = e^x$ is between the graphs of $y = 2^x$ and $y = 3^x$ as shown in Figure 4.11 at the top of the next page.

Discover for yourself

Use a graphing utility to reproduce the graphs shown in Figure 4.11.

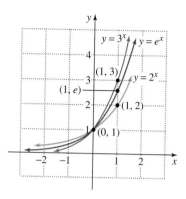

Figure 4.11

Graphs of three exponential functions

Since the number e is related to compounding periods increasing infinitely, or *continuous compounding*, the number appears in the formula for the balance in an account subject to this type of compounding. The formulas for both types of compounding are given as follows.

Formulas for compound interest

After t years, the balance A in an account with principal P and annual interest rate r (in decimal form) is given by the following mathematical models.

1. For n compoundings per year: $A = P\left(1 + \dfrac{r}{n}\right)^{nt}$
2. For continuous compounding: $A = Pe^{rt}$

EXAMPLE 6 Choosing Between Investments

You want to invest $8000 for 6 years, and you have a choice between two accounts. The first pays 7% per year, compounded monthly. The second pays 6.85% per year, compounded continuously. Which is the better investment?

Solution

The better investment is the one with the greater balance in the account after 6 years. Let's begin with the account with monthly compounding. We use the compound interest model with $P = 8000$, $r = 0.07$, $n = 12$ (monthly compounding, means 12 compoundings per year), and $t = 6$.

$$A = P\left(1 + \frac{r}{n}\right)^{nt} = 8000\left(1 + \frac{0.07}{12}\right)^{12 \cdot 6} \approx 12{,}160.84$$

The balance in this account after 6 years is $12,160.84. For the second investment option, we use the model for continuous compounding with $P = 8000$, $r = 6.85\% = 0.0685$, and $t = 6$.

$$A = Pe^{rt} = 8000\, e^{0.0685(6)} \approx 12{,}066.60$$

The balance in this account after 6 years is $12,066.60, slightly less than the previous amount. Thus, the better investment is the 7% monthly compounding option. ∎

Using technology

Here's the graphing calculator keystroke sequence for the expression $8000e^{0.0685(6)}$.

8000 $\boxed{e^\wedge}$ $\boxed{(}$ .0685 $\boxed{\times}$ 6 $\boxed{)}$

$\boxed{\text{ENTER}}$

Discover for yourself

Write an example similar to Example 6 in which continuous compounding at a slightly lower yearly interest rate is a better investment than compounding n times per year.

4 Solve applied problems using exponential functions.

Applications of Exponential Functions

Exponential functions involving base e describe a wide variety of situations in addition to continuous compounding. Frequently encountered are *growth* and *decay* models.

Exponential growth and decay models

The mathematical model for exponential growth or decay is given by

$$f(t) = A_0 e^{kt} \quad \text{or} \quad A = A_0 e^{kt}.$$

Within this model, t represents time, A_0 is the original amount (or size) of the growing (or decaying) quantity, and A or $f(t)$ represents the amount (or size) of the quantity at time t. The number k represents a constant that depends on the rate of growth or decay. If $k > 0$, the formula represents *exponential growth*; if $k < 0$, the formula represents *exponential decay*.

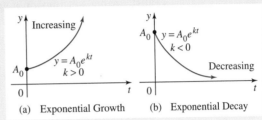

(a) Exponential Growth   (b) Exponential Decay

> **Study tip**
>
> With exponential growth and decay, quantities grow or decay at a rate directly proportional to their size. Populations that are growing exponentially grow extremely rapidly as they get larger because there are more adults to have offspring.

<hr>

EXAMPLE 7 Carbon-14 Dating

Archaeologists, anthropologists, and geologists use a technique called *radiocarbon dating* to estimate when a particular organism died. Carbon-14 is a radioactive substance that is absorbed by an organism while it is alive. Once an organism dies, carbon-14 is no longer replaced in its tissues, but continues to decay. The mathematical model

$$A = A_0 e^{-0.000121t}$$

describes the amount A of carbon-14 present after t years, where A_0 is the amount present at time $t = 0$. If an artifact originally had 16 grams of carbon-14 present, how many grams will be present in:

a. 5715 years?   **b.** 11,430 years?   **c.** 17,145 years?

> **Study tip**
>
> Living beings continually receive carbon-14 that balances the carbon-14 that decays. Thus, the level of carbon-14 is constant in living organisms.

After generations of controversy, the shroud of Turin, long believed to be the burial cloth of Jesus Christ, was dated by carbon-14 techniques to centuries after the death of Christ.

Gianni Tortoli / Science Source / Photo Researchers, Inc.

Solution

a. $A = A_0 e^{-0.000121t}$ This is the given model.

$\quad = 16 e^{-0.000121(5715)}$ A_0 (the initial amount) = 16 grams and t = 5715 years.

$\quad \approx 8$ Use a calculator.

After 5715 years, approximately 8 grams of carbon-14 will be present.

b. $A = A_0 e^{-0.000121t}$ This is the given model.

$\quad = 16 e^{-0.000121(11,430)}$ A_0 = 16 grams and t = 11,430 years.

$\quad \approx 4$ Use a calculator.

After 11,430 years, approximately 4 grams of carbon-14 will be present.

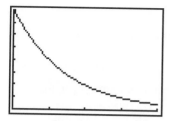

Figure 4.12

The graph of the exponential decay model for carbon-14

(a)

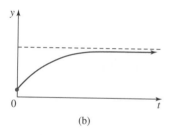

(b)

Figure 4.13

Limits to growth: The learning curve (b) illustrates that when we learn new tasks, learning is initially quite rapid but tends to taper off as time increases.

c. $A = A_0 e^{-0.000121t}$ We'll repeat the same procedure.

$= 16e^{-0.000121(17,145)}$ $A_0 = 16$ grams and $t = 17,145$ years.

≈ 2 Use a calculator.

After 17,145 years, approximately 2 grams of carbon-14 will be present.   ■

The *half-life* of a substance that is decaying exponentially is the time required for half of the atoms in the substance to disintegrate. As we saw in Example 7, every 5715 years half of the carbon-14 decays. Thus, carbon-14 decays exponentially with a half-life of approximately 5715 years.

As always, an understanding of a function's behavior enables us to choose realistic range settings on a graphing utility. The graph of $A = 16e^{-0.000121t}$ or, equivalently, $y = 16e^{-0.000121x}$ is shown in Figure 4.12. We've selected Xmin = 0, Xmax = 22,860 (four multiples of 5715, the half-life), and Xscl = 5715. We chose Ymin = 0, Ymax = 16 (the original amount of carbon-14 present), and Yscl = 2 as range settings for y. If you know the amount of carbon-14 present, how might you use the graph to determine an artifact's age? We'll discuss this in more detail in Section 4.5.

Exponential functions can be used to model long-term population growth, the spread of an epidemic, the sales of new products, or learning. However, nothing on Earth (population growth or the spread of an epidemic) can grow exponentially indefinitely. There are always limits to growth, shown in Figure 4.13 by the horizontal asymptote.

EXAMPLE 8   **Spread of an Epidemic**

The function

$$N(t) = \frac{30,000}{1 + 20e^{-1.5t}}$$

describes the number of people $N(t)$ who have become ill with influenza t weeks after its initial outbreak in a town with 30,000 inhabitants.

a. How many people became ill with the flu when the epidemic began?
b. How many people were ill by the end of the fourth week?
c. What is the horizontal asymptote for this function? Describe what this means in practical terms.
d. Use a graphing utility to graph the function.

Solution

a. $N(t) = \dfrac{30,000}{1 + 20e^{-1.5t}}$ This is the given function.

$N(0) = \dfrac{30,000}{1 + 20e^{-1.5(0)}}$ When the epidemic began, $t = 0$.

$= \dfrac{30,000}{1 + 20}$ $e^{-1.5(0)} = e^0 = 1$

≈ 1429

Approximately 1429 people were ill when the epidemic began.

b. $N(t) = \dfrac{30,000}{1 + 20e^{-1.5t}}$ Use the given function.

ENRICHMENT ESSAY

Exponential Growth of Carbon Dioxide; The Nuclear Option

The amount of carbon dioxide (CO_2) in the atmosphere is an environmental issue that we have looked at throughout this book. The present concentration is about 352 parts per million and continues to increase exponentially at 0.4% per year. Using the exponential growth model $A = 352e^{0.004t}$ that describes the concentration of CO_2 (in parts per million) t years after 1990, climatologists forecast a warming trend of about 1°F per decade.

The major sources of carbon dioxide are energy production and deforestation. Today's American household uses an average of 3200 kilowatts-hours of electricity a year, accounting for emissions of nearly three tons of CO_2, the leading greenhouse gas, and 60 pounds of sulfur dioxide, a major cause of acid rain.

One solution might be nuclear power plants, which do not generate greenhouse gases during operation. However, numerous problems stand in the way of nuclear power expansion, not the least of which is what to do with nuclear waste. By mid-1990 more than 23,000 tons of intensely radioactive nuclear waste had accumulated around the 111 operating nuclear power plants in the United States.

Bill Woodrow "Self Portrait in the Nuclear Age" 1986, shelving unit, wall map, coat, globe, acrylic paint, 205 × 145 × 265 cm. Saatchi Collection, London. Photo credit: Bill Woodrow.

$$N(4) = \frac{30,000}{1 + 20e^{-1.5(4)}}$$

To find the number of people ill by the end of week four, let $t = 4$.

$$\approx 28,583$$

Use a calculator.

Approximately 28,583 people were ill by the end of the fourth week. Compared with the number of people who were ill initially, this illustrates the virulence of the epidemic.

c. The horizontal asymptote is determined by finding out what happens to $N(t)$ as t increases without bound (as $t \to \infty$).

$$N(t) = \frac{30,000}{1 + 20e^{-1.5t}}$$

Again, use the given function.

$$= \frac{30,000}{1 + \dfrac{20}{e^{1.5t}}}$$

$e^{-1.5t} = \dfrac{1}{e^{1.5t}}$, by the definition of a negative exponent.

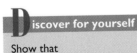

Discover for yourself

Show that

$$\frac{20}{e^{1.5t}}$$

approaches 0 as t gets larger by using your calculator to evaluate the expression for $t = 10, 50, 100,$ and 1000.

As $t \to \infty$ (time increases), $\dfrac{20}{e^{1.5t}}$ gets smaller and smaller $\left(\dfrac{20}{e^{1.5t}} \to 0\right)$ because the numerator (20) is staying the same size and the denominator ($e^{1.5t}$) is getting larger without bound. Consequently, we see that $\dfrac{20}{e^{1.5t}}$ is approximately equal to 0 as t grows increasingly larger. Thus, the function gets

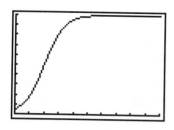

Figure 4.14

The graph of a function modeling the spread of an epidemic

closer and closer to $\dfrac{30{,}000}{1 + 0}$, indicating that $y = 30{,}000$ is the function's horizontal asymptote. In practical terms, this indicates that 30,000 is the limiting size of the population that becomes ill.

d. The graph of Y = 30,000/(1 + 20 $\boxed{e^{\wedge}}$ (−1.5X)), obtained with a graphing utility, is shown in Figure 4.14. Based on our previous results, we used the following range settings: Xmin = 0, Xmax = 10 (This takes us to week 10, and by week 4 approximately 28,583 people were ill), Xscl = 1. We also know that 30,000 is the limiting size, so we select Ymin = 0, Ymax = 30,000 (the limiting size), and Yscl = 3000. As always, other range settings are possible.   ■

PROBLEM SET 4.1

Practice Problems

In Problems 1–8, sketch by hand the graph of each function by making a table of coordinates. Then use a graphing utility to confirm your results.

1. $f(x) = 4^x$

2. $g(x) = 5^x$

3. $h(x) = \left(\frac{1}{3}\right)^x$

4. $f(x) = \left(\frac{1}{4}\right)^x$

5. $y = \left(\frac{3}{2}\right)^x$

6. $y = \left(\frac{4}{3}\right)^x$

7. $g(x) = (1.2)^x$

8. $h(x) = (0.6)^x$

In Problems 9–20, sketch by hand the graph of each function by using transformations of the graph of $f(x) = 2^x$ and a table of coordinates. State each function's domain and range. Then use a graphing utility to confirm your results.

9. $g(x) = 2^{x-1}$

10. $h(x) = 2^{x-2}$

11. $y = 2^x + 3$

12. $y = 2^x - 1$

13. $j(x) = 2^{x+1} - 1$

14. $k(x) = 2^{x+2} - 1$

15. $r(x) = 3 \cdot 2^{x+1} - 2$

16. $v(x) = 3 \cdot 2^{x+2} - 2$

17. $y = -2^x$

18. $y = -2^{x-2}$

19. $y = 2^{-x} + 3$

20. $y = 2^{-x} + 4$

In Problems 21–30, use transformations to graph each function. Then use a graphing utility to confirm your graph.

21. $f(x) = 3^{x-1}$

22. $g(x) = \frac{1}{2} \cdot 3^{x+1}$

23. $y = 3^{x+2} - 1$

24. $y = 4^{x+1} - 3$

25. $h(x) = \left(\frac{1}{2}\right)^{x+1}$

26. $j(x) = \left(\frac{1}{2}\right)^{x+2}$

27. $k(x) = \left(\frac{3}{2}\right)^{x-1}$

28. $r(x) = \left(\frac{3}{2}\right)^{x-2}$

29. $y = 1 - 5^x$

30. $y = -1 - 5^{-x}$

Application Problems

31. The exponential function $f(t) = 67.38(1.026)^t$ describes the population (in millions) of Mexico t years after 1980.

 a. What was the 1980 population?

 b. Predict Mexico's population in 2007, 2034, and 2061.

 c. How many years does it take for Mexico's population to double?

32. The model $N(t) = 2000(2)^{\frac{t}{20}}$ describes the growth of the bacteria Escherichi coli often found in the human bladder. The formula indicates that 2000 of the bacteria are in the bladder at time $t = 0$. If t is measured in minutes, sketch by hand the function for $0 \leqslant t \leqslant 80$.

Use the compound interest models

$$A = P\left(1 + \frac{r}{n}\right)^{nt} \quad and \quad A = Pe^{rt}$$

to answer Problems 33–37.

33. In 1626 Peter Minuit convinced the Wappinger Indians to sell him Manhattan Island for $24. If the Native Americans had put the $24 into a bank account paying

5% interest, how much would the investment be worth in the year 2000 if interest were compounded

 a. Monthly?   **b.** Daily?   **c.** Continuously?

Dan V. Lomahaftewa "Spring
Arrival" Collagraph, 42 × 30.

34. Suppose that you have $8000 to invest. What investment yields the greater return over 3 years: 7% compounded monthly or 6.85% compounded continuously?

35. Suppose that you have $7000 to invest. What investment yields the greater return over 5 years: 8.25% compounded quarterly or 8.3% compounded semiannually?

36. Complete the following table, which indicates what happens to $5000 invested at 5.5% for different time periods and different compounding periods. (Round each entry to the nearest dollar.)

	1 year	5 years	10 years	20 years
Compounded Semiannually				
Compounded Monthly				
Compounded 365 Times per Year				
Compounded Continuously				

37. Repeat Problem 36 for 30,000 invested at 6.5%.

38. The exponential growth model $A = A_0 e^{kt}$ $(k > 0)$ describes the number of AIDS cases in the United States among intravenous drug users. In 1989, there were 24,000 cases of AIDS among intravenous drug users $(A_0 = 24{,}000)$ with a growth rate of 21% $(k = 0.21)$. If this growth rate doesn't change, how many cases of AIDS will be expected by the end of

a. 2000?   **b.** 2020?

39. Take a moment to reread the chapter introduction. At the time *Resources and Man* was issued in 1969, the world population was approximately 3.6 billion, with a relative growth rate of 2% per year. If exponential growth continues at this rate, use the model $A = 3.6e^{0.02t}$, where A is the world population in billions t years after 1969, to show that Earth's carrying capacity will be reached in the year 2020.

40. Polonium-210 has a half-life of 140 days. This means that the rate of decay is proportional to the amount present, and half of any given quantity will disintegrate in 140 days. The mathematical model $A = A_0 e^{-0.004951t}$ describes the amount A of polonium-210 present after t days, where A_0 is the amount present at time $t = 0$.

a. A sample has a mass of 100 milligrams. How many milligrams of polonium-210 will be present in 140 days? 210 days? 280 days? 420 days? 630 days?

b. Display your computations in part (a) graphically, with time (in days) along the horizontal axis, and the amount of polonium-210 present (in milligrams) along the vertical axis. Connect the data points with a smooth curve. Write the equation of the function that you have graphed.

The model $A = A_0 \left(\frac{1}{2}\right)^{\frac{t}{h}}$ is also used to describe exponential decay. If there is an initial amount, A_0, of a radioactive substance with a half-life of h, the formula describes the amount of substance remaining, A, after a period of time t. Units of measure for t and h should be the same. Use this formula to answer Problem 41.

41. The half-life of iodine-131 is 8 years. An island is contaminated with debris from illegal above-ground nuclear testing. The debris contains 3000 grams of iodine-131, which is considered 30,000 times above a safe level for a team of scientists to visit the island and possibly identify the country violating the ban. Assuming that they must wait until there is only 0.1 gram of iodine-131, can the scientists safely visit the island after 80 years?

42. In a learning theory project, psychologists discovered that

$$f(x) = \frac{0.8}{1 + e^{-0.2x}}$$

is a model for describing the *proportion* of correct responses after x learning trials.

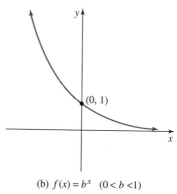

(a) $f(x) = b^x$ $(b > 1)$

(b) $f(x) = b^x$ $(0 < b < 1)$

Figure 4.15

Exponential functions have inverses that are functions.

Evaluate logarithms.

the general shapes shown in Figure 4.15. Because no horizontal line intersects the graph of $f(x) = b^x$ in more than one point, the exponential function is one-to-one. Thus, $f(x) = b^x$ has an inverse that is also a function. We can use the procedure of Section 2.7 to find a formula for f^{-1}.

$$f(x) = b^x$$

1. Replace $f(x)$ by y: $y = b^x$
2. Interchange x and y: $x = b^y$
3. Solve for y: ?

The question mark indicates that we need some sort of notation to solve $x = b^y$ for y. In words, we can write

y = the power on b that gives x.

We solve for y with the following definition.

Definition of the logarithmic function

For $x > 0$ and $b > 0$, $b \neq 1$,

$y = \log_b x$ is equivalent to $b^y = x$.

The function $f(x) = \log_b x$ is the *logarithmic function with base b*.

Some logarithms can be evaluated by inspection.

EXAMPLE 1 **Evaluating Logarithms**

Evaluate:

a. $\log_2 16$ **b.** $\log_3 9$ **c.** $\log_{25} 5$
d. $\log_{10} \frac{1}{1000}$ **e.** $\log_7 1$ **f.** $\log_{\frac{1}{3}} 9$ **g.** $\log_3 3$

Solution

Logarithmic Expression	Question Needed for Evaluation	Logarithmic Expression Evaluated
a. $\log_2 16$	2 to what power gives 16?	$\log_2 16 = 4$ because $2^4 = 16$.
b. $\log_3 9$	3 to what power gives 9?	$\log_3 9 = 2$ because $3^2 = 9$.
c. $\log_{25} 5$	25 to what power gives 5?	$\log_{25} 5 = \frac{1}{2}$ because $25^{1/2} = \sqrt{25} = 5$.
d. $\log_{10} \frac{1}{1000}$	10 to what power gives $\frac{1}{1000}$?	$\log_{10} \frac{1}{1000} = -3$ because $10^{-3} = \frac{1}{10^3} = \frac{1}{1000}$.
e. $\log_7 1$	7 to what power gives 1?	$\log_7 1 = 0$ because $7^0 = 1$.
f. $\log_{\frac{1}{3}} 9$	$\frac{1}{3}$ to what power gives 9?	$\log_{\frac{1}{3}} 9 = -2$ because $\left(\frac{1}{3}\right)^{-2} = \frac{1}{\left(\frac{1}{3}\right)^2} = \frac{1}{\left(\frac{1}{9}\right)} = 9$.
g. $\log_3 3$	3 to what power gives 3?	$\log_3 3 = 1$ because $3^1 = 3$.

We can generalize from Example 1 and obtain the following logarithmic properties.

Basic logarithmic properties

1. $\log_b b = 1$ because 1 is the exponent to which b must be raised to obtain b. $(b^1 = b)$
2. $\log_b 1 = 0$ because 0 is the exponent to which b must be raised to obtain 1. $(b^0 = 1)$
3. $\log_b b^x = x$ because x is the exponent to which b must be raised to obtain b^x. $(b^x = b^x)$

---

2 Graph logarithmic functions.

Graphs of Logarithmic Functions

Figure 4.16 illustrates the fact that the graphs of $y = \log_b x$ and $y = b^x$ $(b > 0)$ are reflections of each other in the line $y = x$ because $y = \log_b x$ is the inverse of $y = b^x$. Let's see specifically what this means for $b = 2$.

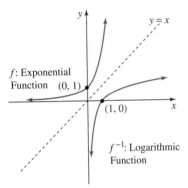

f: Exponential Function (0, 1)

(1, 0)

f^{-1}: Logarithmic Function

Figure 4.16

An exponential function and its inverse logarithmic function are reflections in the line $y = x$.

EXAMPLE 2   **Graphing an Exponential Function and Its Inverse Logarithmic Function**

Graph $y = 2^x$ [or $f(x) = 2^x$] and $y = \log_2 x$ [or $f^{-1}(x) = \log_2 x$] on the same set of axes.

Solution

We first set up a table of coordinates for $f(x) = 2^x$. Reversing these coordinates gives the coordinates for the inverse function $f^{-1}(x) = \log_2 x$.

$f(x) = 2^x$ or $y = 2^x$

x	-2	-1	0	1	2	3
y	$\frac{1}{4}$	$\frac{1}{2}$	1	2	4	8
(x, y)	$(-2, \frac{1}{4})$	$(-1, \frac{1}{2})$	$(0, 1)$	$(1, 2)$	$(2, 4)$	$(3, 8)$

Reverse coordinates

$f^{-1}(x) = \log_2 x$ or $y = \log_2 x$

x	$\frac{1}{4}$	$\frac{1}{2}$	1	2	4	8
y	-2	-1	0	1	2	3
(x, y)	$(\frac{1}{4}, -2)$	$(\frac{1}{2}, -1)$	$(1, 0)$	$(2, 1)$	$(4, 2)$	$(8, 3)$

We now plot the ordered pairs in both tables, connecting them with smooth curves. Figure 4.17 at the top of the next page shows the graphs of $f(x) = 2^x$ and its inverse function $f^{-1}(x) = \log_2 x$. The graph of the inverse can also be drawn by reflecting the graph of $f(x) = 2^x$ in the line $y = x$. ∎

If we generalize the results of this example from base 2 to base b (with $b > 1$) we see that the inverse of $f(x) = b^x$ is $f^{-1}(x) = \log_b x$, as shown in Figure 4.18 on page 454. These graphs illustrate characteristics of $y = b^x$ and $y = \log_b x$ that are listed in the box on page 454.

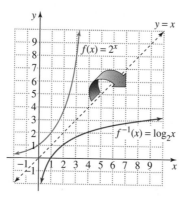

Figure 4.17

The graphs of $f(x) = 2^x$ and its inverse function

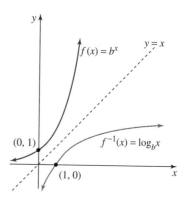

Figure 4.18

Shapes for the graphs of exponential and logarithmic functions, $b > 1$

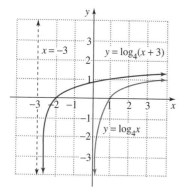

Figure 4.19

A horizontal translation

Characteristics of exponential and logarithmic functions

1. The domain of $y = b^x$ is the set of all real numbers, and the range is the set of all real numbers > 0. Domain $= (-\infty, \infty)$ and range $= (0, \infty)$.

2. The domain of $y = \log_b x$ is the set of all real numbers > 0, and the range of $y = \log_b x$ is the set of all real numbers. Domain $= (0, \infty)$ and range $= (-\infty, \infty)$.

3. The graph of $y = b^x$ passes through $(0, 1)$, and the graph of $y = \log_b x$ passes through $(1, 0)$.

4. The x-axis is a horizontal asymptote of the graph of $y = b^x$ for $b > 1$. ($b^x \to 0$ as $x \to -\infty$)

5. The y-axis is a vertical asymptote of the graph of $y = \log_b x$ for $b > 1$. ($\log_b x \to -\infty$ as $x \to 0^+$)

The graph of $y = \log_b x$ can be transformed through translations, reflections, stretchings, or shrinkings. For example, the graph of $y = \log_4 (x + 3)$ lies three units to the left of the graph of $y = \log_4 x$ (Figure 4.19). The graph of $y = \log_4 x + 3$ lies three units above the graph of $y = \log_4 x$ (Figure 4.20.)

tudy tip

The graph of $y = \log_b (x + a) + c$ with $a > 0$ and $c > 0$, lies a units to the left and c units above the graph of $y = \log_b x$. The domain of $f(x) = \log_b (x + a) + c$ consists of all x for which $x + a > 0$. The vertical asymptote is $x = -a$.

Figure 4.20

A vertical translation

EXAMPLE 3 **Transformations of Logarithmic Functions**

Sketch the graph of each function using transformations of the graph of $f(x) = \log_2 x$. State each function's domain and range.

Study tip

If a logarithmic function is translated horizontally, its vertical asymptote will change. Figure 4.21 shows that the vertical asymptote for

$g(x) = \log_2(x + 2) - 3$

is $x = -2$.

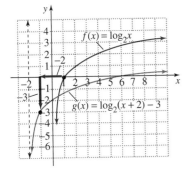

Figure 4.21

The graph of g shifts the graph of f to the left two units and downward three units.

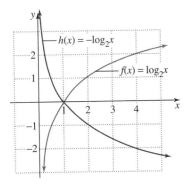

Figure 4.22

The graph of h reflects the graph of f in the x-axis. The line $x = 0$ is the vertical asymptote of h.

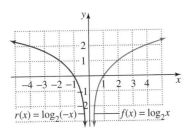

Figure 4.23

The graph of r reflects the graph of f in the y-axis. The y-axis ($x = 0$) is a vertical asymptote of f and r.

a. $g(x) = \log_2(x + 2) - 3$
b. $h(x) = -\log_2 x$
c. $r(x) = \log_2(-x)$

Solution

a. The graph of $g(x) = \log_2(x + 2) - 3$ is obtained from the graph of $f(x) = \log_2 x$ using the following transformations.
  1. A horizontal translation two units to the left: $y = \log_2(x + 2)$.
  2. A vertical translation three units downward: $y = \log_2(x + 2) - 3$.
The graph of $g(x) = \log_2(x + 2) - 3$ is shown in Figure 4.21. As a check, we can find a few ordered pairs satisfying $g(x) = \log_2(x + 2) - 3$.

x	$g(x) = \log_2(x + 2) - 3$	$(x, g(x))$
-1	$g(-1) = \log_2(-1 + 2) - 3$ $= \log_2 1 - 3 = 0 - 3 = -3$	$(-1, -3)$
2	$g(2) = \log_2(2 + 2) - 3$ $= \log_2 4 - 3 = 2 - 3 = -1$	$(2, -1)$
6	$g(6) = \log_2(6 + 2) - 3$ $= \log_2 8 - 3 = 3 - 3 = 0$	$(6, 0)$

The domain of g consists of all x such that $x + 2 > 0$. Thus, $x > -2$ and the domain is $(-2, \infty)$. The range of g is $(-\infty, \infty)$.
b. Since $h(x) = -\log_2 x = -f(x)$, the graph of h can be obtained from the graph of f by reflecting in the x-axis, as shown in Figure 4.22. The domain of h is $(0, \infty)$ and the range is $(-\infty, \infty)$.

Discover for yourself

Check the graph of h in Figure 4.22 by finding three ordered pairs satisfying

$h(x) = -\log_2 x$.

In particular, let $x = 1, 2$, and 4, and find corresponding values for y. Locate these points on the graph.

c. Since $r(x) = \log_2(-x) = f(-x)$, the graph of r can be obtained from the graph of f by reflecting in the y-axis, as shown in Figure 4.23. The domain of r is $(-\infty, 0)$ and the range is $(-\infty, \infty)$.

Discover for yourself

Check the graph of r in Figure 4.23 by finding three ordered pairs satisfying

$r(x) = \log_2(-x)$.

In particular, let $x = -4, -2$, and -1, and find corresponding values for y. Locate these points on the graph.

3 Evaluate common and natural logarithms.

Common Logarithms and Natural Logarithms

The bases that most frequently appear on logarithmic functions are e and 10. If $f(x) = 10^x$, then $f^{-1}(x) = \log_{10}x$. Similarly, if $f(x) = e^x$, then $f^{-1}(x) = \log_e x$.

Notations for common and natural logarithms

We write $y = \log_{10}x$ as $y = \log x$. Logarithms to the base 10 are called *common logarithms*. We write $y = \log_e x$ as $y = \ln x$. Logarithms to the base e are called *natural logarithms*. The symbol $\ln x$ is read as "el en of x."

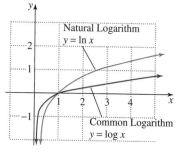

Figure 4.24

Graphs of $y = \log x$ and $y = \ln x$

Figure 4.24 shows the graphs of $y = \log x$ and $y = \ln x$.

You will need to use a calculator to evaluate most common and natural logarithms. Here are some examples obtained by using the common logarithm key $\boxed{\log}$ and the natural logarithm key $\boxed{\ln}$.

Logarithm	Keystrokes	Approximate Display
log 1.75	$\boxed{\log}$ 1.75 $\boxed{\text{ENTER}}$	0.24304
ln 1.6	$\boxed{\ln}$ 1.6 $\boxed{\text{ENTER}}$	0.47000
ln(−3)	$\boxed{\ln}$ $\boxed{(-)}$ 3 $\boxed{\text{ENTER}}$	ERROR

Although we write log 1.75 = 0.24304, it turns out that 0.24304 is only an *approximate* value. We can reinforce this fact by writing

$$\log 1.75 \approx 0.24304.$$

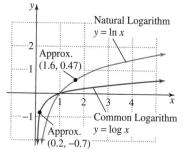

Figure 4.25

Similarly, although our calculator tells us that ln 1.75 ≈ 0.5596, a more accurate statement is ln 1.75 ≈ 0.5596.

We can use a calculator to find, say, log 0.192 and ln 2.4 and then locate points on the graph corresponding to these values.

log 0.192 ≈ −0.7167 and the point (0.2, −0.7) can be approximately located on the graph of $y = \log x$. (See Figure 4.25.)
ln 1.6 ≈ 0.47 and the point (1.6, 0.47) can be approximately located on the graph of $y = \ln x$. (See Figure 4.25.)

You can also use a graphing utility's $\boxed{\text{TRACE}}$ feature with the graphs of $y = \log x$ and $y = \ln x$ to verify these values.

Notice that ln(−3) results in an error message in a calculator's display. Remember that the domain of $y = \log_b x$ is the set of positive real numbers, which means that ln(−3) is undefined. There is no graph for $y = \ln x$ at $x = -3$ (see Figure 4.25). Since −3 is not in the domain of the natural log function, there is no corresponding range value.

The basic properties of logarithms can be applied to common and natural logarithms.

Properties of common and natural logarithms

General Properties	Common Logarithms	Natural Logarithms
1. $\log_b 1 = 0$	**1.** $\log 1 = 0$	**1.** $\ln 1 = 0$
2. $\log_b b = 1$	**2.** $\log 10 = 1$	**2.** $\ln e = 1$
3. $\log_b b^x = x$	**3.** $\log 10^x = x$	**3.** $\ln e^x = x$

We can use the property $\ln e^x = x$ to identify points on the graph of the natural logarithmic function.

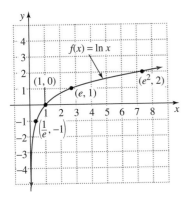

Figure 4.26

Identifying points on the graph of the natural logarithm function

x	$f(x) = \ln x$	$(x, f(x))$	Conclusion (see Figure 4.26)
$\dfrac{1}{e}$	$f\left(\dfrac{1}{e}\right) = \ln \dfrac{1}{e} = \ln e^{-1} = -1$	$\left(\dfrac{1}{e}, -1\right)$	$\left(\dfrac{1}{e}, -1\right) \approx (0.37, -1)$ lies on the graph of $f(x) = \ln x$.
e	$f(e) = \ln e = \ln e^1 = 1$	$(e, 1)$	$(e, 1) \approx (2.72, 1)$ lies on the graph of $f(x) = \ln x$.
e^2	$f(e^2) = \ln e^2 = 2$	$(e^2, 2)$	$(e^2, 2) \approx (7.4, 2)$ lies on the graph of $f(x) = \ln x$.

EXAMPLE 4 **Graphing Utilities and Natural Logarithmic Functions**

Find the domain for each function and verify the domain by graphing the function with a graphing utility.

a. $f(x) = \ln (x + 3)$ **b.** $g(x) = \ln (3 - x)$ **c.** $r(x) = \ln (x - 3)^2$

Solution

a. We know that $\ln (x + 3)$ is defined only if $x + 3 > 0$. The domain of f is $(-3, \infty)$ verified by the graph in Figure 4.27.

b. Since $\ln (3 - x)$ is defined only if $3 - x > 0$, the domain of g is $(-\infty, 3)$. This is verified by the graph in Figure 4.28.

c. We know that $\ln (x - 3)^2$ is defined only if $(x - 3)^2 > 0$. The domain of r is all real numbers except $x = 3$, represented by $(-\infty, 3) \cup (3, \infty)$. This is shown by the graph in Figure 4.29. If it is not obvious that 3 is excluded from the domain, try using a $\boxed{\text{DOT}}$ format.

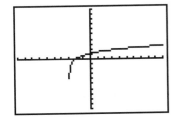

Figure 4.27

The domain of $f(x) = \ln (x + 3)$ is $(-3, \infty)$.

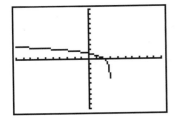

Figure 4.28

The domain of $g(x) = \ln (3 - x)$ is $(-\infty, 3)$.

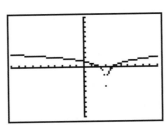

Figure 4.29

The domain of $r(x) = \ln (x - 3)^2$ is $(-\infty, 3) \cup (3, \infty)$. ∎

4 Use logarithmic functions in applications.

Modeling with Logarithmic Functions

Numerous mathematical models contain natural and common logarithmic functions, illustrated in Table 4.4.

TABLE 4.4 Mathematical Models Containing Logarithms

Area Being Described	Model	Variables in Model
Walking speed and city population	$W = 0.35 \ln P + 2.74$	P: population of a city (in thousands) W: average walking speed (in feet per second) for a resident of the city
Cooling time	$t = k \ln \left(\dfrac{T_0 - C}{T - C} \right)$ called Newton's Law of Cooling	t: time it takes for an object to cool from an initial temperature T_0 to a temperature T C: temperature of the surrounding air k: a constant
The pH of a solution (An acid solution has a pH < 7; those with pH > 7 are called basic.)	$\text{pH} = -\log[\text{H}^+]$	$[\text{H}^+]$: concentration of the hydrogen ion in moles per liter pH: pH of the solution
Human memory	$f(t) = A - B \ln(t + 1)$	$f(t)$: Average score on a test for a group of students who take the test t months after learning the material A: average test score on the original test (when $t = 0$) B: a constant
Earthquake magnitude **Magnitude on Richter scale** / **Destructive power** $R < 4.5$ / Small $4.5 \leqslant R < 5.5$ / Moderate $5.5 \leqslant R < 6.5$ / Large $6.5 \leqslant R < 7.5$ / Major $7.5 \leqslant R$ / Greatest	$R = \log \dfrac{I}{I_0}$	I: intensity of the earthquake I_0: intensity of a barely felt zero-level earthquake R: magnitude of the earthquake on the Richter scale

---

EXAMPLE 5 Walking Speed and City Population

a. Find the average walking speed of people living in the cities shown in the table.

City	Population (in thousands)
Tulsa, Oklahoma	367
San Diego, California	1111
New York, New York	7323

Jeff Wall "The Stumbling Block" Digitally manipulated cibachrome transparency, 229 × 337 cm. Courtesy Ydessa Hendeles Art Foundation, Toronto.

Figure 4.30

The graph of $W = 0.35 \ln P + 2.74$, a model for walking speed as a function of a city's population

Energy (ergs)

Roger Brown "San Andreas Fault Line" 1995. Photo courtesy Phyllis Kind Gallery, New York & Chicago.

b. Choose an appropriate viewing rectangle and graph the model on a graphing utility.

Solution

$W = 0.35 \ln P + 2.74$ This is the model from Table 4.4.

a. $W = 0.35 \ln(367) + 2.74$ Tulsa: $P = 367$ (thousand)

≈ 4.8 Average walking speed is 4.8 feet per second.

$W = 0.35 \ln(1111) + 2.74$ San Diego: $P = 1111$ (thousand)

≈ 5.2 Average walking speed is 5.2 feet per second.

$W = 0.35 \ln(7323) + 2.74$ New York: $P = 7323$ (thousand)

≈ 5.9 Average walking speed is 5.9 feet per second.

b. The graph of $y = 0.35 \ln x + 2.74$, shown in Figure 4.30, was obtained using the following range setting (suggested by our prior computations):

Xmin = 0, Xmax = 7500, Xscl = 375, Ymin = 0,

Ymax = 6, Yscl = 0.5   ∎

EXAMPLE 6   **Earthquake Intensity**

The Richter scale, used to measure magnitude of earthquakes, is named for U.S. seismologist Charles Richter (1900–1985). The scale is a common logarithmic scale: For each increase of one unit on the Richter scale, there is a tenfold increase in the energy in an earthquake, as shown in the figure on the left.

The magnitude R on the Richter scale of an earthquake of intensity I is given by

$$R = \log \frac{I}{I_0}$$

where I_0 is the intensity of a barely felt zero-level earthquake.

a. Compare the magnitudes on the Richter scale of earthquakes that are 10 times, 100 times, 1000 times, and 10,000 times as intense as a zero-level earthquake.

b. Northern California's 1989 earthquake was $10^{7.1}$ times as intense as a zero-level earthquake. What was its magnitude on the Richter scale?

Solution

a. $R = \log \frac{I}{I_0}$ This is the given model.

$= \log \frac{10 I_0}{I_0}$ $I = 10 I_0$ for an earthquake 10 times as intense as a zero-level quake. I_0 is the intensity of the weakest earthquake that can be recorded on a seismograph.

ENRICHMENT ESSAY

Earthquakes and the Richter scale

Earthquakes release an enormous amount of energy. Northern California's 1989 earthquake, measuring 7.1 on the Richter scale, released as much energy as 30 million tons of high explosives, nearly ten times the explosive power of all bombs used in World War II (including the two atomic bombs). Magnitude and energy released by an earthquake are not the same thing. The energy released by an earthquake's motion is approximately 30 times greater for each increase of 1 on the Richter scale.

San Francisco's Marina District, built on landfill, was seriously damaged in California's 1989 earthquake.
Gordon L. Kallio/The Image Bank

Magnitude	Energy Released (million of ergs)	Earthquake Magnitude
9	20,000,000,000,000,000,000	8.9 Japan 1933
8	600,000,000,000,000,000	7.9 San Francisco 1906
7	20,000,000,000,000,000	6.9 Armenia 1988
6	600,000,000,000,000	
5	20,000,000,000,000	
4	600,000,000,000	
3	20,000,000,000	3.0 Smallest earth-
2	600,000,000	quakes commonly
1	20,000,000	felt
0	600,000	

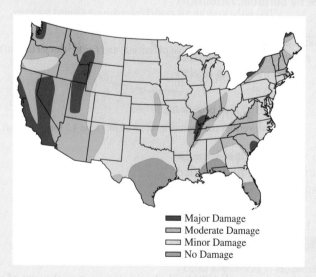

■ Major Damage
■ Moderate Damage
□ Minor Damage
▨ No Damage

This map shows potential earthquake damage for the 48 contiguous states.

PROBLEM SET 4.2

Practice Problems

In Problems 1–32, evaluate the expression without the use of a calculator.

1. $\log_3 9$

2. $\log_9 81$

3. $\log_2 64$

4. $\log_3 27$

5. $\log_7 \sqrt{7}$

6. $\log_6 \sqrt{6}$

7. $\log_2 \frac{1}{32}$

8. $\log_3 \frac{1}{81}$

9. $\log_{36} 6$

10. $\log_{81} 9$

11. $\log_{12} 12$

12. $\log_7 7$

13. $\log_4 1$

14. $\log_5 1$

15. $\log_{16} 8$

16. $\log_{125} 5$

17. $\log 10{,}000$

18. $\log 100{,}000$

19. $\log 0.01$

20. $\log 0.001$

21. $\ln e^7$

22. $\ln e^{13}$

23. $\ln \sqrt[3]{e}$

24. $\ln \sqrt[5]{e}$

25. $\log_5 5^7$

26. $\log_4 4^6$

27. $\log 10^{19}$

28. $\log 10^{34}$

29. $\log_b b^7$

30. $\log_b \frac{1}{b^2}$

31. $\log_3 (\log_7 7)$

32. $\log_5 (\log_2 32)$

33. Graph $y = 3^x$ [or $f(x) = 3^x$] and $y = \log_3 x$ [or $f^{-1}(x) = \log_3 x$] on the same set of axes.

34. Graph $y = \left(\frac{1}{2}\right)^x$ [or $f(x) = \left(\frac{1}{2}\right)^x$] and $y = \log_{\frac{1}{2}} x$ [or $f^{-1}(x) = \log_{\frac{1}{2}} x$] on the same set of axes.

In Problems 35–44, sketch the graph of each function by using transformations of the graph of $f(x) = \log_2 x$. State each function's domain and range.

35. $g(x) = \log_2 x + 3$

36. $g(x) = \log_2 x - 1$

37. $g(x) = \log_2 (x + 3)$

38. $g(x) = \log_2 (x - 1)$

39. $g(x) = \log_2 (x - 1) + 3$

40. $g(x) = \log_2 (x - 2) - 1$

41. $h(x) = -\log_2 (x + 1)$

42. $h(x) = -\log_2 (x + 2)$

43. $r(x) = -\frac{1}{2} \log_2 (-x)$

44. $r(x) = -2 \log_2 (-x)$

In Problems 45–48, use the graph of $y = \ln x$ to match the function with the appropriate graph.

45. $f(x) = 2 - \ln x$

46. $f(x) = \frac{1}{2} \ln x$

47. $f(x) = 4 \ln x$

48. $f(x) = \ln (x - 2)$

a.

b.

c.

d.

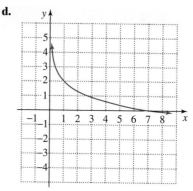

In Problems 49–52, match the function with the appropriate graph.

49. $f(x) = \log_2 x + 1$ **50.** $f(x) = \log_2(x + 1)$ **51.** $f(x) = \log_2 x - 2$ **52.** $f(x) = \log_2(x - 2)$

a.

b.

c.

d.

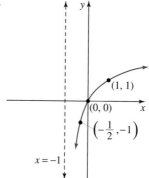

In Problems 53–58, use the property ln $e^x = x$ to simplify each expression.

53. $\ln\left(\frac{1}{e}\right)$ **54.** $\ln e$ **55.** $\ln \sqrt{e}$

56. $\sqrt{\ln e}$ **57.** $\ln e^{-3}$ **58.** $(\ln e)^{-3}$

In Problems 59–66, find the domain, vertical asymptote, and x-intercept for each logarithmic function. Verify your results by graphing each function with a graphing utility.

59. $f(x) = \ln(x + 2)$ **60.** $f(x) = \ln(x - 1)$ **61.** $f(x) = \ln(2 - x)$ **62.** $f(x) = \ln(1 - x)$
63. $f(x) = \ln x^2$ **64.** $f(x) = \ln(x + 1)^2$ **65.** $f(x) = -\log(x - 2)$ **66.** $f(x) = -\log(x + 3)$

Application Problems

Use the appropriate model from Table 4.4 on page 458 to answer Problems 67–74. In Problems 69–70, assume cooling time is measured in hours.

67. How much faster do residents of Chicago (population: 2,784,000) walk than those of Madison, Wisconsin (population: 191,000)?

68. What is the difference in walking speed for residents of Buffalo (population: 328,000) and Philadelphia (population: 1,586,000)?

69. A bottle of wine at a room temperature of 72° Fahrenheit is placed into a refrigerator. If the temperature of the refrigerator is 40° Fahrenheit and $k = 0.4$, how long will it take the wine to cool to 50° Fahrenheit?

70. The police discover the body of a murder victim at 1:00 P.M. The victim's body temperature is 81.2° Fahrenheit. If the victim is in a room with a temperature of 75° Fahrenheit and $k = 10$, at what time was the murder committed? (Assume temperature at the time of death to be 98.6°.)

71. Find the pH of the following substances, classifying each as acid or basic. (See the figure in the next column.)

   a. Milk: $[H^+] = 3.97 \times 10^{-7}$ mole per liter

   b. Orange juice: $[H^+] = 2.8 \times 10^{-4}$ mole per liter

72. Find the pH of the following substances, classifying each as acid or basic. (See the figure in the next column.)

   a. Beer: $[H^+] = 3.16 \times 10^{-5}$ mole per liter

   b. Vinegar: $[H^+] = 9.32 \times 10^{-4}$ mole per liter

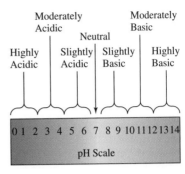

73. Find the Richter scale ratings of earthquakes having the following intensities:

   a. $100,000I_0$ **b.** $1,000,000I_0$

   c. $10,000,000I_0$ **d.** $100,000,000I_0$

74. Compute the magnitude on the Richter scale for the following earthquakes:

   a. Iran, 1978: $10^{7.7}$ times as intense as a zero-level earthquake

   b. San Francisco, 1906: $10^{8.25}$ times as intense as a zero-level earthquake

   c. An earthquake that is 10^k times as intense as a zero-level earthquake

Use the model for sound intensity

$$D = 10 \log \frac{I}{I_0}$$

to answer Problems 75–76.

75. What is the decibel level of a normal conversation, 3.2×10^{-6} watt per meter^2? ($I_0 = 10^{-12}$)

76. People should not be exposed to sound intensities of 3.16×10^{-4} watt per meter^2 for extended periods without ear protection. What decibel level does this represent? ($I_0 = 10^{-12}$)

77. Students in a psychology class took a final examination. As part of an experiment to see how much of the course content they remembered over time, they took equivalent forms of the exam in monthly intervals thereafter. The average score for the group, $f(t)$, after t months was given by the human memory model

$$f(t) = 88 - 15 \ln (t + 1), \qquad 0 \leqslant t \leqslant 12$$

   a. What was the average score on the original exam?

   b. What was the average score after 2 months? 4 months? 6 months? 8 months? 10 months? one year?

   c. Sketch the graph of f (either by hand or with a graphing utility). Describe what the graph indicates in terms of the material retained by the students.

78. Recall that a prime number is a natural number greater than 1 divisible only by itself and 1. The number of prime numbers less than or equal to a given number x can be approximated by the expressions

$$\frac{x}{\ln x} \quad \text{and} \quad \frac{x}{\ln x - 1.08366}$$

when x is large. Fill in the last two columns of the table on page 464, rounding results to the nearest whole number. Then answer the following questions:

   Which of the two expressions provides a better approximation for the numbers in the second column?

What happens to each expression, compared with the numbers in the second column, as x gets larger?

x	Number of Prime Numbers That Are Less Than x	$\dfrac{x}{\ln x}$	$\dfrac{x}{\ln x - 1.083\,66}$
100	25		
10,000	1229		
10^6	78,498		
10^8	5,761,455		
10^9	50,847,534		
10^{10}	455,052,512		

79. The number $n!$ (n factorial) is defined by

$$n! = n(n-1)(n-2) \cdot \cdots \cdot 3 \cdot 2 \cdot 1$$

where n is a positive integer. For example,

$$6! = 6 \cdot 5 \cdot 4 \cdot 3 \cdot 2 \cdot 1 = 720.$$

Very large factorials can be approximated by $n! \approx \left(\frac{n}{e}\right)^n \sqrt{2\pi n}$, called Stirling's formula. Use the formula to approximate 12! and compare it to the actual value.

True–False Critical Thinking Problems

80. Which one of the following is true?

  a. If (a, b) satisfies $y = 2^x$, then (a, b) satisfies $y = \log_2 x$.

  b. $\log(-100) = -2$.

  c. The domain of $f(x) = \log_2 x$ is $(-\infty, \infty)$.

  d. $\log_b x$ is the exponent to which b must be raised to obtain x.

81. Which one of the following is true?

  a. $\log_{36} 6 = 2$

  b. There is no relationship between the graphs of $f(x) = 3^x$ and $g(x) = \log_3 x$.

  c. $\dfrac{\log_2 8}{\log_2 4} = \dfrac{8}{4}$

  d. $\log_{1/2} 32 = -5$

82. Which one of the following is true?

  a. $\log_b 0 = 0$, for $b > 0$ and $b \neq 1$.

  b. If $\log_b 9 = 2$, then $b = 3$ or $b = -3$.

  c. $\log_5 5^7 = 7$

  d. The inverse of $y = 4^x$ is $y = x^4$.

Technology Problems

In Problems 83–87, graph f and g in the same viewing rectangle. Then describe the transformations needed on the graph of f to obtain the graph of g.

83. $f(x) = \ln x \qquad g(x) = \ln(x + 3)$
85. $f(x) = \ln x \qquad g(x) = \ln(-x) - 2$
87. $f(x) = \ln x \qquad g(x) = \ln(x - 2) + 1$

84. $f(x) = \ln x \qquad g(x) = \ln x + 3$
86. $f(x) = \ln x \qquad g(x) = -\ln(x + 1)$

In Problems 88–93, use a graphing utility to graph each function. Use the graph to determine the function's domain and range, as well as intervals in which the function is increasing and decreasing. Where applicable, approximate any relative maximum or minimum values for the function.

88. $f(x) = x \ln x$

89. $f(x) = \dfrac{\ln x}{x}$

90. $f(x) = \log(x^2 + 1)$

91. $f(x) = \log(\log x)$

92. $f(x) = \sqrt{\ln x}$

93. $f(x) = \ln|x|$

94. Students in a mathematics class took a final examination. As part of an experiment to see how much of the course content they remembered over time, they took equivalent forms of the exam in monthly intervals thereafter. The average score for the group, $f(t)$, after t months was given by the human memory model

$$f(t) = 75 - 10 \log(t + 1), \qquad 0 \leq t \leq 12.$$

Use a graphing utility to graph the model. Then determine how many months will elapse before the average score falls below 65.

95. Graph f and g in the same viewing rectangle.

  a. $f(x) = \ln(3x) \qquad g(x) = \ln 3 + \ln x$

  b. $f(x) = \log(5x^2) \qquad g(x) = \log 5 + \log x^2$

c. $f(x) = \ln(2x^3)$ $g(x) = \ln 2 + \ln x^3$

d. Describe what you observe in parts (a)–(c). Generalize this observation by writing an equivalent expression for $\log_b(MN)$, where $M > 0$ and $N > 0$.

e. Complete this statement: The log of a product is equal to _____.

96. Graph f and g in the same viewing rectangle.

a. $f(x) = \ln \dfrac{x}{2}$ $g(x) = \ln x - \ln 2$

b. $f(x) = \log \dfrac{x}{5}$ $g(x) = \log x - \log 5$

c. $f(x) = \ln \dfrac{x^2}{3}$ $g(x) = \ln x^2 - \ln 3$

d. Describe what you observe in parts (a)–(c). Generalize this observation by writing an equivalent expression for $\log_b\left(\dfrac{M}{N}\right)$, where $M > 0$ and $N > 0$.

e. Complete this statement: The log of a quotient is equal to _____.

97. Graph f and g in the same viewing rectangle.

a. $f(x) = \ln x^2$ $g(x) = 2 \ln x$

b. $f(x) = \log x^3$ $g(x) = 3 \log x$

c. $f(x) = \ln \sqrt{x} = \ln x^{1/2}$ $g(x) = \frac{1}{2} \ln x$

d. Describe what you observe in parts (a)–(c). Generalize this observation by writing an equivalent expression for $\log_b M^p$, where $M > 0$.

e. Complete this statement: The log of a number with an exponent is equal to _____.

In Problems 98–106, graph the functions on each side of the = sign in the same viewing rectangle to determine whether each statement is true or false.

98. $\ln(x + 3) = \ln x + \ln 3$ (Graph $y = \ln(x + 3)$ and $y = \ln x + \ln 3$.)

99. $\log \dfrac{x}{2} = \dfrac{\log x}{\log 2}$

100. $\log \dfrac{x}{2} = \log x - \log 2$

101. $\ln x^3 = (\ln x)^3$

102. $x + \ln x^{-1} = x - \ln x$

103. $x^x = e^{x \ln x}$

104. $\ln e^x = x$

105. $(\log x)(\log 2) = \log 2x$

106. $\log x + \log 2 = \log 2x$

107. Graph each of the following pairs of functions in the same viewing rectangle, $-1 \leq x \leq 3$; $-2 \leq y \leq 2$.

a. $y = \ln(1 + x)$ and $y = x - \dfrac{x^2}{2}$

b. $y = \ln(1 + x)$ and $y = x - \dfrac{x^2}{2} + \dfrac{x^3}{3}$

c. $y = \ln(1 + x)$ and $y = x - \dfrac{x^2}{2} + \dfrac{x^3}{3} - \dfrac{x^4}{4}$

d. Describe the emerging pattern.

108. Graph each of the following functions in the same viewing rectangle and then place the functions in order from the one that increases most slowly to the one that increases most rapidly.

$$y = x, y = \sqrt{x}, y = e^x, y = \ln x, y = x^x, y = x^2$$

Writing in Mathematics

109. Suppose that we use the model $W = 0.35 \ln P + 2.74$ relating population (P) of a city and average walking speed (W) of the city's residents. If we know the average walking speed is 2.4 feet per second, what difficulty will we encounter by attempting to approximate the city's population? What skill is needed to overcome this difficulty?

110. Select a mathematical model from Table 4.4 and write a verbal problem that can be solved using the formula. Solve the problem.

111. Without using a calculator, how can you determine the greater number: $\log_4 60$ or $\log_3 40$?

Critical Thinking Problems

112. Without using a calculator, find the exact value of

$$\dfrac{\log_3 81 - \log_\pi 1}{\log_{2\sqrt{2}} 8 - \log 0.001}.$$

113. Without using a calculator, find the exact value of

$$\log \sqrt[3]{10\sqrt{1000}} - \log \dfrac{1}{100}\sqrt{\dfrac{1}{10}\sqrt[3]{100}}.$$

114. Solve for x: $\log_4[\log_3(\log_2 x)] = 0$.

115. Write the point-slope equation of the line passing through $(3 \ln e + \ln(\frac{1}{e}), \ln(\ln e))$, and $(3 \ln(e \ln e), \ln e^2)$.

116. If $f(x) = \ln(\ln x)$, find $f^{-1}(x)$.

SECTION 4.3 **Properties of Logarithmic Functions**

Solutions Manual   Tutorial   Video 8

Objectives

1 Expand logarithmic expressions.
2 Condense logarithmic expressions.
3 Use the inverse properties of logarithms.
4 Use the change-of-base property.

In this section, we consider six important properties of logarithms. These properties can be used to answer questions about variables that appear in logarithmic models.

Three Basic Logarithmic Properties

iscover for yourself

You can discover three basic logarithmic properties on your own with your graphing utility. To do so work Problems 95–97 in Problem Set 4.2 before continuing.

There are three properties of exponents that have corresponding logarithmic properties:

1. $b^M \cdot b^N = b^{M+N}$
2. $\dfrac{b^M}{b^N} = b^{M-N}$
3. $(b^M)^p = b^{Mp}$

These identities, coupled with an awareness that a logarithm is an exponent, suggest the following properties.

Properties of logarithms

Let b, M, and N be positive real numbers with $b \neq 1$, and let p be any real number.

Property	The Property in Words	Example
The Product Rule $\log_b(MN) = \log_b M + \log_b N$	The log of a product is the sum of the logs.	$\ln(4x) = \ln 4 + \ln x$
The Quotient Rule $\log_b\left(\dfrac{M}{N}\right) = \log_b M - \log_b N$	The log of a quotient is the difference of the logs.	$\log \dfrac{x}{2} = \log x - \log 2$
The Power Rule $\log_b M^p = p \log_b M$	The log of a number raised to the power p is the product of p and the log of that number.	$\ln \sqrt{x} = \ln x^{1/2} = \dfrac{1}{2}\ln x$

sing technology

The relationships in the examples given in the preceding box can be confirmed using a graphing utility. The graphs on each side of the three equalities are the same, verifying these special cases of the product, quotient, and power rules.

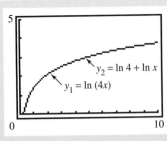

$\ln(4x) = \ln 4 + \ln x$

$\log \dfrac{x}{2} = \log x - \log 2$

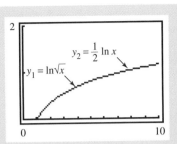

$\ln x^{1/2} = \frac{1}{2} \ln x$

Proving the Logarithmic Properties

All three of the properties of logarithms can be proved in the same way, Let's look at the proof for the product rule

$$\log_b(MN) = \log_b M + \log_b N.$$

We begin by letting $\log_b M = R$ and $\log_b N = S$.

Now we write each logarithm in exponential form.

$$\log_b M = R \quad \text{means} \quad b^R = M$$

$$\log_b N = S \quad \text{means} \quad b^S = N$$

By substituting and using a property of exponents, we see that

$$MN = b^R b^S = b^{R+S}.$$

Now we change $MN = b^{R+S}$ to logarithmic form.

$$MN = b^{R+S} \quad \text{means} \quad \log_b(MN) = R + S.$$

Finally, substituting $\log_b M$ for R and $\log_b N$ for S gives us

$$\log_b(MN) = \log_b M + \log_b N$$

the property that we wanted to prove.

The proofs of the quotient and power rules are nearly identical and are left for the problem set.

Using the Properties Together to Expand Logarithmic Expressions

When we expand a logarithmic expression, it is possible to change the domain of a function. For example, the power rule tells us that

$$\log_b x^2 = 2 \log_b x.$$

If $f(x) = \log_b x^2$, then the domain of f is the set of all nonzero real numbers. However, if $g(x) = 2 \log_b x$, the domain is the set of positive real numbers. Consequently, we should write

$$\log_b x^2 = 2 \log_b x, \quad \text{if } x > 0.$$

In short, when expanding or condensing a logarithmic expression, you might want to observe whether the rewriting has changed the domain of the expression.

Example 1 involves expanding logarithmic expressions. In summary, most of our work will be based on the following three properties.

The graphs of $y = \ln x^2$ and $y = 2 \ln x$ have different domains.

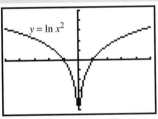

Domain: $(-\infty, 0) \cup (0, \infty)$

Domain: $(0, \infty)$

Notice that the graphs are only the same if $x > 0$. Thus, we should write

$$\ln x^2 = 2 \ln x \quad \text{for} \quad x > 0.$$

Expand logarithmic
expressions.

Properties for expanding logarithmic expressions

1. $\log_b(MN) = \log_b M + \log_b N$ Product rule

2. $\log_b\left(\dfrac{M}{N}\right) = \log_b M - \log_b N$ Quotient rule

3. $\log_b M^p = p \log_b M$ Power rule

In all cases, $M > 0$ and $N > 0$.

EXAMPLE I   **Expanding Logarithmic Expressions**

Use logarithmic properties to expand each expression as much as possible.
Expanded forms should involve logarithms of x, y, and z.

a. $\log_b x^2 \sqrt{y}$ **b.** $\log_6\left(\dfrac{\sqrt[3]{x}}{36y^4}\right)$ **c.** $\log \sqrt[5]{\dfrac{1000x}{y^3 z^2}}$

Solution

We will have to use two or more of the properties of logarithms in each part of
this example.

a. $\log_b x^2 \sqrt{y} = \log_b x^2 y^{1/2}$ Use exponential notation.

$\qquad\qquad = \log_b x^2 + \log_b y^{1/2}$ Use the product rule.

$\qquad\qquad = 2 \log_b x + \dfrac{1}{2} \log_b y$ Use the power rule.

b. $\log_6\left(\dfrac{\sqrt[3]{x}}{36y^4}\right) = \log_6 \dfrac{x^{1/3}}{36y^4}$ Use exponential notation.

$\qquad\qquad = \log_6 x^{1/3} - \log_6 36y^4$ Use the quotient rule.

$\qquad\qquad = \log_6 x^{1/3} - (\log_6 36 + \log_6 y^4)$ Use the product rule on $\log_6 36y^4$.

$\qquad\qquad = \dfrac{1}{3} \log_6 x - (\log_6 36 + 4 \log_6 y)$ Use the power rule.

$\qquad\qquad = \dfrac{1}{3} \log_6 x - \log_6 36 - 4 \log_6 y$ Apply the distributive property.

$\qquad\qquad = \dfrac{1}{3} \log_6 x - 2 - 4 \log_6 y$ $\log_6 36 = 2$ because 2 is the power to which we must raise 6 to get 36. $(6^2 = 36)$

c. $\log \sqrt[5]{\dfrac{1000x}{y^3 z^2}} = \log\left(\dfrac{1000x}{y^3 z^2}\right)^{\frac{1}{5}}$ Use exponential notation.

$\qquad\qquad = \dfrac{1}{5} \log\left(\dfrac{1000x}{y^3 z^2}\right)$ Use the power rule.

$\qquad\qquad = \dfrac{1}{5} (\log 1000x - \log y^3 z^2)$ Use the quotient rule.

$\qquad\qquad = \dfrac{1}{5} [\log 1000 + \log x - (\log y^3 + \log z^2)]$ Use the product rule.

$\qquad\qquad = \dfrac{1}{5} (\log 1000 + \log x - \log y^3 - \log z^2)$ Apply the distributive property.

$\qquad\qquad = \dfrac{1}{5} (\log 1000 + \log x - 3\log y - 2\log z)$ Use the power rule.

$$= \frac{1}{5}(3 + \log x - 3 \log y - 2 \log z)$$

log 1000 means $\log_{10} 1000$, which is 3, because $10^3 = 1000$.

∎

2 Condense logarithmic expressions.

Using the Properties Together to Condense Logarithmic Expressions

In Example 1, we wrote each expression as the sum and the difference of simpler logarithmic expressions. We can also use the logarithmic properties to reverse the direction of this procedure, writing the sum and/or difference of logarithms as a single logarithm. Most of our work will use the following three properties.

Properties for condensing logarithmic expressions

1. $\log_b M + \log_b N = \log_b(MN)$ Product rule

2. $\log_b M - \log_b N = \log_b\left(\frac{M}{N}\right)$ Quotient rule

3. $p \log_b M = \log_b M^p$ Power rule

In all cases, $M > 0$ and $N > 0$.

EXAMPLE 2   Condensing Logarithmic Expressions

Write as a single logarithm:

a. $\log_4 2 + \log_4 32$ **b.** $\ln 5 - 5 \ln x$ **c.** $4 \log_b x - 2 \log_b 6 + \frac{1}{2} \log_b y$

Solution

a. $\log_4 2 + \log_4 32 = \log_4(2 \cdot 32)$ Use the product rule.

$= \log_4 64$ We now have a single logarithm. However, we can simplify.

$= 3$ $\log_4 64 = 3$ because $4^3 = 64$.

Study tip

Coefficients of logarithms must be 1 before you can condense them using the product and quotient rules. Thus, we must write 5 ln x as ln x^5.

b. $\ln 5 - 5 \ln x = \ln 5 - \ln x^5$ Use the power rule.

$= \ln \frac{5}{x^5}$ Use the quotient rule.

c. $4 \log_b x - 2 \log_b 6 + \frac{1}{2} \log_b y$

$= \log_b x^4 - \log_b 6^2 + \log_b y^{1/2}$ Use the power rule so that log coefficients are all 1.

$= (\log_b x^4 - \log_b 36) + \log_b y^{1/2}$ This optional step emphasizes the order of operations.

$= \log_b \frac{x^4}{36} + \log_b y^{1/2}$ Use the quotient rule.

$= \log_b \frac{x^4}{36} \cdot y^{1/2}$ or $\log_b \frac{x^4 \sqrt{y}}{36}$ Use the product rule.   ∎

Study tip

Shown on the next page are the graphs of $y_1 = \ln(x + 3)$ and $y_2 = \ln x + \ln 3$. Our graphing utility indicates that the graphs are *not the same*. The graph of $y_1 = \ln(x + 3)$ is

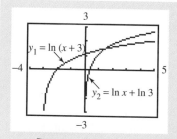

actually the graph of the natural log function shifted 3 units to the left. The graph of $y_2 = \ln x + \ln 3$ is the graph of the natural log function shifted upward by ln 3, which is an approximate vertical shift of 1.1 units.

We see, then, that $\ln(x + 3) \neq \ln x + \ln 3$. In general,

$$\log_b(M + N) \neq \log_b M + \log_b N.$$

Try to avoid each of the following incorrect procedures.

INCORRECT

$$\log_b(M + N) = \log_b M + \log_b N \qquad \log_b(M - N) = \log_b M - \log_b N \qquad \log_b(M \cdot N) = (\log_b M)(\log_b N)$$

$$\log_b \frac{M}{N} = \frac{\log_b M}{\log_b N} \qquad \frac{\log_b M}{\log_b N} = \log_b M - \log_b N$$

Use your graphing utility, replacing $\log_b$ by ln, M by x, and N by 3 to show that all five of these equations are not true in general.

3 Use the inverse properties of logarithms.

"True–False" 1992. Rimma Gerlovina and Valeriy Gerlovina

The Inverse Properties

The inverse properties are a result of the fact that the exponential and logarithmic functions are inverses.

Discover for yourself

We previously learned that $f(f^{-1}(x)) = x$ and $f^{-1}(f(x)) = x$. Apply these relationships to $f(x) = b^x$ and $f^{-1}(x) = \log_b x$ and write two inverse properties involving logarithms.

In the Discover for yourself, were you able to write the following properties?

Inverse properties of logarithms

For $b > 0, b \neq 1$:

(a) $\log_b b^x = x$ for all real numbers (b) $b^{\log_b x} = x$ for $x > 0$

Notice the domain restriction in part (b). This is necessary since the domain of $\log_b x$ is $(0, \infty)$.

We have already introduced the second of these properties, stating that $\log_b b^x = x$ because x is the exponent to which b must be raised to obtain b^x. To prove the first part of this property, let

$$y = \log_b x.$$

$$b^y = x \qquad \text{Rewrite the logarithmic expression in its equivalent exponential form.}$$

$$b^{\log_b x} = x \qquad \text{Substitute } \log_b x \text{ for } y \text{ (from the first equation) into the equation in the previous step. This is precisely what we wanted to prove.}$$

The inverse properties for logarithms can be applied to common and natural logarithms, as shown in Table 4.6.

TABLE 4.6 Inverse Properties Applied to Common and Natural Logarithms		
Inverse Property	**Base 10**	**Base e**
$b^{\log_b x} = x$	$10^{\log x} = x$	$e^{\ln x} = x$
$\log_b b^x = x$	$\log 10^x = x$	$\ln e^x = x$

EXAMPLE 3 **Expanding Logarithmic Expressions**

Use the properties of logarithms to expand each expression, simplifying terms where possible.

a. $\log(A \cdot 10^{7t})$ **b.** $\ln\left(\dfrac{B}{e^{7a}}\right)$ $(A > 0, B > 0)$

Solution

a. $\log(A \cdot 10^{7t}) = \log A + \log 10^{7t}$ $\log_b(MN) = \log_b M + \log_b N$

$\qquad\qquad\qquad\quad = \log A + 7t$ $\log 10^x = x$

b. $\quad \ln\left(\dfrac{B}{e^{7a}}\right) = \ln B - \ln e^{7a}$ $\log_b \dfrac{M}{N} = \log_b M - \log_b N$

$\qquad\qquad\qquad = \ln B - 7a$ $\ln e^x = x$ ∎

EXAMPLE 4 **Condensing Logarithmic Expressions**

Use the properties of logarithms to write each expression as a single term that does not contain a logarithm.

a. $10^{\log 4x + \log 3x}$ **b.** $e^{\ln 8x^5 - \ln 2x^2}$

Solution

a. $10^{\log 4x + \log 3x} = 10^{\log[(4x)(3x)]}$ Condense the log expression in the exponent using $\log_b M + \log_b N = \log_b(MN)$.

$\qquad\qquad\qquad = 10^{\log 12x^2}$ Multiply.

$\qquad\qquad\qquad = 12x^2$ $10^{\log x} = x$

b. $e^{\ln 8x^5 - \ln 2x^2} = e^{\ln(8x^5/2x^2)}$ Condense the log expression in exponent using $\log_b M - \log_b N = \log_b \dfrac{M}{N}$.

$\qquad\qquad\qquad = e^{\ln 4x^3}$ Divide.

$\qquad\qquad\qquad = 4x^3$ $e^{\ln x} = x$ ∎

In the next section we will use the inverse properties to solve exponential equations, gaining further insight into the mathematical models that we have already discussed.

4 Use the change-of-base property.

The Change-of-Base Property

We have seen that calculators give the values of both common logarithms (base 10) and natural logarithms (base e). To find a logarithm with any other base, we can use the following change-of-base property.

The change-of-base property

For any logarithmic bases a and b, and any positive number M,

$$\log_b M = \frac{\log_a M}{\log_a b}.$$

Base a is a new base that we introduce. The logarithm on the left side has a base of b, allowing us to change from base b to any other base a, as long as the newly introduced base is a positive number not equal to 1.

To prove the change-of-base property, we let x equal the logarithm on the left side:

$$\log_b M = x.$$

Now we rewrite this logarithm in exponential form.

$$\log_b M = x \quad \text{means} \quad b^x = M.$$

Since b^x and M are equal, the logarithms with base a for each of these expressions must be equal. This means that

$$\log_a b^x = \log_a M$$

$$x \log_a b = \log_a M \qquad \text{Apply the power rule for logarithms on the left side.}$$

$$x = \frac{\log_a M}{\log_a b} \qquad \text{Solve for } x \text{ dividing both sides by } \log_a b.$$

In our first step we let x equal $\log_b M$. Replacing x on the left side by $\log_b M$ gives us

$$\log_b M = \frac{\log_a M}{\log_a b}$$

which is the change-of-base property.

Because calculators contain keys for common and natural logarithms, we will frequently introduce base 10 or base e.

EXAMPLE 5 **Changing Base to Common Logarithms**

Use common logarithms to evaluate: $\log_5 140$

Discover for yourself

Let $\log_5 140 = y$. Since this means that $5^y = 140$, what is a reasonable estimate for y, to the nearest whole number? Now compare this estimate to the value given in the solution.

Study tip

Since the change-of-base property usually involves introducing base 10 or base e, here's what the property looks like in each of these situations.

Introducing Common Logarithms (Base 10)

$$\log_b M = \frac{\log M}{\log b}$$

Introducing Natural Logarithms (Base e)

$$\log_b M = \frac{\ln M}{\ln b}$$

Solution

$$\log_5 140 = \frac{\log_{10} 140}{\log_{10} 5} \qquad \text{Use } \log_b M = \frac{\log_a M}{\log_a b}. \text{ The newly introduced base is 10.}$$

$$= \frac{\log 140}{\log 5} \qquad \text{We omit the 10 with common logs, writing } \log_{10} \text{ as log.}$$

$$\approx 3.07 \qquad \text{Use a calculator: } \boxed{\log} \; 140 \; \boxed{\div} \; \boxed{\log} \; 5 \; \boxed{\text{ENTER}}$$

This means that $\log_7 50 \approx 3.07$. ∎

EXAMPLE 6 **Changing Base to Natural Logarithms**

Use natural logarithms to evaluate: $\log_5 140$

Solution

$$\log_5 140 = \frac{\log_e 140}{\log_e 5}$$

Use $\log_b M = \dfrac{\log_a M}{\log_a b}$. The newly introduced base is e.

$$= \frac{\ln 140}{\ln 5}$$

We write $\log_e$ as ln to designate natural logarithms.

$$\approx 3.07$$

Use a calculator: $\boxed{\ln}$ 140 $\boxed{\div}$ $\boxed{\ln}$ 5 $\boxed{\text{ENTER}}$

We have again shown that $\log_5 140 \approx 3.07$. ■

Figure 4.31

Partial graphs of natural and

We can use the change-of-base property to determine a relationship between $y = \ln x$ and $y = \log x$, whose graphs are shown partially in Figure 4.31. We begin with

$$\log_{10} x = \frac{\log_e x}{\log_e 10}$$

We've introduced base e.

Using the agreed-upon notation for common and natural logarithms, we can write

$$\log x = \frac{\ln x}{\ln 10}.$$

Multiplying both sides by ln 10 results in

$$(\log x)(\ln 10) = \ln x.$$

Because ln 10 is approximately 2.3026, this equation gives us a relationship between the natural and common logarithmic functions:

$$\ln x \approx (\log x)(2.3026).$$

In terms of the graphs in Figure 4.31, the natural logarithm of any (positive) number is approximately equal to the common logarithm of that number multiplied by 2.3026. Thus, the graph of $y = \ln x$ stretches the graph of $y = \log x$ by a factor of approximately 2.3.

The change-of-base property is useful when a graphing utility is used to graph logarithmic functions with bases other than 10 or e.

EXAMPLE 7 **Using a Graphing Utility to Graph Logarithmic Functions**

Graph $y = \log_2 x$ and $y = \log_{20} x$ in the same viewing rectangle.

Solution

Since $\log_2 x = \dfrac{\ln x}{\ln 2}$ and $\log_{20} x = \dfrac{\ln x}{\ln 20}$, the functions are entered as

$$Y_1 \boxed{=} \ln X / \ln 2 \text{ and } Y_2 \boxed{=} \ln X / \ln 20$$

using

$$\text{Xmin} = 0, \text{Xmax} = 10, \text{Xscl} = 1, \text{Ymin} = -3, \text{Ymax} = 3, \text{and Yscl} = 1.$$

The graphs are shown in Figure 4.32. ■

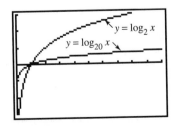

Figure 4.32

Using the change-of-base property to graph logarithmic functions

ENRICHMENT ESSAY

The Curious Number e

- The number e was named by the Swiss mathematician Leonhard Euler (1707–1783), who proved that it is the limit as N tends to infinity of $\left(1 + \dfrac{1}{N}\right)^{N}$.

- e features in Euler's remarkable relationship $e^{i\pi} = -1$.

- The first few decimal places of e are fairly easy to remember: $e = 2.7\ 1828\ 1828\ 45\ 90\ 45\ \ldots$.

- The best approximation of e using numbers less than 1000 is also easy to remember: $e \approx \dfrac{878}{323} \approx 2.71826\ldots$.

- Newton showed that $e^{x} = 1 + x + \dfrac{x^2}{2!} + \dfrac{x^3}{3!} + \dfrac{x^4}{4!} + \cdots$, from which we obtain $e = 1 + 1 + \dfrac{1}{2!} + \dfrac{1}{3!} + \dfrac{1}{4!}\cdots$, an infinite sum suitable for calculation because its terms decrease so rapidly. (*Note:* $n!$ (n factorial) is the product of all the consecutive integers from n down to 1: $n! = n(n-1)(n-2)(n-3) \cdot \cdots \cdot 3 \cdot 2 \cdot 1$.)

- The area of the region bounded by $y = \dfrac{1}{x}$, the x-axis, $x = 1$ and $x = t$ (shown in orange in Figure 4.33) is a function of t, designated by $A(t)$. Grégoire de Saint-Vincent, a Belgian Jesuit (1584–1667), spent his entire professional life attempting to find a formula for $A(t)$. With his student, he showed that $A(t) = \ln t$, becoming one of the first mathematicians to make use of the logarithmic function for something other than a computational device.

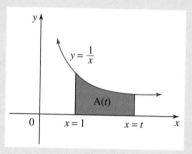

Figure 4.33

EXAMPLE 8 Logarithmic Properties and Transformations

Describe the relationship between the graphs of $y = \log_3 x$ and $y = \log_3 \dfrac{1}{(x+1)^3}$. Then use a graphing utility to verify your description.

Solution

We begin by using the power rule to rewrite the second equation.

$$y = \log_3 \frac{1}{(x+1)^3}$$

$$= \log_3(x+1)^{-3} \qquad \frac{1}{b^3} = b^{-3}$$

$$= -3\log_3(x+1) \qquad \log_b M^p = p\log_b M$$

We can obtain the graph of $y = -3\log_3(x+1)$ from the graph of $y = \log_3 x$ by translating one unit to the left ($y = \log_3(x+1)$), stretching by multiplying by a factor of 3 ($y = 3\log_3(x+1)$), and reflecting in the x-axis ($y = -3\log_3(x+1)$). Using a $[-2, 5]$ by $[-4, 4]$ range setting and entering

$$y_1 = \log_3 x \quad \text{as} \quad Y_1 = \ln X / \ln 3$$

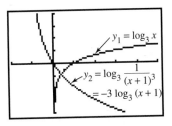

Figure 4.34

The graph of y_2 moves the graph of y_1 to the left one unit, stretches it by a factor of 3, and reflects it in the x-axis.

and

$$y_2 = \log_3 \frac{1}{(x+1)^3} \quad \text{as} \quad Y_2 = \ln(1/(X+1) \;\boxed{\wedge}\; 3)/\ln 3$$

we obtain the graphs shown in Figure 4.34. The graphs verify our description of the transformations. Observe that the domain of $y = \log_3 x$ is $(0, \infty)$ and the domain of $y = \log_3 \dfrac{1}{(x+1)^3}$ is $(-1, \infty)$. Both functions have a range of $(-\infty, \infty)$.   ■

PROBLEM SET 4.3

Practice Problems

In Problems 1–18, use logarithmic properties to expand each expression as much as possible. Where possible, evaluate logarithmic expressions without the use of a calculator.

1. $\log_7(7x)$

2. $\log(100x)$

3. $\ln(x^3 y^2)$

4. $\ln(x^5 y^4)$

5. $\log_4\left(\dfrac{\sqrt{x}}{64}\right)$

6. $\log_5\left(\dfrac{\sqrt[3]{x}}{25}\right)$

7. $\log_6\left(\dfrac{36}{\sqrt{3x-2}}\right)$

8. $\log_8\left(\dfrac{64}{\sqrt{x^2+1}}\right)$

9. $\ln\left(\dfrac{9}{e^4}\right)$

10. $\ln\left(\dfrac{23}{e^7}\right)$

11. $\log\sqrt[3]{\dfrac{x}{y}}$

12. $\log\sqrt[5]{\dfrac{x}{y}}$

13. $\log_b\left(\dfrac{\sqrt{x}\,y^3}{z^3}\right)$

14. $\log_b\left(\dfrac{\sqrt[3]{x}\,y^4}{z^5}\right)$

15. $\log_5\sqrt[3]{\dfrac{x^2 y}{25}}$

16. $\log_2\sqrt[5]{\dfrac{xy^4}{16}}$

17. $\ln\left(\sqrt{\sqrt{xy^3}}\right)$

18. $\log_4\left(2\sqrt[3]{x\sqrt{y}}\right)$

In Problems 19–38, write each expression as a single logarithm whose coefficient is 1.

19. $\ln x + \ln 7$

20. $\ln y + \ln 3$

21. $\log_5 x - \log_5 y$

22. $\log_4 7 - \log_4 y$

23. $2\log_3(x+1)$

24. $2\log_3(x-1)$

25. $\frac{1}{2}\log_2(5x)$

26. $\frac{1}{3}\log_2(7x)$

27. $\log_3(x^2-9) - \log_3(x-3)$

28. $\log_5(x^3+8) - \log_5(x+2)$

29. $\frac{1}{2}\log x + 3\log y$

30. $\frac{1}{3}\log x + 2\log y$

31. $\frac{1}{3}\log_4 x + 2\log_4(3x+2)$

32. $\frac{1}{4}\log_6 x + 2\log_6(x-7)$

33. $3\ln x + 5\ln y - 6\ln z$

34. $4\ln x + 7\ln y - 3\ln z$

35. $\frac{1}{2}(\log x + \log y)$

36. $\frac{1}{3}(\log_4 x - \log_4 y)$

37. $\frac{1}{2}(\log_5 x + \log_5 y) - 2\log_5(x+1)$

38. $\frac{1}{3}(\log_4 x - \log_4 y) + 2\log_4(x+1)$

In Problems 39–44, use properties of logarithms to expand each expression, simplifying terms where possible.

39. $\log(c \cdot 10^{9t})$

40. $\log\left(\dfrac{B}{10^{14a}}\right)$

41. $\ln(A \cdot e^{7x^2})$

42. $\ln\left(\dfrac{10^3}{e^7}\right)$

43. $\ln(A\sqrt[4]{e^3})$

44. $\ln\left(\dfrac{\sqrt[7]{e^4}}{B}\right)$

In Problems 45–50, use properties of logarithms to write each expression as a single term that does not contain a logarithm.

45. $10^{\log 6x^2 + \log 3x^4}$

46. $e^{\ln 7x^3 + \ln 2x^5}$

47. $10^{\log 18y^7 - \log 2y^4}$

48. $e^{\ln 25x^5 y^3 - \ln 5x^2 y}$

49. $e^{-2 + \ln y^2}$

50. $e^{5 + \ln y^4}$

In Problems 51–58, evaluate each logarithm using the change-of-base property. Work each problem twice, first using common logarithms and then using natural logarithms. Round each expression to three decimal places.

51. $\log_3 17$

52. $\log_7 3$

53. $\log_{\frac{1}{2}} 6$

54. $\log_4 0.65$

55. $\log_6 0.8$

56. $\log_{30} 1365$

57. $\log_{15} 195$

58. $\log_{\frac{1}{4}} 0.025$

Application Problem

59. The pH of a solution is a measure of its acidity. A low pH indicates an acidic solution, and a high pH indicates a basic solution. Neutral water has a pH of 7. Most people have a blood pH of approximately 7.4. The precise pH of a person's blood is modeled by the Henderson–Hasselbach formula, $\text{pH} = 6.1 + \log B - \log C$. In the model, B represents the concentration of bicarbonate, which is a base, and C represents the concentration of carbonic acid, which is acidic.

a. Rewrite the model so that the common logarithm appears only once.

b. Use the form of the model in part (a) and a calculator to answer this question: If the concentration of bicarbonate is 25 and the concentration of carbonic acid is 2, what is the pH for this person's blood?

True–False Critical Thinking Problems

60. Which of the following is true?

a. $\dfrac{\log_8 64}{\log_8 8} = \log_8 64 - \log_8 8$

b. $(\log 10)^3 = 3 \log 10$

c. $\ln(7e^{10}) = 10 + \ln 7$

d. $\frac{1}{5} \log_5 x = \sqrt[x]{x}, x > 0$

61. Which one of the following is true?

a. Because $\ln x^2 = 2 \ln x$, we can obtain a complete graph of $y = \ln x^2$ by doubling all the values on the graph of $y = \ln x$.

b. There is a value of x for which $(\log x)^3 = 3 \log x$.

c. There is no value of x for which $\log(x + 3) = \log x + \log 3$.

d. None of the above is true.

Technology Problems

62. a. Use a graphing utility (and the change-of-base property) to graph $y = \log_3 x$.

b. Graph $y = (\log_3 x) + 2$, $y = \log_3 (x + 2)$, and $y = -\log_3 x$ in the same viewing rectangle as $y = \log_3 x$. Then describe the transformation(s) of the graph of $y = \log_3 x$ needed to obtain each of these three graphs.

63. a. Use a graphing utility (and the change-of-base property) to graph $y = \log_{\frac{1}{2}} x$.

b. Graph $y = (\log_{\frac{1}{2}} x) - 1$, $y = \log_{\frac{1}{2}} (x - 1)$, and $y = -\log_{\frac{1}{2}} (x - 1) + 1$ in the same viewing rectangle as $y = \log_{\frac{1}{2}} x$. Then describe the transformations of the graph of $y = \log_{\frac{1}{2}} x$ needed to obtain each of these three graphs.

64. Graph $y = \log x$, $y = \log(10x)$, and $y = \log(0.1x)$ in the same viewing rectangle. Describe the relationship among the three graphs. What logarithmic property accounts for this relationship?

65. a. Use a graphing utility and the change-of-base property to graph $y = \log_b x$ with $b = 3, 25$, and 100 in the same viewing rectangle.

b. Which graph is on the top in the interval $(0, 1)$? Which is on the bottom?

c. Which graph is on the top in the interval $(1, \infty)$? Which is on the bottom?

d. Repeat parts (a)–(c) with $b = \frac{1}{2}$, $b = \frac{1}{4}$, and $b = \frac{1}{10}$.

e. Generalize by writing a statement about which graph is on top, which is on the bottom, and in which intervals for $y = \log_b x$ for $b > 1$ and $b < 1$.

66. a. Use the power rule to rewrite $\log_4 \dfrac{1}{(x - 2)^3}$.

b. Describe the relationship between the graphs of $y = \log_4 x$ and $y = \log_4 \dfrac{1}{(x - 2)^3}$.

c. Use a graphing utility to verify your description.

67. a. Use a graphing utility to graph $y = \log_2 x$ and $y = \log_2 \sqrt{\dfrac{x}{8}}$ in the same viewing rectangle.

b. Show that $\log_2 \sqrt{\dfrac{x}{8}} = \frac{1}{2} \log_2 \left(\dfrac{x}{8}\right)$. Describe the transformations of the graph of $y = \log_2 x$ needed to obtain the graph of $y = \frac{1}{2} \log_2 \left(\frac{x}{8}\right)$. Visually reinforce these transformations with the two graphs that appear in the viewing rectangle.

68. By letting y equal a positive constant of your choice, use a graphing utility to *disprove* each of the following statements.

a. $\log_3 (xy) = (\log_3 x)(\log_3 y)$ (*Hint:* If $y = 2$, first graph $y_1 = \log_3 (2x)$. Then graph $y_2 = (\log_3 x)(\log_3 2)$, the right side of the given statement, and show that y_1 and y_2 do not have the same graphs.)

b. $\log_5 \dfrac{x}{y} = \dfrac{\log_5 x}{\log_5 y}$

c. $\dfrac{\log_4 x}{\log_4 y} = \log_4 x - \log_4 y$

69. Graph $y = \ln(e^2 x)$. Now graph $y = k + \ln x$ so that the two graphs are identical. (First you will need to determine a value for k.)

‑ting in Mathematics _____

In Problem 68a, you disproved the property $\log_3(xy) = (\log_3 x)(\log_3 y)$ using a graphing utility. (Take a moment to reread the problem.) If the property $\log_3(xy) = \log_3 x + \log_3 y$ can be visually verified with a graphing utility for, say, fifty different choices for y (where $y = a$ positive constant), is this a *proof* that $\log_3(xy) = \log_3 x + \log_3 y$? Explain. How does this compare with the proof given on page 467?

Why is there no logarithmic property for $\log_b(M + N)$?

72. Describe the error in the following argument:

$$4 > 2$$
$$4 \log \tfrac{1}{3} > 2 \log \tfrac{1}{3} \qquad \text{Multiply both sides by } \log \tfrac{1}{3}.$$
$$\log \left(\tfrac{1}{3}\right)^4 > \log \left(\tfrac{1}{3}\right)^2 \qquad p \log_b M = \log_b M^p$$
$$\left(\tfrac{1}{3}\right)^4 > \left(\tfrac{1}{3}\right)^2$$
$$\tfrac{1}{81} > \tfrac{1}{9}$$
$$1 > 9 \qquad \text{Multiply both sides by 81.}$$

‑tical Thinking Problems _____

Use the change-of-base property to prove that
$$\log e = \frac{1}{\ln 10}.$$

If $f(x) = e^x$, find the value of $f(\ln 4) + f(\ln 3^2) - f(\ln \tfrac{1}{e})$.

Prove that
$$\log_b\left(\frac{M}{N}\right) = \log_b M - \log_b N$$
by letting $R = \log_b M$ and $S = \log_b N$ and following the procedure used to prove logarithmic property 1 on page 467.

Prove that $\log_b M^p = p \log_b M.$

77. Logarithms were conceived by John Napier (1550–1617), a Scots mathematician who was searching for easier methods of computation with large numbers. Napier's logarithms were neither common nor natural, defined instead by Nap $\log x = 10^7 \log_{\frac{1}{e}}\left(\dfrac{x}{10^7}\right)$. Use logarithmic properties to prove that
$$\text{Nap } \log x = 10^7 \, (7 \ln 10 - \ln x).$$

78. Simplify: $\log_b x + \log_{\frac{1}{b}} x.$

79. Show that $\ln \dfrac{\sqrt{3} + \sqrt{2}}{\sqrt{3} - \sqrt{2}} = 2 \ln(\sqrt{3} + \sqrt{2})$. Do not use a calculator.

SECTION 4.4   ## Exponential and Logarithmic Equations

Objectives

‑lutions Manual   **Tutorial**   **Video 8**

1 Solve exponential equations.
2 Solve applied problems involving exponential equations.
3 Solve logarithmic equations.
4 Solve applied problems involving logarithmic equations.

In Section 4.1, we considered exponential models that described the number of AIDS cases in the United States, the accumulated value of an interest-bearing account, and the age of an artifact. These models contained variable exponents. Techniques for solving equations with variable exponents will enable us to work in more meaningful ways with exponential models.

Solve exponential equations.

Exponential Equations

An exponential equation is an equation containing a variable in an exponent. Examples of exponential equations include
$$10^x = 5.71, \quad e^{7-4x} - 3 = 10, \quad \text{and} \quad 2^{x+2} = 3^{2x+1}.$$

These equations can be solved by isolating the exponential expression, taking the natural logarithm on both sides, simplifying, and then solving for the variable.

Discover for yourself

Solve

$$10^x = 5.71$$

by taking the common logarithm on both sides. Use the change-of-base property to show that the answer is the same as the one in Example I.

EXAMPLE I Solving an Exponential Equation

Solve: $10^x = 5.71$

Solution

$10^x = 5.71$	This is the given equation.
$\ln 10^x = \ln 5.71$	Take the natural logarithm on both sides.
$x \ln 10 = \ln 5.71$	Use the power rule for logarithms.
$x = \dfrac{\ln 5.71}{\ln 10}$	Solve for x by dividing both sides by $\ln 10$.

We now have an exact value for x. We can obtain a decimal approximation using a calculator.

$x \approx 0.757$ Calculator keystroke sequence: $\boxed{\ln}$ 5.71 $\boxed{\div}$ $\boxed{\ln}$ 10 $\boxed{\text{ENTER}}$

Since $10^0 = 1$ and $10^1 = 10$, it seems reasonable that the solution to $10^x = 5.71$ is approximately 0.757. The equation's solution set is $\left\{ \dfrac{\ln 5.71}{\ln 10} \right\}$. We use the exact value for x in expressing the solution set.

We can verify this solution with a graphing utility. Using methods discussed in Section 1.1, enter

$Y_1 = 10 \boxed{\wedge} X$

$Y_2 = 5.71$

$Y_3 \boxed{=} Y_1 - Y_2$.

Figure 4.35

The x-intercept for $y_3 = 10^x$ $- 5.71$ is approximately 0.757. This value is the approximate solution for $10^x = 5.71$.

Deselect y_1 and y_2. The graph of y_3 is shown in Figure 4.35. It appears that the x-intercept for y_3 is approximately 0.7. The more accurate approximation of 0.757 can be obtained using the $\boxed{\text{TRACE}}$ and $\boxed{\text{ZOOM}}$ features. ∎

EXAMPLE 2 Solving Exponential Equations

Solve:

a. $7e^{3x} = 312$ **b.** $e^{7-4x} - 3 = 10$ **c.** $2^{x+2} = 3^{2x+1}$

Discover for yourself

Since e is approximately equal to 2.72, what is a reasonable estimate (to the nearest whole number) of the solution to $7e^{3x} = 312$? Experiment with a few integers for x. When the integer is multiplied by 3 and e is raised to this power, multiplication of this result by 7 should give 312. Now use this approach to find a reasonable estimate (to the nearest whole number) of the solution to the equation in Example 2b.

Solution

a. We begin by dividing both sides by 7 to isolate the exponential expression.

$$7e^{3x} = 312 \qquad \text{This is the given equation.}$$

$$e^{3x} = \frac{312}{7} \qquad \text{Divide both sides by 7.}$$

$$\ln e^{3x} = \ln\left(\frac{312}{7}\right) \qquad \text{Take the natural logarithm on both sides.}$$

$$3x = \ln\left(\frac{312}{7}\right) \qquad \text{Use the inverse property: } \ln e^{\square} = \square$$

$$x = \frac{\ln\left(\dfrac{312}{7}\right)}{3} \qquad \text{Divide both sides by 3.}$$

$$\approx 1.266 \qquad \text{Use a calculator.}$$

The solution set is $\left\{ \dfrac{\ln\left(\dfrac{312}{7}\right)}{3} \right\}.$

b. We begin by adding 3 on both sides to isolate the exponential expression.

$$e^{7-4x} - 3 = 10 \qquad \text{This is the given equation.}$$

$$e^{7-4x} = 13 \qquad \text{Add 3 on both sides.}$$

$$\ln e^{7-4x} = \ln 13 \qquad \text{Take the natural logarithm on both sides.}$$

$$7 - 4x = \ln 13 \qquad \text{Use the inverse property: } \ln e^{\square} = \square$$

$$4x = 7 - \ln 13$$

$$x = \frac{7 - \ln 13}{4} \qquad \text{Divide both sides by 4.}$$

$$\approx 1.109 \qquad \text{Use a calculator.}$$

The solution set is $\left\{ \dfrac{7 - \ln 13}{4} \right\}.$

c.

$$2^{x+2} = 3^{2x+1} \qquad \text{This is the given equation.}$$

$$\ln 2^{x+2} = \ln 3^{2x+1} \qquad \text{Take the natural log on both sides: If } M = N, \text{ then } \ln M = \ln N.$$

$$(x + 2)\ln 2 = (2x + 1)\ln 3 \qquad \ln b^x = x \ln b$$

$$x \ln 2 + 2 \ln 2 = 2x \ln 3 + \ln 3 \qquad \text{Apply the distributive property.}$$

$$2 \ln 2 - \ln 3 = 2x \ln 3 - x \ln 2 \qquad \text{Isolate terms with the variable on one side of the equation.}$$

$$2 \ln 2 - \ln 3 = x(2 \ln 3 - \ln 2) \qquad \text{Factor } x \text{ on the right.}$$

$$\frac{2 \ln 2 - \ln 3}{2 \ln 3 - \ln 2} = x \qquad \text{Solve for } x.$$

The solution set is $\left\{ \dfrac{2 \ln 2 - \ln 3}{2 \ln 3 - \ln 2} \right\}$, approximately 0.191.

Figure 4.36

The x-intercept for $y_3 = 2^{x+2} - 3^{2x+1}$ is approximately 0.191. This value is the approximate solution for $2^{x+2} = 3^{2x+1}$.

Using technology

Shown below is the graph of $y = e^{2x} - 4e^x + 3$. There are two x-intercepts, one at 0 and one (using the [TRACE] and [ZOOM] features) approximately at 1.099, verifying our algebraic solution.

2 Solve applied problems involving exponential equations.

Barton Lidice Benes "Penny dreaming of becoming a dollar." Photo by Karen Furth.

Figure 4.36 shows the graph of y_3, where $y_1 = 2^{x+2}$, $y_2 = 3^{2x+1}$, and $y_3 \boxed{=}$ $y_1 - y_2$.

Use the [TRACE] and [ZOOM] features to approximate the x-intercept as 0.191, verifying the algebraic solution. ∎

EXAMPLE 3 **Solving an Exponential Equation**

Solve: $e^{2x} - 4e^x + 3 = 0$

Solution

The given equation is quadratic in form. If $t = e^x$, the equation can be expressed as $t^2 - 4t + 3 = 0$. Since this equation can be solved by factoring, we factor to isolate the exponential term.

$e^{2x} - 4e^x + 3 = 0$	This is the given equation.
$(e^x - 3)(e^x - 1) = 0$	Factor on the left. Notice that if $t = e^x$, $t^2 - 4t + 3 = (t - 3)(t - 1)$.
$e^x - 3 = 0$ or $e^x - 1 = 0$	Set each factor equal to 0.
$e^x = 3$ $e^x = 1$	Solve for e^x.
$\ln e^x = \ln 3$ $x = 0$	Take the natural log on both sides of the first equation. The second equation can be solved by inspection.
$x = \ln 3$ $x = 0$	$\ln e^x = x$

The solution set is $\{0, \ln 3\}$. The solutions are 0 and (approximately) 1.099. ∎

Modeling Applications

Knowing how to solve exponential equations enables us to work with exponential models and solve applied problems.

EXAMPLE 4 **Revisiting the Continuous Compounding Model**

The model $A = Pe^{rt}$ describes the accumulated value A of a sum of money P after t years at an annual percentage rate r (in decimal form) compounded continuously. Suppose that $1250 is invested at 5.5% compounded continuously.

a. How long will it take the investment to triple in value?
b. What interest rate is required for the investment to double in 10 years time?

Solution

a. $A = Pe^{rt}$	Use the model for continuous compounding.
$3750 = 1250\, e^{0.055t}$	$P = 1250$ (the amount invested), $A = 3750$ (accumulated amount is the triple of $1250 = 3 \cdot 1250 = 3750$), and r (the interest rate) $= 0.055$.
$3 = e^{0.055t}$	Divide both sides of the equation by 1250, isolating the exponential term.

$$\ln 3 = \ln e^{0.055t}$$ Take the natural logarithm on both sides.

$$\ln 3 = 0.055t$$ $\ln e^x = x$

$$t = \frac{\ln 3}{0.055}$$ Solve for t.

$$\approx 20$$ Use a calculator.

We see that the investment will triple in value in approximately 20 years.

b. $A = Pe^{rt}$ Once again, use the model for continuous compounding.

$$2500 = 1250 \, e^{r(10)}$$ $P = 1250$ (the amount invested) $A = 2500$ (we want the investment to double), and $t = 10$ (the doubling is to happen in 10 years).

$$2 = e^{10r}$$ Isolate the exponential term.

$$\ln 2 = \ln e^{10r}$$ Take the natural logarithm on both sides.

$$\ln 2 = 10r$$ $\ln e^x = x$

$$r = \frac{\ln 2}{10}$$ Solve for r.

$$\approx 0.069$$ Use a calculator.

An interest rate of approximately 6.9% is required for the investment to double over a period of 10 years.   ∎

EXAMPLE 5   **Revisiting the Formula for Compound Interest**

The model

$$A = P\left(1 + \frac{r}{n}\right)^{nt}$$

describes the accumulated value A of a sum of money P, the principal, after t years at annual percentage rate r (in decimal form), compounded n times a year (rather than compounded continuously). How long will it take $1000 to grow to $3600 at 8% annual interest compounded quarterly?

Solution

$$A = P\left(1 + \frac{r}{n}\right)^{nt}$$ This is the given model.

$$3600 = 1000\left(1 + \frac{0.08}{4}\right)^{4t}$$ A (the desired accumulated value) = \$3600, P (the principal) = \$1000, r (the interest rate) = 8% = 0.08, and $n = 4$ (quarterly compounding).

Our goal is to solve for t. Let's first simplify within parentheses and reverse the two sides of the equation.

$$1000(1.02)^{4t} = 3600$$

$$(1.02)^{4t} = 3.6$$ Isolate the exponential expression by dividing both sides by 1000.

The model

$$y = 1000 (1.02)^{4x}$$

representing the balance in the account, y, after x years is graphed below. The point with approximate coordinates (16.2, 3600) verifies a balance of $3600 after 16.2 years.

I am directing the Council on Environmental Quality and the Department of State, working in cooperation with ... other appropriate agencies, to make a one-year study of the probable changes in the world's population, natural resources, and environment through the end of the century.

President Jimmy Carter,
May 23, 1977

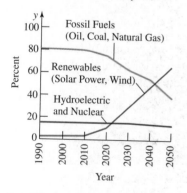

Year

Fossil fuels supply about 80% of the energy used in industrialized countries. Supplies are diminishing, and they could be replaced by cleaner renewable resources such as wind and solar power.

Source: World Bank

$$\ln (1.02)^{4t} = \ln 3.6$$ Take the natural logarithm on both sides.

$$4t \ln 1.02 = \ln 3.6$$ Use the power rule for logarithms.

$$t = \frac{\ln 3.6}{4 \ln 1.02}$$ Solve for t, dividing both sides by $4 \ln 1.02$.

$$\approx 16.2$$ Use a calculator.

After (approximately) 16.2 years, the $1000 will grow to an accumulated value of $3600.

One aim of algebra is to use mathematical models to predict the behavior of variables. The model in the next example, taken from a report to former president Jimmy Carter, involves a prediction that is cause for alarm.

EXAMPLE 6 **Depletion of Nonrenewable Energy Resources**

The model

$$A = \frac{A_0}{k} (e^{kt} - 1)$$

describes the amount of nonrenewable energy resources A (oil, natural gas, coal, uranium) from time $t = 0$ to time t, where A_0 is the amount of the resource consumed during the year $t = 0$ and k is the relative growth rate of annual consumption. In the Global 2000 Report to former president Jimmy Carter, the 1976 worldwide consumption of oil was 21.7 billion barrels, and the predicted growth rate for oil consumption was 3% per year ($k = 0.03$). At that time, the total known remaining oil resources ultimately available were 1661 billion barrels. Using these figures, by what year will the planet be depleted of its oil resources that were known at the time?

Solution

$$A = \frac{A_0}{k} (e^{kt} - 1)$$ This is the given model.

$$1661 = \frac{21.7}{0.03} (e^{0.03t} - 1)$$ $A_0 = 21.7$ (billion barrels) in $t = 0$ (1976). $k = 0.03$. We must find t corresponding to $A = 1661$ (billion barrels).

$$1661 \left(\frac{0.03}{21.7}\right) = e^{0.03t} - 1$$ Our goal is to isolate $e^{0.03t}$.

$$1661 \left(\frac{0.03}{21.7}\right) + 1 = e^{0.03t}$$ Add 1 to both sides.

$$\ln \left[1661 \left(\frac{0.03}{21.7}\right) + 1\right] = \ln e^{0.03t}$$ Take the natural logarithm on both sides.

$$\ln \left[1661 \left(\frac{0.03}{21.7}\right) + 1\right] = 0.03t$$ On the right: $\ln e^x = x$

$$\frac{\ln\left[1661\left(\dfrac{0.03}{21.7}\right) + 1\right]}{0.03} = t \qquad \text{Solve for } t.$$

Using a calculator, we find $t \approx 40$. The planet will be depleted of its then-known oil resources 40 years after 1976, in 2016. ∎

Logarithmic Equations

Just as exponential equations contain a variable in an exponent, logarithmic equations contain a variable in a logarithmic expression. Examples of logarithmic equations include

$$\log_4(x + 3) = 2 \quad \text{and} \quad \log(2x - 1) = \log(4x - 3) - \log x.$$

The first equation contains a logarithmic expression and a constant. The second equation contains only logarithmic expressions. We now consider methods for solving both kinds of logarithmic equations. These methods will enable us to work in more meaningful ways with logarithmic models.

3 Solve logarithmic equations.

Logarithmic Equations Containing Logarithmic Expressions and Constants

The equation

$$\log_4(x + 3) = 2$$

contains the logarithmic expression $\log_4(x + 3)$ and the constant 2. We can solve this equation by rewriting it as an equivalent exponential equation. Example 7 illustrates how this is done.

EXAMPLE 7   **Solving a Logarithmic Equation**

Solve: $\log_4(x + 3) = 2$

Solution

We first rewrite the equation as an equivalent exponential equation.

$$\log_b M = N \qquad \text{means} \qquad b^N = M$$

$$\log_4(x + 3) = 2 \quad \text{means} \quad 4^2 = x + 3$$

Now we solve the equivalent exponential equation for x.

$$4^2 = x + 3$$

$$16 = x + 3$$

$$13 = x$$

Check

$$\log_4(x + 3) = 2 \qquad \text{This is the given logarithmic equation.}$$

$$\log_4(13 + 3) \overset{?}{=} 2 \qquad \text{Substitute 13 for } x.$$

$$\log_4 16 \overset{?}{=} 2 \qquad \text{Substitute 13 for } x.$$

$$2 = 2 \checkmark \qquad \log_4 16 = 2 \text{ because } 4^2 = 16.$$

This true statement indicates that the solution set is $\{13\}$. ∎

The solution method used in Example 7 works when one side of the equation contains a single logarithm and the other side contains a constant. Once the equation is in the form $\log_b M = N$, we rewrite it in the exponential form $b^N = M$. In the next example we use the product rule for logarithms to obtain a single logarithmic expression on the left side.

EXAMPLE 8 Using the Product Rule to Solve a Logarithmic Equation

Solve: $\log_2 x + \log_2(x - 7) = 3$

Solution

$$\log_2 x + \log_2(x - 7) = 3 \qquad \text{This is the given equation.}$$

$$\log_2 x(x - 7) = 3 \qquad \text{Use the product rule to obtain a single logarithm.}$$

$$2^3 = x(x - 7) \qquad \text{If } \log_b M = N, \text{ then } b^N = M.$$

$$8 = x^2 - 7x \qquad \text{Apply the distributive property on the right.}$$

$$0 = x^2 - 7x - 8 \qquad \text{Set the equation equal to 0.}$$

$$0 = (x - 8)(x + 1) \qquad \text{Factor.}$$

$$x - 8 = 0 \quad \text{or} \quad x + 1 = 0 \qquad \text{Set each factor equal to 0.}$$

$$x = 8 \qquad\qquad x = -1 \qquad \text{Solve for } x.$$

Check

Checking 8:

$$\log_2 x + \log_2(x - 7) = 3$$

$$\log_2 8 + \log_2(8 - 7) \overset{?}{=} 3$$

$$\log_2 8 + \log_2 1 \overset{?}{=} 3$$

$$3 + 0 \overset{?}{=} 3$$

$$3 = 3 \checkmark$$

The solution set is $\{8\}$.

Checking -1:

$$\log_2 x + \log_2(x - 7) = 3$$

$$\log_2(-1) + \log_2(-1 - 7) \overset{?}{=} 3$$

The number -1 does not check. Negative numbers do not have logarithms.

∎

Solving an equation containing logarithmic expressions and constants

1. Combine all logarithmic expressions on one side and all constants on the other side of the equation.
2. Use logarithmic properties to rewrite the logarithmic expression as a single logarithm whose coefficient is 1. The form of the equation is $\log_b M = N$.
3. Rewrite step 2 in exponential form $b^N = M$ and solve the resulting equation for the variable.
4. Check each solution in the original equation, rejecting values that produce the logarithm of a negative number or the logarithm of 0.

Logarithmic Equations Containing Only Logarithmic Expressions

We continue our discussion with the solution of equations such as

$$\log(2x - 1) = \log(4x - 3) - \log x.$$

Notice that every term contains a logarithmic expression. The fact that the logarithmic function is one-to-one is very important in solving such equations. Stated symbolically, this means that

If $\log_b M = \log_b N$ ($M > 0$, $N > 0$), then $M = N$.

Consequently, we can solve these equations by using logarithmic properties to rewrite each side as the logarithm of a single quantity. We then set the quantities equal to each other and solve for the variable. Example 9 illustrates this process.

EXAMPLE 9   A Logarithmic Equation Containing Only Logarithmic Expressions

Solve: $\log(2x - 1) = \log(4x - 3) - \log x$

Solution

$$\log(2x - 1) = \log(4x - 3) - \log x \qquad \text{This is the given equation.}$$

$$\log(2x - 1) = \log\left(\frac{4x - 3}{x}\right) \qquad \log_b M - \log_b N = \log_b \frac{M}{N}$$

$$2x - 1 = \frac{4x - 3}{x} \qquad \text{If } \log_b M = \log_b N, \text{ then } M = N.$$

$$(2x - 1)x = 4x - 3 \qquad \text{Clear fractions by multiplying both sides by } x.$$

$$2x^2 - 5x + 3 = 0 \qquad \text{Write the quadratic equation in standard form.}$$

$$(2x - 3)(x - 1) = 0 \qquad \text{Factor.}$$

Using

$$y_1 = \log(2x - 1)$$

$$y_2 = \log(4x - 3) - \log x$$

and

$$y_3 \boxed{=} y_1 - y_2$$

we obtain the graph of y_3 shown below. The range setting

$\text{Xmin} = 0$, $\text{Xmax} = 2$, $\text{Xscl} = 1$, $\text{Ymin} = -0.2$, $\text{Ymax} = 0.2$, $\text{Yscl} = 1$

makes it fairly easy to see that y_3 has x-intercepts at 1 and $\frac{3}{2}$, verifying the solution set.

$$2x - 3 = 0 \quad \text{or} \quad x - 1 = 0 \qquad \text{Set each factor equal to 0.}$$

$$x = \frac{3}{2} \qquad\qquad x = 1 \qquad \text{Solve for } x.$$

Both proposed solutions are valid, since neither causes the logarithm of 0 or the logarithm of a negative number in the given equation. The solution set is $\{1, \frac{3}{2}\}$. ∎

> **Solving an equation containing only logarithmic expressions**
>
> 1. Use properties of logarithms to rewrite each side of the equation as the logarithm of a single quantity. (Be sure that the coefficient of each logarithm is 1.)
> 2. Set the quantities equal to each other and solve for the variable.
> 3. Check each solution in the original equation, rejecting values that produce the logarithm of a negative number or the logarithm of 0.

4 Solve applied problems involving logarithmic equations.

Modeling Applications

Solving logarithmic equations enables us to work with logarithmic models and solve applied problems.

The graph of

$$y = \frac{1}{0.03} \ln \left(\frac{65}{65 - x} \right)$$

continues increasing at a faster and faster rate. This shows that as the number of signs to be learned increases, more and more time is needed to achieve the maximum mastery of 65 signs.

Number of signs to be mastered
$[0, 60] \times [0, 65]$
Xscl = 5 Yscl = 5

The utility's TRACE feature confirms that approximately 30 signs can be mastered in 21 weeks.

X=30.476190476 Y=21.091268425

EXAMPLE 10   A Learning Model

The model

$$t = \frac{1}{c} \ln \left(\frac{A}{A - N} \right)$$

describes the time (t, in weeks) that it takes to achieve mastery of a portion of a task, in which

A = Maximum learning possible

N = Portion of the learning that is to be achieved

c = Constant used to measure an individual's learning style

The formula is also used to determine how long it will take chimpanzees and apes to master a task. For example, a typical chimpanzee learning sign language can master a maximum of 65 signs. How many signs can a chimpanzee master in 21 weeks if c for that chimp is 0.03?

Solution

$$t = \frac{1}{c} \ln \left(\frac{A}{A - N} \right) \qquad \text{This is the given model.}$$

$$21 = \frac{1}{0.03} \ln \left(\frac{65}{65 - N} \right) \qquad \begin{array}{l} t(\text{time}) = 21 \text{ weeks}, c = 0.03, \text{ and } A \\ (\text{maximum learning possible}) = 65. \text{ We} \\ \text{must solve for } N, \text{ the portion (or the} \\ \text{number of signs) to be learned.} \end{array}$$

$$0.63 = \ln\left(\frac{65}{65 - N}\right)$$

Multiply both sides of the equation by 0.03.

$$e^{0.63} = \frac{65}{65 - N}$$

Since $\log_b M = N$ is equivalent to $b^N = M$, then $\ln M = N$ is equivalent to $e^N = M$.

$$e^{0.63}(65 - N) = 65$$

Multiply both sides of the equation by $65 - N$.

$$e^{0.63}(65) - e^{0.63}N = 65$$

Apply the distributive property on the left.

$$e^{0.63}(65) - 65 = e^{0.63}N$$

Collect the term containing N on the right and all other terms on the left.

$$\frac{e^{0.63}(65) - 65}{e^{0.63}} = N$$

Solve for N by dividing both sides of the equation by $e^{0.63}$.

$$N \approx 30$$

Use a calculator.

The chimpanzee can master approximately 30 signs in 21 weeks.   ∎

PROBLEM SET 4.4

Practice Problems

Solve each equation in Problems 1–26 by taking the natural logarithm on both sides. Express the answer in terms of natural logarithms. Then use a calculator to obtain a decimal approximation, correct to the nearest thousandth, for the solution.

1. $10^x = 3.91$

2. $10^x = 8.07$

3. $e^x = 5.7$

4. $e^x = 0.83$

5. $5^x = 17$

6. $19^x = 143$

7. $5e^x = 23$

8. $9e^x = 107$

9. $3e^{5x} = 1977$

10. $4e^{7x} = 10{,}273$

11. $e^{1-5x} = 793$

12. $e^{1-8x} = 7957$

13. $e^{5x-3} - 2 = 10{,}476$

14. $e^{4x-5} - 7 = 11{,}243$

15. $7^{x+2} = 410$

16. $5^{x-3} = 137$

17. $7^{0.3x} = 813$

18. $3^{x/7} = 0.2$

19. $5^x = 3^{x+1}$

20. $11^{1-x} = 4^x$

21. $5^{2x+3} = 3^{x-1}$

22. $7^{2x+1} = 3^{x+2}$

23. $e^{2x} - 3e^x + 2 = 0$

24. $e^{2x} - 2e^x - 3 = 0$

25. $e^{4x} + 5e^{2x} - 24 = 0$

26. $e^{4x} - 3e^{2x} - 18 = 0$

In Problems 27–56, solve each logarithmic equation algebraically. Check each proposed solution by direct substitution or with a graphing utility, eliminating values that produce the logarithm of a negative number or the logarithm of 0.

Problems 27–40 involve logarithmic equations containing logarithmic expressions and constants.

27. $\log_3 x = 4$

28. $\log_5 x = 3$

29. $\log_4(x + 5) = 3$

30. $\log_5(x - 7) = 2$

31. $\log_3(x - 4) = -3$

32. $\log_7(x + 2) = -2$

33. $\log_4(3x + 2) = 3$

34. $\log_2(4x + 1) = 5$

35. $\log_5 x + \log_5(4x - 1) = 1$

36. $\log_6(x + 5) + \log_6 x = 2$

37. $\log_3(x - 5) + \log_3(x + 3) = 2$

38. $\log_2(x - 1) + \log_2(x + 1) = 3$

39. $\log_2(x + 2) - \log_2(x - 5) = 3$

40. $\log_4(x + 2) - \log_4(x - 1) = 1$

Problems 41–56 involve logarithmic equations containing only logarithmic expressions.

41. $\log (x + 2) = \log (3x - 4)$

42. $\log \left(\dfrac{3x - 9}{3} \right) = \log \left(\dfrac{2x - 6}{6} \right)$

43. $\log_3 x + \log_3 2 = \log_3 6$

44. $\log_6 3x + \log_6 4 = \log_6 24$

45. $\log (9x + 2) - \log (3x - 1) = \log 4$

46. $\log_2 (x + 5) - \log_2 x = \log_2 4$

47. $\log x + \log (x + 3) = \log 4$

48. $\log_3 x + \log_3 (x + 6) = \log_3 27$

49. $\log_2 (x + 1) + \log_2 (x - 2) = \log_2 (x + 6)$

50. $\ln (x + 2) + \ln (x + 6) = \ln (x + 20)$

51. $\ln (7x + 12) - \ln (x + 3) = \ln x$

52. $\ln (12 - x) - \ln (x + 2) = \ln 2x$

53. $2 \log x - \log 4 = \log 100$

54. $2 \log x - \log 5 = \log 1000$

55. $\ln (2x - 3) = 2 \ln x - \ln (x - 2)$

56. $2 \log x = \log (2 - x) + \log (4 - x)$

Application Problems

In Problems 57–60, complete the table for a savings account subjected to continuous compounding ($A = Pe^{rt}$).

	Amount Invested	Annual Interest Rate	Accumulated Amount	Time t in Years
57.	$8000	8%	Double the amount invested	
58.	$8000		$12,000	2
59.	$2350		Triple the amount invested	7
60.	$17,425	4.25%	$25,000	

In Problems 61–64, complete the table for a savings account subjected to n compoundings yearly $\left(A = P \left(1 + \dfrac{r}{n} \right)^{nt} \right)$.

	Amount Invested	Number of Compounding Periods	Annual Interest Rate	Accumulated Amount	Time t in Years
61.	$12,500	4	5.75%	$20,000	
62.	$7250	12	6.5%	$15,000	
63.	$1000	360		$1400	2
64.	$5000	360		$9000	4

65. In the Global 2000 Report to former president Jimmy Carter, the 1976 worldwide consumption of natural gas was 50 trillion cubic feet, and the growth rate for natural gas consumption was 2% per year ($k = 0.02$). At that time, the remaining known natural gas resources ultimately available were 8493 trillion cubic feet. Using these figures and the model in Example 6 (page 484), find the year the planet will be depleted of its then-known natural gas resources.

66. In the Global 2000 Report to former president Jimmy Carter, the 1976 consumption of nonrenewable energy resources (petroleum, natural gas, coal, shale oil, and uranium) was 250 quadrillion Btu, and the predicted growth rate for consumption was 2% per year ($k = 0.02$). At that time, the total remaining known resources ultimately available were 161,241 quadrillion Btu. Using these figures and the model in Example 6 (page 484), find the year the planet will be depleted of its then-known nonrenewable energy resources.

Use the exponential growth model $A = A_0 e^{kt}$ to solve Problems 67–69.

67. These statistics were issued in 1995 by the Population Reference Bureau in Washington, D.C.:

Region	1995 Population (in billions)	Percentage of Population in 1995	Growth Rate (k)
World	5.702	100	1.5% = 0.015
More developed regions	1.169	20.5	0.2% = 0.002
Less developed regions	4.533	79.5	1.9% = 0.019

Let $t = 0$ correspond to 1995 and assume that the indicated growth rates are valid for at least 15 years. By what year (that is, how many years after 1995) will the world population be 6.37 billion? At that time, what will be the percentage of the world's population for less developed regions?

68. These statistics were issued in 1995 by the Population Reference Bureau in Washington, D.C.:

Country	1995 Population (in millions)	Growth Rate (k)
United Kingdom	58.6	0.2% = 0.002
Iraq	20.6	3.7% = 0.037

The given growth rates (percentage per year) indicate that the United Kingdom has one of the lowest growth rates in the world and Iraq has one of the highest. Let $t = 0$ correspond to 1995 and assume that the indicated growth rates are valid for at least 15 years. By what year (that is, how many years after 1995) will the United Kingdom have a population of 59.2 million? What will be Iraq's population at that time?

69. In a report entitled *Resources and Man*, the U.S. National Academy of Sciences concluded that a world population of 10 billion "is close to (if not above) the maximum that an intensely managed world might hope to support with some degree of comfort and individual choice." For this reason, 10 billion is called the carrying capacity of Earth. In the 1969 report, world population figures for 1975 were projected at 4.043 billion (low) and 4.134 billion (high), with a relative growth rate of 1.5% per year (low) and 2% per year (high).

 a. Use the low figures and the exponential growth model to estimate the year in which the carrying capacity might be reached.

 b. Repeat part (a) using the high figures.

70. The model $V(t) = C\left(1 - \dfrac{2}{n}\right)^t$ describes the value of a piece of equipment after t years, where C is the original cost and n is the life expectancy in years. How long will it take a piece of equipment that costs \$50,000 and has an expected life of 20 years to be worth \$20,000?

Chemists have defined the pH (hydrogen potential) of a solution by $pH = -\log[H^+]$, where $[H^+]$ represents the concentration of the hydrogen ion in moles per liter. The pH scale ranges from 0 to 14, depending on a solution's acidity or alkalinity. Values below 7 indicate progressively greater acidity, while those above 7 are progressively more alkaline. Use this model to answer Problems 71–72.

71. Normal, unpolluted rain has a pH of about 5.6. An environmental concern involves the destructive effects of acid rain, which is caused primarily by sulfur dioxide emissions. The most acidic rainfall ever had a pH of 2.4. What was the hydrogen ion concentration of that rainfall?

72. The pH of human blood ranges between 7.37 and 7.44. What are the corresponding bounds for hydrogen ion concentration?

73. We have seen that the magnitude R on the Richter scale of an earthquake of intensity I is given by

$$R = \log \frac{I}{I_0}$$

where I_0 is the intensity of a barely felt zero-level earthquake.

 a. Northern California's 1989 earthquake measured 7.1 on the Richter scale. How many times more intense was this earthquake than a zero-level earthquake?

 b. One of the largest earthquakes ever recorded was the 8.9 magnitude quake that struck Japan in 1933. How many times more intense was the earthquake than a zero-level earthquake?

 c. How many times greater in intensity was Japan's 1933 earthquake than California's 1989 earthquake?

 d. Earthquakes release an enormous amount of energy. The model $\log E = 11.4 + 1.5R$ describes the relationship between the energy released by an earthquake (measured in ergs) and the earthquake's magnitude on the Richter scale. How many ergs of energy were released by California's 1989 earthquake and Japan's 1933 earthquake?

74. The total TNT equivalent of all nuclear weapons is 25,000 megatons. Given that 1 megaton = 1 million tons and one ton of TNT releases 4.2×10^6 ergs of energy, use the formula in Problem 73 (d) to find the Richter scale reading for the simultaneous release of all nuclear weapons.

75. The brightness of stars, as seen by the naked eye and measured in magnitudes M, is given by

$$M = 6 - 2.5 \log \frac{I}{I_0}$$

where

I = the intensity of light from the star

and

I_0 = the intensity of light from a just-visible star

The ancient Greek astronomer Ptolemy used six categories for the magnitude M of a star: 6 for the dimmest stars and 1 for the brightest stars.

a. How many times more intense is the light from a star of magnitude 1 than the light from a just-visible star?

b. How many times more intense is the light from a star of magnitude 4 than the light from a just-visible star?

c. How many times more intense is the light from a star of magnitude 1 than the light from a star of magnitude 4?

Ptolemy's six categories for the brightness of stars has been expanded to negative magnitudes for bright bodies such as the sun and to positive magnitudes for stars visible only with telescopes. Two stars of magnitudes M_1 and M_2 and intensity I_1 and I_2 are related by

$$M_2 - M_1 = 2.5 \log \frac{I_1}{I_2}.$$

Use this model to answer Problems 76–77.

76. How many times more intense is the light from Sirius (magnitude = -1.5) than the light from Polaris (magnitude = 2)?

77. How many times more intense is the light from the sun (magnitude = -26) than the light from the full moon (magnitude = -13)?

True–False Critical Thinking Problems

78. Which one of the following is true?

a. The solution of the equation $3^{x+2} = 5$ must be a positive number.

b. A reasonable estimate for the solution of the equation $8^{0.4x} = 5$ is 2.

c. A reasonable estimate for the solution of the equation $e^{1-4x} = 2$ is 10.

d. Examples of exponential equations include $10^x = 5.71$, $e^x = 0.72$, and $x^{10} = 5.71$.

79. Which one of the following is true?

a. If $\log (x + 3) = 2$, then $e^2 = x + 3$.

b. If $\log (7x + 3) - \log (2x + 5) = 4$, then in exponential form $10^4 = (7x + 3) - (2x + 5)$.

c. If $x = \frac{1}{k} \ln y$, then $y = e^{kx}$.

d. An earthquake measuring 8.6 on the Richter scale is twice as intense as one measuring 4.3 on the Richter scale.

80. Which one of the following is true?

a. Models involving logarithmic functions can be expressed in exponential form and vice versa.

b. If $\log (x + 2) + \log (x + 6) = \log (x + 20)$, then $(x + 2) + (x + 6) = x + 20$.

c. $\log (-4) + \log (-5) = \log 20$

d. If $\log 4 + \log (x + 1) = 2 \log x + \log 3$, then $4(x + 1) = (2x)(3)$.

Technology Problems

In Problems 81–84, use a graphing utility to find the solution set for each exponential equation, expressing solutions to the nearest tenth.

81. $\dfrac{e^x + e^{-x}}{2} = 2$

82. $\dfrac{3^x - 3^{-x}}{2} = 5$

83. $3^x = 2x + 3$

84. $5^x = 3x + 4$

85. The model $W = 2600(1 - 0.51e^{-0.075t})^3$ describes the weight (in kilograms) of a female African elephant at age t (in years). Use a graphing utility to graph the weight function. Then trace along the curve to estimate the age of an adult female elephant weighing 1800 kilograms.

Renée Young / Photo Researchers, Inc.

86. The model $h = 79.041 + 6.39x - e^{3.261 - 0.993x}$ is used to predict the height h in centimeters for a preschooler who is x years old, $\frac{1}{4} \le x \le 6$. Graph the model and trace along the graph to predict the age for a preschooler with a height of 75.8 centimeters. What difficulties would you encounter if you attempted to make this prediction using algebraic methods?

87. The model $P = 145e^{-0.092t}$ describes a runner's pulse rate (P, in beats per minute) t minutes after a race ($0 \le t \le 15$). Graph the equation with a graphing utility. Trace along the graph and determine after how many minutes the runner's pulse rate will be 70 beats per minute.

Use a graphing utility to solve each logarithmic equation in Problems 88–91. Round your solutions to two decimal places.

88. $\ln(2x + 1) - \ln(x - 3) = 2\ln 3$

89. $\log(x - 1) = x - 5$

90. $(\log x)^2 - 3x = 1$

91. $\log_3 x + 7 = 4 - \log_5 x$

92. The model $P(t) = 95 - 30\log_2 t$ is a hypothetical formula describing the percentage of students ($P(t)$) who could recall the important features of a lecture as a function of time, where t represents the number of days that have elapsed since the lecture was given.

    a. Enter the function on your graphing utility as

$$y_1 = 95 - 30\frac{\ln x}{\ln 2},$$ using the change-of-base property, with

Xmin = 0, Xmax = 10, Xscl = 1,

Ymin = 0, Ymax = 100, Yscl = 10

    b. Use the graph to solve the equation

$$95 - 30\log_2 t = 0.$$

Describe what the solution means in practical terms.

    c. Use the graph to solve the equation

$$95 - 30\log_2 t = 50.$$

Describe what the solution means in practical terms.

Writing in Mathematics

93. The exponential equation $2^{4-5x} = 8$ can be solved by taking the natural logarithm on both sides. Since $2^3 = 8$, the equation can also be solved by writing each side with a common base, $2^{4-5x} = 2^3$, and then equating exponents, resulting in $4 - 5x = 3$. Solve the equation using both methods and then compare and contrast the two methods. Explain why we did not use the second

method in solving the exponential equations that appeared in this section.

94. Describe similarities and differences in the procedures needed to solve $\log_2 x + \log_2 (x - 7) = 3$ and $\log_2 x + \log_2 (x - 7) = \log_2 8$.

95. In Example 6 we used the model

$$A = \frac{A_0}{k}(e^{kt} - 1)$$

to describe the amount of nonrenewable energy resources from time $t = 0$ to time t, where A_0 is the amount of the resource consumed during the year $t = 0$ and k is the relative growth rate of annual consumption. Using principles for solving logarithmic equations, this model can be solved for t, resulting in

$$t = \frac{\ln\left(\frac{kA}{A_0} + 1\right)}{k}.$$

Under what applied conditions would it be easier to work with the logarithmic form of the model? Which form of the model would be easier to work with to solve Example 6?

Critical Thinking Problems

96. If $4000 is deposited into an account paying 3% interest compounded annually and at the same time $2000 is deposited into an account paying 5% interest com-pounded annually, after how long will the two accounts have the same balance?

Some populations exhibit an increasing rate of growth, followed by a declining rate as the population levels off and approaches the maximum level that can be supported by the habitat. Illustrated by the growth in the figure shown, this growth is described by the logistic model

$$N = \frac{N_0 N_{\max}}{N_0 + (N_{\max} - N_0)e^{-kt}}$$

where

N_0 = the initial population size

$N_{\max}$ = the maximum population that can be supported by the habitat

N = the population at time t

k = the population rate of growth

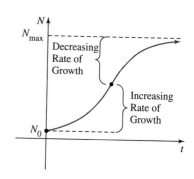

Use this model to solve Problem 97.

97. A student carrying a contagious influenza virus enrolls at a school with 6000 students. The spread of the virus follows the logistics growth model with $k = 0.3$ and time t measured in days. In how many days will half of the students be infected?

98. Use the model $A = \frac{A_0}{k}(e^{kt} - 1)$ and show that

$$t = \frac{\ln\left(\frac{kA}{A_0} + 1\right)}{k}.$$

99. We have seen that the perceived loudness of a sound (D, in decibels) at the eardrum is described by

$$D = 10 \log \frac{I}{I_0}$$

where

I = the intensity of the sound (in watts per meter²)

I_0 = the intensity of a sound barely audible to the human ear

A worker uses a machine that produces 90 decibels. A second machine in the same area produces 80 decibels. Union regulations prohibit exposure to sound levels greater than 100 decibels. What is the combined decibel level of the two machines? Does this situation violate union regulations? (Hint: In measuring sound, we add intensities but not decibels.)

Solve the logarithmic equations in Problems 100–103 algebraically. Check each proposed solution by direct substitution or with a graphing utility.

100. $(\ln x)^2 = \ln x^2$

101. $(\ln x)^2 - 3 \ln x + 1 = 0$

102. $\log x(2 \log x + 1) = 6$

103. $\ln(\ln x) = 0$

Group Activity Problem

104. This problem is appropriate for discussion in a small group.

India is currently one of the world's fastest-growing countries, with a growth rate of about 2.6% annually. Assuming that the relative growth rate is constant, the population will reach 1.5 billion sometime in the year 2010. Treating the year 1974 as year 0, the growth model is $y = 574,220,000e^{0.026t}$.

One problem with this model is that nothing can grow exponentially indefinitely. Although India grew at an average rate of 2.6% per year from 1974 to 1984, the model is based on the assumption that India's growth rate will remain the same at least until the year 2010.

Is this a likely assumption? Can you suggest factors that influence population growth rates for India and other countries? What factors might limit the size of a population? Can you suggest factors that might lead to a greater population growth rate than the one predicted by an exponential growth model? How might these factors be accounted for in a mathematical model predicting population growth or in the model's graph? (In answering this last question, consider the model

$$y = \frac{5000}{1 + e^{-t/6}}$$

which describes the population y of a certain species t years after it is introduced into a new habitat.)

If the assumption of an indefinite growth at a constant rate is unrealistic, why do you think models based on this assumption are widely used? What does this tell you about making predictions based on mathematical models?

SECTION 4.5   Modeling with Exponential and Logarithmic Functions

Solutions Manual   **Tutorial**   **Video 8**

Objectives

1 Model exponential growth and decay.
2 Model cooling and heating times.
3 Fit exponential functions to data.
4 Fit logarithmic functions to data.

In this section, we continue our work with applications of exponential and logarithmic functions. All examples and problems involve modeling actual real world situations.

1 Model exponential growth and decay.

Growth and Decay Models

In Section 4.1, we introduced the exponential growth and decay models

$$A = A_0 e^{kt}$$

where A_0 is the original amount (or size) of a growing (or decaying) entity at $t = 0$, A is the amount at time t, and k is a growth ($k > 0$) or decay ($k < 0$) constant. Some situations require us to use given data in growth and decay models to determine k. Once this value is computed, the model $A = A_0 e^{kt}$ can be used to solve problems and make predictions. This idea is illustrated in our first two examples.

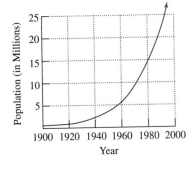

Figure 4.37

Mexico City's population has grown exponentially.

EXAMPLE I   Modeling Mexico City's Growth

The graph in Figure 4.37 shows the growth of the Mexico City metropolitan area from 1900 through 2000. In 1970, the population of Mexico City was 9.4 million and by 1990 it had grown to 20.2 million.

a. Find the exponential growth function that models the data.
b. By what year will the population reach 100 million?

Solution

a. We use the exponential growth model

$$A = A_0 e^{kt}$$

in which t is the number of years since 1970. This means that 1970 corresponds to $t = 0$. At that time there were 9.4 million inhabitants, so we substitute 9.4 for A_0 in the growth model.

$$A = 9.4 e^{kt}$$

We are given that there were 20.2 million inhabitants in 1990. Since 1990 is 20 years after 1970, when $t = 20$ the value of A is 20.2. Substituting these numbers into the growth model will enable us to find k, the growth constant or the growth rate.

$A = 9.4 e^{kt}$	Use the growth model with $A_0 = 9.4$
$20.2 = 9.4 e^{k \cdot 20}$	When $t = 20$, $A = 20.2$. Substitute these numbers into the model.
$e^{20k} = \dfrac{20.2}{9.4}$	Isolate the exponential term by dividing both sides by 9.4. We also reversed the sides.
$\ln e^{20k} = \ln \dfrac{20.2}{9.4}$	Take the natural logarithm on both sides.
$20k = \ln \dfrac{20.2}{9.4}$	Simplify the left side using $\ln e^x = x$
$k = \dfrac{\ln \dfrac{20.2}{9.4}}{20} \approx 0.038$	Divide both sides by 20 and solve for k.

The exponential growth function is

$$A = 9.4 e^{0.038t}$$

where t is measured in years since 1970.

b. To find the year in which the population will reach 100 million, we substitute 100 for A in the model from part (a) and solve for t.

$A = 9.4 e^{0.038t}$	This is the model from part (a).
$100 = 9.4 e^{0.038t}$	Substitute 100 for A.
$e^{0.038t} = \dfrac{100}{9.4}$	Divide both sides by 9.4.
$\ln e^{0.038t} = \ln \dfrac{100}{9.4}$	Take the natural logarithm on both sides.
$0.038t = \ln \dfrac{100}{9.4}$	Simplify on the left using $\ln e^x = x$.
$t = \dfrac{\ln \dfrac{100}{9.4}}{0.038} \approx 62$	Solve for t by dividing both sides by 0.038.

George Segal "Rush Hour" 1983, plaster, acrylic paint, 72 × 96 × 96 in. (182.9 × 243.8 × 243.8 cm). Courtesy Sidney Janis Gallery, New York. © George Segal / Licensed by VAGA, New York 1998.

Since 62 is the number of years after 1970, the model indicates that the population of Mexico City will reach 100 million by 1970 + 62, or in the year 2032. ∎

Study tip

The half-life of a radioactive substance is the time required for half of a given sample to disintegrate. Half-life is a property of the substance and does not depend on its size.

EXAMPLE 2   Carbon-14 Dating: The Dead Sea Scrolls

Carbon-14 (C-14) decays exponentially with a half-life of approximately 5715 years, meaning that after 5715 years a given amount of C-14 will have decayed to half the original amount.

a. Find the exponential decay model for C-14.
b. In 1947 earthenware jars containing what are known as the Dead Sea Scrolls were found by an Arab Bedouin herdsman. Analysis indicated that the scroll wrappings contained 76% of their original C-14. Estimate the age of the Dead Sea Scrolls.

Shrine of the Book, a portion of the Dead Sea Scrolls. Robert Slosser / Israel Museum

Solution

a. We use the exponential decay model and the information about the half-life of C-14 to find k.

$$A = A_0 e^{kt}$$

This is the exponential decay model.

$$\frac{A_0}{2} = A_0 e^{k5715}$$

After 5715 years ($t = 5715$), $A = \frac{A_0}{2}$ (since the amount present (A) is half the original amount (A_0).)

$$\frac{1}{2} = e^{5715k}$$

Divide both sides of the equation by A_0.

$$\ln \frac{1}{2} = \ln e^{5715k}$$

Take the natural logarithm of both sides.

$$\ln \frac{1}{2} = 5715k$$

$\ln e^x = x$

$$k = \frac{\ln \frac{1}{2}}{5715} \approx -0.000121$$

Solve for k.

Substituting for k in the decay model, the model for C-14 is $A = A_0 e^{-0.000121t}$.

b.

$$A = A_0 e^{-0.000121t}$$

This is the decay model for C-14.

$$0.76A_0 = A_0 e^{-0.000121t}$$

A, the amount present, is 76% of the original amount, so $A = 0.76A_0$.

$$0.76 = e^{-0.000121t}$$

Divide both sides of the equation by A_0.

$$\ln 0.76 = \ln e^{-0.000121t}$$

Take the natural logarithm on both sides.

$$\ln 0.76 = -0.000121t$$

$\ln e^x = x$

$$t = \frac{\ln 0.76}{-0.000121} \approx 2268$$

Solve for t.

The Dead Sea Scrolls are approximately 2268 years old plus the number of years between 1947 and the current year. ∎

ENRICHMENT ESSAY

Carbon Dating and Artistic Development

Carbon dating is a method for estimating the age of organic material. Until recently, the oldest prehistoric cave paintings known were from the Lascaux cave in France. Charcoal from the site was analyzed, and the paintings were estimated to be 15,505 years old.

The artistic community was electrified by the discovery in 1995 of spectacular cave paintings in a limestone cavern near Lascaux. Carbon dating showed that the images, created by artists of remarkable talent, were 30,000 years old, making them the oldest cave paintings ever found. The artists seemed to have used the cavern's natural contours to heighten a sense of perspective. The quality of the painting suggests that the art of early humans did not mature steadily from primitive to sophisticated in any simple linear fashion.

Jean Clottes, France's foremost expert on prehistoric cave art, was moved by the sophisticated imagery of the 30,000-year-old work. "I remember standing in front of the paintings and being profoundly moved by the artistry," he exclaimed. "Tears were running down my cheeks. I was witnessing one of the world's great masterpieces."

Jean-Marie Chauvet / Sygma

---

2 Model cooling and heating times.

Alexis Rockman "Thaw" 1996. Envirotex, soil, oil & spray paint, glaciated gravel, modelling paste, clay, plaster bones, digitized photograph, plastic plants, plexiglas, kosher salt on two wood panels. 56 in. H × 88 in. W × 3.5 in. Courtesy of Jay Gorney Modern Art, New York. Photographer: Oren Slor, New York.

Modeling Cooling & Heating Times

Over a period of time, a cup of hot coffee cools to the temperature of the surrounding air. The rate of cooling of an object is proportional to the difference between the object's temperature and the temperature of the surrounding medium. The difference between the two temperatures decreases exponentially, given by

$$T = C + (T_0 - C)e^{-kt}$$

where t is the time it takes for an object to cool from an initial temperature T_0 to a temperature T, C is the temperature of the surrounding medium, and k is a positive constant that is associated with the cooling object. This model, called Newton's Law of Cooling, applies to warming as well. Earlier we encountered Newton's Law in which the formula was solved for t.

EXAMPLE 3 Using Newton's Law of Cooling

A cake removed from the oven has a temperature of 210°F and is left to cool in a room that has a temperature of 70°F. After 30 minutes the temperature of the cake is 140°F.

a. What is the temperature of the cake after 40 minutes?
b. When will the temperature of the cake be 90°F?
c. Illustrate the problem by using a graphing utility to sketch the temperature function.

Solution

a.
$$T = C + (T_0 - C)e^{-kt}$$

Use Newton's cooling model. Our first step will be to determine k.

$$140 = 70 + (210 - 70)e^{-k(30)}$$

Since the cake's temperature after 30 minutes is 140°F, $T = 140$, $C = 70$ (room temperature), $T_0 = 210$ (initial temperature), and $t = 30$ (30 minutes to cool to 140°F).

$$70 = 140e^{-30k}$$

First isolate the exponential term by substracting 70 from both sides.

$$0.5 = e^{-30k}$$

Now divide both sides by 140. The exponential term is isolated.

$$\ln 0.5 = \ln e^{-30k}$$

Take the natural logarithm on both sides.

$$\ln 0.5 = -30k$$

$\ln e^x = x$

$$\frac{\ln 0.5}{-30} = k$$

Solve for k.

Now we substitute this value for k into Newton's formula.

$$T = C + (T_0 - C)e^{-kt}$$

Once again, this is Newton's cooling model.

$$T = 70 + (210 - 70)e^{-\left(\frac{\ln 0.5}{-30}\right)t}$$

$C = 70$ (room temperature), $T_0 = 210$ (cake's initial temperature), and $k = \dfrac{\ln 0.5}{-30}$ (from above).

$$= 70 + (210 - 70)e^{\frac{\ln 0.5}{30}t}$$

We can now answer the question and determine the cake's temperature after 40 minutes.

$$T = 70 + (210 - 70)e^{\frac{\ln 0.5}{30}(40)}$$

Substitute 40 for t.

$$\approx 126$$

Use a calculator.

After 40 minutes the temperature of the cake will be approximately 126°F.

b. The temperature of the cake will be 90°F when

$$70 + (210 - 70)e^{\frac{\ln 0.5}{30}t} = 90$$

Substitute 90 for T in the model and solve for t (time).

$$140e^{\frac{\ln 0.5}{30}t} = 20$$

Once again, isolate the exponential term. Subtract 70 from both sides.

$$e^{\frac{\ln 0.5}{30}t} = \frac{1}{7}$$

Divide both sides by 140. The exponential term is isolated.

$$\ln e^{\frac{\ln 0.5}{30}t} = \ln \frac{1}{7}$$

Take the natural logarithm on both sides.

$$\frac{\ln 0.5}{30}t = \ln \frac{1}{7}$$

$\ln e^x = x$

$$t = \frac{\ln \dfrac{1}{7}}{\dfrac{\ln 0.5}{30}}$$

Divide both sides by $\dfrac{\ln 0.5}{30}$.

$$\approx 84$$

Use a calculator.

Figure 4.38

The graph of the cake's cooling model using a [0, 120] by [0, 250] viewing rectangle and Xscl = 12, Yscl = 25

3 Fit exponential functions to data.

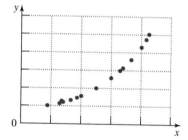

Figure 4.39

Data points suggest an exponential model.

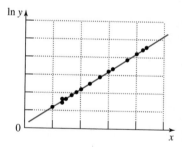

Figure 4.40

Data points suggest a linear model.

The temperature of the cake will be 90°F after approximately 84 minutes.

c. Figure 4.38 shows the graph of the cooling model, entered as

$$Y_1 = 70 + 140e\char94((\ln 0.5)\,X/30).$$

Also graphed is $y_2 = 70$, which serves as a horizontal asymptote. Why is $y = 70$ the horizontal asymptote? ∎

Fitting Exponential Functions to Data

Throughout this chapter, we have been working with models that were given. However, we can create models that fit data by observing patterns in the graph of the data points.

For example, the data in Figure 4.39 suggest that we model it with an exponential function. Since $\ln e^y = y$, if ordered pairs (x, y) lie on an exponential curve, then the ordered pairs $(x, \ln y)$ will lie on a straight line. This is shown in Figure 4.40, where we transformed the data in Figure 4.39 by taking the natural logarithm of each y value.

These observations give us a procedure for fitting exponential functions to data such as the points shown in Figure 4.39.

> ### Modeling with exponential functions
>
> **1.** Represent all data points using (x, y).
> **2.** Take the natural logarithm of each y-coordinate.
> **3.** Write an equation of the line that best fits the data points $(x, \ln y)$. The equation for this line, called the regression line, can be obtained with a graphing utility.
> **4.** Since exponential and logarithmic functions are inverses, then $e^{\ln y} = y$. Use this relationship to find y by taking the equation in step 3 and writing each side as an exponent with base e.

EXAMPLE 4 Fitting an Exponential Model to Data

The data below indicate world population (in billions) for five years.

Year	World Population (in billions)
1950	2.6
1960	3.1
1970	3.7
1980	4.5
1989	5.3

Find a model for the data. Then use the model to predict world population in the year 2020.

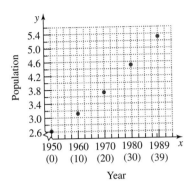

Figure 4.41

The graph of world population over time suggests an exponential model.

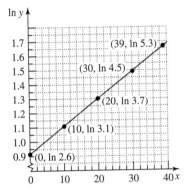

Figure 4.42

Data points suggest a linear model.

Solution

The graph of the five data points in Figure 4.41 has a shape that suggests modeling with an exponential function.

Letting $x = 0$ represent 1950, we transform the points by taking the natural logarithm of each y-coordinate.

Year (x)	World Population y	ln y
1950 (0)	2.6	0.9555
1960 (10)	3.1	1.1314
1970 (20)	3.7	1.3083
1980 (30)	4.5	1.5041
1989 (39)	5.3	1.6677

The five points for $(x, \ln y)$ suggest using a linear model, as shown in Figure 4.42. Using the linear regression option on a graphing utility, the equation of the line that best fits the $(x, \ln y)$ transformed data is

$$\ln y = 0.0183x + 0.9504.$$

Since we are interested in a model with y on the left, we use the property for inverse functions

$$e^{\ln y} = y$$

and write both sides of the equation as an exponent on base e.

$$e^{\ln y} = e^{0.0183x + 0.9504}$$

$$e^{\ln y} = e^{0.0183x} \cdot e^{0.9504} \qquad b^{M+N} = b^M \cdot b^N$$

$$y = e^{0.0183x} \cdot 2.5867 \qquad e^{\ln y} = y. \text{ Use a calculator to approximate } e^{0.9504}.$$

$$= 2.5867e^{0.0183x} \qquad \text{Apply the commutative property on the right.}$$

The exponential model that fits the given data is

$$y = 2.5867e^{0.0183x}.$$

Since we often use t as the variable standing for time, we can equivalently write the model as

$$y = 2.5867e^{0.0183t} \quad \text{or} \quad f(t) = 2.5867e^{0.0183t}.$$

We are now ready to use the model to predict population in the year 2020.

$$f(t) = 2.5867e^{0.0183t} \qquad \text{This is one of the forms of the model obtained from above.}$$

$$f(70) = 2.5867e^{0.0183(70)} \qquad \text{The year 2020 is 70 years after 1950, so substitute 70 for } t.$$

$$\approx 9.3 \qquad \text{Use a calculator.}$$

Using the model that we constructed from the data, predicted world population in the year 2020 is approximately 9.3 billion. ∎

4 Fit logarithmic functions to data.

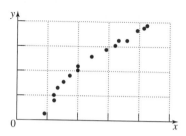

Figure 4.43

Data points suggest a logarithmic model.

Fitting Logarithmic Functions to Data

Suppose that the data we are attempting to model falls into a pattern like the one in Figure 4.43. The graph is increasing, although increasing at a slower and slower rate, but does not seem to be leveling out to approach a horizontal asymptote. The shape suggests a logarithmic function, so we will attempt to model the data with such a curve. We can fit a logarithmic model to a set of points of the form (x, y) by fitting a linear model to points of the form $(\ln x, y)$. This idea is illustrated in our next example.

EXAMPLE 5   **Fitting a Logarithmic Model to Data**

Earlier in the chapter we encountered a model relating the size of a city with the average walking speed, in feet per second, of pedestrians. A study collected the following data.

Population (in thousands)	Walking Speed (in feet per second)
5.5	3.3
14	3.7
71	4.3
138	4.4
342	4.8

Source: Mark and Helen Bornstein, "The Pace of Life," *Nature*, 259 (19 Feb. 1976) 557–559

Find a model that fits the given data.

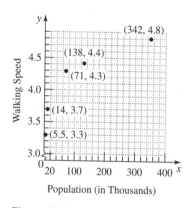

Figure 4.44

The graph of walking speed as a function of population suggests a logarithmic model.

Solution

The graph of the five data points in Figure 4.44 has a shape that suggests modeling the data with a logarithmic function. Represent each data value by (x, y) and transform the points by taking the natural logarithm of each x coordinate.

x	$\ln x$	y
5.5	1.7047	3.3
14	2.6391	3.7
71	4.2627	4.3
138	4.9273	4.4
342	5.8348	4.8

The five points for $(\ln x, y)$ are graphed in Figure 4.45. The points approximately fall along a line, suggesting a linear model.

Using the linear regression option on a graphing utility, the equation of the regression line that models the transformed $(\ln x, y)$ data is

$$y = 0.3525 \ln x + 2.735.$$

This is the logarithmic model that fits the data. Compare this model with the one in Example 5 on pages 458–459.

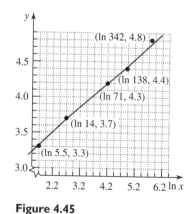

Figure 4.45

Data points suggest a linear model.

Study tip

If any data values fall approximately along a line, the equation of the regression line (or the line of best fit) can be obtained without a graphing utility using the following formulas.

Regression Line: $y = mx + b$

$$m = \frac{n(\sum xy) - (\sum x)(\sum y)}{n(\sum x^2) - (\sum x)^2}$$

$$b = \frac{(\sum y)(\sum x^2) - (\sum x)(\sum xy)}{n(\sum x^2) - (\sum x)^2}$$

where

n = the number of data points (x, y)

$\sum x$ = the sum of the x-values

$\sum y$ = the sum of the y-values

$\sum (xy)$ = the sum of the product of x and y in each pair

$\sum x^2$ = the sum of the squares of the x-values

$(\sum x)^2$ = the square of the sum of the x-values

Summary of curve-fitting procedures

1. If a graph of the data points appears to follow an exponential pattern, fit an exponential model to the set of points of the form (x, y) by fitting a *linear* model to points of the form $(x, \ln y)$. Write the equation of the regression line for $(x, \ln y)$ and then exponentiate both sides to find the model for the data points (x, y).
2. If a graph of the data points appears to follow a logarithmic model, fit a logarithmic model to the set of points of the form (x, y) by fitting a *linear* model to points of the form $(\ln x, y)$. The model for the data points (x, y) is the equation of the regression line for $(\ln x, y)$.

Using technology

Using the statistical menu of a graphing utility, you can immediately draw data points as coordinates. The resulting drawing is called a *scatter plot* of the data. The shape of the scatter plot determines what sort of function best fits the data. Using a graphing utility, it is not necessary to first linearize the data and write an equation for a regression line. Instead, you can use the utility's EXPonential REGression option ($y = ab^x$) to fit exponential functions to data, or its logarithmic regression (LnReg) option ($y = a + b \ln x$) to fit logarithmic functions to data. By telling your graphing utility the regression option you want to use to model the data, the utility will print the equation of the function for you.

Use your graphing utility's exponential regression option to model the data in Example 4 and its logarithmic regression option to model the data in Example 5.

In this era of technology, since graphing utilities have capabilities that fit linear and nonlinear functions to data, the process of creating mathematical models involves decision-making more than computation.

> $\mathcal{S}$**tudy tip**
>
> When using a graphing utility to model data, first draw a scatter diagram to obtain a general picture for the shape of the data. If necessary, fit several models to the data. The number r that appears with each model is called the *correlation coefficient* and is a measure of how well the model fits the data. The value of r is such that $0 \leqslant |r| \leqslant 1$. The best model is the one which yields the value r for which $|r|$ is closest to 1.

PROBLEM SET 4.5

Practice and Application Problems

Use the exponential growth and decay model $A = A_0 e^{kt}$, where A_0 is the original amount (or size) of a growing (or decaying) entity at $t = 0$, A is the amount at time t, and k is a growth $(k > 0)$ or decay $(k < 0)$ constant to answer Problems 1–5.

1. Through the end of 1991, 200,000 cases of AIDS in the United States had been reported to the Center for Disease Control. By the end of 1995, the number had grown to 513,000. Let $t = 0$ correspond to the year 1991.

   a. Since 1991 corresponds to $t = 0$, at that time there were 200,000 cases. This means that A_0, the original number in the growth model, is 200,000. Now use the fact that there were 513,000 cases by 1995 (when $t = 4$, $A = 513,000$) to find k, the growth rate or the growth constant.

   b. Substitute the values for A_0 and k into the exponential growth model and write the function that models the data.

   c. Using this model, in what year will the cumulative number of AIDS cases in the United States reach one million?

   d. The model in this problem and your answer in part (c) is based on uninhibited exponential growth. Is this a realistic assumption?

   e. The World Health Organization makes predictions about the number of AIDS cases based on a compromise between a conservative linear model and an uninhibited exponential growth model. Use the data in this problem, shown again in the table, to write the point-slope formula and the slope-intercept formula for the line modeling the data. Then use your linear model to predict the year in which the cumulative number of AIDS cases will reach one million.

x (Years after 1991)	y (Cumulative Reported AIDS Cases)
0	200,000
4	513,000

   f. What year would be a good compromise between the predictions made by the exponential and the linear models to determine when the number of AIDS cases in the United States will reach one million?

Frank Moore "Hospital" 1992, oil on wood with frame and attachments, 49 × 58 in. (124.5 × 147.3 cm) SW 92637. Private Collection. Courtesy Sperone Westerwater, New York.

2. The 1940 population of New York was 13,479,142 and in 1950 the population was 14,830,192. Let $t = 0$ correspond to the year 1940.

   a. Since 1940 corresponds to $t = 0$, at that time there were 13,479,142 people in New York. This means that A_0, the original amount in the growth model, is 13,479,142. Now use the fact that there were 14,830,192 people in 1950 (when $t = 10$, $A = 14,830,192$) to find k, the growth rate for New York during this decade.

   b. Substitute the values for A_0 and k into the exponential growth model and write the function that models New York's population t years after 1940.

   c. Use the model in part (c) to determine New York's 1994 population ($t = 54$) if the growth rate from 1940 through 1950 had remained in effect from 1940 through 1994. How does this compare with the actual 1994 population of 18,169,000?

   d. What are some of the factors that might account for the difference between the number predicted by the exponential growth model and the actual population?

3. Strontium-90 is a waste product from nuclear fission reactors. Its half-life is 28 years.

   a. Show that the decay model for strontiun-90 is $A = A_0e^{-0.024755t}$.

   b. Strontium-90 in the atmosphere enters the food chain and is absorbed into our bones. As a consequence of fallout from atmospheric nuclear tests, we all have a measurable amount of strontium-90 in our bones. Suppose a nuclear accident occurs and releases 60 grams of strontium-90 into the biosphere. How long will it take for strontium-90 to decay to a level of 10 grams?

   c. Graph (by hand or with a graphing utility) the model in part (a) with $A_0 = 60$ for $0 \le t \le 112$ and $0 \le A \le 60$. Show the solution of part (b) on the graph.

4. The August 1978 issue of *National Geographic* described the 1964 find of dinosaur bones of a newly discovered dinosaur weighing 170 pounds, measuring 9 feet, and having a 6-inch claw on one toe of each hind foot. The age of the dinosaur, called *Deinonychus* ("terrible claw"),was estimated using potassium-40 dating of rocks surrounding the bones.

   a. Potassium-40 decays exponentially with a half-life of approximately 1.31 billion years, meaning that after 1.31 billion years a given amount of potassium-40 will have decayed to half the original amount. Use this information to show that the decay model for potassium-40 is given by $A = A_0e^{-0.52912t}$, where t is given in billions of years.

   b. Analysis of the surrounding rock indicated that 94.5% of the original amount of potassium-40 was still present. Let $A = 0.945A_0$ in the model in part (a) and estimate the age of the bones of *Deinonychus*.

5. A bird species in danger of extinction has a population that is decreasing exponentially ($A = A_0e^{kt}$). Five years ago the population was at 1400 and today only 1000 of the birds are still alive. Once the population drops below 100, the situation will be irreversible. When will this happen?

Use Newton's model $T = C + (T_0 - C)e^{-kt}$, where t is the time it takes for an object to cool from an initial temperature T_0 to a temperature T, C is the temperature of the surrounding medium, and k is a positive constant that is associated with the cooling object, to answer Problems 6–7.

6. A bottle of juice has a temperature of 70°F and is left to cool in a refrigerator that has a temperature of 45°F. After 10 minutes, the temperature of the juice is 55°F.

   a. What is the temperature of the juice after 15 minutes?

   b. When will the temperature of the juice be 50°F?

   c. Illustrate the problem by using a graphing utility to sketch the temperature function. According to the graph, will the temperature of the juice ever reach 45°F? Explain.

7. A pie removed from the oven has a temperature of 375°F and is left to cool in a room that has a temperature of 72°F. After 60 minutes, the temperature of the pie is 75°F.

   a. What is the temperature of the pie after 30 minutes?

   b. When will the temperature of the pie be 250°F?

   c. Illustrate the problem by using a graphing utility to sketch the temperature function. According to the graph, will the temperature of the pie ever reach 72°F? Explain.

8. The intensity of light entering water is reduced according to the model $I = I_0e^{-kd}$, where I is the intensity at a depth of d feet, I_0 is the intensity at the surface, and k is a constant called the *constant of extinction*. In a body of water, half the surface light remained at a depth of 26 feet. Find the depth at which 10% of the surface light remains.

Suppose a set of data in the form (x, y) is graphed as a set of points. The resulting shape of the graph suggests modeling with an exponential function. The natural logarithm of each y-coordinate is taken and an equation of the line that best fits the data *points $(x, \ln y)$ is obtained. The equation of this line is given in Problems 9–10. Write each side of the equation as an exponent with base e, simplify, and find the exponential function that fits the original data.*

9. $\ln y = 0.3782 + 1.0745x$

10. $\ln y = -1.2074 + 0.873x$

11. The amount of carbon dioxide (CO_2) in the atmosphere has increased by over 25% of its original amount since 1900, as a result of the burning of oil and coal. The burning of these fossil fuels results in a buildup of gases and particles that can trap heat and raise the planet's temperature. The resultant gradually increasing temperature is called the greenhouse effect. Carbon dioxide accounts for about half of the warming.

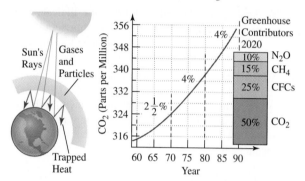

The data below shows the average CO_2 concentration in parts per million (ppm) x years after 1900.

x (Year)	y (Average CO_2 Concentration in ppm)
1900 (0)	280
1950 (50)	310
1975 (75)	331
1980 (80)	338
1988 (88)	351

a. Take the natural logarithm of each y-value.

b. Graph the five data points $(x, \ln y)$. Notice that the points lie nearly on a straight line, suggesting the use of a linear model.

c. Use the linear regression option on a graphing utility or the procedure outlined in the Study Tip on page 501 to write the equation of the line that best fits the $(x, \ln y)$ transformed data.

d. Write both sides of the equation in part (c) as exponents on base e. Simplify and obtain a model for

CO_2 concentration in parts per million x years after 1900.

e. Use your model from part (d) to estimate when the CO_2 concentration might reach 600 ppm. (This would be approximately double the level estimated to exist prior to the Industrial Revolution.)

12. The data below shows the national debt in billions of dollars x years after 1980.

Year x	Debt: y
1980 (0)	907.7
1981 (1)	997.9
1982 (2)	1142.0
1983 (3)	1377.2
1984 (4)	1572.3
1985 (5)	1823.1
1986 (6)	2153.3
1987 (7)	2350.3
1988 (8)	2602.3
1989 (9)	2857.4
1990 (10)	3233.3
1991 (11)	3502.0
1992 (12)	4002.1
1993 (13)	4351.4
1994 (14)	4643.7
1995 (15)	4961.5

a. Take the natural logarithm of each y-value.

b. Graph the 16 data points $(x, \ln y)$. Notice that the points lie nearly on a straight line, suggesting the use of a linear model.

c. Use the linear regression option on a graphing utility or the procedure outlined in the Study Tip on page 501 to write the equation of the line that best fits the $(x, \ln y)$ transformed data.

d. Write both sides of the equation in part (c) as exponents on base e. Simplify and obtain a model for the national debt x years after 1980.

e. Use your model from part (d) to predict the national debt in the year 2000.

13. In a study entitled "Reaction Time and Speed of Movement of Males and Females of Various Ages,"

(*Research Quarterly:* American Assocation of Health and Physical Education and Recreation, 1963), the following data appeared.

x (Age)	19	27	45	60
y (Reflex Time, in seconds)	0.18	0.20	0.23	0.25

a. Graph the four data points. What function might reasonably model the data?

b. Take the natural logarithm of each *x*-value and graph the four data points (ln *x*, *y*). Notice that the points lie nearly on a straight line, suggesting the use of a linear model.

c. Use the linear regression option on a graphing utility or the procedure outlined in the Study Tip on page 501 to find the logarithmic model for the given data.

d. Use the model from part (c) to predict the reflex time for a 75-year-old.

14. The space shuttle *Challenger* exploded approximately 73 seconds into flight on January 28, 1986. The tragedy involved O-rings used to seal the connections between different sections of the shuttle engines. The data below indicate Fahrenheit temperature and the number of damaged O-rings during 26 space shuttle flights.

x Temperature	y (Number of Damaged O-rings)	x Temperature	y (Number of Damaged O-rings)
53	3	70	0
57	1	70	0
58	1	72	0
63	1	73	0
66	0	75	2
67	0	75	0
67	0	76	0
67	0	76	0
68	0	78	0
69	0	79	0
70	1	80	0
70	1	81	0

Find a logarithmic model for the data. Then use the model to predict the number of O-ring problems on the morning the *Challenger* was launched, when the temperature was 31°F.

UPI / Vince Mannino / Corbis–Bettmann

The following table gives the number of deaths from AIDS in the United States for men and for women from 1988 through 1993.

Year	1988	1989	1990	1991	1992	1993
AIDS Deaths among Men	17,947	23,742	26,752	30,725	34,072	35,551
AIDS Deaths among Women	2050	2613	3182	3926	4741	5526

Source: U.S. Center for Disease Control

Use this data to answer Problems 15–16.

15. In order to avoid ln 0, let *x* represent the number of years after 1987 and let *y* represent AIDS deaths among men. Model the data with a linear model, an exponential model, and a logarithmic model. If the actual number of AIDS deaths among men for 1994 was 37,360, which of the three models most accurately makes this prediction?

16. Let *x* represent the number of years after 1987 and let *y* represent AIDS deaths among women. Model the data with a linear model, an exponential model, and a logarithmic model. If the actual number of AIDS deaths among women for 1994 was 6615, which of the three models most accurately makes this prediction?

17. The following table gives per capita health-care expenditures (in dollars) in the United States from 1988 through 1993.

Year	1988	1989	1990	1991	1992	1993
Per Capita Health-care Expenditures	2201	2422	2688	2902	3144	3331

Source: U.S. Health-Care Financing Administration

Let *x* represent the number of years after 1987 and let *y* represent per capita health-care expenditures. Model the data with a linear model, an exponential model, and a logarithmic model. If the actual per capita health-care expenditures for 1994 were $3510, which of the three models most accurately makes this prediction?

We have seen that a logarithmic model can be fitted to a set of data points of the form (x, y) by fitting a linear model to points of the form (ln x, y). However, if x = 0, a problem occurs because ln 0 is undefined. We can avoid this problem by increasing each value of x by 1, fitting a linear model to points of the form (ln (x + 1), y). Use this approach to solve Problem 18.

18. Students in a psychology class were given a final examination. As part of an experiment to see how much of the course content they remembered over time, they took equivalent forms of the exam in monthly intervals thereafter. The average score for the group (y) after x months is given by the following data.

x (Month)	0	1	2	3	4	5	6	7
y (Average Score)	88	78	72	67	64	61	59	57

Find a model for the data in the form

$$y = a + b \ln (x + 1).$$

Use the model to predict the avervage score for months 8 through 12.

True–False Critical Thinking Problems

19. A hot object is left to cool in a room. The graph of the cooling model is shown in the figure below. Time (t) is measured in minutes and temperature (T) is measured in degrees Celsius. Which one of the following is true based on the information conveyed by the graph?

  a. The temperature of the hot object was 20° Celsius when it was first left to cool in the room.

  b. After 15 minutes, the object has cooled to approximately 27° Celsius.

  c. The room is kept at 10° Celsius.

  d. The object will cool down to 21° Celsius after about 27 minutes.

20. Which one of the following is true?

  a. The data points (1, 2), (2, 3), (3, 3.5), (4, 4), (5, 4.1), (6, 4.2), and (7, 4.4) should be modeled using an exponential function.

  b. The data points (1, 4.4), (1.5, 4.7), (2, 5.5), (4, 9.9), (6, 18.1), and (8, 34) should be modeled using a logarithmic function.

  c. The points shown in the figure can be modeled by an exponential function, taking the set of points of the form (x, y) and fitting a linear model to points of the form (ln x, ln y).

  d. The points shown in the figure can be modeled by a logarithmic function, taking the set of points of the form (x, y) and fitting a linear model to points of the form (ln x, y).

Technology Problems

21. Use a graphing utility to solve Problem 11. In particular:

   a. Draw a scatter diagram for the data.

   b. Use the exponential regression option to fit an exponential model to the data.

   c. Use the utility to graph the model from part (b).

   d. Trace along the curve and estimate when the concentration might reach 600 ppm.

22. Use a graphing utility to solve Problem 12. In particular:

   a. Draw a scatter diagram for the data.

   b. Use the exponential regression option to fit an exponential model to the data.

   c. Use the utility to graph the model from part (b).

   d. Trace along the curve and estimate the national debt in the year 2000.

23. Use a graphing utility to solve Problem 13. In particular:

   a. Draw a scatter diagram for the data.

   b. Use the logarithmic regression option to fit a logarithmic model to the data.

   c. Use the utility to graph the model from part (b).

   d. Trace along the curve and estimate the reflex time for a 75-year-old.

24. Use a graphing utility to solve Problem 14. In particular:

   a. Draw a scatter diagram for the data.

   b. Use the logarithmic regression option to fit a logarithmic model to the data.

   c. Use the utility to graph the model from part (b).

   d. Trace along the curve and predict the number of damaged O-rings on the morning the *Challenger* was launched, when the temperature was 31°F.

25. Use a graphing utility to solve Problem 15. In particular:

   a. Draw a scatter diagram for the data.

   b. Use the linear, exponential, and logarithmic regression options to fit a linear model, an exponential model, and a logarithmic model to the data.

   c. The number r that appears measures how good the fit is. The closer $|r|$ is to 1, the better the fit. What is the best model for AIDS deaths among men over time? How closely does this model predict the actual number of 37,360 deaths in 1994?.

26. Use a graphing utility to solve Problem 16. In particular:

   a. Draw a scatter diagram for the data.

   b. Use the linear, exponential, and logarithmic regression options to fit a linear model, an exponential model, and a logarithmic model to the data.

   c. The number r that appears measures how good the fit is. The closer $|r|$ is to 1, the better the fit. What is the best model for AIDS deaths among women over time? How closely does this model predict the actual number of 6615 deaths in 1994?

27. Use a graphing utility to solve Problem 17. In particular:

   a. Draw a scatter diagram for the data.

   b. Use the linear, exponential, and logarithmic regression options to fit a linear model, an exponential model, and a logarithmic model to the data.

   c. The number r that appears measures how good the fit is. The closer $|r|$ is to 1, the better the fit. What is the best model for per capita health-care expenditures over time? How closely does this model predict the per capita health-care expenditures for 1994, which was $3510?

28. The following table shows the gross federal debt (money borrowed by the Treasury and by various federal agencies) from 1980 through 1995.

Year	Gross Federal Debt (in millions)
1980	909,050
1981	994,845
1982	1,137,345
1983	1,371,710
1984	1,564,657
1985	1,817,521
1986	2,120,629
1987	2,346,125
1988	2,601,307
1989	2,868,039
1990	3,206,564
1991	3,598,498
1992	4,002,136
1993	4,351,416
1994	4,643,711
1995	4,921,025

Source: U.S. Office of Management and Budget

   a. Use a graphing utility to draw a scatter diagram for the data, with values of x representing the number of years after 1979 and values of y representing federal debt.

   b. Use the linear, exponential, and logarithmic regression options to fit a linear model, an exponential model, and a logarithmic model to the data.

   c. Use the model with the value of r closest to 1 as the model of best fit. How well does this model predict the 1996 debt of $5,207,298 million?

Writing in Mathematics

29. Describe some of the decisions that must be made in modeling data.

30. Suppose that $(60, 250)$ and $(70, 300)$ are two points for a set of data that can be modeled exponentially. Explain why $(65, 400)$ cannot be a data point in the scatter plot.

31. What does the model in Example 5 on page 500 imply about urban growth and stress?

32. The strength of a habit H is a function of the number of times the habit is repeated N, modeled by $H = 1000(1 - e^{-kN})$. Suppose that an ordered pair (H, N) is known and that you want to predict habit strength for another value of N. Describe how you would do this using the given model.

33. Describe how you would create a mathematical model to fit the data in the graph.

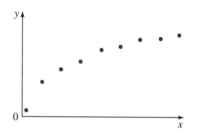

Group Activity Problem

34. Group members should consult the current edition of *The World Almanac* or an equivalent reference. Select data that is of interest to the group that can be modeled with an exponential or logarithmic function. Model the data. Each group member should make one prediction based on the model, and then discuss a consequence of this prediction. What factors might change the accuracy of each prediction?

CHAPTER PROJECT

Helices and Spirals

Although there are numerous types of spirals mathematicians study, we commonly find the Archimedian spiral and the logarithmic spiral around us. An Archimedian spiral resembles the shape of a tightly coiled rope neatly laid out on a dock. We find the distinctive shape of a logarithmic spiral in nature. This is the spiral we see in the cut-a-way view of a nautilus shell. If we pull a spiral up, out of a two-dimensional flat plane and into three dimensions, we have a helix. We see the rising form of a helix in the double-helix of a DNA molecule and the swirl of an antelope's horns. Mathematically speaking, the twisting staircase known as a "spiral" staircase is actually a helix.

To understand why a spiral is referred to as "logarithmic" we need to see the equation of the spiral written in a *polar* coordinate system. In this coordinate system, the equation would be written as

$$\ln r = a\theta$$

where r is a radial length measured out from the origin (pole), a is a constant, and θ is an angle measure. The angle needs to be measured not in degrees, but in *radians*, a real number.

One radian is approximately 57 degrees. The logarithmic spiral is also referred to as the *equiangular* spiral because a line radiating outward from the origin of the spiral always intersects the spiral at the same angle.

1. In modern times, we usually solve for r and rewrite the logarithmic equation $\ln r = a\theta$ in exponential form. What is the equation in exponential form?
2. One simple way to see the difference between an Archimedian and logarithmic spiral is to create a pair of them by folding paper. Take two long strips of paper and mark off measurements in the following way:
  • For the Archimedian spiral, mark off a distance measuring one inch in length. Place the next mark after measuring two inches in length, then mark off three inches, and so on.

- For the logarithmic spiral, mark off inches measured by using the sequence of numbers 1, 1, 2, 3, 5, 8, 13, 21. Thus, the first mark is made at one inch, the second mark is placed after measuring another inch, the third mark is made after measuring two inches further, and so on.
- Bend each strip of paper in a right angle at the mark and study the curves.

3. As an experiment, draw some spirals on a piece of paper, as if you were doodling. Switch hands and draw a few more. How do the two sets of spirals compare? Are they turning in the same direction? How does the distance between the coils compare? Which style of spiral discussed do your sketches resemble?

4. Use a cardboard cylinder from a paper towel roll to investigate a helical curve on the surface of a cylinder. Cut open the cylinder, and lay it out flat. Using a protractor, measure the angle made by the spiral on different levels of the flattened cylinder. What do you observe? Wrap a piece of wire around the cylinder, following the original outline of the helix. Take the wire off and press it flat to the table. What kind of spiral do you see?

5. You can reverse the procedure in the above problem to create the double helix of a DNA molecule. Begin with the flattened cylinder and draw another set of lines duplicating the lines already on the cylinder, but slanted in the opposite direction. When the cylinder is closed, you will see the distinct form of the double helix.

   Compare the spiral on the paper core to the spirals found on different styles of common screws. What do you observe? Notice that some screws are basically cylindrical and others are conical in shape. How does this affect the helix you observe? Make your own versions by wrapping wire around two forms, one cone and one cylinder, and compare the shapes. Florist shops and craft stores sell many varieties of forms and wire suitable for this experiment. Using resources in the library or on the Worldwide Web, find out what is meant by an *Archimedian water screw*.

7. The logarithmic spiral may be drawn by geometric means using a Golden Rectangle. This rectangle is discussed in Problem 43 on page 157. Using resources in the library or on the Worldwide Web, discover how to create a logarithmic spiral by geometric construction. After completing the drawing, use a protractor to check for the equal angle property of the spiral. What effect does the initial size of the Golden Rectangle have on the logarithmic spiral?

Worldwide Web Resources

Go to the Prentice Hall website (http://www.prenhall.com/blitzer) to access other locations on the Internet that will allow you to further explore the concepts presented in this project.

Chapter Review

SUMMARY

1. **Exponential Functions**

   a. The exponential function f with base b is defined by $f(x) = b^x$, where $b > 0$ and $b \neq 1$.

   b. Graphs for $f(x) = b^x$ are shown on the right and on the next page.

   Graph of $f(x) = b^x, b > 1$
   - Domain: $(-\infty, \infty)$
   - Range: $(0, \infty)$
   - y-Intercept: 1

- Increasing
- Horizontal asymptote: x-axis

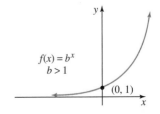

Graph of $f(x) = b^x$, $0 < b < 1$

- Domain: $(-\infty, \infty)$

- Range: $(0, \infty)$

- y-Intercept: 1

- Decreasing

- Horizontal asymptote: x-axis

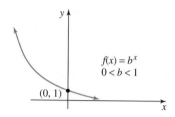

c. Transformations Involving Exponential Functions

1. *Horizontal Translation:* $y = b^{x+c}$ shifts $y = b^x$ to the left c units if $c > 0$ and to the right c units if $c < 0$.

2. *Stretching or Shrinking:* $y = cb^x$ stretches $y = b^x$ for $c > 1$ and shrinks $y = b^x$ for $0 < c < 1$.

3. *Reflecting:* $y = -b^x$ reflects $y = b^x$ in the x-axis and $y = b^{-x}$ reflects $y = b^x$ in the y-axis.

4. *Vertical Translation:* $y = b^x + c$ shifts $y = b^x$ upward c units if $c > 0$ and downward c units if $c < 0$.

d. The Natural Exponential Function: $f(x) = e^x$
The irrational number e is called the natural base, where $e \approx 2.7183$.

2. **Formulas for Compound Interest**
After t years, the balance A in an account with principal P and annual interest rate r (in decimal form) is given by the following mathematical models.

a. For n compoundings per year: $A = P\left(1 + \frac{r}{n}\right)^{nt}$

b. For continuous compounding: $A = Pe^{rt}$

3. **Growth and Decay Models**

a. *Exponential Growth:* $A = A_0 e^{kt}$, $k > 0$

b. *Exponential Decay:* $A = A_0 e^{kt}$, $k < 0$. In both models, t represents time, A_0 is the amount present at $t = 0$, and A is the amount present at time t.

4. **Logarithmic Functions**

a. $y = \log_b x$ is equivalent to $b^y = x$ where $x > 0$, $b > 0$, and $b \neq 1$. The function $f(x) = \log_b x$ is the logarith-

mic function with base b. Thus, a logarithm is an exponent.

b. $y = b^x$ and $y = \log_b x$ are inverses. Thus if $f(x) = b^x$, then $f^{-1}(x) = \log_b x$.

c. The graphs of $f(x) = b^x$ and $f^{-1}(x) = \log_b x$ are shown below (with $b > 1$).

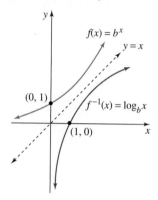

For $f(x) = b^x$:

Domain $= (-\infty, \infty)$ and range $= (0, \infty)$

As $x \to -\infty$, $b^x \to 0$.

The x-axis is a horizontal asymptote.

For $f^{-1}(x) = \log_b x$:

Domain $= (0, \infty)$ and range $= (-\infty, \infty)$

As $x \to 0^+$, $\log_b x \to -\infty$.

The y-axis is a vertical asymptote.

d. *Transformations Involving Logarithmic Functions:*
The graph of $y = \log_b(x + a) + c$, with $a > 0$ and $c > 0$, lies a units to the left and c units above the graph of $y = \log_b x$. The domain of $f(x) = \log_b(x + a) + c$ consists of all x for which $x + a > 0$. The vertical asymptote is $x = -a$.

e. *Common and Natural Logarithms:*
$y = \log x$ means $y = \log_{10} x$ and is called the common logarithmic function. $y = \ln x$ means $y = \log_e x$ and is called the natural logarithmic function. If $f(x) = 10^x$, then $f^{-1}(x) = \log x$. If $f(x) = e^x$, then $f^{-1}(x) = \ln x$.

5. **Properties of Logarithmic Functions**

a. *Basic Properties:*

Base b ($b > 0$, $b \neq 1$)	Base 10 (Common Logarithms)	Base e (Natural Logarithms)
$\log_b 1 = 0$	$\log 1 = 0$	$\ln 1 = 0$
$\log_b b = 1$	$\log 10 = 1$	$\ln e = 1$
$\log_b b^x = x$	$\log 10^x = x$	$\ln e^x = x$

b. *The Product Rule:* $\log_b(MN) = \log_b M + \log_b N$

c. *The Quotient Rule:* $\log_b\left(\dfrac{M}{N}\right) = \log_b M - \log_b N$

d. *The Power Rule:* $\log_b M^p = p\log_b M$

e. *The Inverse Properties:*

Base b	Base 10	Base e
$b^{\log_b x} = x$	$10^{\log x} = x$	$e^{\ln x} = x$
$\log_b b^x = x$	$\log 10^x = x$	$\ln e^x = x$

f. *The Change-of Base Property:*

The General Property	Introducing Common Logarithms	Introducing Natural Logarithms
$\log_b M = \dfrac{\log_a M}{\log_a b}$	$\log_b M = \dfrac{\log M}{\log b}$	$\log_b M = \dfrac{\ln M}{\ln b}$

6. Exponential Equations

a. Exponential equations contain a variable in an exponent.

b. To solve an exponential equation:
1. Isolate the exponential expression.
2. Take the natural logarithm on both sides of the equation.
3. Simplify using one of the following properties:
$$\ln b^x = x\ln b \quad \text{or} \quad \ln e^x = x$$
4. Solve for the variable.

7. Logarithmic Equations

a. Logarithmic equations contain a variable in a logarithmic expression.

b. Equations containing logarithmic expressions and nonlogarithmic constants can be solved by using properties of logarithms to write the equation in the form $\log_b M = N$ and then solving $b^N = M$ for the desired variable.

c. Equations containing only logarithmic expressions can be solved by using properties of logarithms to write the equation in the form $\log_b M = \log_b N$ and then setting $M = N$.

d. Be sure to reject values that produce the logarithm of a negative number or the logarithm of 0 in the original equation.

8. Modeling with Exponential and Logarithmic Functions

a. If the graph of the data points appears to follow an exponential pattern, fit a linear model to $(x, \ln y)$ and then exponentiate both sides to find the model for the data points (x, y). Or use a graphing utility's exponential regression option ($y = ab^x$).

b. If the graph of the data points appears to follow a logarithmic pattern, fit a linear model to $(\ln x, y)$. The model for the data points (x, y) is the equation of the regression line for $(\ln x, y)$. Or use a graphing utility's logarithmic regression option ($y = a + b\ln x$).

c. When using a graphing utility to model data, first draw a scatter diagram to obtain a general picture for the shape of the data. If necessary, fit several models to the data. The model that best fits the data is the one with the value of r closest to 1.

REVIEW PROBLEMS

In Problems 1–8, match each function with its graph.

1. $f(x) = 4^x$

2. $f(x) = 4^{-x}$

3. $f(x) = -4^{-x}$

4. $f(x) = -4^{-x} + 3$

5. $f(x) = \log x$

6. $f(x) = \log(-x)$

7. $f(x) = \log(2 - x)$

8. $f(x) = 1 + \log(2 - x)$

a.

b.

c.

d.

e.

f.

g.

h.

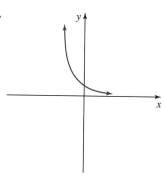

In Problems 9–15, sketch by hand the graphs of the two functions in the same rectangular coordinate system. Use a table of coordinates to sketch the first given function and transformations of the first function plus a table of coordinates to graph the second function. State each function's domain and range. Then use a graphing utility to confirm your results.

9. $y = 2^x$ and $y = 2^{x+1}$

10. $f(x) = 3^x$ and $g(x) = 3^{x-1} - 2$

11. $f(x) = 2^x$ and $y = 2^{-x}$

12. $y = 3^x$ and $y = -3^{-x} + 2$

13. $y = (\frac{1}{2})^x$ and $y = (\frac{1}{2})^{-x} - 1$

14. $f(x) = \log_2 x$ and $g(x) = \log_2(x - 2) + 3$

15. $y = \log_2 x$ and $y = -\log_2(-x)$

Use the compound interest models

$$A = P(1 + \tfrac{r}{n})^{nt} \quad \text{and} \quad A = Pe^{rt}$$

to answer Problems 16–17.

16. Suppose that you have $5000 to invest. What investment yields the greater return over 5 years: 5.5% compounded semiannually or 5.25% compounded monthly?

17. Suppose that you have $14,000 to invest. What investment yields the greater return over 10 years: 7% compounded monthly or 6.85% compounded continuously?

18. Use the exponential growth model $A = A_0 e^{kt}$ (where $k > 0$) to answer this question. In 1990 China had a population of 1119.9 million with a growth rate of 1.3% per year ($k = 0.013$). India's 1990 population was 853.4 million with a growth rate of 2.1% per year. In their 1990 *World Population Profile*, the United States Bureau of the Census stated that "The latest projections suggest that India's population may surpass China's in less than 60 years." Estimate the population of the two countries in the year 2050. Do these estimations reinforce the prediction by the Bureau of the Census?

19. The function

$$N(t) = \frac{200,000}{1 + 1999e^{-0.06t}}$$

describes the number of people $N(t)$ who become ill with an infectious disease t days after its initial outbreak.

a. How many people became ill with the disease when the outbreak began?

b. How many people were ill by the end of the fourth day?

c. What is the horizontal asymptote for this function? Describe what this means in practical terms.

d. Use a graphing utility to graph the function.

In Problems 20–22, evaluate each expression without the use of a calculator.

20. $\log_3 9 + \log_2 32$

21. $\log_3 \frac{1}{27} - \ln e^5$

22. $\log_3 (\log_8 8) + \log_3 (\log_2 8)$

In Problems 23–25, find the domain, the vertical asymptote, and the x-intercept for each function. Verify your results by graphing the function with a graphing utility.

23. $f(x) = \ln(x - 2)$

24. $g(x) = \ln(4 - x)$

25. $r(x) = \ln(x - 2)^2$

26. The model

$$t = \frac{1}{c} \ln \left(\frac{A}{A - N} \right)$$

describes the time (t, in weeks) that it takes to achieve mastery of a portion of a task. In the model, A represents maximum learning possible, N is the portion of the learning that is to be achieved, and c is a constant used to measure an individual's learning style. A 50-year-old man decides to start running as a way to maintain good health. He feels that the maximum rate he could ever hope to achieve is 12 miles per hour. How many weeks will it take before the man can run 5 miles in 1 hour if $c = 0.06$ for this person?

In Problems 27–31, use logarithmic properties to expand each expression as much as possible. Where possible, evaluate or simplify logarithmic expressions without the use of a calculator.

27. $\log_7 \left(\frac{\sqrt{x}}{49y^2} \right)$

28. $\log \dfrac{10,000}{\sqrt[3]{3x + 1}}$

29. $\ln \sqrt{\dfrac{x^3 y}{e^4}}$

30. $\ln(9e^{5t})$

31. $\log_b (\sqrt{x^3} \sqrt{y})^{-1/5}$

In Problems 32–34, write the expression as a single logarithm whose coefficient is 1.

32. $5 \log(x - 4) + \log 7 - 3 \log x$

33. $\frac{1}{2} \ln x - \frac{1}{7} \ln y$

34. $\ln(x^2 - 9) - \ln(x + 3) + \frac{2}{3} \ln(x - 3)$

35. Rewrite as a single term that does not contain a logarithm: $10^{\log 5x^2 + \log 3x} + e^{\ln 16x^7 - \ln 2x^4}$

In Problems 36–37, evaluate the logarithm using the change-of-base property. Work each problem twice, first using common logarithms and then using natural logarithms. Round each approximation to three decimal places.

36. $\log_5 17$

37. $\log_{15} 3000$

On the Richter scale, the magnitude R of an earthquake of intensity I is given by

$$R = \log \frac{I}{I_0}$$

where I_0 is the intensity of a barely felt zero-level earthquake. Use this model to answer Problems 38–39.

38. What is the magnitude on the Richter scale of an earthquake that is $10^{6.7}$ times as intense as a zero-level earthquake?

39. Compare the intensity of Colombia's 1906 earthquake measuring 8.6 on the Richter scale to Northern California's 1989 earthquake that measured 7.1. Calculate the ratio of their intensities and determine how many times greater in intensity was Colombia's 1906 earthquake than California's 1989 earthquake.

40. Another form of Richter's equation is

$$R = 0.67 \log E - 2.9,$$

where E is the energy in joules of an earthquake and R is its magnitude on the Richter scale. What is the difference between the energy released in the two earthquakes described in Problem 39?

41. Describe the relationship between the graphs of $y = \log_4 x$ and $y = \log_4 \dfrac{1}{(x - 1)^2}$. Then use a graphing utility to verify your description.

42. The relationship between the number of decibels (D) and the intensity of a sound (I) in watts per meter^2 is given by

$$D = 10 \log \frac{I}{I_0}$$

where I_0 is the intensity of sound barely audible to the human ear. If damage to the average ear occurs at 90 decibels or greater, will a jet aircraft from 500 feet with an intensity of 1×10^2 watts per meter^2 cause ear damage? (Assume I_0, the threshold of hearing, to be 10^{-12} watt per meter^2.)

Solve the exponential equations in Problems 43–47 by taking the natural logarithm of both sides. Express the answer in terms of natural logarithms. Then use a calculator to obtain a decimal approximation, correct to the nearest thousandth, for the solution.

43. $8^x = 12,143$

44. $9e^{5x} = 1268$

45. $e^{12-5x} - 7 = 123$

46. $7^{x-3} = 5^{4x+2}$

47. $e^{2x} - e^x - 6 = 0$

48. The model $A = Pe^{rt}$ describes the accumulated value (A) of a sum of money (P) after t years at an annual percentage rate (r, in decimal form) compounded continuously. Suppose that $5500 is invested at 4.5% compounded continuously.

   a. How long will it take the investment to triple in value?

   b. What interest rate is required for the investment to double in 8 years time?

49. The model $A = P(1 + \frac{r}{n})^{nt}$ describes the accumulated value (A) of a sum of money (P) after t years at an annual percentage rate (r, in decimal form) compounded n times a year. How long will it take $12,500 to

grow to $20,000 at 6.5% annual interest compounded quarterly?

50. The model

$$A = \frac{A_0}{k}(e^{kt} - 1)$$

describes the amount of nonrenewable energy resources (A) from time $t = 0$ to time t, where A_0 is the amount of the resource consumed during the year $t = 0$ and k is the relative growth rate of annual consumption. In 1990, the total remaining known oil resources ultimately available were 983.4 billion barrels. There were 21.3 billion barrels consumed that year. With a rate of growth in oil consumption of 2.5%, by what year will the planet be depleted of its known oil resources?

51. Use the exponential growth model $A = A_0 e^{kt}$ (where $k > 0$) to solve this problem. In 1995 the United States had a population of 263.2 million and a relative growth rate of 0.7% per year. Brazil's 1995 population was 157 million with a growth rate of 1.9% per year. In what year will the two countries have the same population?

In Problems 52–56, solve the logarithmic equation algebraically. Check each proposed solution by direct substitution or with a graphing utility, eliminating values that produce the logarithm of a negative number or the logarithm of 0 from the equation's solution set.

52. $\log_4(3x - 5) = 3$

53. $\log_2(x + 3) + \log_2(x - 3) = 4$

54. $\log_3(x - 1) = 2 + \log_3(x + 2)$

55. $\ln x + \ln(x - 4) = \ln(2x - 5)$

56. $\log(x + 7) - \log(x + 2) = \log(x + 1)$

57. The formula $W = 0.35 \ln P + 2.74$ is a model for the average walking speed (W, in feet per second) for a resident of a city whose population is P thousand. What is New York City's population (to the nearest thousand) if the average walking speed is 5.9 feet per second?

58. The brightness of stars (or planets), measured in magnitudes (M), is given by

$$M = 6 - 2.5 \log \frac{I}{I_0}$$

where

   I = the intensity of light from the star

   I_0 = the intensity of light from a just-visible star

How many times more intense is the light from the planet Jupiter (magnitude $= -2.9$) than the light from Polaris, the north star (magnitude $= 2$)?

Use the exponential growth and decay models

$$A = A_0 e^{kt} \quad \text{or} \quad f(t) = A_0 e^{kt}$$

where A_0 is the original amount (or size) of a growing (or decaying) entity at $t = 0$, A is the amount at time t, and k is a growth ($k > 0$) or decay ($k < 0$) constant, to answer Problems 59–60.

59. According to the U.S. Bureau of the Census, in 1980 there were 14,609 thousand residents of Hispanic origin living in the United States. By 1994, the number had increased to 26,077 thousand.

   a. Let $t = 0$ correspond to 1980. This means that A_0, the original amount in the growth model, is 14,609.

Now use the fact that in 1994 the number was 26,077 (when $t = 14$, $A = 26,077$) to find k, the growth rate.

   b. Substitute the values for A_0 and k into the exponential growth model and write the function that models the Hispanic resident population of the United States t years after 1980.

c. Use the model in part (c) to project the Hispanic resident population (in thousands) for the years 2005, 2010, and 2025.

60. Carbon-14 decays exponentially with a half-life of approximately 5715 years, meaning that after 5715 years a given amount of carbon-14 will have decayed to half the original amount. Prehistoric cave paintings were discovered in the Lascaux cave in France. The paint contained 15% of the original Carbon-14. Estimate the age of the paintings.

61. A cup of hot coffee is taken out of a microwave oven and placed in a room. The temperature (T, in degrees Fahrenheit) after t minutes is modeled by the function $T = 70 + 130e^{-0.04855t}$. The graph of the function is shown in the figure below. Use the graph to answer each of the following questions.

a. What was the temperature of the coffee when it was first taken out of the microwave?

b. What is a reasonable estimate of the temperature of the coffee after 20 minutes? Use your calculator to verify this estimate.

c. What is the limit of the temperature to which the coffee will cool? What does this tell you about the temperature of the room?

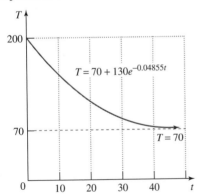

62. Use Newton's Law of Cooling, $T = C + (T_0 - C)e^{-kt}$, where t is the time it takes for an object to cool from an initial temperature T_0 to a temperature T, C is the temperature of the surrounding medium, and k is a positive constant associated with the cooling object, to answer this question. At 9:00 A.M., a coroner arrived at the home of a person who had died during the night. The temperature of the room was 70°F, and at the time of death the person had a body temperature of 98.6°F. The coroner took the body's temperature at 9:30 A.M., at which time it was 85.6°F, and again at 10:00 A.M., when it was 82.7°F. At what time did the person die?

63. The figure at the top of the next column shows world population projections through the year 2150. The data is from the United Nations Family Planning Program and is based on optimistic or pessimistic expectations for suc-

cessful control of human population growth. Suppose that you are interested in modeling this data using exponential, linear, and quadratic functions. Which one of these functions would you use to model each of the projections? Explain your choices. For the choice corresponding to a quadratic model, would your formula involve one with a positive or negative leading coefficient? Explain.

64. The figure shows the number of people in the United States age 65 and over, with projected figures for the year 2000 and beyond.

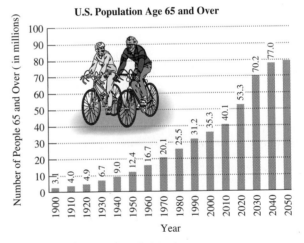

Source: U.S. Bureau of the Census

a. Let x represent the number of decades after 1900, and let y represent the number of people 65 and over. Use the exponential regression option of a graphing utility to model the data from 1900 through 2040, or follow these steps:

1. Take the natural logarithm of each y-value.

2. Graph the 15 data points $(x, \ln y)$. Notice that the points lie nearly on a straight line, suggesting the use of a linear model.

3. Use the linear regression option on a graphing utility or the procedure outlined in the Study Tip on page 501 to write the equation of the line that best fits the $(x, \ln y)$ transformed data.

4. Write both sides of the equation from step 3 as exponents on base e. Simplify and obtain a model for U.S. population 65 and over x decades after 1900.

b. Use the model to predict the U.S. population age 65 and over for the year 2050.

c. In 1990 the United States had a population of 263.2 million. The projected population for the year 2050 is 392.7 million. What is the percentage of U.S. population 65 and over for each of these years?

65. The data below indicate the amount of rain forest cleared for cattle ranching in the indicated year.

x Year	y Rain Forest Cleared (in millions of hectares) (1 hectare = 247 acres)
1960 (1)	0.30
1970 (11)	0.95
1980 (21)	1.36
1988 (29)	1.40

a. Graph the four data points. What function might reasonably model the data?

b. Use the appropriate regression option on a graphing utility to find a function that models the data, or follow these steps:

1. Take the natural logarithm of each x-value and graph the four data points $(\ln x, y)$. Notice that the points lie nearly on a straight line, suggesting the use of a linear model.

2. Use the linear regression option on a graphing utility or the procedure outlined in the Study Tip on page 501 to find the logarithmic model for the given data.

c. Use the model from part (b) to determine the year in which 1.5 million hectares will be cleared for cattle ranching.

66. The data below show consumer expenditures on books in the United States.

x (Year)	y (Consumer Expenditures on Books, in millions of dollars)
1982	9869
1985	12,611
1990	19,043
1992	21,244
1993	22,635
1994	23,798

a. Use a graphing utility to draw a scatter diagram of the data.

b. Use a graphing utility to model the data with a linear model, an exponential model, and a logarithmic model. Which model best describes book expenditures as a function of time?

c. Use the best of the three models to predict the amount that consumers in the United States will spend on books in the year 2005.

CHAPTER 4 TEST

1. Graph $y = 2^x$ and $y = 2^{x-1} + 1$ in the same rectangular coordinate system.

2. Use the compound interest models

$$A = P\left(1 + \frac{r}{n}\right)^{nt} \quad \text{and} \quad A = Pe^{rt}$$

to answer this question. Suppose you have $9000 to invest. What investment yields the greater return over 10 years: 6.5% compounded semiannually or 6% compounded continuously? How much more, to the nearest dollar, is yielded by the better investment?

3. A cup of coffee at 180° Fahrenheit is cooling in a room at a rate of 5°F per minute. The function $f(t) = 72 +$ $112e^{-0.05t}$ describes the coffee's temperature $(f(t))$ after t minutes.

a. What is the temperature, to the nearest degree, after 10 minutes?

b. What is the horizontal asymptote for this function? Describe what this means in practical terms.

4. Evaluate without using a calculator: $\log_2 16 - \log_{1/3} 9$.

5. Graph $y = \log_2 x$ and $y = \log_2(x - 1)$ in the same rectangular coordinate system.

6. Find the domain of $f(x) = \ln(3 - x)$.

Use logarithmic properties to expand the expressions in Problems 7–8 as much as possible. Where possible, evaluate logarithmic expressions.

7. $\log_5\left(\dfrac{\sqrt[3]{x}}{125y^2}\right)$

8. $\ln(10e^{7t})$

Write each expression in Problems 9–10 as a single logarithm.

9. $6 \log x + 2 \log y$

10. $\ln 7 - 3 \ln x$

Solve each exponential equation in Problems 11–12. Express your answers in terms of natural logarithms. Then use a calculator to find a decimal approximation of each answer, correct to the nearest thousandth.

11. $e^{9-3x} - 17 = 25$

12. $e^{2x} - 6e^x + 5 = 0$

13. Use the compound interest model $A = Pe^{rt}$ to answer this question. If \$4000 is invested at 6% annually, compounded continuously, how long will it take (to the nearest tenth of a year) for the investment to double in value?

14. Use the exponential decay model $A = A_0 e^{kt}$ to answer this question. A radioactive substance that initially contains 200 grams decays at the rate of 8% per year. How long will it take until 100 grams of the substance remain?

Solve each logarithmic equation in Problems 15–16.

15. $\log_5 (x - 2) = \log_5 x - \log_5 8$
16. $\log_{16} (10x + 3) + \log_{16} x = \frac{1}{2}$
17. The perceived loudness of a sound (D, in decibels) at the eardrum is described by

$$D = 10 \log \frac{I}{I_0}$$

where

$I =$ the intensity of the sound (in watts per meter^2)

$I_0 =$ the intensity of a sound barely audible to the human ear

An intensity level of 120 decibels is potentially damaging to the ear. How many times louder than I_0 is a level of 120 decibels?

18. Use the exponential growth model $A = A_0 e^{kt}$ to answer this problem.

a. In 1992, world population was approximately 5.5 billion and in 1995 it was approximately 5.8 billion. Find the exponential growth function that models the data t years after 1992.

b. In what year will world population reach 10 billion?

19. The model $T = C + (T_0 - C)e^{-kt}$ describes the time t it takes for an object to cool from an initial temperature T_0 to a temperature T when the surrounding temperature is C.

a. A house whose temperature is 68° Fahrenheit loses power because of an ice storm. The temperature outside the house is 28°F and the temperature of the house drops from 68° to 64° in an hour. Find k and write the model for the temperature T of the house after t hours.

b. After how long will the temperature in the house be 50°F?

20. Use a graphing utility to graph $f(x) = 5 \ln x - \frac{x}{2}$ in an appropriate viewing rectangle. Use the graph to answer each of the following.

a. What is the vertical asymptote of f?

b. Find, correct to two decimal places, the maximum value of f and the value of x at which this occurs.

c. Find the range of f.

d. Solve the equation $5 \ln x - \frac{1}{2}x = 0$. Express each solution correct to two decimal places.

CUMULATIVE REVIEW PROBLEMS (CHAPTERS P–4)

In Problems 1–2, simplify.

1. $\dfrac{3}{4x^2 + 4x + 1} + \dfrac{x + 3}{2x^2 - x - 1} - \dfrac{2}{x - 1}$

2. $\dfrac{1 - \dfrac{2}{x}}{1 - \dfrac{3}{x} + \dfrac{2}{x^2}}$

Solve Problems 3–7.

3. $|3x - 4| = 2$

4. $\sqrt{2x - 5} - \sqrt{x - 3} = 1$

5. $x^4 + x^3 - 3x^2 - x + 2 = 0$

6. $e^{11-5x} - 32 = 96$

7. $\log_2(x + 5) + \log_2(x - 1) = 4$

8. Multiply: $[3y - (2x + 5)][3y + (2x - 5)]$.

9. Graph: $f(x) = \begin{cases} \sqrt{x - 2} & \text{if } x \geq 2 \\ 2 - x & \text{if } x < 2. \end{cases}$

10. Use the graph of $f(x) = x^2$ to graph $g(x) = -(x + 2)^2 + 4$.

11. If $2 - i$ is a solution of $x^4 - 4x^3 + 6x^2 - 4x + 5 = 0$, find the complete solution set.

12. Graph: $f(x) = \dfrac{x^2 - 4}{x - 1}$.

13. The model $F = 1 - k \ln(t + 1)$ describes the fraction of people (F) who remember all the words in a list of nonsense words t hours after memorizing the list. After 3 hours only half the people could remember all the words. Determine the value of k and then predict the fraction of people in the group who will remember all the words after 6 hours.

14. Expand and evaluate logarithms where possible: $\log_3(81 \sqrt[3]{x})$.

15. Factor completely: $x^3 - 5x^2 - 25x + 125$.

16. Solve for n: $I = \dfrac{nE}{R + nr}$.

17. The life expectancy for women born in the United States in 1950 is 71 years. This amount has increased by about 0.2 years for each year of birth after 1950. What is the year of birth for which a woman in the United States can expect to live 81.8 years?

18. A water tank has the shape of an inverted right circular cone of altitude 8 feet and base radius 4 feet. How much water is in the tank when the water is 3 feet deep?

19. What number exceeds its square by a maximum amount?

20. The cost (C) of removing $p\%$ of a river's pollutants is given by the model

$$C = \frac{60,000p}{100 - p}.$$

What is the vertical asymptote for this function? What does this mean in practical terms?

Appendix

Review Problems Covering the Entire Book

Use your graphing utility to verify as many answers as possible.

Solving Equations and Inequalities

Systematic procedures for solving certain equations and inequalities are an important component of algebra. Problems 1–21 give you the opportunity to review these procedures. Solve each problem, expressing irrational solutions in simplified form and imaginary solutions in the form $a + bi$.

1. $\dfrac{2}{x+1} + \dfrac{3}{2x-3} = \dfrac{6x+1}{2x^2-x-3}$

2. $x(4x-11) = 3$

3. $(x^2-5)^2 - 3(x^2-5) - 4 = 0$

4. $\sqrt{2x+3} - \sqrt{4x-1} = 1$

5. $x^{1/2} - 6x^{1/4} + 8 = 0$

6. $\dfrac{x-3}{4} + \dfrac{x+2}{3} \leqslant 2$

7. $-2 < 8 - 5x < 7$

8. $|2x+1| \leqslant 1$

9. $6x^2 - 6 < 5x$

10. $\dfrac{1-x}{3+x} < 4$

11. $x^3 - x^2 - 4x + 4 = 0$

12. $3x^3 + 4x^2 - 7x + 2 = 0$

13. $e^{14-7x} - 53 = 24$

14. $e^{2x} - 10e^x + 9 = 0$

15. $\log_2(x+1) + \log_2(x-1) = 3$

16. $\ln(3x) + \ln(x+2) = \ln 9$

17. (Solve using matrices.)
$$\begin{aligned} x - y + z &= 17 \\ -4x + y + 5z &= -2 \\ 2x + 3y + z &= 8 \end{aligned}$$

18. (Solve for x only using Cramer's rule.)
$$\begin{aligned} x + 2y - z &= 1 \\ x + 3y - 2z &= -1 \\ 2x - y + z &= 6 \end{aligned}$$

19. $\dfrac{x^2}{4} + \dfrac{y^2}{16} = 1$
$$x - y = 2$$

20. $4x^2 + 3y^2 = 48$
$$3x^2 + 2y^2 = 35$$

21. $3x^2 - 2xy + 3y^2 = 34$
$$x^2 + y^2 = 17$$

Graphs and Graphing

Throughout the book, we have used graphs to help visualize a problem's solution. We have also studied graphing equations and inequalities in the rectangular coordinate system. Problems 22–36 focus on problem solving with graphs.

22. Use the graphs shown in the figure to describe how the graph of $h(x) = (x + 2)^3 + 1$ is obtained from the graph of $f(x) = x^3$. Include the graph of g in your description.

23. The graph shown in the figure is based on the distance traveled by a car over a 30-minute period.

   a. Describe what happened to the car over the six-minute interval from $t = 14$ to $t = 20$.

   b. What is a reasonable estimate for how far the car traveled during the last five minutes?

Time (minutes)

24. The graph on the top of the right column shows gender ratios in the United States, with future projections. For males age 65 and over:

   a. In what time interval is the number of males per 100 females constant?

   b. In what time interval is the number of males per 100 females increasing?

   c. In what time interval is the number of males per 100 females decreasing?

For all ages:

   d. Write a constant function $f(x)$ that approximately models the data shown for x in the interval [1950, 2025].

   e. What is misleading about the scale on the horizontal axis?

Gender Ratios in the U.S.

Source: U.S. Bureau of the Census, Statistical Abstract of the United States

25. Sketch the graph of the function f defined by
$$f(x) = \begin{cases} x^2 & \text{if} & x \leq 0 \\ x + 1 & \text{if} & 0 < x < 4 \\ \sqrt{x} & \text{if} & x \geq 4 \end{cases}$$

26. a. List all possible rational roots to
$$32x^3 - 52x^2 + 17x + 3 = 0.$$

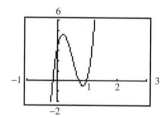

   b. The graph of $f(x) = 32x^3 - 52x^2 + 17x + 3$ is shown in the figure. Use the graph of f and synthetic division to solve the equation in part (a).

27. Use the graph of $f(x) = 2x^3 + 7x^2 - 4x - 14$ shown in the figure to find the smallest positive integer that is an upper bound and the largest negative integer that is a lower bound for the roots of $2x^3 + 7x^2 - 4x - 14 = 0$. Then use synthetic division to verify your observation.

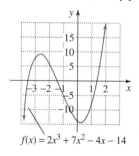

$f(x) = 2x^3 + 7x^2 - 4x - 14$

Graph each rational function in Problems 28–29.

28. $f(x) = \dfrac{x^2 + 3x - 40}{x^2 - x - 20}$

29. $f(x) = \dfrac{x^2 - 1}{x - 2}$

30. Graph $y = 2^x$ and $y = 2^{x-2} + 1$ in the same rectangular coordinate system.

31. Graph $y = \log_2 x$ and $y = \log_2(x + 2)$ in the same rectangular coordinate system.

32. Graph the solution set for this system of inequalities:

$$5x + y \leq 10$$

$$y \geq \frac{1}{4}x + 2.$$

In Problems 33–35, identify each conic section and sketch its graph. For ellipses and hyperbolas, find the foci. For parabolas, identify the vertex, focus, and directrix.

33. $100x^2 + y^2 = 25$

34. $4x^2 - 9y^2 - 16x + 54y - 29 = 0$

35. $x + 2 = 4(y - 3)^2$

36. Graph the solution set for this system of inequalities:

$$x^2 + 9y^2 \leq 9$$

$$x^2 - y^2 \leq 1.$$

Mathematical Models

Describing the world compactly and symbolically using formulas is one of the most important aspects of algebra. Problems 37–44 concentrate on mathematical models.

37. The model $d = 0.01v^2 + 0.16v$ describes the average stopping distance, (d, in meters) for a car traveling v kilometers per hour. If a car stops in 45.6 meters, how fast was it traveling?

38. The function $f(x) = 3.14x + 64.98$ models a woman's height ($f(x)$, in centimeters) in terms of the length of the humerus, also in centimeters. If a woman is 159.18 centimeters tall, find the length of her humerus.

Humerus

39. The data points (3, 5.13) and (8, 8.03), shown and described below, fall on a straight line.

x (Number of Years after 1985)	3	8
y (Total Prize Money [in millions of dollars] Awarded at the Indianapolis 500 Car Race)	5.13	8.03

a. Write the equation of the line on which these measurements fall in point-slope form and slope-intercept form.

b. Use the slope-intercept model from part (a) to find the anticipated total prize money in the Indianapolis 500 race for the year 2010.

40. The model

$$C = \frac{350p}{100 - p}$$

describes the cost (C, in millions of dollars) for removing p percent of the industrial pollutants discharged into a river.

a. Find the cost of removing 60% of the pollutants.

b. According to this model, would it be possible to remove 100% of the pollutants? Explain.

41. Use the compound interest model, $A = Pe^{rt}$, to solve this problem. At what annual rate, compounded continuously, must $7000 be invested to grow to $14,000 in 10 years?

42. The perceived loudness of a sound (D, in decibels) at the eardrum is described by

$$D = 10 \log \frac{I}{I_0}$$

where

I = the intensity of the sound

   (in watts per meter squared)

I_0 = the intensity of a sound

   barely audible to the human ear

How much more intense is a sound of 80 decibels than a sound of 40 decibels?

43. Use the exponential growth model, $A = A_0 e^{kt}$, to solve this problem. In 1930, world population was approximately 2 billion, and by 1960 it had grown to approximately 3 billion.

a. Write the exponential growth function that models this data t years after 1930.

b. Use the model from part (a) to predict the year in which the world will reach its carrying capacity of 20 billion.

44. A ball is thrown directly upward. The ball's height above the ground at various times is given as follows.

Time t (in seconds)	1	2	3
Position $s(t)$ above the ground (in feet)	108	140	140

a. Use the three data values and the position function $s(t) = \frac{1}{2}at^2 + v_0 t + s_0$ to find values for a, v_0, and s_0, thereby modeling the height of the ball above the ground at any time t.

b. What is the ball's maximum height above the ground? After how many seconds does this occur?

c. How long does it take for the ball to strike the ground?

d. Use parts (b) and (c) to graph the position function.

A Potpourri of Skills

Problems 45–65 give you the opportunity to review a number of course objectives presented throughout the book.

45. Factor completely: $x^4 + 3x^3 - 8x - 24$.

46. Simplify: $\dfrac{x^2 - 9}{x^2 - x - 20} \div \dfrac{4x^2 - 12x}{4x^2 - 20x}$.

47. Simplify: $\dfrac{\dfrac{x+2}{x-2} - \dfrac{x}{x+2}}{3 - \dfrac{4}{x+2}}$.

48. Solve for a: $S = \dfrac{a - ar^n}{1 - r}$.

49. If $f(x) = 17x^2 - 11x + 23$, find $\dfrac{f(a+h) - f(a)}{h}$.

50. Write the point-slope, slope-intercept, and general forms of the equation of the line passing through $(-1, 7)$ and perpendicular to the line whose equation is $x - 6y - 4 = 0$.

51. Find $f^{-1}(x)$ if $f(x) = \sqrt[3]{x + 4}$.

52. If $f(x) = x^2 - 3x + 9$ and $g(x) = 5x - 7$, find

a. $f \circ g$

b. $g \circ f$.

53. Expand and evaluate logarithmic expressions where possible: $\log_8 \dfrac{\sqrt[3]{x^5}}{64y^2}$.

54. Write as a single logarithm: $3 \ln x + \frac{1}{2} \ln y - 6 \ln z$.

55. If $A = \begin{bmatrix} 4 & 2 \\ 1 & -1 \\ 0 & 5 \end{bmatrix}$ and $B = \begin{bmatrix} 2 & 4 \\ 3 & 1 \end{bmatrix}$, find $AB - 4A$.

56. Find the partial fraction decomposition for $\dfrac{2x^2 - 10x + 2}{(x-2)(x^2 + 2x + 2)}$.

In Problems 57–59, find the standard form of the equation for each conic section with the given conditions.

57. Ellipse: foci: $(-12, 0)$, $(12, 0)$; vertices: $(-13, 0)$, $(13, 0)$

58. Hyperbola: vertices: $(-7, 0)$, $(7, 0)$; asymptotes: $y = \pm \frac{2}{7}x$

59. Parabola: focus: $(0, -6)$; directrix: $y = 6$

60. Write a formula for the nth term of the arithmetic sequence $2, -3, -8, -13, \ldots$. Do not use a recursion formula. Then use the formula for a_n to find the 19th term.

61. Use the formula for the sum of the first n terms of an arithmetic sequence to find $\sum_{i=1}^{50} (4i - 25)$.

62. Find the sum: $\sum_{i=1}^{10} 20(\frac{3}{2})^{i-1}$.

63. Find the sum: $\sum_{i=1}^{\infty} 10(-0.4)^{i-1}$.

64. Use mathematical induction to prove that, for all natural numbers n,

$$3 + 7 + 11 + 15 + \cdots + (4n - 1) = n(2n + 1).$$

65. Use the Binomial Theorem to expand and simplify: $(x^3 + 2y)^5$.

Problem Solving

Problem solving is the central theme of algebra. Some problems can be solved by modeling conditions with linear equations, systems of equations, functions, or equations of conics. Problems 66–79 give you a chance to review some of the problem-solving situations that have appeared throughout the book.

66. Yearly income for men increases by $1600 with each year of education. Men with no education can expect to earn about $6300 yearly. For women, a comparable model suggests a $1200 increase for each year of education. Women at the zero-education level earn about $2100 yearly. How many years of education, to the nearest tenth of a year, must a woman achieve to earn the same yearly income as a man with 14 years of education?

67. A rectangular room measures 15 by 20 feet. A rectangular rug with an area of 126 square feet is to be placed in the center of the room so that a strip of flooring of uniform width is left uncovered around the room's edges. How wide will this strip be?

68. A chemical is sold in bulk to manufacturers at $800 per ton for orders up to 12 tons. If an order exceeds 12 tons, the charge is discounted 2% per ton based on the number of tons sold. How many tons should be sold to produce a maximum income of $10,000?

69. The price of a VCR is reduced by 20%. When the VCR still does not sell, it is reduced by 20% of the reduced price. If the price of the VCR after both reductions is $224, what was the original price?

70. A box with no top is to be made from a rectangular piece of aluminum. Squares of the same size are cut from each corner and folded up the sides. The box is to be 2 inches deep and the length of its base is to be 5 inches more than the width. If the volume is to be 352 cubic inches, what dimensions should the piece of aluminum have?

71. The rectangular plot of land shown in the figure is to be fenced along three sides using 800 feet of fencing. No fencing is to be placed along the river's edge. Find the dimensions that maximize the enclosed area. What is the maximum area?

72. The following nutritional values are given for three types of foods.

Nutritional Component per Ounce	Food *A*	Food *B*	Food *C*
Calories	200	50	10
Protein (in grams)	0.2	3	1
Vitamin C (in milligrams)	0	10	30

Suppose a dietician wants to prepare a meal that consists of foods *A*, *B*, and *C* with 600 calories, 20 grams of protein, and 200 milligrams of vitamin C. Model the situation with a system of three linear equations and determine how many ounces of each type of food must be used.

73. You are about to take a test that contains computation problems worth 6 points each and word problems worth 10 points each. You can do a computation problem in 2 minutes and a word problem in 4 minutes. You have forty minutes to take the test and may answer no more than 12 problems. Assuming you answer all the problems attempted correctly, how many of each type of problem must you do to maximize your score? What is the maximum score?

74. The figure shows a semielliptic archway that has a height of 10 feet at the center and a width of 30 feet. How high is the arch 8 feet from the center?

75. A small television has a picture with a diagonal measure of 10 inches and a viewing area of 48 square inches. Find the length and width of the screen.

76. Carpets are purchased for two square rooms with a combined area of 65 square yards. The price of the first carpet was $16 per square yard, and the carpet for the larger room was $20 per square yard. If the total cost was $1236, what are the dimensions of the smaller and larger square rooms?

77. A college graduate is considering a job that pays $28,000 the first year, with a 6% raise each year after that. The graduate plans to put aside half of all money earned toward the purchase of a house and wants at least $160,000 at the end of 10 years for this purpose. What is the total salary that will be paid by this job over a 10-year period? Can the desired amount be saved for purchasing a house?

78. You have forgotten a friend's telephone number, but you do remember the first three digits and the last two digits, namely, 451-??71. If you randomly dial a number with these digits and select any two digits where the question marks now appear, what is the probability that you will dial your friend?

79. A committee contains seven women and three men. Three people are randomly selected to write the committee report. Find the probability of selecting three men for this task.

Using Technology

Use of a graphing utility enhances problem solving and exploration, often building greater appreciation of algebraic techniques. Problems 80 and 81 integrate technology into problem solving and developing mathematical models.

80. The rate of a stream is 4 miles per hour. A boat is rowed 9 miles downstream (with the current) and then returns 9 miles upstream (against the current) to the starting point of the excursion.

a. If x represents the rowing rate in still water, write a rational function containing the sum of two rational expressions that models the total time for the round trip.

b. Use a graphing utility to graph the function. Then trace along the curve and determine the rate in still water that one must row to make the round trip in 10 hours.

c. Verify part (b) algebraically.

81. The data below indicate national expenditures for health care in billions of dollars for eight selected years.

Year	1960	1965	1970	1975	1980	1985	1990	1993
Health-Care Expenditures (in billions of dollars)	27.1	41.6	74.3	132.9	251.1	434.5	696.6	884.2

Source: U.S. Dept. of Health and Human Services

a. Let $x = 0$ correspond to 1960 and let y correspond to each of the figures for health-care expenditure. Take the natural logarithm of each y-value.

b. Graph the eight data points $(x, \ln y)$. Notice that the points lie nearly on a straight line, suggesting the use of a linear model.

c. Use the linear regression option on a graphing utility to write the equation of the line that best fits the $(x, \ln y)$ transformed data.

d. Write both sides of the equation in part (c) as exponents on base e. Simplify and obtain a model for health-care expenditures x years after 1960.

e. Use the model from part (d) to predict health-care expenditures for the year 2000.

Answers to Selected Chapter Exercises

Chapter P

1. a. $\sqrt{4}, 7, \dfrac{18}{2}, 100$ **b.** $0, \sqrt{4}, 7, \dfrac{18}{2}, 100$ **c.** $-10, 0, \sqrt{4}, 7, \dfrac{18}{2}, 100$ **d.** $-10, -\dfrac{3}{4}, 0, \dfrac{4}{5}, \sqrt{4}, 7, \dfrac{18}{2}, 100$

e. $-\sqrt{2}, \pi$ **3. a.** None **b.** $\dfrac{0}{3}$ **c.** $-\sqrt[3]{8}, \dfrac{0}{3}$ **d.** $-\sqrt[3]{8}, \dfrac{0}{3}, \sqrt{\dfrac{4}{9}}, 1.\overline{126}$ **e.** $\sqrt[3]{7}$

5. $1 < x \le 6$

7. $-5 \le x < 2$

9. $-3 \le x \le 1$

11. $2 < x < \infty$

13. $-3 \le x < \infty$

15. $-\infty < x < 3$

17. $-\infty < x < 5.5$

19. $\{x \mid x < 6\}; (-\infty, 6)$
23. $\{x \mid 5 < x < 12\}; (5, 12)$

21. $\{x \mid x \ge -1\}; [-1, \infty)$
25. $\{x \mid 2 < x \le 13\}; (2, 13]$

27. $\{x \mid x \le 6\}; (-\infty, 6]$ **29.** $\{x \mid 2 \le x \le 5\}; [2, 5]$ **31.** $\{x \mid x \le 60\}; (-\infty, 60]$ **33.** $\{x \mid -2 \le x < 0\}; [-2, 0)$
35. $[2, 5)$ **37.** $(5, \infty)$ **39.** $(-\infty, 2)$ **41.** $(-\infty, 3]$ **43.** $\varnothing$ **45.** $(1, 7)$ **47.** $(-1, \infty)$ **49.** $(-\infty, 4)$
51. $(-\infty, 6)$ **53.** $(-3, -1) \cup [2, 4]$ **55.** 300 **57.** 203 **59.** $12 - \pi$ **61.** $12 - \pi$ **63.** $5 - \sqrt{2}$

65. -1 **67.** 4 **69.** 15 **71.** 7 **73.** 15 **75.** 2.2 **77.** $\dfrac{7}{10}$ **79.** $\dfrac{11}{4}$ **81.** $|x| = 7$ **83.** $|x| \ge 6$

85. $|72 - 99| = 27$ miles **87.** $|y - 7| \le 3$ **89.** 80; 100 **91.** 65; 35 **93.** 27; 25
95. General medical examination, cough, routine prenatal examination, progress visit.
97. Ear ache or infection, back symptoms, vision dysfunctions, skin rash.
99. General medical examination, cough, routine prenatal examination, progress visit, throat, postoperative visit.
101. Routine prenatal examination, progress visit, throat, postoperative visit, ear ache or infection.

103. d **105.** $\dfrac{112}{80}, \dfrac{873}{618}, \sqrt{2}, \dfrac{4243}{3000}, \dfrac{55}{37}$ **107.** $\dfrac{a}{b}$ gets close to zero. **109.** Answers may vary.

PROBLEM SET P.2

1. 45   **3.** 35   **5.** −36   **7.** 0   **9.** $-\dfrac{2}{3}$ **11.** $\dfrac{5}{2}$ **13.** Commutative Property of Multiplication

15. Commutative Property of Multiplication   **17.** Distributive Property   **19.** Distributive Property
21. Additive Identity Property   **23.** Multiplicative Identity Property   **25.** $7x + 21y$
27. $-4x$ **29.** $12x^5 - 8x^3$ **31.** $13x$ **33.** $20ab$ **35.** $-2x^2 + 5x + 6$ **37.** x **39.** 50   **41.** -32

43. -16 **45.** 32   **47.** 64   **49.** 64   **51.** 32   **53.** $\dfrac{1}{3}$ **55.** 1   **57.** $64x^6$ **59.** $6x^{11}$ **61.** $5a^6$ **63.** $\dfrac{2}{b^7}$

65. $2x^3$ **67.** $-\dfrac{x^6}{729}$ **69.** $-32x^{15}y^{20}$ **71.** $24x^3y^8$ **73.** $-5a^{11}b$ **75.** $-32x^3$ **77.** $\dfrac{y^4}{25x^6}$

79. $\dfrac{y^{10}}{9x^4}$ **81.** $-75x^{13}y^{19}$ **83.** $-\dfrac{192b^{17}}{a^2}$ **85.** $-\dfrac{2s^{21}}{r^3}$ **87.** $-\dfrac{b^6c^{13}}{a^5}$ **89.** $-\dfrac{729z^{17}}{x^{11}y^{22}}$ **91.** $-\dfrac{9z^5}{5x^{12}}$

93. $16x^{10}y^6$ **95.** 713,000   **97.** 0.0000000307   **99.** 9.65×10^7 **101.** 7.361×10^{12} **103.** 7.53×10^0

105. 1.6×10^{-4} **107.** 7.253×10^{-3} **109.** 3.071×10^3 **111.** 3×10^8 **113.** 4.466; A person who earns
\$10,000 annually contributes 4.466% to charity.   **115.** 192π in.^{2} **117.** 5.88×10^{12} **119.** 1.016×10^{-7}
121. 3.6×10^{51} hydrogen atoms   **123.** 1.5×10^9 trees   **125.** 25,350 years   **127.** c   **129.** c
131–133. Answers may vary.   **135.** The pair 10^7 and 10^{43} is closer together.

PROBLEM SET P.3

1. a.
b. $\sqrt{125} \approx 11.18$
c. $\left(-1, -\dfrac{1}{2}\right)$

3. a.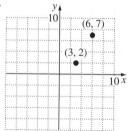
b. $\sqrt{34} \approx 5.83$
c. $\left(\dfrac{9}{2}, \dfrac{9}{2}\right)$

5. a.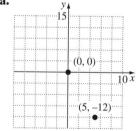
b. 13
c. $\left(\dfrac{5}{2}, -6\right)$

7. a.
b. $\sqrt{45} \approx 6.71$
c. $\left(-\dfrac{3}{2}, 0\right)$

9. a.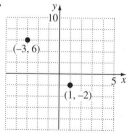
b. $\sqrt{80} \approx 8.94$
c. $(-1, 2)$

11.
40.44 units

13. 8.49 units   **15.**

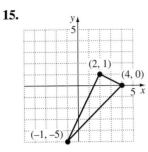

17. $AB = \sqrt{61}, BC = 2\sqrt{61}, AC = 3\sqrt{61}$ so $AB + BC = AC$

Area = 7.5 square units

19. x-intercept: $(2, 0)$
y-intercept: $(0, -6)$

21. x-intercept: $(2, 0)$
y-intercept: $(0, 4)$

23. x-intercepts: $(1, 0), (-1, 0)$
y-intercept: $(0, -1)$

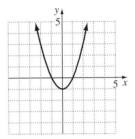

25. x-intercepts: $(-3, 0), (3, 0)$
y-intercept: $(0, 9)$

27. x-intercepts: $(-3, 0), (2, 0)$
y-intercept: $(0, -6)$

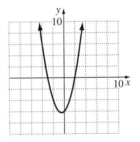

29. x-intercepts: $(0, 0), (2, 0)$
y-intercept: $(0, 0)$

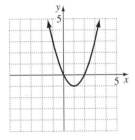

31. x-intercepts:

$$\left(\frac{1 - \sqrt{5}}{2}, 0\right), \left(\frac{1 + \sqrt{5}}{2}, 0\right)$$

y-intercept: $(0, 1)$

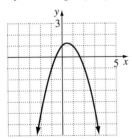

33. x-intercept: $(0, 0)$

y-intercept: $(0, 0)$

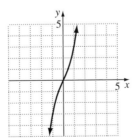

35. x-intercept: $(0, 0)$

y-intercept: $(0, 0)$

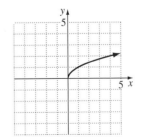

37. x-intercept: $(2, 0)$
y-intercept: none

39. x-intercept: $(0, 0)$
y-intercept: $(0, 0)$

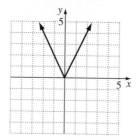

41. x-intercept: $(-1, 0)$
y-intercept: $(0, 1)$

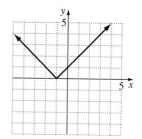

43. x-intercept: $(-1, 0)$
y-intercept: $(0, 1)$

45. x-intercept: $(1, 0)$
y-intercept: $(0, 1)$

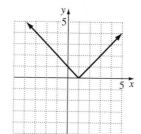

47. x-intercept: $(1, 0)$
y-intercept: $(0, -1)$

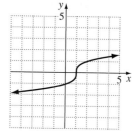

49. $(1977, 2200)$; In 1977 about 2,000,000 women participated in high-school athletics.

51. 33,000; 1945   **53.** Decreasing   **55.** $x \approx 4.1$; the ball hits the ground after approximately 4.1 seconds.

57. $\dfrac{1}{4}$ **59.** c

61. Answers may vary.

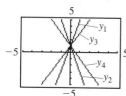

63. $[-10, 10]$ by $[-50, 50]$ **65.** $[-50, 50]$ by $[-10, 10]$

67.

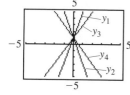

69.

71. a. $y = 5.25$ **b.** $x = 0, x = 4$

73. a. $y \approx 7.81$ **b.** $x \approx -1.13, x \approx 2.35$

75. a. 100   **b.** $y_1 \approx 75.79$; $y_2 \approx 81.24$; a 40-year-old white male can expect to live about 76 years; a 40-year-old white female can expect to live about 81 years.
c. The corresponding value for y increases in each graph as the value for x increases.

77. Answers may vary.   **79.** $AB = 2\sqrt{2}$; $BC = 3\sqrt{2}$; $AC = 5\sqrt{2}$

PROBLEM SET P.4

1. 7   **3.** 3   **5.** -2 **7.** Not a real number   **9.** $\dfrac{2}{5}$ **11.** -1 **13.** $-\dfrac{2}{3}$ **15.** $-\dfrac{1}{2}$ **17.** -8 **19.** $2\sqrt[3]{2}$

21. $2\sqrt[5]{2}$ **23.** $10|y|\sqrt{2y}$ **25.** $2|y|\sqrt{5xy}$ **27.** $5|y|z^2\sqrt{3xz}$ **29.** $2x\sqrt[3]{4}$ **31.** $-2yz^2\sqrt[3]{4xy^2}$ **33.** $2|y|\sqrt[4]{3y^3}$

35. $\dfrac{\sqrt{7}}{7}$ **37.** $\dfrac{\sqrt{15}}{5}$ **39.** $\dfrac{\sqrt[3]{28}}{2}$ **41.** $3\sqrt[3]{4}$ **43.** $-3\sqrt[5]{4}$ **45.** $\dfrac{50 + 10\sqrt{3}}{11}$ **47.** $\dfrac{13\sqrt{11} - 39}{2}$

49. $3\sqrt{5} - 3\sqrt{3}$ **51.** $\dfrac{11\sqrt{7} + 11\sqrt{3}}{4}$ **53.** $8\sqrt{2}$ **55.** $-16\sqrt{2}$ **57.** $20\sqrt{2} - 5\sqrt{3}$ **59.** $3\sqrt{2}$ **61.** $7\sqrt{10}$

63. 6   **65.** 2   **67.** 25   **69.** 81   **71.** $\dfrac{1}{16}$ **73.** $14y^{7/12}$ **75.** $-15x^{1/4}$ **77.** $4x^{1/4}$ **79.** $\dfrac{8}{y^{1/12}}$

81. $32xy^{10}z^2$ **83.** $5x^2y^3$ **85.** $2x^{1/4}y^{1/16}z^{1/6}$ **87.** $\dfrac{8x^{3/4}}{125y}$ **89.** $\dfrac{y^{5/2}}{x^{3/2}}$ **91.** $\dfrac{4a}{3b}$ **93.** $\sqrt{b}$ **95.** $\sqrt[3]{(x-1)^2}$

97. $\sqrt{xy}$ **99.** $\sqrt[3]{2xy^2}$ **101.** $\sqrt[3]{3xy^2}$ **103.** $11\sqrt[3]{2}$ **105.** $\sqrt{5}$ **107.** $f = \dfrac{\sqrt{Pm}}{2Lm}$ **109.** 275.52 mg

111. 5.9%   **113.** c   **115.** 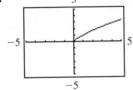   **117.**

119. Numbers are decreasing and are approaching 1.   **121.** $\dfrac{7 + 3\sqrt{3} - \sqrt{5} - 2\sqrt{15}}{11}$

PROBLEM SET P.5

1. $11x^3 + 7x^2 - 12x - 4$; degree 3   **3.** $12x^3 + 4x^2 + 12x - 14$; degree 3   **5.** $6x^2 - 6x + 2$; degree 2
7. $3x^2 - 2xy + 5y^2$; degree 2   **9.** $x^3 + 1$ **11.** $3y^4 + 20y^3 - 14y^2 + 17y - 6$ **13.** $2z^5 + z^4 + 2z^2 - 8z$
15. $x^3y^3 + 8$ **17.** $35x^2 + 26x + 3$ **19.** $18y^6 + 53y^3 - 35$ **21.** $6x^4y^2 - 7x^3y^2 - 20x^2y^2$
23. $81x^5 + 36x^3 - 36x^2 - 16$ **25.** $-2x^3 + 5x^2 - x - 2$ **27.** $25y^2 - 9$ **29.** $16x^4y^2 - 25x^2$
31. $y^2 - 4x^2$ **33.** $x^2 + 12x + 36$ **35.** $x^3 - 18x^2 + 108x - 216$ **37.** $9x^4y^2 + 12x^3y^2 + 4x^2y^2$
39. $27x^3 + 54x^2y + 36xy^2 + 8y^3$ **41.** $8x^6y^3 - 12x^5y^3 + 6x^4y^3 - x^3y^3$ **43.** $8x^{15} + 12x^{14} + 6x^{13} + x^{12}$
45. $9x^2 - 25y^2 + 42x + 49$ **47.** $-4x^2 + 25y^2 - 12x - 9$ **49.** $4x^2 + 4xy + y^2 + 4x + 2y + 1$
51. $9x^2 + 6xy + y^2 - 6x - 2y + 1$ **53.** $9x^2 - y^2 - 6x + 1$ **55.** $x^2 - y^2 + 6y - 9$ **57.** $5x^2 + 9x$
59. $20x^2 + 16x$ **61.** $x^2 + 7x + 6$ **63.** $6x^2 + 26x$ **65.** $4x^3 - 32x^2 + 80x - 80$ **67.** $13.3t^2$ **69.** b
71. They are equivalent expressions.   **73.** Let $y_1 = (x-1)^3$ and $y_2 = x^3 - 1$ **75.** $x^3 + 7x^2 - 3x$

77. a. $24, 35, 48$; $x^2 - 1$ **b.** $130, 222, 350$; $x^3 + x$

PROBLEM SET P.6

1. $9(2x + 3)$ **3.** $3x(x + 2)$ **5.** $9x^2(x^2 - 2x + 3)$ **7.** $4xy(3x - 2y)$ **9.** $7xy(x^2y + 2x - 6x^4y^2 + 3y^3)$
11. $(x - 3)(x^2 + 12)$ **13.** $(x - 5)[2x(x - 5) - 3y]$ **15.** $(x^2 + 5)(x - 2)$ **17.** $(x - 1)(x^2 + 2)$
19. $(3x - 2)(x^2 - 2)$ **21.** $(a + 5)(ac + 2)$ **23.** $(x + 4)(4xy - 1)$ **25.** $(x - 10)(x + 10)$
27. $(6x - 7)(6x + 7)$ **29.** $(3x - 5y)(3x + 5y)$ **31.** $(3y - 2x - 1)(3y + 2x + 1)$
33. $(x^2 + 9)(x + 3)(x - 3)$ **35.** $(3x^2 - y^3)(3x^2 + y^3)$ **37.** $(x - 2)(x^2 + 2x + 4)$ **39.** $(y + 3)(y^2 - 3y + 9)$
41. $(4d + 5)(16d^2 - 20d + 25)$ **43.** $(5 - 2pd)(25 + 10pd + 4p^2d^2)$ **45.** $(x + 5)(x + 3)$
47. $(x - 5)(x - 3)$ **49.** $(x + 6)(x - 5)$ **51.** $(x - 7)(x + 4)$ **53.** $(x + 2)^2$ **55.** $(x - 4)^2$ **57.** $(5x - 2)^2$
59. $(2x + 7)(x + 1)$ **61.** $(4y + 1)(y + 2)$ **63.** $(5x + 2)(2x + 3)$ **65.** $(4y - 3)(2y - 3)$
67. $(4y - 3)(y - 6)$ **69.** $(4y + 3)(3y - 7)$ **71.** Prime   **73.** $2y(y + 2)^2$ **75.** $4(x - 5)(x + 1)$
77. $3x(x + 2)(x^2 - 2x + 4)$ **79.** $(x - 5)(x - 2)(x + 2)$ **81.** $(x + 5 - 6a)(x + 5 + 6a)$ **83.** $c(c - 4)(c + 4)$
85. $(3b - 4)(3b + 4)(x + y)$ **87.** Prime   **89.** $(y - 2)^2(y + 2)$ **91.** $-2x(x - 2)(x^2 + 2x + 4)$
93. $2(2x + 5)^2$ **95.** $(x + y)(x^2 - xy + y^2)(x - z)(x + z)$ **97.** $(3a + 4b)(x - 5)$ **99.** $(r - s)(r^2 + rs + s^2 + 1)$
101. $a^3b^3(ab - 1)(a^2b^2 + ab + 1)$ **103.** $x^{1/2}(x - 1)$ **105.** $\dfrac{4(2x + 1)}{x^{2/3}}$ **107.** $\dfrac{3(x - 2)(x - 1)}{x^{1/2}}$
109. $-(x + 3)^{1/2}(x + 2)$ **111.** $\dfrac{x + 4}{(x + 5)^{3/2}}$ **113.** $-\dfrac{4}{3}(4x - 1)^{1/2}(x - 1)$ **115.** $\dfrac{x(x^2 + 6)}{(x^2 + 3)^{3/2}}$ **117.** d
119. Not correct   **121.** Correct   **123.** $(x - 3)^2$ **125.** $(x + 1)(x^2 - x + 1)$ **127–129.** Answers may vary.
131. a. $(x^2 + y^2)^2$ **b.** $(x^2 - xy + y^2)(x^2 + xy + y^2)$ **133.** $(x + y)(x - y)^3$ **135.** $(x^2 + 1)(2x^2 + x + 2)$

PROBLEM SET P.7

1. $\dfrac{3}{x - 3}$ $(x \neq 3)$ **3.** $\dfrac{x - 6}{4}$ $(x \neq 6)$ **5.** $\dfrac{y + 9}{y - 1}$ $(x \neq 1, 2)$ **7.** $\dfrac{y - 6}{y^2 + 3y + 9}$ $(y \neq 3)$ **9.** $\dfrac{x - 4}{x - 3}$ $(x \neq -5, 0, 3)$
11. $\dfrac{x - 1}{x + 2}$ $(x \neq -2, -1, 2, 3)$ **13.** $\dfrac{x^2 + 2x + 4}{3x}$ $(x \neq -2, 0, 2)$ **15.** $x^2 + x + 1$ $(x \neq -1, 1)$
17. 1 $\left(x \neq -7, -3, -\dfrac{1}{3}, \dfrac{5}{2}\right)$ **19.** $\dfrac{x - 5}{2}$ $(x \neq -5, 1)$ **21.** $x^2(x + 5)(x - 5)$ $(x \neq -5, 0, 5)$
23. $\dfrac{(x - 1)(x + 1)}{2}$ $(x \neq 0)$ **25.** 3 **27.** $\dfrac{9x + 39}{(x + 4)(x + 5)}$ **29.** $-\dfrac{3}{x(x + 1)}$ **31.** $\dfrac{3x^2 + 4}{(x + 2)(x - 2)}$
33. $\dfrac{2x^2 + 50}{(x - 5)(x + 5)}$ **35.** $\dfrac{4x + 16}{(x + 3)^2}$ **37.** $\dfrac{x^2 - x}{(x - 2)(x + 3)(x + 5)}$ **39.** $\dfrac{7y + 1}{(y - 2)(y + 1)^2}$
41. $\dfrac{3y^2 - 25y + 26}{(y - 2)^2(y - 1)(y + 2)}$ **43.** $\dfrac{x - 1}{x + 2}$ $(x \neq -1)$ **45.** $\dfrac{1}{3}$ $(x \neq 3)$ **47.** $\dfrac{x + 1}{3x - 1}$ $(x \neq 0)$
49. $\dfrac{1}{xy}$ $(x \neq y)$ **51.** $\dfrac{c}{c + 3}$ $(c \neq -2)$ **53.** $-\dfrac{y - 14}{7}$ $(y \neq -2, 2)$ **55.** $\dfrac{x - 3}{x + 2}$ $(x \neq -1, 3)$
57. $\dfrac{1}{x^2 + xy + y^2 - x + y}$ $(x \neq y)$ **59.** $-\dfrac{2x + h}{x^2(x + h)^2}$ $(h \neq 0)$ **61.** $\dfrac{x + 2y}{x^2y^2}$ **63.** $\dfrac{\sqrt{x} - \sqrt{x + h}}{h\sqrt{x}\sqrt{x + h}}$
65. $-\dfrac{2}{y^2\sqrt{y^2 + 2}}$ **67.** $\dfrac{2(y^2 - 9)(y^2 + 9)}{y^{5/3}}$ **69.** $\dfrac{540t^2 + 12,640t + 107,100}{-0.14t^2 + 0.51t + 31.6}$ (in dollars per person); $5997 per
person, $6833 per person, $7843 per person, $9086 per person   **71.** $\dfrac{R_1R_2R_3}{R_2R_3 + R_1R_3 + R_1R_2}$; $2.\overline{18}$ ohms
73. $\dfrac{8y + 4}{\pi y}$ **75.** d   **77.** $\dfrac{2x + 1}{6}$ **79.** $-x - 2$ **81.** $\dfrac{7x}{10}$ **83.** $\dfrac{x + 5}{x - 5}$ **85.** -8
87. $(1 + b^{x - y})^{-1} + (1 + b^{y - x})^{-1} = 1$

PROBLEM SET P.8

1. 1   **3.** $-i$ **5.** i **7.** $8 - 2i$ **9.** $-2 + 9i$ **11.** $24 + 7i$ **13.** $-10 + 18i\sqrt{2}$ **15.** $21 + 15i$

17. $-43 - 23i$ **19.** $-29 - 11i$ **21.** 34 **23.** 34 **25.** $-5 + 12i$ **27.** $-\dfrac{1}{2} + \dfrac{\sqrt{3}}{2}i$ **29.** $\dfrac{3}{5} + \dfrac{1}{5}i$

31. $1 + i$ **33.** $-\dfrac{24}{25} + \dfrac{32}{25}i$ **35.** $\dfrac{7}{5} + \dfrac{4}{5}i$ **37.** $-\dfrac{27}{29} - \dfrac{34}{29}i$ **39.** $-\dfrac{1}{2} - \dfrac{3}{2}i$ **41.** $-\dfrac{7}{5} - \dfrac{4}{5}i$ **43.** $23 + 10i$

45. $\dfrac{14}{25} - \dfrac{2}{25}i$ **47.** $-26 + 18i$ **49.** $1 - i$ **51.** $-i$ **53.** $3i$ **55.** $47i$ **57.** $-8i$ **59.** $2 + 6i\sqrt{7}$

61. $-\dfrac{1}{3} + \dfrac{\sqrt{2}}{6}i$ **63.** $-\dfrac{1}{8} - \dfrac{\sqrt{3}}{24}i$ **65.** $-2\sqrt{6} - 2i\sqrt{10}$ **67.** $24\sqrt{15}$

69.

71.

73.

75.

77. d   **79.** $\sqrt{-100} = 10i$ **81.** $\sqrt{-9} + \sqrt{-16} = 7i$

83. $\left(-\dfrac{1}{2} + \dfrac{\sqrt{3}}{2}i\right)^3 = \left(-\dfrac{1}{2} + \dfrac{\sqrt{3}}{2}i\right)\left(-\dfrac{1}{2} + \dfrac{\sqrt{3}}{2}i\right)\left(-\dfrac{1}{2} + \dfrac{\sqrt{3}}{2}i\right)$

$= \left(\dfrac{1}{4} - \dfrac{\sqrt{3}}{2}i + \dfrac{3}{4}i^2\right)\left(-\dfrac{1}{2} + \dfrac{\sqrt{3}}{2}i\right)$

$= \left(-\dfrac{1}{2} - \dfrac{\sqrt{3}}{2}i\right)\left(-\dfrac{1}{2} + \dfrac{\sqrt{3}}{2}i\right)$

$= \dfrac{1}{4} - \dfrac{3}{4}i^2 = \dfrac{1}{4} + \dfrac{3}{4} = 1$

85. $-i$ when n is odd; i when n is even   **87. a.** Correct   **b.** Incorrect   **c.** Incorrect   **d.** Correct
e. Incorrect   **f.** Correct   **g.** Correct

CHAPTER P REVIEW PROBLEMS

1. a. $\sqrt[4]{16}$ **b.** $0, \sqrt[4]{16}$ **c.** $-13, -\sqrt{16}, 0, \sqrt[4]{16}$ **d.** $-13, -\sqrt{16}, -\dfrac{2}{3}, 0, 1.\overline{27}, \sqrt[4]{16}$ **e.** $-\sqrt{5}, \dfrac{\pi}{3}$

2. $-2 < x \le 3$

3. $-1.5 \le x \le 2$

4. $x > -1$

5. $[2, 3)$ **6.** $(5, \infty)$ **7.** $(1, 7]$ **8.** $(-1, \infty)$ **9. a.** $\sqrt{2} - 1$ **b.** $-3 + \sqrt{17}$ **10.** $|-17 - 4| = 21$

11. -45 **12.** Multiplicative inverse   **13.** Associative property of addition   **14.** 7   **15.** $-8x^{12}y^9$

16. $\dfrac{250y^3}{x^2}$ **17.** $\dfrac{81x^8y^{12}}{16}$ **18.** $-\dfrac{8}{x^3y^9}$ **19.** 9.8×10^{13} **20.** 3.62×10^{-4}

21. a. $(1985, 50{,}000)$; 50,000 juveniles were arrested for marajuana possession in 1985.   **b.** $1990; 18{,}000$

22.

$8; (1, 7)$ **23.**

24.

25.

26.

27.

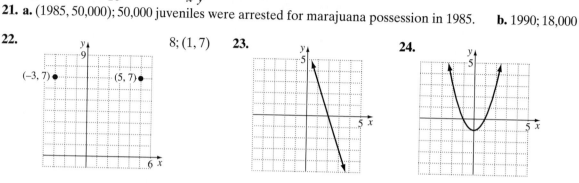

28. -1 **29.** $2xy^2\sqrt[3]{2y^2}$ **30.** $\dfrac{3\sqrt{5}}{2}$ **31.** $\dfrac{\sqrt[3]{9}}{3}$ **32.** $7\sqrt{7} + 7\sqrt{5}$ **33.** $20\sqrt{2}$ **34.** $7\sqrt{10}$ **35.** $\dfrac{63}{16}$

36. $28x^{7/12}$ **37.** $-4y^{11/20}$ **38.** $\sqrt[4]{4x^3y}$ **39.** $12\sqrt[4]{2}$ **40.** $21x^3 - 8x^2 - 10x + 5$, degree 3

41. $2x^4 + 5x^3 - 9x^2 + 17x - 20$ **42.** $36x^2 - x - 21$ **43.** $64x^3 - 144x^2y + 108xy^2 - 27y^3$

44. $-4x^2 + 25y^2 - 4x - 1$ **45.** $10xy^2(6x^5y - 2x^3 + y^3)$ **46.** $(x - 7)(x^2 + 9)$

47. $(x^2 + 9y^2)(x - 3y)(x + 3y)$ **48.** $(x - 10)(x^2 + 10x + 100)$ **49.** $(2x - 5)^2$

50. $(x + 3 - 2a)(x + 3 + 2a)$ **51.** $(4x - 5)(2x + 3)$ **52.** $4(a + 2)(a^2 - 2a + 4)$ **53.** $(x + 3)(x - 3)^2$

54. $-2xy(x - 1)(x^2 + x + 1)(x^6 + x^3 + 1)$ **55.** $(x - 1)^2(x^2 + x + 1)$ **56.** $\dfrac{16(1 + 2x)}{x^{3/4}}$

57. $\dfrac{7(x - 2)(x + 2)}{(x^2 + 3)^{3/2}}$ **58.** $\dfrac{3x + 2}{x - 5}\left(x \neq -\dfrac{1}{2}\right)$ **59.** $4(y + 3)\ (y \neq 3, 5)$ **60.** $\dfrac{4}{x}\ (x \neq -5, -4, 4)$

61. $\dfrac{4x^2 - 4x}{(x + 2)(x - 2)}$ **62.** $\dfrac{2x^2 - 3}{(x - 3)(x + 3)(x - 2)}$ **63.** $\dfrac{5a^2 - 7a + 6}{(a + 2)(a - 1)(a - 2)^2}$ **64.** $-\dfrac{y^2 + 3y - 18}{y - 1}$

65. $\dfrac{25}{\sqrt{(25 - x^2)^3}}$ **66.** $-i$ **67.** $-9 - 7i$ **68.** $29 + 11i$ **69.** $\dfrac{1}{5} - \dfrac{11}{10}i$ **70.** $\dfrac{1}{3} - \dfrac{5}{3}i$ **71.** $i\sqrt{2}$

72. $-7 - 4i\sqrt{11}$ **73.** $-\dfrac{3}{5} - \dfrac{\sqrt{43}}{30}i$ **74.**

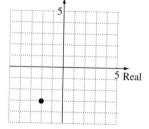

CHAPTER P TEST

1. $x \le 3$

2. $[3, 5)$ **3.** $2\sqrt{13}$

4.

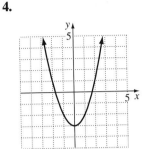

5. Commutative Property of Addition   **6.** $\dfrac{27y^6}{x^6}$ **7.** $\sqrt{2} - 1$ **8.** $2\sqrt[3]{4}$ **9.** $11\sqrt{2}$ **10.** $\dfrac{4\sqrt{3}}{3}$

11. $\sqrt[3]{4x^2 y}$ **12.** $15xy + 39y^2$ **13.** $49y^2 - 16x^2 - 8x - 1$ **14.** $-\dfrac{x}{3x + 5} \ (x \ne 4)$ **15.** $(x - 2)(x + 2)(x^2 + 4)$

16. $2(x + 4y)(x^2 - 4xy + 16y^2)$ **17.** $(x - 4)(x - 1)(x + 1)$ **18.** $\dfrac{(x - 3)(x + 3)x^2}{(x^2 + 1)^{3/2}}$ **19.** $\dfrac{(3y - 7)(y - 2)}{3}$

20. $-\dfrac{2}{x(x - 1)(x + 1)}$ **21.** $\dfrac{2x}{(x + 1)(x + 2)}$ **22.** $\dfrac{10x}{\sqrt{(x^2 + 5)^3}}$ **23.** $47 + 16i$ **24.** $2 + i$ **25.** -3

Chapter 1

PROBLEM SET 1.1

1. $\{16\}$ **3.** $\{7\}$ **5.** $\{13\}$ **7.** $\{2\}$ **9.** $\{9\}$ **11.** $\{-5\}$ **13.** $\{6\}$ **15.** $\{-2\}$ **17.** $\{-15\}$

19. $\{-12\}$ **21.** $\left\{\dfrac{46}{5}\right\}$ **23.** $\left\{\dfrac{1}{2}\right\}$ **25.** $\{20\}$ **27.** $\{4\}$ **29.** $\{-2\}$ **31.** $\{0\}$ **33.** $\{-9\}$ **35.** $\{4\}$

37. $\varnothing$ **39.** $\varnothing$ **41.** $\{-4, 9\}$ **43.** $\{-10, 7\}$ **45.** $\left\{-\dfrac{16}{5}, \dfrac{32}{5}\right\}$ **47.** $\{-1, 9\}$ **49.** $\{-1, 5\}$

51. $\left\{-\dfrac{5}{4}, \dfrac{3}{2}\right\}$ **53.** $P = \dfrac{S}{1 + rt}$ **55.** $n = \dfrac{IR}{E - Ir}$ **57.** $y = \dfrac{e(c - d)}{cd}$ **59.** $f = \dfrac{p - s}{s(p - 1)}$ **61.** 2036

63. Yes   **65.** 205; 125,000   **67.** c   **69.** $\{-5\}$ **71.** $\{4.5\}$ **73.** $\{-2, 5\}$ **75.** $\varnothing$

77. a. The equation has infinitely many solutions.   **b.** The equation has infinitely many solutions.

c.

Only the axes appears on the screen.

d.

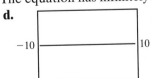

This is the graph of the x-axis.

The equation is true for all values of x.

79–81. Answers may vary.   **83.** $\varnothing$ **85.** 2007   **87.** The answer checks.

PROBLEM SET 1.2

1. $\{-2, 5\}$ **3.** $\{3, 5\}$ **5.** $\left\{-\dfrac{5}{2}, \dfrac{2}{3}\right\}$ **7.** $\left\{-\dfrac{4}{3}, 2\right\}$ **9.** $\left\{-\dfrac{7}{3}, 0\right\}$ **11.** $\left\{0, \dfrac{1}{3}\right\}$ **13.** $\{-3, 1\}$ **15.** $\{-3, 3\}$

17. $\{-\sqrt{10}, \sqrt{10}\}$ **19.** $\{-7, 3\}$ **21.** $\left\{-\dfrac{5}{3}, \dfrac{1}{3}\right\}$ **23.** $\left\{\dfrac{1-\sqrt{7}}{5}, \dfrac{1+\sqrt{7}}{5}\right\}$ **25.** $\left\{\dfrac{4-2\sqrt{2}}{3}, \dfrac{4+2\sqrt{2}}{3}\right\}$

27. $\{-3 - 4i, -3 + 4i\}$ **29.** $\{2 - \sqrt{15}, 2 + \sqrt{15}\}$ **31.** $\left\{\dfrac{7-\sqrt{17}}{4}, \dfrac{7+\sqrt{17}}{4}\right\}$ **33.** $\left\{-\dfrac{1}{2}, \dfrac{3}{2}\right\}$

35. $\left\{\dfrac{3-i}{2}, \dfrac{3+i}{2}\right\}$ **37.** $\left\{\dfrac{3-\sqrt{57}}{6}, \dfrac{3+\sqrt{57}}{6}\right\}$ **39.** $\left\{\dfrac{1-\sqrt{29}}{4}, \dfrac{1+\sqrt{29}}{4}\right\}$ **41.** $\{3 - i, 3 + i\}$

43. $\{2, 4\}$ **45.** $\{1 - 2\sqrt{2}, 1 + 2\sqrt{2}\}$ **47.** $\left\{-\dfrac{\sqrt{105}}{3}, \dfrac{\sqrt{105}}{3}\right\}$ **49.** $\{-\sqrt{21}, \sqrt{21}\}$ **51.** $\left\{-\dfrac{\sqrt{6}}{4}, \dfrac{\sqrt{6}}{4}\right\}$

53. $\{-1, 0\}$ **55.** $\{-\sqrt{6}, \sqrt{6}\}$ **57.** $\left\{-\dfrac{5}{3}, \dfrac{13}{3}\right\}$ **59.** $\{0.3, 5\}$ **61.** $\left\{\dfrac{2-i\sqrt{2}}{3}, \dfrac{2+i\sqrt{2}}{3}\right\}$

63. $\{-\sqrt{7}, \sqrt{7}\}$ **65.** $\left\{\dfrac{5-\sqrt{73}}{6}, \dfrac{5+\sqrt{73}}{6}\right\}$ **67.** $\left\{-\dfrac{13}{4}, -2\right\}$ **69.** $\{-10\}$ **71.** $\left\{\dfrac{-5\sqrt{2}}{2}, 2\sqrt{2}\right\}$ **73.** $\{1\}$

75. $\left\{-\dfrac{1}{4}, \dfrac{1}{2}\right\}$ **77.** $\{-3, 0\}$ **79.** $\{-1, 3\}$ **81.** $\{-8, -6, 4, 6\}$ **83.** 2000   **85. a.** $D = 20$ **b.** No

87. 2024   **89. a.** No   **b.** Yes; twice; going up and going down.   **c.** Yes; once; at the maximum height
91. No   **93.** b   **95.**

240

0 ⌐ 5
0

97–103. Answers may vary.

105. b. The product of the solutions is $\dfrac{c}{a}$. The sum of the solutions is $-\dfrac{b}{a}$.   **c.** Check that the product is $\dfrac{c}{a} = 4$,
and the sum is $-\dfrac{b}{a} = 7$; yes   **107.** $\left\{\dfrac{72}{25}\right\}$ **111.** $\left\{\sqrt{\dfrac{d}{e}}, \sqrt{\dfrac{e}{d}}\right\}$ **113.** Students should show equalities.

PROBLEM SET 1.3

1. 2003   **3.** 115.4 months; $1620   **5.** $489.72   **7. a.** $-10x^2 + 40x + 3200$ **b.** 17 or 19 trees   **9.** $1350
11. Black male: $34,340; white male: $43,690   **13.** *Coach*: $290,000; *Seinfeld*: $295,000;

Home Improvement: $325,000   **15. a.** $2\dfrac{1}{2}$ seconds   **b.** 5 seconds   **c.** $\left(\dfrac{5}{2}, 200\right)$; $(5, 0)$ **17.** 5 or 7 ovens

19. Width: 6 feet; length: 9 feet   **21.** 3 yards   **23.** 2 yards   **25.** 3 yards   **27.** 3 inches   **29.** 2 cm
31. 8.18 feet   **33.** 33.51 cubic feet   **35.** 6 meters   **37.** 5 m   **39.** 522 cm   **41.** 24 feet

43. a. $\dfrac{1 + \sqrt{5}}{2}$ **b.** (d)   **45. a.** 300 m by 400 m or 200 m by 600 m   **b.**

15,000

0 ⌐ 500
0

c. 125,000 m^2; 250 meters by 500 meters   **d.** No   **47. a.** 225

b. The moon graph shows a larger parabola due to lower gravity.   **c.** 119.7 feet

49. No   **51–53.** Answers may vary.   **55. a.** $\dfrac{(4 + \pi)x^2 - 32x + 64}{16\pi}$

b. Side of the square is 0 m; Radius is $\dfrac{2}{\pi}$ m.   **57.** 144 ft/sec

---

PROBLEM SET 1.4

1. $\{-4, 0, 4\}$ **3.** $\left\{-2, -\dfrac{2}{3}, 2\right\}$ **5.** $\left\{-\dfrac{1}{2}, \dfrac{1}{2}, \dfrac{3}{2}\right\}$ **7.** $\left\{-2, -\dfrac{1}{2}, \dfrac{1}{2}\right\}$ **9.** $\{-3, -1, 1, 3\}$

11. $\left\{-\dfrac{\sqrt{6}}{3}, -\dfrac{\sqrt{2}}{2}, \dfrac{\sqrt{2}}{2}, \dfrac{\sqrt{6}}{3}\right\}$ **13.** $\{-1, 0, 5\}$ **15.** $\{-3, -1, 2, 4\}$ **17.** $\{-8, -2, 1, 4\}$ **19.** $\left\{-9, \dfrac{3}{4}\right\}$

21. $\{6\}$ **23.** $\{10\}$ **25.** $\{2, 6\}$ **27.** $\left\{\dfrac{13 + \sqrt{105}}{6}\right\}$ **29.** $\left\{\dfrac{1}{2}\right\}$ **31.** $\{7\}$ **33.** $\{8\}$ **35.** $\{-60, 68\}$

37. $\{-4, 5\}$ **39.** $\{-\sqrt{3494}, \sqrt{3494}\}$ **41.** $\left\{\dfrac{9}{2}\right\}$ **43.** $\left\{-8, \dfrac{1}{8}\right\}$ **45.** $\left\{\dfrac{1}{4}, 1\right\}$ **47.** $\{18, 6563\}$

49. 208.33 feet   **51.** 161,081 miles/second   **53.** 161,081 miles/second   **55. a.** $29   **b.** 402 CD sets

57. 12%   **59. a.** $\dfrac{12}{7}$ miles or 12 miles   **b.** Answers may vary.   **61.** $\sqrt{3}$ ft by $(\sqrt{3} + 3)$ ft by $(\sqrt{3} - 1)$ ft

63. $6(\sqrt[3]{2} - 1)$ in.   **65.** 7.5 miles or about 7.13 miles   **67.** a   **69.** $\{-2, -1, 2\}$ **71.** $\{-4, -0.33, 2\}$

73. $\{-2.28, -0.32\}$ **75. a.** 50,000

b. Increased each year   **c.** 1990

e. Answers may vary.   **77.** $x = 7.5$ miles (road length ≈ 14.4 miles)

d.

79. a. Verification is left to the student.   **b.**

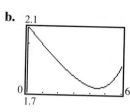

$x = 4.5$; The person should come ashore 4.5 miles from the house. This path gives the minimum amount of time.
c. Verification is left to the student.

81–83. Answers may vary.   **85.** $\{3, 4\}$ **87.** $\{8\}$ **89.** $\{c + d\}$

PROBLEM SET 1.5

1. $(-\infty, 3)$

3. $\left[\dfrac{20}{3}, \infty\right)$

5. $(-\infty, -4]$

7. $\left(-\infty, -\dfrac{2}{5}\right]$

9. $[0, \infty)$

11. $(-\infty, 1)$

13. $[6, \infty)$

15. $\left[-\dfrac{32}{5}, \infty\right)$

17. $(-\infty, -6)$

19. $(-\infty, \infty)$

21. $(3, 5)$

23. $[-1, 3)$

25. $(-3, -2]$

27. $[2, 3]$

29. $(-5, -2]$

31. $[3, 6)$

33. $\left(-\dfrac{8}{3}, \dfrac{10}{3}\right)$

35. $\left(-\dfrac{15}{2}, 4\right]$

37. $\left[-\dfrac{1}{2}, 1\right)$

39. $(-3, 3)$

41. $[-1, 3]$

43. $(-1, 7)$

45. $[-5, 3]$

47. $(-6, 0)$

49. $(-\infty, -3) \cup (3, \infty)$

51. $(-\infty, -1] \cup [3, \infty)$

53. $\left(-\infty, \dfrac{1}{3}\right) \cup (5, \infty)$

55. $(-\infty, -5] \cup [3, \infty)$

57. $(-\infty, -3) \cup (12, \infty)$

59. $(-\infty, -1] \cup [3, \infty)$

61. $(-\infty, -1) \cup (2, \infty)$

63. $\left(-\infty, -\dfrac{75}{14}\right) \cup \left(\dfrac{87}{14}, \infty\right)$

65. $(-\infty, -6] \cup [24, \infty)$

67. $[-11, 1]$

69. $25,000   **71.** $16,400   **73.** 61 or more   **75.** 82 hours or more

77. 5001 or more   **79.** $2 \le k \le 3$ **81.** 2,695,000 barrels; 2,425,000 barrels   **83.** $2 \le x \le 5$

85. Severe cognitive impairment, substance abuse disorders, and depressive: manic, major depression

87. $500 \le$ cost $\le 2500   **89.** c   **91.** $(-\infty, 2)$ **93.** $\left(-\infty, -\dfrac{5}{2}\right] \cup [4, \infty)$ **95.** $(-\infty, -1)$

97. $(-\infty, 3)$ **99.** $\varnothing$ **101.** $C > 25$ **103–105.** Answers may vary.   **107.** Verification is left to the student.

PROBLEM SET 1.6

1. $(-\infty, 3) \cup (5, \infty)$

3. $\left[-3, \dfrac{1}{2}\right]$

5. $(-\infty, -4 - \sqrt{3}] \cup [-4 + \sqrt{3}, \infty)$

7. $\left(\dfrac{4 - \sqrt{6}}{2}, \dfrac{4 + \sqrt{6}}{2}\right)$

9. $[-\sqrt{6}, \sqrt{6}]$

11. $(-\infty, \infty)$

13. $\varnothing$

15. $(-\infty, -3) \cup (6, \infty)$

17. $(-\infty, \infty)$

19. $[-2, -1] \cup [1, \infty)$

21. $(-\infty, -3)$

23. $\left(-\dfrac{2}{3}, \dfrac{2}{3}\right) \cup (2, \infty)$

25. $(-1, \infty)$

27. $(2, \infty)$

29. $(-\infty, -3) \cup (7, \infty)$

31. $(-4, -3)$

33. $(-\infty, 2) \cup [7, \infty)$

35. $\left(\dfrac{1}{2}, \dfrac{7}{5}\right]$

37. $(-3, 2)$

39. $(-1, 1 - \sqrt{3}) \cup (1, 1 + \sqrt{3})$

41. $(-1, 1) \cup (3, 4)$

43. $[-\sqrt{10}, -1) \cup (2, \sqrt{10}]$

$-\sqrt{10}\ -1 \qquad 2\ \sqrt{10}$

45. $(-\infty, -1) \cup (1, 2) \cup (3, \infty)$

$-1\ \ 0\ \ 1\ \ 2\ \ 3$

47. $(-\infty, -8) \cup (-6, 4) \cup (6, \infty)$

$-8\ -4\ \ 0\ \ 4\ \ 8$

49. Between 2 and 3 seconds, exclusive.   **51.** $2\sqrt{3}$ seconds   **53.** $\{1, 2, 3, \ldots, 9, 10\}$
55. Less than 60%   **57.** No more than 3 feet.   **59.** c   **61.** $(-1.5, 1) \cup (1, \infty)$ **63.** $(-4, -3)$
65. $(-\infty, -1] \cup [1, \infty)$
67. a. Less than 80%   **b.** $\quad$ **c.** It is impossible to remove all of the pollutants.

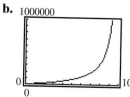

69. a.   **b.** $(0.27, 3.73)$ **c.** Never reaches zero

71. $(-\infty, 2] \cup [5, \infty)$ **73.** $(-\infty, 2) \cup (5, \infty)$ **75.** $(-\infty, \infty)$ **77.** $(-\infty, -2] \cup (5, \infty)$ **79.** $(-\infty, -3) \cup (0, \infty)$
81. $\left(-\infty, -\dfrac{3}{4}\right) \cup \left(-\dfrac{3}{4}, \infty\right)$ **83.** $(-\infty, 2) \cup (2, \infty)$ **85.** $(-\infty, \infty)$ **87.** $(-5, \infty)$ **89.** Answers may vary.
91. $(-\infty, 1) \cup (1, \infty)$

CHAPTER 1 REVIEW PROBLEMS

1. $\{1\}$ **2.** $\left\{\dfrac{3}{2}\right\}$ **3.** $\left\{\dfrac{22}{3}\right\}$ **4.** $\{2\}$ **5.** $\varnothing$ **6.** $(-\infty, -1) \cup (-1, 1) \cup (1, \infty)$ **7.** $\{3\}$ **8.** $\left\{-\dfrac{2}{3}, 2\right\}$

9. $\left\{-\dfrac{8}{3}, \dfrac{16}{3}\right\}$ **10.** $\left\{-4, \dfrac{1}{4}\right\}$ **11.** $\{-4, -3\}$ **12.** $\{-3, 4\}$ **13.** $\{0, 2\}$ **14.** $\left\{-\dfrac{\sqrt{30}}{6}, \dfrac{\sqrt{30}}{6}\right\}$

15. $\{2 - \sqrt{3}, 2 + \sqrt{3}\}$ **16.** $\left\{\dfrac{1 - \sqrt{11}}{2}, \dfrac{1 + \sqrt{11}}{2}\right\}$ **17.** $\left\{\dfrac{-5 - \sqrt{33}}{2}, \dfrac{-5 + \sqrt{33}}{2}\right\}$

18. $\left\{\dfrac{-1 - i\sqrt{5}}{2}, \dfrac{-1 + i\sqrt{5}}{2}\right\}$ **19.** $\{-5, 0, 5\}$ **20.** $\left\{-3, \dfrac{1}{2}, 3\right\}$ **21.** $\{-2, -1, 1, 2\}$

22. $\{-3, -1 - \sqrt{3}, -1 + \sqrt{3}, 1\}$ **23.** $\{13\}$ **24.** $\{5\}$ **25.** $\{0\}$ **26.** $\{-27, 27\}$ **27.** $\{16\}$ **28.** $\{-4, 5\}$

29. $\{16\}$ **30.** $\left\{-1, -\dfrac{2\sqrt{6}}{9}, \dfrac{2\sqrt{6}}{9}, 1\right\}$ **31.** $\{2, 3, 4, 6\}$

32. $(-\infty, 4]$

4

33. $\left(-\infty, \dfrac{15}{4}\right)$

$\dfrac{15}{4}$

34. $\left(-\infty, -\dfrac{21}{2}\right)$

$-\dfrac{21}{2}$

35. $(2, 3]$

$2 \qquad 3$

36. $\left(-\dfrac{8}{5}, \dfrac{2}{5}\right]$

$-\dfrac{8}{5} \qquad \dfrac{2}{5}$

37. $\left(-\dfrac{19}{3}, 7\right)$

$-\dfrac{19}{3} \qquad 7$

38. $(-\infty, -3] \cup \left[\frac{9}{2}, \infty\right)$

39. $\left(-\frac{9}{2}, \frac{15}{2}\right)$

40. $\left[-4, \frac{1}{2}\right]$

41. $\left(-\infty, \frac{3 - \sqrt{3}}{2}\right) \cup \left(\frac{3 + \sqrt{3}}{2}, \infty\right)$

42. $\varnothing$

43. $(-\infty, \infty)$

44. $(-3, -2) \cup (3, \infty)$

45. $(-3, -1)$

46. $(-\infty, 4) \cup \left(\frac{23}{4}, \infty\right)$

47. $\left(-3, -\frac{5}{3}\right] \cup (-1, \infty)$

48. $\dfrac{A - 2LW}{2(W + L)}$

49. $\dfrac{R_2 R_T}{R_2 - R_T}$

50. a. $\dfrac{NDPM}{NDP - MC}$ **b.** Answers may vary.   **51.** 2012 and 2030   **52.** 50 mph   **53.** 2 seconds

54. a. $s = -16t^2 + 64t + 80$ **b.** No   **c.**   **55.** 17.5 years; \$24,250   **56.** 7.1 years

57. \$400 per week   **58.** 19 or 31   **59. a.** About 21.4 million   **b.** About 114.2 million   **60.** 6000 books
61. 12 ft by 27 ft   **62.** 30 ft by 75 ft   **63. a.** 600 ft by 1200 ft   **b.** Yes   **64.** 12 in. by 12 in.

65. 21.5 cm by 21.5 cm   **66.** 285 in^3 **67.** 56.5 ft^3 **68.** 182,200 miles/second   **69.** $33\frac{1}{3}$ seconds

70. 800 units   **71. a.** $\sqrt{25 + x^2}$; 6   **b.** $x \approx 4.8$; 1.2 miles   **72. a.** Males
b. $A \approx 75.1$ or $A \approx 92.4$; a person who has 10 years remaining to live in 1993 is about 75 years old.
73. \$6250   **74.** 1987   **75.** From 1 to 2 seconds   **76.** $(-\infty, -5] \cup [-2, \infty)$
77. Canada, Former Soviet Union   **78.** Australia, Canada, U.S.

CHAPTER I TEST

1. $\{-1\}$ **2.** $\left\{-\frac{4}{3}, 2\right\}$ **3.** $\left\{-\frac{1}{2}, 2\right\}$ **4.** $\left\{\frac{1 - 5\sqrt{3}}{3}, \frac{1 + 5\sqrt{3}}{3}\right\}$ **5.** $\{1 - \sqrt{5}, 1 + \sqrt{5}\}$

6. $\{-2 - \sqrt{5}, -2 + \sqrt{5}\}$ **7.** $\left\{\frac{2 - i}{2}, \frac{2 + i}{2}\right\}$ **8.** $\{-1, 1, 4\}$ **9.** $\{-1, 1, 2, 4\}$ **10.** $\{23\}$ **11.** $\{1, \ 262,144\}$

12. $\{\sqrt[3]{4}\}$

13. $\left(-\infty, -\dfrac{1}{3}\right]$

$-\dfrac{1}{3}$

14. $\left[-7, \dfrac{13}{2}\right)$

-7　$\dfrac{13}{2}$

15. $\left(-\infty, -\dfrac{5}{3}\right] \cup \left[\dfrac{1}{3}, \infty\right)$

$-\dfrac{5}{3}$　$\dfrac{1}{3}$

16. $(-3, 4)$

-3　4

17. $(3, 10)$

3　10

18. a. $125B - 50w$　**b.** 24,000 years!　**19.** 2050　**20.** 60 hours　**21.** \$32,000　**22.** 15 in. by 15 in.

23. 100 m and 240 m　**24.** $\dfrac{9\pi}{4}$ ft^3　**25.** $19 \le x \le 23$; the length for x must be between 19 ft and 23 ft, inclusive.

Chapter 2

PROBLEM SET 2.1

1. Function; domain: $\{1, 3, 5\}$; range: $\{2, 4, 5\}$　**3.** Not a function; domain: $\{3, 4\}$; range: $\{4, 5\}$
5. Function; domain: $\{-3, -2, -1, 0\}$; range: $\{-3, -2, -1, 0\}$　**7.** Not a function; domain: $\{1\}$; range: $\{4, 5, 6\}$
9. a. -6　**b.** -14　**c.** -4　**d.** $4a - 6$　**e.** $-4a - 6$　**f.** $8a - 6$　**11. a.** 7　**b.** 11　**c.** 35
d. $x^2 + 3x + 7$　**e.** $a^2 + 2ah + h^2 - 3a - 3h + 7$　**13. a.** 2　**b.** $\dfrac{17}{4}$　**c.** $a^2 + \dfrac{1}{a^2}$　**d.** $a^2 + \dfrac{1}{a^2}$
15. a. $4a + 2$　**b.** $4a + 4h + 2$　**c.** 4　**d.** $4a + 4h + 4$　**17. a.** $2a^2 - 3a + 5$
b. $2a^2 + 4ah + 2h^2 - 3a - 3h + 5$　**c.** $4a + 2h - 3$　**d.** $2a^2 + 2h^2 - 3a - 3h + 10$
19. a. 6　**b.** 6　**c.** 0　**d.** 12　**21. a.** $\dfrac{1}{a}$　**b.** $\dfrac{1}{a + h}$　**c.** $-\dfrac{1}{a(a + h)}$　**d.** $\dfrac{a + h}{ah}$
23. a. $-6x - 5$　**b.** $6x + 6h - 5$　**c.** 6　**25. a.** $2x^2 + 4x - 1$　**b.** $2x^2 + 4xh + 2h^2 - 4x - 4h - 1$
c. $4x + 2h - 4$　**27. a.** 3　**b.** 3　**c.** 0　**d.** $\pi - 3$　**29.** $(-\infty, \infty)$　**31.** $(-\infty, 4) \cup (4, \infty)$
33. $(-\infty, -8) \cup (-8, -3) \cup (-3, \infty)$　**35.** $(-\infty, \infty)$　**37.** $[3, \infty)$　**39.** $(-\infty, \infty)$　**41.** $(3, \infty)$
43. $(-\infty, -4] \cup [2, \infty)$　**45.** $[1, 3) \cup (3, \infty)$　**47.** $\left(-\infty, \dfrac{1}{3}\right) \cup (2, \infty)$　**49.** $[-1, 1]$
51. 28,771; the number of new AIDS cases in the United States in 1988 was 28,771.
53. 170; the difference in income for a diving boat with 40 and 50 passengers is \$170.
55. 240; the length of a 400-meter tall starship moving at 148,800 miles/second from the perspective of an
observer is 240 meters.　**57.** 33; the average velocity between 2 and 4 seconds is 33 units/seconds
59. 8507.84; the difference in the average price of a mobile home in the United States between 1986 and 1996 is
\$8507.84.　**61.** d　**63.** c　**65.** d　**67.** $(-\infty, 2) \cup (2, 6) \cup (6, \infty)$　**69.** $(-\infty, 5]$
71. $(-\infty, -4) \cup (-1, \infty)$　**73.** $(-\infty, 2) \cup (2, \infty)$
75. a. $P(x) = x(6 - x)$　**b.**　**c.** Answers may vary.

77. Not a function　**79.** Function　**81. a.** No　**b.** Answers may vary.　**83. a–c.** Answers may vary.　**85.** x
87. $g(t) = t + 1$

PROBLEM SET 2.2

1. -6 **3.** 2 **5.** 0 **7.** $L_1: \dfrac{2}{3}; L_2: -\dfrac{3}{4}; L_3: 0$ **9. a.** m_1, m_2, m_4, m_3 **b.** b_3, b_2, b_4, b_1

11. $y - 6 = 5(x + 5); y = 5x + 31; 5x - y + 31 = 0$ **13.** $y + 1 = -(x - 6); y = -x + 5; x + y - 5 = 0$

15. $y + 3 = \dfrac{1}{8}(x + 1); y = \dfrac{1}{8}x - \dfrac{23}{8}; x - 8y - 23 = 0$ **17.** $y + 10 = -4(x + 8); y = -4x - 42; 4x + y + 42 = 0$

19. $y + 7 = -2(x - 4); y = -2x + 1; 2x + y - 1 = 0$ **21.** $y - 0 = 3(x + 3); y = 3x + 9; 3x - y + 9 = 0$

23. $m = 2, b = 1$ **25.** $m = -2; b = 1$ **27.** $m = \dfrac{3}{4}; b = -2$ **29.** $m = -3; b = 2$

      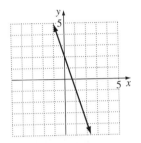

31. $m = -\dfrac{3}{2}; b = 0$ **33.** $m = 3; b = 2$ **35.** Slope is undefined; no y-intercept

37. $m = 0; b = -2$ **39.** $m = 0; y = 0$

41. a. 23.4; U.S. health-care costs between 1975 and 1980 increased at a rate of \$23.4 billion per year.
b. 50.2; U.S. health-care costs between 1985 and 1990 increased at a rate of \$50.2 billion per year
43. a. Answers may vary: 1975 and 1980 or 1985 and 1987; 1500; the number of motor-vehicle deaths between 1975 and 1980 and between 1985 and 1987 increased at a rate of approximately 1500 per year.
b. Answers may vary: 1988 and 1989; -2000; the number of motor-vehicle deaths between 1988 and 1989 decreased at a rate of 2000 per year.   **c.** The horizontal axis is not evenly scaled.

45. $y = \dfrac{424,000}{3}x - \dfrac{843,752,000}{3}; 1,416,000$ **47.** $y = 0.109x - 215.579; \$2.421$ billion; $\$1.113$ billion

49. $y = 2500x + 26,500$ **51. a.** $C = \dfrac{4}{30}M$ **b.** 150 miles   **53.** 7.5 miles   **55.** d

57.

59.

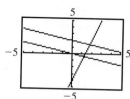

61. a. $y = -\dfrac{2}{3}x + 2$ **b.** $y = -\dfrac{2}{3}x - 2$ **c.** $y = -\dfrac{7}{4}x + 7$ **d.** $y = -\dfrac{7}{4}x - 7$

x-intercept: $(3, 0)$ x-intercept: $(-3, 0)$ x-intercept: $(4, 0)$ x-intercept: $(-4, 0)$
y-intercept: $(0, 2)$ y-intercept: $(0, -2)$ y-intercept: $(0, 7)$ y-intercept: $(0, -7)$

e. Line with x-intercept $(a, 0)$ and y-intercept $(0, b)$

63. b.

c. $y = 0.1907x + 67.7404$
$r = 0.9882$

d.

e. 79.2   **f.** 2067

65. Answers may vary.

67. Yes; no; it is not reasonable to expect that jumping ability is directly proportional to body length.

69. a. $y = \dfrac{b}{a - 2c}x - \dfrac{bc}{a - 2c}$ **b.** $y = \dfrac{a}{b}x - \dfrac{ac}{b}$ **c.** $y = \dfrac{a}{b}x - \dfrac{a^2 - b^2}{2b}$

d. $y = -\dfrac{a + c}{2b}x + b;\ y = \dfrac{b}{a - 2c}x - \dfrac{ab}{c - 2a}$ **e.** $x = 0;\ y = \dfrac{c}{b}x - \dfrac{ac}{b}$ **f.** $x = \dfrac{a + c}{2};\ y = \dfrac{a}{b}x - \dfrac{b^2 - c^2}{2b}$

71. $y - 5 = -\dfrac{5}{6}(x - 0);\ y = -\dfrac{5}{6}x + 5$ **73.** Group activity

---

PROBLEM SET 2.3

1.

Domain: $(-\infty, \infty)$
Range: $[-2, \infty)$

3.

Domain: $(-\infty, \infty)$
Range: $[0, \infty)$

5.

Domain: $(-\infty, \infty)$
Range: $(-\infty, \infty)$

7.

Domain: $(-\infty, \infty)$
Range: $(-\infty, \infty)$

9.

Domain: $[0, \infty)$
Range: $[1, \infty)$

11.

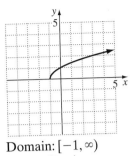

Domain: $[-1, \infty)$
Range: $[0, \infty)$

13.

Domain: $(-\infty, \infty)$
Range: $[0, \infty)$

15.

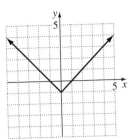

Domain: $(-\infty, \infty)$
Range: $[-1, \infty)$

17.

Domain: $(-\infty, \infty)$
Range: $[0, \infty)$

19.

Domain: $(-\infty, \infty)$
Range: $[0, \infty)$

21.

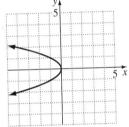

Domain: $(-\infty, 2) \cup (2, \infty)$
Range: $(-\infty, 4) \cup (4, \infty)$

23.

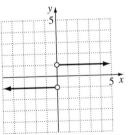

Domain: $(-\infty, -1) \cup (-1, \infty)$
Range: $(-\infty, -2) \cup (-2, \infty)$

25.

Domain: $[0, \infty)$
Range: $(-\infty, \infty)$

27.

Domain: $(-\infty, 0]$
Range: $(-\infty, \infty)$

29.

Domain: $(-\infty, 0) \cup (0, \infty)$
Range: $\{-1, 1\}$

31. Not a function
Domain: $[-5, 5]$
Range: $[-2, 2]$

33. Function
Domain: $(-\infty, \infty)$
Range: $(-\infty, \infty)$

35. Function
Domain: $(-\infty, \infty)$
Range: $(-\infty, 3]$

37. Not a function
Domain: $\{2\}$
Range: $\{-2, 1, 3, 5\}$

39. Function; Domain: $\{-6, -5, -4, -3, -2, -1, 0, 1, 2, 3, 4, 5, 6\}$; Range: $\{0, 1, 2, 3, 4, 5, 6\}$
41. Function; Domain: $(-\infty, \infty)$; Range: $(-\infty, -2]$ **43.** $x^2 + y^2 = 49$ **45.** $(x - 3)^2 + (y - 2)^2 = 25$
47. $(x + 1)^2 + (y - 4)^2 = 4$ **49.** $(x + 3)^2 + (y + 1)^2 = 3$ **51.** $(x + 4)^2 + (y - 0)^2 = 0$

53. Center: $(0, 0)$; radius: 4

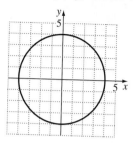

55. Center: $(3, 1)$; radius: 6

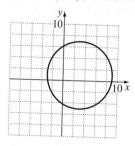

57. Center: $(-3, 2)$; radius: 2

59. Center: $(-2, -2)$; radius: 2

61. $(x + 3)^2 + (y + 1)^2 = 4$
Center: $(-3, -1)$; radius: 2

63. $(x - 5)^2 + (y - 3)^2 = 64$
Center: $(5, 3)$; radius: 8

65. $(x + 4)^2 + (y - 1)^2 = 25$
Center: $(-4, 1)$; radius: 5

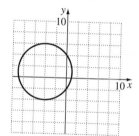

67. $(x - 1)^2 + (y - 0)^2 = 16$
Center: $(1, 0)$; radius: 4

69.

71.

73.

75.

77.

79. $0, 85, 112, 117, 112, 85, 0$

The drugs concentration increases from zero to 117 ppm at 3 hours and then decreases to zero at 6 hours.

81.

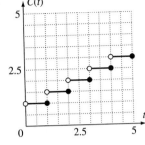

83. c   **85.** d

87.

89.

91.

93.

95.

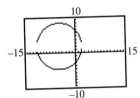

97. No; consider the left or right semicircle.   **99.** No; there is no graph.

101. (a)   **103.** (g)

PROBLEM SET 2.4

1. a. $f(-6) = 6; f(0) = 1; f(3) = 4$ **b.** Increasing: $(0, \infty)$; decreasing: $(-\infty, 0)$
c. Minimum value is 1 at $x = 0$.   **d.** $[1, \infty)$ **3. a.** $f(-2) = 0; f(-1) = 2; f(5) = 3$
b. Increasing: $(4, 6)$; decreasing: $(-5, -1)$; Constant: $(-1, 4)$ **c.** $(-2, 4]$

5. Possible answer: **7.** Possible answer: **9.** Possible answer: **11.** Possible answer:

13. Possible answer: **15. a.** 1967–1975, 1980–1990   **b.** 1975–1980   **c.** 1975; approximately 13%
d. 1978; 15%

17. a. Increasing: $(45, 74)$; decreasing: $(16, 45)$ **b.** 45; 190   **c.** $[190, 526.4]$

19. Possible answer:

21. $A(x) = x(50 - x);$ (b)   **23.** d

25.

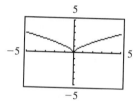

Increasing: $(-\infty, 1) \cup (3, \infty)$
Decreasing: $(1, 3)$
Relative minimum: 1
Relative maximum: 5

27.

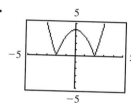

Increasing: $(-2, 0) \cup (2, \infty)$
Decreasing: $(-\infty, -2) \cup (0, 2)$
Relative maximum: 4
Relative minimum: 0

29.

Increasing: $(1, \infty)$
Decreasing: $(-\infty, 1)$
Relative minimum: -3

31.

Increasing: $(0, \infty)$
Decreasing: $(-\infty, 0)$
Relative minimum: 0

33. a.

b.

c. Increasing: $(0, \infty)$; decreasing: $(-\infty, 0)$
d. $f(x) = x^n$ is increasing from $(-\infty, \infty)$ when n is odd.
e. As n increases, the steepness increases.
c. 20.25

35. a. $P(x) = x(9 - x)$ **b.**

c. 20.25

37. a. $P(x) = -0.01x^2 + 150x - 20,000$ **b.**

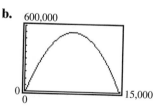

c. 7500 items; $5425

39–41. Answers may vary.   **43.** Group activity

PROBLEM SET 2.5

1.

3.

5.

7.

9.

11.

13.

15.

17.

19.

21.

23.

25.

27. $g(x) = -(x-3)^2$

29. $g(x) = -\sqrt{x-2} + 2$

31. $g(x) = -|x-4| + 1$

33. $g(x) = -\sqrt{9 - (x-1)^2} - 1$

35.

37.

39.

41.

43.

f   *g*

45. a.

b.

c.

d.

e.

f.

47. a.

b.

c.

d.

49. a.

b

c.

d.

e.

f.

51. a.   **b.**   **c.**   **d.**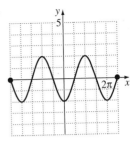

53. Even   **55.** Odd   **57.** Neither   **59.** Even   **61.** Even

63. Possible answer: **65.** Possible answer: **67.** Possible answer: **69.** c

71.   **73.**   **75.**

77. a, b.   **c.** Answers may vary.

d. Stretch the graph of f by multiplying each of its x-coordinates by $\dfrac{1}{c}$.

e. Answers may vary.

79–81. Answers may vary.   **83.** No   **85.** $(a, 2b)$ **87.** $(a, b - 3)$ **89.** $(a + 5, -b)$

91. Increasing on $(-\infty, -6)$; decreasing on $(-6, -1)$; increasing on $(-1, \infty)$

93. Decreasing on $(-\infty, -6)$; increasing on $(-6, -1)$; decreasing on $(-1, \infty)$

95. $mx - y - mx_1 + y_1 = 0$

PROBLEM SET 2.6

1. $(f + g)(x) = 2x^2 - 2$, domain: $(-\infty, \infty)$; $(f - g)(x) = 2x^2 - 2x - 4$, domain: $(-\infty, \infty)$;

$(fg)(x) = 2x^3 + x^2 - 4x - 3$, domain: $(-\infty, \infty)$; $\left(\dfrac{f}{g}\right)(x) = 2x - 3$, domain: $(-\infty, -1) \cup (-1, \infty)$

3. $(f + g)(x) = \sqrt{x + 4} + \sqrt{x - 1}$, domain: $[1, \infty)$; $(f - g)(x) = \sqrt{x + 4} - \sqrt{x - 1}$, domain: $[1, \infty)$;

$(fg)(x) = \sqrt{x^2 + 3x - 4}$, domain: $[1, \infty)$; $\left(\dfrac{f}{g}\right)(x) = \dfrac{\sqrt{x + 4}}{\sqrt{x - 1}}$, domain: $(1, \infty)$

5. $(f + g)(x) = \dfrac{x^2 + 1}{x^3}$, domain: $(-\infty, 0) \cup (0, \infty)$; $(f - g)(x) = \dfrac{x^2 - 1}{x^3}$, domain: $(-\infty, 0) \cup (0, \infty)$;

$(fg)(x) = \dfrac{1}{x^4}$, domain: $(-\infty, 0) \cup (0, \infty)$; $\left(\dfrac{f}{g}\right)(x) = x^2$, domain: $(-\infty, 0) \cup (0, \infty)$

7. $(f + g)(x) = \dfrac{x\sqrt{2x - 6} + 1}{x}$, domain: $[3, \infty)$; $(f - g)(x) = \dfrac{x\sqrt{2x - 6} - 1}{x}$, domain: $[3, \infty)$;

$(fg)(x) = \dfrac{\sqrt{2x - 6}}{x}$, domain: $[3, \infty)$; $\left(\dfrac{f}{g}\right)(x) = x\sqrt{x - 6}$, domain: $[3, \infty)$

9.

11.

13. $\left(\dfrac{f}{g}\right)(x) = 2x - 5 \ (x \neq -2)$

15.a. $(f \circ g)(x) = x^2 + 4x + 4$ **b.** $(g \circ f)(x) = x^2 + 2$ **c.** $(f \circ f)(x) = x^4$ **17. a.** $(f \circ g)(x) = -2x + 11$
b. $(g \circ f)(x) = -2x + 1$ **c.** $(f \circ f)(x) = 4x + 9$ **19. a.** $(f \circ g)(x) = x$ **b.** $(g \circ f)(x) = x$
c. $(f \circ f)(x) = 256x^9 - 192x^6 + 48x^3 - 5$ **21. a.** $(f \circ g)(x) = \sqrt{2x + 1}; \left[-\dfrac{1}{2}, \infty\right)$
b. $(g \circ f)(x) = 2\sqrt{x} + 1; [0, \infty)$ **23. a.** $(f \circ g)(x) = 2x; (-\infty, 0) \cup (0, \infty)$ **b.** $(g \circ f)(x) = \dfrac{x}{2}; (-\infty, 0) \cup (0, \infty)$
25. a. $(f \circ g)(x) = -x^2; [-3, 3]$ **b.** $(g \circ f)(x) = \sqrt{-x^4 + 18x^2 - 72}; [-\sqrt{12}, -\sqrt{6}] \cup [\sqrt{6}, \sqrt{12}]$
27. a. $(f \circ g)(x) = x^2; (-\infty, \infty)$ **b.** $(g \circ f)(x) = x^2; (-\infty, \infty)$ **29. a.** $(f \circ g)(x) = |3x - 1|; (-\infty, \infty)$
b. $(g \circ f)(x) = 3|x| - 1; (-\infty, \infty)$ **31. a.** $(f \circ g)(x) = x; (-\infty, 3) \cup (3, \infty)$ **b.** $(g \circ f)(x) = x; (-\infty, 1) \cup (1, \infty)$
33. a. $(f \circ g)(x) = x; (-\infty, \infty)$ **b.** $(g \circ f)(x) = x; (-\infty, \infty)$ **35.** undefined   **37.** 4.5   **39.** 4.5   **41.** 2
43. -3 **45.** $f(x) = x^4; g(x) = 3x - 1$ **47.** $f(x) = \sqrt[3]{x}; g(x) = x^2 - 9$ **49.** $f(x) = |x|; g(x) = 2x - 5$
51. $f(x) = \dfrac{1}{x}; g(x) = 2x - 3$ **53.** $f(x) = x^{2/3}; g(x) = 2x^2 - 5x + 1$ **55.** $f(x) = 3x^2 + 5x; g(x) = x - 1$
57. $k(x) = (g \circ f)(x)$ **59.** $k(x) = (f \circ h)(x)$ **61.** $k(x) = (g \circ f \circ h)(x)$ **63.** $f^3(x) = 8x - 21$
65. $f^3(x) = x^8 + 4x^6 + 8x^4 + 8x^2 + 5$ **67.** $f^3(x) = x^{27}$ **69.** $f^4(x) = \dfrac{5x + 3}{3x + 2}$

71. a. -0.44; profit is decreasing.   **b.** 0.51; profit is increasing.
c. $(f + g)(x) = 0.07x + 24.76; 0.07$; profit is increasing.
73. $(A \circ r)(t) = 0.16\pi t^2$; area of the circle as a function of time
75. a. The cost of the car to the consumer is the selling price with a \$2000 rebate.
b. The cost of the car is 85% of the selling price, a 15% discount to the consumer.
c. $(f \circ g)(x) = 0.85x - 2000$; the cost of the car is 85% of the selling price with a \$2000 rebate.
d. $(g \circ f)(x) = 0.85x - 1700$; the cost of the car is 85% of the selling price less \$1700.
e. The cost in part (c) is less.
77. $0, 0, 0, 0$; yes   **79.** $-i, -1 -i, -1 + i, -1 -i$; yes   **81.** $1 - i, 1 - 3i, -7 - 9i, -39 + 117i$; no   **83.** c

85. Domain of f: $(-\infty, \infty)$
Domain of g: $[-2, 2]$
Domain of $f \circ g$: $[-2, 2]$

87. Domain of f: $(-\infty, -1] \cup [1, \infty)$
Domain of g: $(-\infty, 1]$
Domain of $f \circ g$: $(-\infty, 0]$

89. Domain of f: $[1, \infty)$
Domain of g: $(-\infty, 1]$
Domain of $f \circ g$: $(-\infty, 0]$

91. a.

b. The y-coordinates of $f + g$ are equal to the sum of the corresponding y-coordinates of f and g.
c. Answers may vary.

d.

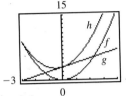

93. $f^n(0.96)$ approaches zero. $f^n(1.04)$ gets very large.

95. $g(x) = 4x - 1$ or $g(x) = -4x - 4$ **97.** Answers may vary.   **99.** Verification is left to the student.

101. Odd   **103.** Odd   **105.** $m = -\dfrac{1}{2}; b = \dfrac{1}{2}$ **107.** Group activity

---

PROBLEM SET 2.7

1. Function; not one-to-one   **3.** Not a function   **5.** Not a function   **7.** Function; not one-to-one
9. Function; one-to-one   **11.** $[1, \infty)$ **13.** $[2, \infty)$ **15. a.** 13   **b.** 7   **17.** 5
19. $(-4, 0), (0, 2), (4, 4)$ **21.** $(1, 0), (2, 1), (4, 2)$

23–27. Verification is left to the student.

29. $f^{-1}(x) = \dfrac{x - 7}{3}$ **31.** $f^{-1}(x) = 6 - 2x$ **33.** $f^{-1}(x) = \dfrac{x^2 - 7}{2}, x \geq 0$ **35.** $f^{-1}(x) = \dfrac{x^3 + 3}{2}$

37. $f^{-1}(x) = \sqrt[3]{\dfrac{x + 7}{5}}$ **39.** $f^{-1}(x) = \dfrac{3x + 1}{x - 2}$ **41.** $f^{-1}(x) = \sqrt{x} + 3$ **43.** $f^{-1}(x) = (x - 3)^3 + 4$

45. $f^{-1}(x) = \dfrac{1}{x-3}$ **47.** $f^{-1}(x) = x^{5/3}$

49.

51.

53.

55.

57.

59.

61.

63. $(f^{-1} \circ g^{-1})(x) = \dfrac{x-5}{2}$ **65.** $(f \circ g)^{-1}(x) = \dfrac{x-2}{2}$

67. a. f is increasing on its domain.   **b.** Number of people in a room for a 25% probability of two people sharing a birthday; number of people in a room for a 50% probability of two people sharing a birthday; number of people in a room for a 70% probability of two people sharing a birthday

69. a. Yes   **b.** No; time is not a function of arts endowment.   **71.** $5D + 5$ **75.** a

77. $f^{-1}(x) = \sqrt[3]{x-2}$ **79.** $f^{-1}(x) = \sqrt{9-x^2}, 0 \le x \le 3$ **81.** $f^{-1}(x) = x^3 + 2$

83. Not one-to-one   **85.** Not one-to-one   **87.** One-to-one

89. Not one-to-one   **91.** One-to-one   **93.** Inverses

95. Not inverses

97. a.

b. No; $\left[-\dfrac{\pi}{2}, \dfrac{\pi}{2}\right]$ **c.** Answers may vary.

99. Answers may vary.   **101.** $f^{-1}(x) = \dfrac{Ax + B}{Cx - A}$ **103.** 8   **105.** Verification is left to the student.

CHAPTER 2 REVIEW PROBLEMS

1. 824.9; from the perspective of an observer at rest, the length is approximately 824.9 meters.

2. -0.095; the average distance each automobile was driven in 1950 was greater than in 1985 by 95 miles.

3. a. -3 **b.** -17 **c.** $7a - 3$ **d.** $7a + 7h - 3$ **e.** 7   **f.** $7a + 7h - 6$ **g.** $14a - 3$ **4. a.** 11   **b.** 37

c. $4a^2 - 5a + 11$ **d.** $4a^2 + 8ah + 4h^2 - 5a - 5h + 11$ **e.** $8a + 4h - 5$ **f.** $4a^2 - 5a + 4h^2 - 5h + 22$

g. $16a^2 - 10a + 11$ **5.** $(-\infty, 4]$ **6.** $(-\infty, \infty)$ **7.** $(-\infty, 1] \cup [4, \infty)$ **8.** $(-\infty, 1) \cup (4, \infty)$ **9.** $[-2, 2]$

10. $[2, 5) \cup (5, \infty)$ **11.** $y - 2 = -6(x + 3); y = -6x - 16; 6x + y + 16 = 0$

12. $y - 6 = 2(x - 1)$ or $y - 2 = 2(x + 1); y = 2x + 4; 2x - y + 4 = 0$

13. $y + 7 = -3(x - 4); y = -3x + 5; 3x + y - 5 = 0$ **14.** $y - 6 = -3(x + 3); y = -3x - 3; 3x + y + 3 = 0$

15. a. 6.6 million; $m = 0.12$; from 1975 to 1980, the number of victims increased at an average rate of 120,000
per year.   **b.** $m = -0.08$; from 1980 to 1985, the number of victims decreased at an average rate of
80,000 per year.   **16.** Answers may vary: $y = 16x - 31,108$; 892 nurses

17. a. $y - 666.2 = 60.1(x - 5)$ or $y - 546 = 60.1(x - 3); y = 60.1x + 365.7$ **b.** \$485.9 billion

c. \$1267.2 billion   **18.**

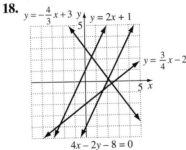

19. $\dfrac{1}{50}, \dfrac{1}{100}, \dfrac{1}{150}$ **20. a.** Drive On Rental Company: $y = 0.15x + 30$; Hit the Road Rental: $y = 0.10x + 40$

b.

21. a. $y = \dfrac{2}{115}x$ **b.** \$608.70

22.

Domain: $(-\infty, \infty)$

Range: $\left[-\dfrac{1}{4}, \infty\right)$

23.

Domain: $(-\infty, \infty)$

Range: $(-\infty, \infty)$

24.

Domain: $(-\infty, 5) \cup (5, \infty)$

Range: $(-\infty, 10) \cup (10, \infty)$

25.

Domain: $(-\infty, \infty)$

Range: $[0, \infty)$

26.

Domain: $[-3, \infty)$

Range: $[0, \infty)$

27.

Domain: $(-\infty, 0]$

Range: $(-\infty, \infty)$

28.

Domain: $(-\infty, \infty)$

Range: $[0, \infty)$

29.

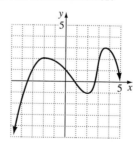

Domain: $(-\infty, \infty)$

Range: $[0, \infty)$

30. a. $[-3, 5)$

b. $[-5, 0]$

c. 3

31. Center: $(2, -1)$; $r = 3$ **32.** Center: $(-1, 2)$; $r = 3$ **33. a.** $-5; 0; -3$

b. Increasing: $(-5, 0)$; decreasing: $(-\infty, -5) \cup (0, \infty)$ **c.** Relative maximum: 3 at $x = 0$; relative minimum: -6 at $x = -5$ **d.** Not one-to-one; $[0, \infty)$ **34. a.** Answers may vary.   **b.** $(3, 12)$ **c.** $(0, 3), (12, 17)$

d. $(17, 30)$ **e.** No   **35. a.** Maximum $= 13.5$ at $x = 25$ **b.** Range: $[1, 13.5]$

36. Possible answer: **37.** Possible answer: **38. a.** Possible answer: **b.** 4

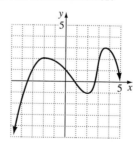

c. $(-\infty, -2)$ and $(2, 3.5)$

d. $(-2, 2)$ and $(3.5, \infty)$

39. Possible answer:

40. Possible answer:

41.

42–43. Answers may vary.

44.

a. Increasing: $(-1, 1)$
Constant: $(-\infty, -1), (1, \infty)$
b. Relative maximum: 1
Relative minimum: -1
c. Odd function

45.

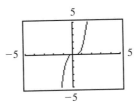

a. Increasing: $(-\infty, 0), (0.33, \infty)$
Decreasing: $(0, 0.33)$
b. Relative maximum: 0
Relative minimum: -0.04
c. Neither

46.

a. Increasing: $(0, \infty)$
Decreasing: $(-\infty, 0)$
b. Relative minimum: 1
c. Even function

47.

a. Increasing: $(-\infty, 0.67)$ and $(2, \infty)$
Decreasing: $(0.67, 2)$
b. Relative maximum: 1.06
Relative minimum: 0
c. Neither

48. a. $f(x) = x(18 - 2x)^2$
b.

c. 3; 432 cubic inches

49. a. $f(x) = (200 + 25x)(400 - x)$
b.

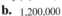

c. 204 people; $1,040,400

50. a. $A = 4x$ **b.** $A = \dfrac{x\sqrt{64 - x^2}}{4}$ **c.** $f(x) = 4x + \dfrac{x\sqrt{64 - x^2}}{4}$

d.

$x \approx 7.44$; 35.23 square feet

51. a. Shift 3 units up   **b.** Shift left 3 units   **c.** Stretch by a factor of 2
d. Shift 1 unit to the right and 3 units down   **e.** Reflect in the y-axis
f. Reflect in the x-axis   **g.** Reflect in the y-axis and then in the x-axis   **h.** Reflect in the line $y = x$

52.

53.

54.

55.

56.

57.

58.
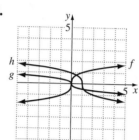

59. $g(x) = |x - 3| - 1$

$h(x) = -\dfrac{1}{2}|x| + 2$

60.

61.

62.

63.

64.

65.

66.

67.
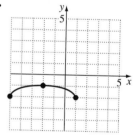

68. $g(x) = -\dfrac{1}{2}\sqrt{16 - x^2} - 1$ **69.** Odd   **70.** Even   **71.** Odd   **72. a.** $(f + g)(x) = x^2 - 9x + 13$

b. $(f - g)(x) = x^2 - 5x + 3$ **c.** $(fg)(x) = -2x^3 + 19x^2 - 51x + 40$ **d.** $\left(\dfrac{f}{g}\right)(x) = \dfrac{x^2 - 7x + 8}{5 - 2x}$

e. $(f \circ g)(x) = 4x^2 - 6x - 2$ **f.** $(g \circ f)(x) = -2x^2 + 14x - 11$ **73. a.** $(f + g)(x) = \sqrt{x + 4} + \sqrt{x - 1}; [1, \infty)$

b. $(f - g)(x) = \sqrt{x + 4} - \sqrt{x - 1}; [1, \infty)$ **c.** $(fg)(x) = \sqrt{x^2 + 3x - 4}; [1, \infty)$ **d.** $\left(\dfrac{f}{g}\right)(x) = \dfrac{\sqrt{x + 4}}{\sqrt{x - 1}}; (1, \infty)$

74. a. $(f \circ g)(x) = \sqrt{2x + 1}$ **b.** $(g \circ f) = 2\sqrt{x} + 1$ **c.** 3   **d.** 11

e. Domain of $f \circ g$: $\left[-\dfrac{1}{2}, \infty\right)$; domain of $g \circ f$: $[0, \infty)$ **75.** $(f \circ g)(x) = -x^2; [-5, 5]$

76. a. $(L \circ p)(t) = 0.7\sqrt{0.0001t^6 + 0.02t^3 + 4}$ **b.** 7.8; the level of carbon monoxide in 2000 is approximately
7.8 ppm.   **77.** $f(x) = x^4; g(x) = 2x + 7$ **78.** $f(x) = \sqrt{x}; g(x) = 3x^2 - 7$
79. $f(x) = 3x^2 + 5x; g(x) = x - 4$ **80.** $f^3(x) = 27x - 26$ **81.** $f^3(x) = x^8 - 4x^6 + 4x^4 - 1$

82. $f^3(x) = 0.857375x$; at the start of 2000 the area of the rain forest will be approximately 86% of the area at the start of 1997.   **83.** Not a function   **84.** Function; not one-to-one   **85.** Function; one-to-one

86. Not a function   **87.** $f^{-1}(x) = 2x + 8$ **88.** $f^{-1}(x) = \dfrac{x + 3}{4}$ **89.** $f^{-1}(x) = x^2 - 2$

90. $f^{-1}(x) = \dfrac{\sqrt[3]{x - 1}}{2}$ **91.** $f^{-1}(x) = \sqrt{x + 4}$ **92.** $f^{-1}(x) = \dfrac{x^3 + 1}{2}$

93. a. Yes   **b.** The number of compounding periods needed to get a balance of $11,250
   c. The statement is false.

94. a.   **b.** $[2, \infty)$ **c.** $f^{-1}(x) = \sqrt{x} + 2$ **d.**

95. a.   **b.** $[-3, \infty)$ **c.** $f^{-1}(x) = x - 3$ **d.**

96. a.   **b.** $[3, \infty)$ **c.** $f^{-1}(x) = \sqrt{x^2 + 9}$ **d.**

97.   **98.**   **99.**

100.   **101. a.** $f(T) = 4T - 160$
   b. 200; at a temperature of 90°, the cricket chirps 200 times per minute.
   c. $(40, 136)$
   d. $(0, 384)$
   e. $T = \dfrac{C + 160}{4}$

102.

x	$f(x)$	$g(x)$	$h(x)$
-3	0	0	0
-2	5	5	undefined
-1	5	5	undefined
0	0	0	0
1	-5	5	undefined
2	-5	5	undefined
3	0	0	0

CHAPTER 2 TEST

1. 11.64; 11.64% of the U.S. population graduated from college in 1970
2. $14a + 7h - 9$ **3.** $(-\infty, 4]$ **4.** $y - 1 = 3(x - 2)$ or $y + 8 = 3(x + 1)$; $y = 3x - 5$; $3x - y - 5 = 0$
5. $y - 6 = 4(x + 4)$; $y = 4x + 22$; $4x - y + 22 = 0$
6. a. $y - 401.1 = 14.9(x - 4)$ or $y - 475.6 = 14.9(x - 9)$; $y = 14.9x + 341.5$ **b.** $639.50
7.

8.

9. a. 5   **b.** $(-1, 2)$
c. $(-\infty, -1), (2, \infty)$
d. 5 at $x = 2$
e. -3 at $x = -1$

10. 128 cubic inches
11. Possible answer:

12. $g(x) = (x - 2)^3$
13. The graph of f is shifted 3 units to the right to obtain the graph of g. Then the graph g is stretched by a factor of two and reflected in the x-axis to obtain the graph of h.

14. Even; the graph in the figure does not have y-axis symmetry.
15. $(f - g)(x) = x^2 - 2x - 2$ **16.** $(f \circ g)(x) = 25x^2 - 5x - 6$ **17.** $(g \circ f)(x) = 5x^2 + 15x - 22$ **18.** 84
19. 28   **20.** $f^{-1}(x) = x^2 + 2$ **21. a.** Yes; the graph of f passes the horizontal line test.
b. The height of a man who has the recommended weight of 170 pounds.   **22. a.** No   **b.** Neither
c. Relative maximum: 3.23 at $x \approx 1.22$; relative minimum: 0 at $x = 0$; relative minimum: -9.91 at $x \approx 3.28$
d. $[-9.91, \infty)$ **e.** $(0, 1.22), (3.28, \infty)$ **f.** $(-\infty, 0), (1.22, 3.28)$

CUMULATIVE REVIEW PROBLEMS (CHAPTERS P–2)

1. $\dfrac{x^9}{8y^{12}}$ **2.** $-14\sqrt{2y}$ **3.** $(x - 1 - y)(x - 1 + y)$ **4.** $\dfrac{1}{(x - 3)(x - 2)}$ **5.** $\sqrt{x + 1} + \sqrt{2}$
6. $\left\{-\dfrac{1}{4}, \dfrac{5}{3}\right\}$ **7.** $\{-1 + \sqrt{6}\}$ **8.** $\{4\}$ **9.** $\{-8, 27\}$ **10.** $\left[-\dfrac{11}{2}, \dfrac{7}{2}\right)$

11. $y - 5 = -2(x + 2); y = -2x + 1; 2x + y - 1 = 0$ **12.**

13. $f^{-1}(x) = \sqrt[5]{2x + 3}$ **14.** $[1, \infty)$ or $(-\infty, 1]$ **15.** m **16.** $r = \dfrac{G - a}{G}$

17. 15 sides   **18.** 1993   **19.** 3 ft by 8 ft   **20.** \$3.00 or \$9.50

Chapter 3

PROBLEM SET 3.1

1. Vertex: $(4, -1)$
  x-intercepts: $(3, 0)$ and $(5, 0)$
  y-intercept: $(0, 15)$
  axis of symmetry: $x = 4$

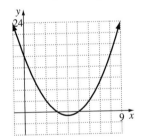

3. Vertex: $(1, 2)$
  x-intercepts: none
  y-intercept: $(0, 3)$
  axis of symmetry: $x = 1$

5. Vertex: $(3, 1)$
  x-intercepts: none
  y-intercept: $(0, 10)$
  axis of symmetry: $x = 3$

7. Vertex: $(-2, -1)$

  x-intercepts: $\left(-2 + \dfrac{\sqrt{2}}{2}, 0\right)$

  and $\left(-2 - \dfrac{\sqrt{2}}{2}, 0\right)$

  y-intercept: $(0, 7)$
  axis of symmetry: $x = -2$

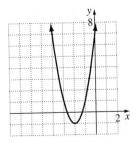

9. Vertex: $(1, 4)$

  x-intercepts: $(-1, 0)$ and $(3, 0)$

  y-intercept: $(0, 3)$
  axis of symmetry: $x = 1$

11. Vertex: $(1, -4)$

  x-intercepts: $(-1, 0)$ and $(3, 0)$

  y-intercept: $(0, -3)$
  axis of symmetry: $x = 1$

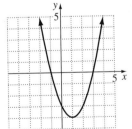

13. Vertex: $\left(-\dfrac{3}{2}, -\dfrac{49}{4}\right)$

x-intercepts: $(2, 0)$ and $(-5, 0)$
y-intercept: $(0, -10)$

axis of symmetry: $x = -\dfrac{3}{2}$

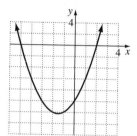

15. Vertex: $(1, 4)$

x-intercepts: $(-1, 0)$ and $(3, 0)$
y-intercept: $(0, 3)$

axis of symmetry: $x = 1$

17. Vertex: $(1, -1)$

x-intercepts: none
y-intercept: $(0, -2)$

axis of symmetry: $x = 1$

19. Year: 1968   **21.** Pair: 8 and 8; Product is 64.   **23.** Dimensions: 5 yds $\times$ 5 yds

25. Dimensions: 120 ft $\times$ 260 ft; Area: 31,200 sq ft   **27.** $\left(\dfrac{1}{2}, \dfrac{\sqrt{2}}{2}\right)$ **29.** $\dfrac{1}{2}$ **31.** 20, 20

33. 200 people, $800   **35.** 5 inches   **37.** $r \approx 35.01$ yards, $x = 110$ yards   **39.** c   **41.** d   **43.** a

45. a.

b.

c.

47. The graph is unrealistic because after peaking around $x = 8$ (1991), the graph rapidly drops below the x-axis indicating that a negative number of cases would be reported. Polynomial functions are best used to model behavior over short periods of time.

49. The midpoint and the value of $-\dfrac{b}{2a}$ are equal when $b^2 - 4ac > 0$. When $b^2 - 4ac = 0$, only one x-intercept exists; when $b^2 - 4ac < 0$, no x-intercept exists.   **51.** $x = 3$; $(0, 11)$ **53.** $y = -(x - 3)^2 + 1$
55. Verification is left to the student.   **57.** 3 square units
59. Vertex: $[-(d + e), (d^2 - 2de + e^2)]$; No, $b^2 - 4ac \le 0$ **61.** Verification is left to the student.

PROBLEM SET 3.2

1. d   **3.** f   **5.** e

7. **a.** Rises to right, falls to left
  b. $x = -2, x = -1, x = 2$
  c.

9. **a.** Rises to the left and the right
  b. $x = -1, x = 0, x = 1$
  c.

11. **a.** Falls to the left and the right
  b. $x = 0, x = -2, x = 2$
  c.

13. **a.** Rises to the left and the right
  b. $x = 0, x = 3$
  c.

15. **a.** Falls to the left and the right
  b. $x = 0, x = 1$
  c.

17. **a.** Rises to the left and falls to the right
  b. $x = 0, x = -\sqrt{2}, x = \sqrt{2}$
  c.
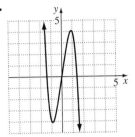

19. **a.** Falls to the left and the right
  b. $x = -1, x = 1$
  c.

21. **a.** Falls to the left and the right
  b. $x = 4, x = -5, x = 5$
  c.

23. **a.** Most of the data points lie very close to the model.   **b.** For 1988, $f(5) = 104{,}706$.
  c. For 1991, $f(8) = 256{,}568.1$ **d.** Leading coefficient is negative.

25. **a.** $V(x) = 216x - 60x^2 + 4x^3$ **b.**   **27.** 320 feet

29. $y = 0.1x^5$ **31.** b   **33.** Possible answer: $f(x) = -x^6$ **35.** Possible answer: $f(x) = x^5$
37. $g(x)$ falls to the left and to the right.   **39.** $h(t)$ rises to the left and to the right.

41. a.

b. The graph does not fall to the right.

c.

43. a.

b. The graph does not rise to the left.

c.

45.

47.

49.

Answers may vary.

51. A fifth-degree polynomial function will never rise on both ends.

53. a. $N(t) = -0.25t^4 - 0.5t^3 + 7t^2 - 4t + 5$ **b.** The model's graph indicates that the patient will feel sickest on the 69th hour.

PROBLEM SET 3.3

1. $x^2 - 3x + 2$; $x = -1, x = 2, x = 1$ **3.** $\left\{-2, \dfrac{1}{2}, 3\right\}$ **5.** $\left\{-4, -\dfrac{1}{3}, 2\right\}$ **7.** $\pm 1, \pm 2, \pm 3, \pm 6, \pm\dfrac{1}{3}, \pm\dfrac{2}{3}$

9. $\pm 1, \pm 2, \pm 3, \pm 6, \pm\dfrac{1}{2}, \pm\dfrac{1}{4}, \pm\dfrac{3}{2}, \pm\dfrac{3}{4}$ **11.** No positive real roots exist; 3 or 1 negative real roots exist.

13. 3 or 1 positive real roots exist; No negative real roots exist.

15. 2 or 0 positive real roots exist; No negative real roots exist.

17. a. $\pm 1, \pm 2, \pm 3, \pm 4, \pm 6, \pm 12, \pm\dfrac{1}{5}, \pm\dfrac{1}{2}, \pm\dfrac{2}{5}, \pm\dfrac{3}{2}, \pm\dfrac{3}{5}, \pm\dfrac{4}{5}, \pm\dfrac{6}{5}, \pm\dfrac{12}{5}$ **b.** 2 is a zero.

c. $2, \dfrac{-5 + \sqrt{265}}{20}, \dfrac{-5 - \sqrt{265}}{20}$ **19. a.** $\pm 1, \pm 3, \pm\dfrac{1}{2}, \pm\dfrac{1}{4}, \pm\dfrac{3}{2}, \pm\dfrac{3}{4}$ **b.** Answers may vary. **c.** $1, \dfrac{1}{2}, \dfrac{3}{2}$

21. Verification is left to the student. (Use the Upper and Lower Bound Theorem.)

23. a. $\pm 1, \pm 2, \pm 3, \pm 4, \pm 6, \pm 12$ **b–e.** 1 is not a root; −3 is not a root; Remaining answers may vary.

25. $\{1, 12\}$ **27.** $\left\{\dfrac{1}{6}, \dfrac{1}{2}, -3\right\}$ **29.** $\{-4, -2, -1, 1\}$ **31.** $\left\{-1, -\dfrac{2}{3}, 1\right\}$ **33.** $\left\{-2, -1, \dfrac{1}{5}, 1, 2\right\}$

35. $\left\{-2, \dfrac{1}{3}, -\sqrt{3}, \sqrt{3}\right\}$ **37.** $\left\{-1, -\dfrac{1}{2}, \dfrac{3}{2}, 2, 4\right\}$ **39.** $\left\{-4, \dfrac{1}{2}, 6\right\}$ **41.** $x = 1$ inch or $x \approx 1.1$ inch

43. $x = 3$ in. **45.** 2 days **47.** d **49.** $\pm 1, \pm 3, \pm 5, \pm 15, \pm\dfrac{1}{2}, \pm\dfrac{3}{2}, \pm\dfrac{5}{2}, \pm\dfrac{15}{2}$; solutions: $-\dfrac{1}{2}, 3, 5$

51. $\pm 1, \pm 2, \pm 3, \pm 6, \pm 9, \pm 18, \pm\dfrac{1}{2}, \pm\dfrac{3}{2}, \pm\dfrac{9}{2}$; solutions: $-3, -\dfrac{3}{2}, -1, 2$

53. $f(x)$ has no sign variations, so $f(x)$ has no positive real roots. $f(-x)$ has no sign variations, so no negative

roots exist. The polynomial graph doesn't intersect the x-axis.   **55.** Polynomials of odd degree must cross the x-axis (leading term test). Polynomials of even degree may sometimes have no real zeros.
57. -3 is a lower bound; 3 is an upper bound.   **59.** Answers may vary.
61. $x^5 + x + 1 = 0$ has one real solution; Answers may vary.   **63.** Answers may vary.
65. By rational root theorem, the possible rational roots of the equation are ± 1 and ± 3. Since $\sqrt{3}$ is a root of the equation, it cannot be a rational number.

PROBLEM SET 3.4

1. $f(1) = -1$, $f(2) = 5$; To the nearest tenth, the zero is 1.3.
3. $f(-1) = -1$, $f(0) = 1$; To the nearest tenth, the zero is -0.5.
5. $f(-3) = -11$, $f(-2) = 1$; To the nearest tenth, the zero is -2.1.
7. $f(-3) = -42$, $f(-2) = 5$; To the nearest tenth, the zero is -2.2.

9. $f(x) = x^3 - 3x^2 - 15x + 125$ **11.** $f(x) = x^4 + 10x^2 + 9$ **13.** $\{-2i, 2i, 2\}$ **15.** $\left\{1 + i, 1 - i, \dfrac{1}{3}\right\}$

17. $\{2 - i, 2 + i, -2 + i, -2 - i\}$ **19.** $\left\{1 - i, 1 + i, -3, \dfrac{1}{3}\right\}$ **21.** $\{3 - i\sqrt{3}, 3 + i\sqrt{3}, 2, 4\}$

23. $\{2 - 3i, 2 + 3i, -i, i, -2\}$ **25.** $f(x) = (x - 1)(x - 5i)(x + 5i)$ **27.** $p(x) = (x - 6i)(x + 6i)(x - i)(x + i)$
29. $p(x) = (x + 2)(4x - 3)(2x + 1 - 2i)(2x + 1 + 2i)$
31. $g(r) = (r + 2)(3r - 1)(r + 1 + i\sqrt{3})(r + 1 - i\sqrt{3})(r - 1 + i\sqrt{3})(r - 1 - i\sqrt{3})$ **33.** $x \approx 1.7$

35. a. 10.3%   **b.** 1980 and 1990   **37.** 9 cm $\times$ 9 cm $\times$ 9 cm   **39.** $f(x) = -\dfrac{1}{3}x^3 + \dfrac{20}{3}x^2 - \dfrac{121}{3}x + 70$

41. b   **43.** Relative minimum ≈ -6.9 feet; Relative maximum ≈ 4.2 feet
45. 3 real zeros (counting multiplicity); 2 complex zeros   **47.** 2 real zeros; 2 complex zeros
49. 1 real zero; 4 complex zeros (counting multiplicity)   **51.** 3 real zeros; 2 complex zeros   **53.** 3   **55.** 6
57. Because of the leading term test which states the polynomial rises to the left and the right, if the polynomial crosses the x-axis once, it must cross it again. A polynomial of degree 20 may be tangent to the x-axis in one place however.   **59.** Yes, a third-degree polynomial has at most 2 turns. A relative maximum occurs at one of these turns.   **61. a–d.** Answers may vary.   **e.** No, the polynomial falls to the left and rises to the right. It must cross the x-axis at least once.   **63.** $(-\infty, -1] \cup [1, 4]$ **65. a–b.** Verification is left to the student.
c. The conjugate roots theorem only refers to polynomials having real coefficients.   **67.** Group activity

PROBLEM SET 3.5

1.

Vertical asymptote: $x = 2$
Horizontal asymptote: $y = 0$

3.

Vertical asymptote: $x = -2$
Horizontal asymptote: $y = 0$

5.

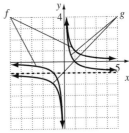

Vertical asymptote: $x = 0$
Horizontal asymptote: $y = -1$

7.

Vertical asymptote: $x = 0$
Horizontal asymptote: $y = 2$

9.

Vertical asymptote: $x = 0$
Horizontal asymptote: $y = 0$

11.

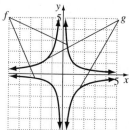

Vertical asymptote: $x = 0$
Horizontal asymptote: $y = 0$

13.

Vertical asymptote: $x = -2$
Horizontal asymptote: $y = -1$

15.

Vertical asymptote: $x = -2$
Horizontal asymptote: $y = -1$

17.

Vertical asymptote: $x = 2$
Horizontal asymptote: $y = 1$

19.

21.

23.

25.

27.

29.

31.

33.

35.

37.

39.

41.

43.   **45.**   **47.**   **49.**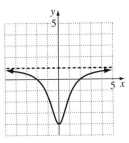

51. d   **53.** Anwers may vary.

55. a.

b. The higher the level of education, the lower the unemployment.
c. $f^{-1}(3.6) \approx 13.97$; The unemployment rate was 3.6% for people with about 14 years of education.
d. Because the x-axis is an asymptote, zero unemployment cannot be fully achieved in spite of higher education levels.
57. No; the graphing utility indicates the domain is $(-\infty, \infty)$.

59. The graph of f has a "hole" at $x = a$ if $p(a) = 0$, provided that the factor $(x - a)$ occurs at least as many times in the factored form of $p(x)$ as it occurs in the factored form of $q(x)$. The graph of f has a vertical asymptote whose equation is $x = a$ if $p(a) \neq 0$ or if the factor $(x - a)$ occurs more often in the factored form of $q(x)$ than in the factored form of $p(x)$.

61.   **63. a.**

b. f will have a parabolic asymptote if the degree of p is two greater. Answers may vary. than the degree of q.

c. Answers may vary.

65. The graph of g will approach the x-axis more rapidly as values of x increase.

67. No; Yes; Verification is left to the student.   **69.** $f(x) = \dfrac{3}{x - 3}$ **71.** $f(x) = \dfrac{x^2 - x - 2}{x - 1}$

PROBLEM SET 3.6

1. a. $220; $40; $22; $20.2   **b.** $y = 20$; As more canoes are manufactured, the average cost approaches $20.
3. a. $100,000   **b.** No; the model indicates that no amount of money can remove 100% of the pollutants since $C(p)$ increases without bound as p approaches 100.
5. a. $F(0) = 80$; When the dessert was placed in the icebox, its temperature was 80°F.
b. Approximately 13.3°F; 6.2°F; 3.6°F; 2.4°F; 1.7°F   **c.** $y = 0$; the temperature will approach but not reach 0°F.
d.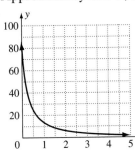

7. Approximately 8885.4 newtons

9. $y = \dfrac{400}{x^2}$; The intensity of the illumination on a surface varies inversely with the square of the distance of the light source from the surface.

11. $y = \dfrac{216,000}{x^3}$

13. a. $T(x) = \dfrac{600}{x} + \dfrac{600}{x - 10}$ **b.**

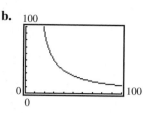

c. $T^{-1}(22) = 60$; If the total time was 22 hours, then the average rate on the outgoing trip was 60 mph.
d. Answers may vary.

15. a.

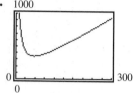

b. 58 cases; Approximately \$346
17. Answers may vary.
19. Verification is left to the student.

CHAPTER 3 REVIEW PROBLEMS

1.

2.

3.

4.

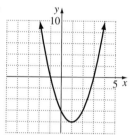

Axis of symmetry: $x = 1$ Axis of symmetry: $x = -4$ Axis of symmetry: $x = 1$ Axis of symmetry: $x = 1$

5. \$54,607   **6.** (17.84, 12.413008); between 1957 and 1958 fuel efficiency of passenger cars was at an all time low of approximately 12.4 miles per gallon.

7. a. $s(t) = -16t^2 + 64t + 80$ **b.** 2 seconds; 144 feet   **c.**

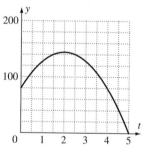

8. 250 ft by 500 ft; 125,000 ft^2 **9.** 40 divers; \$360   **10.** $\left(\dfrac{4}{5}, \dfrac{2}{5}\right)$

11. a. Falls to the left and rises to the right   **c.**
    b. $x = -1, 1, 5$

d.

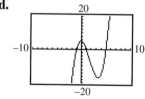

12. a. Falls to the left and to the right   **b.** $-5, 0, 5$ **c.**

d.

13. a. Falls to the left and to the right   **b.** $0, 3$ **c.**

d.
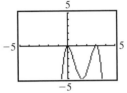

14. a. Rises to the left and to the right   **b.** $0, 5$ **c.**

d.

15. Because the degree is odd and the leading coefficient is negative, the graph falls to the right. Therefore, the model indicates that the percentage of families below the poverty level will eventually be negative, which is impossible.   **16.** c   **17.** b   **18.** a   **19.** d   **20.** $f(x) = 30{,}000x^4$ **21.** 2 or 0 positive solutions; no negative solutions
22. 3 or 1 positive solutions; 2 or 0 negative solutions   **23.** $f(x) = f(-x) = 2x^4 + 2x^2 + 8$ has no sign changes.

24. a. $\pm 1, \pm 3, \pm 5, \pm 15, \pm\dfrac{1}{2}, \pm\dfrac{1}{4}, \pm\dfrac{1}{8}, \pm\dfrac{3}{2}, \pm\dfrac{3}{4}, \pm\dfrac{3}{8}, \pm\dfrac{5}{2}, \pm\dfrac{5}{4}, \pm\dfrac{5}{8}, \pm\dfrac{15}{2}, \pm\dfrac{15}{4}, \pm\dfrac{15}{8}$

   b. 3 or 1 positive real solutions; no negative real solutions   **d.** $\left\{\dfrac{1}{2}, \dfrac{3}{2}, \dfrac{5}{2}\right\}$ **25. a.** $\pm 1, \pm 2, \pm 3, \pm 6$

   b. 2 or 0 positive real solutions; 2 or 0 negative real solutions   **d.** $\{-2, -1, 1, 3\}$

26. a. $\pm 1, \pm 2 \pm 5 \pm 10, \pm\dfrac{1}{2}, \pm\dfrac{5}{2}$ **b.** 3 or 1 positive real solutions; 1 negative real solution   **d.** $\left\{\dfrac{1}{2}, 2, \pm\sqrt{5}\right\}$

27. a. $\pm 1, \pm 2, \pm 3, \pm 4, \pm 5, \pm 6, \pm 10, \pm 12, \pm 15, \pm 20, \pm 30, \pm 60, \pm\dfrac{1}{2}, \pm\dfrac{1}{4}, \pm\dfrac{3}{2}, \pm\dfrac{3}{4}, \pm\dfrac{5}{2}, \pm\dfrac{5}{4}, \pm\dfrac{15}{2}, \pm\dfrac{15}{4}$

   b. 2 or 0 positive real solutions; 2 or 0 negative real solutions   **d.** $\left\{-\dfrac{5}{2}, -1, \dfrac{3}{2}, 4\right\}$

28. a. $\pm 1, \pm 2, \pm 4, \pm 8, \pm\dfrac{1}{3}, \pm\dfrac{2}{3}, \pm\dfrac{4}{3}, \pm\dfrac{8}{3}$ **b.** 3 or 1 positive real solutions; 2 or 0 negative real solutions

   d. $\left\{-2, -1, \dfrac{2}{3}, 1, 2\right\}$ **29. a.** $\pm 1, \pm\dfrac{1}{2}, \pm\dfrac{1}{3}, \pm\dfrac{1}{6}$ **b.** 2 or 0 positive real zeros; 1 negative real zero

   d. $-1, \dfrac{1}{3}, \dfrac{1}{2}$ **30.** $\pm 1, \pm 3, \pm\dfrac{1}{2}, \pm\dfrac{3}{2}$ **b.** 1 positive real zero; 3 or 1 negative real zeros

d. $-1, \dfrac{3}{2}, \dfrac{-1 + i\sqrt{3}}{2}, \dfrac{-1 - i\sqrt{3}}{2}$ **31.** $\pm 1, \pm 2, \pm 3, \pm 4, \pm 6, \pm 8, \pm 12, \pm 24, \pm \dfrac{1}{3}, \pm \dfrac{2}{3}, \pm \dfrac{4}{3}, \pm \dfrac{8}{3}$

b. 3 or 1 positive real zeros; 1 negative real zero   **d.** $-\dfrac{2}{3}, 3, \pm 2i$ **32. a.** $\pm 1, \pm 2, \pm 3, \pm 4, \pm 6, \pm 12, \pm \dfrac{1}{2}, \pm \dfrac{3}{2}$

b. 2 is not a root but is an upper bound.   **c.** -2 is not a root but is a lower bound.   **d.** $\pm 1, \pm \dfrac{1}{2}, \pm \dfrac{3}{2}$

33. $\pm 1, 2, 3, 4, \pm \dfrac{1}{2}, \pm \dfrac{3}{2}$ **34.** 7   **35.** 3 mm   **36.** 4   **37.** $f(1) = -2, f(2) = 3; 1.6$

38. $f(-3) = -32, f(-2) = 7; -2.3$ **39.** $f(x) = x^3 - 6x^2 + 21x - 26$ **40.** $f(x) = 2x^4 + 12x^3 + 20x^2 + 12x + 18$

41. $f(x) = x^4 - 3x^3 + 6x^2 + 2x - 60$ **42.** $\left\{ -\dfrac{1}{4}, 6 \pm 5i \right\}$ **43.** $\{1 \pm i, 1 \pm 3i\}$ **44.** $\left\{ -\dfrac{1}{2}, 1, 4 \pm 7i \right\}$

45. $\{-3, -1, 1 \pm 2i\}$ **46.** $-2, \dfrac{1}{2}, \pm i; f(x) = (x - i)(x + i)(x + 2)\left(x - \dfrac{1}{2} \right)$ **47.** $4, -1; f(x) = (x + 1)^2(x - 4)^2$

48. 4 real zeros, one with multiplicity two   **49.** 3 real zeros; 2 nonreal complex zeros

50. 2 real zeros, one with multiplicity two; 2 nonreal complex zeros   **51.** 1 real zero; 4 nonreal complex zeros

52. Verification is left to the student; $0.47, -1.40$ **53.** Original length of cube = 8 inches.

54.

Horizontal asymptote: $y = 0$
Vertical asymptote: $x = 4$

55.

Horizontal asymptote: $y = -4$
Vertical asymptote: $x = 0$

56.

Horizontal asymptote: $y = -1$
Vertical asymptote: $x = -3$

57.

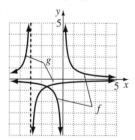

Horizontal asymptote: $y = 0$
Vertical asymptote: $x = -3$

58.

Horizontal asymptote: $y = 1$
Vertical asymptote: $x = 1$

59.

60.

61.

62.

63.

64.

65.

66.

67. $y = 60$; The maximum number of words a person can type per minute approaches 60.

68. $y = 3000$; The number of fish available in the pond approaches 3,000,000.

69. $y = 0$; As the number of years of education increases the percentage rate of unemployment approaches zero.

70. a. $\overline{C}(50) = \$1620$; $\overline{C}(100) = \$820$; $\overline{C}(1000) = \$100$; $\overline{C}(100,000) = \$20.80$

b. $y = 20$; as more calculators are manufactured, the cost per calculator approaches $20.

c.

71. 1600; the difference in cost of removing 90% versus 50% of the contaminants is 16 million dollars.

b.

c. No amount of money can remove 100% of the contaminants since $C(x)$ increases without bound as x approaches 100.

72. Answers may vary.   **73.** Approximately 1.8×10^{20} newtons

74. $y = \dfrac{1200}{x^2}$; 1.3 lumens; Intensity decreases to zero.

75. a. $T(x) = \dfrac{60}{x} + \dfrac{60}{x + 30}$ **b.**   **c.** 30 mph

76. a. $C(x) = \dfrac{100x + 1750}{x + 50}$

b. Answers may vary.   **c.** 80 ounces

C H A P T E R   3   T E S T

1. Axis of symmetry: $x = 1$ **2.** Axis of symmetry: $x = 1$

3. 23 VCRs; \$16,900   **4.** 150 ft by 300; 45,000 sq ft   **5. a.** $5, 2, -2$ **b.**

6. The graph should fall to the left and rises to the right; x-intercepts should be -1 and 1.   **7. a.** 2   **b.** $\dfrac{2}{3}, \dfrac{1}{2}$

8. $\pm 1, \pm 2, \pm 3, \pm 6, \pm\dfrac{1}{2}, \pm\dfrac{3}{2}$ **9.** 3 or 1 positive real solutions; no negative real solutions   **10.** $\{-5, -3, 2\}$

11. a. $\pm 1, \pm 3, \pm 5, \pm 15, \pm\dfrac{1}{2}, \pm\dfrac{3}{2}, \pm\dfrac{5}{2}, \pm\dfrac{15}{2}$ **b.** $\left\{ -1, \dfrac{3}{2}, \pm\sqrt{5} \right\}$ **12.** -3 is a lower bound; 2 is an upper bound; Verification is left to the student.   **13.** $\{2, 3, 1 \pm i\}$ **14.** $(x + 2)^2(x - 1)$

15.   **16.**   **17.**   **18.**

19. a. 750 manuals   **b.** $y = 6$; As more manuals are produced, the cost per manual approaches \$6.
20. $H = 81,000$ **21. a.** $-0.92, -0.38, 0.38, 0.92$ **b.** Minimum: $(0.71, -1)$ and $(-0.71, -1)$, maximum: $(0, 1)$

CUMULATIVE REVIEW PROBLEMS (CHAPTERS P – 3)

1. $2 + \sqrt{3}$ **2.** $26\sqrt[3]{2}$ **3.** $(x - y)(x + y)^2$ **4.** $\{-2, 2, -i\sqrt{2}, i\sqrt{2}\}$ **5.** $\{-4, -2, -1, -3\}$

6. $(-\infty, -1) \cup \left(\dfrac{5}{3}, \infty\right)$ **7.** $\{-3, -1, 2\}$ **8.** $t = \dfrac{15C - 15V}{c}$ **9.** $(-\infty, 5]$ **10.** $g(x) = \sqrt{x - 1}$

11. $f^{-1}(x) = \sqrt[3]{x - 4}$ **12.** $(f \circ g)(x) = 49x^2 - 91x + 42; (g \circ f)(x) = 7x^2 - 35x + 38$

13. Possible answer:

14.

15. a. $-1, 1, 4$ **b.**

16.

17.

18. 3 ft   **19.** 5 trees; 12,250 apples
20. 11.1 foot-candles

Chapter 4

PROBLEM SET 4.1

1.

3.

5.

7.

9. Domain: $(-\infty, \infty)$;
Range: $(0, \infty)$

11. Domain: $(-\infty, \infty)$;
Range: $(3, \infty)$

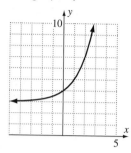

13. Domain: $(-\infty, \infty)$;
Range: $(-1, \infty)$

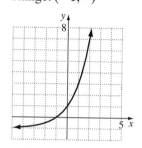

15. Domain: $(-\infty, \infty)$;
Range: $(-2, \infty)$

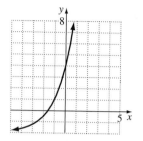

17. Domain: $(-\infty, \infty)$;
Range: $(-\infty, 0)$

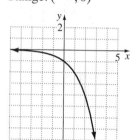

19. Domain: $(-\infty, \infty)$;
Range: $(3, \infty)$

21.

23.

25.

27.

29.

31. a. 67.38 million people   **b.** 134.74 million people; 269.46 million people; 538.85 million people
c. Approximately 27 years
33. a. $3,052,428,614   **b.** $3,169,289,064   **c.** $3,173,350,575   **35.** 8.25% compounded quarterly
37. Compounded semiannually: $31,982, $41,307, $56,875, $107,826;
Compounded monthly: $32,009, $41,485, $57,366, $109,693;
Compounded 365 times per year: $32,015, $41,520, $57,463, $110,066;
Compounded continuously: $32,015, $41,521, $57,466, $110,079
39. $A = 9.98350115$ billion   **41.** No, they cannot safely visit.
43. a. about 0.05   **b.** Horizontal asymptote: $y = 100$. This means that the percent of pilots who suffer from
bends will approach 100% as the altitude increases.   **45.** $S = $143,605.71$ **47.** d
49.

Increasing: $(-\infty, 0)$
Decreasing: $(0, \infty)$
Relative max: 1

51.

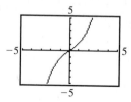

Increasing: $(-\infty, \infty)$
No relative max. or min.

53. a.

b. $x < 0$ **c.** $x > 0$ **d.** Yes, $x = 0$
e. When graphing several functions of the form $y = b^x$ where $b > 1$, the graphs will be ordered with the largest b on the bottom in the interval $(-\infty, 0)$ and the largest b on top in the interval $(0, \infty)$. At $x = 0$ the graphs will intersect.

f.

$x > 0, x < 0, x = 0$. When graphing several functions of the form $y = b^x$ where $0 < b < 1$, the graphs will be ordered with the largest b on the bottom in the interval $(-\infty, 0)$ and the largest b on the top in the interval $(0, \infty)$. At $x = 0$ graphs will intersect.

55. a. $f(-x) = f(x)$ **b.** $y = 0$; When $|x|$ gets large, the likely occurrence approaches zero.

c.

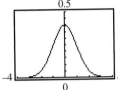

57. a. $A_1 = 10{,}000\left(1 + \dfrac{0.05}{4}\right)^{4t}$, $A_2 = 10{,}000\left(1 + \dfrac{0.045}{12}\right)^{12t}$ **b.**

The bank paying 5% interest compounded quarterly offers the better return.

59.

y approaches e as x approaches infinity.

61.

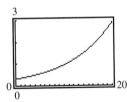

After ten days the tumor is nearly 1 cubic centimeter.
After twenty days the tumor is nearly 3 cubic centimeters.

63. a.   **b.**   **c.**

d. For values of $x < 0$, the second function alternates between being an increasing and decreasing function. As the degree of the polynomial increases, the two functions appear to approach the same values for $x > 0$.

65. A means for isolating the variable y must be used.

67. $y = 3^x$ is graph d, $y = 5^x$ is graph c, $y = \left(\frac{1}{3}\right)^x$ is graph a, $y = \left(\frac{1}{5}\right)^x$ is graph b, Use the facts that when $b > 1$, $f(x)$ is increasing and when $0 < b < 1$, $f(x)$ is decreasing. **69.** A problem involving the decay of a substance would be appropriate. **71.** A problem involving heights of a population would be appropriate. **73.** $\frac{3^{x+h} - 3^x}{h}$ simplifies to $3^x\left(\frac{3^h - 1}{h}\right)$. **75.** Approximately $2\frac{1}{2}$ years

PROBLEM SET 4.2

1. 2 **3.** 6 **5.** $\frac{1}{2}$ **7.** -5 **9.** $\frac{1}{2}$ **11.** 1 **13.** 0 **15.** $\frac{3}{4}$ **17.** 4 **19.** -2 **21.** 7 **23.** $\frac{1}{3}$ **25.** 7
27. 19 **29.** 7 **31.** 0

33.

35. Domain: $(0, \infty)$; Range: $(-\infty, \infty)$

37. Domain: $(-3, \infty)$;
Range: $(-\infty, \infty)$

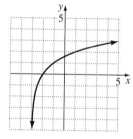

39. Domain: $(1, \infty)$;
Range: $(-\infty, \infty)$

41. Domain: $(-1, \infty)$;
Range: $(-\infty, \infty)$

43. Domain: $(-\infty, 0)$;
Range: $(-\infty, \infty)$

45. d **47.** a **49.** b **51.** c **53.** -1 **55.** $\frac{1}{2}$ **57.** -3

59. Domain: $(-2, \infty)$
Vertical asymptote: $x = -2$
x-intercept: $(-1, 0)$

61. Domain: $(-\infty, 2)$
Vertical asymptote: $x = 2$
x-intercept: $(1, 0)$

63. Domain: $(-\infty, 0) \cup (0, \infty)$
Vertical asymptote: $x = 0$
x-intercept: $(-1, 0)$ and $(1, 0)$

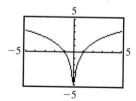

65. Domain: $(2, \infty)$
Vertical asymptote: $x = 2$
x-intercept: $(3, 0)$

67. 0.94 feet per second
71. a. about 6.4; acid
73. a. 5, moderate   **b.** 6, large
75. about 65.1 decibels

69. 28 minutes
     b. about 3.55; acid
     c. 7, major   **d.** 8, greatest

77. a. 88%   **b.** about 71.5%; about 63.9%; about 58.8%; about 55%; about 52%; about 49.5%

c.

The amount of material retained decreases with time.

79. 479,001,600 actual value; 475,687,486.5 (by Stirling's formula)   **81.** d

83.

Shift the graph of f to
the left 3 units.

85.

Shift the graph of f down two
units and reflect the resulting
graph across the y-axis.

87.

Shift the graph of f to
the right 2 units and
upward 1 unit.

89. Domain: $(0, \infty)$
Range: approximately $(-\infty, 0.4)$
Increasing: $(0, e)$
Decreasing: (e, ∞)

91. Domain: $(1, \infty)$
Range: $(-\infty, \infty)$
Increasing: $(1, \infty)$

93. Domain: $(-\infty, 0) \cup (0, \infty)$
Range: $(-\infty, \infty)$
Decreasing: $(-\infty, 0)$
Increasing: $(0, \infty)$

95. a.

b.

c.

d. $\log_b(MN) = \log_b(M) + \log_b(N)$ **e.** "...the sum of the logs of each of the product's factors."

97. a.

b.

c.

d. $\log_b M^p = p\log_b M$ **e.** "...the value of the exponent times the log of the number."

99. False   **101.** False   **103.** True   **105.** False

107. a.

b.

c.

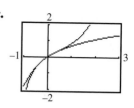

d. As terms are added, the end behavior of the graph of $y = x - \dfrac{x^2}{2} + \ldots$ is flipping above and below the graph of $\ln(1 + x)$.   **109.** The city's population, in thousands, is less than one. We need to multiply our answer by 1000 to find the population (about 379).   **111.** Answers may vary.   **113.** 3   **115.** $y = 2x - 4$

PROBLEM SET 4.3

1. $1 + \log_7 x$ **3.** $3 \ln x + 2 \ln y$ **5.** $\dfrac{1}{2}\log_4 x - 3$ **7.** $2 - \dfrac{1}{2}\log(3x - 2)$ **9.** $\ln 9 - 4$ **11.** $\dfrac{1}{3}\log x - \dfrac{1}{3}\log y$

13. $\dfrac{1}{2}\log_b x + 3\log_b y - 3\log_b z$ **15.** $\dfrac{2}{3}\log_5 x + \dfrac{1}{3}\log_5 y - \dfrac{2}{3}$ **17.** $\dfrac{1}{4}\ln x + \dfrac{3}{4}\ln y$ **19.** $\ln(7x)$

21. $\log_5\left(\dfrac{x}{y}\right)$ **23.** $\log_3(x + 1)^2$ **25.** $\log_2\sqrt{(5x)}$ **27.** $\log_3(x + 3)$ **29.** $\log(\sqrt{x}y^3)$ **31.** $\log_4[\sqrt[3]{x}(3x + 2)^2]$

33. $\ln\left(\dfrac{x^3 y^5}{z^6}\right)$ **35.** $\log\sqrt{xy}$ **37.** $\log_5\left[\dfrac{\sqrt{xy}}{(x + 1)^2}\right]$ **39.** $\log c + 9t$ **41.** $\ln A + 7x^2$ **43.** $\ln A + \dfrac{3}{4}$

45. $18x^6$ **47.** $9y^3$ **49.** $\dfrac{y^2}{e^2}$ **51.** 2.579   **53.** -2.585 **55.** -0.125 **57.** 1.947

59. a. $\text{pH} = 6.1 + \log\left(\dfrac{B}{C}\right)$ **b.** $\text{pH} \approx 7.197$ **61.** b

63. a.

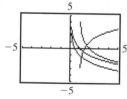

b. $y = \log_{1/2} x$ has been shifted down 1 unit to obtain $y = (\log_{1/2} x) - 1$; $y = \log_{1/2} x$ has been shifted 1 unit to the right to obtain $y = \log_{1/2}(x - 1)$; $y = \log_{1/2} x$ has been reflected across the x-axis, shifted 1 unit to the right and 1 unit upward to obtain $y = -\log_{1/2}(x - 1) + 1$.

65. a.

b. top graph is $\log_{100} x$; bottom graph is $y = \log_3 x$
c. top graph is $y = \log_3 x$; bottom graph is $y = \log_{100} x$
d. $(0, 1)$: top graph is $y = \log_{1/2} x$, bottom graph is $y = \log_{1/10} x$; $(1, \infty)$: top graph is $y = \log_{1/10} x$, bottom graph is $y = \log_{1/2} x$

e. Comparing graphs of $\log_b x$ for $b > 1$, the graph of the equation with the largest b will be on the top in the interval $(0, 1)$ and on the bottom in the interval $(1, \infty)$. Comparing graphs of $\log_b x$ for $b < 1$, the graphs of the equations with the largest b will be on the top in the interval $(0, 1)$ and on the bottom in the interval $(1, \infty)$.

67. a. 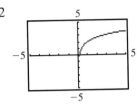 **b.** $y = \log_2 x$ has been shrunk by a factor of $\frac{1}{2}$ and shifted downward.

69. $k = 2$ **71.** Answers may vary.   **73.** $\log e = \dfrac{\ln e}{\ln 10} = \dfrac{1}{\ln 10}$

75. Since $R = \log_b M$ and $S = \log_b N$, $b^R = M$ and $b^S = N$. $\dfrac{M}{N} = \dfrac{b^R}{b^S}$;

$\log_b \dfrac{M}{N} = \log_b \left(\dfrac{b^R}{b^S} \right) = \log_b (b^{R-S}) = R - S = \log_b M - \log_b N$

77. Nap $\log x = 10^7 \log_{1/e} \left(\dfrac{x}{10^7} \right) = 10^7 (\log_{1/e} x - \log_{1/e} 10^7) = 10^7 \left(\dfrac{\ln x}{\ln \frac{1}{e}} - \dfrac{\ln 10^7}{\ln \frac{1}{e}} \right) = 10^7 \left(\dfrac{\ln x}{\ln e^{-1}} - \dfrac{\ln 10^7}{\ln e^{-1}} \right)$

$= 10^7 \left(\dfrac{\ln x}{-\ln e} - \dfrac{7 \ln 10}{-\ln e} \right) = 10^7 (-\ln x + 7 \ln 10) = 10^7 (7 \ln 10 - \ln x)$

79. $\ln \left(\dfrac{\sqrt{3} + \sqrt{2}}{\sqrt{3} - \sqrt{2}} \right) = \ln \left[\dfrac{(\sqrt{3} + \sqrt{2})(\sqrt{3} + \sqrt{2})}{(\sqrt{3} - \sqrt{2})(\sqrt{3} + \sqrt{2})} \right] = \ln [(\sqrt{3} + \sqrt{2})^2] = 2 \ln (\sqrt{3} + \sqrt{2})$

PROBLEM SET 4.4

1. $\left\{ \dfrac{\ln 3.91}{\ln 10} \right\}$; 0.592   **3.** $\{\ln 5.7\}$; 1.740   **5.** $\left\{ \dfrac{\ln 17}{\ln 5} \right\}$; 1.760   **7.** $\left\{ \ln \dfrac{23}{5} \right\}$; 1.526   **9.** $\left\{ \dfrac{\ln 659}{5} \right\}$; 1.298

11. $\left\{ \dfrac{1 - \ln 793}{5} \right\}$; -1.135 **13.** $\left\{ \dfrac{\ln 10{,}476 + 3}{5} \right\}$; 2.451   **15.** $\left\{ \dfrac{\ln 410}{\ln 7} - 2 \right\}$; 1.092   **17.** $\left\{ \dfrac{\ln 813}{0.3 \ln 7} \right\}$; 11.478

19. $\left\{ \dfrac{\ln 3}{\ln 5 - \ln 3} \right\}$; 2.151   **21.** $\left\{ \dfrac{-3 \ln 5 - \ln 3}{2 \ln 5 - \ln 3} \right\}$; -2.795 **23.** $\{0, \ln 2\}$; 0, 0.693   **25.** $\left\{ \dfrac{\ln 3}{2} \right\}$; 0.549

27. $\{81\}$ **29.** $\{59\}$ **31.** $\left\{ \dfrac{109}{27} \right\}$ **33.** $\left\{ \dfrac{62}{3} \right\}$ **35.** $\left\{ \dfrac{5}{4} \right\}$ **37.** $\{6\}$ **39.** $\{6\}$ **41.** $\{3\}$ **43.** $\{3\}$ **45.** $\{2\}$

47. $\{1\}$ **49.** $\{4\}$ **51.** $\{6\}$ **53.** $\{20\}$ **55.** $\{6\}$ **57.** 8.7 years   **59.** 15.7%   **61.** 8.2 years   **63.** 16.8%

65. 2050   **67.** 7.4 years after 1995; 81.9%   **69. a.** 2035   **b.** 2019   **71.** 0.004 moles per liter
73. a. $10^{7.1}$ times   **b.** $10^{8.9}$ times   **c.** 63 times   **d.** $10^{22.05}$ergs; $10^{24.75}$ ergs   **75. a.** 100 times   **b.** 6.3 times
c. 15.9 times   **77.** 158,489 times   **79.** c   **81.** $\{-1.3, 1.3\}$ **83.** $\{-1.4, 1.7\}$
89. $\{1.0001, 5.67\}$ **91.** $\{0.14\}$

85.   **87.**

93–95. Answers may vary. **97.** 29 days **99.** 90.4 **101.** $\{e^{(3-\sqrt{5})/2}, e^{(3+\sqrt{5})/2}\}$ **103.** $\{e\}$

P R O B L E M   S E T   4 . 5

1. a. $k = \dfrac{\ln 2.565}{4}$ **b.** $A = 200{,}000e^{[(\ln 2.565)/4]t}$ **c.** 1998 **d.** No **e.** $y = 78{,}250x + 200{,}000$; 2001

f. Answers may vary. **3. a.** $k = \dfrac{1}{28}\ln\dfrac{1}{2} \approx -0.024755$ **b.** 72.4 years **c.**

5. 34.4 years from today **7. a.** 102°F **b.** 6.9 minutes **c.**

No

9. $y = 1.4597e^{1.0745x}$

11. a. 5.6348; 5.7366; 5.8021; 5.8230; 5.8608 **b.**

c. $\ln y = 0.00246x + 5.6273$
d. $y = 277.91e^{0.00246x}$
e. 2213

13. a. **b.**

c. $y = 0.06044 \ln x + 0.00131$
d. 0.26 seconds

Logarithmic function

15. Linear model: $y = 3513.8x + 15{,}833.2$; exponential model: $y = 17{,}235e^{0.1326x}$; logarithmic model: $y = 9971.42 \ln x + 17{,}197.42$; logarithmic model. **17.** Linear model: $y = 229.43x + 1978.33$; exponential model: $y = 2053.7e^{0.08375x}$; logarithmic model: $y = 630.49 \ln x + 2089.97$; linear model **19.** b

21. a.

b. $y = 277.9195(1.0025)^x$ **c.**   **d.** 313 years after 1900

23. a.

b. $y = 0.001313 + 0.06044 \ln x$ **c.** 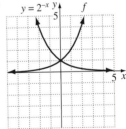 **d.** 0.26 seconds

25. a.

b. Linear model: $y = 3513.8x + 15{,}833.2$;
exponential model: $y = 17{,}235.6(1.1418)^x$;
logarithmic model: $y = 17{,}197.4 + 9971.4 \ln x$
c. Logarithmic model; 36,601 deaths

27. a.

b. Linear model: $y = 229.4x + 1978.3$; exponential model: $y = 2053.7(1.0874)^x$;
logarithmic model: $y = 2090 + 630.49 \ln x$
c. Linear model; $3584

29–33. Answers may vary.

CHAPTER 4 REVIEW PROBLEMS

1. d   **2.** h   **3.** b   **4.** e   **5.** f   **6.** a   **7.** g   **8.** c

9.

$y = 2^x$
  Domain: $(-\infty, \infty)$
  Range: $(0, \infty)$
$y = 2^{x+1}$
  Domain: $(-\infty, \infty)$
  Range: $(0, \infty)$

10.

$f(x) = 3^x$
  Domain: $(-\infty, \infty)$
  Range: $(0, \infty)$
$g(x) = 3^{x-1} - 2$
  Domain: $(-\infty, \infty)$
  Range: $(-2, \infty)$

11.

$f(x) = 2^x$
  Domain: $(-\infty, \infty)$
  Range: $(0, \infty)$
$y = 2^{-x}$
  Domain: $(-\infty, \infty)$
  Range: $(0, \infty)$

12.

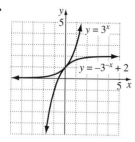

$y = 3^x$

Domain: $(-\infty, \infty)$
Range: $(0, \infty)$

$y = -3^{-x} + 2$

Domain: $(-\infty, \infty)$
Range: $(-\infty, 2)$

13.

$y = \left(\dfrac{1}{2}\right)^x$

Domain: $(-\infty, \infty)$
Range: $(0, \infty)$

$y = \left(\dfrac{1}{2}\right)^{-x} - 1$

Domain: $(-\infty, \infty)$
Range: $(-1, \infty)$

14.

$y = \log_2 x$

Domain: $(0, \infty)$
Range: $(-\infty, \infty)$

$y = \log_2(x - 2) + 3$

Domain: $(2, \infty)$
Range: $(-\infty, \infty)$

15.

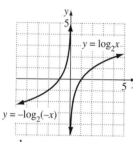

$y = \log_2 x$
Domain: $(0, \infty)$
Range: $(-\infty, \infty)$
$y = -\log_2(-x)$
Domain: $(-\infty, 0)$
Range: $(-\infty, \infty)$

16. 5.5% compounded semiannually   **17.** 7% compounded monthly
18. China: 2443 million; India: 3009 million; yes
19. a. 100 people   **b.** 127 people   **c.** $y = 200{,}000$; 200,000 is the limiting size of the population that becomes ill.   **d.**

250,000

0 |_____| 300`
0

20. 7   **21.** -8 **22.** 1
23. Domain: $(2, \infty)$
Vertical asymptote: $x = 2$
x-intercept: $(3, 0)$

24. Domain: $(-\infty, 4)$
Vertical asymptote: $x = 4$
x-intercept: $(3, 0)$

25. Domain: $(-\infty, 2) \cup (2, \infty)$
Vertical asymptote: $x = 2$
x-intercepts: $(1, 0), (3, 0)$

26. 9 weeks   **27.** $\dfrac{1}{2}\log_7 x - 2 - 2\log_7 y$ **28.** $4 - \dfrac{1}{3}\log(3x + 1)$ **29.** $\dfrac{3}{2}\ln x + \dfrac{1}{2}\ln y - 2$ **30.** $\ln 9 + 5t$
31. $-\dfrac{3}{10}\log_b x - \dfrac{1}{10}\log_b y$ **32.** $\log\dfrac{7(x - 4)^5}{x^3}$ **33.** $\ln\dfrac{\sqrt{x}}{\sqrt[7]{y}}$ **34.** $\ln(x - 3)^{5/3}$ **35.** $23x^3$ **36.** 1.760

37. 2.957   **38.** 6.7   **39.** 31.6 times as intense   **40. c.** 1.45×10^{17} joules   **41.** Answers may vary.
42. Yes   **43.** $\left\{\dfrac{\ln 12{,}143}{\ln 8}\right\}$; $x = 4.523$ **44.** $\left\{\dfrac{1}{5}\ln\dfrac{1268}{9}\right\}$; 0.990   **45.** $\left\{\dfrac{12 - \ln 130}{5}\right\}$; 1.426
46. $\left\{\dfrac{2\ln 5 + 3\ln 7}{\ln 7 - 4\ln 5}\right\}$; -2.016 **47.** $\{\ln 3\}$; 1.099   **48. a.** 24.4 years   **b.** 8.7%   **49.** 7.3 years
50. 30.7 years   **51.** 2038   **52.** $\{23\}$ **53.** $\{5\}$ **54.** $\varnothing$ **55.** $\{5\}$ **56.** $\{-1 + \sqrt{6}\}$ **57.** 8338 thousand
58. 91 times more intense   **59. a.** 0.041   **b.** $f(t) = 14{,}609e^{0.041t}$ **c.** 40,717; 49,981; 92,447   **60.** 15,642 years
61. a. 200°F   **b.** 119°F   **c.** 70°; the room temperature is 70°.   **62.** 7:30 A.M.

63. High projection: exponential function; medium projection: linear function; low projection: quadratic function   **64. a.** $y = 3.46e^{0.0233x}$ **b.** 114 million   **c.** 12% in 1990; 29% in 2050

65. a.

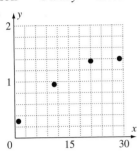

Logarithmic function
b. $y = 0.2738 + 0.3308 \ln x$
c. 2029

66. a.

b. Linear model: $y = 1182.47x - 2,334,123.42$
Exponential model: $y = 1.07 \times 10^{-6}(1.08)^x$
Logarithmic model:
$y = -17,836,653 + 2,350,698 \ln x$
The linear model best describes book expenditures as a function of time.
c. Using the linear model, when $x = 2005$, $y \approx 36726$. Consumers will spend \$36,725 million on books in the year 2005.

CHAPTER 4 TEST

1.

2. 6.5% compounded semiannually; \$663
3. a. 140°F   **b.** $y = 72$; the temperature of the room is 72°F.   **4.** 6

5.

6. $(-\infty, 3)$ **7.** $\dfrac{1}{3}\log_5 x - 3 - 2\log_5 y$ **8.** $\ln 10 + 7t$ **9.** $\log(x^6 y^2)$ **10.** $\ln\left(\dfrac{7}{x^3}\right)$

11. $\left\{\dfrac{9 - \ln 42}{3}\right\}$; 1.754   **12.** $\{0, \ln 5\}$; 0, 1.609   **13.** 11.6 years   **14.** 8.7 years   **15.** $\left\{\dfrac{16}{7}\right\}$ **16.** $\left\{\dfrac{1}{2}\right\}$
17. 10^{12} times louder   **18. a.** $A = 5.5e^{0.0177t}$ **b.** 2022   **19. a.** $T = 28 + 40e^{(\ln 0.9)}$ **b.** 6.6 hours

20. 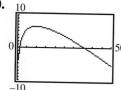   **a.** $x = 0$ **b.** 6.51 at $x = 10$ **c.** Range $(-\infty, 6.51]$ **d.** $\{1.12, 35.77\}$

CUMULATIVE REVIEW PROBLEMS (CHAPTERS P–4)

1. $\dfrac{-6x^2 + 2x - 2}{(2x + 1)^2(x - 1)}$ **2.** $\dfrac{x}{x - 1}$ **3.** $\left\{\dfrac{2}{3}, 2\right\}$ **4.** $\{3, 7\}$ **5.** $\{-1, -2, 1\}$ **6.** $\left\{\dfrac{11 - \ln 128}{5}\right\}$ **7.** $\{3\}$

8. $9y^2 - 4x^2 - 30y - 25$ **9.**

10.

11. $\{2 - i, 2 + i, i, -i\}$ **12.**

13. $\dfrac{0.5}{\ln 4}; 0.3$ **14.** $4 + \dfrac{1}{3}\log_3 x$ **15.** $(x - 5)^2(x + 5)$

16. $n = \dfrac{IR}{E - Ir}$ **17.** 2004   **18.** $\dfrac{9}{4}\pi$ ft^3 **19.** $\dfrac{1}{2}$

20. $p = 100$; it is impossible to remove 100% of the river's pollutants.

Supplementary Problems

Chapter 1

Linear Equations

Solve the following equations.

1. $3[2 - 5(2x - 4)] - 5x = 2 - 3x$

2. $4[1 - 3(2 - 5x)] + 3x = 2(3x - 2)$

3. $|2x + 10| = -3$

4. $|2x + 10| = 6$

5. $|x - 1| = |3x + 5|$

6. $\dfrac{5}{x} - \dfrac{1}{3} = \dfrac{1}{2} + \dfrac{4}{x}$

7. $1 - \dfrac{4}{x} = \dfrac{2}{5} - \dfrac{3}{4x}$

Solve each formula for a specified variable.

8. Solve for d.

$ab + acd = ed$

9. Solve for y.

$xy + 1 = \dfrac{1}{x} + \dfrac{y}{4}$

10. Solve for y.

$\dfrac{2}{x} - \dfrac{3}{y} = \dfrac{x}{3} - \dfrac{1}{2}$

11. Solve for v.

$s - vt - 16t^2 = 0$

Linear Inequalities with Absolute Value

Solve the following linear inequalities. Write your answers using the interval notation.

12. $|2 - x| > -5$

13. $|x + 1| \le -2$

14. $\left| x + \dfrac{1}{5} \right| < 2$

15. $-2 < |x - 1| \le 3$

Quadratic Equations

Solve the following equations by factoring.

16. $3x^2 + 13x - 10 = 0$

17. $2x^2 + x - 21 = 0$

18. $-5x^2 + 2x = 0$

19. $5x^2 + 2x - 3 = 0$

20. $-3x^2 + 2x + 8 = 0$

Solve the following equations by the square root method.

21. $x^2 = \dfrac{1}{9}$

22. $x^2 = -\dfrac{1}{16}$

23. $9x^2 = -25$

24. $(2x + 7)^2 = -5$ $\qquad\qquad$ **25.** $(1 - 3x)^2 = \dfrac{1}{9}$

Solve the following equations using the quadratic formula.

26. $-3x^2 + 5x + 2 = 0$ $\qquad\qquad$ **27.** $-x^2 - 4x + 5 = 0$

Discriminant and nature of roots of quadratic equations.

Without solving the equation determine the number of roots and the nature of these roots (real distinct, real repeated, complex.)

28. $x^2 + x + 1 = 0$ $\qquad$ **29.** $-x^2 + 3x + 4 = 0$ $\qquad$ **30.** $x^2 - 6x + 9 = 0$

Find the value(s) of k for which the following equation will have a repeated solution.

31. $4kx^2 - 3kx + 9 = 0$ $\qquad\qquad$ **32.** $2kx^2 + kx - 1 = 0$

Rational Equations

Solve the following Rational Equations.

Remember, when solving a rational equation, special restrictions need to be made to prevent the occurrence of zeros in the denominator(s).

33. $\dfrac{1}{x + 1} - \dfrac{1}{x^2 - x - 2} = \dfrac{x - 3}{x^2 - 3x + 2}$

34. $\dfrac{1}{x^2 - 3x + 2} + \dfrac{2}{x^2 - 4x + 3} = \dfrac{1}{x^2 - 5x + 6}$

35. $\dfrac{1}{x^2 - 3x + 2} + \dfrac{2}{x^2 - 4x + 3} = \dfrac{x^2 + 3x - 8}{(x - 1)(x - 2)(x - 3)}$

36. $\dfrac{2x - 1}{x - 1} + \dfrac{3}{x - 6} = \dfrac{2x^2 - 10x + 3}{x^2 - 7x + 6}$

37. $\dfrac{x}{x + 5} - \dfrac{2}{x - 2} = \dfrac{-x^2 + x - 8}{x^2 + 3x - 10}$

38. $\dfrac{2}{x - 3} - \dfrac{1}{x + 3} = \dfrac{x^2 - 4x + 15}{x^2 - 9}$

39. $\dfrac{2}{x - 3} - \dfrac{1}{x + 3} = \dfrac{x^2 - 2x + 11}{x^2 - 9}$

40. $\dfrac{5x - 1}{2(x + 3)(x - 1)} - \dfrac{2}{x + 3} = \dfrac{1}{2(x - 1)}$

41. $\dfrac{1}{x^2 - 3x + 2} + \dfrac{2}{x^2 - 4x + 3} = \dfrac{3x - 7}{(x - 1)(x - 2)(x - 3)}$

42. $\dfrac{1}{x^2 - 3x + 2} + \dfrac{2}{x^2 - 4x + 3} = \dfrac{8}{(x - 1)(x - 2)(x - 3)}$

Equations with Radicals

Solve the following equations. Remember, check is MANDATORY when solving equations having a radical with even index.

43. $2x - \sqrt{2x^2 + x + 4} = 1$

44. $5x - 3 - \sqrt{23x^2 - 29x + 10} = 0$

45. $2x = \sqrt{-19x + 28} + 5$

46. $2x - \sqrt{4 - 7x} = -1$

47. $3x + 1 - \sqrt{7x^2 + 13x + 5} = 0$

48. $2 + \sqrt[4]{3x + 1} = 4$

49. $5 - \sqrt[4]{7 - x} = 1$

50. $\sqrt[3]{x - 1} + 2 = 5$

51. $\sqrt[3]{x^2 - 1} = 2$

52. $\sqrt[5]{3x - 1} = 2$

53. $\sqrt[3]{x^2 - 7x - 7} = 1$

54. $\sqrt[6]{10x - 11} + 2 = -1$

55. $\sqrt[3]{x^2 - 9x + 7} = -1$

Chapter 2

Introduction to Functions

Find the domain of each function.

1. $f(x) = \dfrac{\sqrt{x+1}}{x^2+x+1}$

2. $g(x) = \dfrac{\sqrt{x+1}}{x^2-2x+1}$

3. $f(x) = \dfrac{x-3}{x^2+x+1}$

4. $g(x) = \dfrac{x+2}{x^2-5x+6}$

5. $m(x) = \dfrac{x^2-x+2}{\sqrt{x+3}}$

6. $m(x) = \dfrac{x-2}{\sqrt{x-4}}$

7. $f(x) = \begin{cases} x^2 - 2x + 3, & x \le 0 \\ x + 5, & x > 0 \end{cases}$

8. $f(x) = \begin{cases} x - 2, & x < 0 \\ x^3 + 1, & x > 0 \end{cases}$

9. $g(x) = \begin{cases} x - 2, & x < -2 \\ x^3 + 1, & x > -2 \end{cases}$

Given the graph of a function $y = f(x)$. Use the graph to answer the following questions.

10. a) The domain of $f(x)$ is_____

b) The range of $f(x)$ is_____

c) $f(-7) =$ _____

d) $f(3) =$ _____

e) $f(1) - f(-1) =$ _____

f) $f(-6) - f(6) =$ _____

g) Solve the equation $f(x) = 0$

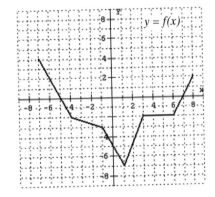

11. a) The domain of $g(x)$ is_____

b) The range of $g(x)$ is_____

c) $g(-8) =$ _____

d) $g(8) =$ _____

e) $g(0) =$ _____

f) $g(3) - g(-2) =$ _____

g) $g(-5) - g(-3) =$ _____

h) Solve the equation $g(x) = 0$

12. For the function

$$f(x) = \begin{cases} x^2 - 2x + 3, & x \le 0 \\ x + 5, & x > 0 \end{cases}$$

find

a) $f(1) - f(-1)$; b) $f(-5)$; c) $f(10)$; d) $f(x)$.

13. For the function

$$f(x) = \begin{cases} x - 2, x < -2 \\ x^3 + 1, x > -2 \end{cases}$$

find

a) $f(1) - f(-1)$; b) $f(-5)$; c) y-intercept; d) $f(-2)$; e) $f(3) - f(-4)$.

Linear Functions and Slope.

14. Find the equation of the vertical line passing through the point $(-2, 3)$.

15. Find the equation of the line passing through the points $(-5, 1)$ and $(5, -8)$.

16. Find the equation of the line passing through the points $(0, -5)$ and $(2, -5)$.

17. A line passes through $(1, -2)$ and has the slope $m = -3$.

Without writing the equation of the line, check if

a) the point $(0, -5)$ is on this line;

b) the point $(2, 1)$ is on the line.

(*Hint: Use geometric meaning of the slope.*)

18. Find the formula of a linear function $h(x)$ if $h(0) = -3$ and $h(2) = 5$.

19. Find the formula of a linear function $r(t)$ if $r(0) = -5$ and $r(3) = 7$.

Modeling with Linear Functions

20. The price of a new car including a 6% sales tax is $18,020. What is the price of the car before the sales tax was added?

21. Find the original price of a computer that was reduced 15% and is now priced at $764.99.

22. The population of a town was 85,000 in 1980 and 124,000 in 1995.

a) Find a linear model that describes the population as a function of time.

b) Use the model to estimate the population in 2003.

c) When will the population reach 163,000?

23. The population of a village was 16,000 in 1970 and 18,400 in 1980.

a) Find a linear model that describes the population as a function of time.

b) Use the model to estimate the population in 2005.

c) When will the population reach 25,000?

24. A farmer wants to fence in a section of his field. The enclosed area will be rectangular with the length $1\frac{2}{3}$ times width. How many yards of fencing will he need to buy if the width is 72 yards?

25. The annual salary of a worker was $25,000 in 1995 and $26,500 in 1997. If the salary follows a linear growth pattern, what will the worker's salary be in 2003?

Increasing and Decreasing Functions

Extreme Values ———————————————————————————————

26. The graph of a function $y = f(x)$ is shown below. Use the graph to determine the function's extrema (locations and extreme values themselves.) State the interval where the function is increasing, decreasing, and constant.

a)

b)

27. Let $f(x) = x^3 - 10x + 8$.

a) Use your calculator to estimate the coordinates of the relative minimum and relative maximum of this function. *Round your answers to five decimal places.*

b) Approximate the intervals on which the function is increasing/decreasing.

28. Let $f(x) = 4x^3 + 7x^2 - 60x + 15$.

a) Use your calculator to estimate the coordinates of the relative minimum and relative maximum of this function. *Round your answers to five decimal places.*

b) Approximate the intervals on which the function is increasing/decreasing.

Transformations of Functions ———————————————————————————————

29. If the point $(-2, 3)$ is on the graph of $f(x)$, what is the corresponding point on the graph of $y = 3f(x) - 11$?

30. If the point $(1, -3)$ is on the graph of $f(x)$, which of the following points $(3, -3), (1, -1), (-1, -3), (1, 5)$ is on the graph of $y = f(x) + 2$?

31. Given the graph of a function $y = f(x)$.

a) State the domain and range for $f(x)$.

b) Sketch the graph of the function
$g(x) = 2f(x - 1) - 3$.
State the domain and range for $g(x)$.

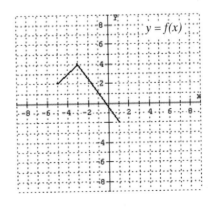

32. Given the graph of a function $y = k(x)$.

  a) State the domain and range for $k(x)$.

  b) Sketch the graph of the function
  $m(x) = -k(x - 3) + 2$.
  State the domain and range for $m(x)$.

  c) Sketch the graph of the function
  $n(x) = k(-x) + 1$.
  State the domain and range for $n(x)$.

33. If points $(0, 1)$ and $(1, 1)$ are on the graph of the function $f(x) = \sqrt{x}$, find the corresponding points on the graph of
$g(x) = 3 - \dfrac{1}{2}\sqrt{x + 2}$

  Hint. Write the sequence of transformations that leads from $f(x)$ to $g(x)$.

34. Given the graph of the function $y = f(x)$,

  sketch the graph of the function $g(x) = -\dfrac{1}{2}f(x - 3) + 1$.

  Write the sequence of transformations you use.
  Label on the graph of $g(x)$ points that correspond
  with points $(-2, 0)$ and $(2, 6)$ on the graph of $f(x)$.
  State the domain and range for $f(x)$ and $g(x)$.

35. Write the sequence of transformations that leads from
  $f(x) = |x|$ to $h(x) = 2|x - 3| - 5$.

  The points $(0, 0)$ and $(-1, 1)$ are on the graph of $f(x)$. Find the corresponding points on the graph of $h(x)$.

Combinations of Functions

36. The graphs of two functions $f(x)$ and $g(x)$ are shown below.

  a) Find the domain of $f + g$.

  b) Find $(f + g)(-4)$.

  c) Find the domain of $\dfrac{f}{g}$ and $\dfrac{g}{f}$.

37. Graphs of two functions $f(x)$ and $g(x)$ are shown below.

   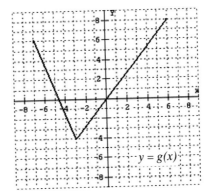

Use the graphs to find the following.

a) $(f \circ g)(0)$; b) $(g \circ f)(0)$; c) $(g \circ g)(-4)$; d) $(f \circ f)(1)$; e) $(f \circ g)(3)$;

f) $(f \circ g)(5)$; g) D_f (the domain of f); h) D_g (the domain of g);

i) $D_{f \circ g}$, the domain of the composition $(f \circ g)(x)$; j) $(f \cdot g)(-3)$;

k) $D_{g/f}$, the domain of the quotient g/f ; l) $(f + g)(-1)$; m) $(f - g)(0)$.

38. Given $f(x) = 4x + 3$ and $g(x) = 2$, find $(f \circ g)(x)$ and $(g \circ f)(x)$.

39. Given $f(x) = \dfrac{x + 1}{2x - 1}$ and $g(x) = 3x + 5$, find $(f \circ g)(x)$ and $(g \circ f)(x)$.

40. Given $f(x) = \dfrac{1}{x + 2}$ and $g(x) = x - 1$, find $(f \circ g)(x)$ and $(g \circ f)(x)$.

41. Given $f(x) = x^2 - 3$ and $g(x) = \sqrt{3 - x^2}$, find $(f \circ g)(x)$ and the domain of $(f \circ g)(x)$.

42. Let $f(x) = \dfrac{x + 1}{2x + 3}$ and $g(x) = x^2 + 1$. Find and simplify $(f \circ g)(x)$.

43. Let $f(x) = x^2 + 4$ and $g(x) = \sqrt{x - 4}$.
Find and simplify $(f \circ g)(x)$ and $(g \circ f)(x)$.

Inverse Functions

44. Let $f(x) = \sqrt{2x - 5}$. Find $f^{-1}(x)$.

45. Consider $f(x) = (x - 1)^2$ for $x \le 1$. Find $f^{-1}(x)$.

46. The graph of a function $y = f(x)$ is shown on the right.

a) Find $f^{-1}(2)$.

b) Find $f^{-1}(0)$

c) Sketch the graph of $y = f^{-1}(x)$.

47. The graph of a function f is shown on the right. Sketch the graph of f^{-1}.

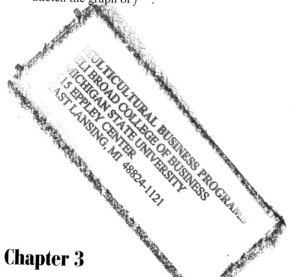

Chapter 3

Quadratic Functions _____

1. Suppose $q(x) = ax^2 + bx + c$ with $q(-2) = 0$ and $-\dfrac{b}{2a} = -0.5$.

What is the solution set of the equation $q(x) = 0$?

2. For what value of c will the minimum value of the function

$f(x) = 2x^2 - 12x + c$ be 23?

3. For what value of c will the maximum value of the function

$f(x) = -2x^2 + 12x + c$ be 6?

4. Find the vertex of the parabola $y = kx^2 + 2x + 4$.

5. Find the vertex of the parabola $y = kx^2 - 4x + 2$.

6. Find the vertex of $y = x^2 - 6x + 1$.

7. Write the equation of the parabola $y = x^2 - 5sx + 3$, s is a real number, in the standard form $y = a(x - h)^2 + k$.

8. For what value(s) of t will the vertex of the parabola $y = 4x^2 - 6tx + 1$ lie on the x-axis?

9. For what value(s) of k will the vertex of the parabola $y = 3x^2 - (k - 1)x + 5$ lie on the y-axis?

10. Find the distance from the origin to the vertex of the parabola $y = -x^2 + 4x - 10$.

11. Find the distance from the point $(1, -1)$ to the vertex of the parabola $y = 3x^2 - 2x + 1$.

Write an equation of the quadratic function whose graph satisfies the given conditions.

12. Vertex: $(-2, 3)$; point on the graph: $(-1, 1)$.

13. Vertex: $(2, -3)$; y-intercept: at $(0, 9)$.

14. Find x-intercept(s) of the graph of the quadratic function with the vertex $(-1, -2)$ and y-intercept at $(0, 7)$.

15. Find x-intercept(s) of the graph of the quadratic function with the vertex $(-1, 2)$ and y-intercept at $(0, -7)$.

16. The graph of the quadratic function $y = f(x)$ is
shown on the right.
Write the equation of this function
a) in standard form; b) in general form;
c) state the intervals over which $f(x)$ is
increasing/decreasing.

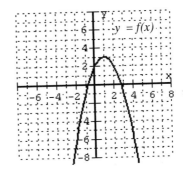

17. The graph of the quadratic function
$y = g(x)$ is shown on the right.
a) Write the equation of this function in general
form $y = ax^2 + bx + c$.
b) State the intervals over which $g(x)$ is
increasing, decreasing.

Quadratic Inequalities

Pattern for solving Quadratic Inequalities $ax^2 + bx + c < 0$ and $ax^2 + bx + c > 0$.

a) Solve the equation $ax^2 + bx + c = 0$. The solutions of this equation are called "critical points".

b) The "critical points" create a partition on the number line.

c) Change of sign of any quadratic function can happen *only* when the function passes through "critical points". Because the quadratic function has the same sign (+ or −) for all points inside of each partial interval, it is enough to check the sign (+ or −) of that function at **one** inner point for each interval in the partition (so-called "trial point").

d) To find where the quadratic function is positive/negative we need to fill out the following table.

Intervals			
Trial points			
Values of the function at the trial point			
Signs of the function's values (+ or −)			

e) The last line allows to write the answer, to pick up the interval(s) where the function takes specified sign (+ or −).

If the original quadratic inequality is not written in the standard form with ZERO on one side, you have to re-write such an inequality in the standard form and then use "test intervals" method.

18. Solve the following quadratic inequalities by "test intervals" method.
   a) $8x^2 + 14x + 3 > 0$
   b) $12x^2 - 5x - 2 < 0$

19. Solve the following quadratic inequalities by "test intervals" method.
   a) $5x^2 - 9x - 2 \leq 0$
   b) $2x^2 - 7x - 4 \geq 0$

If the graph of a quadratic function $y = ax^2 + bx + c$ has **no x-intercepts**, then the discriminant $D < 0$, then

a) the inequality $ax^2 + bx + c < 0$ is true for all real numbers if the coefficient $a < 0$; is never true if $a > 0$;

b) the inequality $ax^2 + bx + c > 0$ is true for all real numbers if the coefficient $a > 0$; is never true if $a < 0$.

Solve the following quadratic inequalities. Sketch by hand the graph of the corresponding quadratic function to illustrate your answer.

20.
   a) $2x^2 - x + 5 > 0$
   b) $-3x^2 + 4x - 5 < 0$

21.
   a) $-5x^2 + 2x + 10 > 0$
   b) $x^2 - x + 5 < 0$
   c) $3x^2 - 2x + 1 \geq 0$

Polynomial Functions _____

22. The graph of a function $y = f(x)$ is shown on the right. State the intervals where f is increasing/decreasing.

23. The graph of a polynomial function
f(x) is shown on the right.

Use the graph to answer the following questions.

    a) Is the degree of the polynomial function $f(x)$ even or odd?

    b) Is the leading coefficient positive or negative?

    c) How many distinct real zero(s) has $f(x)$?

    d) Identify all turning points on the graph of the polynomial $f(x)$.

    e) Is the multiplicity k of the zero $x = 0$ odd or even?

    f) Is the multiplicity k of the zero $x = 6$ equal to 1 or greater than 1?

    g) State the "End behavior" of $f(x)$.

    h) What is the minimum degree of $f(x)$?

24. The graph of a polynomial function $f(x)$ is shown on the right.

Use the graph to answer the following questions.

    a) Is the degree of the polynomial function $f(x)$ even or odd?

    b) Is the leading coefficient of $f(x)$ positive or negative?

    c) How many real zero(s) has $f(x)$?

    d) Identify all turning points on the graph of the polynomial $f(x)$.

    e) Is the multiplicity k of the zero $x = -1$ odd or even?

    f) Is the multiplicity k of the zero $x = -1$ equal to 1 or greater than 1?

    g) State the "End behavior" of $f(x)$.

    h) What is the minimum degree of $f(x)$?

25. The graph of a polynomial function $P(x)$ is shown on the right.

Use the graph to answer the following questions.

    a) Is the degree of the polynomial function $P(x)$
       even or odd?

    b) State the intervals (approximately) where $P(x)$ is
       increasing/decreasing.

26. Sketch the graph of a polynomial function of even degree which
has a negative leading coefficient, $x = 5$ as a zero of multiplicity 2
and $x = 0$ as a zero of multiplicity 1.

27. Sketch the graph of a polynomial function of odd degree which
has a positive leading coefficient, $x = -1$ as a zero of multiplicity
1, $x = 2$ as a zero of multiplicity 2, and y-intercept $(0, -6)$.

28. Find the y-intercept of the polynomial function
$f(x) = 3(x - 1)^3(x + 2)^2(x - 5)$.
State the "End behavior" of $f(x)$.

29. Find the y-intercept of the polynomial function
$f(x) = -2(x - 1)^3(x + 3)^2$.
State the "End behavior" of $f(x)$.

30. Find all zeros of the polynomial
$f(x) = -3x^4 - 3x^2$.
State the multiplicity of each zero.

31. Use factoring to solve the polynomial equation $x^4 + 4x^3 - x - 4 = 0$.

32. Find all zeros of the polynomial $f(x) = x^4 - 4x^3 - 5x^2$.
State the multiplicity of each zero.

33. Use long division to divide $f(x) = x^4 - 3x^3 + 5x^2 - x - 6$ by $d(x) = x^2 + 2$. Write the presentation of the dividend $f(x)$ using the quotient $q(x)$ and remainder $r(x)$.

34. Use long division to divide $f(x) = x^5 - 5x^3 + 2x^2 - x + 5$ by $d(x) = x^3 - x^2 + 2x - 3$. Write the presentation of the dividend $f(x)$ through the quotient $q(x)$ and remainder $r(x)$.

35. Given $x = -1$ is a zero of the polynomial function $f(x) = 2x^4 + 7x^3 + 9x^2 + 5x + 1$, find the multiplicity of this zero.

36. Given $x = -2$ is a zero of the polynomial function $f(x) = x^5 + x^4 - 5x^3 - x^2 + 8x - 4$, find the multiplicity of this zero.

37. Find integer zeros of $f(x) = x^3 + 2x^2 - 15x - 36$ and state the multiplicity of each zero.

38. Find integer zeros of $f(x) = x^3 + 7x^2 + 16x + 12$ and state the multiplicity of each zero.

39. Given $x = -4$ is a zero of $f(x) = x^3 + 3x^2 - 7x - 12$, find other zeros of $f(x)$. State the multiplicity of each zero.

40. Given $x = 3i$ is a zero of $f(x) = x^4 + 13x^2 + 36$, find remaining zeros of $f(x)$. State the multiplicity of each zero.

41. Given $x = -1$ is a zero of $f(x) = x^4 + x^3 - 8x^2 - 15x - 7$, find remaining zeros of $f(x)$. State the multiplicity of each zero.

42. Given $x = 3 + i$ is a zero of $f(x) = x^3 - 7x^2 - +16x - 10$, find remaining zeros of $f(x)$. State the multiplicity of each zero.

Find the formula for a polynomial function of a minimum degree with real coefficients that satisfied the given conditions. Write your answer using the general form of a polynomial.

43. $x = -1, x = 2$, and $x = i$ are zeros; $f(1) = -8$.

44. $x = -2$ and $x = 1 - 3i$ are zeros; $f(1) = 36$.

45. $x = 1$ is a zero of multiplicity $k = 2$, $x = 1 + 2i$ is a zero of multiplicity $k = 1$, and $f(0) = 5$.

46. $x = -2$ is a zero of multiplicity $k = 2$, $x = 1 - i$ is a zero of multiplicity $k = 1$, and $f(0) = 16$.

Chapter 4

Exponential and Logarithmic Functions ⎯⎯⎯⎯⎯⎯⎯⎯⎯⎯⎯⎯⎯⎯

1. Let $f(x) = \log_4(x - 1)$.
    a) State the domain and range of $f(x)$.
    b) Write the equation of the vertical asymptote.
    c) Find the inverse function $f^{-1}(x)$.
    d) State the domain and range of $f^{-1}(x)$.
    e) Write the equation of the asymptote (if any) for $f^{-1}(x)$.
    f) Sketch the graphs of $f(x)$ and $f^{-1}(x)$. Label the asymptote(s).

2. Let $g(x) = \log(x + 2)$.
    a) State the domain and range of $g(x)$.
    b) Write the equation of the vertical asymptote.
    c) Find the inverse function $g^{-1}(x)$.
    d) State the domain and range of $g^{-1}(x)$.
    e) Write the equation of the asymptote (if any) for $g^{-1}(x)$.
    f) Sketch the graphs of $g(x)$ and $g^{-1}(x)$. Label the asymptote(s).

3. Let $f(x) = 2^x - 3$
    a) State the domain and range of $f(x)$.
    b) Write the equation of the horizontal asymptote.
    c) Find the inverse function $f^{-1}(x)$.
    d) State the domain and range of $f^{-1}(x)$.
    e) Write the equation of the asymptote (if any) for $f^{-1}(x)$.
    f) Sketch the graphs of $f(x)$ and $f^{-1}(x)$. Label the asymptote(s).

4. Let $h(x) = 5^x + 2$
    a) State the domain and range of $h(x)$.
    b) Write the equation of the horizontal asymptote.
    c) Find the inverse function $h^{-1}(x)$.
    d) State the domain and range of $h^{-1}(x)$.

5. Find the domain of the function $f(x) = \ln(|x|)$

6. Find the domain of the function $f(x) = \log(-x)$

7. Find the domain of the function $f(x) = \log_2(|x + 1|)$

8. Find the domain of the function $f(x) = \ln(x^2 + x + 1)$

9. Find the domain of the function $f(x) = \log(\sqrt{x^2 + 1})$

10. Find the range of the function $f(x) = -2^x$.

11. Find the range of the function $f(x) = -e^{x-1} + 3$.

12. Find the range of the function $f(x) = \left(\frac{1}{5}\right)^x - 4$

13. Find f^{-1} for each of the following functions.
    Include in your work statements about the domain and range.
    a) $f(x) = \log(x - 4) - 1$
    b) $f(x) = 2^{x+1} - 3$

14. Find the domain and range for each function.
    a) $f(x) = \ln(-x)$;
    b) $f(x) = \log_3(|x - 1|)$

15. Which graph corresponds to f^{-1}, if $f(x) = \log_2(x + 3)$?

a

b

c

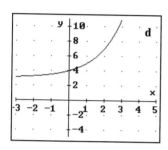

d

e

None of these

16. Which graph corresponds to f^{-1}, if $f(x) = 3^x + 2$?

a

b

c

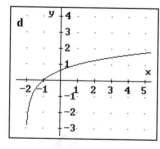

d

e

None of these

Use the properties of the logarithms and given INFO to find the following.

17. Given

$\log_b 3 = 0.6131$	$\log_b 5 = 0.8982$	$\log_b 11 = 1.3383$

$\log_b 55 =$	$\log_b 5\sqrt{11} =$	$\log_b 9 =$	$\log_b \dfrac{3}{5} =$	$\log_b \dfrac{11}{9} =$

18. Given

$\log_b 2 = -0.5757$	$\log_b 13 = -2.13$	$\log_b 0.1 = 1.9125$

$\log_b 0.5$	$\log_b 2\sqrt{13}$	$\log_b 20$	$\log_b \sqrt{10}$	$\log_b\left(\dfrac{13}{2}\right)$

Use properties of the logarithms to write each expression as a single term that does not contain logarithms.

19. $10^{\log 5x^2 + \log 3x} + e^{\ln 16x^7 - \ln 2x^4}$

20. $c^{\frac{1}{3}\log_c 27x - 2\log_c x^2 y}$

Exponential and Logarithmic Equations

Solve the following equations.
Remember, when solving Logarithmic Equations solution(s) check is MANDATORY.
*Find **exact** solutions. Your answers may contain logarithms.*

21. $9^{1-2x} = 81$

22. $4^{3x+2} = \dfrac{1}{8}$

23. $2^{x^2+4x} = \dfrac{1}{16}$

24. $\log_5(x + 2) + \log_5(3x - 1) = \log_5(7x - 1)$

25. $\log_2 x + \log_4 x = \dfrac{2}{3}$

26. $\log_2(\log_2(x + 265)) = 3$

27. $\ln(\ln(x + 3)) = 1$

28. $\log(\log(x - 5)) = 0$

29. $2^{|x|} = 8$

30. $\ln|x - 1| = 0$

31. $\log_3|2x + 1| = 1$

32. $|\log_2(x - 10)| = 1$

Exponential and Logarithmic Inequalities

Use properties of exponential and logarithmic functions to solve algebraically the following inequalities.

33. $3^x > 9$

34. $\left(\dfrac{1}{5}\right)^x > 25$

35. $2^{x-1} \le 16$

36. $\left(\dfrac{1}{3}\right)^x < 1$

37. $\log x \ge 2$

38. $\ln(x + 1) < 0$

39. $\log_{0.5}(x + 1) < 0$

40. $\log_{0.3} x < \log_{0.3} 5$

Supplementary Answers

Chapter 1

1. $\{2\}$ **3.** $\varnothing$ **5.** $\{-3,\ -1\}$ **7.** $\left\{\dfrac{65}{12}\right\}$ **9.** $y = \dfrac{4 - 4x}{4x^2 - x}$ **11.** $v = \dfrac{s}{t} - 16t$ **13.** $\varnothing$ **15.** $[-2, 4]$ **17.** $\left\{-5, \dfrac{2}{3}\right\}$

19. $\left\{-1, \dfrac{3}{5}\right\}$ **21.** $\left\{-\dfrac{1}{3}, \dfrac{1}{3}\right\}$ **23.** $\left\{-\dfrac{5}{3}i,\ \dfrac{5}{3}i\right\}$ **25.** $\left\{\dfrac{2}{9}, \dfrac{4}{9}\right\}$ **27.** $\{-5,\ -1\}$ **29.** Two distinct real roots

31. $k = 16$ **33.** $\{3\}$ **35.** $\{-1\}$ **37.** $\left\{\dfrac{1}{2}\right\}$ **39.** $\{1, 2\}$ **41.** $(-\infty, 1) \bigcup (1, 2) \bigcup (2, 3) \bigcup (3, \infty)$ **43.** $\{3\}$ **45.** $\{0\}$

47. $\left\{-\dfrac{1}{2}, 4\right\}$ **49.** $\{-57\}$ **51.** $\{-3, 3\}$ **53.** $\{1, 6\}$ **55.** $\{1, 8\}$

Chapter 2

1. $[-1, \infty)$ **3.** $(-\infty, \infty)$ **5.** $(-3, \infty)$ **7.** $(-\infty, \infty)$ **9.** $(-\infty, -2) \bigcup (-2, \infty)$
11. a. Domain: $[-8, 8]$ b. Range: $[-6,\ 5]$ c. $g(-8) = -6$ d. $g(8) = 2$ e. $g(0) = -2$

f. $g(3) - g(-2) = 4$ g. $g(-5) - g(-3) = 0$ h. $\{3\}$ **13.** a. $f(1) - f(-1) = 2$ b. $f(-5) = -7$

c. y-intercept: $(0, 1)$ d. $f(-2)$ is undefined e. $f(3) - f(-4) = 34$ **15.** $x = -2$ **19.** $r(t) = 4t - 5$

21. $\$899.99$ **23.** a. $P(t) = 240t + 16{,}000$ b. $24{,}400$ c. In 2008 **25.** $\$31{,}000$

27. a. $f_{\min} = -4.17161$ at $x = 1.82574$ $f_{\max} = 20.17161$ at $x = -1.82574$

b. f is increasing on the interval $(-\infty, 1.82574)$ and on the interval $(1.82574, \infty)$; f is decreasing

on the interval $(-1.82574, 1.82574)$ **29.** $(-2, -2)$ **31.** a. Domain of $f(x)$: $[-5, 1]$; range of $f(x)$: $[-2, 4]$

b. Domain of $g(x)$: $[-4, 2]$; range of $f(x)$: $[-7, 5]$

33. Sequence of transformations:

$$\sqrt{x} \rightarrow \sqrt{x + 2} \rightarrow \dfrac{1}{2}\sqrt{x + 2} \rightarrow -\dfrac{1}{2}\sqrt{x + 2} \rightarrow -\dfrac{1}{2}\sqrt{x + 2} + 3$$

Transformations of coordinates of given points:

$$(0,1) \to (-2,1) \to \left(-2, \frac{1}{2}\right) \to \left(-2, -\frac{1}{2}\right) \to \left(-2, 2\frac{1}{2}\right)$$

$$(1,1) \to (-1,1) \to \left(-1, \frac{1}{2}\right) \to \left(-1, -\frac{1}{2}\right) \to \left(-1, 2\frac{1}{2}\right)$$

37. a. $(f \circ g)(0) = 4$ b. $(g \circ f)(0) = 5$ c. $(g \circ g)(-3) = -2$ d. $(f \circ f)(1) = 4$ e. $(f \circ g)(3)$ is undefined   f. $(f \circ g)(-5) = 0$

g. Domain of $f(x)$: $[-3,2]$ h. Domain of $g(x)$: $[-7,6]$

i. Domain of $(f \circ g)(x)$: $[-5.2, 3.5] \bigcup [-2, 1.5]$ j. $(f \cdot g)(-3) = -4$

k. Domain of the quotient $\left(\dfrac{g}{f}\right)(x)$: $[-3,1) \bigcup (1,2]$ l. $(f + g)(-1) = 4.5$ m. $(f - g)(0) = 4$

39. $(f \circ g)(x) = \dfrac{x+2}{2x+3}, x \neq -\dfrac{3}{2}$; $(g \circ f)(x) = \dfrac{13x-2}{2x-1}, x \neq \dfrac{1}{2}$ **41.** $(f \circ g)(x) = -x^2$; the domain of $(f \circ g)(x)$: $[-3,3]$

43. $(f \circ g)(x) = x, x \geq 4$; $(g \circ f)(x) = |x|, x$ is any real number   **45.** $f^{-1}(x) = 1 - \sqrt{x}, x \geq 0$

47.

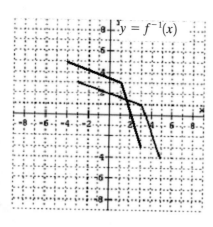

Chapter 3

1. $\{-2, 1\}$ **3.** $c = -12$ **5.** Vertex: $\left(\dfrac{2}{k}, 2 - \dfrac{7}{k}\right)$ **7.** $y = \left(x - \dfrac{5s}{2}\right)^2 + \dfrac{12 - 25s^2}{4}$ **9.** $k = 1$ **11.** $\dfrac{\sqrt{29}}{3}$ **13.** $y = 3(x-2)^2 - 3$

15. Standard form of the parabola is $y = 9(x+1)^2 - 2$. x-intercepts: $\left(-1 - \dfrac{\sqrt{2}}{3}, 0\right)$ and $\left(-1 + \dfrac{\sqrt{2}}{3}, 0\right)$

17. $y = \dfrac{1}{4}x^2 - x$; $g(x)$ decreases on the interval $(-\infty, 2)$ and increases on the interval $(2, \infty)$

19. a. $\left[-\dfrac{1}{5}, \dfrac{2}{3}\right]$ b. $\left(-\infty, -\dfrac{1}{2}\right] \bigcup [4, \infty)$ **21.** a. $\varnothing$ b. $\varnothing$ c. $(-\infty, \infty)$

23. a. Odd degree b. Leading coefficient is positive c. $f(x)$ has two distinct real zeros e. The multiplicity of $x = 0$ is even
f. The multiplicity of $x = 6$ is greater than 1 g. $f(x) \to -\infty$ when $x \to -\infty$ and $f(x) \to \infty$ when $x \to \infty$

h. Minimum degree of the polynomial $f(x)$ is 5   **25.** a. Degree of the polynomial $P(x)$ is odd

b. $P(x)$ increases on the interval $(-\infty, -4)$, on the interval $(-2, 0)$, and on the interval $(4.5, \infty)$; $P(x)$ decreases on

the interval $(-4, -2)$ and on the interval $(0, 4.5)$ **29.** y-intercept: $(0, 18)$; $f(x) \to \infty$ when $x \to -\infty$

and $f(x) \to -\infty$ when $x \to \infty$ **31.** $\{-4, 1\}$ **33.** $f(x) = (x^2 + 2)(x^2 - 3x + 3) + (5x - 12)$

35. $x = -1$ is a zero of the multiplicity $k = 3$ **37.** $x = -3, k = 2$; $x = 4, k = 1$

39. $\left\{-4, \dfrac{1 - \sqrt{13}}{2}, \dfrac{1 + \sqrt{13}}{2}\right\}$, each zero has the multiplicity $k = 1$

41. $x = -1$, $k = 2$; $x = \dfrac{1 - \sqrt{29}}{2}, k = 1$; $x = \dfrac{1 + \sqrt{29}}{2}, k = 1$ **43.** $f(x) = 2x^4 - 2x^3 - 2x^2 - 2x - 4$

45. $f(x) = x^4 - 4x^3 + 10x^2 - 12x + 5$

Chapter 4

1. a. Domain of $f(x)$: $(1, \infty)$; range of $f(x)$: $(-\infty, \infty)$ b. $x = 1$

c. $f^{-1}(x) = 4^x + 1$ d. Domain of $f^{-1}(x)$: $(-\infty, \infty)$; range of $f^{-1}(x)$: $(1, \infty)$

e. $y = 1$ f.

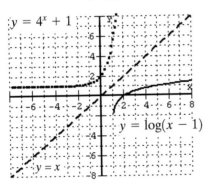

5. Domain: $(-\infty, 0) \cup (0, \infty)$ **7.** Domain: $(-\infty, -1) \cup (-1, \infty)$

9. Domain: $(-\infty, \infty)$ **11.** Range: $(-\infty, 3)$

13. a. $f^{-1}(x) = 10^{x+1} + 4$, x is any real number b. $f^{-1}(x) = \log_2(x + 3), x > -3$ **15.** b

17.

$\log_b 55 =$	$\log_b 5\sqrt{11} =$	$\log_b 9 =$	$\log_b \dfrac{3}{5} =$	$\log_b \dfrac{11}{9} =$
2.2365	1.56735	1.2262	-0.2851	0.1121

19. $120x^5$ **21.** $\left\{-\dfrac{1}{2}\right\}$ **23.** $\{2\}$ **25.** $\{1\}$ **27.** $\{e^e - 3\}$ **29.** $\{-3, 3\}$

31. $\{-2, 1\}$ **33.** $(2, \infty)$ **35.** $(-\infty, 5]$ **37.** $[100, \infty)$ **39.** $(0, \infty)$

Index

Definitions, Rules, and Formulas

The Real Numbers

Natural Numbers: $\{1, 2, 3, \ldots\}$
Whole Numbers: $\{0, 1, 2, 3, \ldots\}$
Integers: $\{\ldots, -3, -2, -1, 0, 1, 2, 3, \ldots\}$
Rational Numbers: $\{\frac{a}{b} \mid a$ and b are integers, $b \neq 0\}$
Irrational Numbers: $\{x \mid x$ is real and not rational$\}$

Basic Rules of Algebra

Commutative: $a + b = b + a;\ ab = ba$
Associative: $(a + b) + c = a + (b + c);\ (ab)\,c = a\,(bc)$
Distributive: $a(b + c) = ab + ac,\ a(b - c) = ab - ac$
Identity: $a + 0 = a;\ a \cdot 1 = a$
Inverse: $a + (-a) = 0;\ a \cdot \frac{1}{a} = 1\ (a \neq 0)$
Multiplication Properties: $(-1)\,a = -a;$
$(-1)(-a) = a;\ a \cdot 0 = 0;\ (-a)(b) = (a)(-b) = -ab;$
$(-a)(-b) = ab$

Set-Builder Notation, Interval Notation, and Graphs

$(a, b) = \{x \mid a < x < b\}$

$[a, b) = \{x \mid a \leq x < b\}$

$(a, b] = \{x \mid a < x \leq b\}$

$[a, b] = \{x \mid a \leq x \leq b\}$

$(-\infty, b) = \{x \mid x < b\}$

$(-\infty, b] = \{x \mid x \leq b\}$

$(a, \infty) = \{x \mid x > a\}$

$[a, \infty) = \{x \mid x \geq a\}$

$(-\infty, \infty) = \{x \mid x$ is a real number$\} = \{x \mid x \in R\}$

Slope Formula

$$\text{slope } (m) = \frac{\text{change in } y}{\text{change in } x} = \frac{y_2 - y_1}{x_2 - x_1} \quad (x_1 \neq x_2)$$

Equations of Lines

1. *Slope-intercept form:* $y = mx + b$
   m is the line's slope and b is its y-intercept.
2. *General form:* $Ax + By + C = 0$
3. *Point-slope form:* $y - y_1 = m(x - x_1)$
   m is the line's slope and (x_1, y_1) is a fixed point on the line.
4. *Horizontal line parallel to the x-axis:* $y = b$
5. *Vertical line parallel to the y-axis:* $x = a$

Absolute Value

1. $|x| = \begin{cases} x & \text{if } x \geq 0 \\ -x & \text{if } x < 0 \end{cases}$
2. If $|x| = c$, then $x = c$ or $x = -c.\ (c > 0)$
3. If $|x| < c$, then $-c < x < c.\ (c > 0)$
4. If $|x| > c$, then $x < -c$ or $x > c.\ (c > 0)$

Special Factorizations

1. *Difference of two squares:*
   $$A^2 - B^2 = (A + B)(A - B)$$
2. *Perfect square trinomials:*
   $$A^2 + 2AB + B^2 = (A + B)^2$$
   $$A^2 - 2AB + B^2 = (A - B)^2$$
3. *Sum of two cubes:*
   $$A^3 + B^3 = (A + B)(A^2 - AB + B^2)$$
4. *Difference of two cubes:*
   $$A^3 - B^3 = (A - B)(A^2 + AB + B^2)$$

Algebra's Common Graphs

Identity Function $f(x) = x$

Standard Quadratic Function
$f(x) = x^2$

Standard Cubic Function
$f(x) = x^3$

Absolute Value Function
$f(x) = |x|$

Square Root Function
$f(x) = \sqrt{x}$

Cube Root Function $f(x) = \sqrt[3]{x}$

Greatest Integer Function
$f(x) = [[x]]$

Transformations

In each case, c represents a positive real number.

Function		How to obtain the graph of g from the graph of f
Vertical translations	$\begin{cases} g(x) = f(x) + c \\ g(x) = f(x) - c \end{cases}$	Shift f upward c units. Shift f downward c units.
Horizontal translations	$\begin{cases} g(x) = f(x - c) \\ g(x) = f(x + c) \end{cases}$	Shift f to the right c units. Shift f to the left c units.
Reflections	$\begin{cases} g(x) = -f(x) \\ g(x) = f(-x) \end{cases}$	Reflect f in the x-axis. Reflect f in the y-axis.
Stretching or Shrinking	$\begin{cases} g(x) = cf(x); c > 1 \\ g(x) = cf(x); 0 < x < 1 \end{cases}$	Stretch f, multiplying each of its y-values by c. Shrink f, multiplying each of its y-values by c.

Distance and Midpoint Formulas

1. The distance from (x_1, y_1) to (x_2, y_2) is

$$\sqrt{(x_2 - x_1)^2 + (y_2 - y_1)^2}.$$

2. The midpoint of the line segment with endpoints (x_1, y_1) and (x_2, y_2) is

$$\left(\frac{x_1 + x_2}{2}, \frac{y_1 + y_2}{2} \right).$$

Quadratic Formula

The solutions to $ax^2 + bx + c = 0$ with $a \neq 0$ are

$$x = \frac{-b \pm \sqrt{b^2 - 4ac}}{2a}.$$

Functions

1. Linear Function: $f(x) = mx + b$
Graph is a line with slope m.

2. Quadratic Function: $f(x) = ax^2 + bx + c, a \neq 0$

Graph is a parabola with vertex at $x = -\dfrac{b}{2a}$.

Quadratic Function: $f(x) = a(x - h)^2 + k$
In this form, the parabola's vertex is (h, k).

3. nth-Degree Polynomial Function: $f(x) =$
$a_n x^n + a_{n-1} x^{n-1} + a_{n-2} x^{n-2} + \cdots + a_1 x + a_0, a_n \neq 0$
For n odd and $a_n > 0$, graph falls to the left and rises to the right.
For n odd and $a_n < 0$, graph rises to the left and falls to the right.
For n even and $a_n > 0$, graph rises to the left and to the right.
For n even and $a_n < 0$, graph falls to the left and to the right.

4. Rational Function: $f(x) = \dfrac{p(x)}{q(x)}, p(x)$ and $q(x)$ are polynomials, $q(x) \neq 0$

5. Exponential Function: $f(x) = b^x, b > 0, b \neq 1$

Graphs:

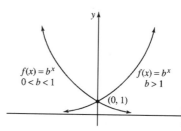

$f(x) = b^x$
$0 < b < 1$

$f(x) = b^x$
$b > 1$

$(0, 1)$

6. Logarithmic Function: $f(x) = \log_b x, b > 0, b \neq 1$
$y = \log_b x$ is equivalent to $x = b^y$.

Graph:

$b > 1$

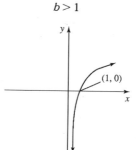

$(1, 0)$

Properties of Logarithms

1. $\log_b (MN) = \log_b M + \log_b N$